TASC PUBLICATIONS

TAMING THE T
Social Exclusion in a Globa
by David Jacobson, Peadar Kirby, and Dei

GRIDLOCK
Dublin's transport crisis and the future of the city
by James Wickham June 2006

OUT OF REACH
Inequalities in the Irish Housing System
by PJ Drudy and Michael Punch December 2005

ENGAGING CITIZENS
The Report of the Democracy Commission
Edited by Clodagh Harris October 2005

POST WASHINGTON
Why America can't rule the World
by Tony Kinsella and Fintan O'Toole June 2005

FOR RICHER, FOR POORER
An investigation of the Irish Pension System
Edited by Jim Stewart May 2005

AN OUTBURST OF FRANKNESS
Community arts in Ireland – a reader
Edited by Sandy Fitzgerald November 2004

SELLING OUT?
Privatisation in Ireland
by Paul Sweeney October 2004

AFTER THE BALL
by Fintan O'Toole October 2003

TASC RESEARCH PAMPHLETS TO DATE

Outsourcing Government
public bodies and accountability
by Paula Clancy and Grainne Murphy May 2006

The Trouble with Northern Ireland
the belfast agreement and democratic governance
by Rick Wilford and Robin Wilson April 2006

tasc
A Think Tank for Action on Social Change
26 Sth Frederick St, Dublin 2.
Ph: 00353 1 6169050
Email:contact@tascnet.ie
www.tascnet.ie

Power to the People?

Assessing Democracy in Ireland

A TASC Report

Written and edited by

Ian Hughes, Paula Clancy,
Clodagh Harris, and David Beetham

With

John Baker, Elaine Byrne, Mark Callanan, Tom Clonan,
Cathal Coleman, Fiona Crowley, Tom Gormley, Tony Kinsella,
Olive Moore, Gráinne Murphy, Aoife Nolan,
Lúghaidh Ó Braonáin, Deiric Ó Broin, Damian Tobin,
Tom Wall and Robin Wilson

Power to the People?
Assessing Democracy in Ireland
First published 2007
by TASC at New Island
an imprint of New Island Press
2 Brookside
Dundrum
Dublin 14

www.newisland.ie

ISBN 978 1 905494 37 8.

British Library Cataloguing in Publication Data.
A CIP catalogue record for this book is available from the British Library.

Typeset by Ashfield Press
Cover design by Public Communications Centre

Printed in Ireland by
Betaprint Limited, Dublin

Contents

Civil Society and Popular Participation

Democracy Beyond the State

Tables

Acknowledgements

It is integral to the design of the democracy audit approach that it is very much a collaborative venture. We have, over the past two and a half years, researched, written and edited this book, with the assistance of a number of people working with TASC at various points. We could not have done so without the contribution of a very large number of people.

Gráinne Murphy from TASC has made a major contribution to the audit in a variety of ways but primarily through researching and writing draft answers across many sections of the audit.

External contributors who wrote or contributed to drafts are as follows:

Nationhood and Citizenship	*Robin Wilson*
Local Government	*Mark Callanan* and *Deiric Ó Broin*
Rule of Law	*Aoife Nolan*
Civil and Political Rights	*Fiona Crowley* and *Olive Moore*
Economic and Social Rights	*Tom Gormley* and *Damian Tobin*
Media	*Lúghaidh Ó Braonáin*
Promoting Integrity	*Elaine Byrne* and *Damian Tobin*
Political Participation	*John Baker, Aoife Nolan*, and *Tom Wall*
The Police and Security Forces	*Tom Clonan*
The International Dimension	*Tony Kinsella, Cathal Coleman* and *Fiona Crowley*

Thanks also to Elaine Byrne who compiled Tables 9.1 and 9.2. In addition, a number of institutions collaborated with us in very specific ways. Amnesty International (Irish section), worked very closely with us on the sections dealing with civil and political rights and the international dimension. Amnesty also co-hosted an expert roundtable on economic and social rights. The School of Communications, Dublin City University hosted a seminar to discuss an early draft of the media section, and provided invaluable commentary and advice. In particular we want to thank Brian Trench, Farrel Corcoran, John Horgan, Colum Kenny and Eddie Holt for their detailed comments on early drafts. The Department of Government in University College Cork hosted a seminar on the Democratic Local Politics section and we want to thank them for the very useful insights and further information that this yielded. Fiachra Kennedy provided very helpful comments and additional information on questions dealing with political parties and we thank him. Joanna McMinn and Orla O'Connor of the National Women's Council of Ireland have supported the process from the outset with advice on the gender proofing of the document, very active participation in one of the consultative round tables and specific input on gender issues where they arise in the audit.

We must also thank the huge number of people who read drafts of sections, very often providing very detailed commentary, amendments and new information. In addition, as part of the audit process we held a total of five expert seminars / roundtables to consider the 14 draft sections of the audit so as to ensure a cross section of commentary and involvement of politicians, public servants, civil society and academics. Because all of these comprise a very large number of people we have listed them in a separate Appendix where they are not otherwise mentioned in the acknowledgements.

From the initiation of the project we have been fortunate to have the advice and support of an advisory steering group comprising Teresa Brannick, John Baker, Elizabeth Meehan, Robin Wilson and Stuart Weir and we wish to thank them for the many and varied ways in which they helped to shape the project as well as providing detailed commentary, advice and input on specific sections and answers.

We would like to acknowledge the valuable advice and input from members of the Democracy Commission and we would particularly like to thank Nora Owen, a member of the Commission, for input at various stages including making very helpful comments on a final draft.

At various points, a number of people working with TASC contributed to the audit research and we would like to take this opportunity to thank Elizabeth Harrington, David Lundy, Lucas Fowler, David McElroy and Cian O'Flaherty. We would like to thank Phill McCaughey for her contribution in organising events associated with the project, compiling the final bibliography and managing the production of the final book. Tony Glavin was far more than a copy editor and we are very appreciative for his work on the text.

Finally, two foundations, the Atlantic Philanthropies and the Joseph Rowntree Charitable Trust, have generously provided funding for this project without which it would not have been possible. We would like to thank them.

Introduction

The continued existence and further development of democracy depends on the vigilance and awareness of its citizens. Indeed, the most significant indicator of a successful democracy is arguably the capacity for critical self-reflection on the part of its citizenry, together with a capacity for self-renewal. The democratic audit methodology which we have used in this study offers a means of engaging a wide range of partners within the public sphere in this very process of critical self-reflection. In addition, a key principle of the audit method holds that assessing democracy should be a responsibility of the citizenry itself, not of outsiders sitting in judgement upon the country. The rationale here is, not only that citizens are best placed to make such an assessment, but also that, unlike an external evaluation, a self-assessment can help to mobilise pressure for change where change is needed. Our objective in undertaking an audit has been to provide a systematic analysis of the strengths and weaknesses of Ireland's democracy that, in turn, might contribute to this self-awareness. At the same time, it will be apparent in reading this book that democracy is not an all-or-nothing affair, but rather a matter of degrees – of the degree to which the people can exercise a controlling influence over public policy and policy makers, enjoy equal treatment at their hands and have their voices equally heard.

There are a number of distinctive features of this report that we hope will be found useful. First, the audit adopts a normative definition of democracy that focuses on popular control over political leaders and decision makers on the one hand, and political equality on the other. Second, within that framework, the audit methodology aims to be objective and to make its findings evidence-based. Third, the audit's methodology, as described, is one which relies greatly on consultation with, and input from, diverse groups of civil and political society.

The report is part of the Democratic Audit Ireland project, a project of TASC – A Think Tank for Action on Social Change. This publication is the outcome of a comprehensive audit of democracy in Ireland, initiated in 2004. As part of the Democratic Audit Ireland project, TASC commissioned the think tank, Democratic Dialogue, to undertake a similar audit in Northern Ireland (Wilford *et al.*, 2007 forthcoming) and to prepare a report on its findings which is published separately. In addition, a number of more detailed investigations of different aspects of democracy in each of the jurisdictions have been published over the past two years: a public-opinion survey on attitudes and behaviour in relation to politics and democracy (Clancy *et al.*, 2005); a report on accountability and public bodies (Clancy and Murphy, 2006); and an in-depth analysis of the Good Friday Agreement of 1998 (Wilson and Wilford, 2006). A further research report dealing with local governance will be published in 2007. (Ó Broin and Waters, 2007 forthcoming) The audit has built on these specialist studies and on the Report of the Democracy Commission. (Harris, 2005)

THE AUDIT METHODOLOGY

The methodology we have used in the audit is based on the International Institute for Democracy and Electoral Assistance (IDEA) Assessment Framework. (Beetham *et al.*, 2001) The methodology was pilot-tested in eight countries representing both new and established democracies across the world. (Beetham *et al.*, 2001) It has by now been used in many countries, most recently in nations as diverse as Mongolia and the Netherlands.

From the perspective of a country's citizens, an audit of democracy can:

- serve to raise public awareness about what democracy entails, and public debate about what standards of performance people should expect from their government;
- provide systematic evidence to substantiate popular concerns about how they are governed, and set these in perspective by identifying both strengths and weaknesses;
- contribute to public debate about ongoing reform, and help to identify priorities for a reform programme; and
- provide an instrument for assessing how effectively reforms are working out in practice.

An audit involves a multifaceted conception of democracy. More specifically, it begins with citizens' rights and responsibilities under the rule of law, examines the institutions of representative and accountable government, looks at the self-organising activity of citizens and social groups within civil society and public life, including the role of the media, and concludes with an analysis of a country's democracy in the light of its international relations and obligations. Furthermore, two central democratic values or principles are used as a guide in making an assessment of each aspect of democracy: the people should have the determining influence over the laws and policies under which they live; and, in doing so, they should treat each other, and be treated, as equals. Only in the light of these principles can we judge how far, and in what respects, the institutions and processes of a country's public life are truly democratic. Such are the principles that democrats in all times and places have struggled for: to render popular control over public decisions both more effective and more inclusive; to remove an elite monopoly over decision making and its benefits; and to overcome obstacles such as those of gender, ethnicity, religion, language, class, wealth etc., to the equal exercise of citizenship rights. Insofar as these principles are embodied in governing arrangements they can be called 'democratic'.

The audit framework comprises 70 areas of investigation across 14 separate sections. The different sections are interrelated, however, given that democracy is a matter of relationships rather than isolated institutions. As such, governmental accountability depends on the independence of the courts, on the media, on popular participation, and so forth, not just on the integrity of office holders or the rules governing their performance in office. At the same time, these different aspects of democratic life have to be treated separately for effective analysis and assessment, as has been done in this audit.

An assessment process across separate sections also allows for a differentiated judgement, since a country may perform better in some areas than others, or better in some respects than others. Nor do all the democratic values or practices necessarily fit together neatly. An electoral system may produce a highly representative legislature, but one that is also less clearly accountable to its electorate. A legislature may have strong checking powers over the executive, but the executive may have difficulty in achieving the policy programme on which it was itself elected. Government may be highly responsive to the public, but some sections of the public may have disproportionate influence over it. In any event, the framework's multisectored structure allows these differentiated judgements to be made.

All of the 70 audit questions share three distinctive features.

- Each question is phrased in the comparative mode (how inclusive…?, how equal….?) with regard to identified benchmarks and international comparators, which further underlines how democracy is always a matter of degree.
- Each question addresses a different aspect of democracy since, as noted above, a country may perform better in some arenas than in others, or in certain facets compared to others. The form of the questions accordingly allows such distinctions to be readily drawn, which in turn encourages more complex or nuanced judgements.
- Each question is phrased in such a way that a more positive answer would indicate a better outcome from a democratic point of view, i.e., they all point in the same direction along the democratic continuum. As such, the questions also entail a judgement about what is better or worse in democratic terms by reference to the key principles outlined earlier.

Data Collection and Analysis.

The purpose of the assessment is to identify strengths as well as weaknesses, and to chart progress as well as identify what most needs improving. The data sources used to answer each question are many and varied, but derive almost entirely from information, analysis and research already in the public domain. These include government statistics, legislation, opinion surveys, non-governmental organisations' (NGO) investigations, academic analyses and so on. Data on best practice as well as past national performance are both used as comparative reference points to establish given benchmarks. In so far as possible, we have attempted to keep the entire audit up to date, but the cut-off points for each section necessarily vary.

Consultation and Collaboration

Questions of what constitutes credible data and what are appropriate standards against which a given country's performance should be assessed are at times contestable. It is in this context that the extensive review and consultative process which the audit framework provides, and which was adopted in our approach, is particularly important.

A wide range of organisations and individuals within civil and political society, including politicians and civil servants, civil society organisations and NGOs, and academics engaged with the project in different ways.

- The Democratic Audit Ireland project itself is part of a series of initiatives by TASC aimed at raising public consciousness and debate about the nature of democracy in Ireland, beginning in June 2003 when TASC and Democratic Dialogue appointed an independent Democracy Commission to examine Irish democracy. This Commission, chaired by the General Secretary of the Irish Congress of Trade Unions, had among its membership representatives of the main political parties, business, and community sectors. The Commission's report, *Engaging Citizens – The case for democratic renewal in Ireland*, published in Autumn 2005, called for significant changes to increase political participation in Ireland. The Democratic Audit Ireland project grew out of the Commission's work and members of the Commission have acted as a standing advisory group to the audit.

- In conducting the audit, we have built partnerships with a number of organisations which have worked with us on different aspects of the audit. These include: the National Women's Council of Ireland, Amnesty International (Irish Section); the School of Communications at Dublin City University (DCU); and the Department of Government at University College Cork (UCC).

- A systematic audit of so many aspects of public life in Ireland could only have been achieved with the collaboration of individual contributors with a wide range of expertise. These commissioned contributions are all acknowledged on page 9.

- Each section was reviewed by one or more subject experts. In many cases, individuals responded to queries and provided further information. All reviewers are listed in Appendix 1.

- Finally, a series of expert conferences took place throughout 2006. These conferences were designed to allow the preliminary findings of the audit to be presented to specialists and practitioners and to allow critical evaluation and external validation. Those who attended are listed in Appendix 1.

This final report incorporates the information and commentary which emerged from this entire process.

HOW A READER MIGHT USE THIS BOOK

The book is set out in the 14 sections of the framework as described above. Each section begins with an introduction which both contextualises the aspects of democracy under consideration and provides a brief overview of the main points that emerge therein. Each section addresses a variable number of questions, each of which carries a stand-alone answer. As a result, while the reader might wish to read the book as a whole, it is also possible to get an overview, section by section, and/or to delve in to a particular aspect of Irish democracy in more detail. The final chapter provides a summary of what we regard as the main strengths and weaknesses of Irish democracy as they have emerged from the detailed analysis contained within each of the 70 measures.

The answer to each question attempts to strike the balance of being both a stand-alone analysis of the issue in question and a part of the narrative of the audit as a whole. Readers should note that, in striking this balance, some repetition across questions is inevitable.

Note for the Future

This is the first time the IDEA Assessment Framework has been applied in Ireland. It is intended that further assessments will be undertaken in the future against the benchmarks set out in this audit. As noted above, the Assessment Framework was designed for application in a variety of social and political contexts. It has proved itself to be a valuable and flexible methodology and is now used by teams of researchers in a large number of countries. This in-built dynamic characteristic of the approach means that it requires constant evaluation and revision. Thus, TASC welcomes critical comment on the framework as a methodological tool as well as on the analysis and conclusions that are contained in this assessment.

The Assessment Framework: Overview

I. Citizenship, Law and Rights

1.0 *Nationhood and Citizenship*
Is there public agreement on a common citizenship without discrimination?

2.0 *The Rule of Law and Access to Justice*
Are state and society consistently subject to the law?

3.0 *Civil and Political Rights*
Are civil and political rights equally guaranteed for all?

4.0 *Economic and Social Rights*
Are economic and social rights equally guaranteed for all?

II. Representative and Accountable Government

5.0 *Free and Fair Elections*
Do elections give the people control over governments and their policies?

6.0 *Democratic role of Political Parties*
Does the party system assist the working of democracy?

7.0 *Government Effectiveness and Accountability*
Is government accountable to the people and their representatives?

8.0 *Civilian Control of the Military and Police*
Are the military and police forces under civilian control?

9.0 *Integrity in Public Life*
Are public officials, elected or appointed, free from corruption?

III. Civil Society and Popular Participation

10.0 *The Media in a Democratic Society*
Do the media operate in a way that sustains democratic values?

11.0 *Political Participation*
Is there full citizen participation in public life?

12.0 *Government Responsiveness*
Is government responsive to the concerns of its citizens?

13.0 *Democratic Local Politics*
Does local politics contribute to the vitality of the country's democracy?

IV Democracy Beyond the State

14.0 *International Dimensions of Democracy*
Are the country's external relations conduct in accordance with democratic norms, and is it itself free from external subordination?

CITIZENSHIP, LAW AND RIGHTS

One: Nationhood and Citizenship

Is there public agreement on a common citizenship without discrimination?

INTRODUCTION AND SUMMARY

Democracy as rule by the people presupposes an agreement on who are "the people" who constitute the democratic subjects, and on the boundaries of the state within which they form a people or nation with a common citizenship and an agreed constitution. The possession of citizenship everywhere brings with it certain rights not available to non-citizens: typically, for adults, they include the right to vote in elections and to stand for public office; to reside permanently in the country and to come and go as one pleases; to enjoy all the benefits of the social security system; and to have one's children registered as citizens. In some countries citizenship also entails the duty to perform military or another equivalent service. Since the Member States of the European Union (EU) agreed to pool an element of their sovereignty, national citizenship within the EU has become more inclusive than heretofore. Citizens of Member States can travel freely across national borders, reside permanently in another EU country, vote in local and European elections, and enjoy employment and social security rights on an equal basis with national citizens.

The concept of a "common citizenship" expresses a twofold idea: first, that all citizens should be treated equally in their rights and responsibilities, without discrimination; second on the basis of this equality, that they should be guaranteed the right to express their different identities and pursue their different ways of living, provided these do not infringe on the fundamental rights of others.

With regard to these basic building blocks of democracy and citizenship, Ireland shows a number of distinctive characteristics. One is the legacy of partition and the historically disputed border with Northern Ireland, whereby it is now the birthright of all the people of Northern Ireland to hold Irish as well as British citizenship. A second is the legacy of past emigration, whereby children born abroad whose parents or grandparents were born in Ireland are eligible for Irish citizenship, though not to vote unless they are resident in the country. On the other hand, the Citizenship Referendum of 2004 removed the previous right of all children born in the Republic to hold Irish citizenship, unless their parents can demonstrate continuity of residence.

Like many other EU countries, Ireland continues to face challenges to ensure non-discriminatory treatment of all social groups under its equality and immigration legislation, for example in employment and services. No comprehensive policy framework for immigration currently exists, although legislation is being introduced, and migrant workers are particularly vulnerable to discriminatory treatment in employment. At the same time, given the extent of immigration over the past ten years and the increased diversity of the population, Ireland shows comparatively low levels of electoral support for far-right or anti-immigrant platforms.

Ireland is one of the few countries where any change to the constitution requires the consent of the people by referendum, though doubts have been expressed about the political motivations with which referendums are introduced and conducted. Among constitutional issues, relations with the North continue to occupy attention. Since the referendum of 1998 endorsed the removal of the Republic's territorial claim to Northern Ireland, there has been agreement between the Irish and British governments on its constitutional position within the UK; and that any change should require the consent of a majority within Northern Ireland. At the same time the Irish government was accorded a role in the governance of Northern Ireland through the North-South Ministerial Council. However, the deep disagreements within Northern Ireland over its own constitutional arrangements continue to influence politics in the South.

Q1.1 How inclusive is the political nation and state citizenship of all who live within the territory?

> *...Irishness is a slippery thing to wrap one's fingers around. Quite a few people who live on the island don't regard themselves as Irish, while a lot of men and women who have never set foot in the place do.* (Eagleton, 2002: 107)

This question addresses issues of eligibility for acquiring Irish citizenship and to what degree laws governing citizenship are impartially applied in practice. This issue is of central importance since both the concept of Irish citizenship and the law with regard to eligibility for citizenship have been significantly changed by two recent events – namely the Good Friday Agreement and the 2004 Citizenship Referendum. Irish citizenship has become both more inclusive under the Good Friday Agreement and more exclusive, following the Citizenship Referendum.

CITIZENSHIP RIGHTS

The Irish Constitution explicitly lists certain rights that it purports to guarantee. These include, for instance, the right to life (Article 40.3), the right to personal liberty (Article 40.4), freedom of expression (Article 40.6.1.i), equal treatment (Article 40.1), and freedom of association (Article 40.6.1.iii). The Supreme Court in Ireland has also recognised that there are, in addition, certain natural rights that exist by virtue of every individual's humanity, which are not listed in the constitution. In fact, it is recognised that an exhaustive list enumerating rights, under either the constitution or other human rights instruments to which Ireland is a party, would be virtually impossible, since it would still lie with the judiciary to decide which further rights are implicit in those listed. (Gallagher, 2005a: 87)

A curious feature of the constitution is that some rights refer explicitly to citizens while others refer to persons. There are competing views as to the significance of this distinction. One view holds that the courts have generally applied fundamental rights universally to Irish citizens and non-citizens alike. The other view holds that the application of constitutional rights to non-Irish citizens has been inconsistent. (Irish Human Rights Commission, 2004a: 3, 6)

Rights under EU Citizenship

Everyone who holds Irish nationality is also a citizen of the European Union. Citizenship of the European Union is complementary to national citizenship and comprises a number of additional rights and duties. (Beetham *et al.*, 2002: 11) These include:

- the right to move and reside freely within the territory of Member States;
- the right to vote and to stand as a candidate in elections to the European Parliament and in municipal elections in the Member State of residence, under the same conditions as its nationals;
- the right to diplomatic protection in the territory of a third country non-EU state by the diplomatic or consular authorities of another Member State, if a national's own country does not have representation there;
- the right to petition the European Parliament; and
- the right to apply to the European Parliament's Ombudsman.

Non-Irish nationals living in Ireland who are nationals of another EU country thus enjoy greater rights and entitlements than nationals of non-EU countries.

Some of the major differences which exist between the rights and entitlements of Irish citizens in comparison to non-Irish citizens living in Ireland, including voting rights, rights to access social welfare, and right to freedom of movement, will be dealt with later in the audit, particularly in Section Three and Section Four and in Q14.3, where some of the major disadvantages which non-Irish citizens resident in Ireland can face are illustrated.

ACQUIRING CITIZENSHIP

Under Article 2 of the Irish Constitution, every person born on the island of Ireland, its islands and its seas has an entitlement to Irish citizenship. In addition, under Article 1(vi) of the British-Irish Agreement, anyone born in Northern Ireland has the right to identify themselves as Irish or British or both as they so choose. The principal legislation governing issues of Irish citizenship is the Irish Nationality and Citizenship Act 1956, the Irish Nationality and Citizenship Act 1986, and the Irish Nationality and Citizenship Acts 1994, 2001 and 2004. The government information website (www.citizensinformation.ie) lists five ways of acquiring citizenship of Ireland. Citizenship can be acquired through birth in Ireland, through descent, through adoption, through marriage, and through naturalisation.

Through Birth

If you are born in Ireland to Irish parent(s), you are also deemed an Irish citizen. On 1 January 2005 the new Irish Nationality and Citizenship Act 2004 came into effect. Children born on or after the 1 January 2005 of non-Irish national parents are not automatically entitled to Irish citizenship. Instead, non-Irish national parents, of children born in Ireland on or after 1 January 2005, must prove that they have a genuine link to Ireland. This will be evidenced by being resident legally in Ireland for three out of the previous four years immediately before the birth of the child. On proof of a genuine link to Ireland, their child will be entitled to Irish citizenship. Time spent in the state as students or asylum seekers are not included in calculating the non-national parents' period of residence in Ireland.

Through Descent

If either of your parents was an Irish citizen at the time of your birth, you are automatically deemed an Irish citizen, irrespective of your place of birth. If you are of the third generation born abroad to an Irish citizen, you may also be entitled to Irish citizenship. Whether your application is successful will depend on whether the parent through whom you claim Irish citizenship had become an Irish citizen by being registered in the Foreign Births Register before you were born. Irish citizenship thus passes through three generations – from grandparents, to parents, to children. You cannot claim Irish citizenship through your great-grandparents.

Through Adoption

Under the Irish Nationality and Citizenship Act 1956, if a child who is not an Irish citizen is adopted by an Irish citizen or a couple where either spouse is an Irish citizen, then the adopted child shall be an Irish citizen. Every deserted infant found in Ireland will, unless the contrary is proved, be considered to have been born in Ireland.

Through Naturalisation

To be eligible to become an Irish citizen through naturalisation, you must:

- be 18 years or older;
- be of good character;
- have had a period of one year's continuous reckonable residence in the state immediately before the date of your application for naturalisation, and during the eight years preceding that have had a total reckonable residence in the state amounting to four years. Periods of study and periods spent awaiting consideration of asylum applications are not allowed as reckonable residence;
- intend in good faith to continue to reside in the state after naturalisation; and
- make a declaration of fidelity to the nation and loyalty to the state.

The Minister for Justice, Equality and Law Reform has power to waive one or more of these conditions under certain circumstances and has discretion over the final disposition of applications for naturalisation. (See also Q14.3)

Through Marriage

Until 2002, under the Irish Nationality and Citizenship Act 1986, a foreign national who married an Irish citizen could automatically acquire Irish citizenship three years after the date of marriage by lodging a declaration "accepting" Irish citizenship.

Fundamental changes were made to the law relating to post-nuptial citizenship by the Irish Nationality and Citizenship Act, 2001. These revisions came into effect on 30 November 2002. The law applicable to couples who married on or after 30 November 2002 no longer allows a foreign spouse married to an Irish citizen to automatically acquire Irish citizenship. The 2001 Act confers on the Minister for Justice, Equality and Law Reform an entitlement to determine post-nuptial citizenship applications in his "absolute discretion". The current provisions have been criticised as unnecessarily complex and open to challenge as being discriminatory and in violation of both the constitution and the European Convention on Human Rights. (*Irish Times*, 26 July 2005)

The current absence of legal recognition for same-sex partnerships in Ireland – such as civil partnership or same-sex marriage – means that within same sex partnerships, a non-Irish citizen has no means of accessing Irish citizenship on the basis of his or her long-term relationship with an Irish citizen This is particularly detrimental to couples in which the non-Irish partner is not an (EEA) European Economic Area citizen. (Mee and Ronayne, 2000) Irish law thus currently discriminates against gay and lesbian couples in this area. (See also Q3.3)

CITIZENSHIP – SHIFTING SANDS

Historically, emigration and the partition of Ireland have been two of the major influences that have shaped concepts of citizenship in Ireland today. Children born abroad whose parents or grandparents were born in Ireland are, and have historically been, eligible for Irish citizenship. Ireland's history of mass emigration has resulted in an unusually large number of people with Irish citizenship who may never have been in Ireland. Government estimates in 2003 indicated there are more than one million Irish-born citizens currently living abroad. In addition, there are millions more people of Irish descent who live abroad, many of whom hold dual citizenship.

The partition of Ireland into two states in 1921 has made citizenship a controversial issue ever since. Many of those born in Northern Ireland consider themselves Irish, even if the majority do not.

Two recent and significant changes regarding the eligibility of those born in Northern Ireland to Irish citizenship, have taken place that involve these issues. The first change has followed the negotiation and implementation of the Good Friday Agreement. (See Q1.3) The second major change, as a result of the 2004 citizenship referendum, has occurred alongside a rapid increase in the numbers of overseas workers coming to live and work in Ireland, and an increase in numbers of people seeking asylum.

Immigration

The scale of immigration in recent years has resulted in significant changes to Ireland's demography. (Ruhs, 2004) (See also Q14.3) As a result, Ireland's demographic profile has rapidly changed from almost entirely Irish-born, white, and predominantly Catholic, to a much more diverse population in terms of nationality, ethnic and religious backgrounds. This increase in immigration has been brought about largely by Ireland's recent economic growth and the need for labour to sustain that expansion. A few figures serve to illustrate the change. In 1999, 6,000 work permits were issued for non-Irish nationals to work in Ireland; by 2003, however, this figure had risen to over 47,500. (www.immigrantcouncil.ie) Moreover, inward migration is set to continue. A recent Central Statistics Office forecast estimates that Ireland will need 50,000 immigrants a year over the next 12 years if current levels of economic growth are to be maintained. (www.cso.ie)

The increase in immigration has not been matched, however, by the development of corresponding policy and legislation to comprehensively manage the ongoing changes. Indeed the current lack of a comprehensive policy framework for immigration, including the absence of a clear entitlement to citizenship or long-term residency provided specific criteria are satisfied, has meant that non-EU migrant workers living and working in Ireland, and contributing to the country's economic success, are unable to live together with their partners and children or plan their long-term futures and experience difficulty in accessing the basic employment rights to which they are entitled under existing Irish law.

The Government's emerging strategy towards immigration appears to involve a twin-track approach to economic migrants, consisting of "a permanent migration system with a primary focus of attracting skilled migrants to Ireland which will select people as potential citizens", and "a fast-track scheme of temporary workers based on sponsorship by employers". A differentiation of rights, such as access to long-term residency and to family reunification, on the basis of educational qualifications and occupational skills is evident in current policy thinking. (Department of Justice, Equality and Law Reform/Department of Enterprise Trade and Employment, 2005) Immigration is further discussed and in greater depth in Q14.3 of this audit.

Increasing numbers of migrant workers arriving in Ireland came at the same time as the government faced a very significant, but quite distinct set of challenges created by a marked increase in the numbers of people seeking asylum and refugee status.

The Citizenship Referendum 2004

In 2004, the government held a Citizenship Referendum which was overwhelmingly passed, with almost 80 per cent of voters in favour. The turnout of 60 per cent was the highest in any referendum since the Referendum on Divorce in 1995 and the Yes vote higher for any referendum, apart from the Good Friday Agreement, since 1979. (The fact that local and European Parliament elections were also held on the same day may have contributed to the high turnout). Despite this resounding support for the government's proposal, the Citizenship Referendum was highly controversial.

Prior to the referendum, under Article 2 of the Constitution, as revised following the Good Friday Agreement, everyone born on the island of Ireland was entitled to Irish citizenship, including children born of non-Irish nationals in Northern Ireland. Allied to this provision was a strong legal claim on the part of non-Irish parents of a child born in Ireland to remain indefinitely in the state. The effect of the referendum was to remove the universal entitlement of those born on the island of Ireland to claim Irish citizenship.

Criticism of the government with regard to the Citizenship Referendum centred on three main issues. The first was the lack of consultation prior to the referendum. Processes which allow for consultation and analysis, such as consideration by the All-Party Oireachtas Committee on the Constitution and the publication of a Green Paper, were bypassed. In its observations on the proposed referendum, the Irish Human Rights Commission stated its concern that "the process which has been adopted in bringing forward the present proposal for constitutional amendment has not facilitated proper consideration of the human rights issues that the proposal raises". (Irish Human Rights Commission, 2004a: 4)

The second criticism centred on the manner in which the government conducted the debate. Arguments justifying the need for the referendum centred on the allegedly large numbers of non-Irish women arriving unannounced late in pregnancy at the country's maternity hospitals, creating an overload on the maternity system. When the government could find no evidence to support these claims, this line of argument was dropped. Some of the political parties in Northern Ireland were also unhappy that the referendum might signify that the Irish government was stepping back from commitments made under the Good Friday Agreement.

A third criticism was that the case for the referendum was never properly made. The Irish Human Rights Commission stated prior to the referendum that "the onus to demonstrate ... pressing social need and the proportionate and non-discriminatory nature of the [removal of automatic citizenship rights] lies with the government. In the view of the Commission, it is questionable whether that burden has been adequately met." (Irish Human Rights Commission, 2004a: 4) William Binchy, Professor of Law at Trinity said before the referendum, the change in the constitution leads us "in a direction opposite from that proposed by the Constitution Review Group and the Council of Europe's Commission on Racism and Intolerance Convention, both of which recommended that the Constitution be amended to extend the protection of its fundamental rights provisions to non-citizens". (*Irish Times*, 27 May 2004)

THE RIGHTS OF THE CHILD IN IRISH LAW

In November 2006, following a period of intense lobbying by children's rights advocates, the government announced its intention to hold a constitutional referendum on the rights of the child in early 2007. This was deemed necessary by the Report of the Constitutional Review Group in 1996 and more recently by the All Party Oireachtas Committee on the Constitution in 2006, both of which recommended amending the constitution to better provide for the specific rights of the child. In essence, the constitution fails to recognise the child as a person with individual rights and has been interpreted as giving a higher value to the rights of parents than to the rights of children. According to the Law Society's Law Reform Committee, the Irish Constitution "is unique" in that the family unit takes precedence over and above that of individual family members. Moreover, "membership of the constitutional family subordinates the rights of the individual members" and "this is specifically true in relation to the rights of the child." (Law Society's Law Reform Committee, 2006: 51-52)

Although used in only a few instances in Irish courts so far, the European Convention on Human Rights (ECHR) includes some protection for children's rights. For example, the European Court of Human Rights has specifically acknowledged in the context of family life the right of a child to a parental relationship with both married and unmarried parents as set out in the Irish case of *Keegan v Ireland*. (Law Society's Law Reform Committee, 2006: 60)

Ireland ratified the UN Convention on the Rights of the Child in 1992, but it has not yet been given effect in Irish law, despite the recommendation of the UN Committee on the Rights of the Child to do so. (United Nations Committee on the Rights of the Child, 2005: 24)

For many children's rights organisations, the recent case of Baby Ann has confirmed the need to amend the constitution to give express recognition to the rights of the child.

In this case, a girl, Baby Ann, was born in 2004 to young, unmarried parents who put her up for adoption. In November 2004, at the age of three months, Baby Ann was placed with foster parents. An important factor influencing the recent Supreme Court's final ruling to return the child to her natural parents was the decision of Baby Ann's natural parents to marry.

The Baby Ann case highlighted a number of issues: first, it confirmed the central position of the family based on marriage in the constitution. Second, the ruling provided 'real evidence of the virtually invisible status of the child in the constitution". (*Irish Times*, 14 November 2006) Indeed, Supreme Court Justice, Ms McGuinness, noted that the 'only person whose particular rights and interests, constitutional and otherwise, were not separately represented" was the child herself. (*Irish Times*, 14 November 2006)

Q1.2 How far are ethnic, cultural, and gender differences acknowledged, and how well are all sections of society protected from discrimination?

Ireland has recently introduced equality legislation that provides protection against discrimination in employment and services. The Employment Equality Act 1998, the Equal Status Act 2000, and the Equality Act 2004 form the basis of this legislation, and cites nine grounds on which it is illegal to discriminate: namely, gender, marital status, family status, sexual orientation, religion, age, disability, race and membership of the Traveller community.

An impartial Equality Tribunal has been established to decide or mediate complaints under the equality legislation. An independent Equality Authority has responsibility for promoting and defending the rights established in the legislation. Independent data, however, shows that persistent systemic discrimination still affects the various groupings named in the legislation.

This answer focuses in particular on discrimination on the basis of ethnicity, culture and gender. It includes discussion of both religious minorities in Ireland (predominantly Islam) and of Travellers. Issues of discrimination are also discussed in Section Three and Section Four.

DISCRIMINATION IN IRELAND

In August 2005, the Central Statistics Office (CSO) published results of a nationally representative survey on equality and discrimination. (Central Statistics Office, 2005b) According to the survey, which was carried out in the fourth quarter of 2004, around 12 per cent of persons aged 18 or over felt they had experienced discrimination in the two-year period prior to the survey.

Within the population as a whole, age and gender were the most widely reported grounds for discrimination. Over 25 per cent of those who experienced discrimination reported age as the basis for that discrimination, while almost 16 per cent attributed the discrimination to gender. The numbers within the survey who reported discrimination on the grounds of sexual orientation, religious belief and membership of the Traveller community were small.

Table 1.1 Rates of Reported Discrimination within Certain Social Groups

	%
Persons from "other ethnic backgrounds"	31.5
Unemployed persons	28.8
Non-Irish nationals	24.4
Non-Catholics	21.6
Persons with a disability	19.6
Young people aged 18-24	17.6

Source: Compiled from Central Statistics Office, 2005b:1

Moreover, Table 1.1 shows that certain social groups reported higher than average rates of discrimination than the general population. The table shows the percentage of persons within each of these social groups who stated they felt discriminated against in the past two years. Persons from "other ethnic backgrounds" reported the highest rate of discrimination of any social group, followed by unemployed persons, non-Irish nationals, and non-Catholics. Persons with a disability and young people aged 18-24 also reported higher than average rates.

Almost 60 per cent of all persons who reported experiencing discrimination took no action in relation to the discrimination experienced. The groups reporting the highest rates of discrimination were also the groups that were least likely to take action.

Almost 25 per cent of persons who reported experiencing discrimination indicated that they had no understanding of their legal rights from an equality perspective. The groups that reported the highest rates of discrimination were also the groups that reported the least understanding of their rights under Irish equality legislation.

Statistics from the Equality Tribunal partially reflect the findings of the CSO Equality Survey. For the period January to September 2005, the highest number of cases referred to the Equality Tribunal under both the Employment Equality Act and the Equal Status Acts were on the grounds of disability, gender, race, age and membership of the Traveller community. (Table 1.2)

Table 1.2 Number of Cases Referred to Equality Tribunal Jan.-Sep. 2005

	Employment Equality	*Equal Status*	*Total*
Disability	56	32	88
Gender	72	11	83
Race	53	12	65
Age	31	28	59
Traveller		27	27
More than 1 ground	79	44	123

Source: www.equalitytribunal.ie

An increasing body of research is beginning to highlight the limitations of single categories as descriptors of the basis for discrimination. This research focuses on the diversity of experiences within social groups as well as acknowledging the differences between said groups.

For example, while women may be discriminated against in comparison to men, women themselves will have multiple experiences depending on their age, sexuality, disability, religion or ethnicity. This research underlines the importance of raising the visibility of individuals experiencing discrimination based on the multiple identities that they hold, e.g., gay and disabled, and to take account of such multiple discrimination in the formulation of anti-discrimination policies. (Zappone, 2003)

ETHNICITY, CULTURE AND GENDER

Race

The Employment Equality and Equal Status legislation prohibits discrimination in the workplace, and in the provision of goods and services, accommodation and education on the basis of race.

The Equal Status Act 2000 is one of the central planks of the Government's anti-racism policy. Although the delivery of services by public bodies can be challenged under the legislation, the Act does not cover government functions such as the arrest and detention powers of gardaí and immigration officials. Reports from NGOs active in anti-racism in Ireland suggest problems of racism within the administration of government in Ireland. These reports are supported by the findings of a recent study by Amnesty International and the Irish Centre for Human Rights (Beirne and Jaichand, 2006) which found examples of discriminatory laws and policies across the four government departments studied. Particular concerns are expressed with regard to the administration of justice, the failure of the police to respond adequately to racist incidents, and the lack of adequate anti-racism training at all levels of the justice system, including the police, the courts and the prisons.

There are also persistent complaints of discrimination by migrant workers in relation to employment, wherein some employers do not consistently comply with legislation. This situation is exacerbated by the fact that work permits are effectively held by employers rather than employees. (See Q14.3)

Certain legislation currently in force discriminates against non-citizens, e.g., in relation to access to third-level education and in the requirement that non-citizens must carry identification at all times.

The Immigration Act 2004 permits the police to stop foreign nationals at any time and ask for such identification.

While Ireland is a party to the Convention on the Elimination of all Forms of Racial Discrimination (CERD), the government has yet to ratify the International Convention on the Protection of the Rights of All Migrant Workers and Members of their Families. Ireland became party to the EU 2000 Race Discrimination Directive in 2004, although problems arose with accurately tranposing the Directive into Irish law. The Directive, which prohibits direct and indirect racial discrimination in the fields of employment, education, training, health, housing, access to goods and services, is a significant enhancement of both the Employment Act and the Equal Status Act.

Compared with the percentage of votes won by explicitly anti-immigrant and racist parties in many European countries, Ireland is at the low end of any spectrum measuring far-right or anti-immigrant electoral support. (Doyle and Connolly, 2002)

In 2006, the Economic and Social Research Institute issued the first large-scale nationally representative sample of immigrants' experience of racism and discrimination in Ireland. (McGinnity *et al.*, 2006) The survey divided the sample into five regional groups: Black South/Central Africans, White South/Central Africans, North Africans, Asians and non-EU East Europeans. Among the report's findings were:

- that Black South/Central Africans experience the most discrimination of all the groups studied;
- that harassment on the street or in public places is the most common form of discrimination in Ireland. 35 per cent of the whole sample experienced this form of discrimination. Over half of the Black South/Central Africans experienced this form of discrimination;
- that insults or other forms of harassment at work were the second most common form of discrimination, with 32 per cent of those entitled to work experiencing this;
- that 21 per cent of those entitled to work reported discrimination in access to employment. This was most common among Black South/Central Africans (34.5 per cent) and White South/Central Africans (37.1 per cent); and
- that 17.6 per cent of those in contact with the immigration

> services reported that they were badly treated or received poor services. This percentile is the highest incidence of institutional discrimination reported in the survey.

This study was part of a wider study on migrants' experiences of racism in 12 EU Member States. (European Monitoring Centre on Racism and Xenophobia, 2006) The results of the twelve country studies show that migrants experience significant discrimination across the EU. One notable finding is the low overall rate of reporting of discrimination to authorities. Overall, 86 per cent of respondents who experienced discriminatory practices did not report their experience to any authority. The study did not allow accurate comparisons of the extent of discrimination and racism between countries.

Religion

Ireland – the state – is overwhelmingly Catholic. According to the 2002 census, the religious affiliation of the population was just over 88 per cent Catholic.

While a separation exists between the Catholic Church and the structures of State in theory, in practice a Catholic ethos continues to pervade large areas of public life, in particular health and education. Due to the country's historical tradition as a predominantly Catholic country, the majority of those in political office are also Catholic. (See also Q3.3)

Recent immigration has had a marked effect on the diversity of religious beliefs within the Irish population. The number of Muslim people in particular in Ireland has grown significantly over the past decade; in 2002 numbers had quadrupled to 19,147 from the 1991 census.

The Employment Equality and Equal Status legislation prohibits discrimination in the workplace, and in the provision of goods and services, accommodation and education on the basis of religion. However, according to the European Commission against Racism and Intolerance (ECRI) report on Ireland in 2001 (ECRI, 2001) Muslims in Ireland encounter both prejudice and discrimination on the basis of their religion. (www.nccri.com) (The Council visited Ireland again in late 2006 and at the time of writing their report was pending.)

The government-appointed National Consultative Committee on Racism and Interculturalism (NCCRI) Racist Incident Reporting Procedure reported an increase in incidents in which Muslims were targeted in 2001 that were directly related to the September 11 attacks on New York and Washington. Incidents were reported of physical assaults and verbal abuse against individual muslims and also against those perceived to be of Middle-Eastern or Asian origin.

Membership of the Traveller Community

There are around 5,500 Traveller families in Ireland, accounting for 0.6 per cent of the population. (Pavee Point Travellers Centre, 2006) Travellers endure racism on a daily basis in Ireland and, despite decades of campaigning for change, anti-discrimination legislation and government initiatives, remain one of the most marginalised groups within Irish society. Widespread negative stereotypes of Travellers lead to discrimination in all areas of life, including access to accommodation, health and education, and employment.

The Employment Equality Act and Equal Status Act prohibit discrimination in the workplace, and in the provision of goods and services, accommodation and education on the basis of membership of the Traveller community. However legislative barriers remain. Among these is the refusal of the government to recognise Travellers as an ethnic minority. Although a contested recommendation, the UN Committee on the Elimination of Racial Discrimination (CERD) has called upon Ireland to recognise Travellers' distinct ethnicity. The government's refusal to do so has consequences, both for the standing of the Traveller community within Irish society and for Government policy decisions. The government's position is that since Travellers "do not constitute a distinct group from the population as a whole in terms of race, colour, descent, or national and ethnic origin", Travellers do not experience racism. It should be noted that Travellers are included in the government's *National Action Plan Against Racism*, the key policy instrument to tackle racism, and other anti-racism activities. (See also Q3.3)

Two legislative setbacks have occurred since the introduction of the equality legislation. The first is that, in response to lobbying from owners of licensed premises, such as pubs, hotels and restaurants, the government transferred responsibility for adjudication on Equal Status grounds involving licensed premises from the Equality Tribunal to the District Court, effectively undermining the equality legislation in this area. The most common claim under the Equal Status Act had been refusal of access to or service in pubs or hotel bars, which affects Travellers disproportionately.

The Housing (Miscellaneous Provisions) Act 2002 allows the Garda to remove caravans that are camped illegally and charge the owners with trespass. This provision was introduced at a time when many local authorities had yet to fulfil their obligations to provide suitable accommodation. Shortly after the Act was passed a local authority in County Clare enforced the legislation against Travellers who were on the council's own housing waiting list. (See Section Three and Section Four for further discussion of discrimination against Travellers in Ireland.)

Gender

Gender and marital status provided the initial focus for debate on equality and discrimination in Ireland. Until as recently as 1973 married women were not permitted to work in the public service. Legislation to allow access to contraception and file for divorce did not appear until 1979 and 1997 respectively. One of the major social changes in Ireland in recent decades has consequently been a real improvement in the choices available to women and in the overall position of women within Irish society.

With regards to legislative protection against discrimination, the Employment Equality and Equal Status statutes prohibit discrimination in the workplace, and in the provision of goods and services, accommodation and education on the basis of gender. Ireland is also a party to CEDAW, the Convention on the Elimination of All Forms of Discrimination against Women. Under the Convention, Ireland is committed to undertake a series of measures to end discrimination against women in all forms. This commitment includes incorporating the principle of equality of men and women in the legal system, abolishing all discriminatory laws and adopting appropriate laws prohibiting discrimination against women. Although Ireland has ratified CEDAW, the Convention has not been fully incorporated into Irish domestic law.

Ireland is also a party to the Beijing Platform for Action (BPfA), a United Nations action plan to address equality between women and men. The Irish government however has yet to draft a National Plan for Women, as required under the terms of the BPfA.

The 2005 Concluding Comments of the UN CEDAW Committee on Ireland's progress on implementing the Convention highlights the progress made by women in Ireland together with a number of areas of ongoing concern. On the positive side, the proportion of women in employment has increased considerably in recent years, and women now comprise the majority of graduates in many fields at third level, while girls outperform boys at Leaving Certificate level. However, women in general remain concentrated in part-time and low-paid employment in comparison to men, and a pay gap persists, with the average earnings of women remaining less than that of men (United Nations, 2005) and women in Ireland also continue to be at higher risk of poverty than men.

Violence against women and girls, particularly domestic violence and rape, resulting from continuing inequality in power relations between women and men, continues to be a major issue. (National Women's Council of Ireland, 2003) (See also Q3.1, Q8.3, Q11.3, and Section Four)

Q1.3 How much consensus is there on state boundaries and constitutional arrangements?

The national question, as the partition of the island of Ireland into two jurisdictions is known, has been a major and divisive issue on the island since 1921. A campaign of violence in Northern Ireland, often referred to as "the Troubles", began in 1969 and continued for thirty years, resulting in over 3,600 deaths in Northern Ireland. In 1998, a constitutional settlement was reached between the British and Irish governments and the political parties in Northern Ireland by means of the Good Friday Agreement. This Agreement was endorsed in referenda by substantial majorities of the electorate North and South. Difficulties in implementation of the Agreement remain due mainly to differences between the Northern parties, and Northern Ireland remains deeply divided along sectarian lines. However, a broad consensus on state boundaries and constitutional arrangements can now be said to exist in Ireland.

HISTORY SINCE PARTITION

The Government of Ireland Act (1920) and the Anglo-Irish Treaty (1922) partitioned the island of Ireland, creating a regional system of government in Northern Ireland within the UK, and the largely independent Irish Free State.

The exclusion of the six north-eastern counties, Antrim, Armagh, Derry, Down, Fermanagh and Tyrone from the newly independent Free State met with strong resistance from Irish nationalists. In the Free State, a bitter civil war ensued. In Northern Ireland, Irish nationalists, who accounted for approximately one-third of the population, refused to recognise partition. Victory by the pro-Treaty forces in the civil war in 1923 led to a *de facto* acceptance of partition during the remainder of the 1920s. In 1932, through the election of Fianna Fáil under de Valera, the anti-Treaty forces came to power with the support of the Labour Party. The new Fianna Fáil government in practice continued a policy of *de facto* acceptance of partition, alongside an official refusal to sanction it.

This official refusal to accept partition took its most concrete form in Articles 2 and 3 of the new 1937 Constitution, which stated:

- Article 2 "The national territory consists of the whole island of Ireland, its islands and the territorial seas"; and
- Article 3 "Pending the reintegration of the national territory, and without prejudice to the right of the Parliament and Government established by this constitution to exercise jurisdiction over the whole of that territory, the laws enacted by that Parliament shall have the like area and extent of application as the laws of Saorstát Éireann and the like extra-territorial effect."

The "right of the Parliament and Government ... to exercise jurisdiction over the whole of that territory", that is the national territory of the whole island of Ireland, was vehemently rejected by the Unionist community in Northern Ireland, which was and remains today, opposed to unification.

In the decades following partition the two territories essentially developed in isolation from each other, on either side of a border that became increasingly fixed. The relationship between the two continued, until recently, to be one of hostility.

Thus, partition has been one of the major issues in politics on the island since 1921. The issue tragically came to the fore with the outbreak of violence in 1969. Two-thirds of the 3,600 persons who died in Northern Ireland since then were under 35 years of age.

The constitutional position of Northern Ireland was at the heart of the multiparty talks between the Irish and UK governments and the political parties in Northern Ireland, which culminated in the Good Friday Agreement in 1998. As part of the negotiated Agreement the Irish government consented to amendments to Articles 2 & 3 of the Irish Constitution, which removed the territorial claim to Northern

Table 1.3 Deaths from 1969 – 1998 in the Northern Ireland Troubles by Age Grouping

Age group deaths	*Number of deaths*	*as % of total %*	*Cumulative*
0-5	23	.64	.64
6-11	24	.67	1.31
12-17	210	5.84	7.15
18-23	898	24.96	32.11
24-29	697	19.37	51.48
30-35	509	14.15	65.63
36-41	344	9.56	75.19
42-47	261	7.25	82.44
48-53	227	6.31	88.75
54-59	156	4.34	93.09
60-65	112	3.11	96.2
66-71	42	1.17	97.37
72-77	31	0.86	98.23
78-80	8	0.22	98.45
81+	8	0.22	98.67
Age unknown	48	1.33	
Total	3598	100	100

Source: Conflict Archive on the Internet at http: //cain.ulst.ac.uk/index.html

Ireland. The new Articles 2 and 3 enshrine the principle of consent reached in the Agreement, which recognises that:

- at the time of the negotiations the majority of people in Northern Ireland wished it to remain part of the UK;

- that it would be wrong to make any change to the constitutional status of Northern Ireland without the consent of the majority of its people;
- that Irish nationalist aspirations for a united Ireland are legitimate; and
- that any change to the constitutional status of Northern Ireland requires the consent of a majority on both parts of the island.

Articles 2 and 3 and the Good Friday Agreement

The new wording of Articles 2 and 3 following the 1998 Referendum reads:

Article 2
It is the entitlement and birthright of every person born in the island of Ireland, which includes its island and seas, to be part of the Irish Nation. That is also the entitlement of all persons otherwise qualified in accordance with law to be citizens of Ireland. Furthermore, the Irish nation cherishes its special affinity with people of Irish identity living abroad who share its cultural identity and heritage.

Article 3
1. It is the firm wish of the Irish nation, in harmony and friendship to unite all the people who share the territory of the island of Ireland, in all the diversity of their identities and traditions, recognising that a united Ireland shall be brought about only by peaceful means with the consent of a majority of the people, democratically expressed, in both jurisdictions on the island. Until then, the laws enacted by the parliament established by this constitution shall have the like area and extent of application as the laws enacted by the parliament that existed immediately before the coming into operation of this constitution

2. Institutions with executive powers and functions that are shared between those jurisdictions may be established by their respective responsible authorities for stated purposes and may exercise powers and functions in respect of all or any part of the island.

These changes were overwhelmingly endorsed in referenda held on the same day in both the Irish Republic and Northern Ireland.

THE GOOD FRIDAY AGREEMENT

The Good Friday Agreement confirmed the acceptance by the Republic's population of the legitimacy, as distinct from the desirability, of the six-county border of the UK state. But within Northern Ireland, matters are not so simple.

The Northern Ireland Life and Times Survey (NILTS) asked respondents in 2005 a question on the future status of the region vis-à-vis the UK and the Irish Republic. The results indicate the ongoing sectarian divisions within Northern Ireland. The survey categorises respondents by perceived religious affiliation. Of the 23 per cent of respondents who favoured reunification (Table 1.4) just 3 per cent of Protestants advocated reunification, compared with 50 per cent of Catholics.

Table 1.4 Public Opinion on Long-Term Policy for Northern Ireland

Do you think the long-term policy for Northern Ireland should be for it …

	%
...to remain part of the United Kingdom	58
Or, to reunify with the rest of Ireland?	23
(Independent state)	7
Other (specify)	2
(Don't know)	11

Source: Northern Ireland Life and Times, 2005 available online at www.ark.ac.uk/nilt

At the time of its drafting in 1998, the Agreement enjoyed the support of majorities within both communities in Northern Ireland. However support within the Protestant community was not as high as support among Catholics. A *Sunday Times* exit poll revealed that 96 per cent of Catholics had voted in favour of the Agreement compared to only 55 per cent of Protestants. (Elliott, 1999: 143) The overwhelming Catholic endorsement brought the overall "Yes" figure in the North to 71 per cent. This compares with the massive 94 per cent "Yes" vote in the republic.

The split within the Protestant community on the Agreement was mirrored a month later in the Assembly elections in which the pro-Agreement unionists won 30 seats while the anti-Agreement unionists took 28. (Elliot, 1999: 143) This balance shifted further towards the anti-Agreement side as some members of the UUP adopted strong anti-Agreement stances.

Successive NILTS annual data have shown a worrying further haemorrhage of support among Protestants for the Good Friday Agreement since 1998. The 2005 NILTS survey found only 36 per cent of Protestants committed to voting Yes if the referendum were rerun, with 38 per cent against, and approximately 26 per cent uncertain or likely to abstain. A sequence of episodes since 1999 that apparently involved the military wing of the republican movement – gun-running in Florida, a break-in at Castlereagh intelligence centre, alleged assistance to FARC guerrillas in Colombia, and a huge raid on the Northern Bank headquarters in Belfast – allied to the failure of both sets of paramilitaries to decommission their weapons as required, were key factors in this collapse in Protestant confidence.

To make matters worse, less than three years after being set up, the devolved institutions in the North were suspended in October 2002 following allegations of a spying operation involving members of Sinn Féin. One of the Sinn Féin members at the centre of the spying allegations was later found to be an agent for British intelligence services.

Attempts to get the institutions up and running again culminated with the St Andrews Agreement in late 2006, the implementation of which is ongoing.

Opponents of the Good Friday Agreement, however, remain convinced for a variety of reasons that the Agreement cannot work. On the positive side, however, changes which have taken place within Northern Ireland make the renewed outbreak of violent conflict much less likely. The Agreement, which has a strong democratic mandate, still enjoys the overall support of public opinion both North and South, while the two governments remain behind it, determined to overcome temporary obstacles no matter how apparently insurmountable they seem.

In addition, substantial ideological shifts have taken place. The removal of the territorial claim over Northern Ireland and an acceptance of the status quo by the population of the South until such time as a majority in the North so wish, have been matched by an official recognition of a role for the Irish government in the governance of Northern Ireland through the North-South Ministerial Council. There has also been official acceptance by both governments of the right for people born in Northern Ireland to identify themselves as either British or Irish or both.

Q1.4 How far do constitutional and political arrangements enable major societal divisions to be moderated or reconciled?

In contrast to the position in Northern Ireland, and many other countries around the world, political parties in the Republic of Ireland do not break down along the lines of major social division such as religion or ethnicity. Parties in the Republic of Ireland are broadly inclusive. (See Q6.7)

As regards the division between the North and South of Ireland, formal institutions aimed at increasing cross-border cooperation are an important element of the Good Friday Agreement reached in 1998. Under the Agreement six new cross-border implementation bodies and six areas of policy cooperation have been established, along with a North/South Ministerial Council. Political difficulties in October 2002 led to the suspension of the power-sharing Assembly in Northern Ireland. This outcome has meant that while the North-South bodies continue to operate, the North/South Ministerial Council has been unable to meet. During the short period of their operation to date, the North-South bodies, despite difficulties, appear to have functioned well. (Coakley *et al.*, 2006) Further details of the structures and functioning of the North-South Bodies is given in the accompanying volume *Power to the People? Assessing Democracy in Northern Ireland.* (Wilford *et al.*, 2007, forthcoming)

Q1.5 How impartial and inclusive are the procedures for amending the constitution?

Ireland is one of the few countries where every constitutional amendment requires the direct consent of the people, in recognition of the fact that the nation's constitution belongs to the people and not to the government of the day. Every time the government wishes to change or amend the constitution, it must do so by holding a referendum. Turnouts in referenda since 1990 have varied between 29 per cent and 68 per cent. An independent Referendum Commission is established by the government for each referendum. The Commission's remit has varied. Its remit in the most recent referendum in 2004 was to make the electorate aware that a referendum was taking place and to familiarise it with the issues at stake. The conduct of some recent referenda, such as that on the Nice Treaty and Citizenship, raise certain questions with regard to the inclusiveness and impartiality of the procedures for amending the constitution in Ireland.

Referenda in Ireland 1992-2004

Date	*Subject*	*Amendment altered*	*For %*	*Against %*	*Turnout %*
18.6.1992	Permit ratification of Maastricht Treaty of European Union	11th amendment	69.1	30.9	57.3
25.11.1992	Restrict availability of abortion	12th amendment	34.6	65.4	68.2
25.11.1992	Guarantee right to travel	13th amendment	62.4	37.6	68.2
25.11.1992	Guarantee right to information	14th amendment	59.9	40.1	68.1
24.11.1995	Permit legalisation of divorce	15th amendment	50.3	49.7	62.2
28.11.1996	Permit refusal of bail to prevent commission of crime	16th amendment	74.8	25.2	29.2
30.10.1997	Allow breaches to cabinet confidentiality	17th amendment	52.6	47.4	47.2
22.5.1998	Permit ratification of the Amsterdam Treaty of the EU	18th amendment	61.7	38.3	56.2
22.5.1998	Permit changes agreed in the Good Friday Agreement	19th amendment	94.4	5.6	56.3
11.6.1999	Recognise local authorities in the constitution	20th amendment	77.8	22.2	51.1
7.6.2001	Prohibit the death penalty	21st amendment	62.1	37.9	34.8
7.6.2001	Ratify the Rome Statute of the International Criminal Court	23rd amendment	64.2	35.8	34.8
7.6.2001	Ratify the Treaty of Nice	24th amendment	46.1	53.9	34.8
6.3.2002	Give constitutional status to the Protection of Human Life in Pregnancy Act	25th amendment	49.6	50.4	42.9
19.10.2002	Ratify the Treaty of Nice and prohibit the state joining an EU common defence	26th amendment	62.9	37.1	49.5
11.6.2004	Restrict the right to citizenship	27th amendment	79.2	20.8	60.0

Source: Institute of Public Administration, 2005 : 432-433.

The number of referenda held in Ireland has increased in recent years. Since 1990, 16 referenda have been held, compared with 12 in the previous five decades since the adoption of the constitution in 1937. (Institute of Public Administration, 2005)

The list of referenda since 1990 gives an indication of the rapid political and social changes that have taken place during that time. (See Box) Ireland's membership within a changing European Union, ratification of international treaties, dramatic political changes in Northern Ireland, the legalisation of divorce, and ongoing debate concerning abortion make up much of the list. Referenda are seldom as clear-cut as that on the Good Friday Agreement in 1998, which saw a record 94 per cent in favour. More often than not they are both controversial and hotly contested, and result in a "No" vote by a substantial proportion of the population, even when passed. Additionally, some referenda since 1990 have raised a number of questions with regard to the procedures for amending the constitution.

PROCEDURES FOR AMENDING THE CONSTITUTION

The government may not introduce legislation that conflicts with the Irish Constitution, Bunreacht na hÉireann. In order to call a constitutional referendum, a proposal to amend the constitution must first be introduced in the Dáil as a Bill, which must then be passed by both the Dáil and the Seanad before being submitted to the people. If the majority of the votes cast at the referendum are in favour, the Bill is signed by the Irish President and the constitution is then amended. Only Irish citizens aged 18 or over named on the Register of Electors are able to vote. Long-term residents who have not become Irish citizens are unable to vote in referenda.

The Referendum Commission

The Referendum Commission is an independent body, set up by the Referendum Act, 1998 as amended by the Referendum Act, 2001, with a judge or former judge of the Supreme Court or the High Court in the chair. The Referendum Commission can be set up for each referendum at the discretion of the Minister for the Environment, Heritage and Local Government. Once the Commission completes its functions, it furnishes a report within six months on its activities to the

Minister, and then dissolves one month after submission of this report.

In referenda held before 1995, the government of the day felt free to use public funds to exclusively promote its side of the issue. This practice changed in 1995 when the Supreme Court in the McKenna judgement found it to be unconstitutional. Successive governments have faced the challenge of creating a level playing field in referenda ever since. Specifically, the McKenna judgement bars the government from funding a single side in any constitutional referendum, on the ground that the government's use of taxpayers' money to promote one side is "an interference with the democratic process" and "an infringement of the concept of equality which is fundamental to the democratic nature of the State". The judgement in no way precludes government leaders from advocating one side, or political parties and others from spending their own money campaigning for one side in a referendum. Only the spending of public money on one side of a referendum debate is forbidden. (*Irish Times*, 25 May 1998)

As a result, the government of the day has set up a referendum commission for each referendum since 1995 in an attempt to comply with the requirement for a more level playing field. From 1995 to 2001, the function of each commission was to provide information to the public on the arguments made for and against in each case. Following the first Nice Referendum in 2001, however, the government decided that a referendum commission would cease presenting both sides of the issue in referendum campaigns. Under amendments in the Referendum Act 2001, a commission's remit is no longer to present the main arguments for and against a proposal, but simply to make the electorate aware that a referendum is taking place and to familiarise it with the issues at stake. (Gallagher, 2005a: 83)

Social Rights Issues

Abortion has historically been one of the most divisive social issues in Ireland. Up until 1992, abortion was deemed to be unlawful under the constitution. In that year, the Supreme Court ruled that abortion was permitted under certain limited circumstances. This ruling arose from the X case, in which the Attorney General was granted a court injunction to prevent a 14-year-old girl, who had become pregnant as a result of rape, from travelling to the UK for an abortion. The Supreme Court overturned this injunction and declared that the constitution did allow abortion if continued pregnancy placed the woman's life at risk. The risk of suicide on the part of the woman was included as a permissible ground for termination. This ruling led to three referenda in 1992 which sought to overturn the Supreme Court's interpretation. (Coakley and Gallagher, 2005: 292) The referenda showed a clear majority against an absolute ban on abortion, in favour of a woman's right to travel to have an abortion, and in favour of information being made available on abortion services outside the state. A subsequent attempt by the government to eliminate the current limited grounds for abortion was again defeated at referendum in 2002. (Coakley and Gallagher 2005: 27)

These four controversial referenda on abortion since 1992 were necessitated by the adoption of a constitutional prohibition on abortion in 1983. The campaign to insert this amendment was spearheaded by a group, the Pro-Life Amendment Campaign (PLAC), whose membership consisted of mostly conservative members of the Catholic church. The impact of this pressure group on the bringing forward of the constitutional amendment in 1983 has been acknowledged by former Taoiseach, Garret Fitzgerald. (Fitzgerald, 2003) Moreover, women were not consulted during the tortuous process of drafting that amendment. The political leaders and deputy leaders of the political parties were all male; the ministers and opposition spokespersons central to the drafting and passing of the amendment, and the lawyers consulted by the government were all male, as were the main medical sponsors of the amendment, and the Supreme Court judges who would later interpret the amendment. And of course the Catholic hierarchy who staunchly supported the amendment were all male. Throughout the preparatory process, the voices of women were excluded. (O'Reilly, 1988: 83)

The situation remains that abortion is lawful where there is "a real and substantial risk" to the life of the woman. Abortion on any other grounds remains illegal. However, the Oireachtas has not defined in legislation what is meant by "a real and substantial risk." This uncertainty leaves medical practitioners open to legal challenge when they perform abortions for what in their professional medical judgement represents a danger to the life of the mother. At present, around 6,000 Irish women travel to the UK for abortions each year. (Kennedy, 2000: 39-42)

Referenda on Europe

Referenda on European treaties were deemed necessary by a Supreme Court ruling in 1987. Without that ruling, the only referendum to date on Europe would have been the 1972 decision on European Economic Community (EEC) membership.

In the referendum on the Maastricht Treaty in 1992 (The Treaty on European Union) 69 per cent in Ireland voted to ratify the treaty. The Amsterdam Treaty of 1997 saw support from all Irish political parties except the Green Party and Sinn Féin. Sixty-two per cent voted Yes in this referendum.

However, the No vote in the 2001 referendum on the Treaty of Nice came as a considerable shock to both the Irish government and its EU partners, in particular those accession states whose entry into the European Union (EU) depended on ratification of the Treaty. Ireland's rejection of the Treaty, within a climate of broad European support, was an embarrassment for the government. The vote was decisive, with the "No" side winning by almost 54 per cent to 46 per cent.

For political reasons, a second referendum was deemed necessary. The government concluded that the first vote on the Treaty was lost due to a broad range of concerns relating to sovereignty, militarisation and other issues that went beyond the Nice Treaty, and that the low turnout of only 35 per cent of eligible voters in the first referendum justified a second. (*Irish Times*, 13 June 2001)

When a referendum to ratify the revised Treaty of Nice was introduced in 2002, almost 50 per cent of voters turned up at the polls, and this time the "Yes" side won. In the period between the two Nice referenda, a cross-party National Forum on Europe had been established, parliamentary scrutiny of Ireland's European policy had increased, and the Seville Declarations on Irish neutrality and a common defence protocol were secured. (Laffan, 2005: 448) Since one of the key factors in the original No vote was deemed to be a perceived threat to Ireland's neutrality, the wording of the second referendum specifically included a provision that prohibited the state from joining a common EU defence protocol. As such, the government made every effort to ensure the second referendum would pass. However, the decision to "try again" in a second referendum following the "unsatisfactory" results of the first poll raises the question as to if and when governments should have the discretion to either abide by the people's democratic decision or not.

Most recently, the rejection of the proposed European Constitution by France and the Netherlands in 2005 has rendered its fate uncertain. A referendum on whether to ratify the constitution by the Irish electorate has been postponed indefinitely.

The Citizenship Referendum

The most recent referendum, the Citizenship Referendum in 2004, raises further concerns that apply to the conduct of referenda in general. (See Q1.1) Of particular concern is the rationale for the Referendum in the first place. The government's stated reasons for holding it have been questioned by human rights groups including the Irish Council of Civil Liberties. There are also concerns as to how the government conducted the Referendum, not only bypassing consultative processes such as the Oireachtas All Party Committee on the Constitution or the preparation of a Green Paper, and ignoring warnings from many groups, including the Irish Human Rights Commission, about possible consequences, but also by granting only the bare minimum of time allowed by law for the campaign.

Accordingly, recent referenda have given grounds for concern on a number of issues: the freedom of government to introduce referenda without adequate consultation; the effect on vulnerable groups of the successful amendment of the constitution without sufficient prior examination of the impact on human rights from such amendments; and the circumstances under which government can decide to ignore the results of a referendum and "try again".

Two: The Rule of Law and Access to Justice

Are state and society consistently subject to the law?

INTRODUCTION AND SUMMARY

The idea of the rule of law is a long-standing concept that predates the advent of democracy. It expresses the important principle that law, not the arbitrary decisions of particular people, whether in government or not, should rule our lives. Law should also be applied and enforced consistently throughout the territory of the country.

Even more specifically, the concept of the rule of law comprises the following elements:

- no one should be above the law, whatever their position or social standing, and everyone should be equal before it;
- all public officials should be subject to the law, and act within the terms of legally prescribed duties, powers and procedures;
- the judiciary should be institutionally and personally independent of both executive and parliament, so that it can interpret and enforce the law without fear or favour;
- all law should be predictable, and its provisions and penalties known in advance;
- no one should be detained or punished without a specific charge and a fair hearing before a duly constituted court; and
- people should themselves respect the law in their daily lives.

In regard to these principles, Ireland has a largely positive record. Citizens are mostly well-protected by the law and the overall crime rate is low by international standards. The constitution guarantees due process and a fair trial for those charged with criminal offences, and the judicial system is independent of the government. Exceptions where the law does not sufficiently reach include the recent rise in so-called "gangland" killings, and the low rates of prosecution and conviction for a range of crimes affecting women, such as rape, domestic violence and illegal trafficking of immigrants for prostitution. The inadequacy of the legal aid system for civil cases, except in the area of family law, discourages many from pursuing their legitimate claims through the courts. On the other hand, the Ombudsman's office provides effective redress in the event of maladministration by public bodies, despite gaps in its oversight.

Overall, the criminal justice system in Ireland contains a paradox. On the one hand the prisons are relatively full of petty criminals, mostly young male offenders from disadvantaged areas, who are inadequately supported through rehabilitation and hence have a high rate of recidivism. On the other hand, public opinion polls show that people think offenders are treated too leniently, while they themselves are not sufficiently protected, despite one of the lowest crime rates in Europe. At the same time, relatively high minorities in the population demonstrate an ambivalence towards complying with the law by means of so-called "victimless" offences, such as evading income tax or falsely claiming benefits.

Q2.1 How far is the rule of law operative throughout the territory?

In the main, the rule of law is respected in Ireland and operates across the country. Although varying crime statistics give rise to different interpretations, it appears that the crime rate is generally low by international standards.

Both homicide and theft are below the EU average, while levels of rape and heroin abuse are close to the EU average. The number of incidents of murder and manslaughter, however, has increased significantly since the mid-1990s, partly because of a sharp increase in so-called "gangland" murders involving members of drug gangs.

CRIME IN IRELAND

While the rule of law is generally respected throughout Ireland, there are significant exceptions which will be summarised here. Crime in Ireland is also discussed in more detail in later questions, particularly Q3.1 and Q8.4.

Together with the aforementioned rise in the number of incidents of murder and manslaughter, prosecutions for drug related offences in Ireland have also increased since the mid-1990s. There has been a sharp increase over the same period in murders involving members of rival drug gangs which has contributed to the overall increase in murders and manslaughters. Between 1972 and 1991, for example, only two incidents of homicide could be attributed to gangland feuding. (Dooley, 2001: 129) In 2005, up to twenty one such murders took place, accounting for approximately one in three of all homicides in that year. (See Q8.4)

Figures from the UN International Drug Control Programme provide estimates of the prevalence of heroin abuse in the late 1990s for various western European countries. Ireland's prevalence of 0.4 per cent of the population aged 15 to 64 compares with figures of 0.2 per cent in Sweden, around 0.3 per cent in the Netherlands, 0.6 per cent in Switzerland, 0.7 per cent in the UK, 0.8 per cent in Italy and 0.9 per cent in Portugal. (United Nations, 2003: 113) Within Western Europe, Ireland and the UK report the highest levels of ecstacy abuse among 15-16 year olds. (United Nations, 2003: 160)

Interpol data suggests that the overall incidence of rape in Ireland is similar to that in other EU countries. Data from 2002 show Ireland's rate as 105 per million compared to 77 per million in Austria, 176 per million in France, and 236 per million in England and Wales. However, cross-country comparisons of data on the incidence of rape need to be treated with caution, given the problem of endemic underreporting and different definitions of the crime within different jurisdictions. Nonetheless, it is accepted that Ireland does compare poorly when it comes to the proportion of cases of sexual violence that result in criminal prosecutions. (Kilcommins *et al.*, 2004: 122) (See also Q3.1)

The rate of theft in Ireland is less than average compared with other European countries. In 2002, Ireland's rate of 1,485 per 100,000 population was low in comparison to that of Germany (3,820 per 100,000), France (4,225 per 100,000), Scotland (4,265 per 100,000), and

England and Wales (4,542 per 100,000). (Kilcommins *et al.*, 2004: 126)

A number of areas give rise to ongoing concern with regard to the reach of the law. These include: the enforcement of health and safety legislation; the enforcement of employment legislation as a protection against exploitation, particularly of migrant workers; the effectiveness of policing in areas marred by drug gangs; the suspected involvement of paramilitary groups in criminality; white collar crime; corruption; and corporate enforcement. These issues are considered in varying degrees of detail in other areas of the audit.

THE IRISH LEGAL SYSTEM

The Irish legal system is rooted in the tradition of common law. In common law systems, the thousands of decisions delivered by the courts over the centuries continue to enjoy binding legal status by virtue of the doctrine of precedent. The Irish legal system is also influenced by that of Britain in so far as many statutes passed by the British parliament before 1921 continue to have the force of law in Ireland because they have not been revised or repealed by the Oireachtas. The two other principal sources of Irish law are the constitution and legislation. The constitution takes precedence over legislation, which in turn takes precedence over common law. (O'Mahony, 2002: 6) Irish law is also increasingly an extension of the framework of European law by virtue of Ireland's membership of the EU.

An important aspect of the Irish legal system is the doctrine of the separation of powers.

Separation of powers is a model of democracy that involves the separation of political power between three branches of the state: the Executive, the Legislature, and the Judiciary. In Ireland, this tripartite separation of powers model is reflected in the fact that legislative power is vested in the Oireachtas, executive power is exercised by, or on the authority of, government, and judicial power is exercised by the courts. (See also Q2.1) However, Ireland's system differs significantly from the separation of powers model in that the legislature and the executive are not separate, nor intended to be. The executive depends formally on the legislature in the sense that the former is both elected by, and can be voted out of office by, the latter. The major separation of powers in the Irish system therefore exists between the Oireachtas and the executive on the one hand and the judiciary on the other.

The separation of powers between the executive and the judiciary in Ireland can be considered on three levels: in the appointment of judges, in the independence of the courts from executive interference during due process, and in safeguards to ensure the enactment of judicial decisions by the executive. In general, the judiciary in Ireland maintains a strong independence from the Executive, and strong safeguards exist to ensure executive compliance with judicial orders. (See also Q2.3)

THE COURT SYSTEM IN IRELAND

Given that the court system is one of the central pillars of democracy, any understanding of democracy consequently requires an understanding of the role of the judiciary and the system through which the rule of law is protected and enforced.

In general terms, there are two types of court cases under Irish law: civil actions involving conflicts between private individuals, and criminal prosecutions involving private individuals and the state. There are also two main types of criminal offences: summary offences, which are minor offences that can be tried before a judge sitting alone, and indictable offences, which are non-minor offences that must be tried by judge and jury. The constitution specifies that all non-minor offences must, in general, involve a trial by jury.

The Irish court system comprises a three-tier system of courts of first instance, each of which has the jurisdiction to rule on a specific range of cases, along with a court of final appeal. In addition to this basic three-tier system plus a court of final appeal, the court system comprises three further courts: the Special Criminal Court, the Court of Criminal Appeal and the Children's Court. (See Box on following pages)

The Court System In Ireland

The District Court

The District Court is the lowest court in the Irish court system. It has both a criminal and a civil jurisdiction. It is organised on a regional basis with 23 District Court Districts throughout the country. It is presided over by the President of the District Court and 54 District Court Judges. The use of the District Court to hear indictable offences, i.e., cases that must be heard by a judge and jury, should be quite restricted and the District Court should be used primarily to hear relatively minor offences. More than 95 per cent of all criminal offences are minor, and are tried summarily, and the majority of these cases are dealt with in the District Court. (Working Group on the Jurisdiction of the courts, 2003: ix) The civil jurisdiction of the District Court is restricted to hearing cases where the claim or award sought does not exceed €6,348. It has power to award up to this amount in damages. The maximum sentence in the District Court is one year.

The Circuit Court

The Circuit Court, sitting with judge and jury, has jurisdiction to hear all serious offences, with the exception of the very serious offences of murder, rape, aggravated sexual assault, treason and piracy, which must be heard in the High Court.

Civil cases in the Circuit Court are tried by a judge sitting without a jury and are restricted to cases where the damages or compensation sought do not exceed an award of €38,092. The country is divided into eight circuits for the purposes of the Circuit Court. The monetary jurisdiction of the District and Circuit Courts is periodically revised upwards to take account of inflation. Where the Circuit Court deals with family law matters, it is referred to as the Circuit Family Court

The High Court / Central Criminal Court

Under the constitution, the High Court is charged with full original jurisdiction and power to determine all matters of civil or criminal law. An important function of the Court is the judicial review of decisions of the lower courts and the determination of cases stated on points of law referred from those courts. In general, civil cases in the High Court are for substantial compensation or damages, and there is no financial limit to the awards which can be made by the High Court in such cases.

The High Court when hearing criminal matters is known as the Central Criminal Court. The offences of treason, murder, attempted murder, conspiracy to murder, rape and aggravated sexual assault must be heard by the Central Criminal Court.

The Supreme Court

The Supreme Court is the court of final appeal as established under Article 34 of the constitution. The Supreme Court consists of the Chief Justice and seven ordinary judges. It has jurisdiction to hear appeals from all decisions of the High Court and from the Court of Criminal Appeal. The Supreme Court also has the power to decide whether any Bill passed by both Houses of the Oireachtas is repugnant to the constitution, once the legislation has been referred to the court by the President. If the Court finds the Bill is contrary or repugnant to the constitution, it cannot be enacted into law. This finding occurred most recently in February 2005 with the Health (Amendment) (No. 2) Bill 2004.

The Special Criminal Court

The constitution allows for the establishment of special courts sitting without juries to try serious crimes where the ordinary courts are inadequate to secure the effective administration of justice and the preservation of public peace and order, usually where intimidation of jury members is likely. The present Special Criminal Court comprises three judges of the ordinary courts – generally one each from the High Court, Circuit Court and District Court. Cases heard in the Special Criminal Court generally involve "subversive crime", most frequently terrorist offences, although it has been used more recently for offences related to organised crime.

While the Special Criminal Court is outside the normal court system, an appeal against a conviction is possible to the Court of Criminal Appeal, and to the Supreme Court on a point of law.

The Court of Criminal Appeal

The Court of Criminal Appeal hears appeals against conviction or sentence from the Circuit Court and from the Central Criminal Court. Under the Court and Court Officers Act 1995, its powers were to be transferred to the Supreme Court. More than ten years later, however, this transfer has yet to happen.

The Children's Court

The Children's Act 2001, changed the old juvenile justice system which had operated in accordance with the Children's Act of 1908, and reformed the Children's Court. Though sections of the 2001 Act await implementation, those sections providing for the establishment of the Children's Court have been enforced. In actuality, the Children's Court is the District Court, but the latter adopts the former name when dealing with cases involving children.

The District Court operates within the overall court system by considering very large numbers of relatively minor offences. Nonetheless, although the offenses may be relatively minor, the outcomes can have serious impacts on people's lives.

The District Court can also hear indictable offences when both the prosecution and the defence opt for summary trial, i.e., trial without jury. In practice this happens perhaps more often than is desirable. In such cases there may be concerns that the standard of trial afforded within the District Court, for reasons of volume of case load for example, may be less than those afforded within the higher courts. It should be noted that the high usage of imprisonment in Ireland by international standards (see Q2.5) can be attributed in large part to sentencing policies in the District Court.

The need for, and the working of, the Special Criminal Court has been criticised by Irish NGOs, while the UN Human Rights Committee has called for its abolition. (United Nations Human Rights Committee, 2000) Of particular concern is the absence of any restraint on whom the Director of Public Procecutions (DPP) can send for trial to the Special Criminal Court. Indeed, according to the Irish Council for Civil Liberties (ICCL), if this practice continues "the authorities will be able to deprive whoever they like – or rather do not like – of the right to trial by jury". (Irish Council for Civil Liberties, 2002: 3) Moreover, the Special Criminal Court is increasingly used to try cases involving no paramilitary or subversive element. As such, the need for the Special Criminal Court has been called into question, particularly as the level of paramilitary violence has declined substantially in recent years.

The Children's Court has the power to deal with both criminal and civil cases involving offenders up to 16 years, and the power to deal summarily, i.e., without jury, with a child charged with most, but not all, indictable offences. Excluded indictable offences include those which are required to be tried by the Circuit Criminal Court or manslaughter. In these cases, young people are treated like their adult counterparts in the adversarial system.

In practice, however, the workings of the Children's Court have come in for much criticism. One central criticism is that few alternatives to the imposition of a custodial sentence exist. While the Children's Act 2001 says that a period of detention should be imposed only as a measure of last resort, in practice detention is in fact the most frequent outcome. (*Sunday Tribune*, 12 November 2006)

Reform of the Court System

In 2002 the Chief Justice set up a working group on the jurisdiction of the courts in Ireland to carry out a root-and-branch examination of the organisation of the courts system in Ireland. This study was the first comprehensive examination of the courts system in Ireland since it was set up in 1924. In 2003, the Working Group published its report, *The Criminal Jurisdiction of the Courts*. This report did not recommend any departure from the existing structure of the courts. (Working Group on the Jurisdiction of the Courts, 2003)

The functioning of the court system with regard to independence from the executive, equality of access to justice, imprisonment, and public confidence will be dealt with in succeeding questions.

Public Attitudes to the Law

A survey was carried out for the Democratic Audit Ireland project aimed at gauging people's attitudes towards a range of issues on democracy. (Clancy *et al.*, 2005) One such issue was public attitudes towards the rule of law. The survey asked which actions, from a list of breaches of the law, people approved or disapproved of. Across all of the issues tested respondents show differing levels of ambivalence towards the law. (See Table 2.1) By categorising as ambivalent to some degree anyone who does not state that they strongly disapprove of a given breach of the law (i.e., including those who disapprove but only slightly), the survey found that between one in ten people to three in ten people demonstrate some ambivalence towards the law on every issue tested.

Perhaps the most striking finding is that evading income tax was only slightly more disapproved of by respondents than dropping litter.

This ambivalence towards the law was even more marked among those who have completed third-level education. Table 2.2 compares the responses for those who completed primary, second-level and third-level education. With just one exception (falsely claiming benefits), those with third-level education were significantly more ambivalent towards the law than those with primary or second-level education only.

Table 2.1 The Rule of Law

To what extent do you approve or disapprove of the following actions?

	Those Who Categorically Disapprove %	Those Who Show Some Degree of Ambivalence %
Dropping litter	67	28
Evading income tax	69	25
Falsely claiming benefits	75	22
Not reporting damage to parked vehicle	75	20
Taking drugs	76	19
Driving over speed limit	77	19
Buying stolen goods	79	18
Making false insurance claims	83	13
Drinking and driving	85	11

Source: Clancy *et al.*, 2005:15

Among those with third-level education, almost 4 in 10 reported something less than outright disapproval towards evasion of income tax, speeding and taking drugs. It would appear that the most educated in Irish society are those most ambivalent towards the law on a wide range of issues. (Clancy *et al.*, 2005)

Table 2.2 Level of Education and Attitudes to the Rule of Law

	Those Who Show Some Degree of Ambivalence		
	% Primary Only	% Second Level	% Third Level
Evading income tax	31	28	39
Dropping litter	30	32	37
Taking drugs	19	21	37
Driving over speed limit	19	20	37
Not reporting damage to vehicle	27	20	36
Falsely claiming benefits	32	21	31
Buying stolen goods	23	18	27
Drinking and driving	17	12	25
Making false insurance claims	16	13	25

Source: Clancy *et al.*, 2005:16

Q2.2 To what extent are all public officials subject to the rule of law and to transparent rules in the performance of their functions?

Recent decades have seen an unprecedented reform of the legislative framework governing the openness and accountability of public officials. This body of legislation and its implementation in practice is the subject of detailed discussion in later parts of this audit. In this answer, the major legislative developments will be summarised briefly. The effectiveness or otherwise of the legislative reforms will be considered in later answers, as indicated throughout.

This legislative framework now includes legislation on corruption, on the financing of political parties and elections, and on the conduct and responsibilities of ministers and senior civil servants. It also includes codes of practice for the governance of state bodies and for the behaviour of civil servants. Various ombudsman offices have been established to oversee the conduct of public officials, including among others the Ombudsman for Children and the Garda Síochána Ombudsman Commission. A Standards in Public Office Commission has also been established to oversee the conduct of politicians and senior public officials.

Parliamentary committees have been reformed to provide additional powers of oversight of the conduct of ministers, senior department officials and CEOs of public bodies. The proceedings and findings of Tribunals of Inquiry have contributed to a climate of greater accountability.

Finally, Freedom of Information legislation which has been introduced has contributed to greater accountability, despite an amending Act which represented a reversal of certain aspects of citizens' right of access to government information. All of this legislation has done much to improve the ways in which the working of public administration is transparent and subject to "good governance" practices.

There is of course a significant difference between the existence of a law and the implementation of a law. In the context of a democratic audit, this difference has particular relevance with regard to the arbitrary exercise of power by persons in positions of public authority. Increased regulation in recent years has not necessarily resulted in increased control of abuses of power. Enforcement has arguably been weak. The situation is further complicated by the fact that arbitrariness can sometimes be concealed behind a veil of apparent legality. Examples where this is still the case will be discussed in Section Seven and Section Nine, where the degree to which recent legislation is effective in practice will be discussed.

LEGISLATIVE REFORM

Among the legislation that has been introduced with regard to accountability of public officials are:

- The Ombudsman's Act 1980;
- The Comptroller and Auditor General Act 1993 ;
- The Ethics in Public Office Act 1995;
- The Public Service Management Act 1997;
- The Freedom of Information Acts 1997 and 2003;
- The Standards in Public Office Act 2001; and
- The Ombudsman for Children Act 2002. (See Q7.3)

In addition to the Ombudsman and the Children's Ombudsman, the Ombudsman for Pensions was established in 2003; the Financial Services Ombudsman in 2004; the Defence Forces Ombudsman in 2005; while the Garda Síochána Act 2005 established a Garda Síochána Ombudsman Commission. (See Q8.2)

The Standards in Public Office Commission was established under the Standards in Public Office 2001 Act as an independent statutory body with the power to investigate and report on contraventions of that Act. (See Q9.1)

A Code of Practice for the Governance of State Bodies was put in place in 2001, while a Code of Standards and Behaviour for the Civil Service was introduced in 2004.

Parliamentary Oversight

The system of parliamentary committees has undergone reform in recent years. (See also Q7.4 and Q7.5) Following the 1997 general election a new set of committees was created, which closely matches the structure of government departments.

The Public Accounts Committee (PAC) has been widely praised as a model for improved oversight by the committee system, and has been successful on a number of occasions in holding the executive to account.

Dáil Committees can call ministers and department officials to answer under certain circumstances. Accountability is limited however as the 1924 Ministers and Secretaries Act has allowed ministers and Department officials to refuse to answer questions on their performance, particularly when reasons of "commercial confidentiality" or "professional autonomy" were cited as justification. (MacCarthaigh, 2005: 211).

While Dáil Committees have the power to require CEOs of public bodies to attend meetings of the select committee for which they are officially responsible, concerns remain as to the effectiveness of the Dáil to scrutinise the work of public bodies. (Clancy and Murphy, 2006: 32) Parliamentary oversight is dealt with more substantively in Section Seven.

Tribunals of Investigations

A number of ongoing tribunals of inquiry are presently seeking to establish the circumstances surrounding allegations of corruption. (See Q9.2) Tribunals are initiated by the government, rather than the legislature, and cannot determine civil or criminal liability. Recent tribunals include:

- The McCracken Tribunal (1997) which investigated payments from leading business-man Ben Dunne to politicians, including former Taoiseach Charles Haughey;
- The Moriarty Tribunal (1997 –) which is investigating illegal offshore accounts held by politicians and business people to evade the payment of tax;
- The Flood/Mahon Tribunal (1997 –) which is investigating political interference in the planning process, including alleged payments by property developers to politicians for planning decisions favourable to them; and
- The Morris Tribunal (2002 –) which is investigating complaints concerning some gardaí of the Donegal Division.

Other tribunals, which have concluded, include:

- The Lindsay Tribunal (1999 – 2002) which investigated practices of the Blood Transfusion Service which resulted in contaminated blood transfusions that infected patients with HIV and Hepatitis C; and

- The Beef Tribunal (1991-94) into allegations regarding fraud and malpractice in connection with the beef processing industry. This Tribunal served as a catalyst for the introduction of legislation and codes of practice designed to regulate the finances of political parties and to provide state funding for parties. (MacCarthaigh, 2005: 210)

Both the proceedings and the findings of the various tribunals are subject to widespread media coverage and have contributed to greater openness and accountability in recent years.

Anti-Corruption Legislation

Many pieces of legislation relating to corruption, both domestic and international, have been introduced in Ireland in recent years. In 2003, Ireland signed the UN Convention on Corruption, which calls for governments to establish as criminal offences the bribery of national public sector officials, bribery of foreign public sector officials, bribery of officials of public international organisations and bribery of private sector decision-makers, although this convention has not yet been ratified. (Dell, 2005)

Ireland, also in 2003, formally ratified the OECD Convention on Combating Bribery of Foreign Public Officials in International Business Transactions and the Council of Europe's Criminal Law Convention on Corruption, which applies to money laundering and bribery in both the private and public sections. Ireland is also a member of the OECD Working Group on Bribery and the Group of States against Corruption (GRECO).

In addition, no less than 25 pieces of domestic legislation which focus directly or indirectly on corruption have been initiated between 1995 and 2005. (See Q9.1) The principal Irish legislation specifically addressing anti-bribery and corruption includes:

- The Public Bodies Corrupt Practices Act 1889;
- The Prevention of Corruption Acts 1906 and 1916;
- The Ethics in Public Office Act 1995; and
- The Prevention of Corruption (Amendment) Act 2001.

Legislation Governing the Financing of Elections
Since 1995, a series of legislative changes have been implemented regarding the regulation of financing elections. (See Q9.3) These include:

- The Electoral Act, 1997;
- The Local Elections (Disclosure of Donations and Expenditure) Act 1999;
- The Oireachtas (Ministerial and Parliamentary Offices) (Amendment) Act 2001;
- The Prevention of Corruption (Amendment) Act 2001;
- The Electoral Amendment Act 2001; and
- The Proceeds of Crime (Amendment) Act 2005.

The legislation, which for the most part embodies international best practice, has introduced greater transparency and reduced the scope for malpractice around party and election financing, although as discussed in Q9.3, problems in relation to enforcement remain.

Freedom of Information Legislation
Ireland has in place a number of legislative measures to increase public access to government information, the most significant of which is the Freedom of Information Act, 1997. (See Q7.7)

The 1997 Act was developed in accordance with the best international practices and the Information Commissioner is widely regarded as operating effectively and independently. However, the potential of the legislation is limited due to various exemptions and exclusions. Moreover, the legislation is not applied across the public sector as a whole.

An amending Act in 2003 represented a retrenchment of citizens' right of access to government information. (See Q7.7) The overall view however is that despite this revison, the legislation has indeed led to increased accountability to the public. (MacCarthaigh, 2005: 245)

Q2.3 How independent are the courts and judiciary from the executive, and how free are they from all kinds of interference?

In Ireland, judges have a high degree of independence from government. This autonomy exists despite the fact that the government effectively controls the appointment of judges, a practice that differs from judicial appointment procedures elsewhere.

Once appointed, judges are obliged under the constitution and legislation to be independent in the exercise of their judicial functions and subject only to the constitution and the law. This independence is safeguarded by the constitutional provision that a judge is not subject to dismissal and can be removed only by resolutions passed by the Dáil and Seanad. The fact that a judge's remuneration is protected provides another constitutional safeguard.

The freedom of the courts and judiciary from executive interference during the judicial process is also safeguarded in Ireland in a number of ways. Under the Irish system, the judicial process is largely inviolable while in operation, i.e., once begun, it must be allowed to run its course. There are generally high levels of government conformity with judicial orders, together with powers of contempt to deal with attempts by the government to disregard or evade judicial orders. As a result, while judges in Ireland are still largely government appointees, this practice has not prevented them from maintaining a strong independence from the executive.

JUDICIAL INDEPENDENCE

The theoretical and practical independence of the Irish judiciary is well established. The separation of the judicial power is by far the most significant aspect of the separation of powers under the constitution. (Morgan, 2003: 29) The judiciary is also strictly separated from the other branches of government in terms of personnel. Article 35 of the Constitution provides that "[a]ll judges shall be independent in the exercise of their judicial functions and subject only to this constitution and the law." Thus, judges are required to be independent from the executive, the legislature, and parties to the litigation. Judges are specifically barred from being members of either House of Elected Representatives. Nor may they hold "any other office or position of emolument" – although they may be appointed to another office, while remaining a judge, so long as no extra remuneration is involved. (Casey, 2000: 305-6)

Appointment

Article 35.1 of the Constitution states that the judges of the Supreme Court, the High Court and the Circuit and District Courts shall be appointed by the President. However, this Presidential function is to be performed "only on the advice of the government". Therefore, it is effectively the government that controls appointments. (Byrne and McCutcheon, 2001: 121)

No necessary qualifications for judicial appointment are set out in the constitution, and are instead set out in statute. The Courts and Courts Officers Act of 1995 set up procedures that must be followed in making appointments to the bench. This reform was introduced following a scandal in 1994 surrounding the then Taoiseach Albert Reynold's insistence on appointing his Attorney General to the post of "President of the High Court", despite revelations that there had been a nine-month delay by the Office of the Attorney General in processing a warrant for the extradition of a suspected paedophile. This appointment was opposed by members of the Labour Party who were in coalition government with Fianna Fáil and resulted in the fall of the government.

The 1995 Act established a Judicial Appointments Advisory Board (JAAB) consisting of the Chief Justice, the Presidents of the High Court, Circuit Court and District Court, the Attorney General, a practising barrister nominated by the chairman of the Bar Council and a practising solicitor nominated by the President of the Law Society. Members of the JAAB also include "not more than three persons appointed by the Minister who shall be persons engaged in, or having knowledge or experience ... of commerce, finance, administration or persons who have experience as consumers of the services provided by the courts that the Minister considers appropriate".

Having considered the suitability of applicants, the JAAB recommends at least seven persons to the minister for appointment to a vacant judicial office. Due to constitutional constraints, the JAAB's recommendations are not binding on the government. However, under the Act, the government must first consider for appointment those persons recommended by the JAAB. Furthermore, notice of every judicial appointment is published in *Iris Oifigiúil* and must state, if applicable, that the appointee was recommended by the Board. As such, any departure by the government from the Board's recommendations becomes a matter of public record. (Casey, 2000) To date, however, the government has made appointments from the list of names given to it by the JAAB.

However, due to constitutional requirements, one of the weaknesses of the 1995 Act is that the JAAB acts as an advisory board only. While the 1995 Act provides that government "shall firstly consider" the seven persons recommended by the commission, the government is not obliged to select one of these individuals. Thus, the power to select judges remains very firmly in the hands of the executive.

The JAAB also has no role to play in relation to the appointment of the Chief Justice, or the Presidents of the High Court, Circuit Court or District Court, as the government must first consider the qualifications and suitability of *serving* judges of the relevant courts in relation to these positions. The JAAB also has no role to play where a serving judge is appointed to another court. The restriction of the function of the JAAB to the appointment of new judges is likewise very significant in the context of appointments to the Supreme Court – candidates for which are nearly always judges already sitting on other courts. As such, the government has a largely free hand in the selection of candidates for the most influential judicial positions.

While the 1995 Act introduced greater transparency to the judicial appointments process and reduced the "political patronage" nature of judicial appointments, it did not remove the party political element. (Forde, 2004) Indeed, the main effect of the JAAB has arguably been to mute political lobbying, rather than end it, in that once a candidate's name is on the list submitted to the government by the JAAB, they are technically in the running as someone who has met the requirements for the job. At this stage the applicant's friends may lobby ministers in hopes that the cabinet will decide in favour of their candidate. The ample list of potentially suitable candidates also preserves the political elements in judicial appointments, so that those in the legal profession seeking to pursue a judicial career likely feel that a political affiliation is of assistance, as it is not unreasonable to assume that a candidate with a political affiliation to the government will be selected over someone who does not.

In practice it does appear that a political affiliation can help those wishing to pursue a judicial career. According to recent research, four of the judges in the Supreme Court have a Fianna Fáil background, with one Progressive Democrat, one Fine Gael and one Labour. In the High Court, 15 of the judges have a Fianna Fáil background, while two have Progressive Democrat, six Fine Gael, one Labour and six non party. (*Sunday Tribune*, 15 August 2004)

Finally it should be noted that there is also provision under legislation for the appointment of "temporary judges" for fixed terms. Temporary judges enjoy all the constitutional guarantees buttressing their independence during their appointment. (Hogan and Whyte, 2003) A judge appointed on such a basis is usually named to fill the next permanent vacancy in the appropriate court. However, such appointments have generally not been made in recent years.

Remuneration

Article 35.5 of the Constitution states that "[t]he remuneration of a judge shall not be reduced during his continuance in office". In this context, "remuneration" also includes pension entitlements. It was held by the Supreme Court in *McMenamin v. Ireland* that the government is constitutionally obliged to keep judges" remuneration under review, so as to ensure that it does not fall out of line with salary levels in the community generally as to undermine judicial independence. The salaries and pensions of judges are provided for by Act of the Oireachtas.

Immunity

Judges in Ireland benefit from the common law principle of immunity which prevents them from being held liable (in damages or otherwise) with respect to acts carried out in the performance of their judicial duties. Furthermore, the constitution's guarantee of judicial independence would also seem to afford judges a degree of constitutional immunity from suit. (Forde, 2004) However the extent of this judicial immunity is unclear. Nor would such immunity extend where judges knowingly act outside their jurisdiction, or where there has been *mala fides* on the part of a judge. It has also been suggested that the state may be required to indemnify members of the judiciary with regard to costs properly awarded against them in situations in which they have exceeded their immunity.

The court's independence is also protected by the law of contempt of court. Under the common law principles of contempt, a judge who becomes aware of any interference with the administration of justice can order the arrest of the alleged offender, try the charges and impose sentence. (Byrne and McCutcheon, 2001) Conduct which could destroy public confidence in the court can come within the offence of criminal contempt. While "fair and free criticism" of the courts is permitted, "scandalising the court" is not.

The courts have no jurisdiction to punish any member of the Oireachtas for a statement made in the course of a parliamentary debate and, since the relaxation of the Oireachtas' self-imposed *sub judice* rule in 1993, issues may be raised so long as, amongst other considerations, they do not appear to be an attempt by Oireachtas to encroach on the functions of the courts. Furthermore, members of the Oireachtas are under an onus to avoid "if at all possible" comment which might prejudice the outcome of court proceedings. A recent incident also suggests that discussion of remarks made by the courts during the hearing of a case will not be permitted in the Dáil on the basis that the judiciary is independent of the Dáil. In this instance, in February 2003, the Ceann Comhairle refused to allow the Dáil to discuss comments made by a District Court Judge in Longford that, "shopping centres in Longford would introduce a ban on "coloured people" entering their premises if a spate of shoplifting did not stop."

Tenure and Removal from Office

High Court and Supreme Court judges enjoy security of tenure under the constitution, while judges appointed to the District Court and Circuit Court acquire security of tenure under statute. In practice, judges appointed on a permanent basis enjoy security of tenure until they reach retirement age.

The threat of the disciplining, or removal from office, of judges has clear potential implications for the independence of the judiciary. Article 35.4.1 provides that "[a] judge of the Supreme Court or the High Court shall not be removed from office except for stated misbehaviour or incapacity, and then only upon resolutions passed by Dáil Éireann and by Seanad Éireann calling for his removal". Similar protection in statutory form has been extended to the judges of the Circuit Court and District Court. (Byrne and McCutcheon, 2001)

The Sheedy affair in 1999 demonstrated the problem of how judicial impropriety should be investigated and, if necessary, punished. In brief, the affair involved the intervention by a Supreme Court judge with the County Registrar in a case, with a view to having the case relisted before the Circuit Court. (Hogan and Whyte, 2003) A report by the Chief Justice concluded that the actions of both judges had compromised the administration of justice and resulted in both judges resigning their positions shortly after its publication, thereby removing the need for impeachment. However, the case illustrated the confusion surrounding Article 35.4.1, both in terms of the definitions of "stated misbehaviour" and "incapacity" as well as the dearth of procedures set out in relation to impeachment. While such cases are rare, they do illustrate the potential for abuse of the system, and the high level of media coverage they attract can potentially have a major influence on public opinion regarding the independence of the courts.

The lack of clarity of the terms of Article 35.4 has also been thrown into sharp relief in the recent Brian Curtin case. In March 2004, Judge Curtin was acquitted on a charge of knowingly having child pornography. The acquittal was directed by a Circuit Criminal Court judge after he found the warrant which allowed a search of Curtin's home, during which a computer and other materials were seized by gardai, was out of date. (*Irish Times,* 28 October 2005) In May 2004, a motion of removal was set down before the Oireachtas, then adjourned while a Joint Committee was established to inquire into and compile a report to be presented to the Oireachtas on the judge's alleged misbehaviour. Brian Curtin subsequently challenged the establishment of the Committee and the rules under which it operates as unconstitutional before the Supreme Court. This challenge was the first time that the Supreme Court had been asked to decide the precise meaning of Article 35, and whether the procedures set up by the Oireachtas for Judge Curtin conform to its provisions for the removal of a judge. (*Irish Times,* 22 October 2005)

The Supreme Court handed down its judgement in March 2006 and rejected that the power to call a judge as a witness or to produce articles as evidence involved any improper or unconstitutional invasion of judicial power or judicial independence. On the contrary, the court observed that the power is included in the constitution for the purpose of ensuring the fitness and the integrity of the judiciary. Judge Curtin has since retired as a judge, thus terminating the Oireachtas investigation.

Draft legislation to provide for dealing with complaints against members of the judiciary and the *disciplining* (as opposed to impeachment) of judges has been promised since 2002. It is understood that the scheme for a bill called the Judicial Council Bill has been prepared and is now the subject of consultation between the minister and the Attorney General and Chief Justice.

A Final Note

It has been noted that the position of judges is not quite as impregnable as a casual reading of the relevant sections of Article 35 of the Constitution might suggest. (Hogan and Whyte, 2003) This potential vulnerability is particularly true in light of Article 36, which provides that certain matters pertaining to the courts are to be regulated in accordance with law. Such matters include the number of judges of the Supreme Court, the High Court, the remuneration, age of retirement and pension of such judges; the number of judges of all the other courts and their terms of appointment; and the constitution and organisation of the courts, the distribution of jurisdiction and business among the courts and judges, and all matter of procedure.

Indeed, the independence of the courts and their immunity from control of the Oireachtas is not absolute, and could hardly be made so, in light of the fact that most of the actual court structure and court procedure is prescribed, immediately or ultimately, by statute, which the Oireachtas can modify. Ultimately, however, the guarantee of judicial independence set out in Article 35.2 makes it likely that any potential intrusion on the independence of the judiciary would encounter constitutional objections. (Hogan and Whyte, 2003)

SOCIO-ECONOMIC DIVERSITY AND THE JUDICIARY

Irish judges, like their counterparts elsewhere in Western Europe, "tend to come from relatively privileged backgrounds" (Gallagher, 2005a: 90).

As cited in a Seanad debate of 29 April 1999, research in the *Sunday Tribune* gives an indication of the select educational background of judges. Of the then thirty two judges of the High and Supreme Courts, twenty two went to one of just seven secondary schools – Clongowes, Blackrock, St. Mary's, Crescent College, Gonzaga, Glenstal and Belvedere (all male-only, private, fee-paying Catholic-run schools). More recent research in 2005 shows that, of the 29 High Court and Supreme Court judges who participated, 75 per cent described themselves as middle class prior to appointment. (*Sunday Business Post*, 25 December 2005)

This finding contrasts with the socio-economic backgrounds of those who find themselves before the law. One survey showed, for example, that 93 per cent of prisoners in Mountjoy prison come from the two lowest socio-economic classes, while a highly disproportionate number of members of the Travelling community are in prison. (See Q2.5)

As Senator David Norris has pointed out, there is a tragic consistency in the courts in terms of the starkly disparate backgrounds of the two principal sides – those who make the judgements and those upon whom the judgements are executed. (Norris, 1999)

It is interesting to contrast the backgrounds and systems for appointment of judges in Ireland with those of lay magistrates (also known as Justices of the Peace) in England and Wales. Unlike judges, lay magistrates come from a wide range of backgrounds and occupations. They are not required to have formal or academic qualifications, nor do they need knowledge of the law because each Bench sits with a court clerk who is legally qualified. Advisory Committees look at the needs of Benches, not only in terms of the numbers required, but also in terms of maintaining a balance of gender, ethnic origin, where people live, occupation, age and social background. Thus, "representativeness" is an explicit aim for those appointing magistrates. The same cannot be said in relation to the appointment of Irish judges.

Q2.4 How equal and secure is the access to justice, to due process and to redress in the event of maladministration for all?

The right to fair trial is protected under the Irish Constitution, including the right to trial by jury for all non-minor offences, and the right to fair procedure. The constitution has been interpreted by the courts as requiring the state to provide criminal legal aid for defendants who cannot afford legal services. Yet Ireland's civil legal aid scheme remains narrowly focused and underresourced. The scheme excludes so many types of legal issues that it effectively renders ineligible many of those most in need of legal aid. The high cost of litigation is also recognised as one of the major barriers in accessing justice in civil cases.

RIGHT TO FAIR TRIAL

The right to fair trial is protected under the Irish Constitution. Article 38.1 of the Constitution states that "no person shall be tried on any criminal charge save in due course of law". The constitution, in Article 38.5, also specifies that all non-minor offences must, in general, involve trial by jury.

Article 38 1 implies the observance of the demands of fair procedure. It has been judicially accepted that failure to observe these precepts means that an accused has not received a fair trial. These fair procedures include that:

- the accused has a right to be informed of the charges against him;
- the accused must be afforded an adequate opportunity to defend himself;
- the prosecution must give advance notice and full disclosure of all the evidence proposed to be adduced against the accused;
- there is an obligation on the prosecution to call all relevant witnesses;
- the accused must be told of the case against him in a language he understands;
- the accused is entitled to be present throughout his trial;
- the accused has a right to silence, which is corollary of the right to freedom of expression;
- the accused has a constitutional right of access to a solicitor while in custody. In Irish law, there is no right to have a solicitor physically present during the actual questioning process, as distinct from having reasonable access to the solicitor on request during detention; and
- the accused has a right to a speedy trial.

In addition, a case cannot proceed if the accused is incapable of giving adequate instructions or incapable of understanding the proceedings; evidence of previous convictions or bad character are generally not admissible; and where evidence is obtained in violation of an accused's constitutional right, such evidence is unconstitutional, save for extraordinary circumstances which can justify the admission of that evidence.

Finally, a trial will not be a trial in the due course of law if the accused can show that there is a real or serious risk that the trial will be unfair, e.g., where the gardaí fail to seek out or preserve missing evidence which is relevant to the case against the accused or where there is adverse pretrial publicity. (Hogan and Whyte, 2003)

The right to fair trial is also protected under the European Convention on Human Rights (ECHR), which was incorporated into Irish law by the European Convention on Human Rights Act 2003. The finality of an acquittal is also recognised by the Irish courts.

It is important to note that while the Irish courts have held that the right to silence is not absolute (*Heaney v Ireland* [1996]; *Rock v Ireland* [1997]), the ECHR has adopted a different position. Although the right to silence is not expressly guaranteed under the ECHR, it has been inferred that such a right exists under Article 6 of the Convention and the ECHR has confirmed such a right exists in successive cases. Indeed, the ECHR has proven much more robust in defending the right to silence than the Irish Courts; Recent ECHR decisions in *Heaney v Ireland* and *McGuinness v Ireland* have shown that the Irish courts tolerated interference with the right to silence (by way of inferences drawn from the silence) which was unacceptable in human rights terms under the ECHR.

CRIMINAL LEGAL AID

Article 38 of the Constitution, which states that no person should be tried on any criminal charge save in due course of law, has been interpreted by the Supreme Court as requiring the state to provide criminal legal aid for defendants in appropriate cases. (*State (Healy) v Donoghue* [1976]) Appropriate cases are those in which (1) the defendant has insufficient means to pay for legal representation and (2) the serious nature of the offence makes it essential in the interests of justice that the defendant has legal aid in preparation of his/her defence. The Irish criminal legal aid scheme is one whereby private legal practitioners who have placed their names on a legal aid panel are assigned by the courts to defend needy defendants and are subsequently reimbursed by the state.

In all cases where there is a possibility that a custodial sentence may be imposed, the defendant must be informed of their right to legal aid. The defendant may then avail of that right if they so choose. (Whyte, 2002: 257) The defendant has the right to choose a solicitor of his/her choice from the legal aid panel and the court should only refuse the defendant's choice for good reason. If the offence is an indictable one, the legal aid certificate will cover the cost of both a barrister and solicitor. Criminal legal aid is entirely free (unlike civil legal aid) which means that the individual does not have to make any financial contribution to costs.

CIVIL LEGAL AID

In contrast to criminal legal aid, which enjoys constitutional status and has been firmly established through successive court decisions, advances in the recognition of the right to civil legal aid have been far more recent. In *O'Donoghue v Legal Aid Board* and the *Minister for Justice Equality & Law Reform*, a constitutional right to civil legal aid was established in certain limited circumstances. This ruling was followed in *Magee v Farrell and Ireland* in October 2005 in relation to legal aid in certain inquests. Despite these developments, Ireland's civil legal aid scheme remains narrowly focused and underresourced. In contrast to their stance on criminal legal aid, the Irish courts have been reluctant to compel the state to provide civil legal aid, even though the establishment of the right to legal aid through the courts is particularly important because there is no express right to legal aid in the Irish Constitution. It has been speculated that this difference in treatment by the courts might possibly be explained in the fact that the right to criminal legal aid is necessary to protect the right to personal liberty, whereas the rights protected by civil legal aid might not be seen by the judiciary as so central a concern. (Whyte, 2002: 263) (See also introduction to Section Four for discussion of social, economic and cultural rights in Ireland.)

The current statutory civil legal aid system was established under the Civil Legal Aid Act 1995. Under the scheme, solicitors are employed full-time by the state – through the Legal Aid Board – to provide services to litigants. A private practitioner scheme is also in operation whereby work can be outsourced to private solicitors.

A major weakness of the current civil legal aid scheme is that large areas of the law are exempt from the scheme. For example, apart from the Refugee Appeals Tribunal, the scheme does not apply to proceedings before any administrative tribunal, including the Social Welfare Appeals Office, the Employment Appeals Tribunal and the Equality

Tribunal. Thus, applicants for child benefit or social assistance payments – including carer's allowance, disability allowance, non-contributory old age pension, unemployment assistance, or supplementary welfare allowance – who are turned down by the Department of Social and Family Affairs for such payments are not entitled to legal aid if they want to appeal their refusal to the Social Welfare Appeals Office, as such appeals are outside the remit of the Legal Aid Board. Similarly, cases of dismissal or maternity protection heard by the Employment Appeals Tribunal, and cases taken under the Employment Equality Act 1998 and the Equal Status Act before the Equality Tribunal or the Labour Court are outside the scope of the civil legal aid scheme. Despite numerous recommendations to government that the remit of the Legal Aid Board should be extended to include all tribunal work, (Law Society of Ireland, 1991) the blanket exclusion of the right to legal aid in all tribunal cases other than the Refugee Appeals Tribunal remains.

As well as the exclusion of tribunals, the 1995 Act also excludes certain types of law from the civil legal aid scheme altogether, regardless of need. Section 28 (9) provides that legal aid or legal advice should not be provided in any of the following cases (1) defamation (2) land disputes (3) civil matters within the jurisdiction of the District Court i.e., small claims (4) licensing (5) conveyancing (6) election petitions (7) claims made in a representative, fiduciary or official capacity (8) claims brought by a person on behalf of a group of persons to establish a precedent on a particular point of law, i.e., test cases (9) any other group or representative action, i.e., class actions. Of particular note is the fact that, despite attempts by citizens through the courts to establish the right to legal aid in defending against eviction, the right of tenants in such circumstances to legal representation is not yet recognised by the Irish courts.

Finally, while certain areas of the law may not be specifically excluded by legislation, in practice the civil legal aid scheme concentrates very heavily on family law, leaving little resources for legal aid in virtually every other area of law. According to statistics from the Legal Aid Board's Annual Reports, the percentage of non-family law cases has never risen above 3.7 per cent since the schemes instigation in 1995. For example, of 4,460 people granted legal aid in 2003, only 81 were for cases of non-family law. (Free Legal Advice Centres, 2005) The Legal Aid Board's predominant role in family law cases is further evident in the fact that it represents parties in two-thirds of all judicial separation cases and one-third of all divorce cases in the state. (*Irish Times*, 12 March 2005)

The predominance of litigants in family law cases among recipients of legal aid is not due to lack of need in other areas of law. Figures compiled by Free Legal Advice Centres (FLAC) show that the issues dealt with in its legal information and advice centres range from tenants' rights and housing issues, employment law, debt and wills to immigration, social welfare, personal injuries and civil litigation. (Free Legal Advice Centres, 2005: 31) A 2002 study on unmet legal need in Ballymun showed that one in every two legal problems related to housing rights. Other areas of major concern were social welfare problems, domestic violence issues and debt. (Gogan, 2002)

Moreover, further obstacles exist even for those in need of legal aid who are eligible to apply. First entitlement to civil legal aid depends on satisfying both a merits test and a means test. The merits test is based on reasonableness and on the chances of winning the case, and does not take the client's need for legal service as a first priority. Meanwhile, FLAC, in its 2005 report *Access to Justice,* found that the means test is unduly harsh, and impacts most heavily on those who are living in the greatest poverty.

A second barrier for eligible applicants is that, unlike in the criminal legal aid scheme, civil legal aid is not free. All individuals, even those on social welfare, have to pay a contribution towards the legal aid they receive, and even the most financially strapped may end up paying the full cost of the services they receive. (Free Legal Advice Centres, 2005: 41)

Waiting times for hearings and decisions is also an access and fair trial issue. In December 2004, of the 30 law centres throughout the State, 15 had a waiting list of over four months, with eight others reporting a waiting period of over nine months. Wicklow and Finglas in Dublin had a waiting time of 15 months while Newbridge had a waiting time of 20 months. (*Irish Times*, 12 February 2005) In the *O'Donoghue v Legal Aid Board* (2004) case, the plaintiff sought compensation as she had experienced a delay of 24 months between contacting the Legal Aid Board and securing the appointment of a solicitor. The High Court found that the plaintiff's constitutional right to civil legal aid had been infringed by the very long delay in granting her a certificate for legal aid.

The recent O'Donoghue case gives some indications that waiting times are being addressed. Indeed, since O'Donoghue, waiting times have fallen. (Free Legal Advice Centres, 2005) In 2006, the longest waiting time in any centre was 4 months, if the case is not priority, and as low as 2 months in some centres. This has been achieved with the assistance of private practitioners with whom files are placed if the queue at a Law Centre is likely to extend beyond the 4 month self-imposed deadline of the Legal Aid Board, as well as an increase in funding to the Legal Aid Board.

Recently, in response to the perception that the legal system currently allows solicitors and barristers to determine their own legal fees, with little regard to public interest, the Government established an expert group to examine the issue of the costs of civil litigation. The subsequent Haran Report on Legal Costs (Haran, 2006) recommended the establishment of a legal costs regulatory body which would be responsible for determining costs based on an assessment of the amount of work reasonably required in typical cases.

The establishment of the Irish Human Rights Commission (IHRC) and the Equality Authority means that some further limited provision for legal aid has been made. The Irish Human Rights Commission may offer legal advice and assistance in cases raising human rights issues where the person concerned cannot obtain assistance from the Legal Aid Board. The Commission also has power to institute proceedings itself in respect of human rights issues. In addition, the Equality Authority may provide free legal assistance to those making complaints under the Employment Equality Act 1998 and the Equal Status Act 2000, where the case is of strategic importance. In practice however, assistance from either the IHRC and the Equality Authority is available in only a small number of cases, and for the vast number of people obtaining civil legal aid, it is obtained from the Legal Aid Board. (Free Legal Advice Centres, 2005: 9)

Two other schemes that allow for legal aid under specific limited circumstances are a scheme by the Attorney General for *habeus corpus* type cases and a scheme run by the Department of Justice, Equality and Law Reform for cases in which death has occurred in custody.

The European Convention on Human Rights and the EU Charter of Fundamental Rights both recognise the right to legal aid where it is necessary to access justice. However, even in the Civil Legal Aid Act 1995, there is no clear statement that legal aid is an entitlement.

REDRESS FOR MALADMINISTRATION – THE OMBUDSMAN

In the event of maladministration, there are various statutory bodies/tribunals which can enquire into wrongdoing, as well provide redress to individuals (See Q2.1). One of the most powerful statutory bodies which provide a mechanism for citizens to have their complaints against state agencies heard is the Office of the Ombudsman. The Ombudsman has a broad mandate to investigate complaints against, for example, government departments, local authorities, and the Health Service Executive.

The Ombudsman's Office was set up in 1984 to examine complaints from members of the public who feel that they have been unfairly treated in their dealings with public bodies. Since its inception, the Office has dealt with over 62,000 such complaints.

Since the Ombudsman's remit covers public bodies only, there is a long list of those the office cannot investigate. These include private individuals or companies, private practitioners, dentists, opticians, pharmacists and doctors. The Ombudsman also has no remit in connection with the gardaí, the prisons or the courts, nor with the reserved functions of local authorities, i.e., those functions exercised by elected representatives.

For those public bodies within its remit, the Ombudsman cannot deal with complaints relating to recruitment, pay and conditions of employment, with matters which are already the subject of court proceedings, or with matters where there is a right of appeal to an independent tribunal or appeal body.

For those bodies that do fall within its remit, the Ombudsman has extensive powers in law. She can demand any information, document or file from a body complained of and can require any official to give information about a complaint. She can look into all administrative actions, including decisions taken, refusal or failure to take action and administrative procedures. The Ombudsman has no power to force a body to accept or act upon her recommendation but if it does not, she may report the matter to the Houses of the Oireachtas. However, there has been only one occasion since 1984 where a public body has refused to implement or accept the formal recommendations of the Ombudsman, and where the Ombudsman submitted a special report on the matter to both Houses of the Oireachtas. (Ombudsman, 2002)

There are approximately 500 non-departmental public bodies in operation at national level. Of this number, only 16 are explicitly covered by the Ombudsman, while approximately 50 are explicitly excluded. Additionally, just 40 agencies are explicitly subject to the remit of the Children's Ombudsman, which was established in 2004, with 9 bodies explicitly excluded. (Clancy and Murphy, 2006) The Legal Aid Board is not subject to the remit of the Ombudsman. While more recently the remit of the Ombudsman's Office has been extended, significant omissions remain. For example, Ireland's Ombudsman is the only Ombudsman in Europe that has no remit over asylum issues, a situation which the current Ombudsman, Emily O'Reilly, has publicly challenged. (O'Reilly, 2005)

In addition to the Ombudsman and the Children's Ombudsman, the following Ombudsman Offices exist to deal with complaints in specific areas.

- The Ombudsman for Pensions investigates complaints concerning occupational pension schemes and personal retirement savings accounts and can award financial compensation.
- The Financial Services Ombudsman deals with complaints about financial institutions.
- The European Ombudsman was established in 1992 by the Maastricht Treaty to deal with complaints regarding maladministration by EU institutions. The role of the European Ombudsman is to safeguard the fundamental rights of EU citizens by ensuring open and accountable administration within the EU.
- A Defence Forces Ombudsman was appointed by the government in 2005 to address complaints regarding the military authorities.
- The Garda Síochána Act 2005 established a Garda Síochána Ombudsman Commission to investigate complaints against the gardaí.

Evidence suggests however that the Ombudsman's services are largely accessed by middle income groups and that access by those in lower income groups and by those living in disadvantaged areas is low.

Tribunals of inquiry, which are not designed to provide redress, are dealt with under Q9.2.

Q2.5 How far do the criminal justice and penal systems observe due rules of impartial and equitable treatment in their operations?

In this response we focus particularly on the criminal justice and penal system's treatment of those who appear before it, in terms of socio-economic status, young offenders and gender. In order to set the context, an overview of the Irish penal system is outlined. The inappropriate use of prisons for people with mental illness and for immigration related detention is also considered.

By European standards, imprisonment in Ireland is overused as a response to crime, particularly for low level non-violent offences. The prison population continues to rise and has increased by almost 50 per cent since 1994. This same overuse of imprisonment for non-serious offenders has contributed to prison overcrowding and unacceptable conditions within the Irish prison system.

Non-serious offences such as criminal damage, public order, crimes against vehicles and traffic-related offences make up the vast majority of juvenile offences. The age of criminal responsibility was raised from seven to ten in 2006, although children up to twelve can still be charged for the most serious crimes. The age of criminal responsibility still remains one of the lowest of any country in Europe. The imprisonment of young persons under 18 in adult prisons continues.

International comparisons suggest that the prison population in Ireland is drawn in a far more concentrated way from the socially, economically and educationally disadvantaged sections of society than is the case elsewhere. Ninety three per cent of prisoners in Mountjoy Prison, Dublin, for example, come from the two lowest socio-economic classes. In addition, a highly disproportionate number of members of the Travelling community are in prison.

Furthermore, Ireland has been criticised internationally for using prisons in inappropriate ways, such as for holding people with severe mental illness, for immigration-related detention, and for incarcerating children alongside adult prisoners.

FAILURE IN INFORMATION GATHERING

Information regarding various aspects of the criminal justice system is difficult to obtain, and the situation regarding the compilation of statistics has deteriorated in recent years. In fact, "massive data deficits persist. For example, there is no information available on arrests, sentencing patterns or recidivism. There are no studies of police or prison culture. How discretion is exercised by prosecutors has never been probed. The cumulative effect is that the criminal justice terrain remains poorly mapped." (Kilcommins *et al.*, 2004: vii)

This means that policy makers must make decisions in the absence of reliable, current and consistent information.

Also as a result, some of the statistics quoted in this answer are of necessity somewhat dated. In most cases, however, the assumption is that the general trends indicated remain valid.

THE IRISH PENAL SYSTEM

According to statistics from the Prison Service, 84 per cent of those sent to prison in 2003 were imprisoned for non-violent offences. (Lines, 2005) The prison system is also used predominantly to incarcerate people from the most disadvantaged sections of Irish society. A substantial number of prisoners are under 21. (McCullagh, 2002: 606)

International comparators present an anomaly. The detention rate in Ireland, i.e., the number of people in prison at a given point in time, is moderate by European standards. This rate was 85 per 100,000 of population in 2004. (www.iprt.ie) However, the imprisonment rate here, i.e., the number of people sent to prison per year, is one of the highest in Europe. The discrepancy between these two comparators can be explained by the fact that while we imprison higher proportions of our population than other European countries, we keep them in prison for shorter periods of time.

While public and media perceptions may be that Irish prisons are full of violent offenders, the facts are that most of the prison population is made up of petty, if persistent, offenders who mainly commit crimes against property, such as burglary and car theft, without violence. (McCullagh, 2002) Fine defaulters, i.e., people whose offences were not enough to merit prison sentences but who were subsequently imprisoned for being unwilling or unable to pay fines imposed by the courts, also make up a sizeable number of the prison population – almost 1,800 in 2005.

It is also still possible to imprison people in Ireland who have failed to pay a debt for contempt of court. The courts also have the power to detain indefinitely those imprisoned for contempt of court for breach of an injunction, as seen for example in a recent highly publicised case of the detention of protestors against the Shell development in Rossport, Co Mayo.

The prison population in Ireland has increased significantly in recent years. The daily average population in detention in 1994 was 2,121; in 2000 2,948; and in 2005 was 3,151 – an increase of almost 50 per cent since 1994. (www.irishprisons.ie) A large proportion of this increase is due to the consequences of the Bail Act 1997 which resulted from a constitutional amendment to allow the courts to deny bail to prevent the commission of offences. (Kilcommins *et al.*, 2004)

PRISON CONDITIONS

Irish prisons, in general, are overcrowded, lock-up times are unacceptably long, and there is a chronic shortage of rehabilitative services, purposeful work, and educational or recreational services. Drug abuse is common. (O'Mahony, 2002: 550) Successive surveys of prisoners in Mountjoy prison carried out in 1986 and 1996 found that on numerous criteria prison conditions had worsened over that time. (O'Mahony, 2002: 626) Most significantly, the percentage of prisoners who were using or had used hard drugs had increased from 37 per cent to 77 per cent.

The Inspectorate of Prisons and Places of Detention (2004) strongly recommended that Mountjoy Prison should be closed down because of its appalling conditions. Additionally, the Inspector is unhappy about the non-statutory basis of the Inspectorate, and has repeatedly called for this situation to be reversed.

The conditions within the Central Mental Hospital in Dublin meanwhile are such that successive Ministers for Health have acknowledged that the institution is substandard. Plans to build a new Central Mental Hospital on a green-field site alongside a new Mountjoy Prison have sparked further controversy about the appropriateness of housing prisoners and people suffering from mental illness in close proximity.

The European Committee for the Prevention of Torture and Inhuman and Degrading Treatment or Punishment (CPT) visited Irish prisons in May 2002. In its report it found:

- appalling sanitary provisions in some prisons;
- inhumane conditions for prisoners suffering from a mental illness;
- that mental health policy and service provision for prisoners did not comply with international human rights standards; and
- generally isolated reports of ill treatment of prisoners by prison officers and of incidents of violence between prisoners. (European Committee for the Prevention of Torture and Inhuman or Degrading Treatment or Punishment, 2002)

Irish prisons however do not appear to be generally violent places. The report of the CPT found that the majority of prison officers treated prisoners in a humane way. An account of a long-term inmate in St Patricks Institution for juvenile offenders and Mountjoy Prison recounts an absence of antagonism between prison officers and prisoners, and only occasional fights between prisoners. More common is self-directed violence, in the form of self-injury and suicide. Boredom, loneliness, depression and drug use, rather than violence, appear to be the dominant features of prison life. (Howard, 1996) Finally, as previously stated, the excessive use of imprisonment for non-serious offenders continues to contribute to both prison overcrowding and the unacceptable conditions within the Irish prison system.

THE COST OF IMPRISONMENT

The Irish prison system is one of the most expensive in Europe. The average cost of keeping a person in prison per annum was around €79,000 in 2001 in Ireland compared with €45,000 in Scotland and €34,000 in England and Wales. (Parliamentary Question, 2003) Moreover, figures from 2005 show that the average cost of keeping a person in prison for one year had risen to €90,900, and ranged from just over €100,000 in Mountjoy Prison to over €240,000 in Portlaoise Prison. (Irish Prison Service, 2005)

Such high costs raise two questions. First, if the cost of imprisonment is high by European standards, why are prison conditions in Ireland still so poor? Second, given the high costs, is incarceration giving Irish society value for money?

A major factor in the high cost of imprisonment in Ireland is prison overtime, an issue that has been a controversial aspect of prison expenditure in recent years. In 2003, for example, overtime cost €214 million, more than two-thirds of the prison service's €300m budget for that year. This was the case even though the ratio of prison guards to prisoners in Ireland is higher than that in either Britain or France. (*Irish Examiner*, 23 December 2004) Such high expenditure on overtime leaves little resources for improving prison conditions.

Furthermore, a recent analysis has compared the costs of imprisonment in Ireland with the estimated costs of around €1,500 for a community service order, just over €4,000 for supervision during deferment of penalty and just over €6,000 for an offender on a probation order, and concluded that "the high numbers of individuals serving short sentences in Irish prisons raises serious questions about the efficacy and effectiveness of the Irish criminal justice system especially when one considers the relative costs of the sanctions". (Seymour, 2006)

Ireland has a strong orientation towards imprisonment and an underdeveloped scheme of community alternatives.

SOCIO-ECONOMIC PROFILE OF PRISONERS

> *...until such time as ...[there are]...effective programmes to incorporate the marginalised and alienated into ....Irish society, our penal policy will continue to be dominated by the objective of protecting those who are included in the social fabric from those who are effectively excluded.* (Riordan, 1994: 360)

A 1996 study of 124 prisoners in Mountjoy Prison suggests that Irish society uses prisons to selectively punish further those already most disadvantaged within our society. (O'Mahony, 1997)

The findings from this study show the prison population to be drawn predominantly from backgrounds of severe personal and social deprivation:

- 56 per cent of prisoners came from just 6 districts in Dublin noted for their socio-economic deprivation;
- only 20 per cent came from owner-occupied housing with the majority coming from rented Dublin City/Council housing;

- only around 15 per cent came from families where the father had held secure well-paid employment; and
- only 10 per cent came from families with less than four children, pointing to severe pressures for parents already on a low income.

The report also found that:

- 79 per cent had left school by age 15 and only 4 per cent had progressed to Leaving Certificate level or beyond;
- 40 per cent had never held a job for more than 3 months;
- 88 per cent had been unemployed prior to being imprisoned;
- 44 per cent had a sibling who had been imprisoned; and
- only 8 per cent were currently married while around 66 per cent were not currently or had never been in a relationship.

And in terms of physical and mental health:

- 66 per cent were heroin users;
- 30 per cent had tried to commit suicide;
- 33 per cent had had a life-threatening drug overdose;
- 33 per cent had HIV, Hepatitis or both; and
- 20 per cent had been in psychiatric care.
  Source: O'Mahony, 1997

International comparisons suggest that the Irish prison population contains a higher precentage of socially, economically and educationally disadvantaged prisoners than elsewhere. In national prison surveys in the UK, only 41 per cent of prisoners in England and Wales hailed from the two lowest socio-economic classes compared with 93 per cent of prisoners in Mountjoy Prison. In England and Wales only 49 per cent of prisoners were unemployed prior to imprisonment compared to 88 per cent in Mountjoy Prison; only 6 per cent had never worked compared to 27 per cent of Mountjoy prisoners; and only 43 per cent had left school before age 16 compared with 80 per cent of Mountjoy prisoners. (O'Mahony, 2002: 627)

In the United States, an African-American male is seven times more likely to end up in prison than his white fellow citizen. Here in Ireland, the odds stacked against the small sector of severely socio-economically deprived persons who disproportionately contribute to the Irish prison population are comparable to those that handicap such socially excluded African-Americans. (O'Mahony, 2002: 627)

These findings are supported by other reports as far back as the 1985 NESC *Report on the Criminal Justice System: Policy and Performance* which found that "a pattern of early school-leavers and marginal employment or unemployment characterised those persons apprehended by the Garda Síochána for indictable criminal offences." More recent studies (Bacik & O'Connell, 1998: 3; Bacik *et al.*, 1997) found that over 73 per cent of district court defendants come from the most socio-economically deprived areas of Dublin. In addition, a highly disproportionate number of members of the Travelling community are in Irish prisons. (Crowley, 2003: 47)

Furthermore, despite the emergence of large numbers of people involved in tax evasion, these types of offenders by way of contrast generally do not go to prison. Employers who tolerate dangerous working conditions that result in the deaths of their employees similarly manage to avoid prison, as do most of those involved in corporate crime. (McCullagh, 2002: 604) Experience of imprisonment for those who are convicted of white collar crime also differs from those from more disadvantaged backgrounds, as white collar offenders are more often sent to open/semi-open prisons than their disadvantaged counterparts. (O'Donnell, 1998: 43)

THE YOUTH JUSTICE SYSTEM

The Irish juvenile justice system is in a period of transition following the replacement of the Children Act 1908 with the Children Act 2001 as the main legislation governing juvenile justice. (Seymour, 2004) The lack of legislative change for nearly a century has been argued as indicative of political indifference towards this issue, since the foundation of the state, until recently.

Ireland's low level of overall crime is reflected in the low level of recorded juvenile crime. Non-serious offences such as criminal damage, public order, crimes against vehicles and traffic-related offences make up the vast majority of juvenile offences. Drink related offences were the most common offence for which young people were referred to the Garda National Juvenile Office in 2002. A study of almost 1,000 cases in Children's Courts found that the majority of juvenile offenders were male (93 per cent), aged 16 and 17 (67 per cent), who tended to come from backgrounds of disadvantage and poverty. A range of problems were prevalent among the children including mental health issues, behavioural problems, substance abuse, and alcohol and drug addiction. (Kilkelly, 2005)

The Children Act 2001 raises the age of criminal responsibility from 7 to 10, albeit still one of the lowest in Europe. Children up to twelve can still be charged for the most serious crimes. Five special industrial / reformatory schools are available to the courts, with places for up to 15 girls and 216 boys. (O'Dea, 2002) These schools are generally used for children up to the age of 16. Due to lack of suitable facilities, almost 150 young persons – one aged 15 and the rest aged 16 and 17 – were placed in adult prisons during the first ten months of 2005. As a matter of course, children consistently continue to be placed in adult prisons in breach of international treaties on the treatment of juvenile offenders. (*Irish Times*, 18 October 2005) Adult places of detention, moreover, are beyond the remit of the Ombudsman for Children.

GENDER

International research on women's crime show crime rates lower than those committed by men across different societies; crimes committed by women also tend to be less serious and in particular less violent than those by men. (Bacik, 2002: 140) Irish research confirms this variance to be the case in Ireland.

In 1999, for example, women offenders accounted for only 13 per cent of all indictable offences. Similarly, only 17 per cent of juvenile offenders in the Garda Juvenile Diversion Programme in 1999 were female. Of all incidents of homicide between 1992-96, the perpetrators were female in only 10 per cent of cases. Statistics from the Irish Prisons Service show that women make up only 3 per cent of the Irish prison population, a very low rate of female imprisonment by international standards. (Bacik, 2002: 136,146) This figure means that even when convicted, women are less likely to go to prison than men. One possible explanation for this discrepancy may be that factors such as marital status, family background and parenthood may be given greater consideration in the sentencing of women than of men. (Farrington and Morris, 1983)

Justice for Women Victims

Turning now to consider women as victims of crime, the discussion that follows on rape, domestic violence and prostitution illustrates how women are systemically disadvantaged in accessing justice under the present criminal justice and penal systems.

The majority of those who perpetrate crime are men. The majority of those who fall victim to crime, particularly violent crime, are also men. Women on the other hand form the majority of victims of rape, sexual assault and domestic violence. For example, in 2005 (www.garda.ie):

- 84 per cent of victims of murder and manslaughter were male; 16 per cent were female;
- 78 per cent of victims of assault causing harm were male; 22 per cent were female;
- 80 per cent of victims of sexual offences were female; 20 per cent were male; and
- 97 per cent of victims of rape were female; 3 per cent were male.

The report of the Committee on the Elimination of Discrimination against Women in 2005 expressed concerns about the prevalence of violence against women and girls, the low prosecution and conviction rates of perpetrators, the high withdrawal rates of complaints and inadequate funding for providers of support services to victims. (United Nations, 2005)

Rape

Ireland has one of the lowest conviction rates in Europe. As many as 95 per cent of rape cases do not result in a conviction. (Kelly and Regan, 2003)

Moreover, the Courts Service has revealed that the number of rape and aggravated sexual assault cases brought to trial at the Central Criminal Court has fallen by 70 per cent over recent years, with just 37 cases heard in 2004, compared to 130 in 1999. This decline comes despite an increase in the number of calls made to women's helplines and the number of cases reported to gardaí. Alongside the high acquittal rates in contested rape trials, it is understandable that few women engage in and stay with the prosecution process as it currently stands.

Long delays in bringing court proceedings, delays in reporting to the gardai and loss of evidence were identified as the main barriers to successful prosecution of rape. (*Irish Examiner*, 7 February 2005)

Domestic Violence

In 2005, the National Crime Council (NCC) and the Economic and Social Research Institute issued a report on domestic violence in Ireland. The NCC Report clearly identifies at least two serious social problems. The first is a not uncommon pattern of isolated incidents of abusive behaviour within a large number of relationships, which affects as many as 17 per cent of the Irish population. A smaller number, 11 per cent according to the NCC, are subject to much more serious physical assaults and severe psychological abuse.

Overall, the NCC Report found that 15 per cent of women and 6 per cent of men experienced severe abuse from an intimate partner. For cases of severe domestic abuse, therefore, women are more than twice as likely as men to be victims. Less than one in three women who are severely abused report the crime to the gardaí. (National Crime Council, 2005) (See also Q3.1)

Prostitution

It is an offence under the 1993 Sexual Offences Act to loiter with intent to solicit another party for sex. Under Irish law, the public display of prostitution is prohibited but not the act of selling sex. As such, the law is chiefly concerned with keeping prostitution hidden from public view. It follows that legislation can be, and is, enforced much more rigorously against those working as prostitutes, mostly women, than against customers, mostly male.(Bacik, 2002: 153) In a study of thirty women working as prostitutes in Dublin, 80 per cent reported as having been victims of violence. (Haughey and Bacik, 2000)

The trafficking of women for sexual exploitation is a rapidly growing phenomenon worldwide. Trafficking generally involves a woman seeking to leave her home country in search of employment who is approached by a trafficker who then offers to assist her in travelling abroad and securing work. The woman, many of whom may be poor and illiterate, is deceived and finds herself forced into prostitution in a foreign country. Control tactics used by traffickers include regularly moving women around the country, along with threats of physical abuse or deportation. (www.ruhama.ie) This trade in human beings has become an extremely lucrative international business, third only to arms and drugs.

In September 2000, Ireland enacted the Illegal Immigrants Trafficking Act, which makes it a criminal offense to knowingly facilitate the entry of illegal immigrants into the state. However, women and children trafficked into Ireland and subsequently forced into prostitution are in an extremely isolated and vulnerable position. Data on trafficked women forced into prostitution in Ireland is currently scarce. The voluntary group Ruhama which offers support to prostitutes says it met or supported 91 women who were trafficked into Ireland between 2003 and 2004. As prostitutes and illegal immigrants both, these women face criminal prosecution and possible deportation, should they come to the attention of the authorities. Forced into sexual slavery, such women consequently find themselves with little or no recourse to the law in Ireland at present. (*Irish Times*, 13 July 2005)

TREATMENT OF MENTALLY ILL PRISONERS

As outlined elsewhere (Q4.3), the mental health services available to people in Ireland are simply not adequate. The Irish Penal Reform Trust estimates that up to 40 per cent of the prison population may be suffering from some level of psychiatric or psychological illness or disturbance. (Bresnihan, 2001) This finding may be attributed at least in part to the inadequacy of psychiatric and psychological services for the mentally ill, some of whom may eventually find themselves first homeless and finally incarcerated.

The inadequacy of treatment services for people with mental illness continues within the prison system. A report by the Irish Penal Reform Trust in 2001 found that solitary confinement is being used within prisons as a means of responding to the disruptive behaviour of mentally ill prisoners. Among the findings of the report were that 78 per cent of the prisoners put into solitary confinement were mentally ill, some of whom are repeatedly put into solitary confinement. (Bresnihan, 2001)

IMMIGRATION-RELATED DETENTION

Until recently it was rare for people to be detained for immigration-related reasons in Ireland. However, a range of statutory detention powers has been introduced in recent years to allow the detention in Garda stations and prisons of people refused permission to land, people detained during the asylum process and people awaiting deportation. A report in 2005, showed an alarming increase in the number of people held in Irish prisons for immigration-related reasons. (Kelly, 2005)

Over 90 per cent of those detained for immigration-related reasons in Ireland are held in Dublin in either Cloverhill Prison, for male detainees, or the Dochas Centre at Mountjoy Prison, for female detainees. In Cloverhill Prison immigration detainees are held in overcrowded conditions, three to a cell, along with people suspected of criminal offences. They are locked in the cells for more than seventeen hours a day, and significant restrictions, including closed visiting arrangements, are imposed on their contacts with the outside world. At the Dochas Centre immigration detainees are held together with others on remand and convicted prisoners. Some two-thirds of those detained in 2004 were held in prison for more than seven weeks at a time, with very restricted family visitation.

The practice of holding immigration detainees in prisons in Ireland has been repeatedly criticised by authorities including the Council of Europe, the Inspector of Prisons and Places of Detention, the National Prison Chaplains, and the Visiting Committees of both the Dochas Centre and Cloverhill Prison. (Kelly, 2005)

Q2.6 How much confidence do people have in the legal system to deliver fair and effective justice?

Data from public opinion polls suggest a decline in public confidence in the legal system over recent years. This decline is also evident in reported levels of public confidence in the gardaí. A decline in the numbers of citizens reporting crime to the gardaí in recent years would also seem to support these opinion poll findings concerning declining public confidence in the legal system.

PUBLIC CONFIDENCE IN THE LEGAL SYSTEM

According to a 2001 Eurobarometer poll, 55 per cent of Irish people had trust in the legal system. This finding compares with an EU average of 49 per cent. In the same poll, 72 per cent of people reported having trust in the gardaí, somewhat higher than the EU average of 65 per cent. (Eurobarometer, 2001: 8-10)

Yet these figures are at odds with more recent opinion polls carried out by Transparency International and Amárach. The Amárach opinion poll "Quality of Life in Ireland 2004" showed public confidence in a range of institutions surveyed, including the gardaí, the media, and the government, to have fallen sharply between 2001 and 2004. (Amárach Consulting, 2004) For example, in 2001, the percentage of the public that trusted the legal system "a great deal" to be "honest and fair" stood at 12 per cent, whereas by 2004 this public confidence had fallen to 5 per cent.

A measure of public confidence in the legal system can also be found in the results of a Transparency International opinion poll in 2004, which found that the legal system/judiciary was perceived to be the second most corrupt institution in Ireland. The gardaí were viewed as the fourth most corrupt institution. (Transparency International, 2004)

Public concern with aspects of the legal system are also evident in a Garda Síochána public opinion survey in 2005. According to this poll, 71 per cent of respondents believe that the criminal justice system is too lenient on offenders. Fifty-two per cent of respondents agreed with the statement that "the better off you are, the better you are treated by the criminal justice system", and 46 per cent of respondents agreed with the statement that "victims of crime get a raw deal from the courts'.

PUBLIC CONFIDENCE IN THE GARDAÍ

Decline in public confidence in the gardaí is also evident from recent opinion poll surveys. According to a Central Statistics Office (CSO) poll in 2003, over half of respondents (56 per cent) rated the work of the gardaí as either good or very good, compared to a figure of 63 per cent in 1998. Older people tend to be more satisfied with the performance of the gardaí, with almost 66 per cent of persons aged 65 or over rating them either good or very good, compared with 47 per cent of those aged between 18 and 24. (Central Statistics Office, 2004b)

However, the level of public satisfaction with the gardaí fell across all age groups between 1998 and 2003. In addition, there is a tendency for victims of any type of crime to be less pleased with the work of the gardaí, with approximately 25 per cent of these respondents rating the gardaí's performance as poor or very poor. (Central Statistics Office, 2004b)

Public confidence in the gardaí can also be gauged by the percentages of the general public who report crimes to the gardaí. In the quarterly national household survey in July 2004, the CSO discovered that "while there were some exceptions, the level of reporting to the gardaí tended to be down in 2003 compared with the situation in 1998". (Central Statistics Office, 2004b: 3)

In 1998, over 78 per cent of burglaries were reported compared with 70 per cent in 2003. The reporting rate for physical assaults has also decreased with only 51 per cent of incidents being reported in 2003 compared with 57 per cent in 1998. A Garda Síochána public opinion survey in 2005 found 42 per cent of respondents said that they would not report a crime because they believed that the gardaí could not have done anything in response, while 29 per cent of respondents believe that the gardaí would not have been interested.

Although public confidence appears to be declining, results of an *Irish Times*/TNS mrbi opinion survey in February 2004 show a majority of voters retain confidence in the fairness and impartiality of the gardaí. (Table 2.3)

Table 2.3 Public Confidence in Gardaí by Age

	All Ages %	*18-24s %*	*Over 65s %*
Confidence in the force	58	40	74
No confidence	37	54	22
No opinion	5	6	4

Source: Compiled by *Irish Times*, TNS mrbi poll, 10 February 2004

Confidence in the force varies with age. Among 18-24 year olds, the numbers expressing no confidence are very much higher than among older age groups. In the 18-24 age group, 40 per cent have confidence in the fairness and impartiality of the gardaí, while 54 per cent do not. Of those aged over 65, 74 per cent have confidence in the force, while 22 per cent do not. Results from the Garda Síochána public opinion-survey in 2005 paint a more optimistic picture. This survey found that 83 per cent of respondents were satisfied or very satisfied with overall garda service, and 72 per cent agreed with the statement "if my rights were infringed, I could rely on gardaí to help me". While there is little statistical evidence concerning levels of confidence in the gardaí among minority communities, the 2005 garda poll did find that 26 per cent of non-EU nationals polled reported racist incidents to the gardaí.

The gardaí are often the first (and possibly only) contact that many members of the public have with the legal system. Evidence suggests that while public confidence in the gardaí is reasonably high, confidence in the garda complaints procedures is not. (For more on public accountability of the gardaí and reforms of the garda complaints procedures see Q8.2).

Three: Civil and Political Rights

Are civil and political rights equally guaranteed for all?

INTRODUCTION AND SUMMARY

Civil and political rights and freedoms are an essential part of democracy, and critical for the full participation of all in social, cultural and political life. People must be able to express their views and share information freely, to associate together for the discussion and solution of common problems, and to organise collectively to influence government and their fellow citizens. Moreover, people must equally enjoy such rights, whatever their gender, religion, language, ethnic origin, sexual orientation, economic or other status. Minorities of all kinds must feel secure in their freedom to use their own language and to practise their own culture or religion, insofar as this freedom does not transgress the rule of law. Only these conditions provide the political equality necessary to ensure that the needs and views of all sections of society are given voice and taken into account in public policy. Above all, people must be free from intimidation and the fear or threat of violence. Physical security and bodily integrity of the person is the basis for the exercise of all other rights.

It is the responsibility of the state, in the first instance, to protect these rights and freedoms, and to ensure redress when they are violated. But it is also the responsibility of citizens themselves to respect the rights and freedoms of others, and to treat others as of equal dignity even when they differ from themselves.

In Ireland, the physical integrity of the person is mainly respected by state personnel, though concerns continue to be raised about the level of protection of those in prison from self-harm and about the independence of investigations into complaints against the gardaí. Most violence against the person occurs within civil society, particularly in domestic contexts against women, while the services supporting those abused are underfunded. The sexual abuse of children of both genders, including abuse perpetrated in publicly-funded institutions, has been described as one of the country's gravest human rights failings, although advances have recently been made in the system of child protection in response to widespread public concern.

The basic civil and political freedoms – of movement, expression, association, and assembly – are guaranteed by the constitution and effectively protected, though not equally so for all minorities. Travellers are subject to discrimination in many areas of life, and are denied recognition as a distinct ethnic group. Non-EU nationals are subject to restrictions on their freedom of movement. Concerns have been raised about the restrictions on freedom of movement for those subject to Anti Social Behaviour Orders (ASBOs), when these come into effect (mainly young people). Lesbians, gays and bi-sexuals experience a climate of fear in education both as pupils and as teachers in a context where most schools remain under religious control although funded by the taxpayer.

Q3.1 How free are all people from physical violation of their person & from fear of it?

The major threats of physical violation for people living in Ireland come from criminal activity and from fellow citizens in the form of homicide, criminal assault, domestic violence and child sexual abuse. Ireland has a low crime rate, including a low rate of homicide as measured by international standards, although homicide rates have increased significantly within the last decade.

Substantive recent advances have been made in the protection of this basic civil right, particularly in relation to the protection of children. Changes have included increases in child protection legislation, the establishment of the Children's Ombudsman, the 1996 Childcare Act and the development of a National Children's Strategy. However, the conviction rates in Ireland for crimes involving sexual violence remain low by international standards.

Incidents of unlawful incarceration and allegations of unwarranted use of lethal force by the police, although rare, do occur. The Morris Tribunal, a recent inquiry into wrongdoing by gardaí in Donegal, has given prominence to police conduct over recent years. Partly in response, the Garda Síochána Act 2005 now provides more stringent accountability mechanisms for the gardaí, including the establishment of an Ombudsman Commission to provide for independent investigation of complaints against the gardaí, and a Garda Inspectorate to monitor the performance of the Irish police.

HOMICIDE

Two comments can be made concerning homicide in Ireland. First, the number of incidents of murder and manslaughter has increased significantly since the mid-1990s; and, second, despite this increase, the rate of homicide in Ireland for the moment remains below the EU average.

Table 3.1 below shows the number of incidents of murder and homicide for each five year period since 1975.

Table 3.1: Recent Trends in Homicide

	Murder	*Manslaughter*	*Total*
1975-79	104	34	138
1980-84	118	29	147
1985-89	105	37	142
1990-94	113	47	160
1995-99	199	51	250
2000-04	225	45	270

Source: Adapted from Kilcommins *et al.*, 2004: 117; Figures from 2000-2004 from www.garda.ie

It can be seen that a significant increase in the homicide rate, that began around 1995, apparently continues.

Table 3.2 shows the average homicide rate for a number of countries, averaged for the three year period 1998-2000. This table shows that despite a rising homicide rate, Ireland still lies below the EU average for this period, and well below countries outside the EU such as the US, Russia and South Africa.

Table 3.2: Average Homicide Rate 1998-2000

Austria	9.0
Switzerland	10.9
Germany	11.9
Ireland	**13.7**
England and Wales	15.0
France	16.8
EU15 Average	17.0
Spain	27.7
Northern Ireland	31.0
United States	59
Russia	205
South Africa	542

Note: Figures are per million population averaged over the three-year period stated.
Source: Adapted from Barclay and Taveres, 2002, cited in Kilcommins *et al.*, 2004: 119

Research shows that men are much more likely to be victims of homicide and serious criminal assault than women. Around three-quarters of the victims of homicide during 1992-96, for example, were male. (Dooley, cited in O'Connell, 2002:120) In certain other categories of crime however, including domestic violence and rape, women are much more likely to be victims than men.

VIOLENCE AGAINST WOMEN

Domestic Violence

The National Crime Council (NCC) and the Economic and Social Research Institute (ESRI) published a report on domestic violence in Ireland in 2005. Based on a questionnaire conducted with 3000 people, this research clearly identified three different groupings with regard to experiences of domestic violence. The largest group, 72 per cent, reported as having experienced no incidents of domestic abuse. An intermediary group, 17 per cent, reported having experienced isolated physical or emotional incidents, but that these incidents did not have a serious impact on them. A third group, 11 per cent, reported having experienced at some point in their lives a pattern of physical, sexual or emotional abuse that seriously impacted on them. This third group can be distinguished clearly from the second group in terms both of the number of different types of incidents experienced and in the severity of the impact of the abusive behaviour on them.

The NCC/ESRI Report not only confirms earlier findings (Arriaga and Oskamp 1999), but also clearly identifies at least two serious social problems. The first is that as many as 17 per cent of the Irish population report isolated incidents of abusive behaviour within their relationships. The second is that a smaller number, 11 per cent according to the NCC/ESRI report, are subject to much more serious physical assaults and severe psychological abuse. Severe domestic abuse usually comprises a pattern of behaviour involving not only physical violence but also other types of abuse such as sexual abuse and emotional abuse, threats, keeping a partner short of money or preventing them from seeing friends and relatives. Severe domestic abuse is the more visible social problem, leading as it often does to victims requiring medical help or hospitalisation and the use of the courts and refuges to escape the abuser.

Overall, the NCC/ESRI Report found that 15 per cent of women and 6 per cent of men experienced severe abuse from an intimate partner. Thus, for cases of severe domestic abuse, women are more than twice as likely as men to be victims. The report however clearly shows that domestic abuse is something that also affects men.

Public awareness of domestic violence in Ireland is high. According to a Eurobarometer survey, *Europeans and their Views on Domestic Violence against Women 1999*, more Irish respondents think that domestic violence against women is very common or fairly common than respondents for any other EU country.

GOVERNMENT RESPONSE

Relevant legislation on domestic violence includes the Family Law (Maintenance of Spouses and Children) Acts 1976 and 1981, the Domestic Violence Act 1996, and the Domestic Violence (Amendment) Act 2002. The Domestic Violence Act 2002 in particular made considerable progress in improving the law. The categories of victims allowed to avail of protection under the law was extended to include cohabitants, parents of abusive children, siblings and same-sex couples. The Act created a new remedy in the form of a safety order which offers protection for those who do not want the perpetrator barred from the home. One issue of concern within the Act, however, is that in order to avail of a barring order, the applicant must possess an equal or greater beneficial or legal interest in the property from which they seek to bar the respondent. This provision means that in a situation where abusive behaviour clearly warrants a barring order, but the victim's ownership of the property is less than the abuser's, the victim of abuse will be prevented from availing of a barring order. In this case, property rights are accorded higher value in law than the fundamental right to protection from physical violation. (Kennedy, 2003)

A government task force on violence against women was set up in 1996 and the report of the task force published in 1997. This report led to the establishment of a National Steering Committee on Violence Against Women, which aims to develop a coherent strategy for responding to domestic abuse, and other forms of violence against women, involving all the relevant government departments. The Committee consists of government departments, gardaí, legal and medical professionals and NGOs, and operates *via* eight regional committees throughout the country. Following its first annual report in 1999, however, no further periodic reports have been published. (Amnesty International, Irish Section, 2004: 7)

In July 2005, the UN Committee on the Elimination of Discrimination Against Women, noting the "prevalence of violence against women and girls in Ireland", expressed concern at the "low prosecution and conviction rates of perpetrators" and "high withdrawal rates of complaints". It also criticised the "inadequate funding for organisations that provide support services to victims". Core government funding for violence against women services – delivered almost exclusively by community and voluntary organisations – is provided by the Department of Health and Children. The 2006 budget for these services remained fixed at the 2003 allocation, representing a drop in real terms. Underfunding of services means that thousands of domestic violence helpline calls go unanswered every year.

Rape

In theory, Ireland currently has some of the severest penalties in Europe for those convicted of sexual assault. In reality, however, Ireland has a very poor record of convicting rapists, coming bottom of the table of 20 European countries in terms of prosecution. Only 5 per cent of reported rape cases result in conviction in Ireland, compared to 25 per cent in Germany. (Kelly and Regan, 2003) The Rape Crisis Network Ireland (RCNI), with partial funding from the Department of Justice, Equality and Law Reform, has commissioned NUI Galway to undertake research on the high rate of attrition in rape cases in Ireland. According to RCNI, fewer than 1 in 10 complainants in cases concerning sexual violence report their experiences to the criminal justice system at all. The results of this study will be published in 2008. (www.rcni.ie)

CHILD SEXUAL ABUSE

Awareness of child sexual abuse has risen dramatically within the past decade and has led to significant social changes in Irish society. While the physical abuse of children was a familiar issue for child protection professionals during the 1970s, and already the subject of Department of Health guidelines at that time, general awareness of child sexual abuse remained low until well into the 1990s. However, a number of high profile scandals during that same decade resulted in child sexual abuse becoming a highly visible issue, particularly in the news media, which raised public awareness to unprecedented levels.

The first of these major public scandals involving child sexual abuse was the Kilkenny Incest case in 1993, in which a young girl was found to have been assaulted and sexually abused by her father over a period of fifteen years. (McGuinness, 1993) Despite repeated contact with hospitals and Department of Health officials over that period, no concerns were raised during that time, nor investigations made into the source of her injuries or the circumstances of her impregnation by her father.

Initial cases were followed by the exposure of a larger number of incidences of child sexual abuse by members of the Catholic clergy. The Brendan Smyth case in the early 1990s led to a public outcry after it emerged that the church authorities, knowing of allegations against him, had failed to take action, preferring instead to hide his actions and move him from parish to parish. This pattern was repeated with other clerical abusers, who as a result were often again placed in direct contact with children upon their relocation to another parish.

Public outrage was further fuelled by the initial refusal of the church authorities to recognise the traumatic effects of child sexual abuse, and by vigorous action on the part of church authorities to protect their financial assets. As an indication of the scale of abuse, the Archdiocese of Dublin alone has recorded complaints against approximately 60 priests over the last 40 years, and had by 2005 paid over €2.5 million in compensation to approximately 40 people. (*Irish Times*, 23 May 2005)

In the late 1990s, the RTÉ television series "States of Fear" uncovered the extent of physical and sexual abuse of children during the 1950s and 1960s in Ireland's Industrial Schools and schools for children with disabilities. The series showed both the scale of the abuse of some of the most vulnerable children in Ireland and the institutional culture which allowed such abuse to continue unchallenged over a period of decades. Most of these schools, while run by religious orders, were funded by the State and were subject to regular statutory inspections. The exposure of the extent of child sexual and physical abuse perpetrated by members of the religious orders has contributed significantly to a dramatic decline in the standing of the Catholic church in Irish society.

As a direct result of the public outcry over the States of Fear series, the government established the Commission to Inquire into Child Abuse. The development of the National Children's Strategy, the implementation in 1996 of the 1991 Child Care Act, the Social Services Inspectorate and the Office of Ombudsman for Children are likewise at least a partial consequence of the public awareness of child sexual abuse that arose from these scandals.

In October 2005, the Ferns Inquiry report on clerical sex abuse in the diocese of Ferns identified more than 100 allegations of child sexual abuse levelled between 1962 and 2002 against 21 priests in the Catholic Church. The report was not only critical of church authorities, the Garda Siochána and the then Health Board in relation to the handling of complaints of sex abuse, but also highlighted ongoing gaps in child protection, and the need for government to place mandatory reporting of child abuse on a legislative basis. In response, the Ombudsman for Children said that changes in policy and practice were required to include interagency working, professional codes of conduct and care in the appointment of staff with unsupervised access to children.

The child sexual abuse scandals involving both church and state uncovered in recent years constitute one of Ireland's gravest human rights failings since the foundation of the State, and constitute a direct violation of the fundamental rights of children under the UN Convention on the Rights of the Child, as ratified by Ireland in 1992. As one commentator has put it, "Any judgement of performance [on the history of Ireland's provision for and treatment of children and young people] is likely to return a verdict that verges on the "appalling." No past government emerges with credit. Successive governments have abandoned, neglected, and utterly failed children." (Keenan 2001)

While public attention has focused largely on sexual abuse by members of the clergy, it has also served to highlight the occurrence of child sexual abuse within society as a whole. The SAVI Report on Sexual Abuse and Violence in Ireland, in a survey of over 3,000 randomly selected adults released in 2002, found that one in five women and one in six men reported experiencing contact sexual abuse in childhood. (Dublin Rape Crisis Centre, 2002)

The survey found that most sexual abuse in childhood and adolescence occurred in the prepubescent period. Sixty-two per cent of boys and 67 per cent of girls who reported abuse in childhood said it occurred before they were 12 years old. Overall, while the risks for men decreased from childhood to adult life, the level of serious sexual crimes committed against women remained similar from childhood through adulthood. One in five women and one in ten men reported experiencing contact sexual assault as adults. More than 4 in 10 women and over a quarter of men reported some form of sexual abuse or assault in their lifetime. In over half the adult cases of abuse, alcohol was involved.

In the SAVI Report, legal redress for sexual crimes was found to be the exception rather than the rule. Of 38 people who reported child sexual abuse to the gardaí, six cases resulted in court proceedings with four convictions.

VIOLENCE AGAINST MINORITY GROUPS

Issues of violence have been raised by groups representing minorities within Irish society, e.g., racial violence, attacks on gay people and violence against Travellers. The issue of bullying within schools is particularly severe for both gay and Traveller youth and is partly responsible for higher rates of early school leaving and subsequent poverty for the individuals affected.

It is questionable whether the balance between freedom of expression and the rights of others not to be subject to incitement to hatred has been correctly struck in Ireland. The Prohibition of Incitement to Hatred Act 1989 is Ireland's only piece of legislation solely devoted to the prohibition of hate crimes. The Act was placed under review in 2000 as no convictions had been made under it at that time. This review was suspended in 2005 and the Department of Justice appears to have changed its mind as to the need for further review. In its report to the Committee on the Elimination of All Forms of Racial Discrimination in 2004, the Department stated that "since [2000] 18 cases have been taken [under the Act] resulting in 7 convictions. This growing body of case law under the Act suggests that application of the legislation is adapting to the growing problem of racism in Ireland".

At the same time, the unavailability for analysis in the public domain of District Court judgements which are not reported, coupled with the lack of an interim report on the effectiveness of this Act, mean that the state's conclusions concerning the effectiveness of the 1989 Act cannot be objectively tested. The government has indicated that it shall review the Act as part of its compliance with the Council of Europe's Framework Decision on Racism and Xenophobia. However, this Framework Decision has yet to be finalised, and Ireland will have a further two years following its adoption to make relevant amendments to Irish law. So revision of the 1989 Act could be as far as five years away. (See also Q1.2)

PHYSICAL VIOLATION BY THE STATE

The failure of safeguards to ensure the lawful conduct of law enforcement officers within the gardaí has been a focus of attention in recent years. In 2006, the Morris Tribunal issued its final report into wrongdoing by gardaí in Donegal. (See Q8.2) The major focus of the Tribunal was an investigation by the gardaí in Donegal of the death of a local man, Richie Barron. The Tribunal found that the gardaí in Donegal both fabricated evidence and conducted a campaign of harassment against a number of men, despite the fact that all evidence in the case pointed to a hit-and-run accident as the cause of Barron's death.

The Tribunal also found, in its first report published in July 2004, that two senior gardaí in Donegal had orchestrated hoax explosive finds in the border region in order to boost their careers. As a result of the inquiry, one garda was sacked by the cabinet, while the second resigned.

The Tribunal was also scathing in its criticism of individual members of the gardaí within the division in Donegal for consistently lying under oath to the Tribunal throughout its investigations. Possible prosecutions of individual garda members for attempting to pervert the course of justice are pending.

The conviction of another Donegal man on charges of knowingly allowing drugs to be sold in his nightclub was overturned in 2002. The man's sentence of three years in prison was also overturned but only after he had been wrongly incarcerated and served 27 months in prison. (*Irish Times*, 28 October 2004)

With regard to unlawful incarceration, Ireland has also been criticized by international human rights monitors for the inappropriate use of prisons for people with mental illness, for immigration-related detention, and for holding children in prison alongside adults. (See Q2.5)

Physical Ill-Treatment of Detainees by Police

In its report of its 2002 visit to Ireland, the European Committee for the Prevention of Torture and Inhuman or Degrading Treatment or Punishment (CPT) found "a not inconsiderable number of persons [who] claimed that they had been physically ill-treated by police officers" and concluded: "The number and consistency of the allegations of ill-treatment heard by the delegation lend them credibility. Moreover, in some cases, the delegation's doctors gathered medical evidence consistent with the allegations received."

The CPT found that legal requirements in the Criminal Justice Act, 1984 (Treatment of Persons in Custody in Garda Síochána Stations) Regulations, 1987 pertaining to the use of force and allegations of ill-treatment, were not always complied with by gardaí. It urged "the Irish authorities to intensify their efforts to prevent ill-treatment by the police", cautioning that, "if the relevant authorities do not take effective action upon complaints referred to them, those minded to ill-treat persons deprived of their liberty will quickly come to believe that they can act with impunity".

Use of Lethal Force by the Police

Amnesty International has expressed concern about several incidents of killings in disputed circumstances by the security forces, in which the police officers may have used excessive force. (Amnesty International (Irish Section), 2000)

The major issue in relation to investigations into such killings concerns the general practice, prior to the Garda Síochána Act 2005, of police officers investigating the actions of other police officers. A recent example was the killing of two men, one of whom was armed, by gardaí during the attempted robbery of a post office in Lusk, Co. Dublin. A third armed man was arrested. No independent inquiry followed this incident; instead a Garda Chief Superintendent was appointed to investigate the circumstances surrounding the shootings.

The introduction of the Garda Síochána Act 2005 established an Ombudsman Commission to investigate complaints against the gardaí. This development is positive, but it remains to be seen how effective the new procedures will be in practice. (See Q8.2 for further discussion.)

Use of Lethal Force in Self Defence

There is currently a focus of public attention on the use of lethal force in self-defence, due in large part to a high-profile case in which a farmer was found guilty of manslaughter of another man who had intruded on his farm. (*Irish Times*, 13 October 2006) The defendant's conviction for manslaughter was quashed on appeal by the Court of Criminal Appeal in late 2006. The retrial returned a verdict of not guilty. This case has highlighted the fact that current Irish law is not clear on a number of issues relating on the one hand to the rights of citizens to protect themselves and their property, and on the other, the rights of all persons (including intruders) not to be subjected to unreasonable (including lethal) force, and has led to concerns about the balance of rights between property and the person.

A recent consultation paper published by the Law Reform Commission points to a number of problems with regard to the use of force in self-defence. (Law Reform Commission, 2006a)

Under the plea of legitimate defence, a person charged with murder who can show that they acted in self-defence will be found not guilty. Legitimate defence accordingly provides a justification for what would otherwise be unlawful actions. Under current Irish law, legitimate defence and the use of lethal force are based on the concept of reasonableness. In addition, Irish law also currently obliges citizens to avail of any opportunity for retreat, and only if this avenue is not available can the right of self-defence be asserted. Additionally, while it is clear that "self-defence applies if the defender themselves or their family is under threat by the attacker", it remains less clear if self-defence can similarly apply when the defender's property is under threat. (Law Reform Commission, 2006a) As a result, the Commission has recommended that this ambiguity be clarified in law and that the extent of force that may legitimately be used be clearly set out.

Q3.2 How effective and equal is the protection of the freedoms of movement, expression, association and assembly?

In general, Irish citizens enjoy extensive rights to freedom of movement, expression, association and assembly. Freedom of movement is a human right enshrined in the Irish Constitution. Indeed Irish citizens enjoy some of the greatest freedoms of movement of any people in the world. Non-EU nationals living in Ireland, by contrast, face a range of restrictions on their rights of freedom to travel.

Freedom of expression is protected under Article 40 of the constitution which guarantees a person's right to freely express their convictions and opinions. According to international monitors, Ireland enjoys one of the freest presses in the world, although this freedom is restricted by the effects of a prohibitive libel law on journalistic freedom.

Freedoms of association and assembly are likewise widely respected, although concerns exist with regard to the application of certain pieces of legislation to Travellers and young people.

FREEDOM OF MOVEMENT

Freedom of movement is a human right that is widely respected in the Irish Constitution. The right to freedom of movement asserts that a citizen of a state has the right to leave that state, travel wherever the citizen is welcome, and, with proper documentation, return to that state at any time. Freedom of movement also includes the right to travel to, reside in, and work in, any part of the state that the citizen so wishes without interference. Under the constitution, enhanced by EU treaties, Irish citizens have a right to move freely within the state, a broader right to travel abroad and return, and a right to obtain a passport for the purpose of travelling.

Freedom of movement is also protected under Article 12 of the International Covenant on Civil and Political Rights, where it is seen as an indispensable condition for the free development of a person.

The freedoms of movement both enjoyed and widely exercised by Irish citizens are on a par with those of any people in the world. As part of the European Union, Irish citizens have the right to travel, reside and work anywhere in the other Member States. Holders of Irish passports enjoy virtually unrestricted access to international travel, and experience no widespread denials for visas on economic or other grounds.

A rare instance of the state attempting to restrict a citizen's freedom of movement was the X case in 1992. In this case, the Attorney General attempted to restrain a pregnant young girl from travelling abroad, to the United Kingdom, for an abortion. This interference by the state was in direct contravention of various international conventions on freedom of movement and the right to travel, and was overturned by the High Court. A constitutional amendment was carried in 1992 to provide that the right to life of the unborn could not be invoked to prevent anyone exercising their freedom to travel.

Freedom of movement for non-EU nationals living and working in Ireland, however, is far more restricted than for Irish and other EU citizens. Non-Irish nationals from within the EU enjoy the full rights of freedom to travel enjoyed by Irish citizens, including rights to travel, work and live in any of the other EU states, and rights to be joined or visited by members of their families. Non-EU nationals by contrast face a range of restrictions on their rights of freedom to travel. For example, non-EU nationals employed on the work permit scheme are effectively tied to a single employer, and accordingly do not have freedom to travel within the state for purposes of work and abode. In addition, non-EU nationals do not enjoy unrestricted access to travel within the EU and must secure separate visas for each EU country they wish to visit. The rights for non-EU nationals in Ireland to be visited by members of their family are also restricted, as applications for such visits remain at the discretion of the Minister for Justice, Equality and Law Reform. In addition, Ireland is not participating in the EU Long Term Residents Directive which came into force in January 2006, and which enables people with long-term residency status (as opposed to citizenship status) within any EU Member State to move between Member States for work, study and other reasons.

FREEDOM OF EXPRESSION

Unlike Ireland, most of the world's citizens do not live in countries that enjoy open, vibrant and unrestricted media.

Every year, the organisation Reporters Without Borders (RWB) establishes a ranking of countries in terms of their freedom of the press. The list is based on responses to surveys sent to journalists who are members of partner organisations of the RWB, as well as related specialists such as researchers, jurists and human rights activists. The survey asks questions about direct attacks on journalists and the media as well as other indirect sources of pressure against the free press, such as pressure on journalists by non-governmental groups. In 2006, Finland, Iceland, the Netherlands and Ireland all shared the top of the list as most free. (Reporters Without Borders, 2006)

A separate study, by Freedom House, confirms Ireland's high level of press freedom by international standards. Entitled *Freedom of the Press 2005: A Global Survey of Media Independence*, the study assesses the degree of print, broadcast, and internet freedom in every country in the world. (Deutsch Karlekar, 2005) Each country is assessed as Free, Partly Free, or Not Free by examining three broad categories: the legal environment in which media operate, political influences on reporting and access to information, and economic pressures on content and the dissemination of news.

Out of the 194 countries and territories examined, 75 (39 per cent) were rated Free, 50 (26 per cent) were rated Partly Free and 69 (35 per cent) were rated Not Free. In terms of population, 17 per cent of the world's inhabitants live in countries that enjoy a Free press, while 38 per cent have a Partly Free press and 45 per cent have a Not Free press. Needless to say, Ireland is rated in the Free category.

Western Europe boasts the highest level of press freedom worldwide, and Ireland, rated at 14th place in the study, enjoys one of the freest media in the world.

Table 3.3 Freedom of the Press 2005

Region	*Free*	*Partly Free*	*Not Free*
Western Europe	23	2	0
Americas	17	14	4
Central & Eastern Europe & Former Soviet Union	8	9	10
Asia Pacific	18	7	15
Sub-Saharan Africa	8	16	24
Middle East & North Africa	1	2	16

Source: Adapted from Deutsch Karlekar, 2005 (www.freedomhouse.org)

Freedom of expression, of which media expression constitutes a major aspect, is set down in Article 40 of the Constitution. Article 40 guarantees a person's right to freely express their convictions and opinions. Freedom of expression is also protected under the International Covenant on Civil and Political Rights.

Limitations

There are some limitations on freedom of expression in Ireland. The Irish Constitution states that the state should try to ensure that the radio, the press and the cinema are not used to undermine public order or morality or the authority of the state, and makes it an offence to publish or utter blasphemous, seditious or indecent matter. The Censorship of Publications Acts and the Censorship of Films Acts allows censorship of publications such as books and films.

Current issues of concern regarding freedom of expression are those of libel law and press regulation, and the rights of citizens to investigate the workings of the state.

Two aspects of current libel law are seen as having a detrimental effect on the freedom of the press in Ireland to operate in the public interest. The first is the assumption in a libel action that a published statement is false until proven otherwise, which places the onus on the media to prove in a court of law the truth of the statement. Yet the production of evidence in a court of law may require journalists to expose their sources, which they very often cannot do. The person suing for libel on the other hand can issue proceedings for defamation in respect of perfectly truthful statements in the knowledge that he does not have to give evidence and face cross-examination. The second problem with existing legislation is that, unlike other areas of civil law, it is not a defence in a libel case to show that reasonable care was taken and that the journalist and the newspaper or broadcaster behaved professionally in attempting to establish the truth of what was said.

Current libel law not only makes the press wary about what it publishes, but can sometimes lead to the non-publication of stories that it knows to be true, but which the press feels it may lose in a court of law if a libel action were to be taken. Specific examples of the imbalance to the current law include the following.

- RTÉ apologised to Larry Goodman's Anglo-Irish Beef company, disciplined two journalists and stated that "no Irish meat company was abusing the export credit insurance scheme". The story later turned out to be true.
- The *Evening Press* carried an apology along with a statement from AIB that a story printed in the paper regarding Charles Haughey being €1 million in debt to the bank was "outlandishly inaccurate". However in later years, as a result of Tribunal inquiries, it emerged that the story was accurate.
- When Labour TD Joan Burton made a speech about planning corruption in Dublin County Council, both she and the *Irish Independent* which covered her speech, received two sets of libel threats. One came from a legal firm representing all of the Fine Gael councillors and the other from a firm acting for all the Fianna Fáil councillors. The letters asked both Joan Burton and the *Irish Independent* to state publicly that "there were absolutely no grounds to suggest bribery or corruption in Dublin County Council". Once again, the story later turned out to be true.

While other attempts to block publication have been unsuccessful, the danger with Irish libel law as it stands is the opportunity it affords wrongdoers to bully the media, political representatives and others into self-censorship with the threat of a libel action that in turn forces them to retract or spike stories even – or perhaps especially – when the stories are true. (*Irish Times*, 20 October 2003; 21 October 2003; 23 October 2003) That said, reform of Ireland's libel law is pending. (See Section Ten)

In their 2004 Annual Report on Ireland, Reporters Without Borders raise both the safety of journalists investigating crime and amendments to the freedom of information law that limit journalists' access to public records as matters of concern. (Reporters Without Borders, 2004) The Democracy Commission Report in 2005 also highlighted the concentration of media ownership in Ireland as an additional issue of concern. (Harris, 2005) (See also Section Ten)

Freedom of expression also includes the right to receive information, and Ireland's legislation with respect to Freedom of Information is discussed in Section Ten. A discussion of recent legislation that restricts charities from advocacy activity is considered in Q3.4.

FREEDOMS OF ASSOCIATION AND ASSEMBLY

Concerns continue to be expressed about the use of the 1994 Public Order Act against political protesters. The most contentious parts of the Act are Sections 6 and 8. Section 6 makes it an offence to "use threatening, abusive or insulting words or behaviour", while Section 8 gives wide powers to the gardaí to remove anyone who is "loitering" or using "threatening, abusive or insulting words". Those convicted under even relatively minor charges can acquire criminal records which in turn can restrict their freedom to travel internationally.

Policing of public demonstrations came under public scrutiny following television footage of excessive use of force by gardaí at a "Reclaim the Streets" rally in 2002. Seven gardaí faced assault charges following the incident and one was convicted. Concerns on the part of the gardaí about the dangers involved in policing civil unrest were highlighted in riots in Dublin in February 2006 when six gardaí were injured and required hospital treatment.

Another issue of concern relates to the law of trespass and how it impacts on the Traveller community. Under Section 24 of the Housing (Miscellaneous Provisions) Act 2002, members of the Traveller community who occupy land without the owner's consent are liable to criminal trespass charges. The Human Rights Commission has warned that this Act may violate key constitutional provisions including the right to travel, and the rights of assembly and association. In addition, a ministerial commitment that the law would not be used against families waiting for accommodation has been broken by evictions in Cork, Lucan and Ennis. Furthermore, these evictions occur even as local councils are in breach of their statutory duty to provide accommodation for Travellers. (*Irish Times*, 2 July 2002; 24 July 2002; 16 November 2002)

Provisions in the Criminal Justice Act 2006 to introduce Anti-Social Behaviour Orders (ASBOs) have also raised concerns about the possible effects of such orders on rights to freedom of assembly and freedom of movement for young people. ASBOs are orders which can be applied for by a local authority or the police against a young person for alleged antisocial behaviour. In practice, the young person can be summoned before a court on a civil rather than a criminal basis and an ASBO can made against them. If the ASBO is breached the young person may then be arrested at which point the matter becomes a criminal one.

Opponents of ASBOs believe they involve a disproportionate interference with personal and private rights and civil liberties, are inconsistent with the European Convention on Human Rights and the Convention of the Rights of the Child, and will be used disproportionately against young people in deprived areas. The introduction of ASBOs in the UK has led to an increase in the numbers of young people in custody there and, while the legislation in Ireland differs, fears have been expressed that they may have a similar effect when introduced in Ireland. The Irish Human Rights Commission has expressed concern that the effect of ASBOs, if used other than in cases of last resort, would be to draw a wider category of children into the formal criminal justice system. (Irish Human Rights Commission, 2006)

Q3.3 How secure is the freedom for all to practise their own religion, language, or culture?

Ireland ranks in the top six countries globally on religious freedom. The free profession and practice of religion are guaranteed to all under the Irish Constitution. Rights to practise religion and culture are also protected in a number of international human rights instruments to which Ireland is a party. Despite these legal protections, the predominance of a single faith, Catholicism, in large areas of public life, most particularly education, raises issues of equality for non-Catholics and for other groups. The predominance of religious schooling means that parents in Ireland effectively cannot choose secular schooling for their children. While the rights of gay, lesbian and bisexual people in Ireland have improved substantially in recent years, the predominance of religious schooling perpetuates negative stereotypes and fails to protect children from homophobic bullying in Irish schools.

The government continues to refuse to recognise Travellers as a distinct ethnic group, despite calls for it to do so by the UN Committee on the Elimination of all forms of Racial Discrimination in 2005.

Irish is recognised in the Irish Constitution as the first official language of the Republic of Ireland, with English being recognised as the second official language. Various legislative protections for the language exist. Language can be a major problem for ethnic minority groups in accessing public services in Ireland and more needs to be done on a national level to ensure equal access to public services for those members of Irish society whose command of English, in particular, is low.

LEGAL PROTECTIONS

The freedom to practice religion is protected in Irish law. Article 44 of the Irish Constitution states the following: that freedom of conscience and the free profession and practice of religion are guaranteed to every citizen; that the state guarantees not to endow any religion; that the state shall not make any discrimination on the ground of religious profession, belief or status; and that legislation providing state aid for schools shall not discriminate between schools under the management of different religious denominations.

In addition, the Employment Equality Act 1998 prohibits discrimination in relation to employment on the basis of nine discriminatory grounds, including religion. The Equal Status Act 2000 prohibits discrimination outside of the employment context, such as in education or provision of goods, based on the same nine grounds.

Rights to practice religion and culture are also protected in a number of international human rights instruments to which Ireland is a party. These include:

- the European Convention on Human Rights;
- the International Covenant on Civil and Political Rights;
- the International Convention on the Elimination of All Forms of Racial Discrimination; and
- the UN Declaration on the Rights of Persons Belonging to National or Ethnic, Religious and Linguistic Minorities.

Protection for minority languages is also covered by the European Charter for Regional or Minority Languages 1992. Under the International Covenant on Civil and Political Rights this protection extends to those professing belief in no religion, including humanist, atheist, rationalist and agnostic beliefs.

According to the UN Special Rapporteur of the Commission on Human Rights on Freedom of Religion or Belief, the recognised International Standards for freedom of religion are the Universal Declaration of Human Rights, the International Covenant on Civil and Political Rights and the Declaration on the Elimination of All Forms of Intolerance and of Discrimination Based on Religion or Belief. The Special Rapporteur of the Commission on Human Rights on freedom of religion or belief has not yet made a country visit to Ireland.

According to the Freedom House millennial survey on global religious freedom, Ireland ranks in the top six countries globally with regard to freedom to practise religion, along with Finland, the Netherlands, Norway, Estonia and the United States. (Freedom House, 2000)

Issues of concern do arise, however, due to the predominant historical role of the Catholic Church in Ireland and the continued dominance of religious-run institutions in large areas of public life, particularly education and health. Although the influence of the Catholic Church has declined markedly in recent years, issues remain with regard to the integration of new non-Catholic migrants to Ireland and on the inequalities affecting gay, lesbian and bisexual people in Ireland. At the same time, the rights of gay, lesbian and bisexual people in Ireland have improved substantially in recent years.

THE PREDOMINANCE OF RELIGIOUS SCHOOLING

According to the 2002 census, the religious affiliation of the population was just over 88 per cent Catholic, around 3 per cent Church of Ireland, 0.5 per cent Presbyterian, 0.25 per cent Methodist, 0.5 per cent Muslim, and less than 0.1 per cent Jewish. Approximately 6 per cent of the population were members of other religions or had no specific religious belief.

Recent years have seen a significant increase in the number of migrants coming to live and work in Ireland. The scale of migration has had a significant impact on the country's population. The proportion of foreign-born persons living in Ireland rose from 6 per cent in 2002 to just under 10 per cent in 2006. (Central Statistics Office, 2006c: 9) The 2002 Census identifies five main regions of origin for non-nationals living here. These are the UK and EU (3.4 per cent of the total population), Asia (0.5 per cent), Africa (0.5 per cent), non EU Europe (0.5 per cent) and the United States (0.3 per cent). As a result, Ireland has over a very short period of time become an ethnically diverse country, with a rising number of non-Catholic immigrants and asylum seekers. Muslim and Orthodox Christian communities in particular continue to grow, especially in Dublin.

At the same time that religious diversity has increased from immigration, the Catholic Church in Ireland has experienced a marked decline in church attendance, and in the number of people professing beliefs in keeping with Catholic teachings.

Most primary and secondary schools are still denominational, and their boards of management are controlled, at least partially, by the Catholic Church. For example, 99 per cent of approximately 3,150 primary schools in Ireland are under the patronage of denominational patrons. Although parents may exempt their children from religious instruction, it is an integral part of the curriculum and is jealously guarded by all religious denominations.

On a practical level, the Catholic Church exerts its power over the school system in three main ways. In the first instance, bishops have control over the appointment of principals and teachers. The local bishop directly appoints the three-member group that interviews and recommends for employment the principals of the schools in his area. He also similarly controls the appointment of all other teachers through his selection of the interview boards for these positions. Since

2002, prior sanction from the Minister for Education is no longer required before successful candidates are notified. However, prior approval from the bishop remains an absolute requirement. The salaries of these teachers are paid entirely by the State.

Second, the Department of Education's rules for boards of management of national schools lay out the powers of the bishops. They "may manage the school personally or may nominate a suitable person or body of persons to act as manager". (www.education.ie) The rules also indicate that the bishop "may at any time resume the direct management of the school or may nominate another manager". In the case where the schools are run by boards of management, the bishops directly appoint the chair of the board and one other member. Recent figures indicate that local priests chair close to three-quarters of these boards. Names of other nominees, e.g., teacher, parents and community representatives, must be forwarded to the bishop, who then formally appoints the entire board.

Third, most of the schools are owned by the Catholic Church, despite the heavy investment by the taxpayer in the buildings.

A further example of the continuing influence of the Catholic Church in education is contained in exemptions from aspects of Ireland's equality legislation for religious-run institutions. The Employment Equality Act 1998 permits educational institutions with a religious ethos to give preferential treatment on the grounds of religion to an employee or prospective employee where it is reasonable to do so in order to maintain the ethos of the institution. The Act also allows religious institutions to take action where it is reasonably necessary to prevent staff from undermining the religious ethos of the institution. In addition, a school whose objective is to provide education that promotes certain religious values is legally allowed to admit a student of a particular religious denomination in preference to other students. Such a school can also refuse to admit a student who is not of that religion, provided it can prove that this refusal is essential to maintain the ethos of the school. (Equality Authority, 2003) The overwhelming majority of schools in the country are therefore legally allowed to discriminate against both staff and pupils on the grounds of religion.

In 2005, the United Nations Committee on the Elimination of All Forms of Racial Discrimination urged the Irish government to amend the existing legislative framework so that no discrimination may take place as regards the admission of pupils of any religions in all schools.

The Committee also urged the Irish government to promote the establishment of non-denominational or multidenominational schools. Under the terms of the constitution, the Department of Education must, and does, provide equal funding to schools of different religious denominations, such as an Islamic school in Dublin. However, the establishment of non-denominational or multidenominational schools is a separate issue. Despite a constitutional imperative under Article 42.1.3 to provide choice for families who do not wish to educate their children in a denominational school, virtually all public funding continues to be channelled into religious-run institutions. (See Q4.3)

Revelations on child sexual abuse by members of the clergy over the past decade would appear to have had a profound effect on public attitudes towards the control of schools by church authorities, and there are signs of an incipient debate on the merits or otherwise of the predominance of religious schooling. Writing in the *Irish Times* following the publication of the Ferns Report, journalist Mary Raftery argues, "when it comes to handing over control of virtually our entire education system to an organisation whose very essence has now been unambiguously identified as a risk factor for children, then it is time to reassess in the most fundamental manner the way in which we as a state organise the education of our young people". (*Irish Times*, 27 October 2005)

A survey undertaken on behalf of the Department of Education in November 2004 showed a strong majority of people in favour of the removal of Catholic Church (and other church) power over education. Almost two-thirds of people (61 per cent) felt schools should be non-denominational. Only 25 per cent favoured maintaining religious control of schools. (Kellaghan *et al.*, 2004) (*Irish Times*, 3 November 2005)

GAY RIGHTS IN IRELAND

Homosexuality was decriminalised in Ireland in 1993. In the relatively short period since, Ireland has passed equality legislation which sees the state now ranked among the top nations worldwide in its legislative protection against discrimination on the grounds of sexual orientation. Ireland is also one of only nine countries with legislation which makes the vilification of homosexual people a criminal offence. (International Lesbian and Gay Association, 2004)

Jeffrey Dudgeon in Northern Ireland and David Norris in the Republic of Ireland have been instrumental in the international gay and lesbian rights movement in their work to establish gay and lesbian rights in European and international law. By taking cases to the European Court of Human Rights, both men succeeded in overturning laws criminalizing gay male sexual activity in the North and South of Ireland respectively. Moreover their cases have established precedence leading to the decriminalisation of homosexuality elsewhere in Europe.

Despite Ireland's generally-positive record with regard to support for international law and its own anti-discrimination legislation at home, concerns remain with regard to non-recognition of same sex partnerships, lack of adoption rights for same sex couples, current exemptions for religious-run institutions from equality legislation, and the conditions for gay and lesbian youth within Ireland's schools. (See also Q3.3)

Moreover, the recent introduction of civil partnerships for same-sex partners in the UK including Northern Ireland under the Civil Partnership Act 2004 has major implications for Ireland. Under the Good Friday Agreement, the Irish Government is required to ensure "at least an equivalent level of protection of human rights as will pertain in Northern Ireland". The government has committed to introducing partnership legislation and a Working Group on Domestic Partnership recommended substantive and comprehensive legal recognition of same-sex relationships in its report issued in late 2006. (Working Group on Domestic Partnership, 2006) (See also Q3.3)

Meanwhile, a same-sex couple, Dr Katherine Zappone and Dr Ann Louise Gilligan, are currently seeking recognition of their marriage in Ireland. The couple, who were married in a civil ceremony in Canada in 2003, took proceedings against the Revenue Commissioners and the Attorney General in 2006. More specifically, the couple sought a declaration that in failing to recognise their Canadian marriage, and in failing to apply the tax law provisions relating to married couples to their own marriage, the State and the Revenue Commissioners have acted unlawfully, in breach of their constitutional rights and in breach of the European Convention on Human Rights. (*Irish Times,* 13 February 2006) A High Court ruling in late 2006 found that the couple do not have the right to marry in Ireland as, under the Irish Constitution marriage is confined to persons of the opposite sex.

Gay and lesbian couples are not alone in being refused equal treatment under Irish law. As Table 3.4 below shows, families and households in Ireland are taking increasingly diverse forms. However, many of these relationships of love and care are not considered families for the purposes of the Irish Constitution. Articles 41-42 of the Constitution, as interpreted by the courts, only affords married families constitutional recognition.

Table 3.4 Families not Recognised by the Irish State

	1996	*2002*
Co-habiting Opposite-Sex Couples	31,300	77,600
Co-habiting Same-Sex Couples	150	1,300
Children Living with Cohabiting Couples	23,000	51,700
Solo Parent Households with Children	60,700*	117,200

Source: Compiled from Irish Council for Civil Liberties, 2006:8
* Figure for 1994 and 2004, Central Statistics Office, 2004a:29

A recent ICCL analysis has found that the European Court of Human Rights adopts a definition of the family that respects a wider range of familial forms than Ireland's domestic law, and that Irish law, especially concerning children and gays and lesbians, falls short of requirements under the UN Convention on the Rights of the Child. This study also found that the constitution's preference for heterosexual married families effectively sanctions unequal treatment for all other family forms and fails to adequately protect children. (Irish Council for Civil Liberties, 2006)

A survey of public opinion carried out in late 2006 showed that nearly two thirds of respondents – 64 per cent – support equality in civil marriage for gays and lesbians, underlining the enormously positive change that has occurred in Irish society on the issue of equality for lesbian and gay people. This finding suggests that a referendum on constitutional change to recognize the equality of the diverse family types in Ireland would not be as divisive as some believe. (*Sunday Tribune*, 22 October 2006)

In relationships involving an Irish citizen and a non-European Economic Area (EEA) partner, immigration policy in Ireland is currently heavily weighted against unmarried couples, both heterosexual and homosexual. There are currently no concessions outside the Immigration Rules for unmarried partners. The Irish situation in this regard differs from a number of other jurisdictions worldwide which make provision in their immigration policies for the entry of non-national partners of citizens of their States. For example, Australia, New Zealand, Canada and the United Kingdom make concessions for unmarried persons to bring their partners to join them in their Home State, including same-sex partners. These provisions can also apply to the granting of Citizenship and long-term residency rights to non-nationals on the basis of long-term relationships with a citizen of the respective country. (Mee and Ronayne, 2000)

Exemptions from Equality Legislation for Religious-run Institutions

The predominance of Catholic-run institutions in primary and second level schooling, along with the exemption for religious-run institutions from equality legislation, results in a climate of fear for gay and lesbian teachers in Ireland and precludes any education on human sexual diversity outside of Catholic doctrine. Gay and lesbian teachers in Ireland by and large must remain silent about their sexuality. The majority of Irish youth are educated about human sexual diversity within a Catholic framework which characterises gay and lesbian people as "objectively disordered", "intrinsically evil" and unable to relate "correctly" to either men or women. The social and psychological effects of this labelling, particularly for gay and lesbian youth in Ireland, are profound.

The Equality Authority report *Implementing Equality for Lesbians, Gays and Bisexuals* (Equality Authority, 2002) reported the following survey results among members of the lesbian and gay community concerning their experiences in school:

- almost 50 per cent of respondents were aware of their sexuality before the age of 15;
- 57 per cent experienced problems in school including isolation, depression, poor self-esteem, harassment and bullying;

- 8 per cent left school earlier than anticipated as a result of problems experienced; and
- 25 per cent had been bullied or beaten because they were assumed to be lesbian, gay or bisexual (LGB).

The Equality Authority report also expressed concern about evidence of elevated rates of suicide amongst gay youth. These concerns proved to be well-founded. A 2003 Report, commissioned by the Department of Education in Northern Ireland, found that young people identifying as LGB, when compared to their heterosexual counterparts, are:

- at least three times more likely to attempt suicide;
- two-and-a-half times more likely to self harm;
- five times more likely to be medicated for depression; and
- twenty times more likely to suffer from an eating disorder. (YouthNet, 2003: 85)

A study published in 2004 gives an equally negative picture of the educational environment that exists for LGB students in Ireland. (Lodge and Lynch, 2004) Their report highlighted the fact that "gay" is the primary term of abuse within the education sector, and concluded that LGB students fare worst among all minorities in the Irish school system.

A study in 2006 surveyed over 700 teachers in every second level school in Ireland and established that homophobic bullying is a common experience in Irish schools and that schools are not providing adequate protection for young gay and lesbian people against discrimination and homophobic bullying. (Norman *et al.*, 2006)

The fear that exists among lesbian and gay teachers can be gauged from the fact that the first support group for lesbian, gay, bisexual and transgendered teachers within the Irish National Teachers Organisation was only established in 2006. Also telling is the fact that the group, which guarantees confidentiality to teachers who avail of its services, holds its meetings in secret. (*Irish Times*, 24 January 2006) Given the religious control of schooling in Ireland, teaching as a profession is simply not an option for many gay and lesbian people.

Understanding of transexuality in Irish society is low. Transexual people desire to live in the opposite gender, to have this gender change facilitated by medical intervention, and for the gender change to be recognised in law. Medical intervention to facilitate transsexualism is now provided in many countries and legal recognition has also increased, with many EU states now allowing changes in birth certificates to acknowledge gender change. In Ireland, medical services for gender reassignment are generally confined to referrals overseas. There is no provision in Irish law for transexual people to be officially recognised in the gender in which they identify. (Collins and Sheehan, 2004)

TRAVELLER CULTURE

Nomadism as a way of life, the family system within the Traveller community, the importance of horses and the existence of the Traveller language, Gammon or Cant, constitute just some of the criteria which support the designation of the Traveller community as an ethnic group.

The recognition of Irish Travellers as a distinct ethnic group in United Kingdom jurisprudence and equality legislation, in addition to the longstanding association between the Traveller community, the Roma and the Sinti, whose ethnicity is not disputed at international level, further support this categorisation. Moreover, the perception of Travellers as an ethnic group by representatives of the Traveller community such as Pavee Point and the Irish Traveller Movement, meets the subjective requirement of self-identification in General Recommendation 8 of the CERD Committee. Travellers are also expressly mentioned in the Declaration and Programme of Action agreed by the international community, including the Irish government, at the 2001 World Conference Against Racism.

In spite of these arguments, the state takes the position that while Travellers possess their own "culture", they are not ethnically different from the rest of the population, as they are not of a different "race", an attitude which is telling in terms of the misunderstanding at state level of the concept of ethnicity. (Beirne and Jaichand, 2006) Despite the fact that the UN CERD Committee has called upon the state to reconsider its position, the government continues to refuse to recognise Travellers' distinct ethnicity.

Recent legislation, such as the Control of Horses Act 1996 has also impacted disproportionately on the freedom of Travellers to practise their culture and on their ability to earn a livelihood. Horses play an immense social and cultural role in Travellers lives and for generations Travellers have kept horses as an alternative method of saving rather than using financial institutions. The Control of Horses Act requires the licencing of horses and includes measures by which local authorities can control horses in urban areas. While legislation is necessary for reasons of public safety and prevention of cruelty, Travellers and Traveller organisations view the way in which it is being enacted as an erosion of their culture. Discrimination experienced by children from the Traveller community within the education system is discussed in Q4.3.

FREEDOM TO PRACTICE OWN LANGUAGE

The Irish Language

Irish is recognised in the Irish Constitution as the first official language of Ireland, with English being recognised as the second official language.

According to the 2002 census, approximately 1.6 million people claim a competence in Irish. Approximately 340,000 people claim to speak Irish on a daily basis. The majority of these, however, are schoolchildren who use it during their classes in Irish. An estimated 70,000 people actually use the language as their first and daily language (Central Statistics Office, 2004c: 67).

Irish has official recognition in Northern Ireland under the Good Friday Agreement, 1998 (Good Friday Agreement 1998, Section 6, paragraph 3) and Foras na Gaeilge was established under the Agreement to promote Irish throughout all of Ireland. (www.gaeilge.ie) From January 2007, the Irish language is recognised as an official working language of the European Union.

Under the Official Languages Act 2003, every act of the Oireachtas must be published in both Irish and English. This Act also places a duty on public bodies to publish public documents, like annual reports, in both languages. In addition, the Act established the office of Language Commissioner, An Coimisinéir Teanga, whose function it is to ensure that the provisions of the Act are being complied with. Irish is a required subject of study in all schools within the Republic that receive public funding.

Irish language broadcast media include Raidió na Gaeltachta and Teilifís na Gaeilge, renamed TG4, both of which are relatively successful. At local level, many local radio stations broadcast programmes in Irish. In Dublin, Raidió na Life, and in Belfast, Raidió Fáilte, broadcast their programmes in Irish.

Within the print media, the first daily Irish-language newspaper *Lá* was launched in 2003 and sells over 5,000 copies each day. There is also an Irish language weekly paper, *Foinse*, while the *Irish Times*, the *Irish News* and *Metro Éireann* have pages in Irish. Among the magazines published in Irish are *Feasta*, *Comhar* and *An tUltach*. In addition, there are also electronic Irish language magazines such as *Beo* and *Gaelport*. (www.gaeilge.ie)

Minority Languages

Language can be a major problem for ethnic minority groups in accessing public services in Ireland. While improvements have been made over recent years, many public services remain difficult to access because of the exclusive use of English and Irish.

Progress has been made in providing information regarding some public services in a variety of minority languages. The Department of Enterprise, Trade and Employment, for example, now provides information on employment rights in ten languages, including Chinese, Latvian, Lithuanian, Polish, Portuguese, Romanian and Russian. Similarly, in 2005, FAS launched a "Know before you go" information resource, available in 12 different languages, which is aimed at prospective migrants to Ireland. (Watt and McGaughey, 2006: 123)

The language barrier is one of the main challenges for ethnic minority groups in accessing education in Ireland. The Department of Education and Science has recently taken steps to address this situation and various documents of interest to parents are being published and made available on-line in a number of languages. (www.education.ie)

In many areas of public service provision, however, language remains a difficulty. For instance, GPs in Ireland currently do not have access to a nationwide interpretation system. This deficit can often result in children acting as interpreters for their parents – a situation which is obviously highly problematic. In addition, the provision of interpreters within hospitals is left to the discretion of hospital management. In practice, hospitals ordinarily contact an interpretation agency which supplies them with interpreters. These interpreters however may have little experience in medical work, which often requires extreme sensitivity. (Watt and McGaughey, 2006)

More needs to be done on a national level to ensure equal access to public services for those members of Irish society whose command of English and Irish is low.

Finally, as part of an initiative to encourage members of Ireland's new ethnic minority communities to join the Garda, the Minister for Justice, Equality and Law Reform announced in January 2005 that the existing requirement of certified proficiency in Irish and English for garda recruits was to be replaced by a requirement of proficiency in two languages, one of which must be either Irish or English. (www.justice.ie) This change was welcomed as a positive step in enhancing employment opportunities within the gardaí for Ireland's immigrant communities.

Q3.4 How free from harassment and intimidation are individuals and groups working to improve human rights?

Organisations in Ireland that work on human rights issues are generally free to organise, lobby, and publish their views without harassment or intimidation.

An issue does arise however regarding the dependence of many such organisations on government funding and the possible effect of this financial dependence on their ability to be vocal in their criticism of government policy or to campaign for legislative change. A recent project involving Traveller organisations, Citizen Traveller – aimed at addressing negative stereotypes of Travellers among the public at large and enhancing the self-esteem of Travellers – had its funding withdrawn largely because the project was campaigning for a change in existing legislation.

Concern also exists among Non-Governmental Organisations (NGOs) over the possible uses of the 1997 Electoral Act to restrict the fundraising activities of Irish NGOs campaigning to change government policy. The vague definition of "political purposes" within the Act means that it could potentially impact negatively on a broad range of organisations, including those campaigning for human rights.

Major legislation on the regulation of charities, the first revision of such legislation in over forty years, is pending. The proposed legislation aims to modernise the legal basis for charity organisations and introduce a charity regulator to oversee such organisations' financial affairs, including fundraising. Human rights organisations have been lobbying government to try to ensure that human rights campaigning remains an activity eligible for charitable status under the new legislation.

NGOS IN IRELAND

A range of NGOs working on human rights issues are active in Ireland. These groups range from the women's movement, campaigners for gay and lesbian rights, for disability rights, organisations working for the rights of Travellers and, more recently, groups addressing migrants' rights and racism. Groups also work on a range of social justice issues, e.g., poverty, homelessness and overseas development. (See also Section Eleven)

A number of NGOs campaign specifically for the incorporation of treaties which Ireland has ratified and for the requirements arising from these treaties. Examples include the Children's Rights Alliance, an umbrella organisation which campaigns for the implementation of Ireland's obligations under the UN Convention on the Rights of the Child, and the Women's Human Rights Alliance which campaigns for the implementation of the UN Beijing Delaration and the UN Convention on the Elimination of all Forms of Discrimination against Women. A number of organisations contribute to the review processes under human rights conventions. In 2005, for example, an NGO alliance of over 40 groups published a Shadow Report in response to the Irish government's First Report to the UN Committee on the Elimination of Racial Discrimination (CERD). In 2006, the European Committee for the Prevention of Torture on its visit to monitor Ireland's compliance with the Council of Europe's European Convention for the Prevention of Torture and Inhuman or Degrading Treatment or Punishment met with representatives of civil society, including Irish NGOs. The committee's findings will be available in 2007.

The Irish Human Rights Commission, a statutory body rather than an NGO, also submitted reports to the UN Committee monitoring Ireland's compliance with the International Convention on the Elimination of All Forms of Discrimination Against Women, to the UN Committee on the Elimination of Discrimination against Women in 2005, and to the UN Committee on the Rights of the Child in 2006. These submissions are considered by the committees alongside the government's official reports.

Organisations describing themselves as human rights organisations comprise a small subset of NGOs in Ireland. The Comhairle Directory of National Voluntary Organisations lists around 30 organisations that refer specifically to human rights in their profile or make reference to their focus on the rights of a particular group. (Comhairle, 2006) At the same time, a number of other organisations would undoubtedly view human rights issues as part of their agenda. For example, the National Women's Council of Ireland and the Irish Family Planning Association do not mention "human rights" in their Comhairle Directory entries, but both organisations highlight human rights issues as central to their work on their own websites.

Human rights language is used in relation to a range of issues from immigration and asylum, housing, prisons, children's rights, people with disabilities, overseas development, gay and lesbian rights, Travellers, housing, crime and mental health.

All organisations working to improve human rights in Ireland are free to organise, lobby, and publish their views without harassment or intimidation. An issue does arise, however, regarding the dependence of all statutory and many voluntary organisations on government funding and the possible effect this funding line may have on their ability to criticise governmental policy or campaign for changes to existing legislation.

The Citizen Traveller Campaign is one instance in recent years where funding was widely believed, within the NGO community at least, to have been withdrawn for essentially political reasons. The campaign, which involved a number of Traveller organisations, was aimed largely at changing common misconceptions regarding Travellers within the public at large, and at empowering and enhancing the self esteem of Travellers. (Department of Justice, Equality and Law Reform, 2002: 21) However, in 2002, the Department suspended funding for the project. One of the grounds for suspension was that continued funding would involve spending public funds to campaign against existing legislation. (Department of Justice, Equality and Law Reform, 2002: 19) In any event, there is clearly no protection in Ireland against the withdrawal by government of public funding for human rights and social justice projects for essentially political reasons, nor any practice of funding NGOs regardless of whether they campaign for legislative change. This situation differs from practices elsewhere, e.g., in the Netherlands, where a well-established culture of government funding exists for organisations who nonetheless campaign actively for changes in the law.

A second area of concern is the effect of the 1997 Electoral Act on the ability of non-profit organisations to engage in public policy debates. The Electoral Act was introduced to regulate donations to political parties and places obligations and restrictions on "third parties" that accept donations for "political purposes." However, the broad definition of political purposes in the Act could be interpreted as including the advocacy and campaigning work of many non-governmental organisations. As such, the provisions of the 1997 Act are capable of placing very extensive restrictions upon the extent to which donors may legitimately fund Irish non-governmental organisations that campaign to change government policy.

The restrictions limit the value of donations from a single donor to around €6,350 per year and no donations may be received from foreign-based organisations or from non-Irish citizens. (Ó Cuanacháin *et al.*, 2004) If applied rigidly in practice, these restrictions would have a crippling effect on the ability of NGOs to engage in campaigning activities in Ireland. (See also Q3.4)

The definition of political purposes within the Act is broad enough to allow for possible interpretations that might apply it to a very wide range of organisations beyond the political parties for which it was intended. According to the Standards in Public Office Commission, the range of bodies which may be deemed to come under the remit of the legislation include: Residents/Tenants Associations, Community Organisations, Tidy Towns Committees, the Credit Union Movement, representative associations such as ICTU, IBEC, IFA, USI, other interest groups such as those representing teachers, accountants, vintners, lawyers, nurses, doctors, as well as NGOs such as Trócaire, Amnesty International, Threshold, and St Vincent de Paul. (Standards in Public Office Commission, 2003)

While the legislation attempts to address a legitimate concern that party political activists might campaign for political purposes under the guise of a charitable organisation, there is clearly an anomaly in the definition of "political activities" that could potentially stymie legitimate human rights and campaigning organisations from carrying out their work.

PROPOSED CHARITIES ACT

A Charities Act being prepared by government will be the first major change to charities legislation since the Charities Act 1961 was passed over 40 years ago. Updated legislation is needed, as no statutory definition of a charity currently exists in Ireland. As a result, there is no reliable information on the number of charities, their financial worth or how they spend their money.

The regulatory reform of charities has been considered by the Law Society in 2002 (Law Society of Ireland, 2002) and the Law Reform Commission in 2006 (Law Reform Commission, 2006b), and the aforementioned draft Charities Bill currently being drawn up is based on a process of widespread consultation over the last number of years. Among the aims of the proposed legislation is the introduction of an integrated system of registration and regulation for the sector, and the introduction of a charities regulator to oversee charities' fundraising and expenditure activities.

Registration as a charity can have a significant impact on an organisation's financial stability, since charities can avail of various tax relief measures, the most significant of which is tax relief on donations received.

A number of legislative changes have been made to bolster the incentives for charitable giving in Ireland in recent years. The 2001 Finance Act simplified and rationalised the tax reliefs for donations to charities, expanded the relief for personal donations to domestic charities and educational establishments, and included sole traders and partnerships as eligible for tax relief on charitable donations. The Finance Act 2005 also reduced the waiting period before tax relief comes into effect after the granting of charitable exempt status by the Revenue Commissioners from three years to two. (Fleming, 2005)

Organisations engaged in human rights campaigning activities have been lobbying to have their current eligibility for charitable status explicitly recognised within the draft Charities Bill. Removal of such status would have severe financial implications for the operation of organisations that campaign for human rights in Ireland and there is sufficient concern within the NGO community for representatives to lobby government on the wording of the proposed Bill.

Four: Economic and Social Rights

Are economic and social rights equally guaranteed for all?

INTRODUCTION AND SUMMARY

Ten to fifteen years ago, few people would have seen much connection between democracy and economic and social rights, or thought that such rights should be subject to legal or constitutional guarantee. Yet, without a minimum level of economic and social wellbeing, health, or the knowledge and skills that come from education, people will be unable to play a part in the democratic life of society, to understand and exercise their civil and political rights, and to make effective use of their personal and political freedoms. This reality is expressed within the international human rights community by the insistence that all human rights – civil, political, economic, social and cultural – are "indivisible". Furthermore, ordinary people everywhere are increasingly coming to expect that a democratic polity should be able to secure their economic, social and physical wellbeing. Indeed the enjoyment of economic, social and cultural rights is demonstrably both a *condition for*, and a *consequence of*, an effectively functioning democracy.

Various public bodies and agencies are charged with protecting and promoting different aspects of socio-economic rights in Ireland. Chief among them are the Human Rights Commission and the Equality Authority. In Ireland, however, most politicians and public officials, including members of the judiciary, do not see economic, social and cultural provision as rights to be enforced through the law or the constitution. This perspective exists despite the fact that Ireland signed the International Covenant on Economic, Social and Cultural Rights (ICE-

SCR) in 1973 and ratified it in 1989. Among the rights contained in the Covenant are the right to work, to social security, to an adequate standard of living, to adequate food, clothing and housing, the right of everyone to enjoy the highest attainable standard of physical and mental health, the right of everyone to education, the right to take part in cultural life, and the right to enjoy the benefits of scientific progress and its applications.

The Convenant entails a number of legal obligations. These include a core minimum for each right; that even limited resources must be equitably applied; and that steps must be taken to advance citizens' rights in these areas. Despite Ireland's ratification of the Convenant, economic, cultural and social rights in Ireland remain "directive principles of social policy" as opposed to rights in law. Successive Irish governments have remained wedded to the position that these issues are essentially political matters that should remain the responsibility of elected officials. Furthermore, in framing various economic, social and cultural policies such as health policy, housing policy, and education policy, governments refuse to be constrained by acknowledging core minimum standards and non-discriminatory distribution of resources as rights that can be enforced and protected in law. (Amnesty International, 2005) Despite the lack of constitutional provision for socio-economic rights there have been a number of court decisions resulting in the direct or indirect protection of these rights. However, the courts have in general displayed a reluctance to recognise and give proper effect to such rights. (Nolan, 2007 forthcoming)

The government position has been challenged by the UN Committee on Economic, Social and Cultural Rights, NGOs such as Amnesty, and by many human rights academics and practitioners. The Government-appointed Human Rights Commission questions the idea that "...the political marketplace necessarily provides a conclusive means of protecting economic, social and cultural rights". Moreover, the Commission contends that "The argument that the promotion of economic, social and cultural rights should emerge naturally through the democratic process overlooks the fact that those suffering extreme disadvantage are largely disenfranchised from the political system in the first instance". (Irish Human Rights Commission, 2005: 22)

In 2005, the IHRC issued a comprehensive discussion document outlining the arguments for incorporating international treaties in this area into domestic law and addressing the issues cited as obstacles by those opposed to such incorporation. (Irish Human Rights Commission, 2005) In its discussion document, the IHRC makes it clear that in its view "much of the opposition to economic, social and cultural rights is based on misunderstandings, not only of the nature of these rights, but also of the relationship between economic and social rights and civil and political rights". It argues that "there are no technical or procedural barriers prohibiting the courts from engaging with economic, social and cultural rights, rather it is a matter of policy to choose whether to make these rights justiciable or not". (Irish Human Rights Commission, 2005: 14)

Similarly, economic, social and cultural rights can be made justiciable, that is capable of being resolved before the courts, at a constitutional level as is the case in countries as diverse as Italy, Spain, Brazil, Columbia, South Africa and India. A survey in 2001 found that an estimated 109 countries recognise the right to health in their national constitutions. Finland has integrated key economic, social and cultural rights into its national constitution, and the European Court of Human Rights and courts in Belgium, Germany, Japan, the United States and elsewhere frequently deal with social and economic rights. Finally there is some movement to work within a human rights framework in Europe, through the laws of the European Union, the European Social Charter, the European Convention on Human Rights and the EU Charter of Fundamental Rights. (Weir, 2006: xv)

Application of Economic and Social Rights in Ireland

The Irish Constitution includes only one socio-economic right, the right to primary education. Legislation obliges a variety of authorities to provide social and welfare entitlements, but gives them a wide degree of discretion over their implementation. As a result, only a limited number of socio-economic rights are legally protected and enforced in Ireland.

At the same time, by signing and ratifying almost the entire range of human rights treaties (See Section Fourteen for details), Ireland has committed itself to be bound by international law. In each case, Ireland has made a legally binding contract with fellow members of the international community, stating that it meets the human rights standards in each treaty. However human rights advocates such as Amnesty argue that the most fundamental domestic law of the state, the constitution, is not in compliance with the obligations regarding socio-economic rights which Ireland has undertaken. For its part, the government has consistently rejected recommendations that the economic, social and cultural rights set out in UN human rights treaties be incorporated into national law, citing the conclusions in the 1996 Report of the Constitution Review Group.

As well as signing up to the UN ICESCR, Ireland has also ratified three further UN treaties – the Convention for the Elimination of Racial Discrimination (CERD); the Convention for the Elimination of Discrimination against Women (CEDAW); and the Convention on the Rights of the Child (CRC) – which provide that there should be no discrimination in the way economic and social rights are met. Ireland has ratified the important ILO conventions and has signed the Revised European Social Charter as well as the Additional Protocol for Collective Complaints. The European Court of Human Rights has been a guiding authority for Ireland's courts since it was ratified in 1953, even before it was incorporated, by legislation, into Irish law in December, 2003. (Amnesty International (Irish Section), 2005b: 21)

A recent survey carried out for the Democratic Audit Ireland project (Clancy *et al.*, 2005) which asked what rights people thought should be included in Irish law found that overwhelming (approximately 90 per cent) support exists for the idea of enshrining social rights such as healthcare, education, and housing in Irish law.

Table 4.1 Inclusion of Social and Economic Rights in Irish Law

Do you think the following rights should or should not be included in Irish law?

	% Yes
Right to education regardless of income	92
Right of homeless to be housed	91
Right to healthcare regardless of income	90
Right to join a trade union	81
Right to childcare for working parents	79
Equal treatment regardless of citizenship	66

Source: Clancy *et al.*, 2005:7

There is also almost as strong a level of support for the concept of employment-related rights, with around 80 per cent agreeing that the right to join a trade union and the right to state support of childcare for children of working parents should be included in Irish law. Moreover, two out of every three respondents supported extending these rights to non-Irish citizens resident here.

Recent years have seen progress in some areas of economic and social rights, for example, the introduction of a minimum wage. However, several specific recommendations from UN and Council of Europe committees have been ignored. (Amnesty International (Irish Section), 2005b)

- Despite the clear recommendation of the UN Committee on Economic, Social and Cultural Rights, the Disability Act (2005) is not human rights based, and does not adequately provide for the core minimum of progressive realisation of economic and social rights of people with disabilities.
- In 2004, the European Committee of Social Rights issued its conclusions on Ireland's first report under the Revised European Social Charter, finding 12 cases of non-conformity with the Charter, including failures to comply with its obligations in the employment of children and towards migrant workers.
- The UN Committee on the Elimination of Racial Discrimination, in its 2005 concluding observations on Ireland's first periodic report, expressed concern about the treatment of asylum seekers, failure to prevent the exploitation of migrant workers and questioned the effectiveness of policies and measures to improve access by the Traveller community to health services, housing, employment and education.
- In 2005, the UN Committee on the Elimination of Discrimination against Women was critical of the persistence of traditional stereotypical views of the social roles and responsibilities of women, reflected in Article 41.2 of the Constitution, in womens' educational choices and employment patterns. For example while the definition of poverty used by the National Anti-Poverty Strategy (NAPS) acknowledges many of the core concepts that underlie human rights based approaches, in 1999, the Committee on Economic,

Social and Cultural Rights expressed concern that Ireland had not adopted a human rights based approach in the NAPS and again in 2002 after Ireland had still not complied. The Committee urged Ireland to integrate human rights into NAPS, in accordance with its statement on poverty; moreover, by refusing to do so, Ireland remains in breach of its essential obligations under the treaty.

Implementation of Economic and Social Rights

Setting aside the constitutional argument, there are three immediate obligations in regard to these binding socio-economic human rights which Ireland has signed up to respect. Each of these human rights, whether health, education or social security requires that:

- a core minimum be guaranteed by the state;
- resources be allocated in a manner that ensures no discrimination; and
- the state has an obligation to take steps to continually improve enjoyment of these human rights.

These obligations have consequences for planning, management of resources, measurable action, and accountability wherein government must demonstrate that it is meeting minimum essential levels of each of the rights for all groups in society, and that it is taking sufficient steps to progressively implement the necessary measures and provide the necessary resources for the full realisation of these rights.

The expert international committees which monitor treaty compliance have repeatedly addressed two issues: first, Ireland's failure to provide national remedies to address violations of economic, social and cultural rights; and second its failure to frame national strategies, plans, programmes and budgets so as to ensure the prevention of such violations. In line with the government's viewpoint that social and economic policies should not be constrained in this latter way, national programmes specifically intended to address social exclusion are inconsistent in their use of rights language. The IHRC expresses concern that Ireland, along with other states, looks to interpret socio-economic rights purely in terms of formal expressions of entitlement to public services. The design and resourcing of public services which takes account of clearly defined rights and obligations would, the

Commission argues, bring "many significant benefits to society and to politics". (Irish Human Rights Commission, 2005: 48)

Government policy emphasises economic development as the key to social and cultural development. Economic development results in higher levels of employment which in turn leads to prosperity and wider social progress. A more recent consensus posits that progress on social and economic developments are complementary goals. However, the language used in the recent Social Partnership Agreement *Towards 2016* makes it clear that using increased resources to accelerate social progress is still officially viewed as dependent on economic progress. (Department of the Taoiseach, 2006)

Many other less wealthy countries have taken steps to ensure compliance with their treaty obligations. In South Africa, for example, relevant organs of the State report to its national Human Rights Commission on measures they have taken towards the realisation of the rights in the Bill of Rights concerning housing, health care, food, water, social security, education, and the environment. In Ireland, there is no similar process to ensure that such steps are taken, and no such reporting to the Irish Human Rights Commission by relevant government departments.

Q4.1 How adequate is the access to income and how far are poor people able to participate in the wider Irish society?

Ireland is now one of the wealthiest societies in the world. The UN Development Programme Report (2006), which assesses countries' performance on wealth, life expectancy and education, ranks Ireland behind only Norway, Iceland and Australia as one of the best places to live, a rise of four places on the previous year. However, the report also ranks the state as 17th out of 18 rich countries for poverty levels, although the measure used has been contested. Arguments that Ireland has had to play catch up in investment in physical and social infrastructure are counterbalanced by a belief that an absence of policy commitment to equality is at least as responsible for this poor record. The substantial decrease in the numbers of people experiencing consistent poverty over the last decade is a positive development. However, there are still around 300,000 people living in poverty in Ireland. Furthermore, using the internationally comparable EU definition of income, the relative income poverty rate in Ireland at 19.7 per cent, is considerably higher than the average EU-25 at risk of poverty rate of 16 per cent. (Central Statistics Office, 2006a) Moreover, a "vulnerable class" of about one in ten of the population is at a heightened risk of income poverty, basic deprivation and self-perceived economic strain. This vulnerability has particularly affected those not in employment and who rely on social welfare payments which have declined relative to average earnings, such as the long-term-unemployed, the elderly, people with disabilities, and those caring within the home; meanwhile asylum seekers are a new vulnerable group in Irish society who are increasingly coming to the attention of organisations such as the Society of the Vincent de Paul.

THE STATUS OF ECONOMIC AND SOCIAL RIGHTS IN RELATION TO POVERTY IN IRELAND

The expectation of "an adequate standard of living" is enshrined in the International Covenant on Economic, Social and Cultural rights (ICESCR) and numerous international and European human rights treaties. Nonetheless many people in Ireland continue to live in poverty, without the sufficient resources to enable them to participate as equal citizens.

Entitlement to social security benefits is an entitlement which is justiciable, that is capable of being resolved before the courts, although access to courts for poor people is itself an almost insuperable challenge. Furthermore Ireland is exceptional within the EU for the high proportion of its social spending which is means tested. (National Economic and Social Council, 2005a: xvi) Anti-discriminatory legislation affords protection to some groups vulnerable to poverty such as disabled people, women and people from ethnic minorities, but no socio-economic rights exist to offer protection against the discrimination emanating from poverty itself.

POVERTY IN IRELAND

The 2005 annual report of the Department of Social and Family Affairs listed one of its goals as follows: "to support and promote families and to attain better outcomes in tackling poverty and achieving a more inclusive society through cooperating, developing and implementing national anti-poverty strategies and through the provision of inclusive and other support services for people in debt or at risk of experiencing hardship".

Poverty and social exclusion have been proactively addressed in Ireland over the last twenty years. The Combat Poverty Agency was established by government in 1986 and in 2002 an Office of Social Inclusion was established. In 1997, Ireland was one of the first countries in Europe to develop a National Anti-Poverty Strategy (NAPS) and the National Action Plan on Poverty and Social Exclusion 2006–2008 is currently in preparation. The NAPS has taken substantial measures to tackle economic and social marginalisation; for example in the introduction of a statutory national minimum wage, the minimum adult rate is fixed at the comparatively high level of above 50 per cent of median earnings, although the continuing high proportion of working poor makes clear its inadequacy.

Consistent poverty is the official Irish government measure of poverty and the one used in the National Anti-Poverty Strategy. By this measure people are living in poverty if their income and resources (material, cultural and social) are so inadequate as to preclude a standard of living which is regarded as acceptable by Irish people. The measure combines income poverty with enforced deprivation which is defined as having to forgo one or more of a specified set of lifestyle items due to lack of money. The eight specified items are: two pairs of strong shoes; roast meat once a week; a meal with meat, chicken or fish every second day; new (not second-hand) clothes; a warm, waterproof coat; not having a substantial meal on at least one day in the past two weeks; going without heating at some stage in the past year; and experiencing debt problems arising from ordinary living expenses. Close to 300,000 people are poor according to this measure, more than 100,000 of whom are children. There has been a major reduction in these numbers in the past decade: a fall from around 15 per cent in 1994 to just over 7 per cent in 2005. There has also been a reduction in the figures for consistent child poverty, from over 17 per cent in 1997 to 6.5 per cent in 2001. (Central Statistics Office, 2006a) The NAPS aims to reduce the numbers of those who are consistently poor to below 2 per cent by 2007, although it is unlikely that this target will be reached.

By the measure used internationally and throughout the EU,

Ireland's poverty record is poor. Against this measure Ireland has 19.7 per cent of its population at risk of poverty, i.e., more than three-quarters of a million people living on an income of just over €10,000 a year. While this shows a marginal improvement on the previous year's figure of just 21 per cent, the only EU countries which match it are Slovakia and Portugal. (Central Statistics Office, 2006a: 5)

Furthermore, a longitudinal study of the period 1994 – 2001 identifies a "vulnerable class" at a heightened risk in relation to income poverty, basic deprivation and self-perceived economic strain. As shown, the size of this class fell sharply over the period: from just over 3 in 10 in 1994 to one in ten in 2001. "At the same time the profile of the vulnerable class changed so that there was an even sharper differentiation between them and the rest of the population". (Whelan *et al.*, 2005: 68) The most critical consequence here is that those not in employment and therefore dependent on social welfare have experienced a decline in their incomes relative to those in employment. This outcome has particularly affected the elderly, lone parents, people with disabilities, and those caring within the home. Other factors include substantial price inflation, particularly in housing, which has increased the risk of poverty for many in Ireland. Economic and Social Research Institute (ESRI) research shows that increasing welfare rates is the key way to reduce poverty. In Ireland, cash transfers are currently 20 per cent less effective in reducing poverty than the EU average. (Combat Poverty Agency, 2006a)

Poverty Traps

A range of anomalies and inconsistencies exist between the income tax and social welfare systems which act as poverty traps. The most obvious of these concerns the "working poor" – those with the lowest incomes from employment. At present more than 7 per cent of those in employment are estimated to be "at risk of poverty". (Central Statistics Office, 2006a: 9) If a person does not earn enough to use up their full tax credit then he or she will not benefit from any tax reductions introduced by government in its annual budget. Under the present system, this in effect means that those with the lowest pay will not benefit at budget time.

The move from tax allowances to tax credits was completed in Budget 2001. This very welcome change put in place a system that had been advocated for a long time by a range of groups including the

Conference of Religious in Ireland (CORI) Justice Commission and the Irish Congress of Trade Unions (ICTU). Still, further changes are required to secure an effective and efficient integration of the income tax and social welfare systems. Mechanisms to secure such an integrated system are not difficult to develop and implement; moreover, such integration would provide government with the capacity to address the "working poor" issue as well as a range of other problems that present themselves when these two systems are not effectively integrated.

INEQUALITY AND SOCIAL EXCLUSION

Consistent with the last number of years, the 2006 United Nations Development Programme (UNDP) report reveals a growing inequality in Irish society in parallel to its growing wealth. Starting from a very low base, Ireland's total accumulated wealth still lags behind many other developed countries and much of Ireland's state revenue in recent years has been invested in developing infrastructure, with close to 5 per cent of GNP being used in a major programme of capital investment by government. (Department of the Taoiseach, 2006) It is arguable, however, that government's goals in relation to poverty are too low and constitute settling for poverty reduction rather than avidly pursuing equality. In any event, the National Economic and Social Forum (established in 1993 by government and comprising the social partners and members of the Oireachtas) pointed out in a 2006 report on social inclusion in the labour market that Ireland has less equality of opportunity than other European countries and that this situation has changed little over the last decade. (National Economic and Social Forum, 2006a: ix) Commentators working in this arena argue that in Ireland we have "resigned ourselves to the least ambitious objectives". (Hegarty, 2006: 114)

Notwithstanding recent marginal improvements, on balance, income inequality in Irish society is widening (O'Donoghue and McDonough, 2006: 58) while the proportion of those at risk of poverty is persisting. In 2005, the CSO data (Central Statistics Office, 2006a: 4) shows that persons in the top income quintile had almost 5 times the equivalised income of those in the bottom quintile, which reflects no change from the 2003 findings. The main explanation for the fact that consistent poverty has decreased while relative poverty has risen is the growth in employment and the rise in incomes for those in employment between 1994 and 2001.

On a positive note, however, according to the Combat Poverty Agency, the redistributive effect of the 2006 budget represents an acceleration of the pro-poor trend in tax/welfare policy since 2003. The Agency concludes that "overall the government is well on its way to reducing income poverty in line with European best practice, a significant achievement in the context of the EU social inclusion strategy and a welcome boost for the forthcoming National Action Plan on Poverty 2006-2008." (Combat Poverty Agency, 2006b) This trend is a welcome shift in implicit if not explicit government policy but one which needs to be sustained into the future. To date, increasing social welfare payments has been the driving mechanism paid for from budget surpluses rather than higher taxation, an option which may not be sustainable into the future.

Social Exclusion – The Inability to Participate

The causes of individual poverty – such as unemployment, illness, discrimination – are also involved with wider deprivations, like bad housing, poor transport, low educational attainment, health and social participation. This broader impact of poverty is known as social exclusion. Demographic data show that social exclusion is often concentrated in specific neighbourhoods. Inhabitants of these neighbourhoods are not only more cut off from basic services such as shops and banks but are also more exposed to crime, drugs and racism. In Ireland there is also evidence of very limited access to public transport. (Wickham, 2006)

The ESRI longitudinal study over the period 1994 to 2001 found that the degree of association between those vulnerable to poverty and social exclusion was modest and that the numbers experiencing multiple deprivation across the entire range of dimensions were very small. They also found "a significant reduction in exclusion levels across the educational spectrum and across age, gender and urban-rural categories". (Whelan *et al.*, 2005: viii)

Nonetheless, there is increasing evidence that inequality in itself has a damaging effect on those who are at the bottom rung of the ladder in ways which materially damage their health, wellbeing and sense of belonging to their society. (Wilkinson, 2005) Critics of the Irish social model argue that "...the neglect of effective mechanisms of redistribution is as serious a defect of Ireland's development model today as was the neglect of sustainable forms of economic growth in the past". (Kirby, 2006: 182)

Q4.2 How effectively is adequate shelter guaranteed to all equally?

Unlike citizens in other EU states such as Belgium, the Netherlands, Portugal and Spain, the Irish population does not have an overall constitutional right to housing, nor is the right to housing inscribed as a "fundamental aim" of the state as is the case in Sweden. (Byrne and Blick, 2006: 182) Along with the remarkable economic growth by international standards in recent years, the construction of infrastructure, including housing, has proceeded at a rapid pace. However, not unlike the UK, Ireland has a policy of selling off its existing public housing stock to existing tenants on advantageous terms at the same time as it faces a growing waiting list for public housing and greater numbers of people who are unable to either buy or rent a house at an affordable price.

ACCESS TO A HOME

A recent study of the Irish housing system (Drudy and Punch, 2005) has highlighted a number of problems in Ireland's current capacity to provide adequate shelter for all. The major deficiency in Ireland is the absence of sufficient affordable housing for rent and the weakness of safeguards for vulnerable households. House prices and rents in Ireland have risen beyond the reach of many, while the state provides far too few houses for those who can neither buy nor rent. Housing in Ireland is characterised by:

- a growing homeless population;
- long waiting lists for public housing and significant housing need;
- unaffordable house prices for a large proportion of the population; and
- prohibitively priced and insecure private rental accommodation.

At the same time, Ireland holds one of the highest rates of home ownership in Europe. Many Irish also own second homes in Ireland and further afield, while others view housing as yet another market-place opportunity for investment and speculation. This state of affairs has developed in a particular policy context as follows.

- The number of houses provided by the state has fallen to 7 per cent of total provision by 2004 compared with 33 per cent of all residences in 1975. Local authorities built just 4,209 homes in 2005 while Housing Associations built 1,350 – a total social housing output of 5,559.
- Local authorities continue to sell off their housing stock. A total of 1,738 were sold off in 2005 at a significant discount, while 918 were acquired at market prices. Despite the prohibitive cost of acquiring land for social housing in the Dublin area, the existing public land bank is being steadily run down through privatisation policies and public private partnerships.
- Current government tax incentive schemes (e.g., Section 23/27 tax incentives) have given an unfair advantage to speculators and investors over struggling first-time buyers. Over 250,000 of these houses/apartments lie vacant around the country.
- Despite legislation many tenants in the private rented sector pay high rents and live insecurely in substandard accommodation.
- Almost 60,000 households in the private rented sector are given rent supplements to subsidise private landlords at an annual cost of €350 million.

Homelessness

Three key groups are known to be at especially high risk of homelessness, namely ex-prisoners, people released from psychiatric care, and young people who have grown up or spent a portion of their lives in residential care. The majority of homeless people are single individuals, mostly men.

Substantial numbers of homeless people will have experienced deeply rooted social problems including mental illness, alcohol and drug dependence, criminal or anti-social behaviour, poverty and loss of contact with family and friends. Ex-prisoners, for example, often find that their shattered family ties mean they have no home to return to on release, whereas children who grow up in care may never have had access to a home outside the care setting. Thus, while a link exists between poverty and homelessness, it is by no means a direct causal relationship. It is estimated that between 30 per cent and 40 per cent of homeless people experience mental illness, with similar numbers suffering drug or alcohol dependence. (Homeless Agency, 2004: 3)

The Health Act 1953 imposes a duty on Health Boards to provide assistance and shelter to people who are homeless and the Childcare Act 1991 makes Health Boards (now the Health Service Executive – HSE) responsible for homeless people under 18. The Housing Act 1998 empowers local authorities to respond to homelessness and requires them to periodically assess the numbers of homeless people in each area.

In the past number of years, the government has developed a cross-departmental strategy to reduce homelessness, (Department of the Environment and Local Government, 2000a) a youth homelessness strategy to eliminate homelessness among under 18s, (Department of Health and Children, 2001a) while the Homeless Preventative Strategy (Department of the Environment, Heritage and Local Government, 2002a) aims to prevent homelessness among people leaving state care, including hospital, prison and childcare. Partly as a result of increased emergency accommodation, the number of people sleeping rough in Dublin has been reduced from around 300 in 2002 to less than 100 in 2005.

In 2005, there were slightly over 2,000 people homeless in Dublin. Noting that it is not entirely appropriate to compare the 2005 figures with earlier dates, the Homeless Agency states that there has been a 19 per cent decrease in the number of homeless people between 2002 and 2005 in Dublin. (Homeless Agency, 2006) A 2005 review found that substantial progress had been made in addressing the problem of homelessness since the launch of *Homelessness: An Integrated Strategy* in 2000. Improvements ranged from the provision of housing and health services to a reduction in the numbers sleeping rough. However, the review also identified further actions needed to implement the Homelessness Strategy fully and made 21 recommendations outlining the need for additional resources and institutional structures to address homelessness. (Fitzpatrick Associates, 2006)

Further progress remains to be made in rehousing homeless people from emergency accommodation into longer term housing. The vast majority of homeless people avail of emergency accommodation such as hostels and Bed and Breakfast accommodation. Accordingly, while those who sleep rough on the streets comprise the most visible proportion of homeless people, they are in fact only a small minority of those who are homeless. (www.homelessagency.ie) Moreover, many homeless people face considerable difficulties in getting back into permanent accommodation. Recent evidence suggests that people are homeless for longer periods than at the commencement of the Government's *Homelessness: An Integrated Strategy* in 2000. Furthermore, the average time spent by the homeless in emergency accommodation has increased from an average of only 20 days in 1993 to an average of 18 months in 2003. Research has also shown that even where homeless people are able to get onto local authority housing waiting lists, they tend to face longer waiting times to get housed than other households – some local authorities reported typical wait times of two to six years. (Drudy and Punch, 2005: 120)

In Ireland, as elsewhere in Europe, there are three main models of housing provision: social housing, the rental sector and owner-occupier.

Public Housing

The number of dwellings rented from local authorities in Ireland steadily increased up to 1961 but since then it has dropped consistently – from 125,000 in that year to 88,000 units in 2002. Consequently the social housing rental sector (local authorities and housing associations) now represents a mere 7 per cent of total housing. As with the other housing tenures, the situation with public housing varies considerably throughout Europe – from less than 3 per cent in Greece, Austria, Spain and Luxembourg to in excess of 20 per cent in the UK, Denmark and Sweden, with a high of 35 per cent in the Netherlands.

Public housing stock has been significantly reduced by a sales policy to tenants at significant discounts of over 230,000 units out of a stock of approximately 330,000 over the last 70 years. Thus while local authorities and other not-for-profit organisations built 33 per cent of all residences in 1975, this proportion had fallen to 7 per cent by 2004 in spite of the growing need for public housing, which has been exacerbated by soaring house prices. The result is a modest net gain of only 2,400 units per annum over the last decade.

The effects of the increase in house prices and rental accommodation can be clearly seen in the increasing numbers of people on local authority waiting lists for social housing throughout the country. In 2005, for example, 43,700 households (approximately 127,000 people) were on local authority waiting lists – a significant increase since 1999. However, recent estimates suggest that the number of people in housing need (i.e., who cannot afford to buy or rent on the private market together with those on the housing waiting list above) is in the region of 250,000. (Drudy and Punch, 2005) Problems with the ability to meet the costs of accommodation are the single greatest contributor to the need for social housing, and accounted for 44 per cent of households included on the waiting list in 2002.

Table 4.2 Local Authority Housing Waiting List, 2002

Category of Need	*Number of Households*	*% of waiting list*
Homeless	2,468	5.1
Travellers	1,583	3.3
Existing accommodation unfit	4,065	8.4
Existing accommodation overcrowded	8,513	17.6
Involuntary sharing of accommodation	4,421	9.1
Young persons leaving institutional care	82	0.17
Medical or compassionate grounds	3,400	7.0
Elderly persons	2,006	4.1
Disabled or handicapped	423	0.1
Not able to meet costs of existing accommodation	21,452	44.3

Source: CORI, 2003: 90 – Calculated from the Dept of the Environment and Local Government Housing Statistics Bulletin, Sept 2002

The lack of an effective policy on social housing has remained one of the government's major policy failures during its successive terms in office. In 2002, the government significantly amended the requirement (set out in the 2000 Planning and Development Act) that developers allocate 20 per cent of all housing to social and affordable housing. The result is that developers can, in effect, avoid complying with the legislation. In August 2005, The Affordable Homes Partnership (AHP) was established in order "to drive and coordinate the delivery of affordable housing in the greater Dublin areas" as part of the government's pledge to provide 10,000 affordable homes as agreed in the last national pay deal. As yet, the Agency has not directly provided any affordable homes, but it is envisaged that 3,000 per annum will be delivered over the next four years. However the national housing organisation, Threshold, has criticised the AHP's performance to date. For example, in 2005, an estimated 81,000 housing units were completed, yet social housing only accounted for approximately 5,500 of these. (Department of the Environment, Heritage and Local Government, 2005: 35)

The Private Rental Sector

Affordability of accommodation in the private rented sector is severely limited. (Fahey *et al.*, 2004) Average rents in Dublin increased by 53 per cent from 1998 to 2001, although the consumer price index for the same period rose by only 12 per cent. Some rents fell for a short period up to 2004 but rents have generally begun to increase again.

Irish tenants have a long way to go before they reach the conditions enjoyed by many of their EU counterparts in relation to security of tenure and accommodation standards; moreover, while landlords continue to receive substantial tax benefits, private tenants receive very little by way of tax relief or legal protection.

While the 2004 Private Residential Tenancies Act represented an improvement on the previous situation, tenants still remain insecure and can be asked to leave a home for a variety of reasons. There is no rent regulation and minimum standards required by law are not observed in a significant proportion of accommodation, especially that occupied by low-income tenants. While there has been a recent growth in the private rental sector, (from 82,000 to 142,000 units since 1992), the Irish figure for privately rented accommodation remains quite small compared to most countries in Western Europe. (Drudy and Punch, 2005: 18)

Home Ownership

Since the 1970s, successive governments have pursued housing policies which have heavily subsidized owner occupation, including tax relief and tenant purchase schemes. As a result, over 77 per cent of the Irish population are owner occupiers, and Ireland now has one of the highest rates of home ownership in Europe, together with Portugal, Italy,

Greece and Spain of the original EU15, although a number of new Member States either equal or exceed this proportion. (Drudy and Punch, 2005: 17)

By comparison, very little emphasis has been placed by successive governments on the development and regulation of either the rental or public housing sectors.

Q4.3 How extensive and inclusive is the right to education, including education in the rights and responsibilities of citizenship?

Investment in education is considerable and policies are in place to extend and improve provision at all levels. Ireland performs well in some international measures of absolute standards of achievement in education but poorly in others. It has a strong record at the upper echelons of academic attainment. However, Ireland is falling well behind in its expenditure on education relative to other countries. The amount invested in each second-level student in Ireland, relative to the country's national income per capita, puts the country at close to the bottom of the 30 countries surveyed. Access to education is provided free of fees at primary, secondary and tertiary levels. However, a series of payments at each level (for example, textbooks, uniforms and extra-curricular activities at primary and secondary level and registration fees at third level) result in considerable difficulties for a proportion of students.

A range of inequalities persist within the educational system in Ireland. Among the children most affected in Irish society are those from disadvantaged backgrounds, children with disabilities and Traveller children.

A major and growing problem is the almost entirely denominational nature of primary education which discriminates against the growing proportion of people who have no religious affiliation, or those who have a different religious affiliation to those catered for, and who do not wish to have their child educated within the ethos of another or any religion. An associated issue is the complete absence of non-denominational teacher training for the primary level. A further significant problem is the class-based nature of the secondary education system which ensures that parents with sufficient resources are able to choose a school (or other form of education) for their child which leads to significant educational and other advantages. Moreover, the state reinforces this inequality through subvention of fee-paying schools and inadequate funding of the public system. A third and growing challenge is the absence of resources to address the particular requirements of children of immigrants.

Both the preschool and adult education sectors remain underdeveloped. Very little development has taken place in infant education in Ireland for decades, despite international evidence that points to the benefits of shifting educational financing from tertiary level to early childhood education and care where returns on investment are greatest. (Organisation for Economic Co-operation and Development, 2004a: 9) The largely informal and unaccredited adult education sector is also a neglected element of educational provision in Ireland, which has high levels of adult literacy problems by OECD standards.

THE RIGHT TO EDUCATION

The framers of the Irish Constitution expressly included only one socio-economic right, namely that of the right to primary education, which is set out in Article 42. In particular 42.2 provides that "the state shall provide for free primary education and shall endeavour to supplement and give reasonable aid to private and corporate educational initiative, and, when the public good requires it provide other educational facilities or institutions with due regard, however, for the rights of parents, especially in the matter of religious and moral formation". In practice, the courts have begun to enforce the provision so as to require the state to provide education facilities and opportunities of a certain quantity as well as quality. However, interpretation of the extent of individual rights under this article reflects the broadly conservative position taken by judges in relation to economic and social rights in general to such an extent that it is arguable "that the way in which the scope of the education right has been progressively curtailed through judicial interpretation in an era of increased resources is out of step with Ireland's obligation under the International Covenant on Economic, Social and Cultural Rights (ICESCR) to progressively realise economic and social rights". (Nolan, 2007, forthcoming: 17)

EXPENDITURE ON EDUCATION IN IRELAND

The ICESCR's General Comment on Article 13 which deals with the right to education indicates that certain conditions, related to the arrangements and resources prevailing in each state, must be met if this right is to be achieved. These conditions are that educational institutions and programmes have to be available in sufficient quantity, the provision must be accessible to everyone without discrimination, the provision must be acceptable (relevant, culturally appropriate and of good quality) to students and the provision must be adaptable to the changing needs of society. The level of resourcing of education moreover will have a bearing on these four criteria. (Fowler, 2006: 220) Ireland's investment in education as a whole remains below the OECD average, and ranked 25th out of 30 OECD countries in terms of public expenditure on education in 2004. (Organisation for Economic Co-operation and Development, 2004b: 13) And while investment in third-level education in Ireland, at 1.3 per cent of GDP, is around the EU average, Ireland by contrast is significantly below the international average when it comes to elementary, primary and secondary education. Total expenditure on education was equivalent to some 4.9 per cent of GNP in the year 2001, lower than that achieved by 7 other countries in the EU15. (National Economic and Social Council, 2005a: 120)

At the same time the level of public spending per student on education has increased in real terms in recent years. In 2001, 15 per cent of GNP per capita was spent per pupil at primary level and 21 per cent per pupil at secondary level, compared to 32 per cent of GNP per capita being spent on each third-level student. More recently there has been a shift to reduce this gap, as seen in the increase in current public spending per student by approximately 30 per cent at primary and secondary level over the period 1998-2002, compared to an increase by only 8 per cent at third level.

Table 4.3 Expenditure on Educational Institutions as % of GDP by Level of Education, 2001.

Country	*Third Level*
USA	2.7
Denmark	1.8
Sweden	1.7
Ireland	**1.3**
UK	1.1
France	1.1
Germany	1.0
Switzerland	-
OECD Average	*1.4*

Country	*Primary & Secondary*
USA	4.1
Switzerland	4.5
Denmark	4.3
Sweden	4.3
France	4.2
UK	3.9
Germany	3.6
Ireland	**3.1**
OECD Average	*3.8*

Source: Adapted from Organisation for Economic Co-operation and Development, 2004b: 14

The primary, secondary and tertiary levels of Ireland's education system show differing demographics over the past two decades. The number of students at primary level has fallen over this time and increased investment has allowed a significant increase in funding per student. At second level where the number of students has remained relatively constant funding per student has more than doubled. At third level, where the number of students has quite significantly risen, increased investment has allowed funding per student to rise as well, although not as fast as at primary and secondary levels.

Table 4.4 Expenditure on Education by Sector 1985-2002

	Primary		*Secondary*		*Third Level*	
	1985	*2002*	*1985*	*2002*	*1985*	*2002*
Absolute Spend*	794M	1,657M	888M	1,880M	320M	1,227M
Number of Students, '000	566.3	441.0	329.0	340.1	50.8	124.5
Spending Per Student	€1,402	€3,756	€2,699	€5,528	€6,300	€8,246

Source: Adapted from National Economic and Social Council, 2005a: 69;
*Figures for Absolute Spend are estimates based on Chart 3.6

These figures suggest that while Ireland's investment at third level, currently at around the OECD average, may need to increase further, a more concentrated investment at primary and second level is needed to bring Ireland up to average levels of spending in these areas.

INEQUALITIES IN ACCESS AND PARTICIPATION IN EDUCATION

Primary Education

In accordance with both the Irish Constitution and in keeping with Article 13 of the ICESCR, primary education is provided free in Ireland, although this does not take account of required expenditure on uniforms, textbooks and other activities.

Similarly in line with this Article and as also stipulated under the Irish Constitution, parents are free to provide education in their homes, in private schools or in schools recognised or established by the state. There is accordingly no obligation on parents to send their children to school, although the state does require that children receive a certain minimum education.

Despite the increased secularisation of many aspects of Irish society in recent years, the national school system remains almost entirely a denominational one, largely financed by the state but controlled by religious bodies, predominantly the Catholic Church. Ninety-eight per cent of all schools are privately owned by religious organisations and recent legislation has strengthened the control of religious organisations over the operational practices of schools. (Educate Together, 2005) The religious or "denominational" nature of the system was enshrined in the "Rules for National Schools" published in 1965. In 1971, the traditional separation of education from religious instruction was contravened in the "New Curriculum", which called for the religious ethos of the school to permeate the entire programme. This change effectively annulled the right of parents to absent their children from specific denominational content in schools. The Education Act (1998) obliged the Board of Management of a national school to promote the religious ethos of its patron. The Equal Status Act (2000) included specific exemptions for schools that allow them to discriminate on religious grounds to maintain their characteristic religious spirit. It is arguable that this provision is a violation of both the Irish Constitution and Article 13(2) (a) of the ICESCR which requires that "primary education shall be compulsory and available free to all" and it has been argued that it is a clear violation of Article 5 (d) (vii) of the Convention on the Elimination of all Forms of Racial Discrimination to which Ireland is a signatory. In that Convention Article, State Parties undertake to guarantee the right of everyone without distinction as to race, colour, or national or ethnic origin...the enjoyment of the following rights...in particular: ...The right to freedom of thought, conscience and religion. An example of the violations involved include instances in which parents holding different views are compelled to send their children to schools that uphold religious views that contradict their own religion, thought or conscience. This practice is taking place in a period of unprecedented increase in ethnic, cultural and religious diversity within the population of the state. The 2002 census recorded a number of religions for the first time and the largest single minority religious identity was that of "no religion". As a result of this increasing diversity, rising numbers of families are being compelled to send their children to schools that promote – and must in law promote – a religious ethos that conflicts with their conscience and lawful preference. They are compelled to do so because the state has not acted to provide reasonable access to schools that provide an alternative. (Educate Together, 2005) (See Section 3)

In 1998, the Education Act – the first such act in the history of the state – obliged the Board of Management of a school to uphold the ethos of its Patron and provided significant penalties for failing to do so.

In 2000, the Education and Welfare Act obliged a parent to ensure that their child was attending a "recognised programme of education" by the age of 6 and provided significant penalties for failing to do so.

In 1998 and 2000 the Employment Equality Act and Equal Status Act allowed schools with religious patronage to discriminate in favour of persons of their religions in order to protect their ethos. This practice is allowed both in the employment of staff, in enrolment policy and in the selection of Board members.

Post-primary Education

Article 13 (2) (b) of the ICESCR states that "secondary education in its different forms including technical and vocational secondary education shall be made generally available and accessible to all by every appropriate means, and in particular by the progressive introduction of free education". Post-primary education has been provided free in Ireland since the 1960s.

Around 85 per cent of 20-24 year olds have completed second level education compared to the EU average of 78 per cent. (Department of Education and Science, 2005) Around 60 per cent of students attend academically oriented secondary schools. Vocational schools and colleges educate just over a quarter of students, while around 14 per cent of students attend comprehensive schools. Secondary schools are generally denominational and single sex. Vocational schools tend to be non-denominational and single sex.

By comparison with other countries such as the UK and Australia, Ireland does not have a market-driven, choice-based education system. Nonetheless, one of the outcomes of increasing income inequality is the resulting inequality of access to educational choice. In the context of a historically flexible system wherein half of all second-level students do not attend their nearest school, middle-class parents increasingly tend to choose fee-paying schooling, pay for private tuition or opt out of the formal school sector entirely and enrol their children in private colleges to gain advantage in the points race for entry to third-level education. Such a trend is arguably proof of "how economically generated inequalities outside of education systematically undermine equality of access, participation and outcome within. (Lynch and Moran, 2006: 221)

Furthermore all schools including private schools in Ireland receive state funding for teachers' salaries and other current costs. The rationale provided for state subsidy of private schools is that of protection of the rights of religious minorities. However a significant proportion of those who attend these schools are not of the same religious denomination. (Lynch and Moran, 2006)

The findings of the *Equality and Power in Schools* (EPS) study show "...schools do not have to have a selective entrance test to be effectively socially selective. Although all the schools were open to applicants from different social classes within their catchment area, in practice some schools had means at their disposal to discourage applicants from social class groups that they did not wish to serve. These included school traditions, extracurricular activities, voluntary contributions (indirect fees) and uniforms." (Lynch and Lodge, 2002: 37-63)

In 2006, 27 grind (or extra tuition) school businesses were identified, 13 of which offer full-time leaving certificate courses. At present there is no way of establishing a comprehensive tally of the numbers attending these schools. (Lynch and Moran, 2006)

Third-Level Education

The third-level sector is made up of a number of different types of institution funded directly by the state and a small private sector. These include 7 universities, 13 institutes of technology, 7 teacher training colleges (all of which are denominational), and a small number of private colleges. A National Qualifications Framework has recently been developed which will introduce a single framework for the standardisation of all qualifications across all providers within the state. One of the intended effects of this measure will be to make it easier for students to build credits for access to educational providers and similarly to progress from one educational provider to another.

The growth in third-level education has been one of Ireland's success stories and is seen by many as having laid the foundation for the country's current economic success. In a single generation, attendance at third-level has risen from just 21,000 in 1965 to over 137,000 in 2003, which represents an over five fold increase in the percentage of the school-leaving age population that continues on to third-level. The national rate of admission to higher education institutions in Ireland was 55 per cent in 2004, an increase of 11 points on the 1998 admission rate of 44 per cent. Indeed, such is the steady increase that the rate of admission in 2004 was more than two-and-a-half times that of the 1980 rate. This increase has also been accompanied by a fall in the numbers leaving second-level schools, whereby the 72,700 school leavers in 1999 had decreased by almost 5,000 to 67,760 in 2004. (O'Connell *et al.*, 2006: 132) The majority of new entrants in 2004 to higher education overall were female (54 per cent), while males accounted for the majority of new entrants to the institutes of technology (53 per cent).

Irish participation rates in higher education are high by European standards; the participation rates for 20 year-olds in Ireland in 2001/2 stood at 38 per cent compared to an average of 32 per cent across the EU25. Moreover, the participation rates among those aged 18 in Ireland are also well ahead of the EU average, though it should be noted that the 20 per cent participation rate of those aged 22 years is substantially lower in Ireland than the 27 per cent EU average. (O'Connell *et al.*, 2006: 12)

INEQUALITIES OF EDUCATIONAL OUTCOMES

Ireland ranks highly in international measures of absolute standards of achievement in education. In the most recent UNICEF league tables on education, Ireland ranks 8th out of 24 countries from across the developed world. Within Europe, only Finland, Austria and the UK fare better. Ireland in turn ranks higher than Sweden, New Zealand, France, the USA and Germany. (United Nations Children's Fund, 2002) The UNICEF rankings are based on the percentage of students in each country scoring fixed standards in reading literacy at 15 years old, maths and science literacy at 15 years old, and maths and science achievement at eighth grade. The OECD's Programme for International Student Assessment (PISA) ranked Ireland as 5th out of 26 countries for reading literacy, 9th for scientific literacy and 15th for mathematical literacy. (National Economic and Social Council, 2005a: 120)

Ireland has a high level of educational disadvantage among certain groups within the school-going population and a poor record of investment in preschool education, in adult education (National Economic and Social Council, 2005a: 122) and in provision for those with disabilities. A useful measure of a country's comparative performance in promoting equality is "relative educational disadvantage". This measure demonstrates how far behind poor performers are compared to the average. Countries which do not allow low-achieving pupils to fall too far behind are doing relatively well in containing inequality. (United Nations Children's Fund, 2002: 2) In the international league table of relative educational disadvantage, Ireland ranks 13th out of 24 countries. (United Nations Children's Fund, 2002)

In Ireland, schools which are classified as disadvantaged on the basis of the socio-economic characteristics of their students are allocated resources accordingly. About 300 of the 3,200 primary schools in the state are designated as disadvantaged. However, while greater attention and resources have been directed towards redressing educational disadvantage, little progress in improving outcomes is actually being made. For example, children in disadvantaged areas are three times more likely to suffer severe literacy problems than children from other schools. (Eivers *et al.*, 2004)

Among the students with poorest educational outcomes in Irish society are those from disadvantaged backgrounds, students with disabilities, and Traveller students.

Social Class

The most recent official analysis of participation rates offers evidence of a trend toward improved equality of access to higher education. School leavers from manual social class backgrounds have greatly increased their share of new entrants since 1998, while the admission rates of those from semi-skilled and unskilled manual workers also increased, although their admission rate was still well below the average in 2004. There has also been an increase in the number of students from disadvantaged areas entering third-level, though there continue to be areas with very low admission rates. All Dublin postal code districts experienced increases in admission rates since 1998. For example, in Finglas-Ballymun, the number of students entering third-level increased from 14 per cent to 28 per cent, while in Tallaght-Firhouse, the number of students increased from 26 per cent to 40 per cent. (O'Connell *et al.*, 2006: 9)

However, young people from professional backgrounds continue to account for a disproportionately higher share of entrants to higher education. Children of higher professionals and farmers are heavily overrepresented among the new entrants, and other socio-economic groups (employers and managers, lower professionals, skilled manual workers) are also overrepresented among new entrants, while those underrepresented include non-manual workers, semi and unskilled manual workers and agricultural workers. (O'Connell *et al.*, 2006: 65)

Social class gradations also exist between types of third-level institutions. For example, more students from disadvantaged backgrounds gain entry to institutes of technology than to the state's universities. Partly as a consequence, the institutes of technology have much higher non-completion rates, with around one third of students leaving without finishing their course, compared to one in ten in the universities.

The consequences of leaving secondary school without qualifications are severe. Of those unemployed in 1997, 63 per cent had not completed secondary education. (Tovey and Share, 2003: 218) Almost 90 per cent of children from families with professional backgrounds left school having completed the Leaving Certificate, compared to just 77 per cent of their counterparts from semi-and unskilled manual family backgrounds. Overall, approximately one fifth of students leave secondary school without reaching Leaving Certificate level. (O'Connell *et al.*, 2006: 56–7)

The government has responded to the various reports on inequality at third-level by setting up the Third-Level Access Fund in 2000, which aims to tackle underrepresentation among three specific target groups: students with disabilities, students from disadvantaged backgrounds, and mature students. The universities and institutes of technology have all appointed access officers and the Higher Education Authority is putting pressure on government to have funding for individual third-level institutions linked to performance targets on access. In 2004, 30 per cent of new entrants to higher education were in receipt of the registration grant. This figure was highest in the institute of technology sector (36 per cent), followed by the colleges of education (32 per cent) and the universities (26 per cent). (O'Connell *et al.*, 2006: 29)

Travellers

Some progress has been made in respect of children from the Traveller community. In recent years a majority of Traveller children complete primary education, and while currently only a small minority from the Traveller community continue on to complete second level education, this is still an improvement, compared with 1995. (Irish Traveller Movement and Combat Poverty Agency, 2002)

Disability

About a quarter of chronically-ill or disabled people aged 25-34 have no educational qualifications compared with only 6 per cent of others in this age group. Those with a chronic illness or disability are also only half as likely among this age group to have a third-level qualification as those without. (Gannon and Nolan, 2005)

Since the mid-1990s a number of cases have come before the Irish courts concerning the rights of individuals with disabilities to access appropriate education. The first significant case addressing the state's duty to protect the right of children with disabilities to free primary education was *O'Donoghue v Minister for Health (1996)*. The judge in the case described the right to free education as involving a right for all children to an education which uses their natural abilities to their fullest potential, no matter how limited these abilities might be. The judge also stated that such education should continue for as long as further development was possible or discernable. (Nolan, 2007, forthcoming)

Another important case concerning the right of individuals with disabilities to education is *Sinnott v Minister for Education (2001)*. Here the applicant was a 23 year-old autistic man. The Supreme Court judgement in this case, which defined the constitutional right to primary education very narrowly by limiting it to those under the age of 18, highlights the general judicial reluctance to become involved in enforcing constitutional rights of a socio-economic nature with particular regard to the doctrine of the separation of powers. According to the Irish Human Rights Commission (Irish Human Rights Commission, 2005: 100), the manner in which the Irish courts have interpreted the right to free primary education under Article 42.4 has ensured that it has not become a strong mechanism for vindicating children's rights. In particular, the failure of the court to vindicate the rights of persons with disabilities over the age of 18 is "indicative of how any attempts to take an expansive interpretation of Article 42.4 have been curtailed". (Nolan, 2007, forthcoming)

The Education for Persons with Special Educational Needs Act, 2004 describes the structures for implementing the provisions of the Act, including the establishment of a National Council for Special Education.

The Act acknowledges that persons with special educational needs have the same right to education as those without special educational needs. The goal of the Act is to ensure that individuals with special educational needs can leave school with the necessary skills to participate in society to the level of their ability.

It is envisaged that the respective Ministers for Education and Science, for Health and Children and for Finance will all have roles in taking government policy into account in discharging special education responsibilities.

One of the key problems of the Act, according to the National Disability Authority, is that resources will be provided to a school for the education of the relevant student subject to available resources. Indeed, the Act makes clear that any decisions made by the Minister for Education or the Minister for Health must be approved by the Minister for Finance.

Moreover, the timeframe of the Act allows the provisions to be implemented over the course of several years, so that the types of delay that have hindered special educational provision to date are likely to continue for several years to come. (National Disability Authority, 2005a)

ADULT EDUCATION

While Article 13 of the ICESCR requires that "Fundamental education shall be encouraged or intensified as far as possible for those persons who have not received or completed the whole period of their primary education", the adult education sector remains one of the more neglected elements of educational provision in Ireland. Approximately only 2 per cent of students enrolled in Irish universities are aged 26 and over, compared with around 20 per cent in the OECD as a whole. Within the non-university sector, including the Institutes of Technology, the figure is around 1 per cent compared with the OECD average of almost 37 per cent. (Tovey and Share, 2003: 198)

While the proportion of Irish adults that have a third-level education attainment is above the OECD average, the proportion that did not complete secondary education is also above the mean. For example, similar proportions of Irish and Swiss 25-64 years olds had a third-level attainment in 2002 but the proportion of Irish 25-64 year olds with less than a completed secondary education was 2.66 times greater in Ireland than in Switzerland. (National Economic and Social Council, 2005a: 123)

The statistics for educational attainment of the adult population in Ireland paint a very different picture of Irish society than that conveyed by the successful performances in international league tables of our second- and third-level students. The table below shows the percentage of the working age population who have completed secondary education. In contrast to the high ranking Ireland achieves in measures of young people's educational performance, Ireland ranks 16th out of the 21 countries for which data is available.

Table 4.5 Proportion of the Population Aged 25-64 who have Completed Secondary Education

Country	*1995*	*2005*
USA	86	88
Germany	84	88
Switzerland	82	86
UK	76	82
Sweden	75	82
France	68	79
Finland	65	74
New Zealand	59	64
Ireland	**47**	**58**
Greece	43	57
Italy	35	48
Spain	28	41
Portugal	20	30

Source: Adapted from Tovey and Share, 2003: 190

This poor performance echoes a 1995 OECD report which showed that Ireland had a level of adult literacy problems second only to Poland among the countries surveyed. One-quarter of Irish adults were found to be restricted to the most basic level of literacy skills. (Tovey and Share, 2003: 197)

Over 90 per cent of the five-fold increase in the numbers of students in third-level education has been generated by the 18-to-20 year-old cohort. Lifelong learning, wider participation and encouragement of mature students to enter third-level education have not been given the same emphasis, (Organisation for Economic Co-operation and Development, 2004b: 8) although under the new social partnership agreement, *Towards 2016*, there is a commitment to investing in lifelong learning and increasing access to training, developing new skills, acquiring recognised qualifications and higher level qualifications. (Department of the Taoiseach, 2006: 23–31)

EARLY CHILDHOOD CARE AND EDUCATION

Childcare

Funding for Early Childhood Care and Education (ECCE) in Ireland is low by international standards. Public spending per child aged 0-6 in Ireland constitutes a smaller part of GDP than in other countries. For example, an estimated expenditure of €2,075 per child aged 0-6 in 2002 compares to $4,050 per child in Austria. (National Economic and Social Council, 2005a) At less than 0.2 per cent of GDP, government investment in childcare is only half of the 0.4 per cent OECD average, and differs substantially from that of 0.7 per cent for France and 0.8 per cent in Denmark. As a consequence Irish parents pay almost three times more for childcare than their EU counterparts, spending on average 20 per cent of their earnings compared to 8 per cent in other EU countries. (National Economic and Social Forum, 2005a: 31; 38)

The childcare sector in Ireland is expensive, fragmented, underregulated and largely privately based. At the same time the increase in employment among women since the mid-1990s has led to an unprecedented increase in demand. Around one-fifth of mothers with full-time jobs and almost half of those with part-time jobs do not use paid childcare at all, relying instead on partner, family, friends or neighbours. (Corrigan, 2002) A recent report on childcare provision in Dublin found that 72 per cent of respondents need access to childcare. In particular the report stressed the need for greater flexibility in the range of childcare services offered. Only 52 per cent of childcare providers indicated that they offered flexibility on full-time and part-time care. (Dublin City Childcare Committee, 2006) Within the political arena childcare is predominantly seen as a means of facilitating women's access to the workforce. For example, the government's

National Childcare Strategy is based on employment policy and seeks to address the needs of children whose parent(s) are at work. The responsibility for delivery of the National Childcare Strategy lies with the Department of Equality, Justice and Law Reform, and not with the Department of Education. Under the strategy a number of measures are provided to improve the level of childcare support including grants for providers and tax relief for employers.

The National Economic and Social Forum (NESF) report notes that it is the children of parents in disadvantaged communities who are most likely to benefit from ECCE. Presently in Ireland, existing government policy provides for childcare and family support in disadvantaged areas, and for Traveller preschool children and children with special educational needs. The success of this policy is, however, open to debate, the OECD report of 2004 concluded that "the further development of early intervention programmes...for Traveller Children ...will be the acid test of national policies to combat poverty and achieve social inclusion". (Organisation for Economic Co-operation and Development, 2004a: 73) Despite the increase in the number of the childcare places, issues of affordable access still apply, particularly in areas of highest disadvantage. For example, in Tallaght West, there were only 300 preschool playgroups for 3,000 children aged 0-4 years. (National Economic and Social Forum, 2005a: 23)

Overall, the NESF report notes that there has been little progress in implementing the policy decisions set out in the government's white paper on *Early Childhood Education* (1999), especially in relation to the structures that are needed to facilitate greater levels of integration of care and education, concluding that "overall...[there is] a picture of relative inaction, peripheral implementation and drift". (National Economic and Social Forum, 2005a: 33)

Early Childhood Education

One consequence of the exorbitant cost of childcare is that it tends to direct the focus of government and public concern away from the issue of early childhood education. The 0-6 age group are not yet seen in Ireland as a cohort of children who have their own cognitive and developmental needs, and there remains an almost total void in policy thinking with regard to issues of pedagogy and childhood development in the early years.

In most OECD countries, between 80 per cent and 100 per cent of children aged 3 to 6 years are in education provided and regulated by education ministries. In Ireland this figure is only 56 per cent which is among the lowest in Europe. (Organisation for Economic Co-operation and Development, 2006) Very little development has taken place in infant education in Ireland in decades. Recent figures from the Department of Education and Science show that 24 per cent of children in infant class are in groups of 30 or more, a child-to-staff ratio which the OECD state would be unacceptable for young children in most European countries. (Corrigan, 2002)

While all children in Ireland suffer the consequences of underinvestment in early childhood education, some of them suffer more than others. For example, children under 4 years of age with disabilities have no entitlement to education provision, although it is recognised internationally that children with special needs should receive structured and regular educational support in the earliest years, and that crucial time is lost if educational intervention only starts at the beginning of infant or primary school. Yet, in Ireland, children under 4 with special needs remain at home without the educational intervention that could act to markedly improve their long-term social and individual development. (Organisation for Economic Co-operation and Development, 2004a)

Many children from disadvantaged backgrounds, along with Traveller children, similarly lack the preschool educational interventions that would enable them to overcome the disadvantage they most likely face at the primary school gates on their first day at school.

While government funded programmes such as *Early Start* and pre-school programmes for children from the Traveller community focus on groups most at risk, government policy remains predominantly focused on childcare rather than on developing a coherent joined–up development-based policy for early childhood education and care. Similarly, there has been little debate on the role of early childhood education and care within society, and the ill effects of current practices on children's development.

International evidence shows that adequate public funding of early childhood education and care is more than compensated by savings in health and social security expenditure, improved educational levels and productivity in the next generation, greater tax returns from larger numbers of women in employment, lower crime and enhanced social cohesion. On the other hand early educational disadvantage is likely to perpetuate itself through educational underachievement and a greater likelihood of economic marginalisation and social exclusion. (United Nations Children's Fund, 2002: 3)

CIVIC EDUCATION

Concepts of citizenship have become more relevant in the context of recent social, economic and demographic changes in Irish society. For the first time in living memory, Ireland is experiencing significant immigration, and an estimated 160 different nationalities are now living here. Modern Irish citizens no longer necessarily share common ethnic or cultural backgrounds, and more diversity exists around moral, religious and ethical perspectives. Other developments, such as the Good Friday Agreement and Ireland's membership of the European Union have also meant that the concept of Irish citizenship has necessarily become more multifaceted. (See Q1.1)

An active democratic citizenry is only possible if people are educated for citizenship and are provided with accessible opportunities and mechanisms for participation. Political literacy, i.e., a critical understanding of democracy and democratic political institutions and systems, is a key component of democratic citizenship education. Tolerance, interdependency, civic self-restraint and openness to deliberative argument are also core components of citizenship education.

At present, neither democratic citizenship, nor political education, is taught as an independent subject to senior cycle, a shortfall which is at odds with most of our European neighbours. This void leaves many people in Ireland at a disadvantage in their awareness of and engagement with many global and national issues, and hinders their ability to participate fully in discussions and decisions on issues as diverse as health care, disadvantage and their rights as residents or citizens of Ireland.

In its recent report, the Democracy Commission recommended the extension of social and political education to the senior cycle at second level. In particular, the Commission favoured the introduction of citizenship studies as a full optional subject to the Leaving Certificate. Additionally, the Commission recommended promoting citizenship issues in primary schools, promoting greater democracy within school structures and providing training and materials to support teachers of democratic citizenship education. (Harris, 2005: 35)

Q4.4 To what extent is the health of the population equally protected, in all spheres and stages of life?

Public spending on health has soared over the last decade to the point where the health budget is over one-quarter of all government current spending. Despite this funding increase health outcomes are universally considered to be poor. For example, waiting times for hospital admission through Accident and Emergency departments have become an issue of considerable concern to the Irish population and significant financial barriers to accessing primary care are an obstacle to improved population health. Moreover, the resources provided to date fall short of those set out in the government's 2001 Health Strategy on which there was widespread consensus. There is also a greater likelihood of ill health for those who are poor, which is compounded by inequalities in access to health services between those who can afford private treatment and those reliant on public provision. Major structural reform of the administration of the health system was carried out in 2005 but it is as yet too early to evaluate its impact.

HEALTH – RIGHT OR COMMODITY?

Article 12 of the IESCR states that each state party "recognises the right of everyone to the enjoyment of the highest attainable standard of physical and mental health", while Article 12.2 outlines the ways in which this right should be realised, including under (d) "The creation of conditions which would assure to all medical service and medical attention in the event of sickness". In 2002, the UN Monitoring Committee, in its review of Ireland, expressed regret about the absence of a human rights framework in the government's health strategy, published in 2001. As yet there is no free-standing recognition of the right to health in Ireland. Unlike many countries including Belgium, Finland, the Netherlands, Portugal and Spain, the Irish Constitution does not contain a provision on the right to health. (Mesquita, 2006: 152) The Committee urged the government to embrace the principles of "non-discrimination and equal access to health facilities and services' and to introduce a single equal waiting list for public and private patients in public hospitals. (Wren, 2003: 17) Similar calls were made by the Commission on Health Funding (1989), and by the National Economic and Social Forum (2002), but there is no indication to date that the government intends to implement this recommendation.

The Health Strategy, if implemented, would provide greater levels of equity in access to healthcare for the most vulnerable groups in Irish society. However, its commitment to reduce public subsidies for the private sector would require the government to take on one of the most powerful groups in the health sector, namely the hospital consultants.

STATE EXPENDITURE ON HEALTH

There have been substantial increases in health funding in recent years, with the total budget estimate for 2007 in excess of €13 billion. The Minister for Finance, Brian Cowen, cited some of the benefits of this spending, including an increase in health service staff together with a concomitant increase in service delivery. (*Irish Times*, 16 November 2006) Recent OECD data show Ireland's current per capita public spending on health at 94 per cent of the EU15 average in 2003. The most recent data which also shows Ireland's capital investment in health care per capita to be the highest in the EU15 must be understood against a background of cutbacks and underinvestment over decades, in particular the reductions in acute hospital beds in the late 1980s and early 1990s. Overall, from 1970 to 1996, Ireland invested on average just over 63 per cent of the EU average in health. (Tussing and Wren, 2006: 8) While it is argued that Ireland needs to spend less than other countries because of its demographics, this view is contested, and, in the context of nationally-set targets, the resources for health provided to date fall short of those contained in government policy as outlined in the 2001 Health Strategy.

INEQUALITIES IN THE HEALTH OF THE POPULATION

Life Expectancy

Life expectancy in Ireland was the lowest of all 15 EU countries in the mid 1990s. Increases in life expectancy have been achieved since 1997, largely due to lower mortality rates for infants and young children. Life expectancy for older people, who are more likely to experience heart disease and cancer, has hardly improved at all. At age 65, Irish male life expectancy was at the bottom jointly with Denmark of the EU15 table. For women at age 65, Irish life expectancy was second from the bottom in the EU15 league table. (Tussing and Wren, 2006: 6)

Deficiencies in the Irish health care system (Tussing and Wren, 2006) are only one reason why Irish life expectancy is lower than the Western European average. Some of the other key factors include obesity, breast cancer and youth suicide. Tackling obesity will require investment in the public health service and linking social welfare incomes to the cost of health foodstuffs. Meantime the national breast screening programme, BreastCheck, is currently confined to the eastern regions of the country, while mental health resources are overstretched and best developed in the areas of greatest affluence, rather than the areas of greatest need.

Poverty and Ill-health

Health services have a prominent place in the public and political agenda in Ireland. Health policy in Ireland, as in many other countries, has for decades been based on the implicit assumption that the greater provision of better health services is the most direct means of improving the health of the population. Issues of equity in the public mind most often focus on a range of inequities that exist in regional access to healthcare. However, as can be seen in the box below, the greatest obstacle in access to health is poverty. There is strong and consistent evidence of a direct relationship between health and socio-economic status in Ireland. The stark reality is that poor people in Ireland get sick more often and die younger.

This reality shows up in the difference in death rates among working age men from different socio-economic backgrounds. Death rates for all causes of death were over three times higher in the lowest occupational class than in the highest. The death rates for cancer are over twice as high as among the highest class, and over six times higher for deaths from respiratory diseases, and for injuries and poisonings. (Institute of Public Health in Ireland, 2001) Further evidence is presented in the box on the following page.

Health Inequalities in Ireland

- Unskilled manual male workers are twice as likely to die prematurely as higher professional men.
- Unskilled manual male workers are eight times more likely to die as a result of accidents than higher professional men.
- Unskilled manual workers are almost four times more likely to be admitted to hospital for the first time for schizophrenia than higher professional workers.
- There is an increasing socio-economic gradient in the incidence of all psychiatric conditions from professional to unskilled manual groups.
- Unemployed women are more than twice as likely to give birth to low-weight babies as women in the higher professional socio-economic group.
- Perinatal and infant mortality rates are higher in families where the father is an unskilled manual worker or is unemployed.
- On average, Traveller women live 12 years less than women in the general population. Traveller men live on average 10 years less than men in the general population. Travellers' babies experience higher rates of still-birth, infant mortality and perinatal mortality.
- The prevalences of specific conditions, such as coronary heart disease and lung cancer, are higher in geographic areas that experience higher levels of socio-economic deprivation.
- Adults and children in lower socio-economic groups have higher levels of smoking, higher body mass index and less healthy eating habits than those in higher socio-economic groups.
- Homeless people experience high incidences of ill health. A study in 1997 found that 40 per cent of hostel dwellers in Cork had serious psychiatric illnesses, 42 per cent had problems of alcohol dependency and 18 per cent had other physical problems.
- The prison population suffers from a disproportionately large rate of psychiatric and drug-related problems. Almost one-quarter of this population suffers from a long-standing disability or illness that limits their activity.
- On average, 39 per cent of men and women surveyed in 2003 identified financial problems as the greatest factor in preventing them from improving their health.

Source: Tussing, and Wren, 2006: 43–4.

The distribution of illness is thus considerably more concentrated towards the bottom of the income distribution. It is not surprising, therefore, that a higher share of total health spending is on people on lower incomes when levels of expenditure are assessed, given that the higher proportion of illness is concentrated in this population. However, when assessed on a per capita basis, the expenditure per person is higher for those who are better off.

TRAVELLERS

The relationship between poverty and ill-health is starkly illustrated in statistics relating to the Traveller community, whose health is significantly worse than the health of those in the settled community. Members of the Traveller community:

- live between 10 and 12 years less than the population as a whole;
- have a sudden-infant-death rate that is 12 times higher than for the general population; and
- many expectant mothers suffer malnutrition, and babies suffer ill-health because of diet and many adults experience hunger. (Pavee Point Travellers Centre, 2005)

Factors influencing the health of members of the Traveller community include poor quality of living conditions, racism, discrimination and lack of health promotion. Many Travellers have difficulty in registering with a general practitioner (GP) and only a small number of GPs were found in many areas who provided services to Travellers. Lack of targeted education and training materials have also contributed to a low uptake of health services. A Traveller health policy unit now exists at department level. At regional level, Traveller health units have been established and primary health care for Traveller projects now exist at local level.

INEQUALITIES IN THE IRISH HEALTH SYSTEM

As we have seen above, one of the main determinants of health inequalities lies in socio-economic conditions, and any overall strategy for lessening health inequalities has to address these socio-economic conditions. A second determinant of inequality is access to healthcare, which may be defined as access on the basis of medical need or capacity to benefit from care, irrespective of other factors such as ability to pay or where one lives. (National Economic and Social Forum, 2002)

The Two-tier System: Private and Public Care in Hospitals

Unequal access for public and private patients to public hospital services is one of the issues of greatest public concern in Ireland. The National Treatment Purchase Fund (NTPF) was established to reduce the length of time public patients are on hospital waiting lists by offering them a choice in obtaining access to treatments. By the end of 2005, over 40,000 patients had been treated under the NTPF and waiting times have been substantially reduced. (www.ntpf.ie) However, it remains the case that people have been offered much faster, sometimes immediate, access when they have indicated that they will opt for treatment as a private patient. An individual's ability to pay and/or access to medical insurance undoubtedly allows them to access treatment more quickly.

For historical reasons, Ireland's health system comprises a mix of public and private services, known as the two-tier system. Both public and private hospitals exist within the hospital system; moreover, all hospital consultants within publicly-funded hospitals are employed under contracts that allow them to treat both public and private patients in beds within the publicly-funded hospital where they work. As a result, approximately 20 per cent of overnight beds and 32 per cent of day beds within each public hospital are designated for consultants' private patients. Furthermore, hospital consultants are paid by salary for public patients and by fee for private patients treated in public hospitals. This practice has led to a number of inequalities in treatment such as the earlier treatment of private patients as noted above. Private patients are also more likely to be treated personally by the consultant, while public patients are more likely to be treated by non-consultant hospital doctors. Irish hospitals also receive revenues for patient care, which are significantly higher for private patients and provide an incentive for hospitals to favour them. (Tussing and Wren, 2006: 128) This two-tier arrangement is unusual compared to other countries, as most states do not provide private services in public hospitals. And in those countries which do, such as Australia, there is a single waiting list for elective surgery and patients are treated on the basis of clinical need. (*Irish Times*, 2 June 2003)

Government proposals to reform consultants' contracts by no longer allowing publicly salaried consultants to work for private hospitals, off the site of their employing public hospital, have met resistance from medical organisations. Although the Minister for Health had appeared to support a public-only contract for consultants on public salaries, it later emerged that she envisaged that they should retain the right to work in private hospitals on the site of public hospitals. Negotiations on contract reform were stalled on these issues in late 2006.

Recently announced government policy to support the provision of private hospitals on the site of public hospitals has met with political and medical opposition and unfavourable critiques from health economists, most recently in the Irish Congress of Trade Unions (ICTU) prebudget 2007 submission. The argument is that the negatives outweigh the positives in the government's plan to permit construction of private hospitals on the grounds of public hospitals. Private hospitals do not offer a complete acute care service, but instead concentrate on elective surgery in less complex and more profitable areas. For that reason, private beds in newly constructed private hospitals on public hospital grounds will not free up private beds in public hospitals for public use on anything like a one-for-one basis. On the contrary, there will be a net increase in private beds, for which taxpayers will pay. (Tussing and Wren, 2006)

Financial Barriers to Accessing Healthcare

Around 25 per cent of the Irish population do not qualify for medical cards nor hold medical insurance. Medical cards provide entitlements to receive services, including GP visits, prescriptions, drugs, and hospital treatment, free of charge. However, the Health Service Executive (HSE) data shows that the proportion of the Irish population covered by medical cards has dropped from 39 per cent in 1977 to 29 per cent in 2006. This includes people aged over 70 who would not qualify on income grounds. The proportion of the population qualifying on income or hardship grounds alone has dropped to 26 per cent in 2006. However, there is evidence that many of those on low incomes, but above the medical card limit, cannot afford to pay for healthcare. More recently a new doctor-only medical card has been introduced but holders must pay for treatment by other professionals such as physiotherapists and also for drug costs. Although the government promised 200,000 of these cards in 2004, uptake has been low and stood at 42,000 or one per cent of the population in November 2006.

Geographic distribution of essential services

The fact that most medical providers, including GPs, dentists, opticians and pharmacists, are self-employed presents a considerable challenge to ensuring an equitable distribution of health services either nationally or within urban areas, given that market demand and personal choice largely determine where medical providers choose to work and live. It is not surprising therefore that research has highlighted considerable variation in the geographic distribution of GP and other services. Regional assessment services for people with physical disability and adolescent psychiatric services are two other examples of services which show substantial regional variation. (Harkin, 2001: 19) Under-funding at a national level, national politics, and even competing county loyalties also play a role in the pattern of such geographical biases.

UNDERDEVELOPMENT OF ESSENTIAL SERVICES

A major issue facing the Irish health system is the problem of underfunding and the underdeveloped nature of many essential services.

Primary Care

While the term primary care is often understood to mean GP services alone, it actually includes a range of professional services also provided by public health nurses, physiotherapists, home helps, speech and language therapists, practice nurses, community pharmacists, psychologists and others. Primary care aims to keep people well through health promotion, screening, assessment, diagnosis and rehabilitation. However, the primary care system in Ireland is acknowledged to be both underdeveloped and fragmented and places a major emphasis on diagnosis and treatment of illness, with little capacity for illness prevention and rehabilitation.

The uneven geographical distribution of health professionals in these various disciplines also means that services are often unavailable, and that individual professionals often work in isolation with limited teamwork across the different medical services. As a result of these limitations, secondary-care institutions, primarily hospitals, very often provide many of the services which are more appropriate for primary care. (Department of Health and Children, 2001b: 15) One effect of this situation can be seen dramatically in the overcrowding of Accident and Emergency (A&E) departments in many of the country's hospitals. Patients are often forced to present at A&E departments simply because there is nowhere else to go to receive attention for what may turn out to be the simplest of medical complaints. The expense associated with GP visits further exacerbates the situation, as many people present at A&E as a means of avoiding that expense. As a result, two significant studies, the Department of Health's Primary Care Strategy and a joint report from the Irish Medical Organisation (IMO) and the Irish College of General Practitioners (ICGP), have advocated major reform in Irish general practice and the broader system of primary care. Both reports said that general practice should move away from isolated smaller practices that focus on diagnosis and treatment of illness to multiphysician team practices with an enhanced capacity for health promotion, prevention of illness and rehabilitation. Nonetheless, the government has since effectively abandoned its widely hailed Primary Care Strategy, neither following up the 10 pilot projects set up therein, nor introducing further legislation or funding to implement the enhanced team practices envisioned in its document. (Tussing and Wren, 2006: 153–74)

Preventative Health

Breast cancer takes the lives of more women than any other cancer in Ireland, with around 600 deaths every year. Meanwhile it is estimated that around one in every 25 Irish women will develop cervical cancer in their lifetime. Around 60 women die of cervical cancer in Ireland every year, despite the fact that it is preventable. There is currently no colon cancer screening programme in Ireland, although this is one of the most commonly diagnosed types of cancer in the country. Those screening programmes that do exist, such as the National Breast Screening Programme, are available only in the Eastern Region although a planned national roll-out of the programme is promised funding in the 2007 budget. A recent vigorous campaign to lobby government for a cervical cancer screening programme also appears to be meeting with some success. Some funding has been allocated to begin a roll-out of this programme in 2007.

Care of the Elderly

There is a chronic lack of respite-care facilities in Ireland. Respite care, which allows carers a period of time away from their care duties, may be either community based, such as home help or day centres, or residential. Requests for home help services appear to be turned down if there seems to be someone else such as a relative or neighbour available to fulfill the role. As a result, this service is largely dependent on volunteers. Similarly, day care centres are largely provided by the voluntary sector and the number of places is widely accepted as being inadequate. (National Council on Ageing and Older People, 2001a) However, the day care sector may be undergoing some privatisation, as a new private franchise system was recently announced.

Long-term care facilities in Ireland comprise health board geriatric homes and hospitals, health board welfare homes, health board district and community hospitals, voluntary sector geriatric homes and hospitals, private nursing homes and psychiatric hospital units. Private nursing homes provide the most common long-stay setting with approximately 14,000 beds, representing about 55 per cent of all long-stay beds. Roughly two-thirds of residents in long-stay settings are women and almost two-thirds of all residents are over eighty years of age. (National Council on Ageing and Older People, 2001b) The private nursing home sector is currently enjoying a period of rapid growth, stimulated by tax incentives, while promised public long-stay facilities have not been delivered as envisaged in the 2001 Health Strategy. (Tussing and Wren, 2006) In December 2006, the Minister for Health and Children announced a new support scheme for nursing home care which aims to make residential nursing home care accessible and affordable to older people. Under the scheme, the state will be allowed to collect a maximum of 15 per cent of the value of an older person's home after their death. The scheme has been criticised by Fine Gael's Leader, Enda Kenny, who claimed it amounted to a "death tax" on the elderly. (*Irish Times*, 13 December 2006)

Outsourcing of Care Services

At a time when public policy is moving increasingly to outsource core public services, the adequacy of systems to assure the quality of the standards is essential. In the health sector, the inadequate provision of the care of the elderly has been highlighted.

Although a recently published report on the inadequacies of care in one particular nursing home created a national scandal, there is neither adequate legislative provision nor resourcing for inspection and maintenance of standards in nursing homes to provide assurance that this was a relatively isolated case. The report, which points the finger at systemic failure by government, health boards and professional bodies to appropriately provide for the care of older people, states that there is an almost complete absence of systematic monitoring of deaths in Irish nursing homes and the nursing home inspection process had also proven to be deficient. (Health Services Executive, 2006)

The Minister for Health has recently announced that The Health Bill 2006, which is before government and will be published imminently, will provide for the first time for an independent, statutory body to set standards and inspect all nursing home places, both public and private. This will also strengthen the registration and de-registration process. New standards for all long-term residential care facilities for older people have already been prepared. The Health Information and Quality Authority (HIQA) was intended to be put in place at the same time as the HSE as a check and balance on its operations and powers. (Tussing and Wren, 2006: 327) However, there has been an unacceptable delay in empowering the HIQA. An interim authority exists but has no legislative empowerment yet. Informed observers have been concerned that HIQA may not be given adequate powers.

Mental Health

The mental health services available to people in Ireland are poor. The 2005 Report of the Inspector of Mental Health Services highlights capital underinvestment in the mental health service, a lack of development of necessary specialist services, resource mismanagement, management deficiencies and lack of accountability for failure to efficiently deliver mental health services. In addition, there is currently no agreed minimum standard of care nationally. The report concludes that "no Health Service Executive area has the full complement of services in sufficient quantity to provide comprehensive mental health care".

The report states that the areas that give cause for most concern are rehabilitative mental health services, forensic mental health services and services for adults and children with intellectual disabilities.

With regard to rehabilitation mental health services, which provide specialist care to those with severe and enduring mental illnesses such as schizophrenia, patients frequently spend many years of their life on long-stay wards. The resulting isolation from family and friends and lack of specialist care sees many patients deteriorate further while in "mental healthcare".

The percentage of the national health budget spent on mental health services has been decreasing steadily from 10.6 per cent of the health budget in 1990 to 6.8 per cent in 2003. (Carey, 2005)

Moreover, while people on low incomes are more likely to suffer mental illness, mental health services are concentrated in areas of greater affluence. (Wren, 2003: 16) Ireland's poor treatment of those with mental illness has in recent years been the focus of a campaign by Amnesty International for measures to redress this as a violation of international human rights law. (Amnesty International, 2003)

Traditionally, mental health services have been governed by the Mental Health Act 1945. It has been acknowledged that such legislation was entirely inappropriate for today's mental health services for a myriad of reasons. The Mental Health Act, 2001 did address many of the issues and established a Mental Health Commission. However, only some sections of the Act have been given effect. It is only since November 2006 that there is now an automatic independent review of decisions to detain people. (*Irish Times*, 15 November 2006)

Disability Services

In 2005, the government passed the Disability Act 2005. The passage of the Act, however, was dogged with controversy as disability groups and others vehemently opposed sections of the Act. One of the core issues of contention was the refusal by the government to include in the Act a guarantee in law of basic minimum standards in services, to which all people with disability are entitled. Instead any services identified as required by an individual under the Act will only be provided where "resources permit" and where "practicable". Accordingly, service providers continue to be permitted wide discretion in the actual provision of resources identified. (Irish Human Rights Commission, 2004b: 2)

This failure to provide a guarantee of basic minimum standards came under criticism from the Irish Human Rights Commission (2004) which called for the Act to be rights-based and to guarantee in law the right for people with disabilities to receive basic services to which they are entitled. Nevertheless the government withstood considerable pressure to change this aspect of the legislation, saying that limited resources and other competing funding priorities mean the government cannot afford to offer people with disabilities such a right. The government's position remains that to do so would be to embed the rights of people with disabilities in legislation, in preference to the rights of the rest of society. (*Irish Times*, 29 April 2005)

HEALTH SERVICE REFORM

There have been numerous commissions, task groups and consultancy reports sought by government in recent years. Three reports in particular, all published in 2003, were designed to inform reform of the health system: namely the Brennan Report on financial management in the Health Service, the Prospectus Report on reforming health structures, and the Hanly Report on medical staffing and the reorganisation of hospital structures.

The extent of the difficulties facing the health system can be appreciated by considering the major recommendations from these reports.

The Prospectus Report (Department of Health and Children, 2003a) recommended the abolition of the Health Boards and their replacement with a single national Health Service Executive, and major reductions in the number of existing agencies, i.e., a reduction in the number of stand-alone agencies by over half and the number of agencies with a direct reporting line to the Department of Health and Children by two-thirds.

The Hanly Report concluded that radical reform of the organisation of acute hospital services was necessary as a matter of urgency. The report found that under the current system, patients have limited access to consultants, and that medical care is delivered mostly by non-consultant doctors who work excessively long hours and have little or no access to formal training. The report recommended that acute care should be concentrated in large hospitals and that regional hospitals should concentrate solely on out-patient clinics and non-emergency elective surgery. (Department of Health and Children, 2003b) The report also recommended a doubling of the number of consultants over the next ten years with acute hospital care moving to a consultant-provided rather than consultant-led service.

The Brennan Report found the absence of any organisation responsible for managing the health service as a unified national system, and systems that provided no incentives to manage costs effectively. Among its recommendations were the establishment of a single national executive to manage the health service, and that all future consultant appointments be on the basis of consultants working exclusively within the public sector. (Government Publications Office, 2003)

In 2004, the government implemented a recommendation of both the Brennan and Prospectus reports with the introduction of a centralised Health Service Executive and the abolition of the eleven regional health boards.

Other recommendations by the reports include radical restructuring of existing regional hospitals. Pressures from local communities to maintain existing services are intense, even though substantial questions have been raised about not only the financial but also the health costs of the current regionalised system. Evidence suggests that bringing severely ill patients to smaller hospitals which lack the proper expertise to treat them is costing patients lives. According to senior surgeons, for example, there are people dying from road accidents whose lives would certainly be saved if brought immediately to a larger and better-equipped hospital. The current practice of bringing emergency patients to smaller ill-suited hospitals also results in more long-term disability, with all the resulting economic, social and personal costs, than would otherwise be the case. (*Irish Times*, 5 June 2003)

Q4.5 How far is equal access to work or social security guaranteed for all?

This question addresses the impact that recent economic change and prevailing European trends have had on employment and social protection in Ireland. Ireland has made commitments to employment rights through the major United Nations economic and social treaties, the International Labour Organisation (ILO), and the Council of Europe's revised European Social Charter (ESC). It is also bound by European Union law to protect core employment rights and has signed up to the EU Charter of the Fundamental Social Rights of Workers which contains a range of work-related rights. It is against this background that Ireland's record on achieving equality of access to employment is assessed. Overall, there has been a remarkable turnaround in prospects for the majority but serious issues of unequal treatment and inequitable outcomes continue to affect a significant proportion of the population. A similar picture emerges with regard to social protection.

GROWTH IN EMPLOYMENT: PROSPECTS FOR THE FUTURE

Access to work is the core employment right under Article 6 of the International Convention on Economic Social and Cultural Rights and articles 1,9,10 and 18 of the European Social Charter (ESC). In Ireland, access to work as indicated by employment statistics increased by 50 per cent between 1993 and 2001, the highest increase in the OECD (National Economic and Social Council, 2005a: 25), and brought about both a considerable reduction in unemployment and an equally significant increase in the active labour force.

Ireland is committed, along with all other EU states, to increase overall employment rates to 70 per cent under the Lisbon Agenda. Only four of the 25 EU states currently exceed this employment rate, namely Denmark, the Netherlands, Sweden, and the UK. (Central Statistics Office, 2005a: 33)

While the phenomenal growth in national employment levels has occurred across the earnings spectrum with increases in highly-paid, medium-and low-paid jobs, a recent report of the NESF (National Economic and Social Forum, 2006a) identify a number of issues of concern.

- The true number of unemployed is quantified at 175,000 when the labour force reserve is included, almost double the 96,700 figure reported as unemployed in the Quarterly National Household Survey.
- While Ireland has continued to create more jobs in recent years, these tended to be lower-value-added jobs which are also less sustainable – for example in construction – compared to those jobs that are being lost.
- The growth is not evenly spread, given that a number of areas have been particularly affected by job losses such as Counties

Donegal, Mayo, Cavan, Carlow, Waterford, Wexford and Limerick. Rural and urban areas exist which have benefited least from recent economic growth and where job losses in manufacturing and in farming and fishing have not been matched by job gains elsewhere. These areas include over 80 "blackspots" where the unemployment rate is three times greater than the national average. Along with high levels of redundancies, there is also a preponderance of lower-paid jobs and levels of infrastructural investment remain poor.
- A high proportion of those who are unemployed are long-term unemployed: 30 per cent of the total, as compared to 21 per cent in the UK and 18 per cent in Sweden.

WORKING RIGHTS AND CONDITIONS

"The right to a fair remuneration" is established as a fundamental right under Article 4 of the European Social Charter while Article 23 of the UN Universal Declaration of Human Rights states that "everyone who works has the right to just and favourable remuneration". The introduction of the National Minimum Wage Act in 2000 was therefore a very significant development in implementing workers' rights. A very positive feature of the minimum wage legislation in Ireland is the fact that it is fixed at above 50 per cent of median earnings, thereby limiting the discretion of government. However, the fact that a relatively high number of the working population experience poverty indicates that the minimum wage level is set too low.

Compliance with this legislation, in particular in relation to the increasing number of working immigrants, has recently become a major contested area, (see Q14.3) and the trade unions made this issue a central plank in their negotiations in the recently-concluded social partnership agreement, *Towards 2016: Ten-Year Framework Social Partnership Agreement 2006-2015*. One major outcome is the stated intention to establish under legislation new regulatory mechanisms, principally a new office of Director for Employment Rights Compliance, a statutory advisory board and increased number of Labour Inspectors. The new office will have considerable powers to investigate complaints and penalise those found to be in breach.

Furthermore, the Agreement adopted a New Compliance Model,

which once again will be institutionalised through new legislation that sets out new principles, procedures and mechanisms for strengthening penalties and redress by an individual employee.

PROTECTION AGAINST DISCRIMINATION

Domestic legislation, namely the Employment Equality Acts 1998 and 2004, has been introduced to prohibit discrimination in employment on the grounds of gender, marital status, family status, sexual orientation, religion, age, disability, race, and membership of the Traveller community. The Equality Authority, which was established in 1999 to combat discrimination and defend the rights established under the Acts, provides legal advice and assistance to individuals taking action against employers under the legislation. In 2005, there were 359 cases before the Equality Authority under the Employment Equality Acts 1998 and 2004. The majority of these cases concerned discrimination on grounds of race (32 per cent), gender (19.5 per cent), disability (15 per cent) and age (12.5 per cent). (Equality Authority, 2006) (See Q1.2)

A recent survey of inequality focussed on the nine grounds of discrimination listed by the equality legislation. In the survey, 100,500 persons – approximately 5 per cent of the population aged 18 and over – reported that they felt discriminated against in the workplace. For those who reported one or more experiences of work-related discrimination, age, gender, family-status and race/skin colour/ethnic group/nationality constituted the top four most frequently reported grounds. A second type of employment-related discrimination, discrimination when looking for work, ranked amongst the top four most frequently reported types of discrimination with 73,900 respondents. While the overall rates of discrimination reported by men and women were very similar, more significant differences between men and women surfaced in their experiences of particular types of discrimination, with the most common type of discrimination reported by women (3.4 per cent) being discrimination in the workplace. (Central Statistics Office, 2005b: 2)

Barriers to Equal Access to Work

International human rights conventions emphasise not only the right to work, but to genuine choice of employment and access to vocational training. The recent report of the National Economic and Social Forum (NESF), *Creating a More Inclusive Labour Market* (2006a), has identified four kinds of barriers which people experience in attempting to move into employment.

- Appropriate skills. The NESF report identifies inadequate investment in infrastructure, including the up-skilling of workers in vulnerable sectors, as a problem. Around 13 per cent of young people leave school early and their subsequent unemployment rate is 18 per cent. Ireland spends €636 million annually in tackling the problems of educational disadvantage, yet the figure for early school leaving is much higher in many disadvantaged areas, where it ranges from 40 to 50 per cent. This finding translates into a figure of 8 per cent unemployment among young people, almost double the national rate.
- High "participation" costs. Childcare, disability and elder-care services (particularly for women returnees and those in lower-paid employment generally) and travel-to-work costs in rural areas, make it difficult or unaffordable for those affected to take up available jobs.
- Labour market barriers. Jobs advertised through "word of mouth" place those out of work at a disadvantage. High minimum entry requirements for jobs, discrimination and prejudice, a lack of employment supports, and a lack of flexible work-life arrangements are also significant barriers to labour-market entry.
- Personal factors which are often related to other inequalities. Poor literacy/numeracy levels (some 23 per cent of our population lack functional literacy skills), homelessness, family-breakdown, previous prison record, addiction; no previous work history and health and disability issues severely hinder individuals attempting to move into employment.

The most marginalised in terms of ability to access employment are those to whom more than one of these types of barriers apply. The EU has recently highlighted the concept of a "labour force reserve" to identify people of working-age who are trapped by these kinds of barriers. The figure in Ireland is 78,500 people. (National Economic and Social Forum, 2006a: xi)

Increasing the employment rate among Ireland's jobless requires reform of the often deeply rooted obstacles which marginalised groups in the working-age population encounter in accessing and remaining in work. The state system of social protection is a critical instrument by which government can tackle these obstacles.

In recent years, many positive changes have occurred both in the scale and priorities of the social welfare budget, as well as in the institutional mechanisms for delivery of services. Comparative Eurostat analysis establishes the rapid growth in spending which has taken place in the decade 1992 – 2001. Excluding unemployment compensation (in recognition of the particularly rapid fall in unemployment in Ireland), the annual percentage rise in total social expenditure on benefits in Ireland was the highest in the EU over the ten years to 2001. Spending on health care, disability and sickness in particular grew strongly. (National Economic and Social Council, 2005a: 104) Excluding social transfers (such as unemployment benefits, child benefit and pensions), the "at risk of poverty" rate was close to 40 per cent in 2005. The inclusion of these transfers however more than halved this risk.. (Central Statistics Office, 2006a) The impact of social transfers is most marked in the case of the elderly, although of all age groups they were still at greatest risk of income poverty in 2004.

Ireland, however, is a particularly low spender on social protection by both EU and OECD standards. The level of social transfers in the Republic is close to the lowest in the OECD countries. (*Irish Times*, 12 October 2006)

Challenges to the Social Protection System

Three sets of social deficits have been identified by the NESC as challenges for Ireland's social protection system. One set is a minority characterised by low educational attainment and extended periods on social assistance, i.e., the long-term unemployed. A core issue here is the persistence of disadvantage from one generation to the next. A second set of social deficits affects those people who are working, but who do not earn enough to afford critical services such as childcare, health care beyond a minimum standard, and adequate pension provision for retirement. This group would include the 7 per cent of workers on low pay who are considered to be in poverty. The third set of social deficits affects groups whose rights have until now been neglected, prominent among them the rights of people with disabilities to access education and employment. Ireland's increased prosperity means that funding is available to address these issues, but it is also clear that funding will not provide sufficient access without changes also in practices that exclude these groups from participating in work without discrimination.

A number of groups in Irish society are particularly vulnerable to exclusion from employment.

Travellers

Members of the Traveller community continue to face significant barriers to accessing, participating in, and progressing from labour market programmes. The 2002 Census highlighted the extent of Travellers' unemployment: 73 per cent of Traveller men in comparison with a 9 per cent national average; 63 per cent for Traveller women in comparison to an 8 per cent national average. The National Economic and Social Forum (2006a) identified a number of the interlinked factors behind these outcomes including discrimination within the labour market, lack of access to good formal education and training, lack of recognition of the skills Travellers have and a subsequent lack of confidence amongst the Traveller community about their employment and progression prospects.

Women

The persistence of traditional stereotypical views of the social roles of men and women continues to be reflected in women's employment patterns. Some of these negative patterns include the following.

- All EU states, including Ireland, have higher male than female employment rates. (Central Statistics Office, 2005a: 33)
- While employment rates grew faster for women than for men between 1995 and 2000 this disparity has recently levelled off. with approximately 79 per cent of working age men currently in employment, compared with 60 per cent of working age women. (Central Statistics Office, 2006b: 3) Ireland ranked sixth highest of the EU25 in employment rate differences between men and women in 2004. (Central Statistics Office, 2005a: 33)
- Women and men's participation rates differ considerably depending on age and family status. Older women and women in the 20-44 age group with children are less likely to partici-

pate in the labour market. (Central Statistics Office, 2004a: 19)

- Lack of access to affordable/subsidised childcare is a huge barrier to labour force participation for women, who generally assume a caring role in younger families. Similarly, the lack of paid parental leave has meant a low uptake of same. In addition, the majority of lower-paid workers are women, who do not have the resources to take unpaid leave.
- Women who take time out of the workforce to care for dependents lose out on social insurance credits, which similarly impacts on their entitlement to Maternity Benefit, Disability Benefit and Contributory Old Age Pensions.
- Despite equal pay legislation now 30 years in place, and despite women's increased participation in work, the gender pay gap persists. The current pay gap is 63 per cent, but when adjustment is made for average hours worked, the pay gap is reduced to approximately 86 per cent. Women's absence from paid employment due to caring responsibilities is the biggest contributor to the pay gap.
- Furthermore, men are more likely than women to have jobs that provide pensions, medical insurance, training and development and fringe benefits. (Central Statistics Office, 2005b)
- Finally, 80 per cent of part-time or temporary workers are women. (www.ncwi.ie)

In summary, "Women are 'crowded' into a narrow range of occupations and along with the costs of childcare and other caring services this limits their potential for advancement. Currently [Ireland] is ranked 51 out of 56 countries in terms of equality of economic opportunity for women". (National Economic and Social Forum, 2006a: xi)

Lone Parents

There are currently some 80,000 lone parents – almost 98 per cent of them women – in receipt of One Parent Family Payments. While there is some provision for lone parents to continue to receive the one parent allowance while accessing either education/training or employment, it is acknowledged that significant barriers exist to lone parents entering full-time employment and there is little support to gain access to good quality employment. Taking up a full-time job on the minimum wage under the current system will result in the loss of rental supplement and the likelihood of childcare costs, which makes it simply unviable for a lone person to take up such work. Overall, the "at risk of poverty" proportion of lone parents and their children is still a phenomenal 41 per cent, albeit a very significant reduction on the previous year's 50 per cent. (Central Statistics Office, 2006a: 2)

Reform of income support measures for lone parents is a central plank of the recently-launched government strategy to improve the employment rate of lone parents. Other measures include an expanded range of available education and training opportunities, extension of the National Employment Action Plan to focus on lone parents, targeted provision of childcare, and improved information services. However, central to the reform is a set of requirements on lone parents which include returning to the workforce while children are still dependent on care, so that unless the whole package of reform is introduced at the same time, lone parents could find themselves in a worse rather than improved position. Furthermore, even if the necessary additional supports (childcare, high-skills training at appropriate times) were put in place, current "welfare to work" provisions mean that an age-related poverty trap will occur if/when the changes are introduced and there are no proposals to address this at present. (www.oneparent.ie)

People with Disabilities

Throughout Europe, people with disabilities are less likely to be in work, or in education and training, compared to people without disabilities. In Ireland, the difference in participation is particularly large: people with disabilities are two and a half times less likely to have a job than non-disabled people. (www.nda.ie) Data from Census 2002 show that only 26 per cent of people of working age with disabilities are in work, compared to 70 per cent of the rest of the population. Furthermore, their employment rate slipped from 40 per cent to 37 per cent over the previous four years. (National Economic and Social Forum, 2006a: xi) It is estimated that 40 per cent of those with a disability do not have a difficulty that precludes them from working, while about 18 per cent of people with disabilities who currently do not work would need assistance to facilitate employment. However, such assistance is far from widespread; in fact, the proportion of people with disabilities who are provided with assistance to work in Ireland is half that for the EU as a whole. This shortfall leaves a substantial number of people with a disability who can work but who are unable to find a job. In 2005, the Disability Act 2005 was passed. Among the provisions of the Act are requirements relating to access to buildings and services, limitations on the use of genetic testing for employment, and a statutory 3 per cent target for the employment of people with disabilities in the public service.

Older People

Those who continue to work after age 65 do not benefit from employee protection legislation such as the Employment Equality Act and the Unfair Dismissals Act. People aged 66 and over are also not eligible for statutory redundancy payments. People on the means-tested Old Age Non-Contributory Pension lose their full payment if they earn more than €7.60 per week.

The biggest issue facing older people, particularly older women, is access to an adequate pension. Only around 52 per cent of people in Ireland have an occupational pension, and Irish pensions as a proportion of final earnings are among the lowest in the developed world. As a result, older people in Ireland are at high risk of poverty, and this risk has increased significantly in recent years. The state pension system is not only the main, but in the majority of cases, the only source of income to retired persons in Ireland. (Stewart, 2005: 35)

The state subsidises private pension schemes to a very significant extent through tax relief. Indeed such tax reliefs have increased to the point where the state is spending almost as much on these tax reliefs as it spends on the two public pension schemes. The highest 20 per cent of earners get 60 per cent tax relief expenditure on private pension. (National Economic and Social Council, 2005a: 59)

Furthermore, the delivery of pensions to those with atypical work patterns is seriously inadequate. Women are especially badly affected because they may have long periods out of the paid labour force and are also more likely to work part-time.

Overall, the current pension system serves to increase inequality by redistributing state resources away from more vulnerable sections of the Irish population and towards the better off.

A NOTE ON THE POLICY SHIFT TOWARDS CONDITIONALITY

Social protection measures are intended in the first instance to provide every person in the society with a basic standard of living below which they should not fall, i.e., a standard at, or ideally above, the poverty line. However, there is a strong case for using the state system of social protection in a proactive manner, by directly tackling the obstacles to participation including, but not confined to, participation in work. For example, people with disabilities require not only higher incomes than those without these disabilities but also changes in the physical environment that promote their inclusion in the activities that others take for granted. (Baker *et al.*, 2004: 21–56) Similarly, through spending on supports such as childcare, public transport, retraining and career-change options, workers can be retained in the labour market who might otherwise leave while others who are currently excluded can be drawn in.

A "developmental welfare model" (National Economic and Social Council, 2005a) has recently been proposed in which social policy is viewed as integral to sustaining economic dynamism and flexibility, while also promoting social justice and a more egalitarian society. An aspect of the proposals which have generated critical comment is a concern that social policies will increasingly reflect a primary emphasis on economic growth. In such an environment, social protection becomes conditional and linked to participation in the labour market. Ireland's spending on active labour market policies designed to get people back to work is already high by international comparisons. (National Economic and Social Council, 2005a: 72) However, the National Economic and Social Forum (2006a: 29) observes that the €1 billion currently spent on these programmes has achieved only limited progress in moving the economically excluded into employment. At the same time, we have seen in Q4.2 that welfare payments have declined relative to average net earnings. Thus the "pauperisation" of segments of society is directly attributable to a policy decision to keep social welfare payments relatively low. (Murphy, 2006: 96)

Furthermore, prioritising employment routes out of poverty and maintaining low welfare rates as a work incentive are likely to have a negative effect on those who are not in a position to participate in the labour market. The elderly, people with disabilities and those involved in "caring" duties at home become even more vulnerable in the "increasing relative gulf between the rich and poor". (Murphy, 2006) Already, in Ireland, those who are not in a position to seek employment are the most likely to be in, or at risk of, consistent poverty. Despite the dramatic increase in overall employment in recent years, welfare receipt for people of working age has not declined, and a significant number of people remain in receipt of welfare benefit for extremely long periods of time. (National Economic and Social Council, 2005a: xv) (See also Q4.1)

As such, Ireland faces a huge challenge to convert the current welfare system into one which can adequately address deep-rooted social disadvantage, promote fair and equal access to work, provide support for those at work to remain employed, and also provide protection against poverty and social exclusion for those who are not in a position to work.

Q4.6 How free are trade unions and other work-related associations to organise and represent their members' interests?

Ireland has committed itself to a range of international instruments protecting the right to trade union representation. Recent figures from the National Centre for Partnership and Performance (NCCP) (2004:10,68) suggest that despite a continuing decline in membership density, unions nevertheless remain a major force in the country's industrial relations system, with almost half of private sector employers – and virtually all of those in the public sector – recognizing employees' rights to independent representation. (Geary, 2007, forthcoming) However, despite recent legislative change the freedom of unions to represent their members in Ireland does not meet the legal standards required by European and international standards. Notwithstanding the evolution of social partnership, the position of trade unions falls considerably short of what we might expect if the terms of international conventions ratified by Ireland in the 1950s, as well as those of the European Social Charter, had been given full effect. This situation is due to a basic contradiction at the heart of judicial views of the employment relationship and to attempts by the social partners, and particularly by trade unions, in response, to maintain and develop what is called a "voluntarist" system of industrial relations.

INTERNATIONAL SUPPORTS FOR THE RIGHT TO BARGAIN

Three relevant international instruments: the European Convention for the Protection of Human Rights and Fundamental Freedoms (Council of Europe, 1950, ratified by Ireland, 1953), the International Labour Organisation convention on the right to organise and collective bargaining (1949, ratified by Ireland, 1955), and the European Social Charter offer support for trade union rights. According to the European Convention:

> Everyone has the right to freedom of peaceful assembly and to freedom of association with others, including the right to form and join trade unions for the protection of his [sic] interests. (Council of Europe, 1950; Article 11.1)

In decisions regarding the application of this article, the European Court of Human Rights has identified trade union freedom as "a form or special aspect of freedom of association" and noted that the reference to protection of interests is not redundant. According to the court, the right of employees to join a trade union for the protection of their interests must include the right to instruct the union to make representations on their behalf; otherwise, the freedom is illusory. It is the role of the state to ensure that trade union members are not prevented or restrained from using their union to represent them in attempts to regulate their relations with their employers.

The ILO convention which seeks to ensure that workers may form independent organisations without interference states that the establishment of workers' organisations under the domination of employers is interference and goes on to provide that trade unions will be more than mere social outlets or welfare institutions:

> Measures appropriate to national conditions shall be taken, where necessary, to encourage and promote the full development and utilisation of machinery for voluntary negotiation between employers or employers' organisations and workers' organisations, with a view to the regulation of terms and conditions of employment by means of collective agreements. (International Labour Organisation, 1949, Article 4)

Article 6 of the European Social Charter, which seeks to secure "the effective exercise of the right to bargain collectively" is, by and large, a reiteration of the above. Ireland has committed itself to all of these instruments but has failed in its laws to ensure that workers are able to exercise their right to collective bargaining. In contrast with the aspirations expressed in these commitments, Irish law has not provided for the independence of worker organisations, and Irish courts have effectively rejected the view that terms and conditions of employment may be regulated by collective agreements, preferring instead to uphold the principle of managerial prerogative.

Some principles of the common law acquire special significance when we consider industrial relations. For example, the law is said to be concerned "directly with the rights of individuals, and only indirectly with the interests of classes". (Erle, cited in McCarthy, 1977: 491) This focus on individuals is the basis of two contradictory views of employment. First, we consider the relationship as one in which one party has a "right to command" and the other a "duty to obey". (O'Donnell, 1952: 584) Based upon this command-and-obey relationship, the common law arrives at a number of conclusions that are important with respect to collective bargaining rights. It has been held, for example, that an employer may terminate a particular work practice, arrived at by a collective bargaining process "unilaterally at any time" without breach of contract of employment. (Byrne, *et al.*, 2003: 53) Whatever is agreed to in the contract of employment "is subject to extensive unilateral alteration by the employer ... largely because the courts wish to preserve the prerogative of management to unilaterally vary the instructions under which employees work". (Honeyball, 1989: 100)

At the same time that they hold this view of employment as a command-and-obey relationship, the courts also see it as a contractual arrangement. Among the rights of individuals under the common law is that to free trade and any restraint of trade is presumed to be unlawful. (Erle, cited in McCarthy, 1977: 495) Based on this doctrine, the law treats employment as a contractual relationship in which two individuals exercise their rights to trade in labour, one to sell, the other to buy. The seller is the employee, a natural person; the buyer, or employer, may be either a natural person or a corporation, i.e., a legal person with similar rights in law to those of a natural person. This relationship is an arrangement between employer and employee as free individuals, equal before the law, either of whom may terminate the contract. In effect, as far as the law is concerned, a worker who does not like the conditions surrounding a particular job is free to leave it, having fulfilled his or her contractual obligations.

On the other side of the bargain, the doctrine of managerial prerogative has been modified by legislation, often derived from EU Directives, to protect workers' rights. However, the law has little to say about it, except where particular forms of unfair treatment are explicitly forbidden by statute. Provided they are not in breach of the Equality Acts (2004), employers are free to treat some employees more favourably than others by offers of promotion, by the allocation of more or less attractive duties or overtime assignments, and within limits imposed by the Unfair Dismissals Act (1977), to dismiss employees they consider unsatisfactory. However, should employees who feel that this represents an imbalance of power join together to form a union, the common law doctrine of restraint of trade takes on importance.

COLLECTIVE ACTION

In the eyes of the common law, a trade union is not an individual but a number of persons conspiring together to restrain free trade.

There continues to be no positive right to strike in Irish law; instead, since 1906, immunity from civil action has been granted to strikers in certain circumstances. In Ireland following independence, these immunities were restricted, by the terms of the 1941 Trade Union Act, to registered unions holding negotiation licences. The 1990 Industrial Relations Act introduced further restrictions, requiring unions to conduct secret ballots prior to industrial action and denying full protection to disputes carried out "in disregard of or contrary to the outcome" of a ballot. At the same time, the Act limited the capacity of employers to secure injunctions preventing picketing. The balloting provisions pose a major barrier to trade unions seeking to organise in the face of employer opposition since it is difficult to ensure that new recruits to the union who are anxious about a hostile employer finding out about their membership actually participate in a ballot.

As well as strikes, collective action by workers may lead to other outcomes. First, an employer may simply refuse to recognise or bargain with organised employees. Irish law now concedes that trade unions have rights, under certain conditions, to organise, to bargain with employers and to represent the interests of their members, but these rights arise from their role as "supporters and advisers of the individual rather than as leaders of collective action". (Byrne *et al.*, 2003: 240) While the workers have a right to organise in unions, courts have found that employers are not required to bargain with them:

> In law an employer is not obliged to meet anybody as a representative of his worker, nor indeed is he obliged to meet the worker himself for the purpose of discussing any demand which the worker may make. (Byrne *et al.*, 2003: 237)

This view is reiterated in a later finding that the constitutional right of employees to join a trade union does not include a constitutional right to compel their employer to negotiate "either with them or with their union". (Byrne *et al.*, 2003: 237) In the current state of Irish law, workers have to rely on a freedom deemed illusory by the European Court of Human Rights: the right to join a union whose ability to bargain on their behalf relies upon the goodwill of their employer.

The second form of outcome is the collective agreement, the legal status of which is uncertain. As we saw above in the case of *Kenny v An Post*, the master-and-servant view of employment allows the employer to make unilateral changes at any time. In the same case, the judge said that collective bargaining was "not normally intended to create legal relations". (Byrne *et al.*, 2003: 53) This had previously been found in a UK case which established that collective agreements "composed largely of optimistic aspirations" are not "contracts in the legal sense and are not enforceable at law". (Byrne *et al.*, 2003: 62) In another Irish case, an agreement containing assurances regarding compulsory redundancies was considered not to "contemplate legal relations" but was intended merely to be binding in honour on the parties. (Byrne *et al.*, 2003: 61) Subsequently, a group of workers with a statutory guarantee that they would not be "brought to less beneficial conditions of service" except by collective agreement, were found to be obliged nevertheless to take on additional duties beyond their established job description, as instructed by management, at times when they would otherwise be "idle and yet remunerated". (Byrne *et al.*, 2003: 56)

In effect, with regard to disputes, union recognition and collective agreements, the principles of the common law have been interpreted instrumentally to uphold the prerogatives of employers. The employment contract is seen as a bargain concluded between two persons with equal rights before the law; at the same time, unlike any other contract, one party is free to change the terms of the bargain in a range of areas while the other has no realistic recourse to law in response. Indeed, the inequality of the parties goes even further. Employers may discuss terms and conditions with their employees or not as they choose, but an employee refusing to meet management is insubordinate and open to disciplinary action.

This situation is far from the terms of the international conventions which call for measures to promote the utilisation of machinery for negotiation and the regulation of terms and conditions of employment by means of collective agreements. The judicial emphasis on the terms of an imagined interpersonal contract over the explicitly agreed contents of collective agreements has led to perverse decisions which at least partially explain the animosity that trade union leaders show towards the law courts and their tendency, when possible, to steer well clear of them and to rely, instead, on maintaining and strengthening the structures of the voluntarist system.

VOLUNTARIST STRUCTURES IN IRISH INDUSTRIAL RELATIONS

The perversity of the legal and common law approach to workers may partly explain why the social partners at national level have been unable to agree on a basic set of rights that could be pursued through the courts but have tried instead to develop and secure what has been called a voluntarist system of industrial relations, in which collective bargaining between employers and organised employees is encouraged and facilitated but in which neither party may be compelled to bargain.

This system is facilitated by two sets of supports: quasi-judicial structures for dispute resolution and the mechanisms of national social partnership itself. The quasi-judicial structures include a panel of Rights Commissioners who deal mainly with individual grievances; advisory and conciliation services of the Labour Relations Commission (LRC); and the arbitration services of the Labour Court, all of which are provided free of charge and usually proceed without the need for legal representation. Traditionally, neither party is obliged to use these structures, though recent legislative changes discussed below may introduce an element of compulsion. In addition, outcomes from the procedures have not normally had the force of law but have been seen as binding in honour on the parties. This situation is dynamic, however, and in a growing range of cases Equality Officers, Rights Commissioners, the Employment Appeals Tribunal and the Labour Court may reach decisions which have the force of law.

The second set of supports is that in use by the parties of social partnership mechanisms at national level in the pursuit of their interests. Unions have sought to secure basic standards and improvements in pay and conditions for all employees. Employers, meanwhile, have sought pay moderation, labour market flexibility and improved productivity through acceptance of changes in work organisation. Since 1987, basic pay increases have been set in the tripartite national agreements, which have also established the national minimum wage and dealt with taxation and a range of social policy issues. These mechanisms have also been used to deal with difficult disputes and the development of legislation.

RECENT LEGISLATIVE DEVELOPMENTS

The trend of recent legislation suggests that trade unions may have been successful in arguing that, while the law courts do not deal effectively with industrial relations, the voluntarist structures are also inadequate. The Industrial Relations (Amendment) Act, 2001, allows the Labour Court to investigate a dispute "if it is not the practice of the employer to engage in collective bargaining negotiations" in respect of the workers concerned. (2001; Section Two) If employees are determined enough to organise in a trade union to seek improvements in terms and conditions, the employer must respond by engaging in collective bargaining negotiations with the employees or the Labour Court may investigate the dispute. If it does so, the Labour Court may first issue a non-binding recommendation and then, at the request of the union, an enforceable determination. It may not provide arrangements for collective bargaining and therefore the "essentially voluntarist nature of the Irish industrial relations system" is maintained. However unions criticised the procedure as ineffective and the level of activity under it was modest. (Roche, 2006)

Subsequent amendments in the Industrial Relations (Miscellaneous Provisions) Act, 2004, were intended to increase the effectiveness of the legislation. It is too early yet to determine their success or not, but the procedure has been challenged. The Labour Court, at the request of the IMPACT union, conducted an enquiry to establish whether or not it was the practice of Ryanair to engage in collective bargaining with its employees who are pilots, and found that it was not. The company sought a judicial review to overturn this decision but was unsuccessful. It then appealed the case to the Supreme Court, claiming that there was no bona fide trade dispute, that its practice was to engage in collective bargaining with the pilots, and that the Labour Court had no jurisdiction in the matter. It further argued that since the Labour Court could now compel an employer to act in a certain way, the informal procedures which it used in the voluntarist system were no longer appropriate. The Supreme Court heard the appeal over three days in May and June 2006 and a decision is awaited at time of writing.

Even if this procedure is upheld by the Supreme Court, however, trade unions will continue to face difficulties arising from the fact that the willingness – indeed often the very ability – of workers to organise in independent trade unions continues to be affected by the extent to which employers will recognise and deal with them.

THE CHALLENGES OF ORGANISING

The image of Ireland's voluntarist industrial relations system as fair and equitable stems from the belief that employees have sufficient power to counterbalance managerial prerogative, if necessary. In reality, the day-to-day implementation of the legal rights of employees continues to depend largely on either the good will of employers or on their own bargaining power. In this respect, workers may rely upon two mechanisms: collective power, usually resulting from independent organisation in trade unions and individual power, resulting for example from the possession of valuable skills or contacts.

Collective action to redress the imbalance of power is less prevalent than it has been in the past, for reasons that may be seen from either an optimistic or a pessimistic perspective. Recent analysis of data from the Quarterly National Household Survey shows that a decreasing proportion of workers tends to join trade unions. (Geary, 2007, forthcoming) Trade union membership among full-time workers fell from a peak of 62 per cent in the early 1980s to 38 per cent in 2004; moreover, the 2004 survey shows that fewer than 20 per cent of part-time workers are in trade unions. The reasons for this decline are complex. Only a small number of workers have actively decided not to join a trade union. Reasons given for this decision were as follows: 57 per cent said they prefer to take up issues directly with management and 51 per cent said there was no need to join a union "given management's care for its employees". These positive explanations are balanced to some extent by 47 per cent who believed that "being a union member might damage a person's career prospects".

The study found that the vast majority of non-union workers in unionised firms have never been approached to consider union membership and that 40 per cent of them would join if invited. In non-union workplaces, however, the employer's attitude is an important factor; in these instances 64 per cent would join if there were management support for union organisation, whereas only 28 per cent would join without the support of management. (Geary, 2007, forthcoming)

Case study research by D'Art and Turner (2005) paints a bleaker picture which provides an insight into the difficulties faced by workers who try to organise trade unions against the wishes of their employers. In a case examined by the authors, for example, 80 of a total of 130 employees in a Dublin-based subsidiary of a multinational company joined a trade union in 2001. The company in question failed to cooperate with the LRC's attempts to resolve the dispute, but adapted its proposal that an in-house committee be elected by the workers to represent their interests. The company established a three-person committee, one of whose members was elected by employees while the other two were appointed by management. After the committee was not permitted to discuss wages and conditions, a general meeting of union members agreed to conduct a ballot for industrial action. The result was in favour of a strike which took place, but the company simply replaced the striking workers and continued to operate. Within a year, all but one of the workers involved in the strike had been "paid off by the company". (D'Art and Turner, 2005)

The implications of this research is that current legislation does not sufficiently redress the imbalance of power that permits a hostile employer to prevent trade union organisation. The weight of available evidence also points to increasing employer resistance to trade union recognition. It seems clear that the rough balance upon which the legitimacy of the voluntarist system relies is illusory and that the quasi-judicial structures within that system do not command sufficient power to redress the imbalance.

Q4.7 How rigorous and transparent are the rules on corporate governance, and how effectively are corporations regulated in the public interest?

In Ireland, there has been growing public concern about corporate governance issues, mainly stemming from the recent high profile corporate failures in the US and Europe. This concern has resulted in amendments to company law and the adoption of the UK's code-based system of governance. There is little doubt that these developments have improved corporate governance practices, at least on the surface. Irish-listed companies must now either comply with the UK's Combined Code or explain non-compliance. However, good corporate governance practices are dependent on more than mere compliance. Recent events such as the cases of overcharging in the banking sector, or the revelations of the interconnections and potential conflicts of interest among listed companies, suggest that many of the fiduciary and ethical elements that underpin good corporate governance may in fact be missing. Moreover, the current code-based system is very much focused on the interests of shareholders, whose interests will frequently not correspond with those of the public. It is therefore reasonable to conclude that from a corporate governance perspective, corporations are not always regulated in the public interest.

WHAT IS CORPORATE GOVERNANCE?

As its name suggests, corporate governance is primarily concerned with regulating the governance of corporations. At its most basic, corporate governance refers to "the ways suppliers of finance to corporations assure themselves of getting return on their investment". (Shleifer and Vishny, 1997) While this definition focuses on the shareholder, corporate governance is also increasingly concerned with the role of stakeholders, and its impact on the collective welfare of society. For example, the OECD views the role of corporate governance as twofold. (Nestor, 2000) First it covers the manner in which shareholders, managers, employees, creditors, customers, and organisational stakeholders interact with one another in shaping corporate strategies. Second it relates to public policy, and an adequate legal regulatory framework, which are essential for the development of good systems of governance. Corporate governance is therefore a key element in improving the microeconomic efficiency of a firm, the functioning of capital markets and the allocation of resources in the economy.

However, achieving a balance between the broad range of stakeholders involved in corporate governance is particularly challenging, as the interests of shareholders, company directors, other organisational stakeholders and the public do not always converge. Recent corporate scandals in the US and Europe, the behaviour of unscrupulous company officers, shareholder expropriation, and the exorbitant remuneration packages often offered to senior executives have highlighted serious problems as regards how large corporations are run and in whose interest.

International capital markets have increasingly responded to the demands of international investors for better protection. The far-reaching Sarbanes-Oxley Act , introduced in 2002 in the US to protect investors by improving the accuracy and reliability of corporate disclosures made pursuant to the securities laws and for other purposes, is a case in point. The Act was a legislative response to the uncovering of large-scale corporate wrongdoing in such large US corporations as Enron and WorldCom. In the UK, a more code-based approach has been followed. Self-regulation in capital markets is where the market voluntarily agrees to bond or commit itself to higher standards of business practice. In the UK, this approach is based on the philosophy of "comply or explain". Corporate governance codes are non-binding; however companies are required by the stock exchange to explain non-compliance. This practice is in contrast to the US (New York Stock Exchange) where the company must certify that it is not aware of any violations of the corporate governance rules.

Ireland's corporate governance rules for listed companies are identical to those in the UK and are based on the "comply or explain" philosophy. The "comply or explain" approach has its origins in the establishment of the Cadbury Committee in 1992, which followed the collapse of several prominent UK companies, such as the Bank of Credit and Commerce International, and Maxwell Communication, that were attributed to weak corporate governance structures. The committee was given a broad mandate to address the financial aspects of corporate governance. The Cadbury Committee developed a list of "best practice" governance standards to which companies were encouraged to aspire, and published a *Code of Best Practice* in 1992. The code was non-binding; however companies were required by the stock exchange to disclose how they measured up to the code and to explain non-compliance. This approach also left companies free to develop their own governance practices. The Cadbury Code formed the basis for dozens of similar advisory codes with a disclosure regime that have been adopted around the world, including Ireland's current Combined Code 2003.

Public listed companies in Ireland are currently required to comply with the Combined Code 2003, or explain their non-compliance. In addition, the code-based approach is backed up by the Company Law Enforcement Act, 2001, which established the Office of Director of Corporate Enforcement (ODCE) with its powers of investigation and prosecution. The legislative approach is primarily based on the common law duty of directors to act in the interest of the company and its shareholders. More far reaching is the Companies (Auditing and Accounting) Act, 2003, which has been described as Ireland's Sarbanes-Oxley Act. (Grace, 2005) Section 45 of the 2003 Act requires directors to take responsibility for compliance with company law, taxation law and other relevant legislation. If it had been implemented as such, its implications for listed companies in Ireland could have been extensive, as it would have brought Ireland much closer to the legislative-based approach that has followed recent developments in the US. However, while it remains on the statute books it is to all intents and purposes a dead provision.

THE COMBINED CODE 2005

The main features of the Combined Code 2005, hereafter referred to as the "Code," are outlined in this section. It is almost certain that the 2005 Code (which updates the 2003 Code) will be accepted in the near future as the benchmark for corporate governance practices in the UK and Ireland. It is worth noting that the Combined Code applies to listed companies, or companies in which the public invest. There is universal recognition that such companies require a greater degree of supervision and regulation than do private companies, whose shares are closely held rather than traded in the market. Section one of the Code deals with companies and covers company directors, remuneration, accountability and audit, and relations with shareholders.

In terms of company directors, the Code addresses the areas of the Board of Directors, the chairman and chief executive, achieving balance and independence within the board, appointments to the board of directors, information and professional development, performance evaluation and re-election. In terms of directors, the main requirements are that an effective board of directors, which provides both entrepreneurial leadership and enables risks to be assessed and managed, should head each company. The company's annual report should identify board members and should contain a statement of how the board operates and the manner in which decisions are taken. The Code recommends a clear division of responsibility between running the board (the chairman) and the executive responsibility of running the company (the chief executive). The objective is to ensure that no one person should have unfettered powers of decision making. Only in exceptional circumstances should the chief executive also become chairman, and even then the company should first consult with major shareholders and the reasons for this decision should be clearly laid out at appointment and in the next annual report. It is worth noting here that for US companies the appointment to the position of chief executive comes with the expectation of appointment as chairman.

Other features of the Code include the following.

- The appointment procedure to the board of directors should be formal, rigorous and transparent. A nomination committee should lead the appointment process and make recommendations. A majority of board members should be independent non-executives. The board should undertake a rigorous annual evaluation of its own performance. All directors should be submitted for re-election at regular intervals.
- Remuneration of directors should be sufficient to attract, retain and motivate directors. A significant proportion should be structured to link rewards to corporate and individual performance. Share options should not be offered at a discount, except where permitted by the listing rules of the relevant

stock exchange. The remuneration of non-executive directors should not include stock options. There should be a formal procedure for deciding remuneration and no director should be involved in deciding his or her own remuneration.

- The board should establish a remuneration committee with at least three independent non-executive directors.
- The board should present a balanced and understandable assessment of the company's financial position and prospects, backed up by a sound system of internal control that safeguards the investment of shareholders and the company's assets. An audit committee consisting of at least three non-executive directors should be established. There should be a separate resolution on each substantially distinct issue at the annual general meeting, and specifically one on the company accounts.

Section two of the Code, which deals specifically with the role of institutional shareholders, advocates a proactive role for institutional shareholders in engaging with the company, evaluating governance practices, and making considered use of their votes.

COMPLIANCE WITH THE CODE

Measuring the level of compliance with the rules of corporate governance is a notoriously time-consuming task, given that a full evaluation requires an in-depth review of individual company annual reports, compliance statements, director appointments, biographical details, committee composition, compensation structures etc. As such, the numbers of reports that have undertaken this task are relatively few. One report on the compliance levels of Irish Stock Exchange (ISE) listed companies was published in 2004. (Brennan and McDermott, 2004) While the report is slightly dated and the research took place before the 2003 Code came into practice, it nevertheless gives a good indication of the ability of Ireland's companies to comply with the code-based approach.

The main finding of Brennan and Mc Dermott's (2004) report are as follows.

- Thirty-two companies (out of a total of 80) did not have majority independent boards.
- Two companies failed to reach the recommended one-third quota of non-executive directors.
- Some companies grant share options to non-executives, but this practice is the exception rather than the norm.
- Thirty-three companies elected not to establish a separate nomination committee.
- Four companies had no remuneration committee and five companies had executive director involvement on this committee.
- Six companies had no separate audit committee and five companies had executive director involvement on the audit committee.
- There were 19 companies that had more than three insufficient disclosures on the independence status of non-executive directors.
- In some cases biographical information clearly revealed circumstances that conflicted with the independence criteria set out in the Code.

The latter finding led the authors to question whether the ISE listed companies was more tolerant of breaches of the combined code than the London Stock Exchange, and the degree of proactivity in its enforcement practices. Their findings also suggest certain challenges facing Irish listed companies in their compliance efforts.

THE EXPECTATIONS OF CORPORATE STAKEHOLDERS

Although codes of governance are typically articulated in terms of the rights of shareholders, some attempts have been made to incorporate the interests of stakeholders. The important role of stakeholders is acknowledged in the OECD Corporate Governance Principles, which state:

> The corporate governance framework should recognise the rights of stakeholders established by law or through mutual agreements and encourage active cooperation between corpora-

tions and stakeholders in creating wealth, jobs, and the sustainability of financially sound enterprises

Many OECD countries, particularly those from continental Europe, give a high priority to corporate stakeholders. Moreover, the fourth OECD principle acknowledges the contribution and function of stakeholders to corporate governance as follows.

- The rights of stakeholders that are established by law or through mutual agreements are to be respected.
- Where stakeholder interests are protected by law, stakeholders should have the opportunity to obtain effective redress for violation of their rights.
- Performance-enhancing mechanisms for employee participation should be permitted to develop.
- Where stakeholders participate in the corporate governance process, they should have access to relevant, sufficient and reliable information on a timely and regular basis.
- Stakeholders, including individual employees and their representative bodies, should be able to freely communicate their concerns about illegal or unethical practices to the board and their rights should not be compromised for doing this.
- The corporate governance framework should be complemented by an effective, efficient insolvency framework and by effective enforcement of creditor rights.

The main problem with the OECD principles is that they are more representative of objectives that Member States should aspire towards than actual codes of practice.

REGULATION OF COMPANIES IN THE PUBLIC INTEREST IN IRELAND?

Since the regulation of corporations is typically based on investor-focused codes it is difficult to say from a corporate governance perspective whether corporations are actually regulated in the public interest. Such codes typically protect shareholder and creditor interests. The codes of corporate governance that matter, e.g., the Combined Code, are essentially shareholder-focused in nature.

Stakeholder codes, such as the OECD Code, ultimately represent compromises between corporate cultures across the different Member States. They are not legally enforceable and are more typically viewed as statements of intent to achieve better corporate practices.

This reality was succinctly illustrated in the case of overcharging by Ireland's two largest banks, AIB and Bank of Ireland. Although overcharging is itself not specifically a corporate governance issue, it serves to illustrate poor systems of internal control and weak transparency, and how such weak governance practices can be detrimental to the public interest. The fact that overcharging of customers was known to take place and tolerated by management indicates that the banks were much more concerned with increasing profit margins for shareholders than looking out for the interests of their own customers and the general public.

There is some evidence of the development of greater accountability towards organisational stakeholders, although this development is usually associated with public pressure. For example, global oil companies have faced increasing demands from shareholders, institutional investors and the public for greater social responsibility. Irish companies will ultimately face this pressure too. In 2006, Tullow Oil, an ISE-listed company with operations in 15 different countries many of which are in Africa, published its first annual Social and Corporate Responsibility Report. The move reflects an increasing trend among global oil companies to invest in local development projects as a key element in promoting good corporate relations and sustainable development. However it must be stressed that good corporate social responsibility practices are non-statutory in nature.

Based on the above discussion, it is possible that a shift towards a post-Enron US style of corporate regulation is justified. Indeed it could be argued that the Sarbanes-Oxley Act in the US was a response in the public interest to the problem of weak corporate governance regulations. However a number of distinguishing features of US equity markets are important when considering the US case. In the US, there are a comparatively higher proportion of individual domestic shareholders than in Europe, and US capital markets typically account for a higher percentage of GDP than European counterparts. US equity markets such as the NYSE have also traditionally been viewed as the guardian of investor interests and compete for business based on reputation. Moreover, although the US system is based on greater compliance in terms of financial reporting, this in itself does not necessarily improve corporate governance practices. For example, the US system is also characterised by high levels of cross directorships, with the board of JP Morgan Chase regarded as the best-connected board in the US.

Corporate governance rules motivated by public interest also create potential conflicts between creating a good corporate environment and over-regulation. Recent reports suggest that many large international companies are being deterred from listing in New York, preferring instead to list in the less regulated London market, precisely because of Section 404 of Sarbanes-Oxley. Recent comments attributed to one of that Act's architects Micheal Oxely also appear to suggest that the legislation may have been drafted in haste and that some of its requirements are too onerous for public companies. In any event, there is no guarantee that stricter legislation will prevent further corporate scandals, which are often the result of deliberate attempts to cover up or deceive shareholders. As such, their uncovering is often dependent on the professionalism and due-diligence of management and gatekeepers such as Audit Committees and external auditors. In this respect many of the traits of good corporate governance are non-statutory in nature and cannot necessarily be legislated for. The legislative approach also tends to avoid specifying in law how companies should go about improving governance practices. For example, Ireland's Companies (Auditing and Accounting) Act 2003, avoids specifying in law that the Audit Committee should be totally independent. The code-based approach on the other hand recommends that such committees should be independent. In addition, one controversial aspect of the Sarbanes-Oxely Act is that the large accounting companies, arguably the chief culprits in the corporate scandals that led to the Act, now look like the largest beneficiaries of the new measures required for compliance. On the other hand, a possible benefit of enshrining corporate governance rules in law is the increased pressure that it puts on non-executive directors and members of the audit committee in terms of their obligations.

REPRESENTATIVE AND ACCOUNTABLE GOVERNMENT

Five: Free and Fair Elections

Do elections give the people control over governments and their policies?

INTRODUCTION AND SUMMARY

The election of representatives to a national parliament constitutes the chief means whereby the two key principles of democracy – popular control over government and political equality – are realised in practice. Popular control is exercised when elections give citizens the effective power to choose in fair and open competition who will represent them, and to retain or dismiss from office their existing representatives and the political parties they stand for. Political equality is realised when each person's vote "counts for one, and none for more than one".

It is now generally accepted that there are three sets of democratic criteria that an electoral process can be expected to meet. The first is that it should be *free and fair* according to international standards: there should be open competition between candidates and parties, and the electoral process should be conducted in a wholly impartial manner. The second criterion is that of *inclusiveness*: procedures for registration and voting should be comprehensive, and ensure that no persons or sections of society are systematically advantaged or disadvantaged as electors or potential electors. The third criterion is that of *representativeness*: the electoral system should ensure that the resulting parliament accurately reflects the distribution of political opinion in the country, and is also broadly socially representative.

In the main, the Irish electoral process satisfies the first of the above criteria. There is open competition between candidates and parties on a reasonably "level playing field", and the supervision of elections is independent of party and government. However, unlike many countries, no single independent Electoral Commission exists to coordinate the supervision of all aspects of the electoral process, and the government of the day has an advantage in being able to determine the timing of elections to the Dáil.

As for *inclusiveness*, the system of regular constituency boundary review is designed to ensure a broadly equivalent weight to each vote across the country despite population changes. On the other hand, serious deficiencies have been identified in the system of voter registration, which overstates some constituency populations while disadvantaging those living in more deprived areas and those lacking a fixed address. Election figures themselves show a significant decline in voter turnout, with relatively low participation rates among the socially disadvantaged and young people.

In terms of *representativeness*, the Single Transferable Vote (STV) electoral system ensures that there is a sufficiently close match between the nationwide electoral support for the different political parties and their proportion of seats in the Dáil. The system also allows the voter a wide range of effective choice between candidates as well as parties. On the other hand, as with most European countries, membership of the Dáil is heavily skewed towards middle-aged males, and middle-class or professional incumbents; in particular. It does not at all reflect the proportion of women and young people in the Irish population.

Q5.1 How far is appointment to government and legislative office determined by popular competitive election, and how frequently do elections lead to change in the governing parties or personnel?

Ireland has been fortunate among European states in having enjoyed uninterrupted democratic government since the foundation of the state. Ireland's system of governance comprises the legislature, the executive, and the judiciary. The legislature comprises two houses, the Dáil and the Seanad. Appointment to the former is *via* popular competitive elections held at least every five years. Members of the upper house, Seanad Éireann, are not directly elected, but rather chosen by a variety of different methods, including direct appointment by the Taoiseach, and elections by specified groupings, including graduates of particular universities, local government representatives, TDs (Members of Dáil Éireann) and outgoing Senators.

Ireland's President plays a limited, but important, role in ensuring government legislation does not violate the Irish constitution. The President is elected through popular competitive election at least every seven years.

The parties in government in Ireland have changed regularly over the course of the history of the state. However, Ireland's largest party, Fianna Fáil has been in government following 22 of the 36 elections since Irish independence, making it one of the most electorally successful political parties in Europe. Such persistence of a single party in office can be seen as damaging for democracy, in that it effectively represents a long-term monopoly of power. On the other hand, it is inherently undemocratic to insist that free and fair elections must necessarily result in a change of government party or parties after a given period of time. In Ireland, the emergence of coalition government in recent decades places some limits on the power which any single party can command.

DÁIL ÉIREANN

The Irish system of governance is based on a variant of the doctrine of the separation of powers. Separation of powers is a model of democracy that involves the separation of political power between three branches of the state: the executive, the legislature, and the judiciary. In Ireland, this tripartite separation of powers model is reflected in the fact that legislative power is vested in the Oireachtas, executive power is exercised by, or on the authority of, government, and judicial power is exercised by the courts. (See also Q2.1) However, Ireland's system differs significantly from the separation of powers model in that the legislature and the executive are not separate, nor intended to be. The executive depends formally on the legislature in the sense that the former is both elected by, and can be voted out of office by, the latter.

Dáil Éireann, as the primary directly-elected forum within Ireland's tripartite system of governance, is what essentially defines Ireland as a democracy. The second house within the legislature, Seanad Éireann, is not directly elected, while the Taoiseach and the government are elected by Dáil Éireann.

The executive branch of the Oireachtas is the government, which consists of not less than seven and not more than 15 drawn from the Dáil and the Seanad. In practice members are rarely drawn from the Seanad. The government is responsible to the Dáil alone. Dáil Éireann comprises 166 seats at present and has a lifespan of a maximum of five years. TDs are directly elected by PR-STV in multimember constituencies. (See Q5.4)

In practice, there is effectively a fusion between the executive and the legislature in Ireland. This fusion is facilitated by the strength of the party whip system and the extent of overlap between government and parliament. Unlike parliamentary systems in many other countries, all government ministers in Ireland are TDs. In fact, only two of the approximately 150 ministers since 1922 in Ireland were never TDs, compared with an average European figure of 25 per cent. (Gallagher, 2005b: 237) (See also Q6.3 & Q7.4)

SEANAD ÉIREANN

Seanad Éireann with 66 members has a subordinate position to the Dáil. It has no veto power but can delay decisions of the Dáil. Senators are not directly elected but rather chosen by a variety of different methods. Eleven members are appointed by the Taoiseach, six are elected by graduates of Dublin University and the National University of Ireland, and 43 are elected from five panels by members of the county and major city councils, the Dáil and the outgoing Seanad. The five panels are Agriculture, Culture and Education, Industry and Commerce, Labour, and Public Administration. The lifespan of the Seanad matches that of the Dáil.

Debates around the unelected nature of the Seanad do occur, but are generally muted by the fact that the Seanad has so little power. In its 2004 report, for example, the Seanad subcommittee on Seanad reform reviewed the composition of Seanad Éireann with a view to reforms which would make the Seanad more democratic. The report recommended that a reformed Seanad should have 65 members and that 32 of the Senators should be directly elected. Of the remaining seats, 20 would be filled through indirect elections by county councillors, Dáil deputies and senators, and 12 by the Taoiseach's nominees. This report has yet to be acted upon and there is no commitment to do so.

For those parliaments within Europe with dual chambers, the method of appointment varies depending on the powers of the second chamber. In Poland and Italy, for example, where the second chamber wields substantial power, all or nearly all seats are directly elected by the people at national elections. However, in most others where the power of the second chamber is weak, indirect election or appointment by local officials plays a major role, as is the case in Ireland. (Gallagher, 2005a: 77) At the same time, a general problem can arise with directly elected second chambers, whereby both bodies have grounds to dispute which best represents the people.

Arguments in favour of the present system of appointment and indirect election in Ireland include the fact that the Seanad is partly elected, albeit indirectly by an electorate comprised mostly of elected officials and the fact that it has such limited powers. In addition, all the members of the Seanad have a limited term of at most 5 years, which precludes grossly undemocratic practices such as hereditary membership or appointment for life. On the other hand, the current system for election and appointment to the Seanad can be criticised on the grounds that the only citizens, as opposed to elected officials, entitled to vote are graduates of Dublin University and the National University of Ireland, who already constitute a privileged constituency.

Nonetheless, the unelected nature of the Seanad is arguably less problematic, given its subordinate position, than the role of the Seanad and its effectiveness in discharging same. In fact, the question of whether there should be a second house at all is an open one. Within Europe, only 12 of the 28 states have a second chamber, while worldwide only around one-third of countries have one. (Massicotte, 2000: 282)

Under current circumstances, strengthening the mechanisms for accountability and consensus within the Dáil should arguably take priority over increased powers for the Seanad, which in turn should only be considered in the context of an increase in direct elections to the Seanad.

CHANGES OF GOVERNMENT

International comparisons show Ireland's party system as being effective in forming and sustaining governments in office. A comparison of the number of governments formed in Ireland between 1945 and 2003 shows that Ireland, with 22 governments, compares well with other European nations in terms of democratic stability. (See Q6.2)

In addition, the parties in government have changed regularly over the course of the history of the state. Of the eleven heads of government since 1922, six have been Fianna Fáil, and five Fine Gael. However this statistic belies the dominant position of Fianna Fáil throughout the history of the state. Twenty-two of the 36 governments formed since Irish independence have included Fianna Fáil. (See Q6.2)

Heads of Government 1922 – 2004

Date	*Head of Government*	*Government Composition*
6/12/1922	William T Cosgrave	Fine Gael
9/3/1932	Eamon de Valera	Fianna Fáil
18/2/1948	John A Costello	Fine Gael led coalition
13/6/1951	Eamon de Valera	Fianna Fáil
2/6/1954	John A Costello	Fine Gael led coalition
20/3/1957	Eamon de Valera	Fianna Fáil
23/6/1959	Sean Lamass	Fianna Fáil
10/11/1966	Jack Lynch	Fianna Fáil
14/3/1973	Liam Cosgrave	Fine Gael led coalition
5/7/1977	Jack Lynch	Fianna Fáil
11/12/1979	Charles Haughey	Fianna Fáil
20/6/1981	Garret FitzGerald	Fine Gael led coalition
9/3/1982	Charles Haughey	Fianna Fáil
14/12/1982	Garret FitzGerald	Fine Gael led coalition
10/3/1987	Charles Haughey	Fianna Fáil
12/7/1989	Charles Haughey	Fianna Fáil led coalition
11/2/1992	Albert Reynolds	Fianna Fáil led coalition
15/12/1994	John Bruton	Fine Gael led coalition
26/6/1997	Bertie Ahern	Fianna Fáil led coalition
17/5/2002	Bertie Ahern	Fianna Fáil led coalition

Source: Combination of Appendices 3b, 3c in Coakley amd Gallagher, 2005: 474–5

THE ROLE OF THE PRESIDENT

The President is the Irish head of state, although he or she plays a mainly ceremonial role in the running of the State. The position is provided for by the constitution in Articles 12-14. The nomination of a presidential candidate requires proposal from 20 members of the Oireachtas or four county or county borough councils. This process generally ensures a candidate from the government party, with some candidates being put forward unopposed. Since the office was instituted in 1938 there have been six uncontested and six contested presidential elections. Presidential election is by secret ballot and based on single transferable vote. The President is elected to a seven-year term and can be re-elected once.

Presidential Power

The Irish presidency is perceived as "the weakest directly elected presidency in Europe". (Elgie and Fitzgerald, 2005: 306) Many of the powers of the President can only be exercised on the advice of the government. This situation means that if the President wishes to exercise a power, he or she must first obtain the advice and agreement of the government. When a Bill has been presented to the President, he or she has the power to refer it to the Supreme Court within 7 days. This power is exercised by the President when there is doubt as to whether the Bill is constitutional. He or she must first consult with the Council of State but the decision to refer the Bill is the President's alone. If a Bill is referred to the Supreme Court, it must decide whether or not the Bill conflicts with the constitution. If the Supreme Court holds that the Bill is unconstitutional, the President will not sign it.

Recent examples of Bills referred to the Supreme Court include the striking down of a law to retrospectively legalise the taking of illegal nursing home charges from the pensions of residents. The President was presented with a Bill which proposed to legalise thirty years of illegal payments taken on behalf of the state from residents' pensions which were applied toward fees. The Bill was struck down as unconstitutional. (*Irish Times*, 17 February 2005)

Another important power is the right of the President to withhold a dissolution from a Taoiseach who has lost majority support in the Dáil. This power has never been formally exercised. If it were to be, the result would be that the outgoing Taoiseach would be obliged to return to the Dáil to see if an alternative government could be formed. In essence, this presidential power recognises that the purpose of an election is to select parliamentarians, whose role in turn is to select the government. The collapse of a government does not therefore automatically necessitate a general election, which can be avoided if the Dáil can agree an alternative government.

The two most recent Presidents, Mary Robinson and Mary McAleese, have changed the image of the presidency in Ireland in a number of ways. While each had demonstrable links to their nominating parties prior to their election, neither emerged from within party ranks or had a history of high-ranking party service, as had traditionally been the case. Moreover, as women, both have presented a very different image to the previous male incumbents, investing their role with an energy and a public profile that was largely absent heretofore. Mary Robinson's election was also notable in that she was nominated by a party other than those then in government.

IRISH POLITICAL DYNASTIES

A relevant issue in regard to changes of personnel at elections is the prevalence of political dynasties within constituencies. While the electoral system is capable of delivering a change of personnel, both expected and unexpected, the presence of political dynasties tends to reduce the degree to which new representatives do in fact get elected.

Family connections within politics are a feature of many constituencies in the country, for example the Collins in Limerick and the Flynns in Mayo, both Fianna Fail, and the Mitchells, Fine Gael, in Dublin. The results of the local council elections that followed the abolition of the dual mandate in 2004 also demonstrated the extent to which such connections feature in Ireland's political culture. (*Irish Times*, 1 June 2004) The three main parties had 94 members of the Oireachtas affected by the dual mandate. Of those positions, 26 were co-opted to family members at its abolition. A high political profile for a local family is clearly a considerable boost to a family member's electoral chances in an electorate that largely focuses on the candidate and on local delivery. While family connections are a feature of politics in many countries, personalism in Irish politics ensures a higher prevalence of family dynasties in Ireland than would be the case in many other countries.

Q5.2 How inclusive and accessible for all citizens are the registration and voting procedures, how independent are they of government and party control, and how free are they from intimidation and abuse?

Open and competitive elections governed by widely accepted rules and procedures are essential to the legitimacy of any political system. In Ireland, judged by international standards, the system of elections is in general free and fair. Voting procedures in Ireland are generally accessible and independent from government and party control, although current procedures can serve to disenfranchise certain groups within society, most notably Travellers and members of disadvantaged communities.

A central element in any parliamentary democracy is the voter registration system, ie. a clear record of who can vote and in which elections. In Ireland, voter registration procedures are hopelessly outdated and ineffective. As a result, the electoral register is in disarray. This disorder leaves the Irish electoral system open to widespread abuse, and makes it impossible to know what proportion of the Irish electorate is actually registered. Fundamental changes to the voter registration system are urgently needed to correct this deficiency.

FREE AND FAIR ELECTIONS

Any election system is comprised of five basic elements: the franchise, electoral districts, election machinery, the electoral system, and voter registration. (Courtney, 2004) On balance, four of these elements of the Irish electoral system are truly democratic: the right to vote is broadly inclusive; the process of redrawing electoral districts is not in the hands of elected officials; those who manage and supervise elections on behalf of all citizens are honest and trustworthy officials; and Ireland's electoral system of PR-STV provides for reasonable proportionality between votes cast and representation in the Dáil. The one area of concern is the inadequacy of the present system for voter registration and the resulting inaccuracy of voter registration lists.

THE RIGHT TO VOTE

Opportunities to vote in Ireland arise in five decision-making procedures:

- the election of the President every seven years;
- Dáil (parliamentary) elections, at least every five years;
- referenda on proposed constitutional amendments;
- the election of representatives to the European Parliament, every five years; and
- elections to local authorities every five years.

The franchise in Ireland extends to all resident adult citizens on a non-discriminatory basis. Resident citizens over the age of 18 years may vote at Dáil, Presidential, local and European elections, and referenda. British citizens living in Ireland may vote at Dáil, European and local elections. The right for British citizens to vote in Ireland actually stems from an Order that enables the right to vote in general elections to be extended to resident nationals of any country that allows Irish nationals to vote in that country's general elections. European Union citizens may vote at European and local elections. All residents, regardless of citizenship, may vote at local elections. In fact, the franchise at local elections in Ireland is the most inclusive of any country in the world. (See Q6.7)

Voting Abroad

Countries worldwide have varying election laws that pertain to their citizens resident in other countries. Ireland does not extend the franchise to Irish citizens living abroad, with the exception of Irish diplomats living overseas. A constitutional amendment has been proposed that would allow three members of the Senate to be elected by Irish emigrants. This proposal has not been acted upon. (*Statesman Journal*, 2005)

Within the European Union, a number of countries, including Britain, Italy, Portugal and France, have extended voting rights in recent years to their citizens residing abroad.

Voting Rights for Resident Non-Irish Nationals

International evidence shows that resident aliens have historically acquired the full panoply of civil, economic and political rights, including the right to vote, only through naturalisation in their country of residence. However, faced with increasing populations of immigrants, democracies have gradually been extending to resident aliens the rights traditionally associated with citizenship, including the right to vote.

While there remain considerable differences among countries, the practice of enfranchising resident aliens is now prevalent among democracies and 22 states currently afford resident aliens at least some voting rights. These rights however differ widely in their scale – for example, the right to vote in local versus national elections – and in their scope, that is, the right to vote of specific alien nationalities versus a general right of all resident aliens. (Earnest, 2003)

The most common form of resident alien voting rights is the right to vote in local elections. Eleven states around the world allow all aliens who satisfy a residency requirement to vote in municipal, provincial or other local elections. These states are: Ireland, Sweden, Denmark, New Zealand, Norway, Finland, Iceland, the Netherlands, Hungary, Venezuela and Belize.

Furthermore, Ireland emerges as having the most liberal residency requirement, allowing non-Irish nationals to vote in local elections after only six months residency. This requirement compares with waiting periods of one year in Denmark, three years in Sweden and Norway, and five years in the Netherlands.

With regard to national elections, only one country – New Zealand – offers universal resident alien voting rights for all elections, local to national, with only a brief residency requirement. At present, any immigrant who has resided in New Zealand for one year may register to vote in national elections. (Earnest, 2003)

Several other states have voting rights for national elections that discriminate on the basis of the resident alien's nationality. Ireland is one such case, in that UK citizens living in Ireland can register to vote in national elections here. As noted earlier (Q5.2), this entitlement stems from an Order that extends the right to vote in general elections to resident nationals of any country that in turn allows Irish nationals to vote in their general elections. Irish citizens have been allowed to vote in national elections in Britain since Irish independence. (Meehan, 2000) No other nationalities however enjoy the right to vote in national elections in Ireland.

As shown above, Ireland has a hybrid system that allows all resident non-Irish nationals to vote in local elections and specific resident non-Irish nationals to vote in national elections.

At least one state, Sweden, has allowed resident aliens to vote in national referenda in addition to local elections. In Ireland, however, non-Irish citizens, even if granted permanent residency, are not permitted to vote in referenda or presidential elections, while only Irish and EU citizens can vote in European elections.

Disenfranchised Groups

Prisoners in Ireland were until recently the social group whose capacity to vote was most severely restricted. Unlike Austria, Belgium, Canada, India, Hungary, Spain and the UK for example, Irish prisoners do retain the right to vote when imprisoned. A series of court cases taken by prisoners within the Irish courts has established that prisoners have a right to be registered in the constituency in which they are normally resident but have no right to be given physical access to a ballot box, or to a postal vote, while they are in custody. As a result, only those prisoners who happen to be on parole or temporary release on any election day may exercise their right to vote, with the vast majority of prisoners therefore being effectively disenfranchised.

This anomalous situation is due to change following a landmark ruling in the European Court of Human Rights in Strasbourg in 2005. In the case of John Hirst, a British prisoner sentenced to life imprisonment for manslaughter, the Court of Human Rights found that any departure from the principle of universal suffrage risked undermining the democratic validity of the elected legislature and its laws. Judgements of the Court of Human Rights are binding on the respondent state, which in this case was the United Kingdom. While strictly speaking, judgements are not binding on the other 46 countries that are signatories to the European Convention on Human Rights, they do indicate to these states as to whether or not their law and practice conforms to the standards set down in the Convention. As such the judgement could have led to similar actions by Irish prisoners. (*Irish Times*, 4 February 2006) In any event, the Irish government has reacted positively to the European Court judgement, and is currently preparing legislation that will give prisoners in Irish jails a postal vote in future elections.

Travellers are another grouping whose members may be denied the vote. The Electoral Act of 1992 makes residence within a constituency a prerequisite for registration, which may disenfranchise some members of the Traveller Community, particularly those not living in established halting sites.

Finally, research on the part of the Vincentian Partnership for Justice uncovered a number of obstacles to voter registration for people living in disadvantaged communities. (Harris, 2005) Specifically, a survey of community leaders/workers in 12 centres across Ireland found that:

- there is a reluctance amongst many people living in socially disadvantaged areas to go to the garda station due to negative perceptions of, and experiences with, the gardaí (Garda authorisation is necessary for people who have missed the date for inclusion on the main electoral register to be included on a supplementary register); and
- the low level of literacy of many people, while not confined to those living in disadvantaged areas, meant that they were embarrassed to admit that they could not fill in the registration form.

These obstacles to voter registration are reflected in the low voter turnouts in disadvantaged areas. (See Q5.6)

In addition, a number of issues, such as the difficulties involved in postal voting and the fact that elections are restricted to a single day, rather than taking place over multiple days, also work against maximising voter participation.

ELECTORAL DISTRICTS

The Irish Constitution requires that the ratio between the number of TDs representing each constituency in the Dáil and the population of that constituency be the same as is possible throughout the country. Article 16.2.2 of the Constitution states: "The total number of members of Dáil Éireann shall not be fixed at less than one member for each 30,000 of the population, or at more than one member for each 20,000 of the population." Article 16.2.3 states: "The ratio between the number of members to be elected at any time for each constituency and the population of each constituency, as ascertained at the last preceding census, shall, so far as is practicable, be the same throughout the country."

As such, changes in population require the regular redrawing of constituency boundaries. The redrawing of constituency boundaries is the responsibility of the Constituency Commission, an independent commission established under the 1997 Electoral Act. With the establishment of the Constituency Commission, the issue of constituency boundaries has formally been removed from the influence of government, which is a positive development. (Sinnott, 2005: 126)

Preliminary census figures released in July 2006, show that dramatic increases in population in the past five years have rendered the current constituency boundaries out of date. According to the preliminary census figures, the four-seat Dublin North constituency, for example, now has a bigger population than the five-seat constituencies of Dún Laoghaire, Limerick East, Wexford and Cavan-Monaghan. In another example, three-seat Dublin West now has more people than four-seat Cork North Central.

The preliminary 2006 census figures also show a number of constituencies with significant fluctuations from the accepted ratio of population to TD due to population changes. This norm was established in the O'Donovan case of 1961, in which the High Court recommended that 5 per cent should be the maximum variation within any one constituency above or below the national average. However, Dublin West, for example, is 21 per cent over the national average, while Dublin North is 17.5 per cent above it, and Meath East 13 per cent over. Other constituencies are well below the average, with Dún Laoghaire and Cork North Central, for example, having a population-to-deputy ratio of almost 11 per cent below the average. (*Irish Times*, 20 July 2006)

Prior to the O'Donovan case, the constitutional requirement that the ratios between the number of elected members to the population of each constituency be the same "so far as is practicable" was not rigorously enforced nationwide. The O'Donovan ruling has resulted in a more frequent redrawing of constituency boundaries which may be unnecessary, since, in many EU countries boundaries are never changed and deputies are simply reallocated between constituencies by mathematical formula. The Constituency Commission is currently obliged to adhere to three- four- and five-member constituencies. Larger constituencies, combined with a relaxation on the rigid enforcement of TDs to constituents for each and every constituency, would reduce the need to continually redraw constituency boundaries and provide a sounder system than at present.

VOTER REGISTRATION

The bedrock of a parliamentary democracy is its voter registration system which provides a clear record of who can vote and in which elections. In Ireland, the electoral register is in disarray and fundamental changes are needed – such as the use of Personal Public Service Numbers (PPSN) – to correct a major deficit in our democratic system.

Since independence, it has been the state's responsibility to ensure the compilation and integrity of the register of electors. Historically this task has been, and continues to be, carried out by local authorities within their catchment area. Each local authority compiles the electoral register on the basis of Application for Registration forms, which are delivered to each household to be completed and returned by post. These forms ask voters for their particulars, comprising surname, forename(s), date of birth, and citizenship status. In practice, many of these forms are not returned and virtually no follow-up process exists. Moreover, all data is accepted without question. Furthermore, the relatively small number of surnames in use in Ireland creates real potential for confusion and difficulty, given the scanty additional information which is required to establish an individual's registration.

The total inadequacy of the present system can be gauged from a 2004 report from Kerry County Council which stated that there was "some difficulty" in removing the names of all those who had died from the register, as fathers and sons with similar names often lived in the same house "and the wrong person could be deleted". The report also stated that the register was becoming increasingly difficult to compile because the degree of "mobility and change within communities is such that local knowledge gathered from parish priests, gardaí and other local contacts is less effective than before". (*Irish Times*, 2 November 2004)

Not surprisingly, the current out-dated system of voter registration results in considerable inaccuracies in the electoral register. Recent research carried out by a political analyst, and published in *The Sunday Tribune* in 2006, suggests that the current register may be wrong by up to as many as 800,000 names. Discrepancies include people who have moved into an area but have never been included on the register, those who are dead, people who are entitled to vote but are not on the register, people who are double registered and those registered in constituencies in which they have no entitlement to a vote. The most recently published electoral register has 3.129 million people on it, which is estimated to be 300,000 more than the number of Irish and British adult citizens in the state entitled to register. (Dáil Debate, 2006)

In response to the publication of these findings, the government launched a campaign, through the local authorities, to update the register. A growing consensus is emerging around the use of PPSN numbers as a means of compiling the register and ensuring against erroneous and fraudulent entries. The Democracy Commission, for example, has recommended automatic registration of 18 year olds on their birthday through their PPSN number. In addition to ensuring the integrity of the electoral register, such a reform would also remove one of the largest procedural obstacles to voting. (Harris, 2005: 47)

ELECTORAL MACHINERY

No single organisation exists in Ireland to oversee the running of elections and referendums in Ireland. A variety of organisations are currently responsible for some of the functions relating to the running of elections and referenda.

The Department of the Environment, Heritage and Local Government has the primary responsibility for overseeing the conduct of elections and referendums in accordance with legislative provisions. A returning officer is appointed by the Minister of the Environment, Heritage and Local Government to oversee and manage the operation of the election process within each constituency. The duties of returning officers range from collating the lists of valid candidates, determining the location of polling stations and the appointment and training of presiding officers, to ensuring the safe custody of the ballot boxes and ballot papers, arranging the vote count and announcing the final result of the election. As such, the returning officers and their counting staff are responsible for the integrity of the counting process and the accuracy and validity of the election results.

Presiding officers are appointed by the returning officer for each polling station and are responsible for the conduct of the election at each polling station. The presiding officers have primary responsibility to prevent personation, which is an indictable offence in Ireland, on the day of the election. The presiding officer may be assisted in this by personation agents, who may be appointed by each candidate. It is widely accepted that those who manage and supervise elections in Ireland are honest and trustworthy officials.

A number of other bodies play a role in the running of elections, including:

- the Constituency Commission – an independent commission, established under the 1997 Electoral Act, for the redrawing of constituency boundaries (see above);
- the Standards in Public Office Commission – an independent body, established by the Standards in Public Office Act 2001, with a role in overseeing election spending (see Section 9); and
- the Referendum Commission – an independent referendum commission, established by the government for each referendum and, while its remit has varied, (See Q1.5) in the most recent referendum in 2004 its role was to make the electorate aware that a referendum was taking place and to familiarise the public with the issues at stake.

A number of bodies, including a recent referendum commission and the Democracy Commission, have called for a single independent electoral commission to be established with the remit to oversee and improve the functioning of the electoral system. Such bodies do exist in other countries, for example, in the UK, with a branch in Northern Ireland.

Voting Methods

In Ireland, voters are required to cast their ballot at an official voting centre. Postal votes are granted to members of the defence forces, the gardaí and to Irish diplomats posted abroad and their spouses. People with a physical illness or disability that prevents them from going to the polling station and those in full-time education away from their address of registration who are likely to be unable to attend their designated polling station may also be eligible for postal votes.

Postal voting facilitates participation by expanding the time frame for voting and allows electors access to voting who may not be able to attend a polling station in person on the day. Currently the option of postal voting is limited and the Democracy Commission among others has recommend that it be extended to all members of the electorate.

Internationally, electronic voting (e-voting) is gaining currency as a mechanism to increase turnout. It is argued that it can make voting more accessible, convenient and attractive through the use of different technologies.

E-voting was used for the first time in Ireland in the 2002 general election. Three pilot constituencies, Dublin North, Dublin West and Meath, were chosen and the government's intent was to implement the system across the country for the 2004 local and European parliament elections. In its proposals the government promoted electronic voting as a means of improving electoral administration, providing earlier and more accurate results, and easier voting for the public. A particular advantage mooted was that it would make spoilt votes a thing of the past.

In the end, however, e-voting was not used in the local and European Parliament elections in 2004. After the Commission on electronic voting, set up by the government to examine the proposed e-voting system, found that it was unable to verify the accuracy and secrecy of the proposed system, the government postponed its introduction. It now appears that e-voting has been dropped for the foreseeable future. If future e-voting initiatives can secure the trust of the electorate, the Democracy Commission has advocated its use as providing the basis for innovations that would facilitate electoral participation – by allowing, for example, voters to cast their ballots in public libraries, post offices, supermarkets etc. (Harris, 2005)

A final criticism of the current method of voting in Ireland is the lack of independent accessibilty for users who are blind or visually impaired. The absence of audio output, tactile features or enlarging features prevents blind/visually impaired voters from casting their ballot in secret. A tactile template can be added over the ballot paper to assist voters who are blind but he/she will still require assistance from a companion or the presiding officer to communicate instructions, the voting options and to confirm the user's voting choice. (National Disability Authority, 2005b)

TIMING OF ELECTIONS

The ability to determine the timing of elections confers an unfair advantage on government within current electoral procedure. The maximum life of a parliament is laid down in Article 16.2.5 of the Irish Constitution which states "the same Dáil Éireann shall not continue for a longer period than seven years from the date of its first meeting: a shorter period may be fixed by law." The constitution however does not specify a minimum duration. The power to set the date for an election is accordingly left in the hands of the Taoiseach of the day, which gives considerable advantage when it comes to contesting a general election.

In some countries, e.g., Norway and Switzerland, parliament has a fixed term and the prime minister does not have the power to call an election. In other countries, prime ministers do retain this power, but it is used sparingly in that elections are only called for grave political or constitutional reasons. Ireland follows the British model in which the prime minister times elections to suit the incumbent government party, a practice which compromises the fairness of the electoral process.

In Ireland, the Taoiseach can, in practice, decide on a polling day that is believed to best suit his or her own party. Government control of the election date also enables the Taoiseach to set the length of the campaign and can give the government parties a head start over the opposition parties in terms of preparation and strategic planning.

According to recent research, elections to the lower house take place at fixed time intervals in 82 per cent of the countries surveyed. In only a minority of countries, including Ireland, France, the Netherlands, Belgium, Canada, India and the UK, does the power to fix the election date rest in the hands of the government. (EPIC Project, 2006)

Ireland's PR-STV electoral system is considered in Q5.4.

Q5.3 How fair are the procedures for the registration of candidates and parties and how far is there fair access for them to the media and other means of communication with the voters?

Procedures for the registration of candidates and parties for elections in Ireland are by and large independent of party and government influence and control. Broadcasters and newspapers generally follow guidelines aimed at providing a fair share of coverage for each of the parties, based on each party's performance in the previous election. Under the Electoral Act of 1997 a new system for controlling and limiting expenditure during an election campaign by political parties and candidates for elections to Dáil Éireann, the European Parliament and to the office of President is in place, aimed at ensuring a fairer electoral system. Provision has been made to apply similar limits to local elections by ministerial order but so far this measure has not been implemented.

PROCEDURES FOR THE REGISTRATION OF CANDIDATES AND POLITICAL PARTIES

The procedures for registration for national, European and local elections in Ireland are the same for party and non-party candidates alike. In order to run for election to Dáil or Seanad Éireann an individual must be an Irish citizen and over 21 years of age. For Dáil elections, an individual may either nominate himself/herself or be nominated by a registered voter. Candidates must either produce a certificate of party affiliation or a document containing 30 signatures of registered voters. The procedures for nomination for election of the European Parliament are similar.

The category of persons who are eligible to run in local government elections is broader than those for the Dáil, Seanad and the European Parliament. Irish nationality is not required; rather, it is sufficient that a potential candidate is ordinarily resident in the state and is 18 or over. A number of grounds exist for disqualification from local government elections, broadly similar to those which apply to prospective candidates for public office at national level. (www.citizensinformation.ie)

Under the Electoral Act 1992, in order to register as a political party, a party must have a constitution or similar type of document, have an executive committee and hold annual or periodic meetings. The party must also have at least one member who is a member of the Dáil or the European Parliament and have more than 300 recorded members aged 18 or over. Alternatively, in order to register to contest elections in part of the state, or in local elections, a party must have at least three members who are members of a local authority, and have more than 300 recorded members aged 18 or over. There is no fee for registering a political party in Ireland. Applications for registration are considered by the Registrar of Political Parties, a function held by the Clerk of the Dáil. Decisions made by the Registrar may be taken to appeal. It should be noted that candidates belonging to groupings which do not qualify for registration as a political party can still contest elections: they simply will not have any party affiliation next to their name on the ballot paper. Parties can include their European Party affiliation on ballot papers in European elections.

The ease with which independent candidates can register is evidenced by the number of independent councillors and TDs in Ireland, a distinctive aspect of Ireland's political system. The electoral success of independents is a function of Ireland's electoral system of PR-STV. (See also Q6.1)

COMMUNICATION WITH VOTERS

The public service broadcaster, RTÉ, the commercial broadcaster TV3, and local radio stations are all regulated by the Broadcasting Commission of Ireland. Broadcasters are not legally obliged to apply exactly proportional coverage to the various political parties. There is a trend, however, to use a rule of thumb that distributes airtime according to the number of first preference votes received in the previous elections.

Live coverage of annual conferences is another means through which political parties communicate with voters. RTÉ carries live coverage of party conferences for all parties with seven or more TDs, or five per cent of the national first preference vote in the last general election. Complaints by political parties regarding the extent or content of coverage around elections can be made to the Irish Broadcasting Authority which regulates both RTÉ, TV3 and local radio.

Newspapers have set up their own guidelines, which state that parties should be covered in proportion to the number of seats held by each of them in the outgoing Dáil. In order to ensure this, editors use the ruler in lieu of the stopwatch and measure the column inches devoted to each party. While there is evidence of some overrepresentation of the government parties, Fianna Fáil and PDs, in the 2002 media coverage of the election, particularly in the British-owned tabloid media. Overall, however, the conclusion is that all parties were treated fairly. (Brandenburg and Hayden, 2003: 193)

Analysis shows that a general lack of partisanship openly expressed in the newspapers is the key difference between the Irish and British press. (Brandenburg and Hayden, 2003: 178) The general election of 1997 stands out as a rare example of a newspaper explicitly taking a political stance and pronouncing its government preference just ahead of polling day. The *Irish Independent*, in an editorial moved to the front page, complained that under the Rainbow coalition "for years we've been bled white. Now it's payback time". In 2002 its election day editorial was more subdued, recommending "a coalition – the preferred option of this paper".

An analysis of Media Coverage of the 2004 European Elections shows that policy issues comprise a minority of press coverage, with greater emphasis placed on more ancillary issues such as poll findings, personalities of candidates and inter-party and intra-party rivalry. Given the dominant role of the media within the democratic process, and particularly the role of the media as the major political educators for the majority of the population, the minimal discussion of issues in the print media is an issue of concern. (See Section Ten for further discussion.)

The increasing role of the internet as a communication tool is not covered by existing rules.

ELECTION CAMPAIGN SPENDING

The Electoral Act of 1997 introduced a new system for controlling and limiting election expenditure by political parties and candidates in Ireland for elections to Dáil Éireann, the European Parliament and to the office of President. Provision was also made to extend application of the legislation to local elections by ministerial order, but this measure has not yet been taken. The 2002 general election saw the imposition for the first time of spending limits in an Irish general election.

The financing of electoral campaigns is also regulated by controls on political donations. All donations in excess of €635 to an individual candidate, or in excess of €5,079 if made to a political party, must be reported to the Standards in Public Office Commission. There are limits to the size of donations that can be received from any one source, and anonymous donations over €127 are prohibited. In addition, parties may not receive donations from outside Ireland unless these come from an Irish citizen or from a body with an office in Ireland. (Sinnott, 2005: 127)

Practices differ for local government elections. Under the Local Elections (Disclosure and Expenditure) Act 1999, all candidates have to provide local authorities with details of expenditure incurred between the government's issuance of the polling day order and the actual polling day, a period of about four weeks. Candidates also have to make returns on donations received. In their analysis of spending by candidates in the 1999 local elections, Michael Marsh and Kenneth Benoit show that spending has a marked influence on outcome, as the candidates who spent a larger share in their districts won a larger share of the district vote. (Marsh and Benoit, 2002: 17) The current lack of limits on election spending at local level accordingly remains undemocratic as current regulations favour political parties and/or individuals with access to large amounts of money. (See Q9.3 for further discussion).

Q5.4 How effective a range of choice does the electoral and party system allow the voters, how equally do their votes count, and how closely does the composition of the legislature and the selection of the executive reflect the choices they make?

Ireland's electoral system, PR-STV, is written into the Irish Constitution. Its use is unusual by international standards, but it does provide reasonable proportionality of representation between the votes cast per party and the number of seats won per party in the Dáil.

In the formation of coalition governments, however, there is no fixed relationship between the votes cast per party and the composition of the executive. This discrepancy is particularly the case, of course, in regard to the minority coalition party's overrepresentation on the executive. In the current Fianna Fáil (FF)/Progressive Democrat (PD) coalition, for example, the PDs have two ministers on the executive, despite achieving only four per cent of the vote in the 2002 Dáil election.

Political parties in Ireland offer a range of choice in terms of party ideologies in that key long-term priorities held by each of the parties do differ significantly. In practice however, party ideologies tend to take a back seat when it comes to the formation of coalition governments, and short-term priorities in practice tend to differ less between all parties. In addition, the number of possible coalitions that might emerge following an election effectively mean that voters have little direct control over the final combination of government coalition partners at the time they vote.

Voter choice is further restricted in that only Fianna Fáil and Fine Gael can claim to be truly national parties which put candidates forward in all constituencies in the country. Moreover, Labour and, more particularly, the smaller parties, currently have limited representation in Dáil Éireann from constituencies outside Dublin.

IRELAND'S ELECTORAL SYSTEM

PR-STV is the electoral system used in Ireland for general, local and European elections. It is not a widely used electoral system, as only Malta and Ireland use it to elect their lower houses of parliament. The unusual nature of Ireland's system can be traced back to preindependence days, when it was designed by the British to ensure minority, and especially unionist, representation. The particular form of PR – proportional representation by single transferable vote – is included in the Irish Constitution and has been endorsed by the Irish electorate on two separate occasions.

In contrast to the PR list systems, where voters chose between various party lists, under PR-STV voters chose candidates as well as parties. Critics of this system have suggested that such an approach fosters personalism, wherein votes tend to be cast on the basis of personality rather than political principle or ideology.

The tables below show the percentages of votes and seats for the three largest parties in each Irish, British and German general election since 1987. An analysis of these tables shows that the Irish system lies between the British first-past-the-post and German mixed electoral systems in terms of proportionality of representation. The differences between the percentage of votes cast and the percentage of seats won are never in double figures, as they often are in the UK, but neither are they as low as the figures in Germany.

Table 5.1 Irish Election Results, 1987–2002, Vote and Seat Percentages

	Fianna Fáil			*Fine Gael*			*Labour*		
	Vote	*Seat*	*Diff*	*Vote*	*Seat*	*Diff*	*Vote*	*Seat*	*Diff*
	(%)	(%)	(%)	(%)	(%)	(%)	(%)	(%)	(%)
1987	44.1	48.8	+4.7	30.7	48.8	+3.6	6.4	7.2	+0.8
1989	44.2	46.4	+2.2	33.1	46.4	+3.8	9.5	9.0	-0.5
1992	39.1	41.0	+1.9	24.5	27.1	+2.6	19.3	19.9	+0.6
1997	39.3	46.4	+7.1	28.0	32.5	+4.5	10.4	10.2	-0.2
2002	41.5	50.6	+9.1	22.5	19.3	-3.2	10.8	13.1	+2.3

Source: Farrell, 2001: 141; results for 2002 calculated from www.environ.ie

Table 5.2 United Kindom (UK) Election Results, 1987-2005, Vote and Seat Percentages

	Conservatives			*Labour*			*Liberal Democrats*		
	Vote	*Seat*	*Diff*	*Vote*	*Seat*	*Diff*	*Vote*	*Seat*	*Diff*
	(%)	(%)	(%)	(%)	(%)	(%)	(%)	(%)	(%)
1987	42.3	57.8	+15.5	30.8	35.2	+4.4	22.6	3.4	-19.2
1992	41.9	51.6	+9.7	34.4	41.6	+7.2	17.8	3.1	-14.7
1997	30.7	25.0	-5.7	43.2	63.4	+20.2	16.8	7.0	-9.8
2001	31.7	25.1	-6.6	40.7	62.6	+21.9	18.3	7.9	-10.4
2005	32.3	30.6	-1.7	35.3	55.1	+19.8	22.1	9.5	-12.6

Source: Farrell, 2001: 27; results for 2005 calculated from www.electoralcommission.gov.uk

Table 5.3 German Federal Elections 1987-2005, Vote and Seat Percentages

	Christian Democratic Union			*Christian Social Union*			*Social Democrats*		
	Vote	*Seat*	*Diff*	*Vote*	*Seat*	*Diff*	*Vote*	*Seat*	*Diff*
	(%)	(%)	(%)	(%)	(%)	(%)	(%)	(%)	(%)
1987	34.5	35.0	+0.5	9.8	9.9	+0.1	37.0	37.4	+0.4
1990	36.7	40.5	+3.8	7.1	7.7	+0.6	33.5	36.1	+2.6
1994	34.2	36.3	+2.1	7.3	7.4	+0.1	36.4	37.5	+1.1
1998	28.4	29.6	+1.2	6.7	7.0	+0.3	40.9	44.5	+3.6
2002	29.5	31.5	+2.0	9.0	9.6	+0.6	38.5	41.6	+3.1
2005	27.8	29.3	+1.5	7.4	7.4	-	34.2	36.1	+1.9

Source: Farrell, 2001: 107; results for 2002 and 2005 calculated from www.bundeswahlleiter.de

Recent debate about Irish electoral reform has focused mainly on the charge that the current system obliges elected TDs to place excessive emphasis on constituency work, and that competition at constituency level tends to be on the basis of services rendered or promised by individuals rather than on party policy differences.

The All-Party Oireachtas Committee on the constitution considered the issue of electoral reform and then reported its findings and recommendations in 2002. The main research undertaken by the Committee examined the consequences of a switch to the additional member system (AMS), a mixed electoral system. Under this system, approximately one half of the seats in the legislature are allocated on a first-past-the-post system to single-seat constituencies and the remainder are filled on the basis of a PR list. Such a system effectively produces two types of deputies, constituency deputies and deputies elected from party lists.

One study has found that if AMS were to be implemented in Ireland, Fianna Fáil would likely win most of the constituency seats with the other parties taking their seats from the PR list element of the election. As a result, Fianna Fáil TDs would face a different set of electoral pressures to TDs of other parties. While there is no intrinsic reason why TDs from different Irish parties should not face different electoral pressures over candidate selection and constituency service, it would be important for people to be aware of this likely key consequence if a decision were made to introduce the AMS system in Ireland. (Laver, 1998: 44-45)

HOW EFFECTIVE A RANGE OF CHOICE DOES PARTY SYSTEM ALLOW THE VOTERS?

The Irish party system differs from that in many other countries in a number of important respects. These variances include the weakness of the left, the weakness of class-based politics and the inherent similarity between the main parties in terms of their perspectives and policies. (Mair and Weeks, 2005; Farrell, 1999; Sinnott, 1995; Chubb, 1982)

Most notably, perhaps, the two largest political parties, Fianna Fáil and Fine Gael, do not identify themselves first and foremost as either centre-right or centre-left parties. Both parties arose from the split, following the foundation of the state, which gave rise to the civil war.

The centre-left in Irish politics is represented by the Labour Party, which is the state's third largest political party. In terms of economic policy, and as reported by candidates of each party in the 2002 general election, the smaller parties on the left are the Socialist Workers' Party, the Workers' Party, the Socialist Party, and Sinn Féin. The right is represented by the Progressive Democrats (PDs), while the Green Party is to the right of Labour and to the left of both Fine Gael and Fianna Fáil. (Gilland Lutz, 2003)

Dáil Éireann is also host to a relatively high number of independent TDs who play an important role in Irish politics, at times supporting minority governments, or governments with slim majorities.

The relative absence of strong ideological underpinnings in Irish politics is demonstrated in the range of coalition governments which have emerged in recent years. Recent elections have seen Fianna Fáil entering coalition with Labour in 1992, followed by Labour entering coalition with Fine Gael and Democratic Left in 1994 (the latter has since merged with the Labour Party), and by Fianna Fáil entering coalition with the Progressive Democrats in 1997 and again in 2002. In general, numbers rather than ideology or policy principles determine who enters government with whom. For this reason, political commentators have characterised Irish political parties as primarily office seeking, (Gilland Lutz, 2003: 43) although political party members would argue that all coalitions are based on programmes which seek to implement key elements of each party's manifesto. This relative absence of ideological divisions between left and right in Ireland is unusual in comparison to other countries, both in Europe and internationally. Perhaps ironically, the biggest exception to the office-seeking nature of Irish political parties is the steadfast refusal of Fianna Fáil and Fine Gael to enter government together under any circumstances, despite being the two parties with the most similar policy positions.

Coalition politics has been particularly useful to Fianna Fáil, which has found it relatively easy to find at least one other party willing to join it in government, a position that is unlikely to change in the short term. Fianna Fáil has, at times, been associated with the centre-left and in coalition with the Labour Party but the party has also been in several coalitions with the economically right-wing Progressive Democrats.

While Fine Gael has often been viewed historically as a broadly centre-right party, such a characterisation is also overly simplistic, given that every past Fine Gael government has involved a coalition with the Labour Party.

Policy Differences between the Major Parties

In a survey of 217 candidates who stood in the 2002 general election, each candidate was asked to name the most important issues facing Ireland during the previous five years. The responses given by most candidates for each party is given in Table 5.4 below and provides a broad indication of the long-term priorities of each of the parties.

Table 5.4 Major Issues Facing Ireland in Recent Years

What do you think has been the most important issue facing Ireland over the last five years?

Party	*Most Mentioned Long Term Policy Priority*
Fianna Fáil	Northern Ireland / peace
Fine Gael	Managing the economy
Labour	Social justice
Progressive Democrats	Managing the economy
Green Party	Environment
Sinn Féin	Northern Ireland / peace
Workers' Party	Health, Social justice
Socialist Party	Social justice
Socialist Workers' Party	Social justice
Christian Solidarity Party	European Union
Independents	Northern Ireland / peace

Source: Adapted from Gilland Lutz, 2003

These answers mirror the long-established perceptions of the core identity of each party, with Fianna Fáil, for example, being strongly associated with Northern Ireland and the Peace Process, while Labour is most strongly associated with social justice.

Each candidate in the survey was also asked a series of questions under the headings morality/religion; environment; tolerance towards minority groups; Northern Ireland; European Union; and economic policy. The results were used to calculate a mean score for each party, which as the following tables show, demonstrate different values on all indicators.

Table 5.5 Values of Irish Political Parties

Morality / Religion	
Most Liberal	Socialist Workers' Party (0.4)
	Socialist Party (0.9)
	Workers' Party (1.4)
	Sinn Féin (2.9)
	Labour (3.9)
	GreenParty (4.5)
	Progressive Democrats (4.9)
	Fine Gael (5.4)
	Independents (5.7)
	Fianna Fáil (5.9)
Most Conservative	Christian Solidarity Party (9.0)

Environment	
High concern	Green Party (8.9)
	Sinn Féin (7.9)
	Workers' Party (7.7)
	Labour (7.3)
	Independents (6.9)
	Progressive Democrats (6.7)
	Socialist Party (6.7)
	Christian Solidarity Party (6.6)
	Fine Gael (6.4)
	Fianna Fáil (6.1)
Low Concern	Socialist Workers' Party (4.9)

Tolerance	
Tolerant	Socialist Workers' Party (10.0)
	Socialist Party (9.9)
	Sinn Féin (8.8)
	Labour (8.0)
	Workers' Party (8.0)
	Green Party (7.8)
	Christian Solidarity Party (7.0)
	Progressive Democrats (6.7)
	Fine Gael (5.6)
	Independents (5.6)
Less tolerant	Fianna Fáil (5.3)

Northern Ireland	
Nationalist	Sinn Féin (9.8)
	Socialist Workers' Party (8.2)
	Fianna Fáil (7.8)
	Christian Solidarity Party (7.8)
	Independents (7.0)
	Workers' Party (7.0)
	Socialist Party (6.3)
	Green Party (5.9)
	Progressive Democrats (5.8)
	Fine Gael (5.7)
Less nationalist	Labour (5.7)
European Union	
Pro-EU	Progressive Democrats (8.5)
	Fine Gael (8.0)
	Fianna Fáil (7.4)
	Labour (7.0)
	Green Party (5.5)
	Independents (5.2)
	Workers' Party (3.9)
	Sinn Féin (3.0)
	Socialist Party (2.6)
	Socialist Workers' Party (2.4)
Anti-EU	Christian Solidarity Party (2.2)
Economic Policy	
Left-wing	Socialist Workers' Party (0.4)
	Workers' Party (0.6)
	Socialist Party (1.1)
	Sinn Féin (2.0)
	Labour (2.7)
	Green Party (3.0)
	Independents (4.3)
	Christian Solidarity Party (5.1)
	Fine Gael (5.2)
	Fianna Fáil (5.7)
Right-wing	Progressive Democrats (6.7)

Source: Adapted from Gilland Lutz, 2003

According to these results, Northern Ireland is the only policy area where Fianna Fáil and Fine Gael differ significantly from each other. Northern Ireland is also the most significant difference in policy between Fianna Fáil and the Progressive Democrats. While this divergence was the source of occasional tension within the Fianna Fáil/ Progressive Democrats coalition government following the 2002 election, the difference has not proved itself irreconcilable in practice.

Labour and the Greens can also be seen to shadow each other quite closely across policy areas and to provide an alternative to certain aspects of Fianna Fáil, Fine Gael and Progressive Democrat policies, particularly in economic policy where they are markedly more left-wing.

Sinn Féin differs significantly from Fianna Fáil and Fine Gael on almost all policy areas, as do the smaller left-wing parties. (Gilland Lutz, 2003: 43) Sinn Féin stands out among the political parties by continuing to provoke controversy and debate with respect to its commitment to exclusively democratic means. The position of all the main parties in the Republic has been one of refusal to share power with Sinn Féin in government until the party has clearly detached itself from the IRA and renounced all violence and criminality. (See the parallel audit of democracy in Northern Ireland, Wilford, *et al* 2007, forthcoming; Q6.1)

As the following table shows, the three largest parties all attract voters across class lines.

Table 5.6 Opinion Poll Support for Parties by Social Group 2002

	All %	*Middle Class %*	*Working Class %*	*Large Farmers %*	*Small Farmers %*
Fianna Fáil	47	47	47	41	61
Fine Gael	18	18	15	42	17
Labour	10	10	11	2	5

Source: Adapted from Coakley and Gallagher, 2005: 472

PARTY REPRESENTATION NATIONWIDE

Another issue affecting voter choice is the degree to which each party is organised nationally across constituencies. The table below shows the number of constituencies which had at least one representative for each party after the 2002 Dáil election. There were 42 constituencies in total nationwide, including the 12 constituencies in County Dublin.

Table 5.7 Party Representation Nationwide

	Number of Constituencies Represented Nationwide	*Number of Constituencies Represented Outside Dublin*
Fianna Fáil	42	30
Fine Gael	29	26
Labour	21	12
Progressive Democrats	8	4
Sinn Féin	6	4
Green Party	6	1
Independents	14	12
Socialist Party	1	0

Source: Compiled from www.ireland.com/focus/election_2002/constituencies

As seen, only Fianna Fáil and Fine Gael can claim to be nationally representative. Labour and the smaller parties currently rely heavily or predominantly on Dublin for their Dáil strengths. *(Irish Times*, 2002)

Q5.5 How far does the legislature reflect the social composition of the electorate?

Neither the Dáil, the Seanad, nor local government are truly representative of Irish society in terms of age, gender, or social class. Young people over 18 and under 30 are sharply underrepresented in Dáil Éireann. Only six TDs aged 30 and under were elected in 2002, representing 3.6 per cent of the total number of deputies. And only 3 per cent of the TDs elected in the 2002 general election were aged 65 or over, although this age group accounts for over 11 per cent of the population.

Lower socio-economic groups are significantly underrepresented.

While 47 per cent of TDs in the 29th Dáil are lower and higher professionals, only 15 per cent of overall Irish society come from these categories.

Women too are significantly underrepresented within the legislature. Women currently comprise 13 per cent of the Dáil and Ireland currently ranks 19th out of the 25 EU states in terms of the percentage of women in its national parliament. At no time in the history of the Dáil has the proportion of women exceeded 14 per cent.

Women's underrepresentation in public office is dealt with in detail in Q11.3. The access of all social groups to public office is likewise dealt with in Q11.4. In this answer, therefore, we deal with the underrepresentation of young people and people from lower socio-economic backgrounds, since these groups are the focus of most concern in regard to low levels of voter participation. In addition, the disengagement of young people from politics is considered by military and security analysts in international literature as one measure of potential threat to democracy and stability.

YOUTH REPRESENTATION

An examination of the age profile of Irish national political representatives shows that they are not representative of young people. According to the 2002 census, around 42 per cent of the Irish population is aged between 18 and 44. An analysis of the figures below reveals that the percentages of Fianna Fáil, Fine Gael and Progressive Democrat TDs aged 44 and under are somewhat representative of this age category, while the Green Party is overrepresentative. The Labour party is the least representative, not having a single TD aged 44 or under at the last election. Thirty year olds and under are, however, grossly underrepresented. Only six TDs aged thirty and under, five of whom are members of Fine Gael, were elected in 2002. This group accounted for 3.6 per cent of the total number of deputies in Dáil Éireann and reinforces young peoples' perceptions of politicians of being "old and grey". (Harris, 2005)

Table 5.8 Age Profile of TDs Per Political Party in 2002

Political Party	*Number of TDs aged 44 and under*	*% of party's total TDs*	*Number of TDs aged 30 and under*	*% of party's TDs*
Fianna Fáil	23	28	0	0
Fine Gael	8	26	5	16
Labour	0	0	0	0
Progressive Democrats	2	25	0	0
Green party	5	83	0	0
Sinn Féin	1	20	0	0
Independents	3	23	1	8

Source: Harris, 2005: 65

REPRESENTATION OF DIFFERENT SOCIO-ECONOMIC GROUPS

Not only are Irish politicians predominantly middle aged, but they also tend to be largely middle class. The overrepresentation of the professional classes in the Dáil as highlighted in the table below reinforces public perceptions of politics as the preserve of the educated and the wealthy.

Table 5.9 Occupation of TDs in the 29th Dáil

Occupation	*Number of TDs*	*% of total TDs*	*% of total population in this occupation*
Manual Employee	3	2	10
Non-manual Employee	35	21	17
Farmer	21	13	6
Lower Professions	37	22	10
Higher Professions	41	25	5

Source: Compiled from Galligan, 2005: 287; and the 2002 Census, www.cso.ie

Q5.6 What proportion of the electorate votes, and how far are the election results accepted by all political forces in the country and outside?

Declining levels of electoral participation over a sustained period of time can weaken democratic systems by eroding mandates, damaging legitimacy, and reducing political equality and the diversity of dialogue. Evidence shows that low and declining turnouts often involve a class bias that leaves the less well-off in society and certain age groups significantly underrepresented. (Lijphart, 1997)

Voter turnout at the 2002 general election was the lowest ever recorded for a parliamentary election in Ireland. On a European ranking of average turnout, only Switzerland shows a lower average than Ireland. Voter turnout for local, European and presidential elections are generally even lower, reflecting the lesser importance the electorate gives to these elections. Moreover, turnout for European elections in Ireland is the most unpredictable of all the member countries, while turnout for presidential elections is the lowest in Western Europe. The low turnout of voters for all elections in economically disadvantaged areas is an issue of particular concern, as is the lower participation rates among young people. In Ireland the results of elections are accepted by all political forces internally and externally.

VOTER TURNOUT

Ireland, like other Western democracies, has been experiencing declining electoral turnout in recent decades. Over a twenty-year period, turnout in general elections has dropped by over 10 percentage points, from 73.8 per cent in 1982 to 62.7 per cent in 2002. A caveat needs to be added, however, in light of the increasing inaccuracy of the electoral register over this period (see Q5.2).

Turnout in second-order elections, that is, elections to the local authorities and European Parliament, has been even lower, for example, dropping as low as 44 per cent in the 1994 election to the European Parliament. The increased level of voter participation in the 2004 local and European elections bucked this trend, and was much higher than the EU average. However, it has been argued that the holding of a contentious citizenship referendum on the same day had a positive impact on the level of turnout. Nonetheless, turnout at 58.8 per cent was still below the lowest turnout for any general election in Ireland.

Table 5.10 Turnout in Dáil Éireann Elections 1969-2002

Year	*Turnout %*
1969	76.9
1973	76.6
1977	76.3
1981	76.2
1982-1	73.8
1982-2	72.9
1987	73.3
1989	68.5
1992	67.5
1997	65.9
2002	62.7

Source: Adapted from Institute of Public Administration, 2005: 430

Table 5.11 Turnout in European Parliament Elections

Member State	*1979*	*1984*	*1989*	*1994*	*1999*	*2004*
Ireland	63.6	47.6	68.3	44.0	50.2	58.8
Average EU	65.9	63.8	62.8	58.4	53.0	45.6

Source: International IDEA, 2004, www.idea.int; Coakley and Gallagher, 2005: 469

Table 5.12 Turnout in Local Elections 1967-2004

Year	Turnout%
1967	69
1974	61.1
1979	63.6
1985	58.2
1991	55.1
1999	49.5
2004	58.8

Source: Adapted from Institute of Public Administration, 2005: 431

It remains to be seen whether the 2004 increase was a once-off event or the beginning of a trend in increased participation at local level. Speculation as to the causes of the increase include the role of Sinn Féin in mobilising the vote, the level of interest in the citizenship referendum, disgruntlement with the government of the day, voter education programmes and extended polling hours. (Harris, 2005: 38)

Turnout Among Young People

Research undertaken by the National Youth Council of Ireland (NYCI) shows that youth participation in the electoral process is declining. In the 1999 local and European elections, almost 67 per cent of young people (aged 18–25) did not vote. (www.youth.ie) This finding is supported by the quarterly national household survey of spring 2003 which revealed that "just over 40 per cent of young adult respondents aged 18-19, and only 53 per cent of those aged 20-24 indicated that they voted" in the 2002 general election. (Central Statistics Office, 2003a: 1) In contrast, almost 90 per cent of those aged 65-74 said they had voted.

Recent Democratic Audit Ireland survey results reveal that young peoples' belief in their ability to influence decisions is weaker than their parents and grandparents. Only half of the 15-24 year olds questioned believed that "ordinary citizens could influence decisions when they made an effort" compared with over two-thirds of older respondents. Only one-fifth of the young respondents disagreed strongly with the statement that "citizens being active in politics is a waste of time" compared with one-third of older respondents. Young people are also far less inclined to discuss politics or political news with someone else, while their parents and grandparents are twice as likely to take part in a political discussion with someone else. (Clancy *et al.*, 2005)

This finding is in keeping with the National Youth Federation's national youth poll of young people aged between 15 and 17 which found that 45 per cent of the respondents had no interest in politics, while a small majority of 55 per cent said they did and 8 per cent indicated that they were very interested. (www.nyf.ie)

Turnout Among People Living in Socially Disadvantaged Areas

Electoral turnout also tends to be lower amongst the less affluent in society. Adrian Kavanagh notes that "class related factors have a large bearing on the geography of turnouts in Dublin and other large urban areas, with large differences in turnout rates generally existing between middle-class and working-class areas". (Kavanagh, 2005: 3)

However, recent analysis shows that turnout figures in a ward may not be a true reflection of socio-economic participation. Kavanagh notes that in the 1999 and 2004 local elections low turnouts in the predominantly middle-class private "gated" apartments in Dublin inner city push down the average turnout in these wards and contribute to a misperception of low political and electoral engagement among the local, mainly working class, inner-city population. (Kavanagh, 2005: 14)

Turnout levels in rural areas tend to be higher than in urban ones. A variety of explanations have been put forward, including a stronger sense of community, stronger political organisations and traditions as well as an older population. Meanwhile high population mobility in the new commuter belts around Dublin has a negative impact on turnout in these areas.

The link between the level of formal education received and the likelihood of voting has been well established. Recent research also reveals the impact of community-based voter education programmes on turnout. In Fatima Mansions, Dublin, turnout levels have increased steadily as a consequence of locally-based voter education programmes and urban regeneration programmes. Voter education programmes run by the Vincentian Partnership for Social Justice were also one of the factors contributing to the high turnout rate for non-EU nationals in the 2004 local elections in the Portlaoise region. (Kavanagh, 2005: 24)

Findings from a survey of public opinion carried out for the Democratic Audit Ireland project support Kavanagh's latest research. The percentage of those who said they had voted at the last general election did not vary significantly between social groups. This was also the case for the last local election. Nonetheless, there were differing perceptions of politics according to socio-economic status. Those who felt most strongly that political activism is not a waste of time are somewhat more likely to be from higher social class groupings. (Clancy *et al.*, 2005:8)

Six: Democratic Role of Political Parties

Does the party system assist the working of democracy?

INTRODUCTION AND SUMMARY

Political parties in most of the world come at the very bottom of the list of public institutions in which people express any confidence and their memberships are in decline. Among other reasons, people dislike parties because they exaggerate public division over policy while stifling internal dissent, and because they appear ready to sell themselves to the highest bidder in the quest for campaign funding. However, if parties did not exist, we would be compelled to reinvent them. In a large society, people can exercise little public influence as individuals but they can have influence if they act in association with others. Political parties bring together like-minded people to frame policy programmes and to campaign both on behalf of issues and for governmental office. In doing so, parties perform several essential functions:

- for the electorate, they simplify the choices that people make at elections by offering them broad policy alternatives and different sets of politicians to choose from and they also make clear who is responsible when policies or politicians fail;
- for governments, they provide a reasonably stable following of political supporters in parliament to enable them to achieve their programmes, if elected, or provide systematic opposition if not; and
- for the more politically active, they provide an opportunity to be involved in public affairs and a channel for influencing public policies and the choice of candidates and leaders.

The Irish party system is distinctive in Europe in that the division between its main parties (Fianna Fáil and Fine Gael) is a product of historical disagreements over the 1921 Treaty rather than a left-right ideological divide. At the same time, party and electoral rules make it relatively easy for new parties to form and to win representation in the Dáil. The PR-STV system also produces more independent representatives than the rest of Europe put together, offering a counterweight to party dominance.

Offsetting this pluralism is the exceedingly tight discipline exercised by the governing party or coalition over its TDs in the Dáil, and the limited possibilities open to opposition parties to influence government policy and legislation. However, the necessity of coalition formation since 1989 has introduced a more consensual approach within government itself, together with an opportunity for enhanced accountability.

In terms of internal party organisation, the recent increase in public funding for political parties, combined with tighter disclosure rules on donations, has substantially reduced the potential for selling favours for donations. The situation regarding internal party democracy, however, is more mixed. Although almost all the political parties assign party members the key role in selecting candidates for elections, only the smaller parties give any role to their members in the selection of the party leader or in influencing the shape of party policy. Meanwhile efforts made across all parties to recruit new members or to increase the low representation of women in public life must be judged inadequate.

Q6.1 How freely are parties able to form and recruit members, engage with the public and campaign for office?

Political parties in Ireland are free to form, recruit members, engage with the public and campaign for office. This state of affairs is evident in the emergence of new parties throughout the history of the state and particularly over recent decades. The regulations for registering a political party are not onerous and unregistered parties are still entitled to fight elections. The relative ease with which individuals not affiliated to any political party can register and contest elections is evidenced by the high number of independent TDs in Dáil Éireann.

REGISTERING A POLITICAL PARTY IN IRELAND

Given the ease with which they can establish themselves, recruit, and campaign, it is not surprising that new parties have emerged throughout the history of the state. A number of new parties have likewise emerged in recent decades, beginning with the Workers' Party in the late 1970s and, following a split in the Workers' Party, the Democratic Left. Currently the Workers' Party are without a sitting TD, while Democratic Left merged with the Labour Party in 1999. The small Socialist Party does enjoy representation in the Dáil through Joe Higgins, TD.

In the 1980s, a split within the Fianna Fáil party led to the defection of a number of TDs to form the Progressive Democrats (PDs), who were also joined by a number of Fine Gael members. The number of parties has increased further with the rise of the Green Party in the late 1980s and more recently with the growth of Sinn Féin. The election of the first Sinn Féin TD in recent times took place in the 1997 general election. (Murphy and Farrell, 2002)

Under the Electoral Act, 1992 and 2001, a political party can apply to register to contest one or more of local, Dáil or European elections. The conditions for registration are outlined in Q5.3. There is no fee for registering a political party.

Unregistered parties are entitled to fight elections but the party's name will not appear on the ballot paper. Candidates at elections who are members of registered parties may add their party name to their own names on the ballot paper and their European party affiliation at European elections. (www.citizensinformation.ie)

AN INDEPENDENT TRADITION

The election of Independent TDs has been remarked upon as one of the distinctive features of the Irish political landscape. (Coakley, 2005a: 28) The 2002 General Election, for example, returned 14 independents or one-person parties to the Dáil, continuing what has been a consistent independent presence since the founding of the state. Indeed the number of non-party TDs in Ireland has often exceeded the total elected to all other Western European parliaments. (Mair and Weeks, 2005: 138)

The success of independents is also reflected at local and European levels where 96 independent councillors and two independent MEPs were elected in the 2004 local and European elections. Some independent representatives do have loyalties to particular parties.

The surge in support for independents, who between them garnered over 10 per cent of the vote in the 2002 general election, has been partly attributed to a decline in voter allegiance to particular political parties. (Mair and Weeks, 2005: 156) Ireland's electoral system of proportional representation and multiseat constituencies also favour independents by lowering the threshold for election to within reach of non-party candidates. (Marsh, 2000) The dominance of candidate-focused voting even within the party system, together with a pronounced focus on local issues and clientelism among the electorate, also contribute to the success of independents.

Studies of the Irish electorate suggest that there is a strong tendency to vote for individual candidates rather than along party lines. Under Ireland's system of PR-STV, voters rank candidates, which means that voters can decide on the basis of candidates, parties or a mix of the two. In one study, 40 per cent of voters said candidates were more important than party affiliation in deciding how to vote, and that they would continue to give a first preference to a particular candidate if she or he were running for a different party. By comparison, only 27 per cent of respondents reported themselves to be strong party voters who would select on the basis of affiliation and would not cross party lines to vote for a particular candidate. (Laver, 2005: 193)

Ireland's independents have a mix of origins. Some independents, such as Catherine Murphy, Jackie Healy-Rae and Niall Blaney had previously been elected as representatives of a political party, but have subsequently stood and won as independent candidates. Still others, such as Jerry Cowley and Liam Twomey (who has since joined Fine Gael) stood as "hospital" or "health" candidates in 2002, and were returned on "single-issue" platforms.

The prime policy goal for independent TDs is generally to maximise delivery to their local constituency base. Furthermore, they have historically proved very effective at doing so when given the opportunity and their willingness to lobby on behalf of "single-issues" such as the retention of hospitals and the provision of infrastructure endears them to their local base.

On the other hand, independents are often accused of having "few goals beyond securing largesse for their constituencies" and are seldom required to engage with national issues. (Weeks, 2004) It must be said, however, that independents are by no means the only TDs expected to deliver for their constituencies.

It has also been argued that independents have at times effectively kept the smaller parties from government, since "rather than conceding a cabinet seat and making cabinet concessions to a small party, the large parties have found the support of independents a more manageable task". (Weeks, 2004) This finding suggests that delivering on the "local largesse" for independents is a more attractive option for the dominant party than compromising on their national policy platform within a coalition government.

THE STABILITY OF ESTABLISHED PARTIES

While new parties are free to form and campaign for office, financial and organisational sustainability, electoral success and achieving government are entirely different matters. Research shows that Western democracies exhibit a remarkable continuity and stability in their party systems. Although new parties are a relatively common phenomenon across developed democracies, they rarely enjoy electoral success either in terms of votes or in government participation. A recent analysis of 13 Western European countries between 1930 and 2000 showed the emergence of 385 new parties during that time. (Golder, 2003) However, less than 8 per cent of these have ever managed to enter government. Moreover, half of those parties that did enter government have since disappeared. As a result, parties that currently dominate elections and governments across Western Europe tend to have been the same dominant parties as far back as the 1920s.

No Irish party that has emerged after Fine Gael formed in 1933 has ever won more than 15 per cent of the vote in national elections and only four formed after 1930 have ever been in government: Family of the Land (Clann na Talmhan) in 1948, Family of the Republic (Clann na Poblachta) in 1948, Democratic Left in 1994, and Progressive Democrats in 1989, 1992, 1997 and 2002. (Golder, 2003: 6) Of these, only the Progressive Democrats still have an independent existence.

Research across Europe suggests that a major consequence of the dominant social divisions at the time of universal suffrage has been their enduring impact ever since on both the shape and remarkable stability of party systems. (Lipset and Rokkan, 1967) As already mentioned, Ireland's case differs from most European countries whose primary divisions in the early years of the 20th century were along class or religious lines, whereas in Ireland at that time the major societal fault line lay between the pro- and anti- treaty forces in the Civil War. This division was the primary electoral focus in the early years of the state and has since had the singular effect of stabilising a system of electoral competition around a difference of opinion concerning a historical treaty rather than differences in class or religion. (Mair and Weeks, 2005: 142) The result has been the observable lack of ideological divide in Irish politics and the relative weakness of the Irish left. Kennedy and Sinnott (2006: 90) conclude that while "the two most important and durable cleavages in Irish society focus on nationalism and religion", they now have only limited influence on support for political parties.

While Ireland can be characterised as having had a markedly stable party system, it is possible that the larger parties have until recently been able to encompass the various cleavages (along the lines of class, urban/rural, left/right etc.) that have existed in Irish politics all along. In any event, changes have also undoubtedly been taking place, as can be seen by the increasing fragmentation of the electorate that has resulted in a greater multiplicity of parties and independents.

The combined electoral support for the two largest parties has been in decline since the 1980s. (Mair and Weeks, 2005: 143) Significantly, declining support for Fianna Fáil and growing support for the smaller parties and independents have resulted in a recent shift to coalition government as the norm. On the basis of the preceding analysis, the most likely outcome is a stabilisation of the current situation with the main parties, particularly Fianna Fáil, maintaining their dominant positions. Other outcomes, however, are also possible. In 2002, the smaller parties and independents represented around 25 per cent of the electorate. (Mair and Weeks, 2005: 143) If this trend were to continue, coalition government which does not involve either of the two major parties, Fianna Fáil or Fine Gael, may become a reality, marking a sea change in Irish politics.

Q6.2 How effective is the party system in forming and sustaining governments in office?

International comparisons show Ireland's party system as being effective in forming and sustaining governments in office. Ireland's largest party, Fianna Fáil, has historically been the dominant party in government, and has been in power on 22 out of 36 possible occasions since the foundation of the state. In recent years an increase in the number of smaller parties and a reduction in Fianna Fáil's share of the vote has partially eroded that party's dominance. As a result, Ireland has moved from a predominantly single party majority form of government to coalition government as the norm. Coalition government in Ireland has proven in the round to be a stable form of government.

STABILITY OF GOVERNMENT

A comparison of the number of governments formed in Ireland between 1945 and 2003 places Ireland between those countries with smaller numbers of governments such as Spain, Portugal and Greece, all of which experienced periods of dictatorship, and countries with high numbers of administrative change such as France and Italy. (Gallagher *et al.*, 2005: 401) Ireland accordingly compares well with other European nations on democratic stability.

The number of parties within a political system critically influences both inter-party competition and the stability of government. International experience shows that stability is enhanced when a country has a limited number of political parties, each of which enjoys broad-based support. Such is the case in Ireland. The extent of polarisation, i.e., the degree of ideological differences between parties, is a second important factor. Political parties here exhibit a low degree of polarisation. (See Q5.4 for more on the ideologies of Ireland's political parties)

Too many parties, accompanied by high levels of polarisation among them, tend to result in political instability, frequent changes of government and the discouragement of a consensual and inclusive approach to politics. (Netherlands Institute for Multiparty Democracy, 2004: 15) This situation is not the case in Ireland.

Table 6.1 Types of Government in Western Europe 1945-2003

	Single-Party Majority	*Single-Party Minority*	*Majority Coalition*	*Minority Coalition*	*Total*
France		4	48	5	57
Italy		11	33	9	53
Finland		4	29	7	40
Belgium	3	1	31	2	37
Denmark		14	4	13	31
Norway	6	13	3	6	28
Sweden	3	16	5	2	26
Iceland		2	22		24
Austria	4	1	18		23
Germany		1	22		23
Ireland	**7**	**4**	**8**	**3**	**22**
UK	20	1			21
Netherlands			19		19
Luxembourg			18		18
Portugal	2	4	5		11
Greece	8		1		9
Malta	9				9
Spain	4	4			8

Source: Adapted from Gallagher *et al*., 2005: 401

The weakness of a left/right divide, the absence of overt class politics and the inherent similarity between the main parties in terms of their policies and standpoints (Gilland Lutz, 2003) has been discussed elsewhere within this audit. (See Q5.4) These aspects of the Irish party system contribute to the stability of government by allowing a large number of possible coalition partners and by the fact that the ideological divides between coalition partners, in practice, are likely to be relatively small. This does not, however, mean that it makes no difference who is elected, since smaller parties in a coalition can ensure a shift to either left or right.

THE PREDOMINANCE OF FIANNA FÁIL

Until as recently as the mid-1980s, Irish party politics was characterised as a two-and-a-half party system – Fianna Fáil, Fine Gael, and the smaller Labour Party – dominated by Fianna Fáil. Of the eleven people who have held the office of Taoiseach since 1922, six have been Fianna Fáil and five Fine Gael. However this finding belies the dominant position which Fianna Fáil has enjoyed throughout the history of the state.

The last number of decades has seen a number of changes. The electoral success of a number of smaller parties and a fall in Fianna Fáil's share of the vote, has partially eroded Fianna Fáil's support and its ability to form single party government.

After failing to win an overall majority in the 1989 election, Fianna Fáil agreed to formally enter coalition with another party for the first time, and formed a coalition government with the Progressive Democrats. This first attempt at coalition government collapsed with the withdrawal of the Progressive Democrats in 1992 and a similar fate befell the succeeding Fianna Fáil/Labour coalition in 1994. Following the 1997 general election, Fianna Fáil entered coalition a third time. This coalition with the Progressive Democrats held and was re-elected to power in 2002. (Mair and Weeks, 2005)

While the party in government changed only four times from 1932 to 1969, a majority single-party government has not been elected since 1977 and coalition governments have become the norm. Moreover, the two most recent Fianna Fáil/Progressive Democrat coalition governments have lasted the full length of their elected terms.

Q6.3 How free are opposition or non-governing parties to organise within the legislature, and how effectively do they contribute to government accountability?

Parliamentary oversight of the executive is a key feature of a democracy. Despite recent reforms to strengthen the role of Dáil committees, the legislature remains limited in its role of overseeing the executive. Opposition parties consequently tend to use the media and public opinion, alongside parliamentary mechanisms, as the principal vehicles for calling the government to account. As in any democracy, of course, national elections provide the ultimate form of government accountability to the people.

ROLE OF OPPOSITION PARTIES IN HOLDING GOVERNMENT TO ACCOUNT

Opposition parties are a crucial part of a democratic system. A brief overview of the core political institution of a democracy – the parliament – shows why.

- Parliament legislates – it adopts the laws that govern a society.
- Parliament oversees the executive – it monitors the performance of the executive, to ensure that the latter performs in a responsible and accountable manner for the overall good of society.
- Parliament allocates financial resources to the executive – through its budgetary function, parliament has responsibility for approving, allocating and monitoring the revenue required by the executive to carry out the policies that it has formulated. (Inter-Parliamentary Union, 2004)

As outlined previously, political parties are the vehicles by which political power is exercised. There are four main roles that political parties play in a democracy.

- Parties are the main vehicle for political representation, in that the vast majority of those elected to public office are representatives of political parties. Independent members of parliament by contrast represent a small minority of the total number of elected representatives.
- Parties are the main mechanism for the organisation of government. Heads of government and government ministers, in whose hands power is centred, are nominated by political parties.
- Parties play an important role in formulating public policy, both in government and as a means of persuading the electorate during election campaigns.

- Parties (principally opposition parties) are key channels for maintaining democratic accountability and providing continuous accountability between elections in their oversight of the executive. (Netherlands Institute for Multiparty Democracy, 2004)

Ireland, however, has along with Britain and Greece one of the most government-dominated parliaments in Europe. (Gallagher *et al.*, 2005: 63) Nearly all legislation consists of Bills introduced by government; the government has nearly complete control over the parliamentary agenda; and Ireland has a strong party system, whereby the government can usually depend on strong party discipline to ensure the support of the government parties in any votes in parliament. The ability of the parliament to hold the government to account in Ireland is accordingly among the weakest in Europe.

Within the Dáil, the opposition parties have three main methods for scrutinising the behaviour of government – debates, parliamentary questions and Dáil committees. Opposition parties and independent TDs can make use of these mechanisms to try to influence legislation and affect policy change, to attempt to scrutinise the actions of government or to deter government from particular courses of action. (See also Q7.4/7.5)

As we shall see in Q7.4/7.5, debates and parliamentary questions are most often used to bring pressure to bear on government by bringing particular issues to the attention of the public *via* the media. Reform of the committee system in the 1990s expanded the number and role of committees, giving them greater powers both in examining legislation and in scrutinising the work of government. As a result the committee system is the most effective mechanism within the Dáil for scrutiny of the executive. Despite these reforms, however, the real power in committees still lies firmly with government parties. (See Q7.4 for further discussion)

POWER OF GOVERNMENT

In theory then, parliament plays a key role in the democratic process by making government accountable for its decisions and by providing a check on the passage of legislation. However, in practice, once a government in Ireland gets into office, parliament has little control over government action and little ability to defeat or even force amendments to legislation. The government majority, combined with the strength of the party whip system and the Taoiseach's power to control and influence backbenchers all serve to ensure that the government executive is the dominant actor in the Oireachtas.

It is the norm in every European country that deputies follow the party line in votes in parliament, and the Dáil is no exception. Each TD generally votes in accordance with the party line on every issue. Government backbenchers consequently see their primary duty as sustaining the government in office rather than acting as independent arbiters of its decisions, which they tend to do in private internal party meetings. Those voting against the party whip face expulsion from the parliamentary party and damage their chances of promotion within the party. (Gallagher, 2005b: 213)

By controlling the allocation of time for debates, the government chief whip can also play a pivotal role in ensuring that the executive controls the Dáil and not the other way around. (MacCarthaigh, 2005: 296)

The fact that the second Chamber, the Senate, has very limited powers, primarily of delay rather than veto, further underlines the power of the government executive. Moreover, the government nearly always has majority support within the Senate, largely because eleven seats are reserved for government appointees.

Parliament in Ireland thus plays a limited role in drafting, or amending, legislation. In practice, each of the mechanisms designed to ensure government accountability – debates, parliamentary questions and Dáil committees – allow opposition parties and independents limited opportunity to effect any real changes in government behaviour, although committees have become more effective in recent years. In general, opposition parties instead use debates and questions to bring issues to public attention *via* the media as a means of bringing pressure to bear on government.

THE EFFECT OF COALITION GOVERNMENT ON EXECUTIVE ACCOUNTABILITY

Coalition governments in parliamentary systems can effectively improve accountability by introducing additional parties into government.

The 1989 coalition government of Fianna Fáil and Progressive

Democrats, which essentially marked the transition to coalition government as the norm, is seen as having fundamentally altered the shape of parliamentary institutions and processes within the Dáil. (Mair, 1993) "Previous Fianna Fáil governments had operated in a manner whereby the party controlled all the vetoes in both houses of parliament, and the decision to enter a coalition necessitated a new system of delegation and oversight... [the effect of coalition was to move the Dáil] closer to the consensual model, in which there is more opportunity for executive oversight. ... Subsequent coalition governments were to contribute to the erosion of the majoritarian nature of governing that had characterised Irish politics". (MacCarthaigh, 2005: 86–7)

The Labour Party's demands for more cooperative government prior to the formation of the 1992 Fianna Fáil/Labour coalition is one example of the erosion of the previous majoritarian style of government. Labour in 1992 insisted on the introduction of both the *Ethics in Public Office* and the *Freedom of Information* legislation as part of the price for entering coalition with Fianna Fáil. Fine Gael's acceptance of more consensual parliamentary practices also became a feature when the Fianna Fáil/Labour Party government ended in 1994. (MacCarthaigh, 2005: 87)

The appeal of coalition government as a means of increasing executive accountability has arguably taken hold of the imagination of the Irish public, given that the Progressive Democrats are widely regarded as having reversed their electoral fortunes in the 2002 general election by using the catch cry, initiated by Michael McDowell, the current Tanáiste and leader of the Progressive Democrats, that Fianna Fáil could not be trusted to govern alone.

OPPOSITION PARTIES AS A GOVERNMENT IN WAITING

In addition to their role in holding government to account, the main opposition party or parties also have a role to play in providing choice for the electorate and by so doing effectively act as a "government in waiting." The Dáil debates and question time in particular allow opportunities for opposition parties and independents to establish their own credibility as an alternative government.

However, the position of opposition parties as "governments in waiting" is weakened in practice by their more limited experience, knowledge and access to expertise. Even the main opposition party, Fine Gael, is at a major disadvantage in terms of resources, in comparison to the government parties that command the civil service and have the advantage of the extensive consultation that has gone into official policy making. These very real differences can become evident, for example, in the level of detail that government parties can include in their manifestos at general elections.

Q6.4 How fair and effective are the rules governing party discipline in the legislature?

Deputies throughout Europe follow the party line in votes in parliament and Ireland is no exception. Government backbenchers regardless of party, see their primary duty as being to sustain the government in office rather than acting as independent arbiters of government decisions. (Gallagher, 2005b: 213)

Strong party discipline aims at ensuring internal party unity and avoiding factionalism and party fragmentation. The desire to impose effective discipline within parliamentary parties, however, can also have undesirable consequences. Chief among these are the fact that the pressures applied on backbench TDs need not necessarily be applied to ensure adherence to the election mandates endorsed at a general election. Potential rebels are unlikely to attain ministerial office or other positions of power within the party, making uncritical loyalty to the party often a precondition for government office. (Beetham *et al.*, 2002: 112)

As a result, rebellion of backbench TDs by voting against a government motion in the Dáil is a rare event. However rebellion is not the only way that backbench TDs can influence and change a government's policies. Governments often give ground and negotiate behind the scenes on issues where it risks losing backbench support. (Beetham *et al.*, 2002: 112)

Parliamentary party meetings, rather than the floor of the Dáil, are therefore where backbenchers in practice air their views more openly. One report of such a meeting, for example, reported how 33 Fianna Fáil TDs stood up and "lambasted" the Taoiseach and Minister for Finance for their stance on a particular issue before "dutifully trooping" into the Dáil to vote for the motion. (*Irish Times*, 22

November 2002) Individual TDs can also influence policy outside of any debating forum through direct negotiations with the Taoiseach. This practice is particularly the case on those occasions when independent TDs have held the balance of power in the Dáil.

Notwithstanding the strength of the party system in Ireland, internal dissent within government parties is not unheard of. A number of TDs, on being expelled from their party, have contested and won elections as independents. This situation has been particularly the case within Fianna Fáil. In fact, the most notable split in Fianna Fáil resulted in the formation of arguably Ireland's most successful smaller party – certainly if measured in terms of participation in government – the Progressive Democrats. (Coakley and Gallagher, 2005: 475)

Q6.5 How far are parties effective membership organisations, and how far are members able to influence party policy and candidate selection.

Less than 3 per cent of the electorate in Ireland are members of a political party; a figure which is well below the EU average. Fianna Fáil is by far the largest party with more members than all other parties combined.

Arguments in favour of increased internal party democracy have been gaining momentum within established democracies in recent years, partly as a response to falling party memberships, a perceived decline in political activism and falling voter turnouts. In Ireland, there have been moves towards greater internal democracy within Ireland's political parties with regard to candidate selection and leader selection. Ordinary party members generally play a significant part in candidate selection for local, general and European elections. These members can also have a real input, in some parties, into leader selection. In general, however, when it comes to policy formation, members have little or no effective input into the development of party policy within the large parties.

PARTY MEMBERSHIP

Only an estimated 80,000 people in Ireland, less than 3 per cent of the electorate, are members of a political party. (Marsh, 2005: 170) This figure compares with 1.5 per cent in France, 1.9 per cent in the UK, 2.9 per cent in Germany, 4.0 per cent in Italy, 7.3 per cent in Norway and 9.6 per cent in Finland. Ireland's membership of political parties is well below the EU average, and membership figures have been declining in recent years. (Gallagher *et al.*, 2005: 312)

Table 6.2 Party Membership and Voters 2002

	Members in 2002	*Members as % of all Members*
Fianna Fáil	47,000	58.8
Fine Gael	21,000	26.2
Progressive Democrats	5,500	6.9
Labour	3,700	4.6
Sinn Féin	2,000	2.5
Greens	800	1.0
Total	80,000	100

Source: Adapted from Marsh, 2005: 169

As the above table shows, Fianna Fáil is by far the largest party in Ireland and accounts for more than half of party members. It has over twice as many members as Fine Gael, and nearly 13 times as many members as the Labour party.

Membership profiles impact on the ability of each of the parties to organise nationally. As was discussed in Q5.4, only Fianna Fáil and Fine Gael have TDs from all, or nearly all, constituencies around the country, and are the only two parties who can claim to be nationally representative. By contrast, Labour and the smaller parties rely heavily or predominantly on Dublin for their strength in the Dáil.

However, despite declining membership, Irish political parties have not shown any great degree of innovation in recent years with regard to recruitment. Efforts by the parties to attract more women into politics, for example, have been particularly lax. The most recent figures, from 2003, show that neither of the two largest political parties spent any of their exchequer funding on the promotion of women in political activity. Of those parties that did, the Labour Party spent 6 per cent of its total funding on promotion of women in politics, while Sinn Féin and the Green Party spent 3.3 per cent and 0.8 per cent respectively. More recently, however, Fianna Fáil has introduced reforms: at its 2005 party conference, Fianna Fáil delegates voted for the introduction of a quota system for women on key party structures alongside a target of one-third of election candidates to be women by 2014. (*Irish Times*, 24 October 2005) While these reforms are welcome, the effectiveness of these measures in practice may be limited. (See Q11.3)

All of the main political parties, with the exception of the Progressive Democrats, allocated funding for the promotion of young people in politics in 2003. The respective amounts ranged from 3.8 per cent for Labour to 1.7 per cent each for Fianna Fáil, Sinn Féin and the Greens. (Harris, 2005: 66)

There has been considerable debate as to whether the decline in party membership matters. For one thing, a fall in membership does not necessarily mean a decline in political activism. (Power Commission, 2006: 41) The decline of political parties has occurred at the same time as the increased popularity of various movements, such as the environmental movement and the Drop the Debt campaign. Other recent examples of political activism are the demonstrations against the Iraq war and the Rossport campaign against the siting of a Shell gas pipeline. These are all examples of the rise of more narrowly-focused groups which concentrate on a single or small number of issues.

A second argument asserts that in an age of mass media, political parties do not need mass memberships. In this view, elections are won or lost through the mass media, so there is less need for a horde of enthusiastic party members when television coverage or articles ghosted in the press do the job as well if not better. Political parties, however, continue to play a central role in the governance of the state, so that declining membership, falling levels of trust and single-issue activism in lieu of engaging with the complexities involved in policy formation and choice can only be detrimental to the functioning of democracy.

PARTY FINANCING

The 1997 and 1998 Electoral Acts brought substantial changes in the way that Irish political parties are financed. As discussed in Q6.6/Q9.3, this legislation, designed in part to reduce the reliance by politicians on political donations, has seen a dramatic increase in the level of state funding for political parties. In 1989, for example, total state funding for political parties was just under half a million pounds. In 1999, this funding had increased fourfold to more than two million pounds. (Murphy and Farrell, 2002: 229)

Under the legislation, parties are required to make full disclosure of payments and political donations above a certain level. However, apart from its intended primary purpose of reducing the potential for corruption, the main effect of the legislation in the longer term may be to substantially strengthen the competency and professionalism of all political parties in Ireland. (See Q9.3 for further discussion) The substantial increase in funding also presents an opportunity for all parties to engage more proactively with the public as well as increase their memberships and improve services to members. Such measures are necessary to counteract falling levels of voter participation, falling party memberships and low levels of trust in political parties. Whether these outcomes happen remains to be seen.

PARTIES AS DEMOCRACIES

Political parties are crucial actors in representative democracies. In short, parties ensure that voters have significant electoral choices, and that such choices effectively translate into policy decisions within the public realm. (Scarrow, 2005: 3) This view of the role of parties in modern democracies is a widely shared one. More disputed, however, is the question of whether it matters how parties arrive at the choices they present to voters, i.e., whether, and to what extent, parties need to be internally democratic. In any event, stable democracies, Ireland included, can have parties which lack guaranteed processes of internal democracy.

Arguments in favour of greater levels of internal party democracy have increased within established democracies in recent years, partly as a response to falling party memberships, a decline in political activism, and falling voter turnouts. One set of arguments sees increased internal democracy as a means of strengthening democratic culture generally and enabling citizens to have a direct input into the choices that parties present – in terms of candidates, leaders and policies – to the electorate at election times. A second set of arguments sees enhanced internal democracy as a way of improving the electoral success of parties, through better choices in the selection of leaders, policies and candidates. (Scarrow, 2005: 4)

Concerns regarding increasing internal democracy tend to posit two opposing views on its potential effects on the power of the party leadership. On the one hand, concern exists that too much democratisation would preclude strong party leadership and undermine the ability of party leadership to formulate and implement electoral promises. There is also concern that measures to involve the party membership as a whole in decision making can empower national leaders at the expense of local and regional party leaders. This second view is strongly influenced by the experience of the British Labour Party in the 1990s, when "democratisation" of the party moved decision making from party activists to the broader membership. This change greatly strengthened the party leadership at the expense of local and factional interests. (Katz, 2001: 293)

There is no convergence on a single set of rules with regard to intra-party democracy. In considering the question, the National Democratic Institute for International Affairs, a US-based think tank, notes that, "Given the diversity of parties' circumstances and political outlooks, there is no single, discrete set of "best practices" for intra-party governance. Party leaders ought instead to … "consider the practical effects of internally-democratic party procedures and assess their respective merits." (Scarrow, 2005: 3)

A diversity of approaches to internal democracy can be seen among the political parties in Ireland, although there is a considerable commonality too. In fact, differences that do exist can often be explained as much by practical necessity as by ideology or design.

Party Structures

In general, political parties have a basic organisational structure comprising of a party conference and an executive committee. In theory, the national conference is the supreme policy-making body of each political party. It is usually held once a year and attended by delegates from local branches of the party around the country, along with elected representatives and party officials. (Marsh, 2005: 163)

Between national conferences, management of the party lies in the hands of an executive committee. The name and precise composition of the executive committee varies from party to party but generally comprises the party leader, elected party officials and TDs. As a result, the parliamentary party plays an often dominant role on each party's executive committee.

Most political parties in Ireland are organised at the grassroots level on the basis of local branches. These branches vary in size depending on the party. For the larger parties, Fianna Fáil and Fine Gael, branches are organised on the parish level. For the other parties, the need to attract a minimum number of members requires that local branches encompass a wider geographical area. For the larger parties, each Dáil constituency would generally comprise a number of local branches. For the other parties, the geographical spread of local branches is more uneven. Fianna Fáil estimates it has 2,500 local branches, and Fine Gael around 1,000. Labour, Sinn Féin, the Green Party and the Progressive Democrats would have fewer still. This finding alone shows that the political parties differ greatly in terms of their organisational capacity.

In terms of a hierarchy of power, the party leader would generally have the greatest level of power, followed by the parliamentary party of individual TDs, senators and MEPs. The national executive, dominated as it usually is by the parliamentary party, would have greater executive power in practice over most issues than the ard-fheis, followed in turn by the local branches and Dáil constituency organisations.

The extent to which parties operate as democratic organisations can be measured in terms of the balance of power between these various parts of the party organisation as well as by consideration of the input individual party members have into party decisions. These measurements are reflected in three main issues: choosing candidates for election, electing the party leader and the influence of party members in determining party policy.

Table 6.3 Internal Party Democracy

Party	*Member Input to Candidate Selection*	*Member Input in Leader Election*	*Member Input into Policy*
Fianna Fáil	Candidates selected by members at constituency conventions; central office can add candidates to the ballot	Parliamentary leader elected by TDs only, who is then *de facto* party leader.	Ard Fheis may give direction, but specific policy development in hands of policy committee / front bench
Fine Gael	As above	Electoral College system: TDs 65%; Party Members 25%; Local representatives 10%.	As above
Labour	As above	Ballot of party members. One member one vote.	As above
Green Party	As above	Election at convention of all party members. One member one vote.	Policy developed through consultative process with high level of input from party members
Progressive Democrats	Alternates between one-member one-vote and block voting for candidate selection	Electoral College: TDs 40%; Party members 30%; National executive & local representatives 30%.	Ard Fheis may give direction but specific policy development in hands of policy committee / front bench
Sinn Féin	Candidates selected by members at constituency conventions; central office may reject candidates thus selected	Party President elected each year at Ard Fheis. Gerry Adams elected unopposed since 1983.	Policy created by party policy committee but has to be passed at Ard Fheis

Source: Compiled from information in Marsh, 2005; Gallagher and Marsh, 2002

Candidate Selection

In general, candidates are selected for both local and national elections in Ireland by a mix of election at constituency level by party members and candidates inserted onto the ballot by the national executive with the consent of the party leader. This mixed system, it could be argued, allows a large measure of local party control of candidate selection with central office retaining ultimate authority. In practice, the majority of candidates across most parties are selected through local constituency elections. It should be noted in passing that this existing system could be used to secure greater representation for underrepresented groups, particularly women. (See also Q11.4)

Given a strong constitutional provision for freedom of political association, parties in Ireland are free to make whatever arrangements they wish for candidate selection. This situation is not the case in some other European countries. In Finland, for example, parties are obliged by law to open up the process of candidate selection to all party members. In Germany and Norway, the law ensures that candidates are selected by local party organisations and that the national party has no power to overturn these selections.

Nonetheless, Ireland's main political parties in practice go further than most European parties in opening candidate selection to party members. (Gallagher *et al.*, 2005: 322) Both Labour and Fine Gael select candidates *via* "party primaries", whereby every paid-up party member is eligible to vote in elections which are held on a constituency basis.

There has also been a move towards greater internal democracy with regard to candidate selection within Fianna Fáil in recent years. For example, the party introduced new selection rules for candidates in the 2002 general election, whereby the previous system of automatic reselection of sitting TDs was removed, requiring incumbents to compete with aspiring candidates for selection in elections organised on a constituency basis. (Galligan, 2003: 38)

Despite the retention by the main parties of the right by the party executive to insert candidates onto the ballot, ordinary party members can still exert very tangible influence. An example of this reality is the selection process within Fianna Fáil for the Connaught/Ulster constituency for the European Parliament elections in 2004. Efforts by Fianna Fáil headquarters to replace the sitting MEP Sean Ó Neachtain with Frank Fahey as its European Parliament election candidate failed when Ó Neachtain was elected by party members at the selection convention. (*Irish Times*, 1 March 2004)

The Progressive Democrats have alternated between one member/one vote and block voting at conventions for candidate selection, while the Greens have made internal democracy a strong plank of party policy. Candidates for the Green Party are proposed by local party members or by the National Executive Committee (NEC). All local party members are entitled to vote and the selected candidate has to be ratified by the NEC. The NEC does not have power to parachute candidates onto the ballot but retains the power to nominate local candidates if there is a snap election and insufficent time to organise the vote.

Sinn Féin candidates are chosen at a local convention from those nominated by polls in various Cumann. Head office has the power to reject a candidate and call for a new vote or impose a candidate. In general, the party prefers to lobby on behalf of its preferred candidate before the selection convention and as a rule does not impose candidates.

Candidate selection is one area where a strong argument can be put forward in favour of greater intra-party democracy. Experience elsewhere shows that where candidate selection is placed in the hands of a selected few, the selectors tend to choose candidates with similar values and priorities. For example, it has become very difficult in recent years for anyone without Eurosceptic views to gain selection as a parliamentary candidate for the Conservative Party in the UK. As a result, the Conservative Party has become overwhelmingly Eurosceptic. Opening the candidate-selection process to the wider party membership may mitigate against this narrowing effect and allow the electorate at national elections a broader and more representative selection of candidates from which to choose. (Gallagher *et al.*, 2005: 323–5)

The effect of candidate-selection processes on the Dáil is an important issue that impacts on the representativeness of a legislative body in which, as shown elsewhere in the audit, women, young people, and increasingly, ethnic minorities are underrepresented. (See Q5.5) In general, the criteria for candidate selection across parties in Ireland are for the most part essentially pragmatic. A track record of electoral success or, failing that, a strong local reputation are the most important attributes. Family dynasties also play their part. (See Q5.1) The political views of the candidate and his potential as a legislator tend to carry less weight. When parties select several candidates, far greater effort is generally made to ensure candidates come from different parts of the constituency than is given to the need to achieve social balance in terms of age, gender, ethnicity or social class.

Choosing the Party Leader

The procedures for selecting the party leader also vary considerably between the parties. For the larger parties, Fianna Fáil and Fine Gael, the selection of the leader of the parliamentary party (and *de facto* party leader) is the preserve of parliamentarians alone. Fianna Fáil restricts the vote to members of the Dáil, while in Fine Gael Senators and MEPs also vote.

By contrast, the Labour Party, the Greens and Sinn Féin have very inclusive methods for electing party leaders. In 2002, Labour, for the first time, held elections for leader and deputy leader in which the membership as a whole could vote. Around 90 per cent of party members eligible to vote cast a ballot. The leader of the Green Party is also elected by the party membership, in this instance through election at a selection convention which all party members are eligible to attend. In 2001, Trevor Sargent became the first party leader to be elected by the ordinary members of the party. Within Sinn Féin, the party president, like all other office holders, 15 elected every year at the annual Ard Fheis. Party president Gerry Adams has not been challenged since his election as leader in 1983 and has been re-elected 23 times.

New rules adopted by the Progressive Democrats in 2004 allow party members a limited input into selection of the party leader. Under these rules, leaders are elected by an electoral college system, whereby the parliamentary party, including MEPs, will account for 40 per cent of the votes, the national executive and local councillors 30 per cent, and rank and file party members 30 per cent.

As shown above, Labour, the Greens and Sinn Féin allow party members a larger role in the selection of party leader than the two bigger parties, while Fine Gael, Labour, and the Greens employ a more democratic process than Fianna Fáil in terms of candidate selection. The Progressive Democrats emerge as less democratic on both counts. This outcome may however simply reflect the practicalities of running a small party with a very small membership base.

Influencing Party Policy

A recent study of Irish political parties observed, "while the ordinary member continues to have a real say in candidate selection and, in some parties, in leader selection, his or her voice may be no more than the faintest of whispers when it comes to deciding the policies on which candidates and their leaders fight elections". (Marsh, 2005: 177)

In general, political parties in Ireland take a top down approach to policy formulation, with little input or influence by either individual members, local branches or the Ard-Fheis. This tendancy is particularly the case after parties move into government and policy making generally becomes a function of the cabinet alone. (See also Section Seven)

Even when a party is in opposition, its parliamentary party designates a set of senior politicians to "shadow" cabinet ministers in the Dáil and to act as party spokespersons on their policy areas. Members of this shadow cabinet develop policy expertise in their respective area and effectively serve as the main drivers of policy development for their party, whatever the party rule book might say.

A survey of members of Fine Gael, for example, showed that three quarters of party members said they had insufficient say in determining party policy. (Gallagher and Marsh, 2002: 116) Within Fine Gael, a policy council, established by the party's executive council, is charged with assisting the front bench and parliamentary party in preparing party policy statements. A similar top down approach is used by Labour.

A more democratic policy development process is that used by the Green Party. The Green Party's constitution provides for standing committees for policy development which circulate policy position papers to all Dáil constituency groups, regional councils, the party leader and public representatives, who then have the right to propose written amendments to national council or national convention meetings. Sinn Féin also has an inclusive policy development process wherein local branches can submit policy proposals to the Ard Fheis to be debated and voted upon.

The variations in approach to the development of policy among political parties in Ireland reflect various differences in party ideologies, the problems of involving large numbers of people in drafting policy, and the sometimes questionable returns that most parties feel such involvement would ultimately yield.

REVITALISING IRELAND'S POLITICAL PARTIES

Political parties play a central role in the governance of the state and declining membership and falling levels of trust can only be detrimental to the democratic process. Ireland's membership of political parties is already well below the EU average and continues to fall. (Gallagher *et al.*, 2005: 312)

Among the issues which political parties need to engage with are:

- the underrepresentation of women;
- the underrepresentation of youth; and
- the human rights of other underrepresented groups.

Ireland's political parties, in general, project an image of exclusionary organisations. Organisational structures are lacking which might help to focus on widening party appeal and attracting members through the provision of events and services – such as public fora for policy debates, international speakers and quality membership magazines.

Instead the image is generally one of parties exclusively focused on local issues, of parties as in-groups whose members need to have a long service record in order to have influence, and where positions of power are closely guarded against newcomers. These outmoded forms of organisation are ill-suited to attracting members and to engaging more widely with civil society.

A continuing decline in party membership however is not inevitable. Recent changes in the legislation governing the funding of political parties has resulted in a significant increase in the monies available to parties in Ireland, so that an opportunity currently exists for substantive reform.

Q6.6 How far does the system of party financing prevent the subordination of parties to special interests?

The financing of political parties is as fundamental an issue as the choice of electoral system, the inclusiveness of the franchise or the voter registration system in the architecture of a country's democratic system. The means by which parties receive funding can, among other things, influence the outcome of elections, determine the relationship between party leaders and members, impact on the number of women elected and condition the level of public trust as a whole.

A substantial amount of legislation has been enacted in recent years that has changed the way in which political parties are funded. This legislation has largely been the result of a series of political scandals involving irregular payments to politicians and the uncovering of corrupt relationships between politicians, businesses and financial institutions. Largely as a result, political parties are rated by the general public as the institution most affected by corruption. (See Q9.2) Among the recent legislative changes have been: a substantial increase in public funding for political parties; restrictions on private donations by a single source; increased transparency on private political donations; stricter requirements for disclosure of interests by elected representatives; limits on campaign spending; and a ban on foreign donations.

The system now in place embodies many of the principles of international best practice, particularly with regard to reducing the possible subordination of parties to special interests; in providing a more level playing field for all political parties; and for minimising corruption. More could be done, however, to amend the system of party financing to encourage small donations by individual citizens, both as a legitimate means of political participation and as a balance to parties' reliance on larger donors; to encourage parties' fundraising activities by matching public funding to private revenues raised; and to encourage all parties to raise funds across a broad spectrum of donors.

There is evidence, however, to support the widespread public perception that certain sectors, particularly the construction and financial services sectors, continue to enjoy significant indirect influence on public-policy as a result of these sectors, priviledged relationship with the political elite.

LEGISLATIVE PROVISIONS

Over the past several years, party financing scandals have shaken public confidence in political parties and politicians throughout the world. As a result, legislation designed to regulate the financing of political parties has been enacted in democracies worldwide. Ireland too has experienced political scandals involving money and legislation has been introduced which has fundamentally changed the ways in which political parties are financed. (See Section Nine)

This new legislation has included:

- the Ethics in Public Office Act 1995;
- the Electoral Act 1997;
- the Local Elections (Disclosure of Donations and Expenditure) Act 1999;
- the Standards in Public Office Act 2001;
- the Prevention of Corruption (Amendment) Act 2001;
- the Local Government Act 2001;
- the Electoral Amendment Act 2001;
- the Oireachtas (Ministerial and Parliamentary Offices) (Amendment) Act 2001; and
- the Proceeds of Crime (Amendment) Act 2005.

Ireland also signed the UN Convention on Corruption in 2003; has ratified both the OECD Convention on Combating Bribery of Foreign Public Officials in International Business Transactions, and the Council of Europe's Criminal Law Convention on Corruption in 2003; and has signed but not ratified the Council of Europe Civil Law Convention on Corruption in 1999.

The intent and effectiveness of these legislative reforms are discussed in more depth in Section Nine. In this answer, we will focus instead on the international context within which these reforms are taking place and on the ways in which reform of the system of party financing can not only prevent the subordination of parties to special interests but also enhance the effectiveness of political parties in performing their vital roles within a democracy.

As outlined earlier, political parties play a central role in every democracy and provide the means through which political power is enacted. (See Q6.3) The introduction of legislation regarding the reform of party financing, in Ireland and elsewhere, has often been driven primarily in response to public disquiet arising from high profile instances of political corruption. Such reform however can serve a number of different purposes. The International Institute for Democracy and Electoral Assistance (IDEA) identifies the following reasons for reforming party financing:

- to prevent abuse and the buying of political influence;
- to enhance fair competition among all parties;
- to empower voters by making party finances open to public scrutiny; and
- to strengthen the effectiveness of political parties as democratic actors.

(International IDEA, 2003)

The existing framework for party financing in a particular country depends in part on the relative importance that is placed on each of these goals. For example, enhancing voter empowerment by making party finances transparent does not necessarily also entail regulations that limit the amounts individual donors can give or that parties can spend. On the other hand, enhancing fair competition among all parties is likely to involve just such limits on donations and election expenditure.

While the systems adopted in practice vary widely between countries, a number of principles have emerged which represent good practice in party financing. These include:

- transparency in sources of income;
- a mixture of private and public funding;
- limits on individual donations to limit the potential for "buying influence";
- prohibitions on sources of funding which may compromise parties in their democratic roles (These prohibitions can include, for example, bans on anonymous donors, on foreign donors, and on corporate and trade union donations, including donations from government contractors);
- incentives, such as tax credits, to encourage private giving by large numbers of individual citizens and to reduce the influence of large corporations and wealthy individuals upon parties;
- provisions for every political party to seek funding from a diversity of sources including members, philanthropic individuals, business, unions etc. and to avoid situations in which parties are identified with particular interests; and
- matching public funding for donations raised from private sources as an incentive for parties' fundraising activities.

(International IDEA, 2005)

Underlying these principles of good practice lie the assumptions that political parties are central to democracy; that public funding of political parties is consequently a legitimate public expenditure; that donations to political parties by individuals and organisations, within limits, are legitimate means of political participation; and that systems of political financing can be designed both to minimise corruption and to maximise public engagement.

PARTY FINANCING IN IRELAND

The major features of the current system of party financing in Ireland include the following:

- irish political parties receive a mixture of public and private funding;
- public funding comes in the form of leader's allowances, funding for annual running costs, and partial reimbursement of election expenses;
- leaders' allowances are allocated to all parliamentary party leaders with distribution weighted in favour of the opposition parties, in acknowledgement that the governing parties are able to draw upon civil service resources (Legislation requires that this money be accounted for in detail and not be used to fund election activities);
- registered political parties which have received over 2 per cent of the vote in the previous election also receive a contribution to their annual running costs, (allocated according to a party's share of the total first preference vote), and the partial reimbursement of election expenses; (Marsh, 2005: 166)
- members of the Oireachtas are required to provide an annual disclosure of interests which could influence them in carrying out their duties;
- an independent statutory body, the Standards in Public Office Commission, is responsible for investigating contraventions of members' disclosure of interests;
- expenditure limits per candidate are in place for election campaigns at general and European elections;

- foreign donations to political parties and candidates are prohibited;
- donations received from a single source in a single year are capped; and
- for political donations above a certain threshold, the names of donors and the amounts contributed must be disclosed.

Ireland's current system of party financing consequently incorporates many of the principles of good practice identified by International IDEA. The legislative provisions provide a framework for minimising corruption, increasing transparency and providing political parties with a sufficient mix of public and private funding to enable them to effectively carry out their democratic functions.

It would appear that less emphasis has been given, however, to the manner in which the system of party financing could be used to encourage giving by ordinary citizens; to encouraging every political party to fundraise among as diverse a range of funders as possible; and to generally encourage fundraising by political parties by providing public monies as matching funding for private funds raised.

The legislative framework governing party financing in Ireland, and the substantial revisions the system has undergone in recent years, are discussed in greater detail in Section Nine.

Q6.7 To what extent does support for parties cross ethnic, religious and linguistic divisions?

Political parties in Ireland do not break down along ethnic, religious or linguistic lines.

Within the context of increased immigration in Ireland, members of new ethnic communities have begun to actively engage in politics. In the 2004 local elections, for example, members of new ethnic minorities stood for election and a number were successful. Most of these candidates stood as independents and not as part of established political parties. The evidence shows that political parties in Ireland have, in general, made little effort to bring members of immigrant or ethnic minority communities into the political mainstream and do not yet see the immigrant and ethnic minority communities as potential voters.

A longstanding hostility to Travellers exists, in local politics in particular, with local politicians often seeking to establish their anti-Traveller credentials for electoral gain. Despite some positive efforts by political parties in Ireland to prevent the exploitation of racism by parties or candidates at election time, more measures are needed to address the political exclusion of Travellers and ensure against the political exclusion of new ethnic communities.

INCLUSION AND EXCLUSION IN POLITICAL PARTIES

The reality in many Western countries is that immigrants and ethnic minorities have been marginalised within politics for generations. In the UK, for example, ethnic minority communities established since the 1950s have only recently become visible in political parties, and remain underrepresented at both local and national level. Meanwhile, in the US, the first African-American cabinet members were appointed as recently as 2000.

At the same time, the very recent and distinctive history of immigration suggests that the errors of exclusion experienced elsewhere need not happen in Ireland. However, the decades-long marginalisation, not only in politics but in wider aspects of economic and social life, of members of the Traveller community shows our own history of excluding minorities. This record, together with the current lack of response from political parties towards new immigrant and ethnic minority communities, points to the need for political parties to take active measures to avoid the exclusion of immigrant and ethnic minority groups from political life and to maintain a political system in which parties do not break down along ethnic, religious or linguistic divisions. International experience, along with the history of sectarian division between political parties in Northern Ireland, shows that such divisions between political parties lead to greater injustice and social unrest.

While many members of immigrant and ethnic-minority communities are not yet eligible to vote in national and European elections, the increasing number of people acquiring citizenship by naturalisation means that the ethnic composition of the Irish electorate is changing rapidly across all election categories. Nonetheless, despite eligibility to vote in local elections, it would appear that the main political parties do not yet see the immigrant and ethnic minority communities as potential voters.

MEASURES TO ENHANCE INCLUSIVENESS BY POLITICAL PARTIES

A survey carried out by the Africa Solidarity Centre in 2003 (Fanning *et al.*, 2003), showed that most political parties in Ireland have no distinct measures designed to encourage immigrants and ethnic minorities to become party members. Prior to the Africa Solidarity Centre's report, one party, the Progressive Democrats, had a constitution that prevented people who were not Irish or EU Member-State citizens from joining the party. However, the adverse publicity generated by the report's findings on this issue saw the party subsequently change its constitution which now allows membership regardless of nationality.

The only parties identified with specific initiatives aimed at inclusion of immigrants and ethnic minority communities were the Green Party, where one candidate from the immigrant community stood for election in the 2004 local election and Sinn Féin, which produced voter registration leaflets in a number of different languages. It is also worth noting that although a number of immigrant candidates did stand in the 2004 local elections, all of them, bar the sole Green Party candidate, stood as independents.

The Africa Solidarity Centre report concluded that political parties in Ireland, for the most part, currently offer a narrow definition of "Irishness" and as a result are poorly positioned to address racism in Irish society. A number of minor initiatives by various parties in the wake of the Africa Solidarity Centre report have not changed this conclusion.

A subsequent report by the Africa Centre in July 2006 presented the results of a survey of the African ethnic community in Ireland with 41 respondents. Although the sample size was small, this survey represents one of the very few pieces of research available on political participation within Ireland's new ethnic communities. (Ejorh, 2006) Among the reports findings were:

- that one person (2 per cent of respondents) belonged to a political association, a figure similar to that of the Irish population as a whole;

- of those who were not a member of a political association, 59 per cent were not members because they felt their non-residency status disqualified them from any form of membership;
- that 27 per cent of respondents had voted in the 2004 local election (although it should be noted that this figure is difficult to use for comparative purposes as it is not clear what proportion of the sample were entitled to vote); and
- that some of the reasons given for not voting were based on mistaken beliefs, for example, that asylum seekers are disqualified from voting in local elections when in fact under Irish law, asylum seekers are permitted to vote in local elections.

On a positive note, prior to the 2002 general election, all the political parties in Ireland endorsed an Anti-Racism Protocol for Political Parties, developed and promoted by the National Consultative Committee on Racism and Interculturalism. This protocol was designed to prevent the exploitation of racism by parties or candidates for political gain.

Political parties who are signatory to this protocol undertook to ensure that election campaigns were conducted in such a way that they do not incite hatred or prejudice on the grounds of "race", colour, nationality or ethnic or national origins, religious belief and membership of the Traveller community. Under the protocol, political parties agreed:

- to send a consistent and clear message to their constituents that they reject racism;
- to condemn any campaign materials or statements susceptible to incite hatred or express prejudice on the grounds of "race", colour, nationality or ethnic or national origins, religious belief and membership of the Traveller community;
- to guarantee that when engaging in ongoing debate in relation to groups which are the potential targets of racism, such as asylum seekers and refugees and Travellers, that such debate is conducted in a responsible way and with respect to the dignity and rights of minority ethnic groups;
- to use appropriate and inclusive language when referring to people of different ethnic backgrounds in order to avoid creating prejudice or confusion; and

- to inform all party campaigners about the intent and contents of this protocol.

In general, the leaderships of political parties in Ireland have indeed been critical of perceived efforts by individual politicians to exploit racism and prejudice for political gain. Despite this, individual politicians have pandered in this fashion, both with respect to new ethnic communities and more widely with respect to the Traveller community. With regard to the latter, individual councillors have often sought to establish their anti-Traveller credentials, or at least be seen for electoral purposes as opposing measures designed to meet the accommodation needs of Travellers. Many local authority debates on Traveller issues have historically been characterised by vehement anti-Traveller rhetoric, illustrating a longstanding acceptance of hostility to Travellers in local politics. Individual politicians too have sought to exploit racism against asylum seekers for political gain. (Fanning, 2002)

Seven: Government Effectiveness and Accountability

Is government effective and accountable to the people and their representatives?

INTRODUCTION AND SUMMARY

The two main requirements of government in a modern democracy are First that it should be *effective* in its delivery of public services, human security and its overall policy programme and, second *publicly accountable* for its performance. Effectiveness is largely dependent on the capacity of resources and personnel, and the way in which they are organised, while the ultimate judge of government effectiveness lies with the citizens themselves. Accountability is ensured through different agencies working in combination: the people through the sanction of the electoral process; the media, through enquiry, report and comment; the scrutiny of independent regulatory bodies; and finally and most importantly, parliament through its various instruments of governmental oversight, i.e., debates, questions, and select committees etc. Effective accountability by any of these agencies is impossible without accurate information about the actions of government and the right to secure such information. Although the need for accountability is sometimes argued to hinder government effectiveness, it should chiefly be seen as essentially contributing to it, given that public exposure of inadequacy typically leads to improvement.

In Ireland, there is certainly some positive evidence of government effectiveness. Sustained economic expansion has resulted in an increasing resource base for government, while departmental management has been modernised through the strategic management initiative. Also, public rating of government performance, though fluctuating, has been more positive than negative over the decade since 1995, and compares favourably with the rest of Europe. On the other hand, the delivery of front line services, such as health, education and transport, where the public is more critical, has not improved overall, and in some respects has even deteriorated. Specific weaknesses have also been identified in the governmental capacity for long-term planning. There are significant gaps in civil service expertise and the continuity of policy is vulnerable to short-term political interventions.

Meanwhile, a major development over the past decade or so has been the expanding number of independent regulatory bodies and codes of conduct that are designed to ensure the greater accountability and impartiality of the public service. However, their reach is incomplete and their operation inconsistent, since many public bodies to which government is now "outsourced" are excluded from their purview, and no public appointments commission exists to ensure the impartiality of appointments across the public sector as a whole. Similar gaps also occur in the application of freedom of information legislation.

Significant weaknesses are likewise to be found in the parliamentary oversight of government. Opposition parties in the Dáil can work effectively with the media and public opinion to highlight serious policy or administrative failures but systematic scrutiny of government by parliamentary committees is limited by their built-in government majorities, and the respective responsibility of ministers and officials for proceedings in their department is not always clear-cut. Compared with other European parliaments, the relative weakness of the Dáil in relation to the executive also extends both to the legislative process and to the scrutiny of EU legislation, though the latter has recently improved in response to the first Nice referendum result.

Q7.1 How far is the elected government able to influence or control those matters that are important to the lives of its people, and how well is it informed, organised and resourced to do so?

It is the task of parties in government to respond to hopes and desires for change that citizens may invest in a particular political party by carrying these wishes through in practice. International comparators (International IDEA, 2002: 90) suggest that the most frequent factors hindering a government's ability to deliver change are a lack of financial resources and poor-quality public administration. In Ireland over the past decade, the government executive, i.e., the cabinet, has enjoyed the economic resources to deliver on vital matters for its people. In that time there has been a major advance in employment and enhanced wellbeing for many, but significant deficiencies still exist in the actual delivery of critical public services and a socially just society. While the government does have considerable power to direct and control the resources of the state, it is at the same time subject to some limitations and constraints in the extent to which it is sufficiently well informed and/or organised, through its public management system, to effectively implement desired change. Moreover, a number of initiatives taken to modernise the public management system in the last decades have shown mixed outcomes. Finally, while a number of public management challenges are institutionally-based, others arise from the policy decisions taken by the present coalition government.

IRELAND IS ECONOMICALLY WELL RESOURCED

Ireland now possesses the economic resources to provide for a secure and decent standard of life for its population. Exceptional economic and employment growth has seen Irish living standards increase significantly over the last decade. According to the OECD, only the US, Norway and Luxembourg had higher GDP per capita in 2003. (Organisation for Economic Co-operation and Development, 2005a) This prosperity is a relatively recent phenomenon which dates from the 1990s and followed a long period of economic and social stagnation.

The strong economic performance has made a huge contribution to social progress, principally by vastly improving employment prospects and reducing enforced emigration, raising real incomes and providing the state with a greater level of resources. Clearly it has allowed government to spend more – current public spending has risen by an average of 5 per cent per annum in real terms since 1993, even while cutting taxes. (Central Bank, 2004, 2006) Consequently, under the present Fianna-Fáil/Progressive Democrat coalition which has been in power since 1997, significant investment in public services and public infrastructure has taken place which is making a real difference. Recent examples include the following.

- Social welfare expenditure has increased in each of the following areas: old age pensions, child benefit payments, illness, disability and caring allowance and lone parent payments. (National Economic and Social Council, 2005a)
- Public educational spending per student at primary, secondary and third-level rose significantly between 1995 and 2002. (National Economic and Social Council, 2005a)
- Total funding in the health service has increased by 220 per cent since 1997. (Department of Health and Children, 2005)
- Infrastructure has been extensively developed following large investments by the government in accordance with the goals set out in the National Development Plan. (Department of Finance, 2006)

Nonetheless, while public spending has risen every year, its proportion of GDP has fallen from 44 per cent in 1994 to 34.1 per cent in 2005. (www.ec.europa.eu/eurostat) Despite its comparative wealth, the level of social protection provided by Ireland's welfare state is low by comparative EU15 standards. (National Economic and Social Council, 2005a) The most recent OECD annual Tax Revenue Trends report ranked Ireland as 27 out of the 30 countries surveyed in level of social transfers as a percentage of GDP. Social transfers are the redistribution of wealth through benefits such as welfare or pensions payments. The percentage for Ireland was 15.8 per cent, while that of Sweden, where transfers were highest, was 31.3 per cent. (*Irish Times*, 12 October 2006)

The period since the early 1990s has been marked by widening inequalities in several areas such as incomes and housing, and has occasioned new forms of social vulnerability, for example, among immigrants. (National Economic and Social Council, 2005a: 198) Ireland also continues to have unacceptably high poverty rates, unequal income distribution, and underequipped health and education systems. There is widespread agreement, including from the National Economic and Social Council (NESC), the government-funded agency chaired by the Secretary-General to the Department of the Taoiseach and representing the main social partners, that a "significant gap remains between what social actors see as necessary and what is accomplished in practice". This applies to public service provision generally, and the addressing of social disadvantage in particular. This gap between expectation and delivery is attributed to a number of factors: the implementation of formally agreed strategies can be weak; leadership is frequently contested; the data that would permit evaluation of the effectiveness of programmes is lacking; and social policy as a whole is not sufficiently aligned with the economic policies being pursued by the state. (National Economic and Social Council, 2005a: 5)

CAPACITY OF GOVERNMENT TO CONTROL POLICY AND IMPLEMENT ITS DECISIONS

In Ireland, the government executive (or cabinet), led by the Taoiseach, is the dominant force in political decision making. In practice, the decision making processes of government are effected through (i) ministerial responsibility for government departments, which are in turn organised on functional lines and (ii) cabinet collective responsibility for governments decisions. Within this system the Taoiseach exerts significant power, mitigated only by the relative strength of a coalition partner, or in times of small majority or even minority status in Dáil representation. The central role played by the Taoiseach's office in the overall formulation of policy has a considerable, and sometimes major, impact on other departments. Moreover, no item can be tabled at cabinet meetings without the Taoiseach's approval. Within the government executive, each minister is appointed by and can be sacked by the Taoiseach. The Minister for Finance, as minister responsible for overall management of the public finances, also exerts significant control over each department of government and thereby wields more influence than other cabinet colleagues. The position of the Tánaiste, under coalition circumstances, also exerts considerable power. All discussions at cabinet are confidential by virtue of Article 28.4.3 of the Constitution, except where the High Court determines that disclosure should be made; and all members of cabinet must publicly support decisions made at cabinet, regardless of each individual's views on particular issues. (Connolly, 2005: 341)

The government executive has wide powers beyond ensuring that its legislative programme be implemented. These prerogatives include the power to reshape the civil service without recourse to the Dáil, and, since 1992, governments have frequently restructured, merged and/or created new departments, functions and responsibilities of ministers. (MacCarthaigh, 2005: 88) Such restructuring reflects the policy priorities of the different parties. For example, following negotiations between Fianna Fáil and the Progressive Democrats in 1997, the Department of Equality and Law Reform (established under the 1993–1994 Fianna Fáil/Labour coalition) was merged with the Department of Justice. (Connolly, 2005: 331) Such revamping is also frequently an outcome of a political trade-off between coalition parties in order to satisfy the parties in question on the balance of ministerial portfolios. Regardless of motivation, such restructuring is carried out apparantly without reference to its impact on civil service efficacy and effectiveness.

Other important government powers include the freedom to establish a wide range of public bodies to undertake important public functions. While the majority of these are set up under legislation and therefore subject to parliamentary scrutiny, certain others are not. The government and individual ministers also have a very considerable degree of freedom with regard to decision making within the EU and other international contexts, notwithstanding the formal powers of the Dáil to scrutinise EU or other international legislation. (See Q 7.6) There has also been an increase in the degree of centralisation of government *vis-à-vis* local authorities, so that Ireland now has one of the most centralised systems of governance and one of the weakest systems of local government in Western Europe. (See Section 13)

New systems and structures were created from 1992 onwards to provide for greater transparency and an enhanced flow of information between government coalition partners that is intended to provide the "junior members" of a coalition with more influence on decision making. The introduction of politically-appointed programme managers whose role is to operate within the civil service in order to coordinate activities between government departments, together with the appointment of special advisors, has had the additional effect of strengthening political rather than administrative control.

Public Management Capacity

Major organisational challenges faced by Ireland's public management system include: the degree of cooperation between civil service departments and with public agencies, the extent of centralised control, and the *ad hoc* growth of public bodies and other third-party agencies. The absence of expertise in key areas within the public management system, and the consequent reliance on external input from private agencies, political advisors and private consultants has also added to the government's operational problems in recent years.

The Strategic Management Initiative (SMI)

The Strategic Management Initiative in 1994 marked the first real attempt by government since the 1970 Devlin Committee report to modernise public service provision in Ireland. The Devlin report had identified two serious defects in the Irish public administration system, namely insufficient attention to policy making and an absence of coordination across departments and other public sector institutions. It was followed in 1985 by a White Paper (1985) *Serving the Country Better* which focused on the need for management systems based on personal responsibility for results and value for money. However, no significant measures were undertaken to implement reform proposals until the launch of the SMI. The objectives of SMI are to make efficient use of resources, to ensure a high standard of service delivery and to contribute to overall national development. (www.bettergov.ie) Subsequently, in 1996, the government published a report, prepared by the group of civil servants charged with managing the SMI process, entitled *Delivering Better Government*. This report highlighted the need to ensure greater openness and accountability, quality customer service and the efficient operation of regulations in the public sector.

A comprehensive and independent evaluation of the SMI modernisation programme in 2002 found the civil service better managed and more effective than it had been a decade previously and that the modernisation programme had contributed critically to this change. (www.bettergov.ie) However, a survey on communicating change and modernisation in the civil service in January 2003 found that overall awareness of SMI initiatives is generally quite poor, with a quarter of civil servants unable to name any reform initiative to implement change in the past five years. Indeed many civil servants do not understand many of the key reform initiatives such as strategy statements, partnership committees and customer action plans. Awareness of SMI initiatives is particularly poor for civil servants in lower and middle grades. Neither is there evidence of significantly improved outcomes for the population. The National Economic and Social Council (2005: 162–3) has warned that "The ability of existing public sector service providers in Ireland to satisfy users and retain the confidence of the public has come under unprecedented strain and there is a real danger that public services will be reduced to a residual role within the state with all the attendant implications for a two-tiered society: those who can afford to purchase services privately and those who are entirely reliant on public provision". The Ombudsman has also questioned the effectiveness of the SMI in improving public service delivery, arguing that those public bodies with which members of the public have most contact and are reliant on for public services are precisely those bodies where the SMI has had the least impact. (Office of the Ombudsman, 2006a)

Coincidental with the internal drive for reform was a renewed political emphasis on addressing deficits of accountability and transparency. Since the launch of the SMI in 1994, issues of serious maladministration have continued to come to light, many of which have required a series of judicial enquiries, tribunals and special reports to Oireachtas Committees. (See Q 7.3 for more detailed discussion)

CHALLENGES TO STRATEGIC PLANNING

In recent years, government has invested hugely in developing strategic and operational plans to address many of Ireland's major developmental issues. These activities include developing multiyear plans for:

- public capital spending through the National Development Plans and the National Spatial Strategy;
- researching and addressing the needs of the 0-17 age group through the National Children's Strategy and National Children's Office;
- researching and addressing the needs of disability groups through the National Disability Authority;
- addressing poverty and social exclusion through the National Anti-Poverty strategy and National Office for Social Inclusion;
- National Partnership Agreements – the current agreement runs for a ten year period to 2016; and
- National Action Plan Against Racism in Ireland.

There is also a range of subnational development exercises which include regional programmes and county development plans among others.

Since 1997, the secretary-general of a government department is required to prepare and submit to the minister a departmental strategy statement based on these plans within six months of the minister coming into office. Nonetheless, a major deficit identified in the Irish public administration system, dating as far back as the Devlin Report, continues to be its capacity to undertake long-term policy planning. Some of the critical structural issues which continue to seriously challenge this capacity include the high degree of centralisation in Ireland (see Section Thirteen), the ability to respond flexibly and effectively to new requirements, and the impact of political interventions. (National Economic and Social Council, 2005a: 165)

A number of further operational constraints on longer-term policy thinking within the civil service have been identified. These include: accountability systems that focus more on apportioning blame than acknowledging deficits and encouraging dialogue on the longer-term implications of policy options and choices; congestion and fragmentation in the system, whereby department officials spend their time dealing with routine matters and with servicing the democratic process (preparing replies to parliamentary questions, responding to representations etc); divisions within and between departments that preclude longer-term thinking on interdepartmental issues; and ongoing concerns about the lack of skills and competencies within the civil service to develop appropriate longer-term policy options. (Boyle *et al.*, 2002)

Problems in Ireland's capacity to plan accurately for major infrastructural projects, such as the National Roads system, also point to poor levels of expertise within certain areas of the public management system. Examples include the following:

- although the M50 took approximately 15 years to build, it is not big enough to sustain the current volumes of traffic in the city;
- the Port Tunnel in Dublin overran on time and on budget;
- the computerised system of public health payment administration had to be revamped after the system was found to have serious flaws, despite over €100 million of public expenditure on the project; and

- an e-voting system which is now deemed not up to standard and effectively redundant, despite over €50 million of public expenditure on the project.

Strategic planning is also hampered by gaps in the knowledge base; for example, the current strategy to address the needs of the increasing numbers of older people is almost 20 years old and wholly inadequate. (National Economic and Social Forum, 2005b)

All strategic plans are, of course, subject to amendment in light of actual developments over time. However, the potential for such plans to be undermined by politically-motivated, short-term changes in policy direction is both extensive and decidedly detrimental to coherent planning. This situation is especially true in countries such as Ireland where there is a strong government executive. A good example is provided by the unexpected introduction in the 2003 budget of the largest Decentralisation Plan (DP) for the public service in the history of the state, which provides for a complete transfer of eight government departments and various state bodies to different locations around the country. Moreover, this DP runs counter to the National Spatial Strategy (NSS), which was introduced in 2002, following an extensive consultation process, and designed to ensure balanced regional development over a twenty-year period. While the stated objective of both the NSS and DP is to strengthen regions outside of Dublin by the strategic amalgamation of population, employment and services, the different locations selected under the DP plan have led to accusations that they were chosen more for electoral advantage and constituency party political reasons than for purposes of national development. Other problems with the DP include the potential loss of experience and expertise that will result from civil servants leaving specialised posts in order to remain in Dublin. Further problems exist specific to a number of specialist agencies; for example, the National Roads Authority (NRA) says it may be unable to deliver major roads programmes on schedule because it faces the loss of experienced personnel who will be difficult to replace. Similar concerns have also been expressed by the Equality Authority. In addition, a real possibility exists that implementation of the plan will lead to both a fragmentation of policy making and a weakening of public services delivery, not least because the disaffection and demoralisation of public servants will likely also impact on delivery of quality public services. These problems have thrown up real obstacles to the implementation of the DP, which in turn have had their own negative impacts on public service management capacity.

GROWING IMPORTANCE OF PUBLIC BODIES AND OTHER THIRD-PARTY AGENCIES

Finally, the role of the central civil service has been emasculated to a certain degree by the increasing scale and importance of a range of public bodies (See Q 7.3 for more discussion of this issue), and by an increasing reliance on consultants and other third-party service providers. The increasing use of the private sector to provide essential services such as hospital and nursing home care in the absence of adequate systems of regulation and protection also raises strong concerns. As a consequence of both this trend toward increasing privatisation and changes in EU law, many largely state-owned companies in the energy and transport sectors have witnessed the transfer of regulatory responsibility from the relevant minister to independent regulators in recent years. At the same time the current regulatory system has come under criticism for a lack of accountability. Opposition TDs cannot table or receive answers to parliamentary questions about any of these regulators, although the regulators may be called before Oireachtas committees.

Q7.2. How much public confidence is there in the effectiveness of government and its political leadership?

Data from opinion polls, such as *Irish Times*/TNS mrbi and the IMS/Lansdowne, which have been tracking public satisfaction in the government since the mid-1970s, shows that satisfaction with governments most frequently hovers below 40 per cent. During the first period of office of the current administration (i.e., 1997–2002) satisfaction levels dramatically increased, only to return to more normal patterns over the course of the current period of office. It can be expected that confidence in a government is likely to be affected by major events affecting thc society, particularly when the population perceives government as having an important impact on their everyday lives.

During the 1990s, the hugely positive change in Ireland's economic performance constituted one such high impact event which helps to explain the high level of public confidence in the first period of the Fianna Fáil/Progressive Democrat administration (1997–2002), as expressed in opinion polls and by their re-election in 2002. The return to pre-mid-90s levels of satisfaction over the last several years supports the argument that popular confidence in government generally registers within a relatively narrow range, regardless of its party composition. Furthermore, Irish people tend to be more positive about their system of government than is the case in the majority of European countries.

PUBLIC CONFIDENCE IN THE EFFECTIVENESS OF GOVERNMENT

From the early 1990s, a general upwards trend in public satisfaction with the government reached an unparalleled high of over 70 per cent in the first years of office of the present administration. (Lyons, 2006) While it slipped from this peak, the Fianna Fáil/Progressive Democrat administration nonetheless generally stayed above the 50 per cent positive rating over the 5 years of its first term of office. Moreover, for the first time since 1976, the proportion of people satisfied with the government was consistently greater than those dissatisfied. This high level of satisfaction was reflected in 2002 when this administration was the first to be re-elected since 1969.

Improvement in public satisfaction with the government coincided with the dramatic upturn in the Irish economy in the mid-1990s. Conversely, the economic crisis of the 1980s coincided with the lowest levels of public satisfaction in the government, which fell as low as circa 15 per cent at one point in 1987.

Public Satisfaction with the Performance of the Government, 2002 to Date

In the year following the 2002 election, the level of public satisfaction with the re-elected Fianna Fáil/Progressive Democrat government declined, with only 27 per cent of those surveyed satisfied with the performance of the government by September 2003. This slide coincided with both a dip in economic performance and with escalating problems in accessing good quality public services. However, the most noteworthy point about opinion polls is their capacity for wide variation in any given time period. For example, in January 2005, the administration achieved an approval rating of 52 per cent, an increase which disappeared by September 2005, when just 37 per cent of people were satisfied with the government but was reinstated by December 2006. (See Table 7.1)

The fluctuations in satisfaction trends have been subject to much media analysis and attributed to a myriad causes, including difficulties in accessing public services, the rising fortunes of the opposition parties, and a general public fatigue with the government. The recent upsurge in satisfaction with the government has confounded many political analysts, as it immediately followed a major political and media storm concerning the Taoiseach's receipt of monies while Minister for Finance during the 1990s. (See Q 9.1)

INTERNATIONAL COMPARISONS

In international terms, more Irish people are positive (36 per cent give a rating of seven or better out of a possible ten) in their assessment of the system of government than the rest of Europe (where 22 per cent of the aggregate give a rating of seven or more). Moreover, at the time of this European Values survey in 2000, Irish people rated the system of government more highly than they had ten years previously. This finding is all the more remarkable when compared with the majority of countries included in the survey, where the people of 19 out of 33 nations, on average, gave a lower rating to the system of government in 1999-2000 than they had ten years previously. Fahey *et al.* (2005) raised the question as to whether the political scandals of the 1990s (see Section Nine) had created a more negative perspective of the system of government or alternatively whether the subsequent economic dynamism had provided a boost in confidence. On balance, they argue that the general trend in public satisfaction has been slightly upwards, and while evidence of some cynicism about the system could be found, there was also a widespread sense that the political process was working better than it had previously.

Table 7.1: The Level of Public Satisfaction with the Government, May 2002–December 2006

	Satisfaction with Government %	Dissatisfaction with Government %	No Opinion %
May-02	61	32	7
Oct-02	33	61	6
Sept-02	36	56	8
Feb-03	31	62	7
May-03	28	65	7
Sep-03	27	67	6
Feb-04	38	55	7
May-04	35	58	7
Jun-04	34	58	8
Oct-04	43	49	8
Jan-05	52	40	8
Feb-05	51	42	7
Jun-05	42	51	7
Sep-05	37	58	5
Jan-06	46	46	8
May-06	40	50	10
Oct-06	46	47	7
Dec-06	52	41	7

Source: Compiled from figures published in the *Irish Times*/TNS mrbi Polls, May 2002-December 2006

Q7.3 How effective and open to scrutiny is the control exercised by elected leaders and their ministers over their administrative staff and other executive agencies?

Clear lines of accountability are essential in a well-functioning democracy if governments and their administrative staff are to act as servants or agents of the people. Openness and transparency are also critical for such accountability, including the degree to which the relationships between government ministers and the civil service and various executive public bodies are exposed to scrutiny and investigation. The extent to which parliamentary, legislative and administrative mechanisms exist to govern the behaviour of public officials, and to monitor and provide for redress, as well as the degree to which these are actually and effectively implemented, are good indicators of accountability and transparency in a democracy.

The non-partisan Irish civil service displays an independence that has been reinforced by its autonomous recruitment process. In addition, senior civil servants are barred from engaging in any form of political activity. The workings of the civil service and executive agencies are also increasingly subject to public scrutiny in light of the introduction of various pieces of legislation that have reduced the likelihood of undue political influence and interference. Problems identified include the potential for political interference and patronage in the system of ministerial appointments to the boards of executive agencies, while the relationship between the minister and the secretary-general and the relationship between the growing number of public bodies and their parent departments as well as their accountability to the Oireachtas continue to prove problematic for the accountability and transparency of the system.

ACCOUNTABILITY AND TRANSPARENCY MECHANISMS

Over the past twenty five years Ireland has developed a body of legislation and regulation to provide transparency and accountability directly to the public. This legislation has been largely in response to concerns over the secretive and opaque nature of the system of public administration, as well as the way in which the role of TDs as broker between voter and state administration undermines the impartiality of the public service. (See Q 12.2 for detailed discussion of the role of personalism and brokerage in Irish political life) In 1980, the Ombudsman's Act was enacted, followed by the Comptroller and Auditor General Act, 1993; the Ethics in Public Office Act, 1995, updated with the Standards in Public Office Act, 2001; the Freedom of Information Acts, 1997 and 2003; and the Ombudsman for Children Act, 2002. A Code of Practice for the Governance of State Bodies was also put in place in 2001. All of this legislation has considerably improved the ways in which the working of public administration remain transparent and subject to "good governance" practices.

Paradoxically, however, the inconsistent and *ad hoc* manner in which this legislation is applied has called into question the value of at least some of these measures. For example, the Information Commissioner has complained in a recent report that "a culture of secrecy" continues, citing the growing number of non-disclosure provisions in individual pieces of legislation, one-third of which have been introduced by various government departments since 1997. (Office of the Information Commissioner, 2005: 5, 30) Moreover, many important public bodies are excluded from coverage by one or more of these aforementioned legislative measures, or are included in an *ad hoc*, inconsistent and or partial way. For example, the Office of the Ombudsman, acting directly on behalf of the citizen, is prevented from investigating complaints in relation to a number of agencies with important public functions. Similarly, the Freedom of Information legislation does not cover bodies like the National Development Finance Agency and the National Pensions Reserve Fund. Rather than establishing through statute the criteria which would automatically include certain types of bodies within the legislation, the Minister for Finance determines, following the recommendation and consent of other government ministers, those agencies that are subject to FOI status. And all of these inconsistencies lead to uncertainty and lack of clarity both within government departments and agencies and for the population at large. Furthermore, the measures themselves have been put in place under a variety of rules and formats which contribute to the inconsistency and confusion.

INDEPENDENCE OF THE PUBLIC SERVICE

There has been a long history of independent service by public servants in Ireland. (Murphy, 2002) The Irish public service is widely acknowledged to be independent from political influence and control. The extent to which this autonomy is taken seriously is underlined in the *Civil Service Code of Standards and Behaviour* which states that all civil servants above clerical officer level are totally debarred from engaging in any form of political activity. (Standards in Public Office, 2005a: 10)

The independent public appointments service in existence since the 1950s ensures that appointments to the public service are made without any political interference or bias. Since 2004, the Commission for Public Service Appointments (CPSA) has been given the power to grant recruitment licences to certain public service bodies which wish to carry out their own recruitment. The secretary-general of government departments can apply for a recruitment licence if she or he decides to avail of the opportunity to recruit directly without using the services of the Public Appointments Service. As yet this power has not been exercised, but when licenses are issued the CPSA code will be applied.

Traditionally, there has been a constructive tension in the relationships between a minister and his/her civil servants. However, this is an area which needs to be monitored, especially if occasional incidents which come to public notice were to increase. A recent example of a minister who put a civil servant in a position where the principal of political neutrality could have been undermined was the controversy surrounding the resignation of Junior Minister at the Department of Transport, Mr Ivor Callely, TD. A contributing factor in his resignation was his request to his private secretary to attend on his behalf a function which she believed was of a political nature. The civil servant in question refused to attend the event on these grounds and subsequently tendered her resignation as private secretary to the minister. (*Irish Times*, 25 November 2005)

Non-Executive Appointments to Public Bodies

There is in the region of 5,000 appointments to public bodies at national level alone in the gift of government. Given both the number and importance of these appointments, the fact that Ireland has no independent system in place to ensure that such appointments are free from undue political influence is a large gap in the provision of accountability. Ministers and senior civil servants are currently responsible for appointing the vast majority of members to public bodies, while the influence of the Oireachtas in making public appointments remains negligible. Such political control of appointments is becoming less common in other countries as governments realise the need for transparent and accountable processes. For example, since 1995 the UK has had a Commissioner for Public Appointments who regulates, monitors and reports on the way ministers make appointments to public sector boards in order to ensure that all government departments "have in place systems which are visible, fair and open, and that all appointments to boards of public bodies are made on merit". (www.ocpa.gov.uk)

The "hit and miss nature" of the selection process is also problematic. It is unmonitored, unsystematic, and potentially suffused with subjective judgements. There is, with some exceptions, an absence of criteria of the required expertise or experience which might objectively merit such appointments. Finally, there is a lack of accountability of those appointed and the power of dismissal is, in practice, rarely used.

THE ROLE OF THE SECRETARY-GENERAL

The secretary-general of each government department is appointed by the government for a normally fixed seven-year term, the fixed term being unique to the role of the secretary-general within the civil service. The top-level appointment committee puts forward three names to government from which an appointment is made. This contract system of appointments is designed to ensure the independence of senior civil servants, and to create mobility at the top. In Ireland, the Civil Service Code of Standards and Behaviour prohibits engaging in any activity which could be seen to give personal benefit because of prior specific knowledge. (Standards in Public Office, 2005a: 14) Furthermore, a one-year moratorium on acceptance of employment outside the civil service has recently been introduced and is based on best practice in other EU Member States where the norm is a one-year restriction, though some countries have a two-year moratorium. After the twelve months moratorium has elapsed, the secretary-general must continue to observe the restrictions imposed by the Official Secrets Act 1963.

Relationship between Government Ministers and Senior Public Servants

Traditionally, control and implementation of public policy was balanced between the relevant senior civil servant and the minister of the day. As such, civil servants such as T.K. Whitaker are acknowledged to have had as much, if not more, influence on public decision making as the governments under which they served. (Connaughton, 2005) However, changes in public management systems in recent decades, and increased provisions for accountability and transparency have contributed to a greater degree of tension in the relationship between minister and secretary-general. Certainly heretofore the nature of the interactions between a minister and his/her civil servants would not have been discussed in the public domain as was the case in the Nursing Home Scandal (see below for full account). And while the manner in which individual civil servants can now be held to account has positive implications for greater openness and accountability, it does create challenges for the civil servant who, unlike the minister, is not covered by privilege in the Dáil.

In Ireland, ministers are responsible to the Parliament for the day-to-day actions of their departments as a "corporation sole" as opposed to in a personal capacity. Under Article 28 of the Constitution the government is collectively responsible for the administration of departments under the control of individual ministers. In Ireland, the secretary-general is responsible for all financial matters to the Dáil, through the Public Accounts Committee (PAC). Although she is fundamentally answerable to the relevant minister for all the affairs of the department, her role as accounting officer is a critical one in terms of scrutiny by Parliament. This accountability is reinforced by virtue of Article 33 of the Constitution, whereby the Comptroller and Auditor General is responsible for conducting an audit of the financial accounts of all government departments. Such reports are put before the Dáil and examined on its behalf by the PAC which considers whether public monies have been properly used. Uniquely to Ireland and the UK, this responsibility is a personal one. On all other matters, civil servants are not directly accountable to the Parliament, but rather held publicly accountable *via* their relevant minister.

Traditionally, civil servants have been protected from political controversy by the Ministers and Secretaries Act 1924, which laid the foundation for the modern Irish civil service. Under this Act, senior officials within the department were afforded no independent role in policy making or in the management of government departments (with the aforementioned exception of the secretary-general as the accounting officer for his/her department) and had no accountability or responsibility for the actions of the civil servants within their department. In essence senior civil servants had no statutory basis for independent action and could act only in the name of the minister. In practice, this situation tended to obscure the role of the senior civil servants. According to Connolly, "ministerial responsibility acted like a shield, behind which the actual policy role of senior civil servants was hidden from the public". (Connolly, 2005: 344) The Ministers and Secretaries Act of 1924 continues to provide the basic framework within which both the minister and the secretary-general operate.

As part of the process of civil service modernisation, the Public Service Management Act 1997 sought to reform the Ministers and Secretaries Act 1924 by clarifying the respective responsibilities of the minister and the secretary-general. (MacCarthaigh, 2005: 16–17; Connaughton, 2005) For the first time the accountability of a secretary-general to his or her minister was put on a statutory basis, wherein the minister is responsible for the performance of functions of the department, while the secretary-general has responsibility for carrying out specified functions including managing the department, preparing and submitting strategy statements, providing progress reports, and importantly advising the minister on any matter connected with the department. With regard to line management and staff accountability, the Act gives secretaries-general the power to assign responsibility for the performance of functions to officers of a department. These officers are deemed accountable for the performance of assigned functions to the secretary-general or head of office, and mechanisms such as personal performance plans have been introduced to assure accountablity for delegated tasks. While these changes in themselves constitute a progressive development, it is too early to evaluate their effectiveness.

Despite these improvements, the question of relative responsibilities and ultimately accountability remains essentially unresolved. On the one hand, the 1997 Act does not address how the minister's will, as mandated through the political process, is to be imposed on the department. (Connaughton, 2005) On the other hand, the effectiveness of the department strategy statement as a key mechanism by which secretaries-general can be held accountable by the minister, remains in question.

Not only has accountability not yet been effectively strengthened, but the changes in the informality which heretofore facilitated the traditional close working relationship between senior civil servants and

Travers Report on Charging of Illegal Nursing Home Fees

The charging of illegal fees for nursing home care came to public attention in 2005 and the subsequent investigation of who knew what within the Department of Health and Children caused a major political row. The Travers Report provides evidence that officials within the Department of Health were aware of legal difficulties surrounding charges for long-term care since the introduction of the In-Patient Services Regulations in 1976. Although successive documents noted the legal uncertainty in regard to the charges and all recommended amending the 1970 Act, no action was taken. The Travers Report effectively lays the blame for the long-stay charges scandal on the civil servants within the department, finding that there has been "overall systemic corporate responsibility and failure within the Department of Health and Children at the highest levels over more than 28 years". (Travers, 2005: 34) However, at a political level, the Travers Report effectively exonerated all previous ministers, stating that "no documentation was made available to demonstrate or to indicate that the minister had been fully and adequately briefed by the department on the serious nature of the issues". (Travers, 2005: 56) It did however point out that "it may be considered that there have been shortcomings over the entire period since 1976 at a political level on the part of Ministers of the Department of Health and Children in not probing... more strongly and assiduously the issues underlying the practice of charges for long-term care in health board institutions". (Travers, 2005: 77) In any event, in the aftermath of the Travers Report, only the secretary general of the Department of Health and Children resigned, and he was subsequently appointed executive chair of the Higher Education Authority.

ministers have also diminished the influence of the civil servant. New positions of programme manager and ministerial advisors which had been introduced by the coalition government of 1992 are now institutionalised, and have provided an independent and alternative flow of information and advice to the minister along with the knowledge and expertise of the secretary-general. (Mitchell, 2003: 438) While this development in turn gives political parties in government, through their ministers, far greater political input into national affairs, it also at the very least has the potential to diminish the influence of the secretary-general. (Connolly, 2005: 343) At the same time, the relative roles of the minister as "corporation sole" and the secretary-general as accounting officer provides an important institutional protection against maladministration, or in extreme cases, the potential for corruption between the minister and the secretary-general. However, it can also provide a source of tension since it potentially puts a secretary-general under pressure to yield to her minister on issues of financial accountability.

Moreover, the 1997 Act has not addressed the way in which individual ministers and governments confine ministerial responsibility only to those actions personally taken by the minister. While it is accepted that that a minister cannot be held responsible for individual acts of each civil servant, she should be held responsible in the case of systemic maladministration in her department. In Ireland, this accountability deficit is illustrated by the debacle surrounding the illegal charging of nursing home subventions, which has had enormous financial implications for the state and for the wellbeing of many elderly people and their families. (See Box above)

ACCOUNTABILITY FOR PUBLIC FUNCTIONS OUTSOURCED TO PUBLIC BODIES AND EXTERNAL SERVICE PROVIDERS

Public bodies, operating at national, regional and local level in Ireland, are now more numerous than ever before, and many of them impact significantly on people's everyday lives. As a result, a growing proportion of public services and functions have effectively been outsourced from the civil service or local and regional authorities to such organisations established by government to perform a specific public role. At the top end of the spectrum is the Health Service Executive (HSE), which in January 2005 replaced eleven democratically accountable regional bodies and which was responsible in that same year for the expenditure of approximately 12 billion euro to deal with the major problems confronting the Irish health care system. Other significant areas of everyday life under the purview of public bodies include the provision of a safe and efficient network of national roads by the National Roads Authority (NRA) set up in 1993, and the onerous task of protecting and improving our natural environment for present and future generations given to the Environmental Protection Agency.

Needless to say, this trend in outsourcing public services touches on a number of democratic questions of transparency, accountability and freedom from political/elite patronage. A separate study conducted for the Democratic Audit Ireland project (Clancy and Murphy, 2006) established a worrying shortfall in transparency in regard to these bodies. Public bodies also have been created in an apparently *ad hoc* and unplanned manner and the absence of any explicitly-stated or debated overarching rationale has resulted in considerable confusion, inconsistency and opacity. A recent survey of non-commercial agencies in Ireland, for example, found that "there is no general set of criteria to help policy makers decide whether or not to establish an agency to carry out a particular public function, or to decide on the appropriate levels of autonomy and accountability for an agency carrying out a particular task. Once agencies are set up, there is then no standard or regular review of their status". (McGauran *et al.,* 2005: xiii) This *ad hoc* process is further reflected in the lack both of a single register of all public bodies and any agreed definitions of what constitutes a different type of body. Consequently, any attempts to gauge the extent of outsourcing of government activity remain extremely difficult, even though many of the more than 500 such bodies at national level are core to the state system of governance. Furthermore, outsourced public functions have long since ceased to be merely an adjunct to the main work of government that is conducted within the central civil service. Indeed many public bodies are extremely significant in the public functions they perform, the scale of public expenditure they control, and in their sheer size as public-sector employers.

Table 7.2 Percentage of Annual Budget Allocated to Public Bodies by Government Department

Department	*Department Budget Estimate, 2005 '000*	*Total Department Budget Estimate allocated to named Public Body '000*	*% of Total Department Budget Estimate allocated to named Public Body*	*No. of Public Bodies listed in Budget Estimates*	*No. of Public Bodies*
Education and Science	€7,120,560	€1,498,547	21	26	80
Health and Children	€10,994,772	€9,553,845	87	30	88
Justice, Equality and Law Reform	€366,732	€97,675	27	12	48
Enterprise, Trade and Employment	€1,292,632	€1,170,573	90	15	29
Communi-cations, Marine and Natural Resources	€503,382	€275,966	55	7	51
Arts, Sport and Tourism	€458,947	€214,113	47	12	25
Environment, Heritage and Local Government	€2,467,767	€52,733	2	6	23
Finance	€102,680	€18,570	18	7	20
Transport	€2,144,613	€20,708	1	4	22
Community, Rural and Gaeltacht Affairs	€342,964	€84,573	25	4	16
Agriculture and Food	€1,426,576	€131,597	9	2	15
Foreign Affairs	€209,697	€360	0.1	3	8
Social and Family Affairs	€6,206,449	€56,909	1	4	9
Taoiseach	€37,495	€3,236	9	4	7
Defence	€758,332	€6,890	1	2	4

Source: Clancy and Murphy, 2006: 22, based on Annual Budget Estimates for Public Services, 2005

Despite their central significance to the state, effective accountability structures for public bodies have historically been poor and if anything have worsened as their number has increased. Accountability to parent departments is poorly developed; judicial interpretations of the legal and constitutional framework combined with strong political control by the government executive means that ministers can avoid responsibility for them, while the various calls for stronger Oireachtas scrutiny have been largely unsuccessful. There also continue to be considerable gaps in the legislative/administrative provision of best practice standards in openness and transparency; for example, no formalised right of the public exists to review agendas and minutes of meetings, observe board or committee meetings or access the register of members' interests.

It is generally accepted that all public bodies should be publicly accountable and that political interference is inimical to the public interest in areas where a non-party political approach is fundamental. There is also a strong convention that ministers do not interfere in day-to-day activities of the executive agencies under his departmental remit. In theory, public bodies are responsible to their ministers and through the ministers to the Dáil, but in practice there are no effective departmental mechanisms for the appraisal of their results. (Institute of Public Administration, 1970: 21) Systems for financial accountability are more strongly developed but paradoxically a lack of autonomy in this area provides few incentives for agencies to economise in their spending and there is also a lack of monitoring and accountability in relation to effective use of funding. (McGauran *et al.*, 2005: 154)

Q7.4 How extensive and effective are the powers of the legislature to initiate, scrutinise and amend legislation?

and

Q7.5 How extensive and effective are the powers of the legislature to scrutinise the executive and hold it to account?

Public opinion supports the view that the Dáil is one of the core public institutions for legitimating political power and the Dáil is perceived to be one of the most important means of holding government to account. Moreover, a variety of mechanisms and institutional structures have been put in place to improve matters in recent decades. At the same time, the Dáil is still judged to be one of the weakest parliaments in Europe. (Gallagher, 2005b: 211) The strength of the government executive and its relationship with government backbenchers means that the legislature is significantly hobbled in its ability to scrutinise the actions of government and hold them to account. The capacity of the members of the Dáil, particularly the opposition, to have a meaningful input into legislative activity, i.e., initiating, scrutinising and amending proposed legislation, is also similarly constrained. At present the system of parliamentary committees is the most effective means of scrutiny available to opposition parties. In particular the Public Accounts Committee (PAC) plays an important role in ensuring administrative probity, not least because it is chaired by a member of an opposition party. However, there are a number of features which limit the usefulness of committees: appointments are made through the office of the government chief whip, positions taken are party political, and a lack of political will exists on the part of governing parties to increase committees' powers.

This situation is somewhat mitigated by the multiparty system, which has seen a decrease in core support for the largest party, Fianna Fáil, and a rise in the number of independent TDs. The consequent increased likelihood of coalition government and/or minority governments also creates the possibility that governments will pay more attention to issues and concerns of their own backbenchers and of opposition TDs in framing legislation and in determining policy. The presence too of a range of extra-parliamentary accountability structures supports TDs in holding government to account. The scrutinising and auditing activities of parliamentary committees, TDs' questions and parliamentary debates, regardless of their formal impact, maintains pressure on government as ministers are vulnerable to public criticism. (Mulgan, 1997)

INPUT OF PARLIAMENT INTO THE FRAMING OF LEGISLATION

While it is possible that legislation will very occasionally be brought forward on the initiative of a member of the opposition through a Private Member's Bill, it is almost always the government of the day that proposes new laws. The protocol for bringing forward new legislation begins with a minister seeking the authority of the government for the drafting of legislation by way of a "memorandum for government" to the cabinet. This memorandum outlines the intended purpose of the Bill, the views of all ministers concerned with the issue, and an outline draft of the Bill. If this memorandum is approved by cabinet, a request is made to the government's legal officer, the Attorney General, to determine that legislation to be drafted is in accordance with the memorandum. Checking that the legislation is compatible with the constitution and EU obligations is one of the functions of the Attorney General.

Ireland's law-making process within parliament is closely based on that of Westminster, and involves a formal five-stage process. (See Box)

Ireland's Law-Making Process

Stage 1:	A Bill is introduced in either the Dáil or the Seanad to secure agreement to proceed to the second stage. Since virtually all Bills are in practice government Bills, this stage is usually a formality and Bills move quickly to the second stage.
Stage 2:	The Dáil debates the broad principle of the Bill. The details of the Bill are not discussed at this stage and the substance of the Bill cannot be amended. It is very rare for a government Bill to be defeated at the second stage and a significant number of Bills are passed at second stage without even the need for a vote. Once passed, the Bill is then referred to the third or committee stage.
Stage 3:	Amendments may be proposed at Stage 3 provided they do not conflict with the principle of the Bill. Such amendments may be accepted by the proposing minister.
Stages 4 & 5:	The decisions made at committee stage are tidied up and the Bill is formally passed in the Dáil. The Bill now goes to the Seanad which can delay, but not veto, its passage.

Strength of Government Control

The parliamentary stages described above occur after the government has evolved a policy on the issue that has received broad approval from its own parliamentary parties. The committee stage provides the greatest opportunity for opposition party input but amendments are limited to those which are deemed not to conflict with the principle of the Bill. Along with Spain and the UK, Ireland is one of only three European legislatures that restrict the committee stage in this manner. Most European legislatures allow committees to alter the shape and scope of legislation significantly before it reaches the House. In Ireland, adequate parliamentary time is rarely given to consider all Bills properly. For example, in a single week before the 2004 Summer recess, twelve substantive Bills were rushed to completion in parliament with rigorous use of the guillotine. Curtailing debate in this manner most frequently occurs in majoritarian-style parliaments such as those in Greece, France and Ireland while most other European parliaments decide the legislative timetable by mutual agreement among the parties. (MacCarthaigh, 2005: 100, 108)

Positive Features

The fact that Ireland has a judicially-interpretable written constitution acts as a check on the power of the executive in the framing of legislation. The actual process of passing legislation also does provides TDs with opportunities to challenge and question the relevant minister (and, by virtue of collective responsibility, the government as a whole) as to his or her intentions and the rationale for the legislation.

While the government need not accept proposed amendments, in practice it frequently does. The reasons for accepting opposition amendments moreover are not always tactical, i.e., concerned with the smooth passage of the legislation, but can in fact reflect a genuine concern for the parliamentary process on the part of the relevant minister. As such, opposition parties can find it worthwhile to propose amendments and the numbers of amendments proposed are on the increase.

A high degree of media attention and interest, especially when associated with popular sentiment, can also give opposition parties an opportunity to influence the outcome of a debate on legislation and force the government to accept amendments. For example, in the 2003 Budget, the government announced cutbacks in various social welfare measures including a cut in the widows' allowances. Following an outcry by the opposition parties and the vocal opposition of the National Association of Widows in Ireland, the government reversed its decision in April 2004. (*Irish Independent*, 12 April 2004)

Finally, it should be noted that backbench government TDs often have more influence in bringing about policy changes to government-sponsored legislation than the opposition parties. This outcome is particularly the case when a number of backbench TDs act in unison in order to extract amendments to proposed legislation as the "price for loyalty". (Gallagher, 2005b: 237)

Delegated Legislation

The steadily increasing use of delegated legislation in recent years is another issue of concern. Delegated legislation, in the form of statutory instruments, arises when the Dáil passes an Act that expresses a broad goal, but allows another authority, usually a specific minister, to make the detailed regulations. In instances where the primary enabling legislation is vague, the subsequent delegated legislation – which needs only to be passively laid before the Dáil – can come into effect without active discussion by the legislature, creating a situation which effectively grants ministers the power to change existing law without recourse to parliament. (Gallagher, 2005b: 218) Indeed there may not even be any public acknowledgement that the law has in fact been changed.

Statutory instruments are particularly common when it comes to transposing EU directives into Irish domestic law. The Supreme Court in 1994 found that the sheer number of EU directives necessitated their implementation by means of statutory instruments rather than by an Act of the Oireachtas, even when this implementation involved the amendment of existing legislation. (Gallagher, 2005b: 219)

ABILITY OF PARLIAMENT TO SCRUTINISE GOVERNMENT

Opposition parties in Dáil Éireann have three main methods at their disposal for scrutinising the behaviour of government: debates, parliamentary questions and parliamentary committees.

Debates

Opposition TDs can propose motions for debate including private members' motions, for which special time is set aside, on topical political issues, motions of no confidence in the government, and formal motions, e.g., the adjournment of the house for recess. On only two occasions in the history of the state have the non-governing parties been successful in removing a government through motions of no-confidence. (Gallagher, 2005b: 227) Debates are also held after the formal introduction of a Bill in the Dáil. After the debate, a vote is taken which determines whether the Bill will proceed or is rejected. In theory, this stage of a Bill provides the opposition parties with the opportunity to question the government. In practice, the strength of the party whip ensures that government proposals are almost always guaranteed success. Consequently, debates tend to serve as rhetorical attacks on the government and attempts by opposition parties to present themselves as a better alternative government.

Parliamentary Questions (PQs)

A total of 75 minutes is allocated three days a week to questions to a minister by members of the opposition parties, and the Taoiseach is questioned at the start of proceedings on two of those days. The aggregate amount of time spent by the Taoiseach answering questions in the Dáil compares favourably with the thirty minutes per week to which the British Prime Minister is committed. (MacCarthaigh, 2005: 117)

The number of PQs put to ministers has steadily increased over the years, so that in 2004 more than 27,568 questions were put, of which less than 10 per cent were answered orally. (MacCarthaigh, 2005: 121) A PQ is frequently used as a means of highlighting an issue by putting it on the record of the Dáil, and members of the public and representatives wishing to put pressure on government or a public body in relation to a particular matter will lobby a TD to put the question on their behalf. A PQ is also used as a tool to gather information not otherwise accessible by either the TD or the constituent on whose behalf she or he is asking the question. For example, a reply can be used as the basis for seeking further information under a freedom of information request. The most serious criticism of the effectiveness of this method of holding government to account is the fact that PQs are submitted in advance. This practice is necessary to allow the Taoiseach or ministers and the respective department the time needed to reply but it also allows time to prepare an evasive reply or one which does not answer the intent behind the question. As Justice Liam Hamilton of Beef Tribunal observed, "I think that if the questions that were asked in the Dáil were answered in the way they are answered here, there would be no necessity for this inquiry and an awful lot of money and time would have been saved." (O'Toole, 1995: 241)

Following an agreement with the Labour Party in 2002, the Taoiseach is no longer required to be present for two of the three days in which questions can be put. Further efforts to confine the Order of Business on Tuesdays and Thursdays to legislative matters to be taken by the government whips as part of proposed reforms to Standing Orders in June 2005 were only withdrawn following vigorous and public opposition.

As it is highly politicised, question time can provide many of the more lively occasions in the Dáil and often receives relatively good media coverage as a result. Indeed it is through the media that accountability can on occasion be realised, as media coverage of a minister failing to answer a question or unable to give a convincing reply can damage his or her public image and, in some cases, the standing of the government. (Gallagher, 2005b: 229) However, media coverage is by its very nature unpredictable, focuses only on particular issues, and can sometimes present stories in ways which gloss over the actual issues at heart.

There are a number of other types of questions available to the opposition in addition to PQs, namely: leaders' questions; questions on the order of business; priority questions and private notice questions. Introduced in 2001, leaders' questions have proved the most significant development in the parliamentary timetable in terms of increasing the opposition's opportunity to raise matters of immediate concern.

Parliamentary Committees

The system of parliamentary committees is the most effective means of scrutiny available to opposition parties and one which is a relatively recent development in the history of the state. After the 1997 general election, a new set of committees was created which closely matches the structure of government departments. Under this system, the activities and estimates of each government department are monitored and discussed by committee. Each committee contains 11 TDs, the majority of whom are normally drawn from the governing parties. Joint committees contain a mix of TDs and Senators.

Some of the positive features of the committee system include: the opportunity provided for greater backbench participation in the legislative process and in parliamentary life overall; serving as a mechanism by which governments can expedite legislation *via* the parallel production of Bills; the facilitation of public participation by offering a forum through which the public can express their opinions; and the development of expertise by TDs in certain areas. (MacCarthaigh, 2005: 139) The Public Accounts Committee (PAC), in particular, has been widely praised as a model for improved oversight provided by the committee system, given its success on a number of occasions (see, for example, the DIRT inquiry and also its work on the Comptroller and Auditor General reports) in holding the executive to account. It is probably not a coincidence that the chair of this committee is a member of the main opposition party. (Gallagher, 2005b: 231) All of the Joint and Select committees are chaired by a representative from the government parties, apart from the Joint and Select committees on European Affairs (chaired by members of the Fine Gael party) and on Social and Family Affairs (which is chaired by a member of the Labour party).

While the current committee system is an overall improvement on previous practice, the ability of the committee system to hold the government to account remains circumscribed. The system suffers from all the limitations resulting from strong executive control over parliament, and is basically constructed to facilitate that same political control by the government executive in some of the following ways: a majority of government party TDs prevents committee work from upsetting the executive agenda; a majority of seats are reserved to the government parties; government controls the appointment of "convenors" and the appointment of committee chair and other paid positions. (MacCarthaigh, 2005: 140–43) Moreover, the positions of committee chair are seen within the government parties as important stepping stones to higher office. In addition, the short space of time available to committees is inadequate for scrutiny of a wide range of departments and public bodies and the essentially retrospective nature of the work is itself a major practical limitation. Furthermore, while some committees may be very active, many others rarely meet, and those that do tend not to pursue detailed investigations of the department they are mirroring. The issue of Dáil reform has long been a matter of debate for political parties in Ireland, especially those on the opposition benches, but less pressure exists to address the deficiencies of Oireachtas committees. For example, a ten-point plan for Dáil reform recently published by Fine Gael and Labour in 2006 did not contain any specific recommendations in respect of Oireachtas committees.

CAPACITY OF PARLIAMENT TO SCRUTINISE PUBLIC BODIES

Given the growth in the numbers and the increasing importance of public bodies, it is important to note the specific constraints on the capacity of the Dáil to effectively monitor the actions of these bodies. For example, the convention of ministerial responsibility laid down in the 1924 Ministers and Secretaries Act has in practice prevented the Oireachtas from attaining direct accountability from state agencies. The convention has similarly allowed ministers and department officials to refuse to answer questions on their performance, particularly when reasons of "commercial confidentiality" or "professional autonomy" were cited as justification. The Blood Transfusion Supply Board (BTSB) is a perfect example of a body which operated outside of parliamentary scrutiny until the scandal, created by revelations about the infection of Irish women with hepatitis C, forced the establishment of a tribunal of enquiry in 1996. (MacCarthaigh, 2005: 211)

There have been various, albeit largely unsuccessful, attempts over the years to address the lack of oversight of public bodies, in response to concerns from opposition parties and from the media and wider community. According to the Standing Orders relative to Public Business (2002), Dáil committees do have the power to require that principal office holders in bodies in the state which are partly or wholly funded by the state, or which are established or appointed by members of government or by the Oireachtas, attend meetings of the committee to discuss issues for which they are officially responsible. Nonetheless, even this limited committee power is only spasmodically exercised, usually in response to a media story which has aroused public concern.

Q7.6 How effective are the Oireachtas powers to subject European legislation and policies to scrutiny?

Traditionally, there has been a high degree of consensus about the positive nature of Ireland's membership of the European Union (EU), and until relatively recently there has been little concern about the level of involvement of the Oireachtas in EU affairs. (Laffan, 2001) The rejection of the Nice Treaty in 2001, however, marked a turning point in Ireland's relationship with the EU, as people began to seriously question the implications of a number of developments associated with EU membership for Ireland. A particular concern has been the retention of parliamentary control over key issues such as defence and neutrality.

Improvements have been made in recent years to strengthen Oireachtas oversight of EU legislation, including the role of the Oireachtas in examining EU proposals before they pass into law. Nonetheless, the absence of an obligation on ministers to account for their decisions at EU level to the Dáil diminishes the effective role of the Oireachtas in EU affairs.

RELATIONSHIP BETWEEN EU LEGISLATIVE PROCESS AND THAT OF NATIONAL PARLIAMENTS

In Ireland as elsewhere, one of the most persistent criticisms of the EU is that it suffers from a democratic deficit. Several factors contribute to this perception, including the weak role given to national parliaments in EU affairs. The three main players in the EU decision-making process are the European Commission, the Council of Ministers and the European Parliament (EP). The Commission initiates almost all proposed European legislation. The Council – representing Member States – and the European Parliament – representing citizens on a pan-European basis – make the laws. The degree to which national parliaments formally examine EU policy as it is being formulated varies between Member States. In practice, national parliaments can select from the Commission's Annual Legislative Work Programme those legislative proposals which they would like to review.

EU legislation consists of directives, regulations and decisions. Within the context of secondary legislation, national parliaments of EU Member States are capable of having a role, albeit limited, in implementing EU legislation.

It is in respect of directives that national parliaments of EU Member States primarily have a role. While directives bind Member States to the objective of the legislation, Member States have a choice as to the form and method they employ to meet such objectives, which is ordinarily realised through implementing national legislation. In Ireland, the legislation required for implementing EU directives is in the vast majority of cases processed by means of secondary legislation. (Laffan, 2001: 256) The sheer number of EU directives necessitates their implementation by means of statutory instruments rather than by an Act of the Oireachtas, even when this implementation involves the amendment of existing legislation.

The weak role attributed to national parliaments is due in part to the historical basis on which the EU (originally the EEC) was established as a mechanism for economic cooperation. However, since the 1950s the role of the EU has expanded greatly, and in the 1960s, the European Court of Justice held that EU law was directly effective and supreme over national law of Member States. At present, the EU governs many areas of public policy including economic, agricultural, defence and foreign affairs, although the extent of its powers varies greatly in each of these areas.

Attempts to Increase Role of National Parliaments

There have been successful efforts over the years to increase the role and powers of national parliaments in the EU policy process, most notably through the Conference of European Affairs Committees (COSAC) and the Amsterdam Protocol on National Parliaments 1997.

COSAC consists of representatives from the European Affairs Committees of EU Member States' national parliaments, along with members from the European Parliament. COSAC can examine any EU legislative proposal concerning issues of freedom, security and justice that might have a direct bearing on the rights of individuals, and its opinions are subsequently forwarded to the European Parliament, the Council and the Commission.

The Amsterdam Protocol meanwhile places an obligation on EU institutions to provide information to national parliaments. Accordingly, all consultation documents (white and green papers) together with drafts of EU legislative acts and agendas and minutes of the Council of Ministers, must be sent to national parliaments.

The proposed EU Constitutional Treaty (2004) seeks to enhance the role of national parliaments in the EU legislative process by directly involving national parliaments in monitoring the proper application of the subsidiarity principle. Under the terms of the Treaty, the Oireachtas would be able to review any proposed EU legislation and submit an opinion to the EU institutions and to their own national government if it believes that the legislation does not comply with the principle of subsidiarity, i.e., the desired results would be better achieved by action at a national, regional or local level. If one-third of the national parliaments of Member States argue that the proposed EU legislation is contrary to the principle of subsidiarity, the Commission must review its proposal. (http://europa.eu) As of now, however, the drive to have the Treaty agreed and implemented has ground to a halt, following its defeat in two Member States, although it should be noted that Germany, during its term as EU President from January 2007 will try to reactivate a debate on the Treaty.

VARIABLE INVOLVEMENT OF NATIONAL PARLIAMENTS OF MEMBER STATES IN EU AFFAIRS

National parliaments have contributed to their own weak engagement in EU affairs. In general, it is the national parliaments across the EU which ratify EU Treaties, and by ratifying such treaties, national parliaments are tacitly accepting their reduced role in the final say over major areas of legislation. (Maurer, 2001: 29) The extent of involvement of national parliaments in scrutinising EU legislation varies across the EU, though all parliaments have established parliamentary committees on European Affairs. (See Box)

Role of National Parliaments in EU Policy

- Denmark's national parliament is considered to exercise the most control *vis-à-vis* EU policy out of the former EU 15 Member States.
- The national parliaments of Denmark, Austria, France and Sweden focus their involvement in EU affairs on the formulation and issuing of voting instructions to government ministers when negotiating EU policy.
- In Austria, the role of parliament in respect to EU affairs is enshrined in the constitution which highlights the importance that is attached to such matters.
- The Netherlands parliament has adopted a more open and consensual approach to monitoring EU affairs.
- In Ireland, the Oireachtas's approach has been classified as being "deliberately supportive" and is similar to the approach adopted by national parliaments in Italy, Belgium, Luxemburg and Greece. In effect, the Irish system is designed to ensure that nationally elected representatives can track EU policies in accordance with constitutional rules.

Source: Maurer and Wessels, 2001; Hegeland and Neuhold, 2002

WEAKNESS OF SCRUTINY OF EU LEGISLATION

Although various mechanisms are in place to ensure that the Oireachtas can scrutinise EU policies, most of these are largely ineffectual. Among the numerous factors accounting for this are (Laffan, 2001):

- the Oireachtas is a comparatively weak parliament;
- the impact of Ireland's membership of the EU on the role of the Oireachtas was not an issue of concern when Ireland joined in 1973;
- the Oireachtas has been relatively unconcerned about the impact of the EU on the nature and operation of Irish parliamentary democracy; and
- Ireland's membership of the EU has not been a divisive political issue and in general has received strong cross-party and public support.

In Ireland, all EU treaties are subject to a referendum – there have been five since 1973. All treaties, with the exception of the referendum on the Nice Treaty in June 2001, have been strongly endorsed by the Irish people. (See Q1.5) Therefore, the decision by Irish citizens to relinquish national power and control to EU institutions has been a democratic choice.

However, this positive, acquiescent and largely uncritical attitude toward the EU is now showing signs of strain. The Nice Referendum, 2001 marked a shift away from the pro-EU sentiment previously displayed in Ireland as people began to question the implications of EU treaties. While a myriad of factors contributed to the No vote in the referendum, concern about the nature and direction of EU governance, and in particular the relinquishing of control over national issues, such as neutrality and defence, to the EU was among the foremost issues.

As a result, more attention is now being paid by TDs to EU affairs. For example, the Oireachtas did play a more proactive role in scrutinising the proposed EU Services Directive.

The EU Services Directive

In January 2004, the European Commission proposed the draft directive to create an internal market for all services provided to consumers and businesses except those public services provided by public authorities. The proposed directive has proved one of the most disputed and controversial pieces of EU legislation in recent years, and in January 2006, the opposition parties expressed concerns about the implications of such a directive on workers' rights and employment standards and recommended a series of amendments. An Oireachtas amendment was passed by 67 votes to 60 which stated that such amendments to the directive would be considered with an open mind by the government. (*Irish Times*, 27 January 2006) In February 2006, the European Parliament voted through a diluted version of the Services Directive, reducing its scope and the range of applicable service sectors. In May 2006, the Council of Ministers overwhelmingly adopted a common position on the Directive, with only Belgium and Lithuania abstaining. The Directive was adopted by the European Parliament at a second reading in November 2006.

MEASURES TO IMPROVE SCRUTINY

Four key initiatives were launched in 2002 to improve Oireachtas oversight of EU affairs in the aftermath of the No vote in the referendum on the Nice Treaty.

Oireachtas Committee System

One of the strongest powers at the disposal of the Oireachtas to examine EU legislation is the committee system. Prior to the 1990s, the committee system in place was weak and ineffectual and there was little urgency to put mechanisms in place to ensure a strong role for the Oireachtas in monitoring EU legislation. (Laffan and Tonra, 2005: 454) In response to these perceived weaknesses, the government in 1993 established a new Joint Oireachtas Committee on Foreign Affairs which subsumed the work previously conducted by the Committee on Secondary Legislation. Meanwhile, a separate Joint Committee on European Affairs was established in 1995 as the work of the Foreign

Affairs Committee meant it had inadequate time to deal effectively with EU legislation. Ireland was among the last of the original 15 Member States of the EU to establish a Committee on European Affairs, and even then problems persisted; attendance by TDs was patchy and a lack of resources to support the committee's work led to an overall reappraisal of the manner in which the Oireachtas scrutinised EU affairs. (Laffan and Tonra, 2005: 455) As a result, the entire Oireachtas committee system underwent further reform in 2002.

In 2002, in response to the outcome of the first referendum on the Nice Treaty, Ireland established two Oireachtas Committees on European Affairs, namely the Joint Oireachtas Committee on European Affairs and a Select Committee on European Affairs. Of the two committees, the Joint Oireachtas Committee which meets frequently plays a stronger role in EU affairs. The Joint Committee has a wide remit in scrutinising EU policies and can examine EU measures taken by the Council of Ministers and acts and regulations made by the EU. The Committee also has the power to request members of the government to appear before it.

Pre-Council of Minister Meetings

Prior to each General Affairs and External Relations Council (GAERC) meeting at EU level, the Joint Oireachtas Committee on European Affairs has an opportunity to meet with the Minister for Foreign Affairs to discuss the agenda of the GAERC. The Minister briefs the Committee both on the proposals for discussion and the government's approach in relation to these matters. Accordingly, the Committee is able to make its views known on the proposals in advance of the minister's participation in Council meetings, thereby ensuring a certain degree of Oireachtas oversight of EU decisions. While the Minister is asked to give consideration to the position of the relevant Oireachtas committee *vis-à-vis* a particular EU proposal, she is under no obligation to be bound by it at Council of Minister meetings, as unlike the Danish national parliament, an Oireachtas committee cannot bind a minister to a particular policy position. As a result, the Oireachtas Committee on European Affairs generally plays "a notional role" in EU policy formulation. (MacCarthaigh 2005: 145)

Nonetheless it is possible, with political will, for the Oireachtas to have more input into the positions taken by the relevant minister at Council meetings, as is already the case in a small number of Member

States. (Mitchell, 2005) This opportunity particularly exists in relation to scrutiny of EU legislative proposals, which are accessible as soon as they go before the European Parliament and Council of Ministers and as the subsequent adoption process generally takes 12 months, there is ample opportunity to analyse and flag concerns.

The government is also required to forward to the Oireachtas all EU legislative proposals including an outline of the content, purpose, significance and implications for Ireland.

A Sub-Committee on European Scrutiny, established under the European Union Scrutiny Act 2002 and operating within the remit of the Joint Oireachtas Committee on European Affairs, then examines EU documents and decides whether parliamentary scrutiny is warranted. In every instance two options are open to the Sub-Committee:

(1) Where the Sub-Committee agrees that a particular document requires additional scrutiny, it is referred to the relevant Joint Oireachtas Sectoral Committee, e.g., those EU proposals which deal mainly with agriculture are referred to the Joint Oireachtas Committee on Agriculture.
(2) Where the Sub-Committee agrees that a particular document does not warrant additional scrutiny, no further action is needed.

In the case of (1) above, the relevant Joint Oireachtas Sectoral Committee considers the proposal forwarded by the Sub-Committee to determine whether further scrutiny is merited. If further scrutiny is merited, a report will be brought before both Houses of the Oireachtas. Similarly, if further scrutiny is not merited, a report is also sent to both Houses of the Oireachtas. In reaching its opinion, the Joint Oireachtas Sectoral Committee can hear concerns and opinions expressed by individuals and groups about a particular EU proposal.

In the case of (2) above, the relevant Joint Oireachtas Sectoral Committee can scrutinise a measure that the Sub-Committee has agreed merits no further scrutiny, but which falls within its remit. Where the relevant Joint Oireachtas Sectoral Committee determines further scrutiny is merited, a report will be forwarded to both Houses of the Oireachtas, where it can be debated and voted upon.

The Sub-Committee also produces an annual report which is furnished to the Joint Oireachtas Committee on European Affairs with the recommendation that it be laid before both Houses of the Oireachtas.

The volume of EU legislation makes clear the need for the Sub-Committee. In 2002, 72 documents were considered. In 2003, the first full year of its operation, this increased to 371. In 2004, the Sub-Committee considered 569 documents, an increase of 53 per cent on the 2003 figure. Despite the increased number of proposals, the majority (54 per cent) were deemed not to warrant referral to the relevant Oireachtas Committee. (Sub-Committee on European Affairs, 2005)

On a positive note, the introduction of a new document tracking system designed to allow the committees to more closely monitor European affairs aids the work of the Oireachtas in monitoring EU legislation and has led to a more systematic scrutiny of EU legislation by Oireachtas committees. (MacCarthaigh, 2005: 145)

National Forum on Europe

In 2002, the National Forum on Europe was established by the government and includes members from all political parties in the Dáil, in proportion to the number of seats they hold. According to Laffan and Tonra, the forum has helped to inform TDs and Senators on major European initiatives, forcing them to engage more seriously with such issues. (Laffan and Tonra, 2005: 455)

Q7.7 How comprehensive and effective is legislation giving citizens the right of access to government information?

Government transparency and openness is essential in order to ensure an effective and vibrant democratic society. Such openness provides checks against mismanagement of public services and corruption. A greater level of openness also ensures a heightened awareness of, and involvement by the citizen with, the governmental system, which in turn brings numerous benefits including enhanced public trust in government. As of 2004, over 50 countries around the world have adopted comprehensive Freedom Of Information (FOI) Acts. In the main, such acts have been adopted in the last decade or so. In general, FOI legislation everywhere shares a number of common features, the primary one being the right to access information from government bodies. Exemptions and exclusions to this right are similarly the norm, as nearly all FOI Acts exempt such areas as international relations, law enforcement and privacy. In practice, internationally, the legislation has been found to be a necessary, but insufficient measure in itself, to ensure openness or provide public access to government records in an effective and meaningful way. (Banisar, 2004: 5) While Ireland has in place a number of legislative measures to increase public access to government information, the most significant of these by far is the Freedom of Information Act 1997.

The 1997 Act was a welcome and progressive move in opening up the government and public administration system to greater public scrutiny. It was developed in accordance with the best international practices and overall is judged to have led to increased accountability to the public. The Information Commissioner is widely regarded as operating effectively and independently. However, the potential of the FOI legislation is limited due to the varying types of exemptions and exclusions, and the legislation is not applied across the public sector as a whole. An amending Act in 2003 represented a retrenchment of citizen's right of access to government information. There is also little evidence of a more open culture in government and the civil service that was one of the main intents of the original legislation. Despite these problems, the legislation is considered to have indeed contributed to accountability. A consultancy report into the progress of public service reform found that the FOI act had "generated additional workloads across Departments/Offices", but significantly the Report added that "it has undoubtedly improved the accountability of the civil service to the wider public". (MacCarthaigh, 2005: 245)

POSITIVE FEATURES OF IRELAND'S FREEDOM OF INFORMATION REGIME

The transition to democracy for most countries has led to the recognition of FOI as a right of citizenship. Other forces for openness also exist in established democracies. In Ireland, for example, the widespread pressure for greater accountability and transparency that followed a period of major political scandals was paramount in the decision to implement the 1997 FOI legislation which came into effect in April, 1998. The FOI

Act in Ireland established new statutory rights: a legal right for a person to have access to information held by public bodies; a legal right for each person to have official information relating to himself/herself amended where it is incomplete, incorrect or misleading; a legal right to obtain reasons for decisions affecting himself/herself; and a legal right to reasons for decisions taken by public bodies which is exercisable by those who have a material interest in the subject matter.

The principle of government-held data as a public asset that was enshrined in the legislation constituted a fundamental shift in the state's approach to the issue of openness and transparency and thereby to accountability. The Act was modelled on the best practices established in Canada, Australia and New Zealand and displays a number of extremely positive features as follows.

- The cornerstone of the Act was the setting up of an independent Information Commissioner, with powers to set aside refusals to disclose official information under a strong appeals system. The Commissioner also enjoys wide powers to summon witnesses and examine documents. The duties of the Commissioner include general oversight of the system, reviewing and proposing changes, training and public awareness. A variety of mechanisms for appeals and enforcement exist worldwide, and in general the jurisdictions that have created an outside monitor such as an ombudsman or information commissioner are more open. Ireland is one of a dozen or so countries with independent Information Commissioners. (Banisar, 2004)
- Ireland, along with New Zealand, is considered to have effective openness laws, and both countries have some of the strongest external appeals systems. (Banisar, 2004)
- The Information Commissioner's decisions in Ireland, as in the UK, are binding on both the public body and appellant, subject only to appeal to the Irish High Court on a point of law. The Commissioner also reviews the operation of the FOI Act and may investigate the compliance of public bodies with its terms.

The enactment of an FOI law is only the first step in creating an open and accountable system, as there is a growing international tendency for governments and their civil servants to resist releasing information, causing long delays in which users can give up hope and cease making requests. (Banisar, 2004: 7) In Ireland, civil society, together with the media and opposition, has played an important role in focusing attention on these practices and thereby providing an important countervailing force. The Information Commissioners also have been very vocal in highlighting problems with the legislation and the manner in which it is implemented.

LIMITATIONS OF THE ACT

The scope of FOI is limited in the Irish context in a number of important ways. However, this situation is not uncommon, as some countries have failed to properly implement FOI laws, while governments elsewhere have abused the exemptions. (Banisar, 2004: 5) In many cases, FOI legislation is hedged with exemptions, including measures to protect the decision-making process for reasons of cost and administrative workload. Resource barriers also constrain citizens who do not have the time, money or expertise to access government data. (Heeks, 2000)

Extent of Exclusions

In Ireland, the Information Commissioner can be refused access to records on three different grounds: on administrative grounds; where the requested records are excluded from the scope of the Act; and where the records in question are exempted. Seven categories of record are the subject of mandatory exclusion from the remit of the Act. Twelve categories of record are subject to exemption from the scope of the Act and operate in respect of: meetings of government; deliberations of public bodies; functions and negotiations of public bodies; parliamentary, court and legal professional privilege, law enforcement and public safety; security, defence and international relations; information obtained in confidence; commercially-sensitive information; personal information; research and natural resources; financial and economic interests of the state and public bodies; and enactments relating to non-disclosure of records. Exempting rather than excluding material means that material referred to in exemption provisions may, in certain circumstances, be disclosed while excluded records can never be. (McDonagh, 2003)

The number of public bodies subject to the remit of the office is limited. Initially, the Act only applied to government departments and a list of about 60 agencies of central government. Since then, the remit of FOI has been gradually extended to over 500 in order to cover a range of public bodies, including local authorities, hospitals, universities and state-funded bodies working with people with physical and intellectual disabilities. Important bodies that remain outside the scope of FOI include the gardaí, the National Development Finance Agency, the National Pensions Reserve Fund, schools and some commercial state-sponsored bodies.

Absence of Criteria for Exclusions

Rather than establishing the criteria through statute which would automatically include certain types of bodies within the legislation, the Minister for Finance determines, on the recommendation and with the consent of other government ministers, those agencies that are subject to FOI status. The Information Commissioner has stated that it is undesirable that the FOI Act should be amended on this piecemeal basis as "such an approach tends to favour the sectional interests of particular public bodies over and above the purpose and principles of the FOI Act generally". (Information Commissioner, 2005) And while the Information Commissioner welcomed the intention announced in October 2005 to extend the FOI Act to a further 109 public bodies (in fact 130 more again have since been added), she nonetheless expressed concern that quite a few significant public bodies will remain outside the scope of the Act without any apparent specific timeframe for their inclusion.

Administrative Provisions Create Opacity and Confusion

There are also problems with the administration of the provisions of FOI which hinder its effectiveness. For example, attempts to identify which public bodies are covered by the Act have uncovered a number of areas of uncertainty and lack of clarity within the Central Unit of the Department of Finance with responsibility for determining FOI status as well as within the FOI office itself. Frequently it is only when an information request is received that an agency not listed on the official list is found to be subject to the FOI, usually under the umbrella of a larger body. Finally, the legislation applies only to records created since April 1998, when the 1997 Act came into force, unless they contain personal information or are necessary to understand other documents covered under the Act.

SHORTFALLS IN CREATING AN OPEN AND ACCOUNTABLE SYSTEM

By far the most serious effort to roll back the intent of the 1997 FOI legislation was the introduction of an amended Act in 2003 on foot of a review undertaken by a group of senior civil servants. This review was undertaken without the involvement of the Information Commissioner, whose statutory duty it is to oversee the functioning of the Act, or indeed of any independent experts or citizen groups. The Irish Council for Civil Liberties (ICCL) has criticised this procedure, remarking that "to enact legislation based on the report without further consultation and input from the many stakeholders affected would be contrary to the principles of participatory democracy". (Irish Council for Civil Liberties, 2003a)

The amended legislation rolled back the terms of the 1997 Act in a number of important ways, the most significant of which is the extension of the protection period of certain cabinet decisions from five to ten years. Since April 2003 would have been the first occasion on which such records could have been disclosed following the 1997 provision, the timing of the amended legislation is widely interpreted as a mechanism to limit access to information on decisions taken during the period of office of the present government.

The public interest test has also been weakened by the 2003 Act. Under the 1997 Act, access to a record concerning deliberations by a public body could only be refused if its disclosure could be shown by a government department of the agency concerned to be contrary to the public interest. The 2003 Act amends this provision to allow for refusal unless the head of the public body concerned believes that the public interest would be better served by granting rather than by refusing access. (McDonagh, 2003)

There is also further recent evidence of successful efforts to resist the full exploitation of the legislation. In her 2004 annual report, the Information Commissioner commented on the importance she attached to Section 32 of the FOI Act which provides that the Joint

Oireachtas Committee on Finance and the Public Service shall review the operation of all secrecy provisions in all statutes to ascertain if any of the actual provisions themselves should be amended, repealed or included in the Third Schedule to the FOI act. Under the FOI Act, the Joint Committee is obliged every five years to prepare and furnish to each House a report in writing of its operational review. Such a report, however, was not presented in 1999. In 2005, the 15 central government departments did provide details on the policy areas where they are not required to disclose information and the Information Commissioner subsequently prepared a review for the Joint Committee. Her report comments critically on the growing number of non-disclosure provisions in individual pieces of legislation, one-third of which have been introduced since 1997 and complains " that a culture of secrecy ...[which]... hinders the achievement of a simple, transparent and consistent approach to the treatment of information in public bodies". (Information Commissioner, 2005)

Standards of Record-Keeping

There has been some debate as to whether or not the application of FOI will result in less recording and documentation of information that is committed to paper by the civil service. However, following an investigation by his office into the progress of the new regulations, the then Information Commissioner found such fears to be unwarranted. Nonetheless, the report on this investigation expressed concern over the inadequate standard of record-keeping in some departments, and queried the consequent "ability of public bodies to conduct their business efficiently", noting that this shortfall "also has implications for accountability". (MacCarthaigh 2005: 245)

Curtailment of Effective Public Access

Excessive fees are charged in some countries to limit or prevent requests. In Australia, for example, the Commonwealth's FOI fees for appeals are so high that few are able to afford them. In Ireland, the amended legislation allowed for higher fees to be imposed for those appealing decisions.

The level of usage is an important measure of the success of FOI in allowing citizens the right of access to government information. In 2002, for example, there were over 17,000 access requests, an increase of over 50 per cent over the number of requests in 1999, which was the first full year of the operation of the Act. (McDonagh, 2003) Following the introduction of higher fees after the 2003 Act, overall usage of the Act between 2003 and 2004 fell by 50 per cent, while media usage declined by 83 per cent and business requests fell by 60 per cent. Of eight comparable jurisdictions, Ireland is the only one which charges for internal review and just one of two jurisdictions, that charges for an appeal to the Information Commissioner. (Information Commissioner, 2004b)

During 2004, the decline in numbers using the legislation continued, with a 32 per cent reduction on the 2003 figure. In 2005, this figure increased, but remained 21 per cent down on the 2003 figure. The majority of FOI requests are made by members of the public or representative organisations. The number of requests from journalists declined significantly to around 7 per cent in 2004 and 2005, down from 12 per cent and 13 per cent in 2002 and 2003 respectively. (www.oic.gov.ie)

OTHER MEASURES FOR ENSURING ACCESS TO PUBLIC INFORMATION

The *National Archives Act 1986* provides that all government and departmental records (including cabinet minutes) over 30 years old must be transferred to the National Archives and be made available to the public. This Act, for the first time, facilitated a closer look at the decision-making process and how various governments since the foundation of the state reached the decisions they did. (MacCarthaigh 2005)

The Official Secrets Act 1963 remains in force in Ireland and criminalises the unauthorised release of restricted information. In addition, the Garda Síochána Act 2005 imposes penalties of a €50,000 fine and five years sentence on current or former Garda employees who disclose information obtained in the course of their duties if the person knows the disclosure is likely to have a harmful effect.

The *Data Protection Acts 1988, 2003* confer a right of access to personal data held by private or public sector bodies.

The *Access to Information on the Environmental Regulations Act 1998*, implements the 1992 EU Directive which confer a right of access to environmental information.

Eight: Civilian Control of the Military and Police

Are the military and police forces under civilian control?

INTRODUCTION AND SUMMARY

Modern states are vulnerable to military intervention in the affairs of the civil government, or even to outright takeover of power. A distinguishing feature of democratic countries is their dedicated civilian control over the armed forces, and the effective accountability of all the agencies of public security to parliament and, in the case of the police, also to their local communities. Citizens of these countries rightly expect that there will be no "No Go" areas for law enforcement, and that the police will act impartially, and with the consent and support of the relevant public sectors with whom they have to deal. To this end, it is important that uniformed appointments should be made on professional, not political, grounds; that recruitment should be representative of a broad cross-section of society; and that there be independent complaints procedures for all the uniformed services, including their staff.

Throughout the history of the Irish Republic, the military have been securely under the control of the civil authorities, and thanks to a strict policy of "garda primacy", their occasional deployment among the civilian population has proved noncontentious. Despite the recent rise in drug-related offences, Ireland continues to enjoy a relatively low crime rate as compared with other European countries.

Opinion surveys show high levels of public confidence in the gardaí, though much less so in the handling of complaints against them. The longstanding lack of an independent police complaints process has recently been addressed with the establishment of an Ombudsman Commission under the 2005 Garda Síochána Act, which also provides for Joint Policing Committees to give local communities a greater say in law enforcement priorities.

However, these reforms do not address the system of political appointments of senior officers and the opportunity has been missed to establish a National Policing Board to manage the gardaí, as has been introduced in Northern Ireland. Funding for the Office of the Northern Ireland Ombudsman is also much higher than that for the Commission in the Republic. In any event, only time will show how effective the positive measures under the 2005 Act prove to be.

Concerns also remain about the quality of policing in disadvantaged areas and policing as experienced by members of minority communities. Neither the armed forces nor the police are notable for being socially representative in composition, especially as regards women, who can sometimes be vulnerable to harassment from their male colleagues.

Q8.1 How effective is civilian control over the armed forces, and how free is political life from military involvement?

Article 13.4.2 of the Irish Constitution vests command of the armed forces in the President of Ireland. Articles 13.5.1 and 13.9 of the Constitution go on to qualify the President's command so as to ensure the exercise of this command is both within the law and only under the explicit direction of the Oireachtas. In this manner, whilst the President enjoys "de jure" command of the Defence Forces, *de facto* command in effect lies firmly in the hands of the Minister for Defence and the Taoiseach of the day. The Defence Acts 1954 – 1998 further bind the Irish military to civilian oversight and control.

Throughout the lifetime of the Irish Republic, the Irish military have not been associated with independent military, political or lobbying activities. Despite the fraught epoch that gave birth to the Free State Army during the War of Independence, and latterly the tensions and challenges thrown up by the Troubles in Northern Ireland, the

Irish military authorities have remained accountable to, and under the control and direction of, the Irish civil authorities at all times.

INDEPENDENCE AND CIVIL WAR: THE ORIGINS OF IRISH DEFENCE FORCES

The Irish armed forces, known as the Permanent Defence Forces (PDF) or "Óglaigh na hÉireann", number approximately 10,000 personnel across the Naval Service, Army and Air Corps. The Defence Forces in Ireland play an active role domestically in "Aid to the Civil Power" Operations (ATCP Ops) with the Irish police force, An Garda Síochána. The Defence Forces are also active internationally in UN peacekeeping and peace enforcement operations in Europe, Asia, Africa and the Middle East. (See also Section Fourteen)

The Defence Forces in Ireland are traditionally associated with compliance to the law and conformity to the twin concepts of accountability and subordination to the civil authorities. The Irish military have not to date been associated with independent military, political or lobbying activities. Neither have they ever been associated with any unilateral show of force, coercion or negative engagement in the democratic process.

As an organisation, the Irish Defence Forces is a direct descendant of the Irish Free State Army – initially formed in 1922 following the Irish War of Independence from Britain. From the inception of the Free State Army until 1954, the Irish armed forces were legislated for under the 1923 Temporary Provisions Act.

This act was repealed by the Defence Act of 1954, and since then the Irish Defence Forces are legislatively regulated by the Defence Acts 1954 – 1998.

Throughout the turbulent years of the Irish Civil War and the remainder of the 1920s, the Irish Free State Army operated under the constitutional authority provided by the Irish Free State Constitution of 1922. This constitutional authority in tandem with the Temporary Provisions Act of 1923 enshrined in law the formal subordination of the Irish military to the civil authorities and the Irish houses of parliament, the Oireachtas.

Throughout the fraught period of the Civil War and subsequent years of World War Two – known in Ireland as "the Emergency" – the

Irish armed forces and the Irish military authorities remained loyal to, and subject to the direction and control of, the civilian authorities regardless of political persuasion. Over time, serving members of the Irish armed forces came to be regarded both internally within the organisation and externally in the public service as generally "non-political servants of the state".

THE IRISH DEFENCE FORCES AND THE LAW

From the point of view of the Irish Constitution, Article 15.6.1 gives the Irish government the sole constitutional premise for raising and maintaining an army within the state:

> The right to raise and maintain military or armed forces is vested exclusively in the Oireachtas.

Article 15.6.2 reiterates this point:

> No military or armed force, other than a military or armed force raised and maintained by the Oireachtas, shall be raised or maintained for that purpose.

The existence of this article in the Irish Constitution unmistakeably refutes the claim made by organisations such as the Provisional Irish Republican Army to the title of "Óglaigh na h'Éireann" and copper-fastens the status of the Irish Defence Forces as the sole, legitimate armed force within the state.

Article 13.4.2 of the Constitution vests command of the armed forces in the President of Ireland. Articles 13.5.1 and 13.9 of the Constitution go on to qualify the President's command so as to ensure the exercise of this command is both within the law – regulated and checked by law – and only under the explicit direction of the government through the Council of Defence.

The Defence Acts 1954 – 1998 further bind the Irish military to civilian oversight and control. With reference to the command and control of the Irish military, Section 17 of the Defence Act 1954 states:

> Under the direction of the President and subject to the provisions

> of this Act, the military command of, and all executive and administrative powers in relation to, the Defence Forces, including the power to delegate command and authority, shall be exercisable by the government and, subject to such exceptions and limitations as the government may from time to time determine, through and by the minister.

This section of the Act explicitly "corrals" control of the military within the civil sphere and makes amenable all aspects of Irish military activity to civilian and government direction and scrutiny.

Section 17(3) of the Act provides the mechanism by which the Minister for Defence oversees the day-to-day management of every aspect of the Irish military. It states:

> The minister may make regulations applying to officers, as to the persons to be invested, as officers, with military command over the Defence Forces or any part thereof or any person belonging thereto and as to the mode in which such command is to be exercised.

This legislative mechanism for control of the Defence Forces finds expression through Defence Forces Regulations (DFRs) and Statutory Instruments (SIs) which are promulgated on an ongoing basis by the Minister for Defence. DFRs govern every aspect of Irish military activity across the full spectrum of command and administration, logistics and supply, operations and intelligence.

THE TROUBLES

Over the last four decades, Ireland has experienced considerable volatility in terms of its internal security associated with the "Troubles" as the conflict in Northern Ireland has been called. The deployment posture of the Defence Forces during this period has been extensive.

For example, in the year 2005 – 7-8 years after the Good Friday Agreement, the Provisional IRA (PIRA) ceasefires and announcement of disarmament – the Irish Defence Forces undertook 2,574 armed cash escorts, 176 armed political prisoner escorts, 81 bomb disposal call outs and operations, 23 armed commercial explosives escorts, 212 armed military escorts of weapons and explosives and 1,242 armed patrols of vital installations such as airports, power stations and broadcasting facilities. This activity was significantly more intensive during the period of the Troubles themselves.

Despite the thousands of daily interactions between armed Irish troops and their fellow citizens within Ireland, relatively few contested exchanges or negative outcomes result. This unproblematic deployment of an army among the civilian population, over such an extended period of time without incident or legal challenge, is possibly unprecedented throughout the EU.

The unproblematic nature of this deployment is due largely to the strict policy of "garda primacy" that has existed within the Irish state even throughout the period of the Troubles. No matter where they are deployed throughout the state, Irish soldiers are normally accompanied by unarmed members of An Garda Síochána, where ever they are likely to interact with the Irish public. As a result, it is normally a member of An Garda Síochána who communicates with members of the public at checkpoints or cordons, during searches or on armed escort duties. This policy differs considerably, for example, from British government policy in Northern Ireland where British soldiers have regularly mounted independent checkpoints and routinely question civilians as to their identity, occupation and movements. However this practice was necessitated in part by the fact that the police force in Northern Ireland, unlike its counterpart in Ireland, did not enjoy almost unanimous support from the population. The replacement of the British army with members of the Police Service of Northern Ireland (PSNI) and on-going efforts to win cross-community support for the PSNI have been key elements in building the peace in Northern Ireland.

Whilst deployed among the general public, the Irish armed forces are subject to both military law and civil law as regards their use of force. Though armed, Irish troops, operating domestically on ATCP Ops, enjoy no special privileges or entitlements in law. According to *Military Law in Ireland,* (Humphreys and Craven, 1997) an Irish soldier on duty in Ireland is simply "a citizen armed in a particular manner … (who) cannot because he is a soldier excuse himself if without necessity he takes human life".

In this regard, the legal basis for Irish soldiers bearing arms in public is predicated on a combination of legal premise, including the common law right of individual citizens to defend themselves, the constitutional right of the government to call upon the military as citizens to assist in the maintenance of public order, and all of the relevant statute legislation governing the use of force. Consequently, the Irish military are fully amenable to the law in instances where force is used.

Among the levels of force open to armed troops are unarmed response by weight of numbers, the use of batons, and *in extremis*, the firing of ammunition in warning or to inflict non-fatal injuries. In terms of justification, the "rules of engagement" for Irish troops are amenable to external scrutiny and are not secret. Irish troops may use force, for example, only in defence of their own lives, or the lives of members of An Garda Síochána or members of the public. In terms of prevention, such force may only be used to prevent loss of life and cannot be employed in a punitive manner after a criminal act has been committed by a third party. The legal requirements incumbent upon Irish soldiers include a broad range of provisions from evidence of proficiency with a weapon to the detailed exigencies of the Non-Fatal Offences Against the Persons Act (1997). In this manner, Irish troops operating in their day-to-day ATCP Ops are fully accountable to civil control and amenable to the law.

The legitimacy of participation by Irish Defence Forces' personnel in ATCP Ops has been challenged in the courts, arising from the arrest of suspected members of the Provisional IRA during boarding operation of the Marita Ann – a trawler carrying an arms shipment for the PIRA into Irish waters in 1984.

In remarks made by Chief Justice Finlay in *The People (D.P.P.) v. Ferris, Crawley and Brown,* the courts have taken the view that

> The gardaí are entitled to call upon the assistance of the Defence Forces in support of the civil power; it would be ludicrous if it were otherwise.

The Chief Justice went on to state

> There is no constitutional rule which rigidly separates the functions of one class of citizen thus uniformed and disciplined, from another such class; and the fact that day-to-day keeping of the peace is conventionally attended to by a police force does not

> prevent any other part of the state's service from being called in to supplement it in need. (Humphreys and Craven, 1997: 21)

It is the key phrase "supplement" that possibly helps to explain the relatively unproblematic operation of the Irish Defence Forces in an intensive, sometimes overactive role alongside the domestic police force. It is precisely because of "garda primacy" and complete subordination to the civil powers that the Irish military have not overstepped their authority or role in civil-military relations. Indeed, in the key area of intelligence gathering – where a negative interface between the military and the civil populace is often most keenly felt – the Irish Defence Forces play a secondary role to that of An Garda Síochána. The Irish military restrict their intelligence-gathering and evaluation role primarily to the international scene, leaving it primarily to the police force to fulfil that role domestically.

Q8.2 How publicly accountable are the police and security services for their activities?

The issue of garda accountability has been the focus of much media and public attention in recent years due to a public tribunal of inquiry, the Morris Tribunal, into complaints against garda officers in Donegal, and to a small number of incidents of lethal force employed by gardaí in situations where the use of such force was open to question. While surveys have consistently shown high levels of public confidence in the gardaí, they have also shown consistently low levels of confidence in the garda complaints procedures. (See Q12.4)

Largely as a result of these recent issues, the systems of accountability for the gardaí are currently undergoing considerable change. In fact, the introduction of the Garda Síochána Act 2005 represents the largest review of the Irish police since 1922. Changes in the systems of accountability being introduced under the Act include the introduction, for the first time, of an independent body, the Garda Ombudsman Commission, for investigating complaints against a garda; the establishment of a Garda Inspectorate to monitor the performance of the gardaí; and the establishment of Joint Policing Committees which, when implemented, will provide local communities with an enhanced role in addressing crime and disorder.

Unlike within Northern Ireland, however, the Garda Síochána Act 2005 does not establish a National Policing Board to manage the gardaí.

While there are very real improvements under the Act, a number of concerns remain. First, in regard to the independence of appointments to and dismissal from senior positions, the Act largely retains the existing systems. Second, the reporting arrangements between the Commissioner and the Minister could potentially pose a threat to garda operational independence. Third, the main concerns regarding the new Garda Síochána Ombudsman Commission are that procedures laid down in the Act for taking complaints are both overly bureaucratic and heavily dependent on the Garda Commissioner for their effectiveness; furthermore, the Ombudsman Commission may have to rely on members of the gardaí to undertake investigations due to lack of funding. The Office of the Northern Ireland Ombudsman currently has around five times the number of personnel and fifteen times the funding compared to that budgeted for the Commission in Ireland.

GARDA ACCOUNTABILITY

The system governing the accountability of the Garda Síochána is currently in a state of flux. The Garda Síochána Act 2005, which was signed into law in July 2005, deals with all aspects of policing, including police functions, personnel and organisation, the creation of a volunteer service, a code of ethics, setting policing priorities and community policing measures. The Act also includes provisions relating to the establishment of a Garda Inspectorate to monitor performance and a Garda Síochána Ombudsman Commission. All those sections of the Act which are concerned with the accountability of the gardaí are, at the time of writing, due to be fully implemented by the end of 2006. A Garda Síochána Implementation Group has been appointed by the Minister for Justice, Equality and Law Reform to oversee the implementation of the Act. The Group will review the Minister's plans to establish an independent Garda Síochána Ombudsman Commission, the creation of a Garda Inspectorate, the drafting of a code of ethics and arrangements for local bodies. (Irish Council for Civil Liberties, 2006)

The accountability of the Garda Síochána has been the subject of intense media and public attention in recent years. In June 2005, the Tribunal of Inquiry (the Morris Tribunal) into complaints against garda officers in the Donegal Division issued its report. This Inquiry received extensive coverage throughout its lifetime. The Tribunal ultimately found culpability ranging from instances of negligence to two officers corruptly orchestrating the planting of ammunition and hoax explosives. It also made a finding of gross negligence, short of actual complicity, on the part of senior management in the division. The Tribunal made recommendations for improved management, recording of incidents, an urgent review of policy on the handling of informants, and greater accountability.

In addition, a number of high-profile cases involving the use of lethal force by members of the service have occurred in recent years, accompanied by extensive media coverage. These have included:

- the killing of John Carthy who was shot dead in April 2000 after being barricaded for 24 hours in his home and surrounded by 60 police officers. John Carthy was reportedly suffering from depression and many people questioned whether the force used by the police was excessive in the circumstances; and
- a number of incidents in which criminals were killed by gardaí, in particular, the Garda Emergency Response Unit, either at, or fleeing from, crime scenes. A recent example was the killing of two men during the attempted robbery of a post office in Lusk, Co. Dublin in 2005.

Lethal force is not the only documented allegation of police abuse. After the 2002 visit to Ireland of the European Committee for the Prevention of Torture and Inhuman or Degrading Treatment or Punishment, the Committee stated that a not inconsiderable number of persons interviewed claimed that they had been physically ill-treated by gardaí. This echoed findings of the Committee from earlier visits. Most of the allegations received concerned the time of arrest or related to ill-treatment in cells or detention areas in police stations. (European Committee for the Prevention of Torture, 2003: 36)

APPOINTMENTS AND DISMISSALS OF SENIOR GARDAÍ

Currently, the Garda Commissioner, Deputy Commissioners and Assistant Commissioners are appointed by the government in accordance with the Police Forces Amalgamation Act 1925. The Garda Commissioner is responsible to the Minister for Justice, who in turn is accountable to the Dáil for the activities of the service. While legislation permits the appointment of a commissioner to be made from outside the garda service, he / she is normally a garda officer who has risen through the ranks.

In addition, the government may appoint, subject to and in accordance with the regulations, "such numbers of persons as the government sees fit to the ranks of superintendent and chief superintendent in the Garda Síochána". In turn, the Garda Commissioner may appoint, in accordance with the regulations, "such numbers of persons as he or she sees fit to the ranks of garda, sergeant and inspector". Thus, as the Irish Human Rights Commission commented in relation to the Garda Bill 2004, the Act "largely retains the existing system of political appointment of senior officers within the police service." (Irish Human Rights Commission, 2004c) In light of the undesirable implications of political patronage on the independence of appointees in the exercise of their function, it is troubling that the provisions of the 2005 Act relating to the appointment of the highest levels of the gardaí would appear to continue to allow for such possible patronage.

Under the 2005 Act, the Garda Commissioner, Deputy Garda Commissioner or Assistant Garda Commissioners may only be removed from office by the government for one of a number of stated reasons, including: (a) where the person fails to perform the functions of the office with due diligence and effectiveness; (b) where the person has engaged in conduct that brings discredit on the office or that may prejudice the proper performance of the functions of the office; or (c) where the person's removal from office would, in the government's opinion, be in the best interests of the Garda Síochána. While it is no doubt important that the Garda Commissioner and Deputy and Assistant Commissioners be in some way accountable for their actions to the government, the wide discretion granted to the government in this context could, in certain circumstances, enable inappropriate political influence to be exerted over the relevant officers.

RELATIONSHIP BETWEEN GARDA COMMISSIONER AND MINISTER FOR JUSTICE

Historically, both Ireland and the United Kingdom have rejected the model of direct ministerial control of policing, which is the norm in many European countries. (Irish Council for Civil Liberties, 2003b) Nonetheless, increased powers and a greater involvement in garda affairs by the Minister for Justice is arguably the thread running through the 2005 Act. The Irish Centre for Civil Liberties has emphasised that, while in a democratic society it is important that the police force remain independent of any government department, which has traditionally been the case in Ireland, the 2005 Act changes the relationship between the gardaí and the minister by requiring the Garda Commissioner to report directly to the Minister for Justice, Equality and Law Reform. This change would appear to pose a potential threat to the Commissioner's independence and freedom from political interference. Section 40(1) of the 2005 Act further provides that the Garda Commissioner shall account fully to the government and the minister through the secretary-general of the Department of Justice, Equality and Law Reform "for any aspect of his or her functions". Of potentially greater concern, however, is the provision in section 40(2) that this duty to account includes the obligation to provide, on request by the secretary-general, any document in the power or control of the Garda Síochána, including material in the form of garda records, statements made by members of the Garda Síochána and by other persons and reports.

As previously stated, unlike Northern Ireland, the Act does not establish a National Policing Board to manage the gardaí. The Northern Ireland Policing Board has wide ranging powers, including the power to hold the Chief Constable accountable, powers of inquiry into police activities, and the power to appoint senior officers. Instead, the 2005 Act runs the risk of over-centralising and politicising the gardaí, by making the Minister for Justice, Equality and Law Reform directly responsible for its management.

Having noted that several sections of the (then) Garda Bill 2004 granted broad discretionary powers to the minister in relation to the operation of the Garda Síochána, the Irish Human Rights Commission stated in its "Observations on the Garda Bill 2004" that "the vesting of oversight and appointment functions with an independent and representative agency, such as a Police Authority as recommended by the Patten Report, could make a valuable contribution to the promotion of human rights within Irish policing. The independence and the public perception of independence of the police service from executive control are central to the credibility and the capacity of the police service to protect human rights and we urge the government to give further consideration to this issue". (Irish Human Rights Commission, 2004c) In the event, this advice has not been heeded.

The government position is that the establishment of a police authority/board would be inappropriate in relation to state security matters, and that much of what has evolved in Northern Ireland was a specific response to the political/security issues there. It has been observed that this rationale overlooks the fact that measures developed in relation to widespread conflict might still have merit in a relatively stable society. Arguments that there is no need to have a garda board in Ireland because Ireland is sufficiently small in size not to require this type of civic oversight ignores the fact that the populations of many of the areas under the scrutiny of English police authorities are in fact smaller than this jurisdiction.

COMPLAINTS PROCEDURES: CHANGES BROUGHT ABOUT BY GARDA SÍOCHÁNA ACT 2005

Prior to the Garda Síochána Act 2005, complaints made against the gardaí were dealt with in accordance with the procedure set out in the Garda Síochána (Complaints) Act 1986. The core difficulty with these prior complaints mechanisms was outlined in 2000 by the UN Human Rights Committee, in its concluding observations on Ireland's state party report under the International Covenant on Civil and Political Rights, which stated that:

> While [the Committee] welcomes the existence of a mechanism to investigate complaints made against the police force, namely the Garda Complaints Board, the Committee regrets that the Board is not fully independent, in that investigations of complaints against the gardaí are often entrusted to members of the gardaí without consultation with the Board. It emphasises that the availability of recourse to the courts to address allegedly

> unlawful conduct by the police does not displace the need for independent and transparent investigation of allegations of abuse. The Committee recommends that, in the context of its current review of the Garda Complaints Act of 1986, the state party take steps to ensure that the Garda Complaints Board is not dependent on the gardaí for the conduct of investigations. Consideration should be given to the establishment of a police ombudsman. In the case of death resulting from action by members of the gardaí, the state party should ensure that allegations are investigated by an independent and public process. (United Nations Human Rights Committee, 2000)

The key problem with the prior procedure was the fact that the Garda Complaints Board which investigated complaints was dependent on the gardaí for the conduct of investigations. Problems in relation to the complaints system included instances in which officers on the investigating team had come from the same police force as the officers against whom a complaint had been lodged. (Amnesty International, (Irish Section), 2000)

The Garda Síochána Complaints Board itself called for its own replacement with an independent investigative body. According to the Irish Council For Civil Liberties (ICCL), "This is not the first time that the Board has fully acknowledged its inadequacies and the lack of public confidence it enjoys...This report is unambiguous in the need for the establishment of a fully independent mechanism with real powers of investigation". (Irish Council for Civil Liberties, 2003c)

Grounds for lack of public confidence in the garda complaints procedures are indicated by the low level of response to those complaints that are made about gardaí. During 2002, three-quarters of complaints were either dismissed or withdrawn. This issue was raised by a member of the UN Human Rights Committee during the Committee's consideration of Ireland's state party report under the ICCPR. The committee member noted that very few complaints made to the Garda Síochána Complaints Board had been referred to the Garda Síochána Complaints Tribunal which rules on breaches of discipline. In 2004 while 1,232 complaints were received about garda conduct, only 27 cases involving serious breaches of discipline were referred to the Complaints Tribunal, and hearings in respect of only 18 members, involving 49 breaches of discipline, were held.

In addition, a very high level of complaints are ultimately withdrawn, or "constructively withdrawn" because of a lack of cooperation from the complainant. In 2003, 350 complaints were withdrawn, while in 2004, 302 were withdrawn. (An Garda Síochána Complaints Board, 2005: 21) The Garda Síochána Complaints Board (GSCB) has stated that three factors play a significant part in many withdrawals. First, many individuals find the formal investigation procedures contained in the Act somewhat daunting; second, the length of time taken to finalise complaints; and third, individuals, at the time of making their complaint, do not envisage it as a formal complaint to be considered under the Act but rather as a matter suitable to be dealt with by local garda management. (An Garda Síochána Complaints Board, 2004)

The first two issues illustrate the ineffectiveness of the complaints procedure then in place, i.e., the "daunting nature" of the investigation procedures which results in cases being withdrawn; and the delay in processing complaints which remains a major issue.

Complaints System After 2005 Act

In its 2004 annual report, the Garda Síochána Complaints Board stated that its belief that three major legislative defects prevented it from carrying out its duties in the best interest of the public. These were:

- the lack of independent investigative resources with the ability to inquire into matters of concern whether or not a complaint had been received;
- the inability of the Board to compel members of the gardaí to answer questions in connection with any complaint; and
- in dealing with complaints, the Board was restricted in terms of the level of supervision it could exercise over garda investigating officers appointed to investigate complaints who, at all times, remained answerable to the Garda Commissioner.

The report concluded that the three person Ombudsman Commission proposed under the 2005 Act will have "virtually all the powers that the Board has for so long sought for itself". (An Garda Síochána Complaints Board, 2005: 8) The 2005 Act has thus changed the complaints system considerably.

The new complaints system has been generally welcomed as a significant improvement although a number of reservations have been voiced. One concern relates to the fact that the members of the Commission are government appointees, raising the issue of the Commission's independence from government. It should be noted, however, that those appointed to the Commission by the Minister for Justice include a judge of the High Court, a former editor of the *Irish Times* and a former Director of Consumer Affairs. The previous professions of these individuals would not appear to suggest an undue susceptibility to government interference. Furthermore, a person is not eligible to be nominated or appointed to the Ombudsman Commission if he or she is a member of either House of the Oireachtas, a member of a local authority, or is or has been a member of the Garda Síochána. This provision serves to strengthen the independence of the Commission from both An Garda Síochána and the government. Moreover, the provisions for dismissal of commissioners further augment the independence of the Commission from the executive. Section 68(2) of the Act provides that the President may remove a member of the Ombudsman Commission from office, but only for stated misbehaviour or for incapacity, and then only on resolutions passed by the Houses of the Oireachtas calling for the member's removal.

The Irish Council for Civil Liberties has highlighted two concerns regarding the new Garda Síochána Ombudsman Commission. First, procedures laid down in the Garda Síochána Act for taking complaints are overly bureaucratic and heavily dependent on the Garda Commissioner if they are to function effectively. Second, that the Ombudsman Commission may have to rely on members of the gardaí to undertake investigations due to lack of funding and will have to seek permission from the Garda Commissioner before conducting searches of garda stations. (Irish Council for Civil Liberties, 2006)

At the time of writing, the Ombudsman Commission is due to begin to receive complaints at the beginning of 2007. (Department of Justice, Equality and Law Reform, 2005a) Where investigations have commenced prior to the repeal of the 1986 Act, the previous complaints procedures will continue to apply.

Accountability of Garda Security Forces

An Garda Síochána is responsible for ensuring the security of the state and in practice a number of sections of the gardaí deal with security issues. The activity of the security and intelligence section involves the monitoring of trends in subversive and criminal activity in the state, while the functions of the liaison and protection section include promoting international law enforcement liaison, protection of resident and visiting dignitaries and VIPs, and the security of key state installations and buildings. The international coordination unit is a focal point for international policy determination and activity on matters covered by European Union working groups, Schengen, Europol, Interpol and liaison officers, while the special detective unit deals with matters relating to the security of the state, and aims at combating the activities of unlawful groups within the state, with a particular focus on anti-terrorism. Finally, the Garda Síochána emergency response unit, which operates within the legal framework of the state and current Garda Síochána regulations, is responsible for resolving any situation where armed resistance is confirmed or anticipated and for providing an effective armed protection service to persons categorised as "high risk".

The members of these units, as well as reservists, are at all times "members" of the gardaí and as such are subject to the same accountability mechanisms and complaints procedure for the gardaí. However, the Act does place qualifications on the Ombudsman Commission's powers in instances where state security may be at issue. While this provision does not necessarily mean that the conduct of members of the gardaí dealing with matters of state security is exempt from complaints procedures or investigations, these restrictions could potentially limit attempts to render gardaí working in areas related to state security publicly accountable for misbehaviour.

Community and Local Authority Involvement in Policing

Another important element of the 2005 Act in terms of the accountability of the Garda Síochána is the provision for the establishment of Joint Policing Committees (JPCs). The primary function of JPCs is to serve as fora for consultations, discussions and recommendations on matters affecting the policing of administrative areas within local authorities. In particular, the JPCs are to keep levels and patterns of crime, disorder and antisocial behaviour (as well as the factors contributing to same) under review. JPCs advise local authorities and the gardaí on how they might best perform their functions. They also arrange and host public meetings concerning matters affecting the policing of the local authority's administrative area. The sections of the Garda Act relating to Joint Policing Committees (Sections 34–36 of the 2005 Act) clearly provide local authorities with an enhanced role in addressing crime and disorder. The public meetings and local policing fora provided for under the Act constitute a concrete means by which communities can help influence the policing they receive. That said, it has also been observed that the relevant provisions involve a diffusion of responsibility without necessarily putting in place a clear framework for how such responsibilities are administered, resourced or reviewed. Under the Act, much of the JPCs structures/actions have been left to ministerial guidelines, which in itself suggests a lack of clear vision concerning their role and development. Furthermore, the fact that the minister is responsible for issuing guidelines concerning the establishment and maintenance of joint policing committees – without any need to even consult with local authorities or the Garda Commissioner – circumscribes the extent to which local authorities may, in fact, be able to influence the policing they receive. To date, pilot committees have been established in a limited number of local authorities, and JPCs will only be established in all local authorities after mid-2007.

Q8.3 To what extent does the composition of the army, police and security services reflect the social composition of society at large?

Neither the armed forces nor the gardaí are representative of wider Irish society today. Women are vastly underrepresented in both organisations, comprising around 17 per cent of gardaí and less than 5 per cent of the armed forces. This underrepresentation has been shown to have very negative consequences in regard to high levels of bullying and harassment of women within both organisations. Underrepresentation of minority and marginalised groups within the gardaí is reflected in the high prevalence of negative stereotyping of various groups within all ranks of the force and difficulties in police relations with these same groups.

A number of positive initiatives undertaken in recent years include: an independent human rights audit of the gardaí; the appointment of ethnic liaison officers; a change in the entry requirements for the police to encourage more applications from ethnic minority groups; the appointment of liaison officers to the lesbian and gay community; and provisions in the Garda Síochána Act 2005 to formalise community policing structures for the first time. No major initiatives have been undertaken to address the underrepresentation of women within either the police or the army.

THE ARMED FORCES

Recruitment for the Defence Forces is open to all EU and non-EU nationals, provided they satisfy the residency/work requirements laid down by the Department of Justice, Equality and Law Reform, and the Department of Enterprise Trade and Employment. In addition, unlike in some other countries, there is no ban on gays and lesbians joining the Defence Forces in Ireland. A code of conduct covers all sexual relations between members of the forces, and applies regardless of sexual orientation. The single greatest issue with regard to the composition of the defence forces is the vast underrepresentation of women.

Women in the Army

The full integration of training for female recruits in the army began only in 1994. At that time women made up less than 1 per cent of the defence forces. This proportion had risen to 4.6 per cent by 2004, and there are now around 500 female officers, non-commissioned officers and privates serving out of a total of around 10,500.

It has been shown that working conditions for women within the army were, at least in the past, extremely difficult. An authoritative report in 2001 into bullying and harassment within the Defence Forces found that all but one of sixty servicewomen questioned had encountered some form of bullying or harassment. The report cites numerous incidents of women soldiers being subjected to obscene phone calls and sexually explicit remarks. Twelve women reported having been victims of sexual assault in the workplace. (Clonan, 2000)

As a result of this report, the then-Minister of Defence, Michael Smith, commissioned a government investigation on the nature and extent of harassment, bullying, discrimination and sexual harassment in the defence forces. The resulting report of the External Advisory Committee on the Defence Forces found that around 35 per cent of females and 27 per cent of males experienced harassment. Furthermore, around 78 per cent of female respondents and 72 per cent of male respondents said the alleged perpetrator was a person who was senior in rank. The perpetrators were alleged to be almost all male: around 96 per cent of females and 98 per cent of males reporting harassment were harassed by males. Bullying was experienced by almost 27 per cent of all respondents. (External Advisory Committee on the Defence Forces, 2002) As a result of these investigations, the defence forces subsequently developed a comprehensive set of guidelines on bullying and harassment. (Irish Defence Forces, 2006)

The report also significantly commented: "This is the first time [in Ireland] that the issues of harassment, bullying, discrimination and sexual harassment have been the focus of research throughout an organisation. The model established ... might become a challenge to other organisations and workplaces to reflect on....". (External Advisory Committee on the Defence Forces, 2002: 2)

THE GARDAÍ

As the experience of women in the Irish military shows, low representation of particular groups may be linked to marginalisation within the organisation, and mistreatment in various ways, especially bullying. However, despite the efforts of police and military forces to deal with these issues in different ways, underrepresentation of minority groups remains a persistent pattern in police forces worldwide.

The persistence of underrepresentation has a number of very significant consequences.

The first is the impact that low representation has on an organisation's ability to respond meaningfully to concerns that specific groups may have. A second issue relates to the level of trust that the police can command within underrepresented communities.

Surveys of public opinion in Ireland consistently record high levels of public confidence in the gardaí. (See Q2.6) However, marginalised groups persistently have the lowest levels of confidence. While support by the majority of the population is vital, most of the population will have had little or no contentious contact with the gardaí. Effective policing and building good community relations with marginalised or minority groups critically depends on the gardaí commanding trust among those groups with whom they are routinely involved in difficult or hostile situations. In this regard, building trust within minority and marginalised communities requires a willingness on the part of the gardaí to demonstrate inclusiveness, and to build confidence among members of these same communities that they too would be welcomed as members of the force.

Composition of the Gardaí

In a recent survey of members of the gardaí, only 15 per cent of members questioned believed the gardaí was representative of Ireland's diverse communities. (An Garda Síochána, 2004: 103)

Table 8.1 Composition of Gardaí December 2005

		Male	*Female*
Commissioner	1	1	
Deputy Commissioner	2	2	
Assistant Commissioner	12	11	1
Chief Superintendent	47	44	3
Superintendent	173	168	5
Inspector	289	271	18
Sergeant	1,926	1,779	147
Garda	9,815	7,809	2,006
Total	12,265	10,085	2,180

Source: An Garda Síochána, 2005: 5

According to the Census 2002, women made up just over 13 per cent of all gardaí, (Central Statistics Office, 2003b) although updated figures from the Garda Annual Report 2005 show that women in 2005 represented around 18 per cent of the force overall. At the same time, however, only 7 per cent of those ranked above Garda were women. Women within the gardaí tend to be younger, reflecting the fact that women have only joined the force in greater numbers in recent years. The first woman Assistant Commissioner was appointed as recently as 2003.

Various international studies raise concerns in regard to the sexist nature of many police forces. Research in the UK on how the British police force dealt with complaints of sexual assault revealed an empowered male, racist culture that was in denial with regard to the prevelance of racism and sexism within the ranks. (Gregory and Lees, 1999) A similar study on English and Welsh police found that nearly all of the 1,800 females surveyed had experienced sexual harassment. Preliminary research in Ireland suggests that female gardaí would not complain about sexual harassment and bullying as no reliable independent complaint mechanisms exists, and those who do complain invariably face negative consequences in return. (An Garda Síochána, 2004: 106) In-depth research into the extent of bullying and harassment as defined by the External Advisory Committee on the Defence Forces has, to date, not been carried out within the gardaí, and the extent of bullying and harassment within the organisation remains a cause for concern.

In addition to the underrepresentation of women, minority communities are underrepresented within the force with demonstrably adverse consequences for policing.

The Consequences of Underrepresentation Within the Gardaí

Efforts have been made within An Garda Síochána to address issues of underrepresentation and the policing of minority and marginalised communities. In 1999, the gardaí established a Human Rights Office and a Human Rights Working Group as part of a Council of Europe programme on Policing and Human Rights. In 2004, an independent human rights audit of An Garda Síochána, commissioned by the Human Rights Working Group, was published. This report in itself is an extremely positive development.

Among the report's main findings were: that many members report bullying and harassment despite the existence of a manifest anti-bullying policy; that despite progress in the recruitment of women in recent years, career development and progression remain imbalanced against women; and that there was an urgent need for diversity and race relations training, starting with senior managers, to address the issue of institutional discrimination. (An Garda Síochána, 2004: 96)

A strong theme which emerged from the human rights audit was the evident degree of antipathy towards various minority groups among garda personnel. In a survey conducted as part of the audit, over 1200 members of the gardaí were asked how they would assess An Garda Síochána's overall relationship with various communities.

As shown below, the results identify Travellers and refugees and asylum seekers as the groups most likely to have a poor relationship with the gardaí.

Table 8.2 Community Relations with the Gardaí

How would you assess An Garda Síochána's overall relationship with the following communities?

	Good	*OK*	*Poor*	*Don't Know*	*No Answer*
Women	73%	23%	1%	2%	1%
People with disabilities	68%	24%	5%	3%	1%
Young people	48%	40%	9%	2%	1%
Black & other ethnic minority groups	35%	45%	13%	6%	1%
Gay & lesbian communities	26%	39%	17%	17%	2%
Faith groups	24%	42%	14%	18%	2%
Refugees & asylum seekers	21%	48%	24%	6%	2%
Travellers	15%	46%	35%	2%	2%

Source: Adapted from An Garda Síochána, 2004: 84

In addition, extremely prejudicial and stereotypical views of certain communities were expressed by members at all ranks within the force which, the auditors concluded, could only impact negatively on the policing of particular minority communities, lead to a disrespect for the rights of those communities, and a failure to protect individuals from those communities from abuse. Allegations about levels of criminality among the Traveller and Nigerian communities in particular were made by individuals at every level within the force, with little hard evidence to substantiate them. Concerns were also expressed by the auditors regarding the views of respondents towards the Muslim community. (An Garda Síochána, 2004: 140)

Descriptions of discrimination described by those community representatives consulted by the auditors were also supported by reports from non-governmental organisations. (An Garda Síochána, 2004: 93) The audit concluded that tackling institutional discrimination must be made a key priority for the organisation. This involves both recruitment of more members of minority and marginalised communities into the force and the provision of training to address the high prevalence of negative stereotypes of various minority communities at all levels within the force.

GARDA RELATIONS WITHIN DISADVANTAGED AREAS

Policing of disadvantaged areas is a particular challenge for all police forces. Many residents living in marginalised areas in cities around Ireland expressed the view to the Human Rights Audit that the police were concerned mainly with the containment of their communities, and that victims of crime within those areas often find themselves either ignored or accorded a low priority by gardaí. Accounts of police misconduct, particularly physical mistreatment of young males, circulate widely, and members of marginalised communities complain of having little opportunity to provide input into the policing they receive.

Critical for the effective policing of disadvantaged communities is the fact that surveys reveal the lowest levels of confidence in the gardaí among young males from working class backgrounds. Residents in disadvantaged areas typically have far higher levels of involvement with the criminal justice agencies, both as victims and offenders, than the general population, while young men from disadvantaged areas are massively overrepresented among the prison population. (See Q2.5)

Illegal drug use has also seriously impacted both on crime levels within socially disadvantaged areas, and on the relations between gardaí and the populations living in those areas over the last several decades.

The resources available for community policing in socially marginalised areas, where they do exist, are low, despite evidence that community policing works. In areas where community policing fora exist, 70 per cent of community respondents believe that garda services have improved, 72 per cent stated they would be more willing to cooperate with the gardaí in relation to drug-related crime, and 59 per cent in relation to non-drug related crime. (Connolly, 2004)

However, aside from underresourced police community fora in some areas, there has been no tradition of formal police-community consultation in Ireland. This pattern is set to change. The Garda Síochána Act 2005 provides for the first time for formal links between the police and the community. This new legislation has the potential to provide the basis for the very consultation and input into policing that marginalised communities have been seeking for decades.

Garda Relations with the Travelling Community

In 2005, only about three officers, in a force of approximately 12,000, came from Traveller backgrounds. (Mulcahy and O'Mahony, 2005: 22)

Relations meanwhile between Travellers and the police are shaped by a historical legacy of conflict and distrust. In the survey of over 1,200 uniformed gardaí and civilian support staff conducted as part of the Human Rights Audit in 2004, 81 per cent of gardaí classified their relationship with the Traveller community as either "ok" or "poor." (An Garda Síochána, 2004: 84)

In an earlier survey carried out by Amnesty International in 2001, 37 per cent of Travellers claimed to have experienced discrimination from the gardaí, while 57 per cent of all ethnic minorities groups surveyed, including Travellers, said they thought they would not be welcome as members of the gardaí. (An Garda Síochána, 2004: 79)

In addition to being over-policed, Travellers persistently complain about being underprotected by the police. In the Human Rights Audit of 2004, members of the Traveller community expressed particular concern about the poor response from gardaí to Traveller women who are victims of domestic violence. (An Garda Síochána, 2004: 91)

Many of the difficulties between gardaí and Travellers are associated with the latter being denied access to, or removed from particular locations, most notably campsites and social venues such as public houses. Moreover, these instances are likely to continue to disrupt relationships between Travellers and the gardaí until such a time as the underlying issues of Traveller accommodation and discrimination against Travellers in access to social venues, in particular, are resolved within the wider Irish society.

Garda Relations with Ethnic Minority Communities

There are very few members of minority ethnic communities in An Garda Síochána at present. As a result, two recent initiatives have been introduced within the gardaí aimed at addressing the deficits with regard to representation for minority ethnic communities. These are changes in recruitment procedures designed to encourage more members of ethnic minorities to apply, and the appointment of ethnic liaison officers to work with ethnic minority communities.

Ethnic minority liaison officers were first appointed in 2002. This position involves no extra pay, but officers do undergo intercultural training before taking on the role. Superintendents are responsible for appointing ethnic liaison officers, with one or more usually being appointed in areas with high immigrant populations. These posts are generally not full-time positions.

It is recognised that the role of members of the gardaí in immigration law enforcement can cause conflict with some minority communities and undermine garda efforts at establishing good community relations. As such, the Human Rights Audit recommended the establishment of a separate immigration enforcement agency as a means of reducing potential conflicts. (An Garda Síochána, 2004: 143)

Despite the recognition of this issue, however, the establishment of ethnic minority liaison officers was seriously mishandled. In 2004, one fifth of those appointed were at the same time members of the Garda National Immigration Bureau (GNIB). This dual responsibility resulted in untenable situations wherein some gardaí assigned to establishing good relations with ethic minorities were simultaneously carrying out immigration crackdowns.

The Irish Council for Civil Liberties among others highlighted this situation as completely inappropriate. Moreover, such dual roles also serve to compound an existing reluctance among immigrants to report racially motivated crime. As a result, appointment of immigration police officers to ethnic liaison roles was to be reviewed to ensure all of the former were removed from the list of ethnic liaison officers. Overall, however, the establishment of ethnic liaison officers represents a necessary and positive development.

A second positive development has occurred in relation to the requirements for recruitment to the gardaí. In 2005 the requirement to hold a qualification in both Irish and English in the Leaving Certificate or equivalent was replaced by a requirement to hold a qualification in two languages, at least one of which must be Irish or English.

This change is designed to open up entry to An Garda Síochána to persons in Ireland from all parts of the community and from all ethnic backgrounds. In introducing the change, the Minister for Justice, Equality and Law Reform said the amended requirement recognised that Irish society was becoming increasingly multiethnic and multicultural, and that the old requirement for garda trainees to hold an academic qualification in Irish was a barrier for many persons. (Department for Justice, Equality and Law Reform, 2005b) The change was widely welcomed as a significant first step by ethnic minority organisations and NGOs.

Garda Relations with the Gay Community

European surveys have shown that levels of violence directed against lesbian, gay and bisexual people are up to three times higher than those experienced by the population as a whole. The likelihood of verbal or physical assault for same-sex couples walking hand in hand down the main street of any Irish town or city is quite high. Research shows that lesbian couples are doubly at risk because of their gender, and that such assaults often take the form of stone throwing and verbal abuse directed towards their home. Non-reporting to the gardaí is particularly prevalent among lesbian, gay and bisexual (LGB) victims of assault. (www.equality.ie)

There has been significant progress in the development of relations between the gardaí and the LGB community in recent years. A submission by the LGB community to the National Crime Forum in 1998 began a formal process of consultation. Liaison officers to the community have been appointed in a number of locations throughout the country and input into the training for these officers has been provided by the LGB community.

However Ireland, unlike the UK and other European countries, does not yet have an officially recognised Gay Police Association to offer support and recognition to lesbian and gay members and represent them at hearings associated with homophobia. Furthermore, homophobic or anti-gay sentiments are rife within the gardaí, according to gay and lesbian garda officers, who also report that overtly homophobic comments from fellow members are commonplace, and homophobia is either accepted or, at best, left unchallenged by senior officers. (*Irish Examiner*, 10 February 2006)

INCREASING THE SAFEGUARDS FOR THE POLICING OF UNDER-REPRESENTED COMMUNITIES

The recommendations of the 2004 Human Rights Audit of An Garda Síochána provide a blueprint for action to ensure greater safeguards in the policing of minority communities.

Its findings of widespread institutional racism highlighted the need for a comprehensive programme of training at all levels within the force. At the time of the audit there was no comprehensive provision of either human rights training or equality and diversity training across the organisation, and while there is some community involvement, e.g., from Pavee Point and the LGB community, this input has yet to become systematic or routine.

The audit also found the Racial and Intercultural Office, which operates within the community relations section of the gardaí with responsibility for the development and implementation of policies on racial, ethnic, religious and cultural diversity, is underresourced.

Among the report's recommendations was the establishment of a high-level strategic advisory committee, including external membership as well as senior garda representation, to implement the audit's core recommendations, and the need to undertake a human rights impact assessment of all existing and forthcoming policy and operational procedures. (An Garda Síochána, 2004: 137) Overall, the findings of the Human Rights Audit provide a clear way forward to more effective minority representation within the gardaí and more effective policing as a result.

Q8.4 How free is the country from the operation of paramilitary units, private armies, warlordism and criminal mafias?

Concerns around criminal gangs in Ireland centre on two issues – drug gangs and paramilitary organisations. Two murders which occurred in 1996, of Detective Garda Jerry McCabe during an attempted robbery by the IRA, and of investigative journalist Veronica Guerin by organised criminals involved in the drugs trade, brought the issue of organised crime centre stage. These murders, which occurred within weeks of each other, and the political reaction to them, have had a lasting effect, both in the enforcement of drugs policy and on exaggerated public perceptions of the prevalence of crime in Ireland.

While Ireland does not yet rank in the top league of countries affected by organised crime, the Europol Report *European Union Organised Crime Situation Report 2005* does point out that Irish criminals are thought to be cooperating in drug trafficking into Ireland in tandem with established groups in other EU countries.

ORGANISED CRIME AND THE EU

Organised criminal activity in the European Union has grown enormously in the past decade. (Europol, 2005) Although organised crime is not a new phenomenon, the fall of Communism and the creation of the European Union have provided increased impetus for organised crime across the continent, with the lack of "internal frontiers" across Europe resulting in the freer movement of increasingly sophisticated organised criminal groups between East and West.

During the early 1990s, established criminal gangs from western Europe moved quickly into eastern Europe and Russia to tap into the emerging markets for drugs and to secure their position in the important drugs-trafficking routes coming out of Asia. Russian organised crime was also quick to exploit the new opportunities and has in turn extended its operations westward, where it is now thought to be heavily involved in the production and trafficking of synthetic designer drugs such as ecstacy in Europe.

Money laundering, the processing of "dirty" money into "clean" untraceable funds, is another key area of organised criminal activity, and essential in concealing the massive profits made from drugs trafficking. It has been estimated that $150 billion is laundered internationally every year, and "legitimate" banks have been reputed to be involved in laundering money for organised criminal groups. (Tupman, 2006)

The social consequences of organised crime are far-reaching. The impact of drugs trafficking on society is especially obvious and destructive. In addition, because of the vast profits made by organised crime, organised criminals can in turn pose a particular threat to the democratic process. This situation is particularly the case, for example, in Russia, Eastern Europe and the transition countries of the

Commonwealth of Independent States, where involvement of organised crime in politics is a source of concern for the functioning of these new democracies.

On an economic level, the amount of revenue that is lost to countries, particularly in eastern Europe and Russia, from non-taxable profits and money laundering by organised crime is immense. (Tupman, 2006)

The drugs trade represents the most important market for organised crime. The scale of the illegal drugs sector is vast and international. A significant proportion of international police cooperation is specifically related to the smuggling of illegal drugs, and the activities of criminal gangs in this sphere have wide-ranging implications for criminal justice policy and the absorption of criminal justice resources that otherwise would be used to deal with various "ordinary" crimes.

Furthermore, the issue of links between criminal gangs and paramilitary organisations – whether in relation to violent competition between them, or cooperation through the sharing of personnel, intelligence, expertise, weaponry etc. – is significant, especially given the need of paramilitary organisations to finance their activites.

ORGANISED CRIME IN IRELAND

Major concerns around criminal gangs in Ireland centre on two issues – drug gangs and paramilitary organisations. The Europol Report *European Union Organised Crime Situation Report 2005* lists the major organised crime groups in Europe as being Albanian, Bulgarian, Dutch, German, Italian, Lithuanian, Polish, Russian, Romanian, and Turkish. Ireland does not yet rank in the top league of countries affected by organised crime. However, the report does point out that organised crime groups are becoming increasingly more heterogeneous, and Irish criminals are thought to be based either temporarily or permanently in Holland and Spain, where they cooperate in drug trafficking into Ireland with Dutch and Belgian groups.

Organised Crime and Paramilitaries

That paramilitary organisations are involved in organised crime in Northern Ireland is widely accepted by law enforcement agencies and the public. A 2006 survey in Northern Ireland found that 96 per cent of those surveyed thought that there was a problem with organised crime, and 77 per cent thought that paramilitary organisations were mainly responsible. (Wilson, 2006)

To address this, the Northern Ireland Organised Crime Task Force was created in 2000 to tackle organised crime and its link to paramilitaries, bringing together the Police Service for Northern Ireland, the Revenue and Customs, the Home Office, the Assets Recovery Agency, the Serious Organised Crime Agency and other UK government agencies.

The signing of the Good Friday Agreement resulted in increased cooperation between law enforcement agencies on each side of the border. A joint report, issued by An Garda Síochána and the Police Service of Northern Ireland in 2004, identified eight key areas of concern with regard to organised crime affecting both jurisdictions: drug trafficking; money laundering; alcohol fraud; tobacco fraud; oils fraud; intellectual properties crime; counterfeiting; vehicle crime; and immigration crime. Of these issues, drug crime is the single most serious threat to law and order.

The report points out a significant difference between the illegal drugs markets on either side of the border. In Ireland, cocaine and heroin represent the most sizeable part of the drugs market, while in Northern Ireland cannabis and ecstacy remain the most commonly used drugs. (An Garda Síochána/Police Service of Northern Ireland, 2004)

Drug Crime in Ireland

The impact of drug trafficking on Irish society has been destructive of both lives and communities. The types of crimes associated with drug distribution include gangland murders and battles over organisational and territorial issues; disputes over transactions and debt collection; and corruption of business and government officials. Third-party violence can include injury or death to bystanders; while drug-related crimes and associated anti-social behaviour can destroy the fabric of entire communities.

Problems associated with drug trafficking and drug use impact disproportionately on certain sections of the population and within certain geographic areas. Research on seven local authority estates, although somewhat dated, highlights the problems of social disorder – through direct experience of anti-social behaviour, loss of sense of personal safety, community-wide loss of safe communal spaces, and negative labelling of the estates in the wider community – which profoundly affect the quality of life of the residents of areas where drug abuse is prevalent. (Fahey, 1999)

Two murders which occurred in 1996, of Detective Garda Jerry McCabe during an attempted robbery by the IRA, and of investigative journalist Veronica Guerin by organised criminals involved in the drug trade, brought the issue of organised crime centre stage. These closely spaced murders and political reaction to them have had a lasting effect, both in the enforcement of a more draconian crime policy and on exaggerated public perceptions of the prevalence of crime in Ireland.

Prosecutions for drug-related offences in Ireland have increased since these murders. Over the same period there has also been a sharp increase in so-called "gangland" murders involving members of drug gangs. Between 1972 and 1991, only two incidents of homicide could be attributed to gangland feuding. (Dooley, 2001) In 2005, up to 21 such murders took place, accounting for around one in three of all homicides that year.

In response to the murders of Guerin and Detective Garda McCabe in 1996, the Oireachtas has enacted a series of measures to protect against drug gangs and organised crime. The Criminal Justice (Drug Trafficking) Act 1996, the Proceeds of Crime Act 1996, and the Criminal Assets Bureau Act 1996 were the principle legislative responses.

The Proceeds of Crime Act allows the state to remove the property of citizens that it believes to be the proceeds of crime, without the requirement of a criminal conviction. The Criminal Assets Bureau Act allowed for the establishment of the Criminal Assets Bureau, a multi-agency body designed to target such assets and staffed by officers from An Garda Síochána, the Revenue Commissioners and the Department of Social, Community & Family Affairs.

The Criminal Assets Bureau (CAB) seized almost €19 million from criminals in 2004 and froze assets and cash worth almost €6 million that same year. (Criminal Assets Bureau, 2004) This total brought to €140 million the value of cash and other assets that the CAB has frozen or secured for the state since its inception in 1996 up to the end of 2004. (*Irish Times*, 21 October 2005)

In 1996, the government also held a referendum to expand the reasons for refusal of bail to include the committing of a serious offence while on bail along with the traditional grounds of the risk of someone accused of a serious offence absconding while on bail. (Daly, 2004)

The referendum was carried in a 75 per cent Yes vote, although less than 30 per cent of the electorate took part. The statutory change effected by this referendum has also contributed significantly to a dramatic increase in the prison population since 1996. (See Section Two)

PUBLIC PERCEPTIONS OF CRIME IN IRELAND

Despite the fact that Ireland is, by international standards, one of the safest countries in which to live, with an average homicide rate below the EU average, crime has grown enough in recent years to become one of the major issues of concern among the Irish public. A Eurobarometer survey of EU public opinion in 2006 found that more than half of Irish people identify crime as one of the two foremost issues of concern facing the country, compared with the EU average of 22 per cent. (Eurobarometer, 2006)

Crime has not always been such a high profile issue in Ireland, as shown in public opinion surveys covering every general election between 1981 and 2006. (Kilcommins *et al.*, 2004: 132) The three foremost issues in the minds of the electorate in each election are shown in Table 8.3 below.

Table 8.3 Public Perceptions of Major Issues of Societal Concern 1981-2001

	Number 1 Issue	Number 2 Issue	Number 3 Issue
1981	Unemployment (41%)	Prices/Cost of Living (25%)	NI/Security (14%)
1982	Unemployment (36%)	Prices/Cost of Living (16%)	National Debt (12%)
1982	Unemployment (45%)	Stable Government (17%)	Cost of Living (16%)
1987	Unemployment (85%)	Taxation (45%)	Cost of Living (26%)
1989	Unemployment (78%)	Health Service (41%)	Emigration (34%)
1992	Unemployment (86%)	Health Service (22%)	Taxation (15%)
1997	Crime (41%)	Unemployment (40%)	Drugs (22%)
2001	Health service (34%)	Prices/Cost of Living (29%)	House Prices (21%)
2006	Crime (50%)*	Health Service (45%)*	Prices/ Inflation (22%)*

Source: Compiled from Kilcommins *et al.*, 2004: 133-139 and Eurobarometer, 2006: 9
* Eurobarometer results where respondents were asked to name top two issues facing their country. Figures show percentages who named these issues as being in top two.

The effects of the economic boom can be clearly seen in the disappearance of unemployment as a major public concern. Of particular note here, however, is the reference to crime for the first time in 1997, shortly after the murders of Veronica Guerin and Jerry McCabe. Crime as an issue of major public concern disappeared in the 2001 surveys and emerged again in 2006.

THE POLITICS OF CRIME

In the 1997 election, Fianna Fáil campaigned as the "zero tolerance" party with a promise to get tough on crime. Since election to office, successive Fianna Fáil/Progressive Democrat governments have pursued such a policy. Prison numbers in Ireland have increased dramatically as a result and further legislative responses, particularly the Criminal Justice Act 2006, continue to introduce tougher measures to deal with criminal behaviour, particularly drug crime.

Some of the legislative measures introduced since 1996 have come under criticism from civil society organisations on the basis that they erode basic civil rights. The Criminal Justice (Drug Trafficking) Act 1996 for example allows for the detention of persons suspected of committing drug trafficking offences for up to seven days, allows possible inferences to be drawn if a suspect exercises the right to remain silent, and allows search warrants to be issued by senior gardaí without recourse to the courts. The Proceeds of Crime Act 1996 and the Criminal Assets Bureau Act 1996 also allow for the forfeiture of private property without any judicial finding of guilt. (Daly, 2004: 17)

The Criminal Justice Act 2006 includes a further range of anti-crime measures designed to enhance the powers of the gardaí in the investigation and prosecution of offences. These measures include increased powers for gardaí in relation to the issue of search warrants; increased detention powers of up to 24 hours for arrestable offences; provision on the admissibility of statements by witnesses who subsequently refuse to testify or retract their original statements; the establishment of a new offence of membership of an organised criminal gang; and provisions to strengthen sentencing for drug trafficking and firearms.

Public support exists for policies which are tough on crime and political mileage is to be gained from highlighting crime as a major issue. Media coverage of crime, particularly drug crime and gangland murders, continues to feed the cycle. Nevertheless, overcrowded prisons, heightened public concern over crime, and more and more repressive legislation all belie the fact that Ireland remains, for most of its citizens, one of the safest countries in the world in which to live.

Being emphatically "tough on crime" also makes it difficult to have a more balanced debate on both the true threats to democracy from drug crime, and the balance of policies – be they dismantling criminal gangs and ensuring that Ireland does not become a major international player in organised crime; initiatives to alleviate the effects of drug crime on communities most affected; enforcing the law for those individuals in breach; initiatives to reduce secondary crimes committed by drug users; and alternatives to prison for individual drug abusers – that is needed to address these threats.

Nine: Integrity in Public Life

Are public officials, elected or appointed, free from corruption?

INTRODUCTION AND SUMMARY

Corruption – the abuse of public office for private, personal or party gain – is particularly damaging to a democracy as it undermines the relationship of trust between the people and their elected government. The purpose of democratic government is to serve the public interest, not the private interests of office holders or their personal circle. Confidence in government can be quickly eroded if people suspect or indeed know that politicians or public officials are using their official position, funded by taxpayers, to further their own interests.

However, the precise parameters of what constitutes "corruption" are difficult to define with certainty. We could distinguish a number of different forms of impropriety, such as "conflicts of interest" on the part of ministers or parliamentarians, lack of impartiality by office holders more generally, the purchase of political influence by private interests through the funding of political parties or other favours, and so on. The UN has also published an international code of conduct for public officials and a convention on corruption; and there are now accepted standards of good practice for legislation to combat these different forms of impropriety.

There is also the question of how well do Irish procedures measure up to these international standards? After a number of high-profile cases of wrongdoing in both the public and private sectors, a substantial body of new legislation has been adopted over the past decade to prevent their recurrence. For example, the Ethics Acts of 1995 and 2001 require the compulsory disclosure of interests that might conflict with the public duties of office holders, including ministers and Oireachtas members, under the supervision of a Standards in Public Office Commission. The Prevention of Corruption (Amendment) Act of 2001 and the Proceeds of Crime (Amendment) Act of 2005 strengthen the legislation against corruption in both public and private sectors. Various independent tribunals have been established to investigate high-profile cases of alleged impropriety; and the Commissions of Investigation Act of 2004 strengthens procedures for the future investigation of such cases. A raft of recent legislation has also served to make the financing of political parties more transparent, to limit donor influence, and to tighten the control of election expenditure.

Most of this legislation conforms to international standards of good practice, and should serve over time to increase public confidence in the integrity of government. Some weaknesses in the legislation have, however, been identified; for example, the Standards Commission can only work reactively, in response to a complaint, and that complaints against members of the Oireachtas are investigated by fellow members. There is also poor protection for "whistle-blowers" who report evidence of corrupt practice. Limits on election expenditure only apply for the immediate electoral period itself, and can impact unevenly on the different political parties. Finally, there remains considerable public concern about the preponderant influence of particular business sectors on government.

Q 9.1 How effective is the separation of public office, elected and unelected, from party advantage and the personal business and family interests of office holders?

The Ethics in Public Office Act 1995 and the Standards in Public Office Act 2001, commonly referred to as "the Ethics Acts", introduced for the first time the compulsory annual disclosure of interests for members of the Oireachtas. The Standards in Public Office Commission was established under the 2001 Act as an independent statutory body with the power to investigate and report on contraventions of the legislation.

Few cases have so far been taken under the legislation and a strong criticism of the current system is that the Standards in Public Office Commission can only initiate an investigation of its own volition on the basis of information in the public domain. Furthermore, the Commission is not empowered to appoint an Inquiry Officer unless a complaint has been received. This situation makes it easier for individuals who do not register their interests to evade detection. Sanctions so far levied against those found to be in breach of the legislation have been lenient, although the public attention which the Commission's investigations have attracted has had very real consequences for the individual TDs involved.

The introduction of legislation for the first time in the history of the state for the compulsory disclosure of interests for members of the Oireachtas, is a significant development in preventing future corruption. Further strenthening of the powers of the Standards in Public Office Commission to allow it to initiate investigations in the absence of the receipt of a complaint would act as a further deterrent to corruption by members of the Oireachtas.

LEGISLATIVE PROVISION TO ENSURE INTEGRITY

The obligation of public officials to declare various interests is set out in the UN Convention on Corruption, which deals extensively with the issue of personal and business interests of office-holders, and requires each state party to adopt systems that promote transparency and prevent conflicts of interest. Ireland signed the convention in December 2003 buts its ratification is still pending.

A raft of domestic legislation has in fact been introduced to combat corruption in recent years, including legislation specifically aimed at preventing conflicts of interest. The primary legislation in this area is the Ethics in Public Office Act 1995 and the Standards in Public Office Act 2001, which are commonly referred to as the Ethics Acts. The broad focus of the Ethics Acts is to provide for disclosure of interests which could influence a government minister or minister of state, a member of the Houses of the Oireachtas or a public servant in performing their official duties. (Standards in Public Office Commission, 2006)

The 2001 Act provided for the establishment of the Standards in

Public Office Commission, an independent statutory body chaired by a judge of the High Court, who is appointed by the President on the recommendation of the government following a resolution of both Houses of Parliament. Its other members include the Comptroller and Auditor General, the Clerk of the Dáil, the Clerk of the Seanad, the Ombudsman (all ex officio members) and a former member of the Dáil who has served as a minister and MEP, all of whom are appointed by the government, following a resolution of both Houses of Parliament.

The principal functions of the Commission are to administer the disclosure of interests and to investigate and report on possible contraventions of the legislation. The Commission has developed guidelines for Office Holders and Public Servants which set out their duties and obligations under the Ethics Acts. It should also be noted that the Commission must pass on any case that concerns corrupt activity to the Director of Public Prosecutions (DPP). According to the guidelines established in the 1995 Act, members of Dáil or Seanad Éireann are required to furnish a statement of registrable interests including:

- occupational income;
- shares in excess of £10,000;
- directorships or shadow directorships;
- interests in land and buildings exceeding £10,000, excluding private home;
- gifts of over £500;
- property or services supplied to the person at a price considerably below the commercial value;
- travel facilities, including living accommodation, meals or entertainment which were supplied at a price below the commercial value; and
- remunerated positions as a political or public affairs lobbyist, consultant or adviser, and contracts with the state.

In addition, all members of the Dáil and Seanad are required to disclose any material interest they or a connected person might have if they are voting or speaking in the proceedings of either House so that:

- where a member proposes to speak, she must make a declaration of the material interest in the proceedings before or during her speech; and

- where he proposes to vote, he must make the necessary declaration in writing and give it to the Clerk of the relevant Committee before voting.

INVESTIGATIONS CARRIED OUT UNDER LEGISLATION

The Ethics in Public Office Act 1995 provided for a Committee for each House of the Oireachtas: the Committee on Members' Interests of Dáil Éireann and the Committee on Members' Interests of Seanad Éireann, respectively.

Only one investigation was conducted by either the Dáil or Seanad Éireann Members' Interests Committees. In September 1997, Denis Foley, then a Fianna Fáil TD, voted on a Dáil motion concerning the investigation into Ansbacher accounts and deposits. At the time he had an Ansbacher account, which allowed individuals to avoid paying tax by locating money in an offshore bank account, yet simultaneously have access to their money here in Ireland. Foley resigned from the Fianna Fáil parliamentary party in early 2000 when it was revealed that he was under investigation. (*Irish Times*, 24 May 2000) A complaint was made by the Labour Party leader Ruairi Quinn under section 7 of the 1995 Act. (*Irish Times*, 11 May 2000) Foley appeared before the Committee and admitted he had breached the Ethics Act.

The Committee presented a report to the Houses of the Oireachtas. According to the Committee, "the potential benefit to Deputy Foley as a result of his contravention [in that he might have avoided investigation by the Moriarty Tribunal and examination by the Revenue Commissioners of his monies held offshore] was of such significance that the contravention cannot be regarded as minor". (Committee on Members' Interests, 2000) The Committee recommended that Foley be suspended for 14 days. A resolution to that effect was put to, and approved by, the Dáil. The brevity of the suspension period was the subject of heavy criticism by both the media and other TDs. (*Irish Times*, 20 May 2000)

Since its establishment, only one full investigation has been conducted by the Standards in Public Office Commission in relation to a contravention of the disclosure of interests-related provisions of the Ethics Acts.

In 2001, the Commission found that Deputy Ned O'Keeffe, while

Minister of State at the Department of Agriculture, Food and Rural Development, failed, either before or during a speech in the Dáil in November, 2000, to declare a material interest which he had in the subject matter of the proceedings before the Dáil. In this case, the contravention was determined by the Commission to be unintentional.

More recently, in 2005, the Commission considered whether a full enquiry should be launched with regard to allegations of impropriety in the awarding of public relations contracts by the then-Minister for the Environment, Martin Cullen. The evidence available to the Standards Commission included a report prepared by Dermot Quigley, who had been charged by the government with investigating contracts between Monica Leech and departments and offices under Minister Cullen's direct political control, and the documentation furnished to the Standards Commission by the Office of Public Works and the Department of the Environment, Heritage and Local Government on foot of orders for discovery made by the Chairman of the Standards Commission. (Standards in Public Office Commission, 2005b) Dermot Quigley's report cleared the Minister of wrong-doing in relation to established procedures but stated that he had left himself open to a "perception of impropriety" by proposing his supporter for the work. *(Irish Times*, 5 February 2005) Following this report, the Taoiseach immediately moved to withdraw from ministers the power to directly hire public relations consultants from the private sector. The Commission concluded that the evidence before it did not establish a *prima facie* case which would have warranted an investigation within the terms of the Ethics Acts. The lack of clarity in the Commission's reasoning in this case is problematic, however, as it remains unclear in what circumstances such an enquiry would be conducted in the future.

That there is still a gap in the current legislation was shown by the recent revelation (*Irish Times*, 27 September 2006) that the current Taoiseach, Bertie Ahern, accepted loans and donations totalling €60,000 in 1993 and 1994. The acceptance of similar loans and donations falls within the current legal parameters, subject to disclosure. Furthermore, the affair raises questions about the continued prevalence of a political culture which argues about the letter of the legislation while avoiding a wholehearted acceptance of its spirit.

As a result of the political scandal caused by the revelations, the government has now announced new legislation to regulate the acceptance by ministers of gifts from friends. The proposed changes to the

Ethics in Public Office Act 1995 will mean that ministers will be prohibited by law from taking any gift unless they can show that its acceptance would not cause a conflict of interest. Ministers will have to brief the Standards in Public Office Commission confidentially before they accept anything of value from friends or anyone else. However, drafting of the legislation is not expected to be easy since the Commission sought a legal definition of "a friend" six years previously from the government without success. (*Irish Times*, 27 September 2006)

SHORTCOMINGS OF THE LEGISLATION

A number of further shortcomings in the existing legislation can be identified based on the experiences of the Standards in Public Office Commission as outlined to date above:

Inability to Initiate Investigations

The Commission can only initiate an investigation of its own volition on the basis of information in the public domain, or once a complaint is made in relation to a specified act or a contravention of the Ethics Acts. Furthermore, the Commission is not empowered to appoint an Inquiry Officer unless a complaint has been received. The system of interest registration is therefore largely based on trust supported by the complaints mechanism.

In its 2004 annual report, the Commission recommended that the legislation should be amended so that an Inquiry Officer can be appointed in cases where the Commission wishes to pursue a matter under the legislation in the absence of a complaint. This amendment would potentially greatly increase the number of investigations that the Commision could carry out and increase the deterrance against wrong-doing, but this recommendation has not been given effect by government.

Peer Culture among Oireachtas Committee Members

There are obvious problems in relation to the provision in the Ethics Acts that investigations in relation to complaints brought against members of the Oireachtas who are non-office holders are to be investigated by a committee made up of other members of the Oireachtas. Perhaps one of the most dramatic illustrations of the problematic situations that can result is illustrated by the fact that Liam Lawlor was a member of the Dáil Committee on Members' Interests which investigated the complaint against Denis Foley at the same time Liam Lawlor himself was being investigated by the Flood Tribunal. (*Irish Times*, 22 April 2000) Anecdotal evidence suggests that TDs do not wish to sit on this Committee because of their reluctance to sit in judgement on their peers.

Another weakness, specific to complaints against ministers is that if enough evidence to form a *prima facie* case ever surfaces against a cabinet minister, that individual is likely to have either resigned or been sacked by the Taoiseach before the Commission completes its investigation.

A similar problem arises in relation to complaints to/investigations by the respective Members' Committees. Namely, if the person under investigation ceases to be a member of the Oireachtas at any time before the Committee produces its report on an investigation, the Committee shall take no further steps in relation to the matter unless the person under investigation requests the Committee to do so. As such, a member may avoid investigation or sanction by resigning his/her post.

It has also been argued that, burdened by increasingly complex legislation that is difficult if not impossible to implement, the Commission is doing little to restore public confidence in the system.

Lack of Deterrents

It can be argued that the sanctions under the Ethics Act do not act as a sufficient deterrent, given their relative weakness and the tendency– as is clear from the cases described above – not to fully apply them in cases brought to date. On the other hand, the primary sanction is arguably that of public opprobrium, seeing that where a full inquiry is launched against a minister, TD, or Senator there will be calls for him or her to step aside. This argument is strengthened by the fact that the two cases investigated under the legislation to date resulted in Deputy Foley resigning from the parliamentary party, while Deputy Ned O'Keeffe resigned as Minister of State.

Restrictions on Subsequent Employment

Another measure under the UN Convention on Corruption aimed at preventing conflicts of interest is the imposition of restrictions, "for a reasonable period of time, on the professional activities of former public officials or on the employment of public officials by the private sector after their resignation or retirement, where such activities or employment relate directly to the functions held or supervised by those public officials during their tenure". Such restrictions are now in place for civil servants and for local authorities.

However, no such restrictions are placed on TDs in Ireland as yet, although certain restrictions are in place with respect to office holders (i.e., ministers, ministers of state, chairman of Dáil Éireann and chairman of Seanad Éireann, chairman of the Dáil and Seanad Committees) under the Code of Conduct for Office Holders which states that "office holders, in taking up appointments on leaving office, should be careful to avoid any real or apparent conflict of interest with the office they formerly occupied. Particular care should be taken in the first few months following departure from office. Office holders should give careful consideration to the type of occupation chosen having left office".

Q9.2 How effective are the arrangements for protecting office holders and the public from involvement in bribery?

The new anti-corruption legislation introduced in recent years significantly strengthens the framework for minimising corruption in Ireland. However, it is difficult to determine its effectiveness as yet. Meanwhile, perceptions of corruption in Ireland have worsened in recent years. The tribunals of inquiry which have been used extensively to investigate allegations of corruption involving politicians, financial institutions, businesses and private individuals have played a major role in focusing public attention on issues of corruption in Irish public life. At time of completing this study the Moriarty Tribunal had just published its first report. It found the incidence and scale of secretive payments from business people to the then-Taoiseach, Charles Haughey "devalued the quality of a modern democracy". (*Irish Times*, 20 December 2006)

Virtually all corruption/bribery-related inquiries opened in recent years have been in the form of tribunals of inquiry. However, time delays, excessive costs and the questionable outcomes in terms of justice being seen to be done have inadvertently contributed further to public cynicism and undermined public confidence in the reforms towards a more ethical political system which the new anti-corruption legislation aims to achieve. Meanwhile, there is little legislative protection for whistle-blowers who bring instances of wrongdoing to the attention of the appropriate authorities.

ENSURING PROTECTION FROM BRIBERY

Many pieces of legislation relating to corruption, both domestic and international, have been introduced in Ireland in recent years. In 2003, Ireland signed the UN Convention on Corruption, which calls for governments to establish as criminal offences the bribery of national public-sector officials, bribery of foreign public-sector officials, bribery of officials of public international organisations and bribery of private-sector decision makers, although this Convention has not yet been ratified. (Dell, 2005)

In 2003, Ireland formally ratified both the OECD Convention on Combating Bribery of Foreign Public Officials in International Business Transactions and the Council of Europe's Criminal Law Convention on Corruption, which applies to money laundering and bribery in both the private and public sectors. Ireland is also a member of the OECD Working Group on Bribery in International Business Transactions and the Group of States against Corruption (GRECO). GRECO was established by the Council of Europe in 1999 to monitor the implementation of international legal instruments adopted in pursuance of the Programme of Action against Corruption. GRECO evaluates and reports on a large number of European countries and the USA on their anti-corruption performance.

Ireland has also signed but not ratified the Council of Europe Civil Law Convention on Corruption (signed November 1999) and the UN Convention against Transnational Organized Crime (signed December 2000).

The principal Irish legislation specifically addressing anti-bribery and corruption includes:

- the Public Bodies Corrupt Practices Act 1889;
- the Prevention of Corruption Acts 1906 and 1916;

- the Ethics in Public Office Act 1995; and
- the Prevention of Corruption (Amendment) Act 2001.

No less than 25 pieces of domestic legislation focused directly or indirectly on corruption were initiated in the ten-year period from 1995 to 2005.

The Ethics in Public Office Act 1995 (See Q9.1) and the Prevention of Corruption (Amendment) Act 2001 have effectively updated Ireland's anti-corruption legislation after an interval of 79 years.

The Prevention of Corruption Act enabled Ireland to ratify the conventions dealing with corruption drawn up by the European Union, the Council of Europe and the OECD, as outlined above. The Act also introduced liability for corruption on the part of a body corporate, stating that where an offence under the Prevention of Corruption Acts, 1889 to 2001, has been committed by a body corporate "and is proved to have been committed with the consent or connivance of or to be attributable to any wilful neglect on the part of a person being a director, manager, secretary or other officer of the body corporate, or a person who was purporting to act in any such capacity", that person as well as the body corporate shall be guilty of an offence and be liable to prosecution and punishment.

Other pieces of corruption/bribery-related legislation include the 1997 Electoral Act, (See Q9.3) and the Local Government Act 2001, which provides the specific legal framework for employees and members of local authorities. In addition, codes of conduct have been drawn up for members of the Oireachtas under the Standards in Public Office Act 2001, while a revised Code of Standards and Behaviour for Civil Servants was introduced in 2004. Amongst other things, this code established a 12-month employment moratorium and an outside appointments board to address possible conflicts of interest when civil servants take positions in the private sector. The Code also prohibits civil servants from engaging in outside business or activities that would conflict with the interests of their departments. (Byrne, 2006a) (See Q7.3)

TRIBUNALS OF INQUIRY

Various methods of inquiry are available to investigate allegations of bribery or corruption in Ireland. These entities include statutory inquiries/commissions, non-statutory inquiries, commissions of investigation, high court inspectors, parliamentary committee inquiries and the law courts. Despite both this range of options and the extensive revision of anti-corruption legislation *via* the Ethics in Public Office Act and the Prevention of Corruption (Amendment) Act, almost all corruption/bribery-related inquiries undertaken in recent years, other than those taken in the criminal system, have been in the form of tribunals of inquiry. As a result, these tribunals have played a transformative role on attitudes to, and knowledge about, corruption since their inception in 1997. (Byrne, 2006b)

A number of tribunals of inquiry which have sought or are presently seeking to establish the circumstances surrounding allegations of corruption include the follwing.

- The McCracken Tribunal (1997) investigated payments from leading businessman Mr Ben Dunne to politicians, including former Taoiseach Charles Haughey. The Tribunal found that Haughey had given unacceptable evidence before the Tribunal in respect of payments he received from Dunne and that former government minister, Mr Michael Lowry, had evaded tax. In the aftermath of the Tribunal Report, the government established the Moriarty Tribunal to provide for extensive follow up.
- The Moriarty Tribunal (1997–) is investigating illegal offshore accounts held by politicians and business people to evade the payment of tax. The early revelations of this Tribunal were responsible for amendments to the Ethics in Public Office Act 1995 as well as new codes of conduct for public representatives.
- The Flood/Mahon Tribunal (1997–) is investigating political interference in the planning process, including payments to politicians for planning decisions favourable to property developers. This Tribunal has already found that former Minister Ray Burke and former Dublin City Manager, George Redmond received corrupt payments.

Other tribunals which have concluded include the Lindsay Tribunal (1999–2002) which investigated malpractice in the Blood Transfusion Supply Board resulting in contaminated blood being transferred into patients and infecting them with HIV and Hepatitus C; and the first of the tribunals, the Beef Tribunal (1991–94), which led to the fall of the

1989-92 Fianna Fáil/Progressive Democrat government and served as a catalyst for the introduction of legislation and codes of practice designed to regulate the finances of political parties and to provide state funding for parties. (MacCarthaigh, 2005: 210)

The tribunals, which are primarily public and generally chaired by members of the judiciary, have been the subject of some considerable criticism. They are "tools of inquiry and interrogation but, unlike judicial courts, are not adversarial and do not determine rights, duties or obligations". (MacCarthaigh, 2005: 210) The fact that they are not involved in the administration of justice and therefore cannot determine civil or criminal liability has seen the tribunals criticised as being unable to deliver justice.

In addition, the Tribunals of Inquiry (Evidence) Act 1921 which provides for the establishment of tribunals predated the evolution of "fair procedures". As a result there have been numerous legal challenges to various aspects of the tribunals' activities, resulting in increased costs and delays. The fact that tribunals are initiated by the government, rather than the legislature, has also been criticised on the grounds that the number of issues that government will "permit" to be investigated by the tribunals are likely to be circumscribed.

Finally, there has been wide variation in the quality of tribunal reports, with charges that the findings of several tribunals have been ambiguous. At the same time the response of the government to the tribunals has also been disappointing, with the government frequently responding to tribunal findings by "distancing" themselves from the subject under investigation.

Improving the Effectiveness of Tribunals

The Commissions of Investigation Act, passed in July 2004, provides for the creation of commissions of investigation that will investigate "matters of significant public concern" including corruption. The commissions of investigation will have powers to compel witnesses to give evidence, search premises and remove documents and will operate alongside the tribunals. A commission of investigation will be primarily a private investigative process, designed to encourage cooperation by moving away from the adversarial approach that applies within the courts and tribunals. (Byrne, 2006a) While one of the major issues arising in relation to tribunals has been the issue of legal representation of those appearing before them, there is less likelihood of a need for legal representation with the commissions of investigation. Furthermore, there is an express obligation on the commission both to submit a report on its findings and to be timely and cost-effective – two adjectives that have rarely applied to the tribunals. Thus far, one commission of inquiry has been set up, relating to the Dublin/Monaghan bombings in 1974.

The tribunal process itself has been streamlined through legislation. For instance, the Tribunal of Inquiry into Certain Planning Matters and Payments Act 2004 removes the obligation of the tribunal to inquire into every matter before it by granting it discretionary power over what it investigates. The Act also granted tribunals greater powers regarding discretion of costs. Furthermore, new provisions under the Proceeds of Crime (Amendment) Act 2005 eliminates existing legislative difficulties that require that a specific instance of corruption must be linked to a specific payment and a specific favour. In addition, the Act increases the powers of the Criminal Assets Bureau (CAB), which now requires a lower burden of proof to confiscate the assets of corrupt individuals and seize a gift suspected of being a bribe. (Byrne, 2006a)

While no individual has successfully been convicted on corruption charges arising from the tribunals, criminal proceedings arising from revelations at the Flood tribunal are ongoing.

GAPS IN ANTI-CORRUPTION LEGISLATION

There is little evidence, as yet, that the new and extensive statutory framework of anti-corruption legislation is resulting in effective detection and punishment of corruption. The Garda Síochána currently investigate allegations of corruption, and if sufficient evidence of criminal activity is found, the Director of Public Prosecutions (DPP) prepares a file for prosecution. A small number of public officials have been convicted of corruption and/or bribery in the past, but this has not been a common occurrence. In fact, 2006 witnessed the first prosecution under the Electoral Act. Liam Cosgrave, a former Leas-Cathaoirleach of the Seanad, who failed to declare a donation of £2,500 was given a community sentence by the Dublin Circuit Criminal Court. The sum was received during the 1997 election period and Cosgrave did not keep a record of the donation, which was spent on the election. This sentence seems lenient considering that the maximum penalties for the offence were either three years imprisonment or a fine of up to €25,000.

In its First Evaluation Report on Ireland in 2001, GRECO highlighted the shortage of detailed statistics on corruption and recommended the development of a detailed analysis of corruption, situated securely outside of any mainstream intelligence system that would more clearly measure the extent of corruption in Ireland. (GRECO, 2001) This recommendation was echoed in GRECO's 2005 report.

An obvious gap in the legislative framework relates to "whistle-blower" protection. This shortfall was criticised by GRECO in its 2001 Evaluation Report on Ireland, as was the lack of a general statutory obligation on civil service employees to report existing signs of corrupt practices to the authorities in charge of detecting, investigating and prosecuting corruption offences. (GRECO, 2001) Nonetheless, no steps to date have been taken to fully address either of these issues. In fact, the government scrapped prospective whistle-blower legislation in 2005 with no explanation. (*Irish Times*, 1 January 2006)

In addition, a recent judicial decision has even served to undermine the position of someone who "whistle-blows" to a TD. (*Howlin v The Hon. Mr. Justice Morris*, [2005]) The case arose from an order by the Morris Tribunal that Brendan Howlin should produce his telephone records (*Irish Times*, 21 December 2005) in order to reveal the identity of the person from whom he received information about the garda internal inquiry into alleged corruption among the Garda Síochána in Donegal. As the informant did not want to be identified, Howlin refused to produce the records, citing his privilege as a member of the Dáil. The Supreme Court held that for the House to exercise the power of protection set out in Article 15 of the Constitution, it must take certain steps which had not occurred here. According to the lead judgement, delivered by Mr Justice Geoghegan, the House would have had to pass a standing order or general rule, which could then apply to these documents, or to others in other circumstances, as and when the Oireachtas considered it necessary. In addition, the common law argument of "public interest" could justify the disclosure. As a result, there exists no absolute guarantee to a constituent, seeking to confide in his TD, that any documents, like correspondence or phone records generated in this exchange, might not become public in certain circumstances if required by the public interest.

PUBLIC PERCEPTIONS OF CORRUPTION

According to Transparency International's Global Corruption Barometer 2005, corruption in political life is of grave concern to people in many countries around the world. In 45 out of 69 countries surveyed, including Ireland, political parties were rated by the general public as the institution most affected by corruption. The police were rated as the institution most affected by corruption in 17 countries internationally. (Transparency International, 2005) In Ireland, political parties were followed by the legal system/judiciary in second place and parliament and the business/private sectors in joint third place, as the sectors perceived to be the most affected by corruption.

Aside from trust in political institutions, the public in Ireland have traditionally shown greater trust in its public institutions than in many other countries as shown by the following. (Coakley, 2005b: 58)

- Eurobarometer surveys carried out regularly since 1973 have consistently shown that the clear majority of Irish people questioned are satisfied with the way democracy works.
- This confidence in "how democracy works" is reflected in the high levels of confidence that the Irish public has in other major institutions. Eurobarometer surveys show consistently higher levels of confidence in the legal system, trade unions, religious institutions, the media, the police, the army, and other major institutions than is the average across the EU. (Eurobarometer, 2006)
- Eurobarometer surveys show high levels of trust in the civil service in Ireland, in sharp contrast to the negative ratings of national civil services across the EU as a whole.

The single biggest issue with regard to public perceptions of corruption is thus the public's lack of confidence in the integrity of political parties. A 2006 Eurobarometer survey shows that only 32 per cent of respondents tend to trust political parties. Remarkably, however, even this level of trust is significantly higher in Ireland than it is in the EU as a whole. (Eurobarometer, 2006)

Q9.3 How far do the rules and procedures for financing elections, candidates and elected representatives prevent their subordination to sectional interests?

Since 1995, an unprecedented proliferation of seminal legislation has been implemented to regulate the financing of elections in Ireland. The legislation which limits the donations that can be received by political parties for the most part embodies international best practice. The legislation has also resulted in a very substantial increase in state funding. As a result, political parties are not now as dependent upon donations as they once were with regard to their basic operations. However, as previously stated, the legislation has not yet fully come to terms with the highly personalised dynamics of Irish campaigning and electioneering.

Perceptions meanwhile persist that political parties are dependent upon sectional interests – for instance, that government housing policy is influenced by property developers, or that business interests prejudice tax policy – and that specific sectors consequently have a disproportionate influence on policy. (See Q9.4) Such perceptions are undoubtedly influenced by the fact that some individuals appointed to state agencies have a history of previous donations to specific political parties.

The identified flaws in the legislation could be specifically addressed by allowing the Standards Commission to control election-spending limits and by introducing spending limits between elections. These reforms would further diminish the need for donations and ensure a genuine level playing field.

LEGISLATIVE REFORMS

Measures to regulate the financing of elections in Ireland include the following.

- The Electoral Act 1997, ended the legislative vacuum that had existed since Irish Independence with regard to the regulation of the expenditures by candidates and political parties, their disclosure of donations and the financing of elections.
- The Local Elections (Disclosure of Donations and Expenditure) Act 1999, introduced legislation similar to the Electoral Act 1997 with regard to local government elections.

- The Oireachtas (Ministerial and Parliamentary Offices) (Amendment) Act 2001 introduced regulations on the expenditure of the annual allowance given to the leaders of parliamentary parties. This amendment addressed the findings of the 1997 McCracken Tribunal which found that Charles Haughey, a former leader of Fianna Fáil and Taoiseach, had used the party leader's allowance for personal expenditure instead of for expenses arising from the parliamentary activities of the political party.
- The Prevention of Corruption (Amendment) Act 2001, amended the archaic definition of corruption within previous legislation. This Act also provides for a presumption of corruption where an undeclared donation, above the limits permitted, is accepted.
- The Proceeds of Crime (Amendment) Act 2005, increased the powers of the Criminal Assets Bureau (CAB), which now requires a lower burden of proof in order to confiscate the assets of corrupt individuals and seize a gift suspected of being a bribe.
- The Electoral Amendment Act 2001, which introduced a cap on the value of donations which could be accepted and prohibited the acceptance of foreign donations. The Act also introduced the requirement to open and maintain a political donations account and a requirement on "third parties" to register with the Standards Commission. A "third party" is an individual or group (other than a candidate or a political party) which accepts a contribution for political purposes in excess of €126.97. (See Q5.3)

IMPACT OF NEW LEGISLATION ON PARTY FINANCING

Table 9.1 below shows the donations received by each of the main political parties in Ireland between 1998 and 2005. As shown, the peaks in donations correspond directly to elections and referenda. Most parties in 2001 saw a jump in donations received as they consolidated their finances in advance of the General Election and in anticipation of the Electoral Amendment Act 2001.

Table 9.1 Annual Disclosure of Donations by Political Parties to the Standards in Public Office Commission 1998-2005

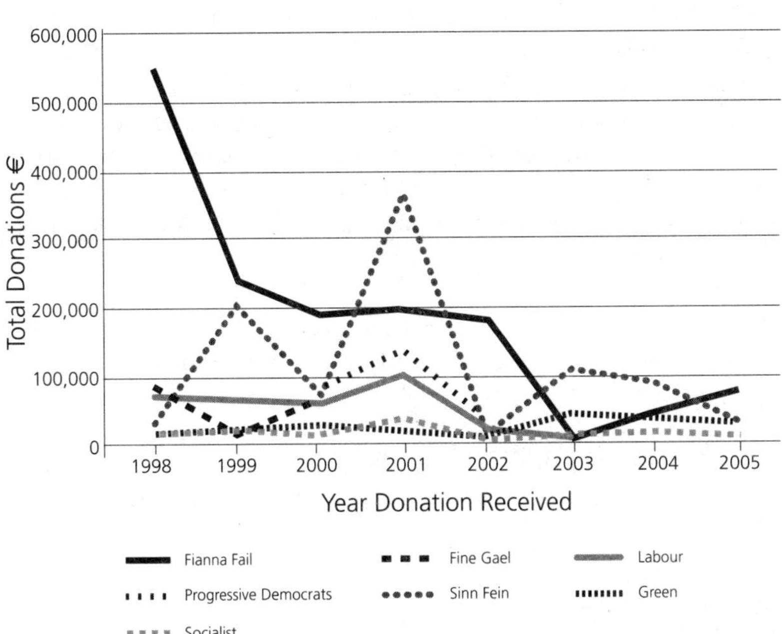

Source: Calculations from Public Office Commission Annual Reports 1998-2001 and Standards in Public Office Commission Annual Reports 2002-2006.

Table Notes: Total figures rounded up to the nearest euro. 1998-2000 figures converted from punt to euro. Converted on the first of January of the year of disclosure. Total figures exclude monies a) returned to donors and b) returned because monies exceeded disclosure limit.

The graph also shows a marked decrease in disclosed donations following the introduction of the Electoral (Amendment) Act 2001. The consequences of these legislative changes have been highly significant, given that Fine Gael disclosed a nil return in donations for the period 2001-2005, as did the Progressive Democrats for 2003-2005, and the Labour Party for 2004-2005.

The impact of the Electoral Acts is further underlined by the fact that the total donations disclosed by all political parties in the 2004 European Parliament and Local Government Elections were less than a third of the disclosed donations received in the equivalent 1999 elections. It should be noted however that Table 9.1 does not represent total donations received by political parties. Individual party representatives disclose separately to the Commission, and donations under the €5,078.95 limit are not required to be disclosed.

While disclosed donations substantially dropped after 2002 with the introduction of the revised Electoral Act, exchequer funding for political parties substantially increased following the implementation of the Oireachtas (Ministerial and Parliamentary Offices) (Amendment) Act 2001. Table 9.2 below underlines the significance of the Act, and clearly shows that political parties are not as dependent upon donations in regard to their basic operations as heretofore.

Table 9.2 Combined Spending by Political Parties of Exchequer Funding Received Under the Electoral Acts and the Party Leaders' Allowance

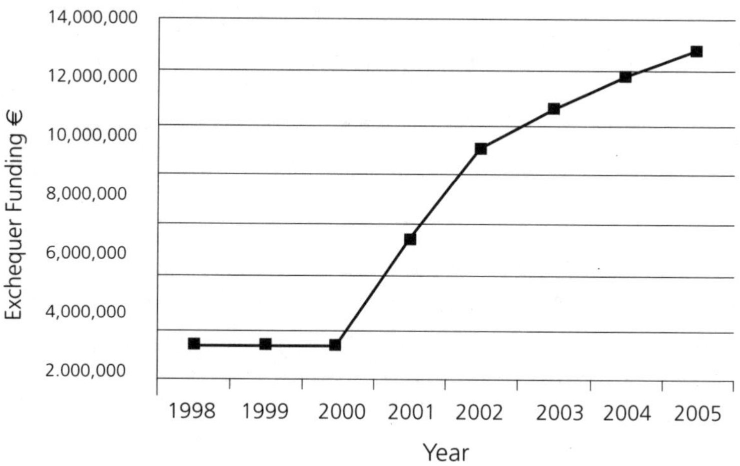

Source: Calculations from Public Office Commission Annual Reports 1998–2001 and Standards in Public Office Commission Annual Reports 2002–2006.

Table Notes: 1998–2000 converted to euro. Amount of total figures has been rounded to the nearest euro. Figures represent exchequer monies spent by political parties each year as opposed to monies received from the exchequer.

However, despite the fact that donations have markedly decreased and exchequer funding cannot be used for election or referendum purposes by parties, the exchequer does reimburse qualified candidates' election expenses to a maximum of €6,348. Overall, more is being spent on election campaigns. For example, in the three-week period before the 2002 Election, the Commission calculated political parties' and candidates' expenditure at €9.24 million. (*Irish Times*, 12 June 2003) Moreover, the *Irish Times* reported that in the three months before the 2002 Election writ was passed, Fianna Fáil alone spent approximately €3.5 million.

SHORTCOMINGS OF THE LEGISLATION

The Electoral Act specifies that election expenditure limits may only be calculated when the election date is officially announced or the writ is passed. As a result, election expenditure is only calculated in the three- or four-week period prior to the election date, while campaigning and electioneering prior to this period are not accounted for at all. This stipulation amounts to a serious flaw within the legislation and renders election expenditure limits essentially redundant and irrelevant: political parties, particularly those in government who have the power to exercise the writ, have duly exploited this legislative loophole. However, there is no easy solution, as it can be difficult to differentiate logistically between appropriate promotion of a department action and the political promotion of a minister.

Successive elections have demonstrated that political parties have engaged in particularly expensive newspaper and billboard advertising in the period immediately before the 2002 election was called and the writ was passed. For example, during this pre-election period Fianna Fáil spent massively on newspaper and outdoor advertising in comparison to the rest of the political parties combined. (*Irish Times*, 12 June 2003) This pattern of expenditure is also the case for specially commissioned focus group surveys and opinion polls, used to determine the attitudes of voters to election policies and is additionally the case regarding the distribution of several different types of glossy leaflets, newsletters and other election material which promote the candidate or the party.

The Number of Candidates and Election Expenditure Limits

The Electoral Act calculates expenditure limits per candidate within a constituency and not per party. Each candidate must separately account for her or his expenditure and not exceed the stated expenditure limits. Notwithstanding these legislative requirements, the more candidates who stand from the same party, the greater the combined expenditure limit available in the critical three-week period prior to the election. (See Table 9.3 below)

Table 9.3 General Election Expenditure Limits for Party Candidates

Number of Seats in Constituency	*Spending Limit per candidate €*	*Combined Spending Limit for Two Candidates €*	*Combined Spending Limit for Three Candidates €*
Three	25,395	50,790	76,185
Four	31,743	63,486	95,229
Five	38,092	76,184	114,276

Source: Compiled from Standards in Public Office Commission, 2002: 21

Initiating an Investigation

Although the Commission has repeatedly raised the matter in its annual reports, it cannot initiate an investigation on breaches of the legislation unless it has explicitly received a complaint. (See also Q9.1) It should be noted, however, that the Standards Commission does not require a complaint before enquiring into a particular matter, and can make whatever enquiries and request whatever information it considers appropriate for the purpose of carrying out its duties. Most enquiries carried out by the Standards Commission under the Electoral Acts have not been the subject of a complaint.

Furthermore, members of the Commission are not full-time members and consequently have other duties. As such, the sheer number of candidates and the diversified nature of their campaign spending in an intensified three-week period clearly preclude the Commission from undertaking any serious monitoring of election spending on the ground. For example, the 2002 General Election required the Commission to monitor and account for election receipts totalling €8,337,780 for 463 candidates, an altogether impressive undertaking by the Commission. However, the Commission is clearly very much dependent upon full disclosure by political parties, election candidates and their agents in this regard.

One area that is particularly open to possible abuse is reimbursing party volunteers around election times. Irish political parties are especially reliant upon party volunteers to engage in face-to-face canvassing, leaflet dropping and similar activities on the candidate's behalf. The potential electoral success of a candidate is often dependent on the number of party volunteers "working on the ground". In response to diminishing party political membership, volunteers are now commonly provided with travel, accommodation and food expenses. This payment is provided for in the Electoral Act and the Commission regards as reasonable an amount of €50 per day per person. It is only when this sum is exceeded that it must be accounted for as an election expense.

DIFFICULTIES IN IMPLEMENTATION

A number of amendments and legal challenges to the legislation governing corruption have been made in recent years, (MacCarthaigh, 2005) while the Standards Commission itself has criticised aspects of the legislation. Indeed, all the evidence suggests that, in practice, the legislation has yet to fully come to terms with the personalised dynamics of Irish campaigning and electioneering.

In particular, a tradition of focusing on the letter and not the spirit of the legislative requirements is both readily evident and inimical to the anti-corruption reform process. This tendency to parse the law is particularly exemplified by the strict definition of certain statutory terms to the detriment of their wider ethical implications. Legislative regulation, no matter how stringent or fine tuned, is no substitute for strong ethical standards or values. (Murphy, 2002)

Finally, the success of this increasingly vast and complex body of legislation is ultimately reliant on the public's engagement with the Commission. And if an information deficit exists around this relatively new regulatory framework, it arguably rests with political and other leadership to address this failing.

Q9.4 How far is the influence of powerful corporations and business interests over public policy kept in check, and how free are they from involvement in corruption, including overseas?

The transformation of Ireland's fortunes in the 1990s has undoubtedly benefited from the contributions to economic growth by large businesses and powerful corporations. Economic growth has also witnessed a decline in the importance of such traditional contributors to a robust economy as agriculture, together with a rise in the importance of multinational corporations, the construction industry and the services sectors of the economy. The growth of these latter sectors has benefited from favourable economic policies, as well as Ireland's strong social, political and legal institutions. At the same time, economic growth has been accompanied by the revelation of a host of poor political and corporate practices, as well a general perception of an unhealthy level of influence brought to bear by vested interests.

In Ireland, big business and large corporations do enjoy significant indirect or implicit influence on the public policy process, and it is clearly evident across major sectors of the economy that large business interests have accumulated significant positions of influence. While these interests have not necessarily resulted in corrupt behaviour, evidence exists that large businesses have abused the powerful positions afforded to them by weak enforcement of regulatory procedures. This has been manifested in the reluctance of government to take on big business interests, although there are exceptions to this, the recent abolition of the Groceries Order in 2006, despite intense lobbying by the retail industry, being a case in point.

The "legislative explosion" since 1995 and the establishment of a range of statutory and regulatory bodies suggest that Ireland is at least moving in the right direction. Meanwhile, one of the paradoxes of economic growth and development is that it often goes hand in hand with increasing levels of revealed corruption. Although there is no evidence in Ireland that large corporations and business interests are corrupt, for example in the numbers of criminal prosecutions being taken against them, there is strong evidence of poor ethical and professional standards, among some.

LEGAL AND REGULATORY FRAMEWORK

Ireland's recent economic development has been accompanied by the increasing importance of large businesses and corporations. On occasion this development has resulted in the emergence of potential conflicts between the state's regulation of the market and the interests of big business. Tribunals of inquiry have brought into the public arena the relative ease with which big business has been able to access government offices. One viewpoint of the exposure of these problems and their subsequent investigation by tribunals of inquiry suggests that Ireland enjoys strong legal and political institutions capable of keeping in check the relationship between business interests and the political system. A less sanguine interpretation is that these scandals are the result of a failure in the system of checks and balances, and that they have been only uncovered as a result of a vigilant press and hasty amendments in the legal and political systems.

In theory, the opportunities for large corporations to influence the public policy process can be diminished by strong institutional structures. From this perspective, there is little doubt that Ireland already has in place an appropriate set of legal and political institutions to regulate the influence of large corporations and business interests on the public policy process and to also mitigate the opportunities for corruption. The establishment of the Standards in Public Office Commission in 2001 has led to improvements in transparency on such issues as the funding of political parties by large businesses. (See Q9.3) Ireland's much admired social partnership approach also provides a formal negotiating platform for all social partners to share their views with government on future economic agreements. Indeed, so successful has the social partnership approach been that the social partners have on occasion been accused of overly influencing government economic policy. (See Q12.2) Ireland also benefits from a free and vigilant press.

In terms of corporate regulation, Ireland enjoys significant advantages as a common law country, given that countries with common law origins are generally regarded as enjoying far greater flexibility in dealing with such corporate governance issues as expropriation and fraud. (La Porta *et al.*, 2000) The Competition Authority was established in 1991 to enforce competition law and investigate uncompetitive practices. Established under the Competition Act 1991, its functions have been strengthened most recently under the Competition (Amendment) Act 2006, which abolished the Groceries Order. The Authority has conducted investigations into such professions as dentists, solicitors and barristers, optometrists, architects and engineers, and has ongoing investigations into medical practitioners and veterinary surgeons. The far-reaching Proceeds of Crime Act 2005, which allows the Criminal Assets Bureau (CAB) to seize assets of corrupt individuals and gifts suspected of being a bribe, also applies to corporate crime, and requires a much lower burden of proof compared to the more adversarial tribunal process. At the supranational level, the European Commission's Competition and Internal Markets Directorates play a proactive role in reducing barriers across the EU and in applying antitrust policy on a European-wide basis. In addition, international organisations including the OECD, GRECO and Transparency International actively monitor the level of corruption, and the political independence and impartiality of these organisations imposes an important source of international oversight on the Irish political system.

An alternative view is that much of the legislative and regulatory changes have only occurred recently. In addition to the implementation of legislation designed to prevent corruption, the recent establishment of such regulatory bodies as Irish Financial Services Regulatory Authority (IFSRA) and the amendments to competition law all indicate important changes in the government's approach to maintaining competitive conditions in the economy. However, while these developments are undoubtedly welcome, the cases highlighted in the following section suggest that the fact that many large business interests have already gained strong positions of influence in the economy throws up considerable challenges for regulation and enforcement.

Indeed a singular dilemma that emerges in the Irish case is the overwhelming perception that, despite our common law origins, the legal and regulatory systems are ill-equipped to deal with such issues as corporate fraud, enforcement and business influence over the political system. The cases that follow illustrate that these issues associated with the relationship between business and politics are of real concern and in fact run deeper than a lack of legislation.

THE INFLUENCE ON THE POLICY PROCESS OF LARGE BUSINESS INTERESTS

Recent developments in the construction, multinational, and financial sectors highlight how large business interests in Ireland have in the past influenced the public policy process. Demonstrably more implicit than explicit in nature, their influence over the policy process tends to be manifested in the apparent reluctance of successive governments to tackle and prosecute powerful corporations and large business interests. As such, influence over the public policy process tends not to occur through explicitly corrupt acts but rather through their ability to exploit strong market positions and weak regulatory enforcement.

The Construction Sector

In no other sector of the Irish economy have the effects of economic growth been so evident than in the construction sector. The sector has become not only economically dominant but also simultaneously dominant within the political sphere. According to figures from the Central Statistics Office, in 1998, the sector employed just over 128,000 workers at that time. In the same year, there were 37,000 planning applications granted and 39,000 private-sector dwelling completions. By 2005, the sector employed over 242,000 workers, making it one of the largest employers by industrial sector, with over 50,000 planning permissions granted, and 75,000 private dwelling completions. (www.cso.ie/statistics) In the same year, figures from the Standards in Public Office Commission show that property developers and construction-related companies were the largest declared source of donations to Ireland's political parties. Specifically, they were the main source of declared donations for the largest partner in the coalition government, the Fianna Fáil party. (www.sipo.gov.ie)

Although the donations made to Fianna Fáil are legitimate and within the guidelines set out by the Standards in Public Office Commission, they are at the same time a continuation of the longstanding close connections between the construction sector and Irish political parties. The revelations at the McCracken Tribunal that former Taoiseach Charles Haughey solicited and received money from large and well-known property developers is a telling case in point. For example, property developer Patrick Gallagher testified to the Tribunal that Haughey personally solicited a donation and received £300,000. (*Sunday Business Post*, 30 July 2000) Although such donations are now much smaller, they fall within the limits set by the Standards in Public Offices Commission, and are more closely scrutinised, usually taking the form of fundraising benefits rather than personal solicitations, the longstanding connection between the largest government party and the construction industry creates an unhealthy perception.

The rapid growth in planning applications often creates a somewhat adversarial relationship between property developers, the public and government institutions. It is not unusual for the property-developer donors to be involved in highly contentious disputes with residents' groups and government planning institutions over prime development lands and properties. The government also faces a trade-off between the need to achieve infrastructural and housing objectives and a sustainable standard of development, although the latter can be much more difficult to achieve in a rapidly growing sector whose major industry interests also provide the primary source of political funding.

The perception that the construction industry has an unhealthy influence over government policy is given further credence by the poor level of regulatory and tax compliance within the sector. A recent report by the Health and Safety Authority (2005) highlighted the construction sector as having one of the highest incidences of work place fatalities. The Authority also noted that over the years the same industries, namely construction and agriculture, had the worst safety records in terms of the number of people being injured and killed in the workplace. In 2004, 15 workers were killed in work-related accidents in the construction sector. By May 2005, nine people had been killed, an increase of two over the same period in the preceding year. And despite the fact that Health and Safety legislation was updated in 2004, the implication is that the problem is not necessarily one of legislation but rather one of enforcement.

A similar situation is evident in the tax compliance practices of the sector. A case highlighted in the media concerned a major construction firm with a turnover of €40 million, yet which for the year ending March 2005 was registered as having only employed 71 operatives and foremen on their sites, along with 50 office workers. (*Village*, 9 March 2006) During the same period the company operated between 10 and 15 large sites with several hundred "subcontracted" workers on them. These "subcontractors" are in fact mostly individual workers. Under the Relevant Contracts Tax (RCT) deductions scheme, tax compliance is essentially the responsibility of individual subcontractors, i.e., individual employees. The RCT scheme was introduced in 1970 to improve revenue compliance in the meat processing, construction and forestry sectors. It also gives greater flexibility to employers in terms of hiring short-term workers.

It would appear however that the scheme has been subject to a high degree of abuse and non-compliance, particularly in the construction sector. A report produced by the Office of the Comptroller and Auditor General (2005) showed that 33,801 principal contractors and 40,329 registered subcontractors had availed of the scheme. The report also found that compliance with the programme in May 2005 was 57 per cent. This low rate was attributed to the rapid growth in the construction sector and also the arrival of large numbers of foreign workers into the sector. In addition, a report by the Department of Enterprise, Trade and Employment found that nearly 130,000 construction workers, almost half the workers in the sector, are not covered by the industry pension scheme. It would appear that the RCT system, which effectively places the onus of tax compliance and pension contributions on subcontractors, has effectively removed responsibility for employee welfare from property developers.

Multinational Corporations

Neither the importance of multinational companies (MNCs), which employ an estimated 100,000 people, nor their political influence can be understated. By 2004, Ireland had attracted over 1,100 multinational companies, exporting goods worth $US60 billion a year. (*The Economist*, 14 October 2004) The Irish government has been to the fore of efforts in Europe to prevent the introduction of tax harmonisation across all Member States in the EU, as harmonisation could potentially remove one of Ireland's perceived competitive advantages in attracting international investment, namely a low rate of corporation tax. Indeed the importance of multinationals, particularly those from the US, has also led to the suspicion that Ireland's foreign policy tends to be more oriented towards Boston than Berlin. The political implications of the dependence on US multinationals became particularly apparent on the Shannon refuelling issue during the Gulf War 2003, when senior figures in the government publicly acknowledged that Ireland's economic interests were an important factor in not being more vocal in Ireland's opposition to US military action in Iraq. (Minister for Enterprise, Trade and Employment, 2003) (See also Q14.4)

Financial Services

There is little doubt that a strong relationship exists between economic growth and the stability of a country's financial institutions. One would therefore expect good adherence to best practices and a strong enforcement of regulatory guidelines by the financial system in a rapidly growing economy like Ireland. However, recent developments in the financial sector suggest exactly the opposite.

There is some evidence of a long-standing relationship between the political and banking systems. The McCracken Tribunal, for example, revealed the ease with which former Taoiseach, Charles Haughey, was able to borrow significant sums from financial institutions during the 1970s. Financial institutions also sanctioned large payments to Fianna Fáil, which often ended up in the party leader's account, from which Haughey made personal drawings. While there is no evidence that the financial institutions involved received any special favours in return, it is clear that banks were willing to extend an unusually large amount of credit to a high-profile political figure. More recently, the most blatant abuse of the power of banking institutions came to light after the revelation of systematic overcharging of customers. Moreover, although the overcharging was indicative of deliberate fraud, astonishingly no member of management at the offending banks was charged with any criminal offence.

The revelation of overcharging at Allied Irish Bank (AIB) which overcharged its customers to the tune of €34.2 million on foreign exchange and other transactions up to 2004 is a case in point. An initial investigation by the Irish Financial Services Regulatory Authority (IFSRA) revealed overcharging on foreign exchange transactions totalling €25.5 million and €0.5 million affecting other transactions also covered by the Consumer Credit Act 1995. The investigation further revealed that, not only were staff aware of overcharging but they also had had ample opportunities over a six-year period between 1998 and 2004 to inform the regulator. The overcharging scandal highlighted two specific problems: failure to comply with legislation and failure to notify non-compliance.

While it is accepted that human error in financial transactions can occur in individual cases, the IFSRA expects to be notified of such problems. Under the Consumer Credit Act 1995, the banks are required to notify the regulator of breaches of guidelines. The IFSRA also expects that these issues will be dealt with in a timely and openly transparent manner. However, AIB failed to comply with either of these conditions. Although AIB's initial problems stemmed from a breach of the retail charging margins notified to the regulator, its problems were compounded by its failure to notify the regulator. As such, AIB's non compliance extended beyond human error.

More worrying is that these problems were not confined to AIB. The IFSRA's 2005 Annual Report highlighted overcharging amounting to €50 million, involving 36 companies in the banking and insurance industries during 2005. This figure brings to €118 million the amount of overcharging involving financial services companies since 2004. The major offenders include Bank of Ireland (repaying €18 million) and National Irish Bank (repaying €11 million).

Corporate Malpractice, Fraud or Corruption?

The problems in Ireland's large banks further indicate the difficulties in separating malpractice from corruption in this sector. In particular, it raises the question: when does a breach of regulatory guidelines become more than poor compliance? The simple answer is that it's impossible to tell, as we have limited legislative guidelines in this regard. A more complex interpretation of the problems in the banking sector however suggests severe problems in the existing system. Management at the offending banks were able to take advantage of weak enforcement to achieve profit targets. These examples show that management were more concerned with profit than with enforcement of regulations.

Prior to the establishment of the IFSRA in 2003, the big banks exercised a large degree of discretion in terms of compliance. The then regulator, the Central Bank, appears to have been much more concerned with the general integrity of the banking system. The Consumer Credit Act also appears to have allowed the banks a high degree of discretion. The establishment of the IFSRA has witnessed a move towards a more customer-focused regulation and an optimistic view of the banking sector might therefore suggest that the current problems are an artefact of years of weak regulatory enforcement and that recent scandals could be excused on the grounds of regulatory failure. However, the widespread nature of non-compliance uncovered, and the fact that management had knowledge of the issues involved, indicates systematic management-level problems in the banking sector. Moreover, it is clear that even the current regulatory environment may not be particularly well-equipped to deal with a large banking scandal. For example, although AIB voluntarily agreed to refund monies, it was not obliged to repay all of the overcharges under existing regulations or legislation.

A less optimistic interpretation of the overcharging scandals suggests that the banks effectively enjoy immunity from criminal prosecution. If Ireland's legal system is as strong as its common law origins suggest, it should be perfectly capable of detecting and prosecuting cases of fraud. Nor should cases of corporate fraud require additional legislation. Nonetheless, no one at either of the banks accused of overcharging has been held criminally responsible, despite admission of culpability. The implications of this situation are that the major banks not only get away with non-compliance but also face little chance of being held accountable. While the banking system may not be corrupt in the strict sense, it is patently affected by poor corporate and managerial practices. Moreover, the suspicion remains that the sector is being regulated with kid gloves. Recent attempts to tighten the regulatory code, which involved detailed consultations with the banks, have been described as a missed opportunity and have been criticised for allowing too many exemptions for the commercial banks. (RTÉ, 25 July 2006)

CIVIL SOCIETY AND POPULAR PARTICIPATION

Ten: The Media in a Democratic Society

Do the media operate in a way that sustains democratic values?

INTRODUCTION AND SUMMARY

For citizens to be properly informed about and engaged with the issues of the day, the media need to provide:

- accurate information and comment;
- a pluralism of viewpoints and opinions, including minority ones;
- investigative journalism to expose error and falsehood in public life; and
- a public sphere in which citizens can freely voice their own opinions to one another and to government.

In addition, the principle of equality in a democratic society requires the media to respect the equal dignity of all persons. How these criteria are met in practice will vary from one country to the next. However, good regulative practice will typically include: legislation to limit concentrations of media ownership and to ensure the independence of public broadcasting from government control or pressure; impartial bodies to provide effective self-regulation of media content and respond to public complaints; strong freedom of expression and information legislation, while at the same time providing of safeguards against so-called "hate-speech".

Besides the traditional media of press and broadcasting, the Internet now provides an important source of news, information and exchange of opinion, especially for young people. Democratic concerns about this new medium include the question of regulation to limit the worst abuses, and how to extend access to those sections of society that are, for a variety of reasons, currently excluded from its use.

How do the Irish media measure up to these democratic criteria? Despite the unusual concentration of press ownership in Ireland, Irish newspapers, both national and local, exemplify considerable diversity and offer a wide range of choice to readers. This diversity is partly due to the very positive readership figures, when compared with other European countries, and the tradition of a strong local newspaper industry. Editorial policy is largely independent of political party and ownership interests. There are no discernable pressures from international corporations or foreign governments on the media in Ireland.

In the field of broadcasting, Radio Telifís Éireann (RTÉ) has by far the largest share of the domestic TV market and has a guaranteed public service remit. Like publicly-owned broadcasters elsewhere, it is potentially vulnerable to government pressure on one hand (through government control of board membership and the level of the licence fee), and to pressure for privatisation from commercial broadcasters, on the other. Irish radio shows much greater diversity than television, with strong regional and local stations and much higher proportions of the population listen to news on the radio every day than the European average.

As regards the wider context of Irish journalism, there has been considerable success over the years in uncovering and publicising wrongdoing in public life. Sufficient variety in the range of Irish media also allows differing opinions to be heard and encourages creative competition between media outlets which provides incentives for the investigation of wrongdoing. At the same time, journalists have to operate within what many regard as unduly restrictive libel laws and freedom of information legislation. On the other hand, concerns have been expressed about gross invasions of personal privacy, especially by the press, and about the manner in which Travellers, immigrants and other minorities are portrayed in the media.

Q10.1 How independent are the media from government, how pluralistic is their ownership, and how free are they from subordination to foreign governments or multinational companies?

While press ownership in Ireland is somewhat concentrated, it is not excessively so when compared to that in other EU countries. Two publishers own, either wholly or partially, eight of Ireland's ten indigenous newspapers. Four of the six national radio stations are operated by the public service broadcaster Radio Telifís Éireann (RTÉ), while indigenous television broadcasting is also dominated by RTÉ. Apart from the Irish language public service broadcaster TG4, the only indigenous competition to RTÉ television are the private commercial television channel TV3, the fledgling entertainment station Channel 6, the sports channel Setanta and the community-style city channels. When non-indigenous stations are excluded, RTÉ's share of the TV audience represents a virtual monopoly in today's terms.

Despite this concentration, there is enough variety of outlets and voices in the Irish media to facilitate democratic debate. In practice, the effect of concentrated ownership of the indigenous national daily newspaper market is offset by the presence of so many Irish editions of UK papers.

Government may exert substantial control over RTÉ through appointment to its governing body, the RTÉ Authority, and through control of its revenue *via* authorisation of licence fee increases. However, in practice it prefers to be seen in recent years to adopt a hands-off approach, wherein it has attempted to influence the media through message management and public criticisms that are democratically appropriate. The degree of dominance of the broadcast media by RTÉ is unusual but does not represent a democratic deficit owing to the plurality of voices that can be heard within the organisation. Where governments in the past have been able to "punish" an unobliging RTÉ through withholding licence fee increases, a proposed index-linking of increases would remove this opportunity for interference.

Issues of concentration of ownership tend not to negatively affect democracy within the media: market pressures, media diversity and professional standards generally mean that interference by owners, governments and corporations with the publication of stories of public concern very rarely occurs.

TELEVISION IN IRELAND

RTÉ operates two national television services: RTÉ 1, a public service channel with an emphasis on news and current affairs programming and RTÉ 2, a channel that has tried to project a more youthful image by broadcasting music programmes and films aimed at a younger market. Ireland has also had a third public service broadcasting channel since 1996, namely the Irish-language TG4 which operates under the statutory and corporate aegis of RTÉ but which was set up as a separate broadcasting authority under the Broadcasting Act 2001. The creation of TG4 was a cultural and language policy decision on the part of the Irish government in response to demands made by Irish language speakers.

As in the rest of Europe, the ownership of the Irish media is a hot topic in any discussion of media democracy. Problems exist with the concentration of indigenous broadcast media under the RTÉ Authority, which at 42 per cent commands a very large share of the TV audience, compared to the independent TV3 which has only 13.4 per cent. (www.agbnmr.com) This situation compares internationally with the overconcentration within the Danish TV market where the public service broadcasters TV2 and DR are watched by 72 per cent of the audience. (International Federation of Journalists, 2005: 45) In the UK, however, the BBC has a 36.6 per cent portion of a much more evenly-divided market in which ITN has a 24 per cent share. (International Federation of Journalists, 2005: 155) Portuguese TV currently has no dominant player with private stations SIC on 28.3 per cent and TV1 on 29.5 per cent and the public service broadcaster RTP1 on 23.2 per cent. (International Federation of Journalists, 2005: 120) The seemingly equitable position in Ireland *vis-à-vis* Denmark takes on another cast entirely, however, when non-indigenous stations are excluded from the figures (as they are for the other countries mentioned here), as the RTÉ share jumps to a remarkable 84 per cent. (www.medialive.ie) It should be noted, moreover, that in Denmark one of the public service broadcasters, TV2, is likely to be privatised while retaining its public service remit, which will end the state's dominant position there.

Apart from TG4, the only serious indigenous competition to RTÉ until very recently has been TV3. Even though the TV3 consortium was awarded a licence to broadcast television as far back as 1988, the channel only commenced in 1998, after it received strong financial backing in 1997 from the Canadian television company, CanWest

Global. (It is now owned by the equity company Doughty Hanson.) One possible explanation for this ten-year delay is the financial viability of four national television channels in a country with a population of just over 3.6 million, most of whom can also receive British television. Most of TV3's programming consists of US, UK or Australian series and films, and advertising, with a minimum of home-produced programmes.

At present, funding for RTÉ comes from a combination of licence fees and advertising revenue. Unlike most public broadcasters throughout the EU, RTÉ does not enjoy independence from commercial interests, since around 65 per cent of its revenue comes from advertising. Nor does it enjoy independence from government, which exerts its power over RTÉ in a number of ways. First the government appoints the nine-member RTÉ Authority which acts as RTÉ's board, making policy and guiding corporate direction. The Authority is directly responsible to the Minister for Communications, Marine and Natural Resources. Second the government has control over a large share of RTÉ's revenue since it retains the power to set the level of the licence fee. (*Irish Times*, 31 August 2002) There have also been suggestions, in the past at least, that RTÉ management has on occasions been responsive to the degree of control by government over RTÉ corporate policy through its ability to set the licence fee. (Quinn, 2001: 236–40)

The *Report of the Forum on Broadcasting* (2002: 24) established by government recommended a system of indexing increases in the licence fee, whereby the licence fee would be granted on the recommendation of the new Broadcasting Authority of Ireland provided it found that RTÉ had met the targets set for it in its business plan and in its public service broadcasting outputs. This recommendation, if implemented, would effectively remove direct government control over licence fee increases and allow RTÉ greater certainty in forward financial planning.

The second challenge to RTÉ's independence comes from the increasingly-commercial climate within which broadcasters must now operate. With changes in technology and an increase in for-profit television, RTÉ, together with other public broadcasters in Europe, has had to justify its very existence against the argument that a need for state ownership of TV no longer exists because of new technologies and increased commercial competition. In addition, TV3 and the commercial radio stations, echoing an argument used by their counterparts in Europe, continually maintain that RTÉ's partial funding through licence fee represents an unfair and uncompetitive subsidy.

In light of this argument, the Amsterdam Treaty has proved vital to the interests of RTÉ. The Treaty defines public service broadcasting as the activity of a public service broadcaster – not as a generic activity which is common to publicly and privately owned broadcasters. This definition remains a valuable bulwark for public service broadcasters and there are no plans to privatize RTÉ at this time. Strong arguments also exist that such a privatisation would contribute little to democratising the media. (Corcoran, 2004: 223)

State Ownership Effects on Editorial Freedom

While the concentration of ownership of broadcast outlets in the hands of the state is not unusual for an EU country, there are issues of concern for the possible effects on editorial policy arising from this level of state control. The issue of "agenda setting" is discussed in Q10.3, the focus is on the amount of government interference with RTÉ at the corporate level.

In the past, government's dominant relationship with RTÉ has tempted it to interfere with the running of the station. The experiences of the 1990s suggest that indirect pressures are possible: "Government supporters who don't balk at exercising their partisan power can pack broadcasting authorities…Financial pressure can be exerted…Public flak can be generated in an attempt to drive a wedge between broadcaster and public" and "Informal and formal accusations about journalistic content can also be applied" and "legislative reorganisation" threatened. However, former Chairperson of the RTÉ Authority, Farrel Corcoran, recalls a hands-off approach to RTÉ in his time on the Authority, from politicians in any case: "Large broadcasting organisations, including those the size of RTÉ, are difficult to control from outside because they are protected by internal systems of checks and balances." (Corcoran, 2004: 71)

Progress has been made in recent years, in offsetting any potential dangers of political interference: the proposed index-linking of RTÉ's licence fee, for example, and the Broadcasting Act 2001, which removed Section 31 that made direct political censorship possible. The Broadcasting Complaints Commission acts as an independent arbiter between complainants and broadcasters, and the annual Statements of Commitments and RTÉ's Audience Council have introduced further transparency to the sector.

RADIO OWNERSHIP IN IRELAND

The percentage of people in Ireland who listen to news on the radio is considerably higher than the EU15 average. 63 per cent of people in Ireland listen to the news on the radio every day, compared with the EU15 average of 38 per cent. Only Denmark at 65 per cent has a higher level of its population who tune in to radio news every day. (Eurobarometer, 2002)

Ireland has 54 radio stations licensed by the regulatory authority, the Broadcasting Commission of Ireland (BCI). Six of these are national stations, four operated by RTÉ (Radio 1, 2FM, Lyric FM and Raidió na Gaeltachta) and two commercial stations (Today FM and Newstalk).

Local and regional radio is strong in Ireland. Listenership figures for November 2006 show that 57 per cent of the population listened to local/regional stations compared with figures of 23 per cent for RTÉ Radio 1 and 18 per cent for 2FM, while 16 per cent listened to Today FM. (www.tnsmrbi.ie)

Ownership of the local and regional radio market is concentrated among four main players: Emap Plc; Denis O'Brien's Communicorp Ltd; UTV; and Thomas Crosbie Holdings.

Table 10.1 Summary of Private Ownership of Radio Stations

Emap Plc	*Communicorp Ltd*	*UTV*	*Thomas Crosbie Holdings*
Highland Radio	98FM	LM FM Dundalk	Midwest Radio (shareholding)
Today FM	Spin 103	Q102 FM	Red FM (shareholding)
FM104 Dublin	Newstalk (majority shareholding) East Coast FM (shareholding)	Limerick Live 95FM Cork 96 and 103 FM	

Source: Compiled from *Irish Times*, 24 June 2005

The Broadcasting Commission of Ireland (BCI) is responsible for ensuring a diversity of ownership and/or control of the TV and radio market (See Q 10.2 below). In 2005, the BCI imposed a temporary cap on ownership and control of the radio sector, such that no one company can own and control more than 17.9 per cent of the sector. Since then, broader operational guidelines have been introduced raising the acceptable share for any one company to between 15 and 25 per cent. (Broadcasting Commission of Ireland, 2006)

Despite the BCI's remit to ensure diversity of ownership, a strong degree of concentration of ownership exists, at least in the Dublin radio market. In 2003, the market was dominated by a combination of RTÉ and Denis O'Brien's Communicorp Ltd., which owned over half of the radio stations broadcasting to the Dublin area. In general, the license winners from the BCI since 1998 have been wealthy individuals and those already involved in the media sector.

Figures from the European Institute for the Media show that seven of the small-to-medium national media markets have a radio broadcaster with a higher share of listenership than that enjoyed by RTÉ.

NEWSPAPER OWNERSHIP

Readers in Ireland have access to a broad range of both Irish and imported newspapers. News readership is higher than the EU15 average with 91 per cent of Irish people reading a newspaper each week, and 57 per cent of the population reading at least some news in the papers every day. (www.jnrs.ie)

Roughly 684,000 national daily newspapers, 1.2 million Sunday newspapers and 650,000 regional newspapers are sold in Ireland. In addition, there is wide availability of British newspapers (not Irish editions) throughout Ireland, which sell approximately 22,000 daily and 49,000 Sunday editions. (www.medialive.ie)

The press in Ireland consists of four Irish-owned national dailies (the *Irish Independent*, *Irish Times*, *Irish Examiner* and the *Star*), two national evening newspapers (the *Evening Herald* and the *Evening Echo*), five national Sunday newspapers, (the *Sunday Independent*, *Sunday Business Post*, *Sunday Tribune*, *The Sunday Star* and the *Sunday World*) and around fifty regional and twelve local newspapers. There are also Irish editions of four British-owned daily and five Sunday papers, all with large locally based staffs which provide extensive coverage of Irish affairs.

There have been some recent positive developments in the magazine sector, namely, the reduction of VAT to 12.5 per cent, and the launch of the weekly *Village* politics magazine. (O'Brien, 2005: 139–40) The most successful magazine with around 114,000 sold copies per issue is the RTÉ Guide, a weekly guide to radio and television, published by RTÉ.

Concerns have been expressed in Ireland in recent years that a diversity of views is being undermined by the increasing concentration of media ownership. Independent News and Media (IN&M) Plc is the dominant actor in the Irish newspaper industry. The group publishes five leading national newspapers, and twelve regional papers. The group also owns the Belfast Telegraph group, the largest newspaper publisher in Northern Ireland. (*Irish Times*, 24 June 2005) In the Republic, ABC figures for June 2006 show IN&M titles account for 43 per cent of national daily paper sales.

Thomas Crosbie Holdings, another heavy hitter in the Irish newspaper industry, has two national titles, eight regional titles and shareholdings in two radio stations. (*Irish Times*, 24 June 2005)

Consequently, of Ireland's 18 national newspapers, only two titles – one daily, (the *Irish Times*) and one evening, (*Evening Echo*) – are not owned wholly or partially by Independent News and Media, Thomas Crosbie Holdings, and Trinity Mirror and News Corporation.

There is also a strong local newspaper industry in Ireland. Local newspapers are by definition very much tied to locale, with close coverage of affairs in specific parishes and neighbourhoods. (Tovey and Share, 2003: 426) In the regional press, ownership is largely concentrated among seven publishers, including the two major newspaper groups above. (*Irish Times*, 24 June 2005)

The degree of concentration in media ownership in Ireland, as compared to the rest of the EU, can be seen from figures compiled by the European Institute for the Media (2004) which show nine EU countries that have a major publisher which controls more than 43 per cent of the daily newspaper market. Excluding the five large media markets (France, Italy, Germany, Poland and the UK), all of which have diverse press ownership, Ireland ranks midway on the table which measures the concentration of press ownership in EU countries.

Table 10.2 Concentration of Newspaper and Radio Ownership in Ireland

Group	*National titles*	*Regional titles*	*Local radio*
Independent News and Media plc	Irish Independent The Star (daily and Sunday version) The Evening Herald The Sunday Independent The Sunday World Sunday Tribune (29.9%)	The Kerryman The Corkman The Wexford People The Wicklow People The Bray People The Enniscorthy Guardian The Carlow People The Gorey Guardian The New Ross Standard The Fingal Independent The Drogheda Independent The Dundalk Argus	
Thomas Crosbie Holdings	The Irish Examiner The Sunday Business Post	The Evening Echo Waterford News and Star The Western Post The Sligo Weekender The Kingdom The Nationalist and Leinster Times The Roscommon Herald	Midwest Radio (shareholding) Red FM Cork (shareholding)

Source: Compiled from *Irish Times*, 24 June 2005 and *Village*, 24–30 June 2005

The Irish government and the Irish Competition Authority have recently conducted reviews into the concentration of press ownership. The Competition Authority notes that considerable barriers to new entrants to the Irish newspaper market exist here as elsewhere. Challenges to the dominance of IN&M from within the press are likely only to come from well-financed corporate-owned titles. And in practice, the effect on IN&M dominance of the indigenous national daily market is somewhat offset by the presence here of Irish editions of UK papers.

Table 10.3 Newspaper Ownership in the Regional Press

Johnston Press	The Kilkenny People
	The Longford Leader
	The Leitrim Observer
	The Tipperary Star
Limerick Leader	The Leinster Leader
	The Limerick Leader
	The Leinster Express
	The Offaly Express
	The Dundalk Democrat
	The Limerick Chronicle
	The Tallaght Echo
Dunfermline Press	The Meath Chronicle
	The Anglo-Celt Cavan
	The Westmeath Examiner Group
Alpha Newspaper Group	The Midland Tribune
	The Roscommon Champion
	The Longford News
	The Tullamore Tribune
	The Athlone Voice
3i group plc	The Derry & Donegal News
	The Donegal Democrat

Source: Compiled from*Irish Times*, 24 June 2005 and *Village*, 24–30 June 2005

At the same time, the concentrated ownership of newspapers in Ireland raises legitimate concerns about impartiality of the Irish media in their examination of government and big business. (See Q10.3)

Effects of Newspaper Ownership on Editorial Freedom

It is in the press that the issue of ownership and its possible impact on editorial and content is most controversial. Depending on who is speaking, owners tend to take one of three perspectives: they have a justifiable right to expect their views to be represented in papers they own; they never interfere in the running of their papers; or they regularly interfere in a manner which could potentially undermine democracy. The *Irish Times* "constitution" from 1922 stated that the title is the property of the owner "to do with as he wants". Former *Irish Times* editor Conor Brady suggests "Editors are generally chosen because they broadly share or reflect the proprietors'/publishers' values...there should be no need for crude interventions in the form of late night telephone calls". (Brady, 2006: 29) However, there have been controversies at the *Irish Times* with stories allegedly being cut when critical of the paper's board of trustees. (*Sunday Independent,* 13 February 2005) There have also been comments that Irish media coverage of a recent dispute involving the Irish Ferries dispute may have been coloured by a pro-union bias, given that most Irish journalists are members of the NUJ. (Ruddock, 2005)

The question of owner influence is most often raised in connection with IN&M. Differing opinions range from there being no clear evidence that Tony O'Reilly has ever abused his position as owner of Independent News and Media for political ends to the opposing view that O'Reilly has used his influence to favour or damage political fortunes and to limit editorial criticism of corporate greed. (See also Q. 10.2)

INTERNET / NEW MEDIA

Access to the Internet in Ireland is less than that in many European countries, particularly in relation to broadband access. Fifty per cent of respondents to a 2006 Comreg survey said that they personally used the Internet from any location. (www.comreg.ie) Broadband take up in Ireland is low also, at just over half the OECD average. (www.oecd.org)

The Internet as a source of news differs from the mass media of newspapers, radio and television in the distinct socio-economic profile of its users. The most significant characteristic of Internet users is their youth.

The main uses of the Internet in Ireland included email (65 per cent), information research (69 per cent) and general browsing (67 per cent). Other uses mentioned included downloading online material (22 per cent), getting news updates (24 per cent) and playing games (16 per cent). (www.comreg.ie)

While levels of Internet usage are still well below those of the traditional news media, they are increasing especially amongst the young and are likely to play an increasingly significant role in the future. The increased popularity of blogging and the spread of Really Simple Syndication (RSS) news feeds are likely to fuel these developments.

INTERFERENCE FROM CORPORATIONS AND FOREIGN GOVERNMENTS

There has been very little discussion about the influence of foreign organisations on the Irish media in general, whether from the absence of such interference or its subtlety. The question of self-enforced censorship on matters concerning foreign investment does arise, however, where coverage of certain issues that might affect the national interest is sparse. For example, it has been suggested that the very limited Irish coverage of a *Wall Street Journal* story on creative accounting practices by US companies operating in Ireland stemmed in large part from a reluctance by the journalists expert enough in the field to cover such controversial tax or productivity anomalies. (Browne, 2005) Such self-censorship, were it widespread, would represent a serious threat to an effective media. However, the extended coverage of controversies involving multinational companies and their operations in Ireland, as seen in the Shell Mayo gas pipeline dispute, suggests that this is not the case.

The influence of foreign governments in Ireland is also not very much in evidence. Claims of an anti-American bias in RTÉ, whether justified or not, indicate a perceived lack of control of the Irish media by the most powerful of Ireland's friendly governments. The coverage of the Irish anti-war movement and the protests at the US use of Shannon is impartial in all media outlets and further demonstrates either an unwillingness, or an inability on the part of foreign governments to control the media in Ireland.

Q10.2. How representative are the media of different opinions and how accessible are they to different sections of society?

This question addresses three issues of representation in the media: how representative of society as a whole is the media workforce in

Ireland; how representative of the diversity of society is the Irish media's output; and what impact does media ownership and regulation have on the diversity of media content?

With regard to the media workforce, the Irish media are quite inequitable in providing access to women and members of minority groups. Two-thirds of members of the National Union of Journalists (NUJ) are male, and this gender imbalance is even worse at management level in media outlets.

Overall, employment of individuals from minority groups in mainstream television, radio and press remains low. In the independent radio sector, programme makers from minority communities have fared better, and newspapers now publish in a variety of languages. Ethnic minorities, however, remain underrepresented on the staff of mainstream Irish newsrooms.

Inequity in employment is sometimes further reflected in media content. Although RTÉ's policy is to reflect Ireland's current diversity of culture, religion, political views, physical ability and disability, age, class, race and ethnicity, and sexual orientation in its programming, putting this policy into practice has proven difficult. As a result, Ireland's ethnic diversity is much better reflected in the press than on television or radio. However, recent research suggests that press coverage of refugees and asylum seekers is biased towards negative stereotyping and may perpetuate racism. (See discussion below)

HOW REPRESENTATIVE OF SOCIETY IS THE MEDIA WORKFORCE IN IRELAND?

Gender

When it comes to gender, journalism reflects many of the inequities that affect Irish society in general. And while some parity of participation is emerging between men and women in the workplace, a far from equitable division of power and control exists at management levels.

Ninety seven per cent of journalists working in the media in Ireland are represented by the NUJ. (Dooley, 2003) Figures from that organisation indicate a total membership of just over three thousand in 2006, only 35 per cent of whom are women. Ireland's poor performance in this area is in keeping with the average across other countries, where 27 per cent of journalists are women, ranging from a high of 50 per cent in Finland and Mexico to a low of 6 per cent in Sri Lanka. (Peters, 2001: 4)

As noted above, the gender imbalance is even worse at management level. Of the 125 newspaper editors in Ireland, 112 (89.6 per cent) are male while 13 (10.4 per cent) are female. (Shaw, 2005: 21–45)

The picture in broadcasting is equally bleak. An analysis of RTÉ figures shows that women in RTÉ made up 83 per cent of administrative workers overall, but only 23 per cent of senior managers. (Moran and Price, 2005: 31) Women in RTÉ represented 66 per cent of bottom pay scale workers (<€30k) but only 16 per cent of top pay scale workers (>€90k). (Moran and Price, 2005: 33) The picture for high-profile broadcasters is similar with only two women on the list of the top ten most highly paid on-air broadcasters for 2003.

While there are no published figures for the gender makeup of broadcasters on independent radio stations, women are also under-represented as presenters, and there are reports of management resistance to granting women equal access to the microphone. For example, of the two national independent radio stations, only two of Today FM's 18 shows are presented by women, while on Newstalk women present five out of 15 shows. Women do produce key radio programmes in the independent sector, but specious arguments about the unsuitability of the timbre of women's voices as presenters are reportedly still made. (Ingle, 2006)

Employment in the media is covered by the terms of the Employment Equality Acts 1998 and 2004, which prohibit discrimination, including discrimination on grounds of gender equality, and permit positive action measures to promote equal opportunities between men and women. One such measure is the Women Active in Diversity Equality programme or WADE, which has resulted in the creation of a database of women who are expert in a wide range of areas which can be drawn upon by journalists and programme makers in order to give gender balance to their work. The WADE project has also examined the barriers to career progression for women working in RTÉ and has produced recommendations to advance their promotion within the organisation. However, it is still too early to assess the effect of these recommendations.

Minority Groups

The participation of members of minority groups within the media varies from television, to radio to the print media.

In regard to television, RTÉ offers only one multiethnic programme *Mono*, which only runs for a short season in the Summer. There are also very low rates of appearance by disabled characters on evening time television in Ireland. Given the estimated 10 per cent prevalence of disability in the population, there appears to be a huge disparity in disability representation. And while City Channel does employ Polish staff to produce its *Oto Polska* programme, no Travellers broadcast regularly on RTÉ television. As such, it would appear overall that few individuals from minority groups are employed in television.

In regard to radio, RTÉ broadcasts minority programmes such as *Audioscope*, *Spectrum*, and *Outside the Box*, but these shows represent a tiny fraction of the overall programming. Instead, it is in the independent radio sector that programme makers from minority communities have fared best, even though progress here has been modest. Some community radio stations have provided air-time to broadcasters from various ethnic backgrounds; Anna Livia FM 103.2 for example, has magazine programmes made by members of the Gaelic-speaking, Korean, Chinese, Russian and African communities. Meanwhile, Sunrise Radio 94.9 FM was recently granted a temporary licence from the Broadcasting Commission of Ireland (BCI) and provides opportunities for broadcasters from a variety of ethnic backgrounds.

Ireland's current ethnic diversity is far better reflected in the press, where various newspapers publish in the Polish, Russian, Mandarin and Irish languages. Web-based publications also exist such as *Metro Éireann*, which publishes in French as well as English. At the same time, ethnic minorities who now constitute approximately 6 per cent of the Irish population remain significantly underrepresented among the staff of mainstream Irish newsrooms. (McGee, 2005)

Speakers of Irish have a greater level of opportunity in the media, as evidenced by both a national television station (TG4), a national radio station (Radió na Gaeltachta), and numerous local stations that produce programmes in Irish, along with some Irish language programming retained on RTÉ Radio 1. Two national Irish-language newspapers (*Foinse* and *Lá*) also exist. As a result, fluency in Irish has become a decided advantage for those seeking a career in the Irish media.

HOW REPRESENTATIVE IS THE IRISH MEDIA'S OUTPUT OF THE DIVERSITY OF IRISH SOCIETY?

Television

Ireland cannot be said to enjoy a wide choice of domestic TV channels, given that RTÉ, TG4 and TV3 were until recently the only players. Setanta Sports and Channel 6 are recent additions, as are the community services, City Channel Dublin, Galway and Cork.

RTÉ's need in general to satisfy the requirements of its majority audience also makes it difficult to meet the demands of minorities, in addition to the minimal participation by members of minority groups in programming discussed above. The failure to date to launch Digital Terrestrial Television (DTT) has similarly closed off the opportunities that medium would afford to smaller communities to access TV broadcasting. However, there are positive indications that DTT is soon to be rolled out on a pilot basis and wider opportunities for more pluralistic inter-cultural programming may finally become available.

Radio

Potential access to radio in Ireland, however, is a different matter. While "there are still far fewer radio choices in Ireland than in most other European countries", the position here is generally quite strong, "community radio in Ireland, unlike the UK is a strong and growing sector, and there is now a community radio network which works together on training and development initiatives". (Shaw, 2005: 77–9) The BCI has recently issued licences to one national station, one regional station, 26 local stations, 15 community stations, four communities of interest stations and one special interest radio station, all of which compete with RTÉ which remains the dominant player with a 40 per cent audience share. (www.tnsmrbi.ie) Overall, private commercial radio stations have a 57 per cent share which continues to grow at the expense of RTÉ, and this trend is likely to continue since Newstalk 106 moved from being a Dublin-only to a national broadcaster.

While the geographical spread of the Irish radio audience has been adequately catered for, Ireland's social and cultural diversity is only now beginning to be reflected on the airwaves. Until recently, Anna Livia FM was a lone voice in intercultural broadcasting and, even then, its schedule devoted only 4.5 per cent of its broadcast output to intercultural programming.

Moreover, previous applications to the BCI for intercultural radio service licences have not fared well. (Onyejelem, 2005: 76) The failure of established broadcasters and regulatory bodies to respond quickly to recent demographic developments are an indication of an inherent conservatism within the broadcasting sector.

Print Media

Ireland's newspaper market thrives by dint of very positive readership figures in comparison to other European countries. ABC figures show that the 47 indigenous titles (including three national daily and five national Sunday papers) sell well and effectively hold their own against the 24 British papers distributed in Ireland, eight of which have Irish editions. All tastes from tabloid to broadsheet are catered for, and coverage in various papers ranges from serious investigative reporting to sports and lifestyle-dominated stories. While new titles wishing to break into the market may face difficulties from the expense involved, new titles do appear to be satisfying most geographical, linguistic and ethnic demands. The nationwide launch of the *Irish Daily Mail* although costly is so far considered successful. *Lá*'s publication shows that the Irish language can still be seen as a potential growth market and *Gazetta*, *Lietuvis* and *Tiao Wang* as well as the *Polska Gazeta* and *Polski Herald* show how enterprise at least recognizes the value of Ireland's immigrant communities. As stated above, Ireland's ethnic diversity is much better reflected in the press than on television or radio.

IMPACT OF OWNERSHIP AND REGULATION ON MEDIA DIVERSITY

Press Ownership and Media Pluralism

As seen in Q10.1, there are concerns about the degree of concentration of ownership in the Irish newspaper sector. It has been suggested, for example, that Independent News and Media's (IN&M) dominant position in the Irish media affords it the ability to influence public and hence political opinion. (Dooley, 2005: 3) This assertion raises the question of whether there is in fact any discernable effects of media ownership on the content of the Irish media.

The *Irish Press* was historically the only national Irish newspaper with an overt link to a particular political party. (Horgan, 2001: 28) And, while the *Irish Times* is sometimes portrayed as having a liberal agenda and the *Irish Independent* has been criticised for having an editorial policy that too closely parallels the interests of its owners, little proof of such biases has been produced.

While front page election editorials are unusual in Ireland, the infamous "Payback Time" editorial on the front of the *Irish Independent* before the 1997 general election has been cited as proof of a newspaper attempting to influence an election on behalf of its owners' business interests. (Walsh, 1997) However, owner Tony O'Reilly, has been adamant that there was no interference from him and has been backed up by the editor in question. O'Reilly claims that: "the general view, I would say, about Independent News & Media, is that governments always feel they are being maligned by it, whatever government, and opposition feel that they are being ignored". (Keena, 2004)

There has also been criticism of the press in its 2002 general election coverage. A lack of balance in pictorial coverage in the national media in favour of government parties during that election saw the Progressive Democrats receiving a disproportional amount of coverage. (Montague, 2002) While this disparity seemed to have little influence on the outcome of the campaign, it further illustrates the need for vigilant objectivity on the part of newspaper editors, media commentators and readers.

The portrayal of refugees, asylum seekers and immigrants in the Irish media represents another order of bias altogether. Research into media coverage of refugees and asylum seekers found that media stories on asylum tend to exclude the voices of minorities, over-simplify complex situations and present stereotypical images of asylum seekers and refugees. Overall, this research found that the media in Ireland, however unconsciously, may effectively be perpetuating racism. (Haynes, Devereux and Breen, 2004: 7)

In addition, less subliminal perpetuations of racism exist: "Travellers and black people are equally misrepresented and negatively portrayed in the Irish media. In particular also various codes and code terms have evolved in the Irish media which are no more than a form of racist shorthand". (Onyejelem, 2005: 76) An earlier study had also suggested that negative public opinion towards immigrants may have been influenced by media coverage. (Pollak, 1999: 42)

According to the NUJ code of conduct, "A journalist shall mention a person's age, sex, race, colour, creed, illegitimacy, disability, marital status, or sexual orientation only if this information is strictly relevant. A journalist shall neither originate nor process material which encourages discrimination, ridicule, prejudice or hatred on any of the abovementioned grounds". In too many instances, however, Irish journalists have not abided by these guidelines. There are also no "agreed mechanisms" of redress below the courts for print journalists and no significant sanctions against those who breach the NUJ code of practice, although the proposed Press Council and the reform of libel law may provide some change in this area. (See below)

Media Regulation

If a medium is to be pluralistic, a balance must be struck between the rights of individuals to be protected from unfair media treatment and the duty of the media to effectively examine society. In broadcasting there are methods by which an equitable balance can be maintained without the need for court intervention. The RTÉ charter, for example, pledges that "RTÉ... shall reflect the democratic, social and cultural values of Irish society and the need to preserve media pluralism." It will "strive to reflect fairly and equally the regional, cultural and political diversity of Ireland and its peoples," and it promises that: "No editorial or programming bias shall be shown in terms of gender, age, disability, race, sexual orientation, religion or membership of a minority community. (Department of Communications, Marine and Natural Resources, 2004: 2)

In addition, the Broadcasting Complaints Commission (BCC) adjudicates on complaints from the public about all broadcasts, including RTÉ. Its rulings, however, are binding only on BCI licensees. A survey of such judgements reveals that since 2004, 200 complaints have been adjudicated by the BCI: 83 per cent of these were rejected, while 17 per cent were upheld. The majority of complaints received related to bias (61 per cent), while the greatest number of successful complaints related to taste and decency (57 per cent). Only eight out of a total of 122 (6.6 per cent) complaints of media bias were upheld. Four complaints that a person's privacy had been violated were upheld. (www.bcc.ie)

This complaints procedure might predict the manner in which a press council could operate, although broadcasters in Ireland in general are not seen as partial in comparison to broadcasters in other countries and are largely perceived to present themselves as impartial and as respectful of the privacy of individuals. (www.rte.ie/about/guidelines) The same perception would not be the case with the press where charges of privacy and bias are more common.

Press Council

There are still no official codes of practice for the press in their dealings with citizens who feel they have been unfairly treated by a newspaper. No press council currently exists in Ireland, although one is to be established as part of a proposed Defamation Bill which is now at draft stage. Supporters of the Bill point to cases where the media have acted with disregard to the right of citizens.

The final version of the press council that emerges will have a significant impact on the ability of the media to practice free from government interference. (Other aspects of the Defamation Bill and the controversy surrounding it are discussed in more detail in Q10.5.)

Q10.3 How effective are the media and other independent bodies in investigating government and powerful corporations?

The major prerequisites for effective investigative journalism are by and large present in Ireland. The market for media is very healthy and journalism has the financial backing it needs to operate effectively. Irish people watch more news on TV, read more news in their papers, and listen to more radio news than is the average across the EU. Trust in radio and television in Ireland are both well above the EU average, while the level of trust for press journalists, although lower, is average for the EU. Irish media is not generally perceived as being corrupt and Irish people believe that the media have an important role in society in ensuring government accountability.

Over recent years, journalists have uncovered many instances of government and corporate wrongdoing. In fact, of 22 instances of corruption which occurred between 1991 and 2000, 13 came to public attention as a result of a media investigation or story. (Collins and O'Shea, 2000)

INVESTIGATIVE JOURNALISM IN IRELAND

Effective investigative media requires firm financial foundations, the respect and attention of its audiences, a regulatory environment which is not oppressive, a lack of interference in editorial decisions from government and corporations, and the cooperation of the public and officials in providing it with its lifeblood: information. These elements are by and large present in Ireland. While Q10.2 explores some aspects of the regulatory environment and the potential for interference in editorial decisions, the focus here will be on the remaining issues cited.

Financial Supports for Journalism

The media landscape in Ireland is varied enough to enable journalists to find outlets for good investigative work. The market for media products is very healthy as a result of the continuing economic boom – so much so that many international corporations have bought into the Irish media with the expectation of profitable returns. In general, journalism in Ireland has the financial backing it needs to operate effectively.

Public Opinion of the Media

Some sections of journalism in Ireland are held in high regard, while others do not enjoy the respect of their public. According to a recent Eurobarometer survey, broadcast journalists enjoy the trust of their audiences while press journalists do not; however, the low level of trust for press journalists is still average for the EU15 (see Table 10.4 below). Trust in both radio and television in Ireland are both well above the EU average. Newspaper readership in Ireland is higher than average, which indicates that whatever about trusting their journalists, Irish readers like to read what they have to say.

Table 10.4 Trust in the Media

For each of the following institutions, please tell me if you tend to trust it or tend not to trust it?

	Tend to Trust % (Ireland)	*Tend to Trust % (EU)*
The Press	47	46
Radio	75	63
Television	74	54

Source: Compiled from Eurobarometer, 2004: b15

There are mixed findings on whether Irish people believe that the media can influence political and social events. A Prime Time/MRBI poll in 2003 found that the media (at 21 per cent) were less-valued members of the community than doctors (90 per cent); teachers (81 per cent); gardaí (78 per cent); priests (49 per cent); solicitors (35 per cent) and politicians (22 per cent). At the same time this finding could partly be explained by the fact that the media have no "community" role.

However, Irish people do believe that the media have an important role in society. In a 2005 survey carried out for the Democratic Audit Ireland project, respondents when asked what they thought was most important in making government answerable for their actions cited the media as one of three effective means of ensuring government accountability. (Clancy *et al.*, 2005: 13)

Table 10.5 Government Accountability and the Media

Which of these do you think is most important in making government answerable for their actions?

	%
The people at election time	32
Opposition parties / Independent TDs	23
The Media	19
Other	26

Source: Adapted from Clancy *et al.*, 2005: 12

Eurobarometer statistics reveal a public decidedly eager for news coverage. Indeed, Irish people watch more news on TV (68 per cent daily), read more news in their papers (47 per cent daily) and listen to more radio news (63 per cent daily) than do their EU15 counterparts (69 per cent, 40 per cent, 38 per cent respectively). (Eurobarometer, 2002) Morever, this news appears to be disseminated by a media not held to be corrupt, as evidenced by the *Global Corruption Barometer, 2005*, in which Irish people give their media a 2.8 score which is below the European average of 3.3 (with 1.0 seen as not corrupt and 5.0 seen as very corrupt).

FREEDOM OF INFORMATION

Initially the Freedom of Information Act 1997 was viewed by journalists as a largely unqualified success. (See also Q7.7) However, the Dáil amended the Act in April 2003, limiting journalists' access to public records, and the introduction of fees for some categories of requests has also had a constraining effect. As a result the amendment of the Freedom of Information Act has been sharply criticised as obstructing journalists' access to public data. There is now a fee of €15 to seek permission to look at government and court documents, including minutes and internal department communications deemed to be of public interest. An appeal against refusal costs €75, whatever the result of the appeal. In addition, under the amendments, material cannot be accessed before it is 10 years old instead of the previous five years, and the authorities are allowed to either deny or not confirm the existence of confidential documents. Former journalist Emily O'Reilly, appointed to oversee the operation of the Act, has expressed her own doubts: "...the imposition of fees has caused a sharp downturn in usage of the Act and has so diluted its guiding principles ... that the policy of charging fees needs to be re-examined". (O'Reilly, 2004: 34) Between 2003 and 2004, usage of the Act fell by 50 per cent; non-personal requests fell by 75 per cent and media usage declined by 83 per cent.

PRIME TIME

"The history of RTÉ tends to suggest that the station's reputation is built primarily, not just on the authenticity of its news coverage, but on the impact made by a flagship current affairs programme...". (Horgan, 2004: 192) At present, this flagship programme is *Prime Time.*

Prime Time plays an unusually significant role in public debate. A survey of the Dáil record between 20 January 2004 and 28 March 2006 shows that *Prime Time* was mentioned as a source in discussion of a public controversy 212 times. An issue covered by *Prime Time* on a Tuesday regularly appears in questions and discussions the following Wednesday or Thursday.

In general, investigative journalism at RTÉ benefits from its improved financial position as the national broadcaster which, since removal of the advertising cap and the proposed index-linking of the licence fee, is more secure. With this security has come an increased willingness on the part of the station to invest resources in investigative journalism, particularly the *Prime Time Investigates* series of programmes.

Q10.4 How free are journalists from restrictive laws, harassment and intimidation?

In general, journalists in Ireland are free from harassment and intimidation. There have been isolated incidences in the past of interference by government, and harassment of individual journalists by criminal gangs does occur. Such incidents, however, are exceptional.

The European Court of Human Rights has accepted that the anonymity of journalists' sources should be protected and that such protection is one of the basic conditions for press freedom. However, there is currently no explicit legal protection for journalists in Ireland with regard to their right to protect sources of confidential information. Although it is extremely rare for journalists in Ireland to be jailed for refusing to reveal sources, there have been recent instances where Tribunals of Inquiry have sought to force journalists to do so.

PRESS FREEDOM

According to international measures, Ireland enjoys one of the freest presses in the world. Freedom House, a US-based non-governmental organisation (NGO), assesses the degree of print, broadcast, and Internet freedom in every country in the world. (Deutsch Karlekar, 2005) Each country is assessed as free, partly free, or not free by examining three broad categories: the legal environment in which media operate; political influences on reporting and access to information; and economic pressures on content and the dissemination of news. Ireland emerged in 18th place in the 2005 Global Press Freedom Ranking. (See also Q3.2)

In general, journalists in Ireland are free from harassment and intimidation. There have, however, been isolated incidences documented in the past of interference by government, for example, the cases of phone tapping of journalists Geraldine Kennedy and Bruce Arnold in the early 1980s.

Cases of harassment of individual journalists by criminal gangs do occur. Moreover, in 1996 investigative journalist Veronica Guerin was murdered by organised criminals involved in drug dealing. Her murder, along with that of Detective Garda Gerry McCabe, (See Q8.4) led to the enactment of a series of measures against drug gangs and organised crime. Organised criminals have also been responsible for a series of incidents of intimidation against the *Sunday World* crime correspondent Paul Williams. These examples, however, are exceptional.

The law on defamation in Ireland has been criticized as creating an overly-restrictive work environment for journalists and thereby a restriction on press freedom. Under the Defamation Act 1961, newspapers and periodicals accused of libel have to prove that defamatory words employed are true. In October 2003, Independent News and Media complained to the European Court of Human Rights that the very heavy fines facing the media in libel and slander cases created a climate of fear that restricted journalists in their work. (*Irish Independent*, 17 October 2003)

The Censorship of Publications Acts 1929 to 1967, although infrequently used, retain the power to limit magazine and newspaper content in Ireland. In the past, Section 31 of the Broadcasting Act permitted the minister responsible to pass an order that "any matter" could not be broadcast. Between 1976 and 1994, a ministerial order under Section 31 decreed that interviews with the IRA and Sinn Féin could not be broadcast. An earlier order, in existence between 1971 and 1976 had a similar effect but did not specifically name any organisation. Journalists, concerned that they might break the law, in practice interpreted this order quite broadly. (Horgan, 2004) The Broadcasting Act of 2001 removed this provision and little danger currently exists to a democratic media from censorship in Ireland.

PROTECTION OF JOURNALISTS' SOURCES

An issue of concern involves cases in which the courts and tribunals seek to force journalists to reveal sources of information. One example is the effort in 1999 by the British authorities to force Ed Moloney, Northern Editor of the Dublin-based *Sunday Tribune*, to surrender to the security forces notes he had made of an interview with a murder suspect in 1989. The judge's decision, while not conceding the journalist's rights to withhold, nonetheless found in his favour in this instance. The judgement was welcomed by the National Union of Journalists (NUJ) as a significant step towards greater protection for journalists' sources. However, there have been more recent cases in Ireland where tribunals of inquiry have sought to force journalists and politicians to reveal the sources of their information.

There is no explicit legal protection for journalists with regard to their right to protect sources of confidential information. The Law Reform Commission considered this issue in 1994 and recommended leaving the law unchanged. However, in its judgement in the case of *Goodwin v U.K.* (1996), the European Court of Human Rights accepted that the anonymity of journalists' sources should be protected. The Court found that:

> Protection of journalistic sources is one of the basic conditions for press freedom, as is reflected in the laws and the professional codes of conduct in a number of Contracting States and is affirmed in several international instruments on journalistic freedoms. (European Court of Human Rights, 1996)

Journalists in Ireland have been jailed twice in the history of the state for refusing to reveal sources, once in 1931 – the Dennigan case, and once in 1972 – the Kevin O'Kelly case, in which a fine was substituted, on appeal, for the original jail sentence. At the same time, a number of cases have occurred more recently where journalists have been threatened with imprisonment. In 1995, journalist Susan O'Keefe of Granada Television was prosecuted for refusing to name her sources to the Beef Tribunal and subsequently acquitted on a technicality. The fact that O'Keefe remains the only person to appear before a court as a result of the Beef Tribunal is richly ironic, given that it was her investigative journalism which was responsible for the Tribunal being established in the first place.

In 1996, journalist Barry O'Kelly, then of *The Star*, was threatened with imprisonment unless he revealed his source for a relatively uncontroversial story he wrote on a breach-of-settlement claim by a former employee of the Garda Representative Association (GRA). O'Kelly avoided prison when the judge, on advice from the Attorney General, continued the trial without insisting that O'Kelly reveal his sources. The same journalist was again threatened with prosecution in 2004 when, on this occasion working for the *Sunday Business Post*, he refused to reveal his sources to the Mahon Tribunal on two stories relating to payments to politicians being investigated by the Tribunal. Recent appearances by Geraldine Kennedy and Colm Keena of the *Irish Times*, also before the Mahon Tribunal, over alleged leaks to the newspaper from the Tribunal which initiated the controversy over payments made to the Taoiseach, Bertie Ahern, in the 1990s is a further example of the difficulties journalists face in protecting their sources.

Politicians have also been at the receiving end of judicial demands to reveal the sources of allegations made to them about gross misconduct in the senior ranks of the gardaí. In 2003, the Morris Tribunal, which is investigating alleged corruption by gardaí in Co Donegal, ordered the Labour Party's Brendan Howlin and Senator Jim Higgins of Fine Gael to reveal their sources, on threat of prosecution. (*Irish Times*, 1 March 2003)

Q10.5 How free are private citizens from intrusion and harassment by the media?

Citizens in Ireland are generally free from intrusion and harassment by the media. Politicians, with some justification, have argued that this reality is less the case for public representatives. Two pieces of draft legislation – a Privacy Bill and a Defamation Bill – are currently being prepared which propose reform of libel law and the establishment of a press council to deal with complaints against the press.

The proposed reforms in the draft Defamation Bill have been broadly welcomed, while the draft Privacy Bill has come in for severe criticism. The major criticisms focus on the proposal within the Bill to establish a press council. The proposed press council differs significantly from that which pertains in many other countries in that it will be both statutory and indirectly appointed by the Minister for Justice, Equality and Law Reform. As a result, there are significant concerns regarding the effect of such a council on press freedom in Ireland.

REFORM OF LIBEL LAW AND PRESS REGULATION

It is widely accepted that libel law in Ireland is in need of reform. At present, taking an action in the court is the only course for those who believe their rights have been infringed by the press. However, High

Court costs average €50,000 per day and are beyond the reach of most. (Bourke, 2004: 10) Those individuals who do not have the resources usually cannot protect their reputations, while those who do are in a position to pressurise newspapers not to go to print, even when stories may be true. While the former situation is inequitable, the latter presents a threat to a democratic and effective media.

There is evidence that libel law has been used on occasion by business and political figures to silence the press. An analysis of libel cases taken in Ireland since 1995 shows that of 73 cases considered, the overwhelming majority of plaintiffs were drawn from elite social groups, particularly from business and politics. Only 10 cases were brought by private citizens.

The issue of libel law reform has been researched extensively. In 1991 the Law Reform Commission reported that Ireland's civil law on defamation was hopelessly out of date and "served neither plaintiff, defendant nor public satisfactorily". Five years later, the government-appointed Commission on the Newspaper Industry added its view that changes to the libel laws were "a matter of considerable urgency".

In 2000, the UN Commission on Human Rights Special Rapporteur in his report on Civil and Political Rights recommended that a new Defamation Bill be introduced. The report urged that under any new law, the onus of proof should be on those claiming to have been defamed, rather than on the defendant as it is at present, and that the damages awarded for defamation should not be so large as to exert a chilling effect on the freedom of expression.

Among the recommendations of the various reports are an end to the presumption of falsity, clearer guidelines for juries on assessing damages, and a provision for the publication of an apology without admission of liability.

The Legal Advisory Group on Defamation, set up by the Minister for Justice, Equality and Law Reform in 2002, reported in March 2003. After making a commitment to reform of libel law in its Programme for Government, the government in 2001 agreed the general scheme of a Defamation Bill. The Legal Advisory Group was subsequently asked to examine this draft Bill with a limited remit to suggest changes or additions. The Advisory Group recommended that, while the presumption of falsity should be retained, all plaintiffs should be cross-examined in court on the particulars of their claims, as a means of providing a degree of balance.

The terms of reference of the Legal Advisory Group on Defamation gives an insight into government thinking on the area of libel law and its use as a means of limiting investigative journalism. The preamble of the Group's report states "The Legal Advisory Group on Defamation was established ... against a background where the agreed programme for government indicated that the government would, in the context of a statutory press council and improved privacy laws, move to implement reforms of libel laws to bring them into line with those of other states."

Another investigation into the use of libel law in Ireland stated that, "This juxtaposition of libel law on one hand and broad statutory regulation of the press on the other amounts to the frankest acknowledgement so far ...[that]...libel law currently substitutes for direct statutory regulation...and is seen to do so by politicians." (Bourke, 2004: 19)

Indeed, the most controversial proposal made by the Legal Advisory Group on Defamation in the Mohan Report was the recommendation to establish a government-appointed statutory press council.

The 2003 Mohan Report on Defamation

The Mohan Report Proposals

- A new defence of reasonable publication should be created.
- Judges would be required to give directions to a jury on the matter of damages.
- There should be no substantive change in the status quo insofar as the presumption of falsity is concerned.
- A statutory press council should be established with functions which would include the preparation of a press code of conduct and the investigation of complaints concerning alleged breaches of that code.
- Defendants in defamation cases should be able to make lodgements without an admission of liability.
- The tort of malicious falsehood should be retained but should be restated in a clearer and more simplified manner.
- As a general rule, the limitation period for defamation actions should be one year.

Two separate Bills – a Privacy Bill and a Defamation Bill – are currently working their way through the legislative process.

Under the terms of the draft Defamation Bill it is proposed to introduce a defence of publication "for the purpose of discussing a subject of public importance". The draft Bill also allows for an apology to be issued without an admission of liability and makes welcome amendments in the area of damages, by proposing increases in the power of the Supreme Court to reduce the amount of awards on appeal. The draft Bill also proposes to reduce the period for actions from six years down to a maximum of two years. These proposed changes have been broadly welcomed.

One caveat is that "issues of public importance" may be judged, of course, to be quite different from those of "public interest". A broad definition of "the public interest" by the Supreme Court may, therefore, be a key in determining that this wording in the draft Defamation Bill does not become an undue restriction on press freedom in the future.

The draft Privacy Bill has come in for more severe criticism. The major criticism focuses on the proposal to establish a statutory press council. The press council which is outlined in the Bill differs significantly from that which pertains in many other countries, in that it will be statutory and indirectly appointed by the Minister for Justice, Equality and Law Reform, whereas most press councils are voluntary and self-regulatory bodies which contain some level of non-owner, non-journalist participation.

The Organisation for Security and Cooperation in Europe (OSCE) has recommended that provision for a press council should be removed from the Bill and such a council established voluntarily, on the grounds that press councils are not suited to statutory regulation. The OSCE continues that "if the statutory press council is not abolished, there must be clear provisions ensuring its administrative and operational independence. These should include the protection of the security of tenure of both the directors of the statutory press council and the press ombudsman." (Article 19, 2006: iii)

There is currently in the draft Bill a kind of "at-arms-length" system of government appointment, wherein the minister will appoint a panel, which will appoint a press council which will in turn appoint an ombudsman with a supervisory role over the council. However, even this indirect process of political appointment may still leave the council and ombudsman open to criticism on the grounds of perceived partiality.

An assessment of the democratic character of the proposed press council can be made by comparing it with the norm elsewhere. Of the 25 EU states, independent press councils exist in eighteen jurisdictions. A small minority of these are statutory councils, while many have a mixed membership drawn from outside the media. These bodies are themselves very critical of what is being proposed for Ireland. According to the Alliance of Independent Press Councils Europe (AIPCE), a government-appointed press council "would not only go against the trend in Europe and throughout much of the world – where independent rather than state-controlled press regulation is the norm – it would also diminish press freedom and undermine the independence of Irish newspapers". (www.pcc.org.uk) The National Newspapers of Ireland, the representative body for Ireland's national newspapers and Irish editions of UK national newspapers, is equally opposed to a statutory press council and has called instead for an independent system.

Achieving a balance between the proposals contained within the draft Privacy Bill and in the Defamation Bill is essential to ensuring freedom of investigative journalism in the public interest.

In December 2006, the newspaper and magazine industry agreed proposals with the government for an independent press council and complaints procedure. The agreed proposals are that a majority on the new press council will be independent of the media and are to be chosen through an independent appointments process. The second stage debate on the Defamation Bill to give effect to these proposals was initiated in December 2006.

Eleven: Political Participation

Is there full citizen participation in public life?

INTRODUCTION AND SUMMARY

The idea of "active citizenship" has received considerable international attention in recent years, and was the focus of a special task force set up by the Taoiseach Bertie Ahern in 2006. The concept moreover encompasses two separate but related ideas – the notion of "social capital" and that of "deliberative democracy".

Social capital, according to the concept's leading proponent Robert Putnam, "refers to the collective value of all 'social networks' and the inclinations that arise from these networks to do things for each other". (Putnam, 2000) According to Putnam, social capital is a key component in building and maintaining democracy. Studies of social capital thereby tend to focus on volunteering and informal social networks, and the ways in which these contribute to the cohesion of society.

Deliberative democracy, on the other hand, focuses mainly on civic participation and mechanisms for citizen input into decision making. While voting is recognised as a central democratic institution, proponents of deliberative democracy argue that legitimate lawmaking can only arise from the ongoing public deliberation of the citizenry between, as well as at, elections.

These two aspects of active citizenship were described in a submission to the Democracy Commission as "the sense of wider social concern and the capacity to participate deliberatively in self-government". (Honohan, 2005: 179) To these definitions we might also add people's readiness to take part in the more formal aspects of public life, such as holding a public office, whether paid or unpaid. Just how widespread active citizenship is in all these senses, and how representative of all sections of society, provides a litmus test of the vitality of a country's democracy.

In this section we examine a number of issues across all these areas of concern, including the range of voluntary associations, citizen groups, social movements, and non-governmental organisations in Ireland, together with their degree of independence from government; citizen participation in voluntary associations and in other voluntary public activity; the extent of women's participation in political life and public office; and the access to and equality of representation within public office for all social groups.

Our "health check" of civic activism in Ireland reveals a wide range of organisations in the non-profit sector, covering every area of social, cultural and economic life, many of which are dependent on volunteers to operate effectively. Their role in public life has become more formalised through the social partnership process at national level, and *via* area-based partnerships at the local level. The close relation that many organisations consequently have with government, and the fact that 60 per cent of the sector's overall income comes from public funds, have led to concerns that their independence in advocacy and agenda setting may become compromised. Such concerns are less evident in membership organisations such as trade unions and professional associations, whose income comes mainly from membership dues.

As regards the extent of people's participation in such associations and their activities, Ireland shows higher levels of engagement in informal social networks and community activism than the UK, higher rates of involvement in membership organisations, and greater confidence that ordinary people can make a difference to public decision making. Non-Irish nationals make up a significant proportion of volunteers in some sectors. Women are more likely than men to be "community activists", and equally involved as men in "political activism". These ratios, however, are not reflected in their presence in public office. Although steps have been taken through positive government action to increase female board membership on public bodies, the proportion of women members in the Oireachtas remains pitifully low, with the process and culture of candidate selection a likely reason. The unrepresentativeness of the Oireachtas applies also to other groups and sectors of Irish society.

Q11.1 How extensive is the range of voluntary associations, citizen groups, social movements, etc, and how independent are they from government?

The non-profit sector in Ireland includes a myriad of organisations engaged in a broad range of activities.

The growing interaction between the state and the voluntary sector has become increasingly formalised over recent years. In the white paper *Supporting Voluntary Activity* in 2000, the government set out a range of practical measures to be taken by the state to enhance the input from community and voluntary organisations into policy formation. However, an analysis of the government's response to the white paper carried out three years after its publication concluded that progress on implementation has been very limited.

The state currently provides around 60 per cent of total funding for the non-profit sector. In contrast, overall private donations in 2006 to the sector amounted to around 10 per cent, while fees constituted around 15 per cent of funding, and corporate donations contributed 1.4 per cent. (Donoghue *et al.*, 2006: 47) Anecdotal evidence suggests that dependence on state funding can result in voluntary groups effectively practising "self-censorship" so as to avoid any risk to funding. A small number of groups specifically involved in advocacy and campaigning for human rights and social change choose not to rely on government funding, as a means of ensuring independence in their work, but these represent a tiny proportion of all groups within the non-profit sector.

Two of the more visible manifestations of the increase in formalised collaboration between the state and organisations within the voluntary sector since the early 1990s are social partnership at national level and area-based partnerships at local level.

The subsector which has seen the greatest growth over recent years is that concerned with ethnic minorities, refugees and asylum-seekers. Perhaps the weakest part of the voluntary sector is the subsector working on environmental issues.

EXTENT OF THE NON-PROFIT SECTOR

A 2006 survey of the non-profit sector in Ireland, *Hidden Landscape,* set out to map non-profit organisations in Ireland. (Donoghue *et al.,* 2006)

As is clear from their findings, the non-profit sector includes organisations engaged in a very wide range of activities including arts, recreation and sports, social service voluntary organisations, charities, community groups, churches, voluntary-run hospitals and schools, area-based partnerships, trade unions and NGOs, among others. (Table 11.1) Moreover, many non-profit organisations are often involved in more than one such activity. Within the non-profit sector, the "voluntary and community" sector is often defined as a subset of the non-profit sector by excluding hospitals, hospices, primary and secondary schools and higher education establishments. (Donoghue, 1998)

Table 11.1 Activities of Irish Non-Profit Organisations

Activities	*% of Respondents Engaged in These Activities*
Culture and arts	35.0
Recreation and social clubs	34.1
Environmental	29.8
Sports	29.0
Economic, social and community development	26.4
Adult education	23.2
Social services	22.4
Primary education	22.2
Employment and training	18.6
Civil rights and advocacy	18.2
Physical health	18.0
Secondary education	14.0
Mental health	13.6
Housing	8.9
Higher education	8.7
International/overseas development	8.3
Religious/faith-based	7.2
Emergency and relief services	7.2
Business and professional	7.0
Hospitals and rehabilitation	6.1
Animal protection	5.4
Law and legal services	5.3
Political	5.1
Trade union	3.5

Source: Adapted from Donoghue *et al.*, 2006: 35

Many organisations within the non-profit sector depend heavily on volunteers to operate effectively. Of the around 4,300 responding organisations to the *Hidden Landscape* survey, almost half (48.7 per cent) stated that volunteers were essential to their organisations. Volunteers were found to be particularly important for groups focusing on sports and recreation, the environment, arts and culture, and religion. (See also Q11.2)

Funding

According to the *Hidden Landscape* survey, the state provides the majority of funding to non-profit organisations (59.8 per cent).

In 2006, the vast majority of public sector funding to the non-profit sector went to organisations working in health (30.2 per cent), social services (16.9 per cent), education and research (15.9 per cent) and development and housing (13.4 per cent). Non-profit organisations working in international development received 7.7 per cent of state funding; organisations working in advocacy, law and politics received 6.8 per cent; arts, culture and heritage groups received about 5.6 per cent of public funds; and those working on issues concerning the environment received only 0.6 per cent.

The pattern of distribution of income from private donations varies greatly from that of state funding. (Table 11.2 overleaf) Non-profit organisations working in international development received 25.1 per cent of private donations; those focusing on social services received 21.6 per cent; philanthropy 10.4 per cent; and arts, culture and heritage 8.4 per cent. In contrast, health received only 8 per cent of private donations; education and research 5.9 per cent; development and housing 5.4 per cent; and organisations focused on advocacy, law and politics 3.5 per cent. (Donoghue *et al.*, 2006: 48) Private donations chiefly consist of individual private contributions from the public at large.

Further data from the *Hidden Landscape* survey shows that membership dues and corporate funding were important sources of funding for some organisations. Membership organisations such as trade unions, business and professional associations received more than half their income from membership dues. Income from fees was of greatest importance to education and research organisations which received over one-third of reported income from this source. Fees were also a significant source of income for health organisations and development and housing organisations.

Table 11.2 Public and Private Funding of Non-Profit Organisations

Public Funding	%	*Private Funding*	%
Health	30.2	International development	25.1
Social services	16.9	Social services	21.6
Education and research	15.9	Philanthropy	10.4
Development and housing	13.4	Arts, culture and heritage	8.4
International development	7.7	Health	8.0
Advocacy, law and politics groups	6.8	Education and research	5.9
Arts, culture and heritage	5.6	Development and housing	5.4
Environment	0.6	Advocacy, law and politics	3.5
Others	2.9	Others	11.7
Total	100	Total	100

Source: Adapted from Donoghue *et al.*, 2006: 47

With regard to corporate funding, philanthropy groups received over 45 per cent of corporate donations, with those focusing on social services, arts, culture and heritage, health, education and research also benefiting from this source of funding at a rate of around 9 per cent each. In contrast, religious groups, trade unions and environmental organisations received relatively low proportions of corporate donations.

According to the *Hidden Landscape* survey, the most vulnerable organisations in terms of financial stability were those working on the environment along with arts and cultural organisations. In contrast, the least vulnerable groups were those groups involved in philanthropy, trade unions and professional associations, and sports and recreation groups. Those working on advocacy, law and politics and development and housing were also relatively resource-secure. (Donoghue *et al.*, 2006)

INDEPENDENCE OF NON-PROFIT ASSOCIATIONS FROM GOVERNMENT

Independence from government within the non-profit sector is of particular importance for those organisations whose remit includes influencing government policy.

Church organisations, primarily schools and hospitals, will not be considered here, although some aspects of government policy which continue to be influenced by religious organisations, particularly education and health, are considered elsewhere in the audit (See, for example, Q3.3 and Q4.4). Organisations which receive little or no funding from government are potentially more independent in their operations than those who depend primarily on government for funding. Even here, though, there are concerns around potential government restrictions on such organisations' activities, for example, through the Electoral Amendment Act 2001. (See Q3.4)

In relation to non-profit organisations whose primary source of funding is from government, two main issues of independence need to be considered: a functional independence in terms of ongoing activities, particularly the freedom to express views to government and lobby for change and the related issue of financial independence.

The collaboration between the state and the voluntary sector has become increasingly formalised over recent years. Area-based partnerships were set up under the government's *Programme for Economic and Social Progress* in 1991. (Donoghue, 1998) The partnership companies were funded by the EU and the Irish government, with the bulk of the funding provided under the EU Local Urban and Regional Development Programme. (See Q13.3)

Community and Voluntary Pillar

The community and voluntary pillar of social partnership in 2006 consisted of:

- Age Action Ireland
- Carers Association
- Children's Rights Alliance
- Congress Centres for the Unemployed
- CORI Justice Commission
- Disability Federation of Ireland
- Irish Council for Social Housing
- Irish National Organisation for the Unemployed
- Irish Rural Link
- Irish Senior Citizens Parliament
- National Association of Building Co-operatives
- National Youth Council of Ireland
- Protestant Aid
- Society of St Vincent de Paul
- The Wheel

Source: (www.cori.ie)

The voluntary sector has also seen an increased formal, albeit consultative, role at national level and organisations from within the sector form the fourth pillar in the social partnership process. (Harvey, 2002) (See Q12.2 for full discussion of social partnership)

Since 1993, selected voluntary organisations have been chosen by government to become full members of the National Economic and Social Forum (NESF), and are also represented on the National Economic and Social Council (NESC), where the sector has five seats.

The National Economic and Social Council and the National Economic and Social Forum

The NESC was established in 1973. Since 1987, a primary function of the Council is to provide the framework for the development of a strategic framework for the conduct of relations and negotiation of national agreements between the government and the social partners. The NESF was established by the government in 1993 to provide advice on policies to achieve greater equality and social inclusion by analysing, monitoring and evaluating relevant programmes and policies in the context of social partnership arrangements, and to facilitate public consultation on policy matters referred to it by the government from time to time. The NESC Council includes nominees of employer and business organisations, community and voluntary organisations, trade unions and secretaries-general of a number of government departments. The NESF membership comprises four broad strands: members of the Oireachtas; employers/business, trade unions and farming bodies; the voluntary and community sector; and central government, local government and independents.

Source: Institute of Public Administration, 2007

Such formalised relationships between the state and voluntary sector function in parallel to longer-standing relationships which the state has maintained for many years with non-profit organisations, primarily church organisations, in the areas of schools and hospitals.

The trend toward this increasing formalisation seems set to continue. In its 2000 white paper *Supporting Voluntary Activity*, the government set out a range of practical measures to be taken by the state to enhance the input from community and voluntary organisations into policy formation. These provisions included:

- introduction of mechanisms in all relevant public service areas for consultation with community and voluntary sector groups and to allow the communities they represent to have an input into policy-making;
- designation of voluntary activity units in relevant government departments to support the relationship with the community and voluntary sector;
- holding of regular policy fora by relevant departments and agencies to allow for wider consultation and participation by the community and voluntary sector in the policy-making process; and
- "best practice" guidelines in relation to consultation by statutory agencies with the community and voluntary sector and in relation to funding mechanisms and systems.

An analysis of the government's response to the white paper undertaken three years after its publication concluded that progress on implementation was very limited. While funding schemes for the community and voluntary sector had been approved, they have come on stream several years late and at a 53 per cent lower level of funding than originally intended. (The Wheel, 2006) Moreover, only one government department had established a voluntary activity unit. Progress had, however, been made on new charities legislation and regulation. (See Q3.4)

Reforms are thus tending to increase both the number, and more formal nature of, relationships between the state and the voluntary sector. At the same time, the limited implementation of the white paper points to the continuation of present practice in many areas of government, whereby it remains relatively easy for voluntary organisations to gain access to meetings with government departments and even with ministers, but where departments resist the formalising of those relationships.

Recent experience has shown that disagreement with government may result in exclusion from consultative processes. The relationship between government and organisations within the community and voluntary pillar, for example, became particularly strained during the social partnership negotiations in 2002. Sixteen members of the community pillar voted against the national agreement *Sustaining Progress 2003-5* which resulted from those negotiations because of what they saw as a lack of social commitments within the agreement. As a consequence, those organisations lost their places, not only within the community and voluntary pillar, but on a broad range of national consultative and negotiating bodies as well. (Acheson *et al.*, 2004)

One of the organisations in the community and voluntary pillar that refused to endorse *Sustaining Progress* was the Community Workers Co-operative (CWC), a national anti-poverty network. In 2005, the CWC had its funding withdrawn, despite the fact that all evaluations of the funding programme showed the CWC to be one of the most active and effective organisations in addressing poverty and exclusion.

Reacting to the withdrawal of funding, the chairperson of the CWC said "The CWC is clearly being punished for its role in bringing the critical voice of disadvantaged communities together and allowing it to be heard. The right to have this independent voice and the role of the government in ensuring that such a voice exists is central to a healthy democracy. By making this decision this government is saying to disadvantaged communities throughout Ireland – "we will support you as long as you do not question our policies". (Community Workers Cooperative, 2005)

This interpretation was contested by government. A statement from the relevant Department said that its commitment was to focus "available resources on support for communities experiencing disadvantage, exclusion and isolation. Because the CWC does not meet this criterion, funding as an anti-poverty network will be discontinued..." (*Irish Times*, 25 January 2005)

A very small number of groups involved specifically in advocacy and campaigning for human rights and social change choose not to rely on government funding as a means of ensuring independence. Such organisations as a result are more dependent on philanthropic organisations than on government.

A 2002 analysis of the voluntary sector in Ireland concluded that while funding for the sector had improved in recent years, the subsector working on human rights and social justice issues received little government funding. The subsector which has seen the greatest growth over recent years is that concerned with ethnic minorities, refugees and asylum seekers, while perhaps the weakest part of the voluntary sector is the subsector working on environmental issues. (Harvey, 2002) This analysis also concluded that the most difficult subsector to identify was that concerned with political accountability and new democratic ideas. The more recent data from the *Hidden Landscape* survey (See Table 11.1 above) suggests that little has changed in this regard.

Q11.2 How extensive is citizen participation in voluntary associations and self-management organisations, and in other voluntary public activity?

Membership of voluntary and community organisations in Ireland is on a par with the OECD average, although well behind that in the US, the Netherlands and Great Britain. Estimates for 2006 show that around 37 per cent of the total population volunteer, an increase of around 4 per cent on the last available figures in 1999, which suggests there has not been any significant drop in the number of volunteers in recent years contrary to what many believe. Non-Irish nationals make up a significant proportion of volunteers in some sectors.

Ireland lies below the OECD average in terms of membership of political parties, local political groups, labour unions and professional associations. At the same time, membership of these groups in Ireland is ahead of that in major EU countries such as Germany, Great Britain and France. Survey findings show that substantial majorities of Irish citizens believe they have a duty to vote and want to have a say in how Ireland is run. These findings also show that most people believe that when ordinary citizens make an effort to influence political decisions, they can truly make a difference. Only one in five respondents think that being active in politics in Ireland is a waste of time.

POLITICAL ENGAGEMENT IN IRELAND

Of particular interest from a democratic point of view is citizen engagement in political activities as broadly defined. Table 11.3, on the following page, looks at the membership of various types of voluntary or community organisations across a number of countries. The figures are ranked by rates of participation in the various activities.

Table 11.3 Membership by Types of Voluntary and Community Organisations

	Political or Unions	*Sports or Cultural*	*Church or Religious*	*Other Groups*
USA	49.6	55.7	57.1	61.1
Netherlands	40.5	69.6	34.7	65.7
OECD Average	28.4	31.6	23.5	29.5
Ireland	**20.7**	**31.7**	**16.2**	**25.0**
Czech Republic	20.1	28.9	6.6	29.1
Germany	13.9	32.1	13.5	15.2
Japan	13.4	21.4	10.6	20.3
Great Britain	13.2	12.0	5.0	21.0
France	9.5	21.5	4.4	17.7
Spain	8.1	12.8	6.6	12.5

Source: Adapted from Organisation for Economic Co-operation and Development, 2005b: 84–5

It can be seen that while Ireland lies below the OECD average in terms of membership of political parties, local political groups, labour unions and professional associations, it is ahead of major EU countries such as Germany, Great Britain and France.

The finding that people in Ireland are more politically engaged in general than those of our nearest neighbour, the UK, finds further support in a survey carried out as part of the Democratic Audit Ireland project. The survey findings show that substantial majorities of Irish citizens want to have a say in how Ireland is run and believe they have a duty to vote. The survey also found that most people believe that when ordinary citizens make an effort to influence political decisions they can really make a difference. (Table 11.4)

While almost two-thirds (64 per cent) of respondents believe that citizens who make an effort can in fact influence political decisions, just over half (55 per cent) feel it is worthwhile to be active in politics. Such a finding suggests that a substantial number of people believe either, that they can influence politics by means other than political activism or, they are simply not interested in engaging.

Table 11.4 Participation in Democracy: Political Activism

To what extent do you agree or disagree with the following statements about citizen's participation in politics in Ireland today?

	Net Agree %	*Net Disagree %*
It is my duty to vote	79	5
I want to have a say in how the country is run	72	7
When ordinary citizens make an effort to influence political decisions, they can really make a difference	64	14
Citizens being active in politics is a waste of time	21	55

Source: Clancy *et al*., 2005: 8

While there is no marked gender difference in attitudes to political activism, age and socio-economic status do play a role. Those who feel most strongly that activism is not a waste of time are somewhat more likely to be aged 35 plus, to be from higher social class groupings and to have higher levels of education. Similar patterns are evident in relation to both the desire to have a say in how the country is run and a belief that an individual's actions can make a difference.

Positive attitudes towards the value of political activism, of course, do not necessarily translate into concrete action. In order to compare the extent of people's involvement in political and community activities respondents were asked about activities in which they had taken part during the past three years.

Table 11.5 Political and Community Activism

Which, if any, of the following have you done at any time in the past three years?

	Ireland %	*UK* %
Donated money or paid a membership fee to a charity or a campaigning organisation	61	44
Done voluntary work	39	28
Taken part in a charity/sponsored event	32	22
Helped organise a charity event	28	21
Been an officer of a voluntary organisation or club	17	13
Served on a school committee	10	NA*
Voted in the last general election	69	61
Voted in the last local authority election	67	50
Urged someone outside my family to vote	26	17
Stood for public office	1	1
Discussed politics or political news with someone else	40	38
Signed a petition	26	44
Urged someone to get in touch with a local councillor or TD	20	16
Attended the clinic of a local councillor or TD	16	NA*
Boycotted certain products for political, ethical or environmental reasons	8	20
Donated money or paid a membership fee to a political party	8	6
Taken part in a political demonstration, picket, march or political meeting	5	6
Taken an active part in a party political campaign	4	NA*
Taken an active part in any political campaign	3	3

Source of Irish figures: Clancy *et al*, 2005: 9
Source of UK figures: Adapted from The Electoral Commission, 2005: 30-31 *NA = Not asked.

Definitions were devised that defined a political activist as someone who has engaged in one or more of the following activities: boycotted certain products; donated money or paid a membership fee to a political party; taken an active part in a party political campaign; taken part in any political campaign; taken part in a political demonstration. A community activist is defined as someone who has engaged in one or more of the following: voluntary work; helping to organise a charity event; acting as an officer of a voluntary organisation.

The findings show that levels of community activity are much higher than levels of political activity. Almost 40 per cent of respondents had done some kind of voluntary work, and 28 per cent had helped to organise a charity event. By comparison, less than 10 per cent had boycotted products, or donated money or paid a membership fee to a political party, the most likely forms of political activism. (Table 11.5)

It is also the case that, women are more likely than men to be community activists. Political activists on the other hand are equally likely to be women or men. This finding is revealing. It demonstrates that the low levels of women's representation in politics is not due to a shortage of grass-roots women activists.

Those who are engaged in community activities are significantly more likely to also be engaged in political activism. More than 30 per cent of those who were very active at community level (i.e., at least two of the three activities) engaged in at least one political activity as well. This finding compares with just 10 per cent of those who were not active at community level at all.

Comparison of the findings from this survey with results from the UK reveals that levels of involvement in community activities are much higher in Ireland. While levels of party political activity are similar in the two countries, people's reported propensity to vote is much higher in Ireland. The two areas where respondents in the UK are more active are in signing petitions and boycotting goods.

VOLUNTEERING

The following key features of volunteering and civic engagement in Ireland were identified by the Task Force on Active Citizenship in (2006):

- Ireland is rich in terms of informal social networks by international comparisons;

- reported group membership and volunteering is around average by international comparisons; and
- there does not seem to have been any dramatic decline in recent decades in the numbers of people claiming to be active in their communities.

That social capital in Ireland is high by international standards can be seen in the responses to the World Values Survey 1999-2002 to the question, "How often do you spend time with friends, or with colleagues from work, or with people from church, sport/cultural groups?", as shown for a number of countries in Table 11.6. Only the Netherlands among the countries surveyed has a more sociable population, by this measure at least, than Ireland.

Table 11.6 International Measures of Sociability

Responses to World Values Survey: Proportion of respondents who rarely or never spend time with friends, colleagues or others in social groups.

	Rarely	*Never*
Japan	15.3	1.7
Czech Republic	10.0	1.2
France	8.1	1.5
Spain	6.8	1.5
OECD Average	6.7	1.2
Great Britain	5.0	1.2
Germany	3.5	0.5
USA	3.1	0.6
Ireland	**2.9**	**1.0**
Netherlands	2.0	0.3

Source: Adapted from Organisation for Economic Co-operation and Development, 2005b: 82–3

The World Values Survey also considered membership of voluntary and community organisations across various countries. The figures in Table 11.7 below show that membership of these organisations in Ireland is on a par with the OECD average, although well behind that in the US, the Netherlands and Great Britain.

Table 11.7 International Comparators of Membership of Voluntary and Community Organisations

	Proportion of respondents who do unpaid work for at least one group	*Average number of groups to which respondent belongs*
USA	64.7	3.26
Netherlands	47.3	3.06
Great Britain	43.1	0.61
OECD Average	31.2	1.34
Czech Republic	29.8	1.02
Ireland	28.4	1.15
France	21.9	0.61
Germany	19.5	0.84
Japan	15.6	0.84
Spain	15.6	0.48

Source: Adapted from Organisation for Economic Co-operation and Development, 2005b: 84–5

According to the National Committee on Volunteering, 33 per cent of the adult population volunteered in some capacity in 1998 – down from 39 per cent in 1992. (Ruddle and Mulvihill, 1999) However, responding organisations to the 2006 *Hidden Landscape* survey reported having a total 1,570,408 volunteers, implying that volunteer numbers were relatively high. Based on the 2006 census figures, this finding suggests that around 37 per cent of the total population (4,234,925) volunteer some of their time – up 4.1 per cent from the last figures in 1999. This suggests an increase rather than a drop in the number of volunteers in recent years.

Volunteering among Non-Irish Nationals

One area that has received less attention from those collecting data on volunteering is the participation of non-Irish nationals in voluntary work. While this sector has only emerged in recent years due to the increase in immigration, the restrictions imposed on non-Irish nationals (especially those from non-EU countries) – and on asylum seekers in particular – mean that, for many non-Irish nationals, the only work available to them is of a voluntary nature. Indeed, it has been observed that volunteering can be a key step in refugees and asylum seekers' resettlement. Figures from the Volunteer Centres of Ireland indicate that a significant proportion of volunteers are non-Irish nationals. (http: //emea.salesforce.com)

- Three hundred and two of the registered volunteers at the South Dublin Volunteer Centre in 2006 were Irish, 141 were non-Irish nationals.
- Of the 134 registered volunteers at the Galway Volunteer Centre, 101 were Irish and, in Sligo, 43 of the 109 registered volunteers were foreign.
- In Dublin City South Volunteer Centre, of the 385 volunteers registered in 2005 and 2006, 68 were foreign, while in Tralee 110 out of 197 registered volunteers were Irish.

The increase over recent years in the numbers of non-Irish nationals involved in volunteering has occurred alongside a marked increase in the numbers of immigrant and minority ethnic-led community and voluntary organisations in Ireland. (Feldman *et al.*, 2005)

Q11.3 How far do women participate in political life and public office at all levels?

The concept of democracy will only assume true and dynamic significance when political policies and national legislation are decided upon jointly by men and women with equitable regard for the interests and aptitudes of both halves of the population.

INTER-PARLIAMENTARY UNION

Women remain vastly underrepresented in political life in the Dáil where, currently, only 13 per cent of representatives are women, in the Seanad, with currently only 17 per cent representation, and in local government, where there is 17 per cent representation on county councils, 22 per cent on city councils and 15 per cent on borough councils respectively. Ireland's female representation at the European Parliament is significantly better at 38 per cent, while the election of female presidents for the last three successive terms is a significant change. Previously all Irish presidents were male. Women's membership of the larger political parties, including participation in their respective national executive committees, is significantly higher at around 30 per cent than women's elected representation. While women's representation within politics has grown, these increases occurred largely in the late 1980s, with little additional change since then. Most worryingly, advances in the equal representation of women in the Dáil have been halted in their tracks since 1992.

Advances by women have been made within the last decade in other areas of public life outside politics. Within the civil service, women now make up 20 per cent of principal officers, 10 per cent of assistant secretaries and 12 per cent of secretaries-general, which represents a significant advance. Similarly, over 25 women now hold positions in the judiciary, compared with six in 1992. Meanwhile, a significant number of boards of state bodies are approaching the government target of 40 per cent. These changes, which have largely occurred within the past decade, would appear to be ongoing.

Overall, despite significant gains in Ireland over recent decades, women remain significantly underrepresented in political life and public office at all levels.

INTERNATIONAL DEVELOPMENTS

Internationally, there have been substantial barriers to women's involvement in politics, which for centuries remained a domain traditionally reserved for men. This situation however has changed slowly, beginning with the extension of suffrage to women in the early twentieth century in Western democracies. As Table 11.8 indicates, the trend in terms of women's representation in politics around the world over the past half century has been one of gradual, but steady, progress. (Inter-Parliamentary Union, 2005)

Within the last decade, there has been a significant increase in the number of parliaments where women account for 30 per cent of representatives. The Beijing Platform for Action (BPA), which resulted from the final outcome of the 4th World Conference on Women held in Beijing, China in 1995 and obliges governments to advance the goals of equality for women around the world, has set a target of 30 per cent of women in parliament as the critical mass necessary to bring about real change. In 1995, women constituted over 30 per cent of the legislature in only five countries, but, by October 2005, the number of countries had increased to 20. (Inter-Parliamentary Union, 2005: 3)

Table 11.8 Percentage of Women in Lower House of Parliament 1945-2005

	1945	*1955*	*1965*	*1975*	*1985*	*1995*	*2000*	*2005*
Number of Parliaments	26	61	94	115	136	176	177	187
% of Women Representatives in Lower House	3.0	7.5	8.1	10.9	12.0	11.6	13.4	16.2

Source: Adapted from Inter-Parliamentary Union, 2005: 2, www.ipu.org

Despite these advances, women continued to represent just over 16 per cent of all elected representatives to international parliaments in 2005; moreover, women have no representation whatsoever in 11 parliaments; and in the lower house of 60 parliaments, the proportion of women is less than 10 per cent. (Inter-Parliamentary Union, 2006a: 19) Clearly, equality of representation for women across the world is still far from reality.

WOMEN IN IRISH POLITICS

Prior to the 1970s, women had a very limited role in political and public life in Ireland. Moreover, in 1970 the importation and sale of artificial contraceptives was illegal; women in the civil service and in many white-collar private-sector jobs were obliged to resign on marriage; and discrimination between men and women (and between married men and single people of both sexes) was blatant and pervasive. All of these prescribed barriers and more were removed by the late 1970s, after the issue of women's rights and women's role in society had forced its way onto the political agenda.

Today, the greater representation of women in political life worldwide is reflected in the changing position of women in Irish politics. (Table 11.9)

Table 11.9 Firsts for Women in Irish Politics

1918	Votes for women over 30; first women elected (Countess Markievicz, Sinn Féin)
1919	First woman government minister (Countess Markievicz)
1923	Votes for all women
1969	First women on a parliamentary committee (Evelyn Owens, Labour)
1979	First woman government minister in modern times (Maire Geoghegan-Quinn, Fianna Fáil)
1982	First woman cathaoirleach of the Seanad (Tras Honan, Fianna Fáil)
1982	First woman chairperson of a parliamentary committee (Nora Owen, Fine Gael)
1990	First woman president (Mary Robinson)
1993	First woman party leader (Mary Harney, Progressive Democrats)
1997	First woman Tánaiste (Mary Harney)
2002	First woman government chief whip (Mary Hanafin, Fianna Fáil)

Source: Galligan, 2005: 274

Women in the Oireachtas

The level of female representation in both Houses of the Oireachtas has remained poor since the foundation of the state. Since 1922, the percentage of women in the Dáil has never exceeded 14 per cent, and currently women constitute 13 per cent of Dáil members. (Galligan, 2005: 275) Internationally, Ireland performs poorly in terms of the representation of women in the national parliament, sharing the 78th position in the classification of 188 countries in 2006. This ranking places Ireland below the average level of female representation in the lower houses of parliament found in the Nordic Countries (41 per cent), the Americas (22 per cent), Europe (20 per cent), and Sub-Saharan Africa (17 per cent). (Inter-Parliamentary Union, 2006b)

The poor level of female representation in the Dáil is mirrored in the low proportion of women in the Seanad. Between 1937 and 1977, there were a total of only 19 female senators. (Galligan, 2005: 275) Since 1977, a slight increase in the number of women has occurred with the current

Seanad comprised of 17 per cent women. This figure is broadly in line with the global average of 16 per cent for female representation in the upper house, though it still compares unfavourably to figures in Belgium (38 per cent), the Netherlands (29 per cent), Austria (27 per cent) and Spain (23 per cent). (Inter-Parliamentary Union, 2006b)

Dáil committees form an important part of the legislative process in Ireland, and the12 per cent female membership on these committees mirrors the overall percentage of women in the Dáil and Seanad. (Galligan, 2005: 277) The number of women on each committee varies, with no female representation on three Dáil select committees, including the Committe for Social and Family Affairs. (Galligan 2005: 278)

Appointment of women as government ministers is a relatively recent phenomenon in Ireland. Prior to 1979, the sole female appointed to a ministerial post was Countess Markievicz 50 years earlier in 1919. In all, a total of only nine women ministers were appointed in the period 1922 to 2002. (Galligan, 2005: 274)

There are currently three women ministers in government along with two junior ministers. Meanwhile, certain government offices continue to elude women ministers, including the Office of the Taoiseach, the Department of Finance and the Department of Foreign Affairs.

The number of women both running for election and winning seats in Dáil Éireann has increased over time. Between 1922 and 2002, for example, 68 women were elected to the Dáil, two-thirds of whom were elected after 1977. Before 1977, the average Dáil contained only four women whereas, since then, the average has increased to fourteen. It would appear, however, that despite increases in the 1980s, and an increased presence at cabinet level since then, women's overall representation in the Dáil has effectively ground to a halt for almost 15 years. (Galligan, 2005: 275)

Ireland's President

I was elected by the women of Ireland, who instead of rocking the cradle, rocked the system.

MARY ROBINSON,
First Female President of Ireland

A change in public attitudes to women in politics is arguably evidenced most dramatically in the election of women as the two most recent presidents of Ireland. In 1990, Mary Robinson was elected as Ireland's first female head of state and, succeeded in 1997 by Mary McAleese. Mary Robinson's victory was particularly significant in making Ireland one of just two European countries, alongside Iceland, to elect a female head of state by popular vote. Moreover, prior to the election of Mary Robinson, the six presidential elections between 1938 and 1997 had been all-male affairs. By contrast, four of the five candidates in the 1997 election campaign were women. (Galligan 2005: 273)

Irish Representation at the European Parliament

The number of women elected as Irish MEPs to the European Parliament has increased since such elections were first introduced in 1979. In the first three European Parliament elections, held respectively in 1979, 1984 and 1989, at most two were elected out of a total of 15 seats on each occasion. In the 1994 election, however, the number of women MEPs elected increased to four, while in 1999 five women were elected out of a possible 15 seats. In the 2004 elections, the number of seats decreased to 13 but the number of women returned remained at five. (Inter-Parliamentary Union, 2006b)

The increase in Irish women MEPs is reflective of the increase in women elected to the European Parliament as a whole. In 1979, women constituted 17 per cent of the total number of members, whereas following the 2004 elections, the level of women's representation had increased to 30 per cent, (Inter-Parliamentary Union, 2006b) making the European Parliament considerably more representative of women than many of the national parliaments of its Member States, including Ireland.

Women in Local Government

In the 2004 local government elections, 122 women (17 per cent) won seats at county council level. This result represented only a marginal increase on the figure for 1999 but almost twice the number elected in 1986. At city and borough council level, women won 22 per cent and 15 per cent of the seats respectively. (www.qub.ac.uk/cawp) As shown by these figures, women remain significantly underrepresented at local government as well as at national level. In comparison, women comprised an average of 22 per cent of local government representatives for the EU overall in the late 1990s. (Galligan, 2005: 279)

Decision-making structures at the local level also include county enterprise boards, area partnership companies, county development boards and regional authorities. While the figures in each of these bodies are better than for elected office, women here too continue, in general, to be underrepresented. In 2004, the percentage of female representation on county enterprise boards stood at around 26 per cent on county development boards at about 21 per cent and on regional authorities at approximately 14 per cent. (Central Statistics Office, 2004a: 26) The proportion of women on the boards of area partnership companies presents the most positive picture of women's participation in decision making at local level with 31 per cent of women board members. (Galligan, 2005: 279)

Women in Irish Political Parties

In 2003, women constituted around 25 per cent, 29 per cent and 35 per cent of the respective membership in Fianna Fáil, Fine Gael and the Labour Party. (Galligan, 2005) Anecdotal evidence further suggests that the number of women joining the main political parties has increased since the early 1980s. For example, in the early 1980s, women constituted around 23 per cent to 25 per cent of total Labour Party membership compared with 33 per cent in 2006.

Additionally, the percentage of women on the national executive of Fianna Fáil and Labour has increased substantially since the 1980s. Fine Gael has consistently had higher female representation on its national executive, dating as far back as 1983. (Table 11.10) By 2004, the percentage of women on the national executives of the three larger political parties was largely proportionate to the percentage of female membership of each party itself.

Women have also achieved success at leadership level in recent years. In 1992, Liz McManus was elected as deputy leader of the Labour Party. In 1993, Nora Owen became the first woman deputy leader of Fine Gael and Mary O'Rourke became the first woman deputy leader of Fianna Fáil. In the same year Mary Harney became the first woman party leader (of the Progressive Democrats) and, in 1997, became the first woman Tánaiste. Also in 1997, Mary Hanafin, of Fianna Fáil, became the first woman government chief whip.

Table 11.10 Percentage of Women on National Executive of the Main Political Parties, 1983-2004 (%)

	Fianna Fáil	*Fine Gael*	*Labour*
1983	16.6	23.5	8.3
1987	16.6	21.6	16.2
1993	12.6	23.7	21.0
1998	30.0	21.4	26.3
2004	26.6	28.6	32.4

Source: Adapted from Galligan, 2005: 280

WOMEN IN PUBLIC OFFICE

Women in the Civil Service

By 2006, women constituted approximately 60 per cent of those employed. (Central Statistics Office, 2006b) This increase has been influenced in some measure by the lifting of the marriage ban in 1973 which had excluded an entire generation of women from continuing to work in the civil service once they married.

As a result, the proportion of women working in the civil service has increased significantly within a generation. Progress has also been made in opening up the senior grades in the civil service to women. In the late 1990s, only one woman (4 per cent) was in charge of a government department, i.e., at secretary-general level, while women comprised 11 per cent of the next most senior grade, assistant secretary, and 12 per cent of principal officers, with the majority of women employed in the civil service filling the lower grades. (Humphreys *et al.*, 1999) In 2003, 12 per cent of the secretaries-general, 10 per cent of the assistant secretaries and 20 per cent of the principal officers were women. Representation at middle-management level, i.e., administrative officer and higher executive officer, was more evenly balanced while women accounted for the majority of those employed at the lower grades, particularly at staff and clerical level. (Central Statistics Office, 2004a: 27)

Women on State Bodies

In 2005, the government renewed its commitment to ensure that a minimum 40 per cent representation from both genders is achieved on the boards of state bodies. Since 2005, nominating bodies must put forward both male and female options for appointment to those state boards for which they are the responsible authority. The government then chooses from among nominees so as to ensure that the 40 per cent minimum representation from both genders is achieved. Data suggests that this affirmative action is having a positive effect.

In a 2002 survey of board membership of 47 public bodies, conducted by the National Women's Council of Ireland, (2002: 17) 12 boards met the government target of 40 per cent minimum representation of women, 18 had less than 20 per cent women members, while female members on the remaining 17 boards ranged from 20 to 40 per cent.

In 2004, CSO data for the appointments to state-sponsored bodies showed the overall proportion of women to be over 25 per cent. (Central Statistics Office, 2004a: 26)

More recent figures suggest that the level of female representation on state boards is moving closer to the 40 per cent requirement, with women making up around 34 per cent of the total membership of state boards in December, 2005. (Department of Justice, Equality and Law Reform, 2006)

In 2005, the government introduced a rule that nominating bodies must put forward both male and female options for those appointments to state boards where they are the responsible authority. This decision was made on foot of figures which showed that where appointments were made on foot of nominations by the government or ministers, the 40 per cent target was achieved. However, where other bodies had the right to nominate members, women made up only 19 per cent of appointments. The fact that these "other bodies" account for 60 per cent of all appointments to state boards is arguably sufficient grounds for the imposition of the nomination rule as a means of ensuring further progress towards achieving the target. (Department of Justice, Equality and Law Reform, 2005c)

Despite criticism that there is no legal requirement to achieve the 40 per cent target and the fact that an overall balance between men and women on state boards has not yet been achieved, the government's action in this area remains the most positive move taken to date to redress gender imbalance in public office.

Women in the Judiciary

The number of female justices has increased substantially throughout the 1990s. In 1992, there were no women on the Supreme Court or Circuit Court, while only two out of 18 High Court judges and four out of 50 District Court judges were women. (www.qub.ac.uk/cawp) In 2003, these figures had increased significantly (Table 11.11), but women still overall account for only 21 per cent of all judicial positions. (Table 11.12)

Table 11.11 Women in the Judiciary – 1992 and 2003

Court	*No. of Women 1992*	*No. of Women 2003*
Supreme Court	0	2
High Court	2	3
Circuit Court	0	9
District Court	4	11
Total	6	25

Source: 1992 figures compiled from the Centre for Advancement of Women, www.qub.ac.uk/cawp and 2003 figures adapted from Galligan, 2005: 284

Table 11.12 Women in the Judiciary – 2003

Court	*No. of Judges*	*No. of Women*	*% of Women*
Supreme Court	8	2	25
High Court	28	3	10.7
Circuit Court	31	9	29
District Court	51	11	20.7
Total	120	25	20.8

Source: Adapted from Galligan, 2005: 284

REDRESSING THE BALANCE

Membership of international organisations, like the EU and the UN, has had a positive effect on the advancement of gender equality in Ireland. The Irish government has signed up to both the UN Convention on the Elimination of All Forms of Discrimination against Women (CEDAW) (1979) and the Beijing Platform for Action (1995).

States under CEDAW commit themselves to end all forms of discrimination against women by abolishing all forms of discriminatory laws; by introducing gender equality legislation; by establishing public bodies to protect women against discrimination; and by eliminating all acts of discrimination against women by individuals and organisations. Countries that have ratified the Convention are legally bound to put its provisions into practice and are also committed to submitting national reports every four years on measures they have taken to comply with the Convention.

Ireland submitted its combined Fourth and Fifth progress report on the implementation of CEDAW in June 2003. The UN CEDAW Committee in 2005 subsequently highlighted the progress that has been made in ensuring greater gender equality in Ireland under the Convention. However, the Committee called on the government to do more in particular to ensure greater representation of women in Irish political life. (United Nations, 2005)

A range of factors can be identified which hinder the ability of women to participate equally in political and public life in Ireland. These include social attitudes towards women, poor childcare facilities and, in the case of women in politics, the selection processes used by political parties in putting forward candidates for election.

In fact, the aforementioned candidate-selection process would appear to be one of the most significant barriers to women's entry into politics. (Galligan, 2005: 289–90) In a survey of Fianna Fáil party members, 84 per cent of female office holders within the party identified the lack of women delegates at selection meetings as a serious obstacle to ensuring equal opportunities for women nominees at conventions. (Centre for the Advancement of Women in Politics, 2004) In addition, anecdotal evidence suggests that it is not only the selection process itself, but also the attitudes of the selectors towards women as candidates that contributes to this barrier. A political culture within many parties, which disproportionately values male political endeavors, effectively ensures that women who go forward for selection are perceived less positively than male candidates, even though they may be just as effective as local councillors.

Growing pressure exists on political parties to adopt measures to redress the imbalance in female representation. The National Women's Council of Ireland has recommended the introduction of legislation to make 50 per cent of state funding for political parties dependent on maintaining a 40:60 gender balance among candidates selected for general and local elections. (National Women's Council of Ireland, 2002: 6) In its submission to the CEDAW committee in May 2005, the Irish Council for Civil Liberties also recommended that the Irish government introduce temporary special measures to increase the number of women who are nominated for election by political parties and for sanctions to be enforced against state boards who fail to meet quotas designed to increase women's participation. (Irish Council for Civil Liberties, 2005) Also in 2005, the Democracy Commission recommended the introduction of obligatory gender quotas (50: 50) for candidates put forward by political parties. (Harris, 2005: 69)

The fact that women's increased representation within politics largely occurred in the late 1980s and, that advances in women's equality of representation, within the Dáil in particular, have effectively halted since 1992, gives added weight to these arguments.

Q11.4 How equal is access for all social groups to public office, and how fairly are they represented within it?

As discussed in Q5.5 and Q5.6, neither the Dáil, the Seanad, nor local government, are truly representative of Irish society in terms of age, gender, or social class. In addition, the protection of the rights and interests of various minority groups are not at present sufficiently embedded in the representative structures of the Oireachtas or local government. No reserved seats exist in either the Dáil or Seanad for minorities, nor is the Seanad used as a means of increasing the overall representativeness of the Oireachtas. As a result the interests of these minorities and other marginalised groups are at present not fairly represented.

REPRESENTATION

While access to public office is relatively equal, on paper at least, for all those who fulfil the eligibility requirements (See Q5.3), there are in practice a number of serious impediments for members of particular social groups.

It is important to focus particularly on the issue of access and representation of minorities and vulnerable groups in relation to public office, bearing in mind the negative impact that an indifferent – or even hostile, majority of office holders may have on their enjoyment of the rights and benefits accorded by Irish society.

One could argue that groups which do not have direct access to public office may be represented by means of "virtual representation", whereby their interests are looked after by other enfranchised members of society. Such virtual representation might occur on the basis of common interests between minority groups and the wider electorate, or else through sympathy for a particular vulnerable group on the part of the wider electorate. However, ample evidence exists that such indirect representation simply does not work to adequately protect the interests of minority groups.

- According to the 2002 census, around 21 per cent of the Irish population is aged between 18 and 30, and almost 42 per cent are aged between 18 and 44. However, all political parties are under-representative of these age categories – only six TDs aged 30 and under were elected in 2002, which is less than 4 per cent of the total number of deputies in Dáil Éireann.
- The picture is similar for older people. Only 3 per cent of the TDs elected in the 2002 general election were aged 65 or over in that election year, whereas this same age group accounts for over 11 per cent of the population.
- Non-nationals cannot run in Dáil or Seanad elections. However, EU citizens living in Ireland are eligible to run for election as MEP and all those normally resident in Ireland are eligible to run for public office in local government, regardless of nationality.
- There are currently no representatives from racial or ethnic minority communities in either the Dáil or the Seanad. One of the few members of ethnic minority communities to have been elected to the Dáil so far was Dr Mosajee Bhamjee, a naturalised Irish citizen originally from South Africa, who was elected as Labour TD from 1992 to 1997. Some members of ethnic minority communities have succeeded in being elected to local councils in recent years. However, information on the representation of religious, racial or ethnic minorities at local government level is extremely difficult to obtain, and when contacted during the course of research for this study, neither

the Central Statistics Office nor other state agencies were able to provide the relevant information.

- No TDs, Senators or MEPs are members of the Traveller community but there is limited representation of the Traveller community at local government level.
- Lower socio-economic groups are significantly underrepresented in both the Dáil and Seanad. While almost 47 per cent of TDs in the 29th Dáil are lower and higher professionals, only 15 per cent of Irish society overall come from these categories. The overrepresentation of these categories is also the case at local government level. (Harris, 2005: 67) The socio-economic background of TDs does not differ significantly across parties.
- Research suggests that socio-economically disadvantaged social groups are less likely to vote than their more affluent counterparts, which consequently results in a further loss in the representation of their interests. (Hardiman, 1998)

INCREASING REPRESENTATION FOR UNDER-REPRESENTED GROUPS

Political reform aimed at achieving greater equality of representation generally takes two approaches, depending on the size of the under-represented group in relation to society as a whole. On the one hand, certain groups are big enough that their interests and perspectives would be adequately represented within the existing elected fora, provided they were represented therein in a roughly proportionate manner. On the other hand, groups exist whose numbers may be so small that elected representation in proportion to their numbers would likely result in few, if any, representatives in elected office.

In the case of women's representation, the aim is generally to improve their representation within all elected fora so that their numbers more closely approximate their proportion of the population as a whole. Quotas, for example, are now used extensively around the world as a means of addressing the underrepresentation of women in elected office. (See Q11.3) Such solutions could also conceivably be applied to other groups which form a large part of the population, such as younger, older, and working class people. In practice, however, such solutions are not yet widely applied in any representative democracy.

The issue with regard to numerically small minorities, however, is how to ensure that their interests are represented in light of the fact that, with or without franchise, their numbers are likely to be so small that even the attainment of a proportional number of elected representatives may not be sufficient to ensure actual electoral representation.

A number of mechanisms have been adopted by parliaments around the world to improve the extent to which such groups are represented.

Two such measures in particular have gained widespread acceptance, and can be employed either to achieve proportionate representation or to enable representation for groups too small to achieve representation through the normal electoral process.

- Reserved seats for representatives of minority communities in the lower house. This provision is the most widely used method, and currently employed by some 25 parliaments from every region of the world, usually for representatives of ethnic or religious minorities. (Beetham, 2006: 25) In India, for example, this measure works by designating certain constituencies wherein only members of scheduled castes can be nominated, whereas in New Zealand, it proceeds by designating a certain number of seats that are filled by means of an election from a separate Maori electoral roll. (Baker *et al.*, 2004: 114)
- The use of the second chamber or upper house of parliament to ensure a greater representation for different communities and social groups, whether through a different electoral system from the lower house, or through direct appointment of minority representatives. (Beetham, 2006) It has been argued, for example, that Travellers should be regarded as a special constituency for the purpose of Seanad elections, but such a provision has not yet taken place.

In fact, in Ireland, neither of these initiatives have been implemented. No reserved seats exist in either the Dáil or Seanad for minorities and the Seanad is not used as a means of increasing the representativeness of the Oireachtas as a whole. More could therefore be done to ensure that both the Oireachtas and local government more fairly represent the diversity of all members of Irish society.

Twelve: Government Responsiveness

Is government responsive to the concerns of its citizens?

INTRODUCTION AND SUMMARY

Whatever the importance of elections, citizens in a democracy expect that they will be able to exercise some ongoing influence over government policy between elections, and that governments will be responsive to their concerns. Such responsiveness differs from accountability. While the mechanisms of accountability typically operate *after* the event, to review or repudiate past government actions, responsiveness requires the government and parliamentarians both to solicit the views of the public *before* policy or legislation is finalised, and to take them into account.

The traditional avenue through which citizens have made their voices heard in a constituency-based representative system is by direct contact with their elected representative(s), whether in writing, by email or by direct face-to-face contact. This avenue remains important for individual citizens, but is typically supplemented by more systematic processes of consultation by government and parliamentarians with relevant interest groups or "organised publics" before policy or legislation is initiated. It is important that such processes be as inclusive and transparent as possible, so that government or parliament is not subject to "capture" by a few powerful and well-organised special interests or lobbies, which benefit from privileged access to ministers or legislators. Citizens also engage with government as users of public services, and another important criterion of government responsiveness is the effectiveness of the consultation process with the public over issues of service delivery, whether these are nationally or locally determined. The combination of all these channels of public "voice" will determine the degree to which citizens believe that they have a significant opportunity to influence public policy, and the degree of confidence they express in democratic government.

Ireland's representative system puts a great deal of weight on elected representatives looking after constituency and local interests, even at the expense of their legislative and oversight functions. This emphasis conforms to the demands of voters themselves, who expect their TDs to be both readily available for consultation with constituents and to bring tangible benefits to the locality. Responsiveness at the governmental level is met by Ireland's relatively open system of consultation and "concertation" through the social partnership arrangements, which aim to achieve a compromise between different organised interests in determining economic and social priorities. Although the system has been criticised for sidelining parliament, it ensures that interests other than those of the dominant business sectors are systematically considered in the preparation and implementation of policy. Less well developed are arrangements for consulting public service users on issues of service delivery, which is only done in a relatively piecemeal fashion compared with best European practice.

Overall, the Irish public maintains a much higher degree of confidence in public institutions and the way the country's democracy works than is typical for Europe as a whole, although, as elsewhere, political parties stand lowest in public esteem. A particularly significant index of government responsiveness is the degree of confidence which voters express in their ability to influence political decisions if they make the effort to do so.

Q12.1 How accessible are elected representatives to their constituents?

Elected representatives in Ireland are readily accessible to their constituents. Concerns have been voiced by many, including TDs themselves, that the workload involved in dealing with local constituency interests is to the detriment of TDs' wider roles as legislators. The recent ending of the dual mandate, whereby members of Dáil Éireann could also serve as local councillors, goes a considerable way towards redressing the large amount of time spent on local political issues by many TDs. However, a number of other factors, including public expectations, mean that for most TDs, the balance between constituency work and parliamentary duties remains weighted in favour of the former.

ROLE OF TDS

The means through which citizens in representative democracies have traditionally had access to their parliament has been through their elected representatives. (Beetham, 2006: 69) As in most democracies, TDs in Ireland are elected on the basis of geographically-based constituencies whereby TDs represent a specific locality. The strengths of constituency based electoral systems are that elected representatives directly experience the concerns of their constituents through personal contact, and that constituents have ready access to their representatives. However, the pressure on elected representatives to balance constituency work with the requirements of their legislative and other parliamentary duties presents a particular challenge in all democracies.

Without question, elected representatives in Ireland do a great deal of constituency work. Indeed, many spend the majority of their time on this task. The role of TD at local level has a number of components, including:

- interceding with the local or central civil service on behalf of an individual constituent or group;
- acting as a local dignitary, attending events within the constituency; and
- advancing the interests of the constituency by helping to attract investment, jobs, infrastructure etc.

Particular attention has been paid to the inordinate amount of time which TDs spend engaged in the first two of these activities, whether holding several clinics a week, exchanging letters or phone calls with constituents and officials to follow up on individual queries, or spending evenings travelling throughout their constituencies to attend meetings and funerals. (Gallagher and Komito, 2005)

The PR-STV electoral system arguably puts additional pressures on TDs to concentrate on constituency work, compared to other systems. Two reasons can be cited for this: first, the number of votes needed to be elected in multimember constituencies is sufficiently small that constituency work can be a decisive factor for individual candidates; and second, PR-STV generates intra-party competition wherein members of the same party are forced to compete against each other at local level and constituency work is where this competition is played out.

Public expectations also play a major role, as shown by a recent survey of public attitudes to democracy undertaken as part of the Democratic Audit Ireland project. When asked to select from a list the most important of TDs' duties, 61 per cent of respondents chose representing constituency and local interests as the single most important duty of a TD. Implementing new laws and policies was seen as the most important duty of a TD by only 15 per cent of respondents. (Clancy *et al.*, 2005)

Despite the misgivings around this issue, concerns about an overemphasis by TDs on constituency work may be overstated. For example, a 1995 survey comparing TDs with British MPs found that MPs did less constituency work than TDs, but not hugely so. A greater difference, however, between the two sets of elected representatives was that while the majority of TDs felt that their chances of re-election would be damaged if they cut back on constituency work, most MPs did not believe this. Nonetheless, MPs still carried out a considerable amount of constituency work. The reasons given for this were personal satisfaction at engaging in constituency work and the belief that such work forms a central part of the role of an elected representative. (Wood and Young, 1997: 221)

ENDING OF THE DUAL MANDATE

Until recently, the pressure on elected representatives to balance constituency work with the requirements of their legislative and other parliamentary duties was further complicated by the fact that TDs could also run in local council elections and, if elected, serve as both TD and local councillor. In 1999, for example, nearly half of TDs were also serving as local councillors. However the Local Government Bill

2003 ended this practice and members of the Oireachtas can no longer also serve as councillors on local authorities.

The end of the dual mandate was designed to bring about a separation of local government from the national legislature for the first time since the foundation of the state. The measure was seen as a necessary step, given the increasing complex roles of both local and national representatives. (Department of the Environment, Heritage and Local Government, 2002b) The increasing complexity of local authority business on issues such as planning, waste and environmental concerns, coupled with increasing demands on local councils following the introduction of the new strategic policy committees (SPCs) and county/city development boards, made it increasingly untenable for individuals to simultaneously perform both national and local roles. The ending of the dual mandate was a difficult step, however, given the opposition which the government faced from its own backbenchers as well as from opposition TDs.

The 2007 election will be the first time the effects of the end of the dual mandate will be tested, when it will be seen whether councillors take seats from sitting TDs as a result of being closer to the voters.

PERSONALISM AND BROKERAGE IN IRISH POLITICAL CULTURE

Personalism and brokerage have been traditionally cited as two distinctive aspects of Irish political culture. Personalism refers to the importance of personal ties between a TD (and his/her family) and constituents, and is evidenced in Irish politics by the large number of people who have had individual contact with their local TD. At the 2002 election, for example, 71 per cent of voters had spoken personally to the candidate to whom they gave their first preference. (Gallagher and Komito, 2005: 257)

Brokerage meanwhile is the process whereby elected representatives act as intermediaries between individual constituents and the state in order to secure services to which the individual constituents are already legally entitled. Personalism is also a prerequisite for brokerage, in that TDs personally known by their constituents are more likely to be approached to act as go-betweens in accessing or expediting their dealings with the state. While there is nothing corrupt about brokerage, given that TDs are acting to secure for constituents what is rightfully theirs and there is no direct gain for the politician since individual constituents may not vote for her in return, brokerage has been criticised on other grounds. These include: its effect in diverting TDs from national issues; its effect on the civil service where, in the words of political scientist Basil Chubb, TDs go around "persecuting civil servants; and on perceptions of the political system wherein TDs are seen as capable of gaining privileged access to services for individual constituents.

At the same time, it has been suggested that most TDs, with the exception of ministers and independent TDs holding the balance of power in the Dáil (See below), lack the power to deliver anything substantive and that brokerage is therefore largely symbolic. (Gallagher and Komito, 2005) However, a counter argument suggests that brokerage actually plays a different, but essential, role in Irish political culture. According to this view, brokerage has effectively afforded the mass of citizens access to their political representatives within Ireland's highly centralised and hierarchical political system. And the fact that this access has made little real difference in their interactions with the state has been secondary to the fact that it allows citizens to feel included in an otherwise exclusionary, hierarchical system. (Cichowski, 2000)

Better service provision by state agencies, the establishment of new ways of accessing information, e.g., community information centres, freedom of information legislation and the Internet, along with new bodies for addressing complaints, e.g., ombudsman, may all act to reduce the incidence of brokerage at constituency level. (Share, 2003) However, representing the interests of constituents will continue to be a central role for TDs, as it is for elected representative in all other democracies.

BROKERAGE IN PRACTICE

In contrast to the limited ability of the vast majority of TDs to deliver to their constituencies, ministers can have substantial power to deliver brokerage to their constituencies. Moreover, Irish political culture is such that TDs and ministers are expected to bring rewards to their electoral base or for their constituency as a whole.

When Dick Spring stepped down as Labour Party leader in 1997, he was praised by one reporter for having delivered to his home town of Tralee, a leisure centre, a heritage project, a marina, hotels, a new sewage treatment plant, a regional college, and a technology park. (*Irish Times*, 6 November 1997) And in December 2003, following the announcement of government plans for decentralisation of government departments from Dublin to locations around the country, the Junior Minister Tom Parlon immediately issued leaflets in his constituency headed "Parlon Delivers! 965 jobs!". (Gallagher and Komito, 2005: 250)

Actual as opposed to "virtual" brokerage can also be the case for independent TDs who hold the balance of power in the Dáil. For example, Fianna Fáil, which lacked an overall majority following the 1997 election, entered into negotiation with the Progressive Democrats and independents in order to form a government. Mildred Fox, one of four independent TDs who reached agreement to support the government in exchange for spending on specific projects in their constituencies, later said that her constituency of Wicklow had gained the following from this deal:

- a CAT scanner for Loughlinstown hospital;
- a District Veterinary Officer for Wicklow town;
- a new secondary school for Kilcoole;
- a new Garda Sstation in Bray;
- improvement on the N81 road in west Wicklow;
- a CCTV system for Bray;
- refurbishment of the courthouse in Baltinglass;
- a new library in Baltinglass; and
- additional funding for Wicklow jail museum.

The other three independent TDs also made similar claims about their own success in getting public spending commitments for their constituents. (Gallagher and Komito, 2005: 250)

Such examples readily illustrate that brokerage is widely viewed, and indeed promoted by some public representatives, as an acceptable activity, and that Irish politics is still largely seen to be influenced by competition between elected representatives to deliver "favours" to their local constituencies

At the same time, it can be difficult to determine the real role which ministers actually have in "delivering for their constituencies".

For example, the new sewage-treatment plant "delivered" by Dick Spring was an essential service, and similarly the establishment of a regional college required to be strategically justified on the basis of demographics, employment opportunities and demand.

The practice of brokerage in Irish politics is further facilitated by the fact that, unlike some other parliamentary systems, wherein some ministers are not elected representatives, all government ministers in Ireland are TDs who also represent local constituencies. (Harris, 2005: 82) Only two of approximately 150 ministers since 1922 in Ireland have never been TDs, compared with an average European figure of 25 per cent over this time. (Gallagher, 2005b: 237)

Q12.2 How open and systematic are the procedures for public consultation on government policy and legislation, and how equal is the access for relevant interests to government?

In many countries in Europe, governments have looked to involve key interests, primarily those of labour and capital, in a more systematic process of policy making. Ireland has developed its own distinctive system of social partnership which has evolved to the extent that it currently includes a wider range of interests and organisations than would generally be the case elsewhere. A significant proportion of the Irish adult population are involved to some degree in the social partnership process, making it by far the most important measure by which conflicting interests are reconciled and government policy influenced.

While a great deal of the social partnership negotiations focuses on the ratification, clarification and implementation of existing government policies, as opposed to new policy initiatives, negotiations on a number of key issues do commit government to measures that it would likely not undertake in the absence of national agreements.

THE EVOLUTION OF SOCIAL PARTNERSHIP

Although centralised bargaining had been a previous feature of the Irish industrial relations system, the *Programme for National Recovery* agreed in late 1987 effectively began the process of social partnership, and the process has greatly expanded since in terms of scope, structure and participation. As the areas for negotiation expanded and the outcomes, particularly for unemployment, were seen to be significant, interest groups other than the union, employer and farming bodies demanded entry. The involvement since 1996 of a range of voluntary and community organisations representing a wide spectrum of civil society interests has further widened the agenda as each organisation sought to have its particular concerns addressed.

Social partnership has developed into an important forum for social dialogue, consensus building and social and employment policy formation within the Irish system of governance. While most see the contribution made by the partnership process in positive terms, it has also been criticised for giving power to unelected insiders to determine matters that are properly the business of members of the Oireachtas (Clinch *et al.*, 2002; Ó Cinéide, 1998; Crotty, 1998). Some go so far as to claim that the process is eroding democracy. Parliamentarians also complain of being sidelined, and a Fine Gael and Labour Party joint policy statement refers to the "inevitable democratic deficit" arising from the partnership process. (Fine Gael and Labour, 2005) However, the involvement of interest groups in governmental policy formation is now a feature of virtually all developed democracies. Furthermore, the Irish model is arguably more open and transparent than alternative systems.

Although an elaborate institutional framework now buttresses the partnership process, the processes of engagement remain fluid and relatively informal. These involve a mix of social dialogue, a more substantive set of engagements which can be defined as "concertation", and pay negotiations. Social dialogue involves a process of representations, consultations and information exchange. A draft text is developed and amended to take account of various representations made by relevant participant groups. Amendments can be significant where a broad consensus is evident but social dialogue is rarely about negotiating new policy initiatives so much as it is about the ratification, clarification and implementation arrangements for existing government policies. The bulk of the text of the final agreements can be viewed as the outcome of this kind of social dialogue, and, indeed, much of it is merely a restatement of government programmes. The comprehensive texts of the agreements, particularly since the *Programme for Prosperity and Fairness* (PPF), can give the misleading impression that the parties are engaged in detailed policy making in areas as diverse as transport infrastructure and development aid, whereas in actuality government departments and ministers are eager to have their already existing programmes acknowledged in national agreements, while relevant participating organisations are happy to be given some ongoing consultative role. Although the social dialogue element of the process does not involve the government sharing its authority to any appreciable degree, it does facilitate ongoing information sharing and consultation with a wide range of voluntary bodies within a myriad of consultative committees and fora. (See Q11.1)

POLITICAL EXCHANGE AND RELATIVE INFLUENCE EXERCISED BY INTEREST GROUPS

At the same time, a substantive level of engagement on a number of key issues takes place during each set of negotiations that often commits government to initiatives that it would likely not undertake in the absence of national agreements. This latter type engagement between government and the social partners is referred to as "concertation" in the academic literature. Concertation is said to apply to situations where the process of resolving interest conflicts gain "systemic" relevance for the essential features of government and the national economy. (Lehmbruch, 1984) It iinvolves the state sharing authority in specified areas with organised interest groups who agree to forgo some degree of their own autonomy "in exchange for political influence". (Visser, 1998) Where concertation becomes embedded in the system of governance, as arguably is the case with social partnership in Ireland, it can be described as a form of "generalised political exchange". (Lehmbruch, 1984; Molina and Rhodes, 2002)

The system of political exchange that surrounds pay determination within social partnership mirrors the consensual approach adapted by unions and employers to the management of economic and social policy elsewhere in Europe. This system also affords unions and employers more leverage with government in that they bring something concrete to the table. Although the pay talks are a distinct set of negotiations within the broader process, confined to unions, employers and government, this process has wider ramifications. The Irish Congress of Trade Unions (ICTU) and Irish Business and Employers Confederation (IBEC) will often make their agreement conditional on particular government actions. For example, during the talks on the recent *Towards 2016: Social Partnership agreement 2006-2015*, the issue of labour standards was so important to the union side of the table that they would not even commence the pay negotiations until they had seen the colour of the government's money on the issue. But this process also works both ways, whereby the prospect of legislation or some other desired government action is used as an incentive by government to secure agreement on pay and other issues. The grand prize meantime is a continuation of the partnership process, valued by all as greater than just the sum of the terms of any particular agreement. Social partnership is widely seen as having contributed to Ireland's economic transformation, and while the extent of the contribution can be debated, it would be foolhardy to discount the value of consensus.

Other participants do not enjoy the same level of exchange opportunities within the system. Voluntary and community organisations rely more on a moral claim (O'Donnell, 2000), although their participation gives additional credibility to the process which, together with the expertise and implementation capabilities they also bring to the table, provides them with sufficient leverage to extract some concessions. In addition, the ongoing access to government afforded them within committees and various forums connected with partnership is prized and encourages constructive engagement.

For its part, the government acts as conciliator, broker, and negotiator within the process. The National Economic and Social Council (NESC) refers to the negotiations as being conducted under the "shadow of hierarchy" whereby the government uses its authority to foster problem solving by threatening to impose solutions in the absence of consensus. The Council goes on to state that government in this way can support weaker groups "in order to even up imbalances in power and resources". (National Economic and Social Council, 2005b: 292)

At the same time, there have been complaints about the disproportionate influence wielded by the traditional social partners. For example, the Simon Community, who were represented on the Community Platform that in turn were part of the Social Pillar during the talks on the 2003 social partnership agreement *Sustaining Progress*, complained that:

> ...the agreement on affordable housing is a critical example of the difference between how the unions and employers as opposed

> to the Community Platform were engaged by government in the "social partnership process". (*Simon News*, 2002)

This complaint related to the fact that the issue of affordable housing was the subject of agreement within the pay and conditions negotiations which involve only employers and unions along with the government. The issue highlights a difficulty of securing a balanced approach within, and between, narrowly focused groups, as Simon who work with the homeless would naturally want greater resources to be applied to sheltered accommodation or social housing than to affordable housing.

A further factor that undermines the negotiating position of the social pillar is their disparate composition and lack of cohesion. Despite attempts to achieve an internal consensus on key issues, the pillar has no secretariat or consolidated decision-making structure. However, they frequently seek and secure the support of the ICTU for their demands, which helps to overcome a certain degree of their organisational and resource limitations.

While the imbalances in leverage within the social partnership process can be explained if not justified, more traditional approaches to interest representation are more inequitable. The pluralist model is even more likely to favour rich and powerful lobbies to the disadvantage of others and relying entirely on the political system would not appear to offer better prospects. Powerful vested interests will always secure access to the corridors of power and such access, whether legitimate or otherwise, is most likely to occur outside of the public gaze. While few would today openly support Edmond Burke's contention that "property must carry influence in every part of the public concerns", no one would deny its continued reality. An important measure of the quality of our democratic institutions is how they manage to address this inherent inequality of access and influence. No evidence exists that the process of social partnership has diminished the level of private representations by vested interests but partnership does provide an alternative and countervailing mechanism for influencing government that can go some way towards redressing the power imbalance.

Unequal influence, moreover, can be justified in certain instances by the relative size and importance to society of particular interests and organisations. The ICTU, with over half a million members, represents by far the largest civil society organisation in the state. Unions moreover remain democratic in structure with regular leadership elections. Almost all unions also conduct membership ballots on the terms of every national agreement and many undertake elaborate membership consultation. While some critics point to the fact that unions only represent a minority of Irish employees, the benefits of any agreement are enjoyed by virtually all. Certainly there is no evidence that non-union workers represent a separate and disaffected employee interest group. On the contrary, recent research indicates that the majority of workers would join a union if the opportunity arose, or if their employers signalled their approval. (Geary, 2007, forthcoming) Meanwhile IBEC's importance lies in its widespread representation within the business sector wherein they carry out extensive consultations, and in the degree to which they facilitate Ireland's version of a structured compromise between capital and labour that underpins the process here.

The scores of other groups invited by government to participate in the social partnership process have varying claims to be democratic representatives for particular constituencies and most of them also engage their members in a widespread consultation and ratification process. However, the legitimacy of the overall partnership process is not dependent on the membership profile of each and every participating organisation, although some, such as the farming organisations, have quite significant memberships. Rather it is the wide range of interests represented in the process that distinguishes the Irish model from other centralised bargaining and consultation systems. While 26 organisations were directly involved in the recent talks leading to *Towards 2016*, many of these are umbrella bodies so that hundreds of other organisations are thereby involved at one remove. Consider, for example, the Wheel which represents more than 200 individual organisations, or the Irish Senior Citizens Parliament which represents 300 separate organisations with a claimed total membership of 80,000. Given that these are just two of the 15 constituent groups within the social pillar, it is likely that a majority of the adult population are engaged to some degree in the social partnership process. The fact that hundreds of thousands of union members and others now vote to accept or reject the draft agreement also demonstrates its democratic nature and comprehensiveness. In similar fashion, the consultation and ratification arrangements put in place by participating organisations constitute a level of civil participation in public policy making that is unparalleled in Ireland or elsewhere.

While the *Towards 2016* agreement commits the government to a dozen pieces of new legislation, this outcome cannot be said to infringe upon parliamentary democracy, as members of the Oireachtas will have the power to amend or reject any text put before them in the normal manner. Nevertheless, enhanced consultation between the political and social partnership systems could be beneficial and the agreement contains provisions for such a process. (Department of the Taoiseach, 2006: 76)

Q12.3 How accessible and reliable are public services for those who need them, and how systematic is consultation with users over delivery?

Significant legislative and administrative reforms have taken place in recent years aimed at improving public input into the design and delivery of public services and at ensuring greater openness and accountability in the public sector in Ireland.

The evidence, however, shows that some areas of the public sector are clearly performing more strongly than others in achieving these goals. Irish public-sector efforts to engage effectively with its service users are still at a comparatively early stage and in general compare unfavourably with international best practice. While there are examples of good practice, the extent to which individuals are consulted with regard to public service delivery is exceedingly *ad hoc*, and operates on a piecemeal basis, particularly at national level.

In general, the consultation process with service users at local level is more organised than at national level, and systems are now in place for consultation with users, including the Strategic Policy Committees and City and County Development Boards. Overall, local authorities have made marked improvements over recent years in the reliability of the services they deliver. However, such success is not yet reflected in the level of public satisfaction with local authorities.

HOW ACCESSIBLE AND RELIABLE ARE PUBLIC SERVICES?

That the accessibility and reliability of public services are issues of public concern in Ireland is evidenced by the large part played by these issues in public discourse. In an opinion poll conducted in October 2006, 56 per cent of respondents stated that improving key public services such as health, transport and education would be a key issue when voting at the next general election. (*Irish Times*, 14 October 2006)

The accessibility and reliability of some of the key public services in Ireland have been addressed in detail in Section Four of this audit. In particular, education is addressed in Q4.3, health in Q4.4, childcare in Q4.3, eldercare in Q4.4, housing in Q4.2, and employment in Q4.5. Consequently, the focus here will be on recent reforms aimed at improving public service delivery and at initiatives to increase consultation with service users.

In Q 7.1, the extent to which the public service is capable of developing and implementing strategic plans so that public services are delivered both efficiently and effectively is considered. In this question, the focus is on the degree to which government consults with the users of these services as a key part of this process. A trend common to the implementation of all public sector reform programmes by OECD countries is the systematic effort being made to seek the views of citizens in order to improve service delivery and to assist in the development of policy initiatives better suited to the needs of those who use them. (Humphreys, 2002) From the perspective of a democratic audit, the important question is the degree to which citizens, as the funders of public services, have a real input into the design and delivery of those services resulting in a positive effect on the public good. As discussed in the introduction to this section, such consultation is both an important mechanism for citizen input into decision making, and a key aspect of "active citizenship" in a vibrant democracy.

NATIONAL PUBLIC SERVICE REFORM

Important legislative and administrative reforms have taken place over recent years, beginning in 1994 with the launch of the Strategic Management Initiative, aimed at ensuring greater consultation with users of public services. (See also Q 7.1) In that same year, the government also established a strategy group, comprising the secretaries-general of all government departments, to consider the development of strategic management processes across the Irish public service. Its report, *Delivering Better Government*, published in 1996, recommended basic principles for reform, including the provision of quality information and advice to service users; the establishment of comprehensive systems for measuring and accessing user satisfaction; a complaints and redress mechanism; and consultation with, and participation by, service users on a structured basis. (Second Report of the Co-ordinating Group of Secretaries, 1996)

In a second initiative, the government in 1997 launched the Quality Customer Service Initiative (QCS) to promote the adoption of improved customer service standards across government departments. In 2000, the government extended the remit of the QCS, by adopting the initiative across all of the civil service. The QCS contains commitments to ensure a high standard of service, timely and courteous delivery and equality of service for all. The QCS initiative also aimed to establish a complaints and appeals system as well as formal structures for consultation and evaluation with users across all public services. (www.bettergov.ie)

In a third initiative, outlined in *Reducing Red Tape: An Action Programme of Regulatory Reform in Ireland* (1999), the government set out a programme of action with regard to regulatory reform in which considerable emphasis is placed on the importance of consultation with users of public services. The report recommends that government departments should consult with service users and, based upon those consultations, departments would identify problems with existing legislation and identify priorities for its consolidation, revision and/or repeal. (Department of the Taoiseach, 1999)

Most recently, the government's white paper, *Regulating Better* (2004), focused on the importance of greater consultation with consumers of public services in order to ensure greater openness and accountability in the public sector. In the white paper, the government commits itself to making public consultation more rigorous and consistent; to establishing norms and standards for the consultation process; and to making better use of web-based technologies as a proactive measure to increase the scope of the consultation process. (Department of the Taoiseach, 2004)

The government has acknowledged that, "historically in Ireland, the consumer voice (and in particular, the domestic consumer) has been weak relative to producer interests. This imbalance has often resulted in a higher priority being placed on promoting the interests of producers/providers of particular goods/services rather than those who consume them". (Department of the Taoiseach, 2002: 25) The same could be said of public service provision. However, since the launch of the Strategic Management Initiative, some progress in ensuring greater user consultation over the delivery of public services at local and national level has been made.

USER CONSULTATION IN PRACTICE

A wide range of different mechanisms are used by OECD countries for consulting with public sector users. These measures include customer satisfaction surveys; local/regional/national opinion polls; referenda; feedback from the frontline of service providers; user boards and suggestion boxes; customer complaints procedures; user advisory boards; user representation on boards; focus groups; brainstorming groups; monitoring of news media reports; as well as public hearings. (Humphreys, 2002)

Many of these consultation mechanisms are currently employed by the Irish public sector to engage with its users. The social partnership model in Ireland, which has led to the involvement of employer and trade union organisations, and voluntary sector organisations, in the development of policy and service delivery initiatives is the most significant example. (See Q 11.1 and Q12.2) Other examples include:

- the Department of Social and Family Affairs, which has for many years sought feedback *via* ongoing consultation with service users and staff, as well as regular customer surveys;
- the Office of the Civil Service and Local Appointments Commissioners, which regularly conducts customer opinion surveys to monitor and improve its service delivery (Humphreys, 2002: 59); and
- the Department of Arts, Sports and Tourism, which has engaged in a major consultative exercise with local community organisations in the development of the National Anti-Drugs Strategy. (Humphreys, 2002: 59)

In addition, a number of public service initiatives make use of information and communication technologies to engage service users online to facilitate improved access to information. A range of sites are currently available which focus upon particular services, including social services (www.reach.ie), business (www.basis.ie), citizen information (www.citizensinformation.ie) and tendering for government contracts (www.tendersireland.com). (Humphreys, 2002)

Citizens or Customers

An important issue in any discussion on user consultation is the use of the term "customer" when referring to service users. The vast majority of service users are of course citizens and residents who, through taxation, are funding the services they are accessing. A fundamental distinction therefore exists between customers of private services and tax-paying citizens and residents as users of public services. A recent positive development which acknowledges this critical distinction is the renaming of the government agency Comhairle as the Citizens Information Board, An Bord um Fhaisnéis do Shaoránaigh. The agency's new name was chosen to more accurately reflect the nature of its functions, which are primarily concerned with the provision of information to the public about social rights and entitlements. (www.comhairle.ie)

Under the Citizens Information Bill 2006, the remit of the Citizens Information Board is to be expanded to include a personal advocacy service for people with disabilities. The role of the personal advocate is to assist people with disabilities who have difficulties accessing or obtaining social services. The Citizens Information Bill forms part of a broader legislative programme to improve the deliver of public services to people with disabilities. The Disability Act 2005 and the Education for Persons with Special Needs Act 2004 are further examples of legislative changes aimed as ensuring equal access to public services for people with disabilities.

However, despite progress on some fronts, ensuring effective and systematic engagement and consultation with the users of the public service has been slow and *ad hoc*. In 1998, one study concluded that "with some notable and noteworthy exceptions…there is still a very long way to go before it can be asserted that Irish public service organisations have taken on board wholeheartedly the need to be [service user] focused throughout the design, planning, implementation, monitoring, evaluation and review of the services delivered...Rarely were [service users'] needs placed centre stage". (Humphreys, 1998: 77)

By 2001, the OECD found that the voices of service users in Ireland were still not adequately heard within the policy process, and that consultation in general tended to come late, often by asking for pro forma comment on the finished product rather than for assistance in creating it. (Organisation for Economic Co-operation and Development, 2001: 105)

In 2002, Irish public sector efforts to engage effectively with its service users were still found to be at a comparatively early stage and, in general, compared unfavourably with international best practice. Where public bodies had made progress in ensuring greater consumer consultation, "these efforts are often not underpinned by statutory or institutional requirements on public bodies to consult". (Humphreys, 2002: 74)

More recently, a 2006 National Economic and Social Forum (NESF) study found that while there has been significant improvements in the delivery of public services, "there are still significant shortcomings as well as new and emerging challenges to be met". (National Economic and Social Forum, 2006b: 105) In particular, the report found that there is a need for stronger connections between those operating at central level who are responsible for policy and resources and the providers and users of public services at local level. (National Economic and Social Forum, 2006c: 1) The report also highlighted the need for public service providers to "more clearly set out the rights and entitlements and standards of services that users can expect to receive...". (National Economic and Social Forum, 2006b: 110)

Local Government Level

To date, greater progress on consultation with service users has been made at local level than at national level. The 1996 report, *Delivering Better Local Government* sought to increase the involvement of civil society in local decision-making processes, and to this end, Strategic Policy Committees (SPC) and City and County Development Boards (CDB) were established. (Department of the Environment and Local Government, 1996) (See Section Thirteen)

As part of *Better Local Government*, local authorities were required to establish standards to measure progress in relation to these goals. Twenty-one service indicators are now in place for each local authority and these are included in local authority annual reports.

A review was carried out on this local government modernisation programme by the Institute of Public Administration in 2003. (Boyle *et al.*, 2003: 104-107) This review found:

- that most local authorities were complying with the request to report performance against service indicators in their annual reports;
- that most local authority customer action plans published service standards;
- that the levels of openness and accountability were well in advance of those at central government level; and
- that there was considerable evidence of local authorities providing complaints and appeals mechanisms and making use of customer surveys.

Overall, the evidence suggests that local authorities have made marked improvements in the reliability of the services they deliver. However, this success is not yet reflected in the level of public satisfaction with local authorities. In a 2004 survey, only 40 percent of respondents rated the service provided by local authorities as good. Additional evidence of public dissatisfaction is attested by the fact that around 33 per cent of all complaints received by the office of the Ombudsman in 2005 were in respect of local authorities. (Office of the Ombudsman, 2006b)

PUBLIC SATISFACTION WITH PUBLIC SERVICE DELIVERY

In general, recent opinion poll surveys show that the public's view of the civil service and the quality of public services provided is improving. For example, according to a 2006 poll for the Department of the Taoiseach, the majority of the public who have had contact with the civil service are satisfied with the service provided. The poll, (IPSOS MORI, 2006) found that:

- 78 per cent of respondents claimed to be very satisfied or fairly satisfied with the service provided by the civil service;
- 62 per cent of respondents viewed the civil service as being very efficient or fairly efficient, up slightly from 58 per cent in 2002;
- 57 per cent of those polled had a favourable opinion of the way

in which the civil service meets the needs of the public, up from 47 per cent in 2002; and

- 65 per cent of respondents who had contact with the civil service stated that they have a very favourable or favourable opinion of the way in which the civil service meets the needs of the public.

The relatively high level of public satisfaction with the civil service in general however is not reflected in the level of public satisfaction with individual public sector organisations. For example, a MORI Ireland survey in 2004, found that only 53 per cent of those surveyed rated the service provided by local hospitals as good (MORI Ireland, 2004) and only 40 per cent of respondents rated the service provided by local authorities as good. Moreover, a sizeable minority of the public tends to see public sector organisations as poorly managed; as providing poor information; and as being unable to admit and respond appropriately to mistakes. (Table 12.1)

Table 12.1: Responsiveness of Public Service Organisations

To what extent do you agree or disagree that public sector organisations, like local gardaí, local hospitals and local councils...

	Disagree %	*Agree %*
Always admit to mistakes they make	65	23
Are more efficient than private sector organisations	52	27
Have less corruption than large private sector organisations	37	38
Do not learn from mistakes they make	29	49
Provide poor information to the public about their performance	33	50
Are poorly managed	30	51

Source: MORI Ireland, 2004: 4

The development of effective processes of public consultation on public-service design and delivery are a key aspect of active citizenship. To be effective, such consultation must be genuinely taken into account in the formation of policy and delivery and such processes must be designed in such a way that they actually lead to improvements in public services. While a start has been made, the evidence shows that more needs to be done to further strengthen this key aspect of Irish democracy.

Q12.4 How much confidence do people have in the ability of the government to solve the main problems confronting society and in their own ability to influence it?

The evidence suggests that the Irish public retains a high degree of confidence in the system of government and the way in which democracy works. The overall level of confidence in a range of public institutions in Ireland is among the highest in Europe, and over two-thirds of people express satisfaction with the way democracy is developing, compared to less than half in the rest of Europe. Indeed, one commentator has stated that "the attitudes towards the political system [in Ireland] could be considered almost enthusiastic, especially when set against the glummer attitudes prevailing in many other countries in Europe". (Fahey *et al.*, 2005: 230)

The Irish public also retain a high belief that citizens can affect political decisions and make a real difference. They believe that their ability to change things is best expressed through voting, which provides them with a clear opportunity to express their satisfaction or otherwise with the government. However, despite these positive attitudes towards the political system, a sizeable minority of the electorate has little confidence in government, whatever its political makeup, to solve major issues such as problems in healthcare, childcare, and controlling consumer prices.

SATISFACTION WITH DEMOCRACY

A series of surveys carried out regularly since 1973 has consistently shown that the clear majority of Irish respondents are satisfied with the way democracy works. Over the period 1973 to 1989, the proportion declaring themselves either very or fairly satisfied has averaged 53 per cent in Ireland compared to 51 per cent in the EU overall. From 1992 to 1998, this proportion averaged 66 per cent, 20 percentage points above that for the EU as a whole. In autumn 2003, the Irish level of satisfaction was 69 per cent, 15 per cent above the EU average. (Coakley, 2005b: 58)

Table 12.2 Satisfaction with Democracy

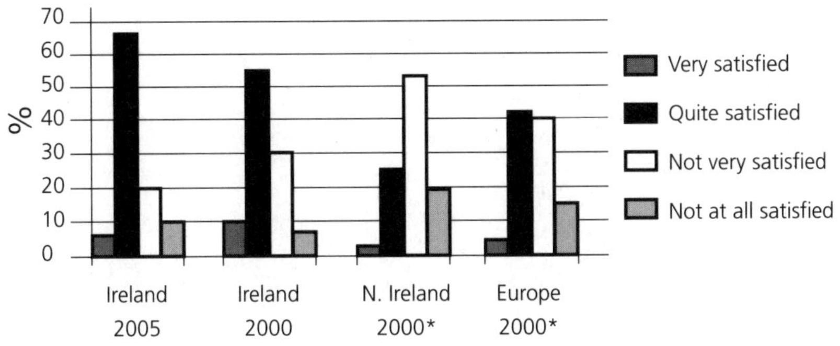

Source: Clancy *et al.*, 2005: 5

In a poll conducted for the Democratic Audit Ireland project in June 2005, 70 per cent of respondents said they are satisfied or quite satisfied with the way democracy is developing. The fact that one quarter say they are either not very satisfied or not at all satisfied, however, is not to be dismissed. Social class is a major determinant of satisfaction. 70 per cent of the highest socio-economic grouping reported being very or quite satisfied, compared with only 53 per cent of the lowest. (Clancy *et al.*, 2005)

The results of another question in this survey, designed to assess public attitudes towards political participation, were presented in Q11.2. (See Table 11.4) The results revealed that a high proportion (79 per cent) of respondents agreed with the statement "it is my duty to vote"; almost two-thirds of respondents believed that when ordinary citizens make an effort to influence political decisions they can really make a difference; and just over half of the population believed that it is worthwhile to be active in politics.

The fact that voter turnout and civic participation have been in decline does not readily marry with these findings. However, they do suggest that a high proportion of the electorate believe they can and do influence the governmental system.

The Irish public also has a higher degree of trust in certain aspects of the political system compared to our European counterparts, as seen in Table 12.3.

Table 12.3 Level of Public Trust in Aspects of the Irish and EU Political System, 2006

	Ireland %	*EU* %
The Justice System	50	48
The Parliament	44	38
The Government	42	35
The Political Parties	32	22

Source: Compiled by Eurobarometer, 2006: 4

CONFIDENCE IN POLITICAL PARTIES TO ADDRESS MAJOR ISSUES

Despite these positive signals, the Irish public has less faith in the ability of political parties to address some of the key issues in society.

A Eurobarometer survey of EU public opinion in 2006 found that more than half of Irish people identify crime as one of the two foremost issues of concern facing the country, compared with the EU average of 22 per cent; around 45 per cent identify healthcare as one of the two top issues, compared to the EU average of 18 per cent. (Eurobarometer, 2006) In similar fashion, 56 per cent of respondents to an *Irish Times*/TNS mrbi poll of October 2006 stated that improving key public services such as health, transport and education would be a key issue when voting at the next general election. (*Irish Times*, 14 October 2006)

However, in an *Irish Times*/TNS mrbi poll in September 2005, a substantial number of people expressed no confidence in either the coalition government or the possible alternative government of Fine Gael, Labour and the Greens, to address these issues. (Table 12.4) In fact, public opinion was equally divided between those who expressed confidence in the current government, the alternative coalition, and those who believed that neither would make a difference in tackling problems in healthcare, childcare, and controlling consumer prices. (*Irish Times*, 24 September 2005)

Table 12.4 Public Confidence in Political Parties

Issue	*Alternative Government of FG, Labour, Greens %*	*Coalition Government %*	*Neither %*	*No Opinion %*
Improving Health Services	33	25	25	18
Access to affordable Childcare	33	23	23	22
Controlling Consumer Prices	35	23	24	18
Keeping Taxes Low	30	30	22	18
Managing the Economy	31	33	19	17

Source: *I*Compiled by *rish Times and TNS mrbi*, 24 September 2005

The overall picture painted by these surveys is a decidedly contradictory one, wherein the Irish public express a high degree of confidence in public institutions, in the system of government and in the way in which democracy works, yet at the same time they express little confidence in political parties to solve major issues facing Irish society.

Thirteen: Democratic Local Politics

Does local politics contribute to the vitality of the country's democracy?

INTRODUCTION AND SUMMARY

The case for a vigorous system of elected local government as an essential part of a country's democracy rests on a number of considerations. One is the simple fact of diversity – between town and country, industry and agriculture, scattered and concentrated populations etc. – and that diverse needs can only be effectively met by sensitivity to local conditions, known best by the people who live there. A second consideration is the development over time of local identities and loyalties which can best be satisfied by local units of government with which people can readily identify and a third is the much greater accessibility of local councillors to their electors than is typical of national parliamentarians. The locality is also the place where the self-organisation of people to meet their various common needs most readily takes place and its natural focus lies with a local elected authority. A final consideration is the fact that elected councillors, typically working on a part-time basis, tend to be much more representative of the electorate in their social composition than is true of national parliamentarians.

In most countries, however, the ability of local councils to frame and implement policies independently to meet the needs of their populations has been substantially eroded by the forces of centralisation. The demand in more mobile societies for equality of service provision as a basic element of citizenship, wherever one happens to live, is partly responsible for a trend towards greater uniformity. There are also powerful pressures from central government for effective management of the national economy and the public budget, and for the delivery of policy programmes without obstruction from localities, especially where these are controlled by opposition parties. A European Charter of Local Self-Government has sought to define some minimum criteria for protecting the autonomy of local elected authorities throughout Europe, though there are no means for ensuring that the states which have signed the Charter actually respect it in practice.

In Ireland, the trend towards centralisation has gone perhaps further than in any other European country. The competence of elected councillors has been eroded over the past decade or more from three different directions simultaneously. Statutory obligations determined by central government are increasingly extensive and regulated in detail, with little discretionary finance left for local decision. There has been the loss of local functions to non-elected public bodies, which are subject to little popular accountability. Finally, the role of council manager has given the chief executive of city and county councils a competence in decision making which has further eroded the political responsibility of elected members. Initiatives under recent legislation to establish effective social partnership arrangements for local authorities, together with bodies for longer-term planning, have been hailed as an attempt to reverse the centralising trend, but have done little to address the limited competences of elected local government itself.

Q13.1 How independent are the tiers of local government from the centre, and how far do they have the powers and resources to carry out their responsibilities?

The Irish system of local government is weak in comparison with other EU states, due to strict central control, a lack of financial independence and a narrow functional range. (Collins and Quinlivan, 2005: 388) Irish local government is also heavily dependent on central government funding and a growing gap between demands on expenditure and expected income is forecast for the coming years. Central control of local government has been a persistent feature of the Irish system, due in part to historical problems as well as more recent issues concerning abuse of planning and other matters. The increased dominance of the centre is in stark contrast to most other systems of local government, which adopt a more "hands-off" approach, and is also contrary to the spirit of the European Charter of Local Self-Government to which Ireland is a party.

WHAT CONSTITUTES LOCAL GOVERNMENT IN IRELAND

Local government in Ireland consists of:

- five city councils – Cork, Dublin, Galway, Limerick and Waterford – which prior to 2001 were known as county borough councils;
- twenty-nine county councils – this number includes the 26 counties that make up the Irish Republic (County Tipperary in fact has two county councils, North Riding and South Riding and County Dublin has three, Fingal, South Dublin, and Dún Laoghaire–Rathdown);
- seventy-five town councils; and
- five borough councils.

Prior to the Local Government Act 2001, which provided for modest salary-type payments, elected members to councils were not paid. They were however entitled to the reimbursement of expenses occurred in carrying out their council duties.

Ireland also has eight regional authorities, established in 1991 in response to the distribution of EU structural funds. Members of these regional authorities and two further super-regional assemblies – Border Midland Western and Southern and Eastern – are not directly elected but are nominated from the constituent local authorities. Functionally speaking, regional authorities are limited to monitoring the implementation of EU structural fund spending in their area and coordinating public service policies at the regional level. The super-regional assemblies, established in 1999, have specific management responsibilities – reporting, evaluating, financial control and monitoring of spending under the two regional operational programmes of the 2000-6 national development plan. (Callanan, 2004: 65)

INDEPENDENCE OF LOCAL GOVERNMENT FROM THE CENTRE

Traditionally, Ireland has had one of the most centrally controlled of local government systems. (Chubb, 1982: 288) Indeed, it was felt at the formation of the Irish state that "a tight rein with strict centralised control was (deemed) appropriate for a small and troubled state". (Collins and Quinlivan, 2005: 389) The *ultra vires* doctrine, which stated that a local authority in Ireland had to be able to adduce legal authority for its action was only removed as recently as 1991. A general competence provision was also introduced in 1991 but subsequently repealed and replaced by the Local Government Act 2001 (Section Sixty-Six). Prior to this legislation, a local authority had to seek specific legal authorisation for every single action.

Part of the reason for this degree of centralisation may be an historical distrust of local politicians by the centre, arising from long-remembered problems with clientelism, jobbery, inefficiency and, in some cases, actual corruption which emerged in the early days of the state. More recent problems include abuse of the physical planning legislation which resulted in the perceived need to establish the Flood Tribunal (Fitzgerald, 2003) and unwillingness at the local level to face up to waste management issues. Whatever the merits of this perspective, the counter-argument is inherently persuasive, that is, the local level is where the best opportunities for participation in decision making for the ordinary citizen reside. (Tierney, 2006)

Government has also said it is committed to the principle of devolution of decision making, which is a central element of *Better Local Government: A Programme for Change* (1996) and has put in place new structures for enhanced participation. However as discussed in more detail in Q13.3, the opportunities provided under these structures for actual decision making are generally held to be more illusory than real. (Tierney, 2006: 66)

Narrowness of Function

The Public Bodies (Amendment) Order, 1975 classifies the functions of local government into the following eight programme groups:

- housing and building;
- road transportation and safety;
- water supply and sewage;

- development incentives and control;
- environmental protection;
- recreation and amenity;
- agriculture, education, health and welfare; and
- miscellaneous.

A comparative study of 15 European countries demonstrates the relatively low level of independence of local government from the centre in Ireland. A further distinguishing feature of the Irish system is the limited range of services provided by local authorities in comparison to other EU Member States. (See Table 13.1) For example, Ireland is exceptional in that its local authorities have no responsibility for primary and secondary education services or for family welfare services, while only Ireland and the UK exclude such aspects of health care as hospitals and convalescence facilities from local and or regional control. (Collins and Quinlivan, 2005: 389) Ireland is also very unusual in its exclusion from local control of areas such as policing, economic development/local development and tourism which in other countries fall within the remit of local or regional authorities. Furthermore, instead of moving to increase the functions of local authorities, areas of activity are being removed from their control. For example, since the establishment of the Health Services Executive (HSE) in 2005, local governments no longer make nominations to local health structures. Prior to the establishment of the HSE, the community was represented on health boards by a mixture of elected representatives from the relevant councils and local people involved in various organisations concerned with public health.

Inadequate Financing of Local Government

The proposition that some power of local taxation is essential for local government to retain a degree of autonomy is generally accepted in the rest of the EU but remains unresolved in Ireland. Approximately 50 per cent of local government funding comes from central coffers, while rates, service charges and development levies account for the remainder. Despite the existence of a substantial subnational governance infrastructure, the vast majority of public expenditure decisions (approximately 94 per cent) continue to be made at national level. This situation substantially reduces the ability of local governments and the communities they serve to address local problems in a flexible and appropriate manner. (Ó Broin and Waters, 2007, forthcoming)

Table 13.1 Functions of Local and Regional Government Within the EU

Functional Classification	*Germany*	*Austria*	*France*	*Sweden*	*UK*	*Netherlands*	*Belgium*	*Denmark*	***Ireland***
Refuse Collection and Disposal	L	L	L	L	L	L	L	L	**L**
Slaughterhouses	L	L	L	L	L	L	L	L	**L**
Theatres/Concerts	L,R	L,R	L	L	L	L	L	X	**X**
Museums, Libraries etc	L,R	L	L,R	L,R	L	L	L,R	L,R	**L**
Parks/Public Spaces	L	L	L,R	L	L	L,R	L,R	L	**L**
Sports and Leisure	L,R	L	L	L	L	L,R	L,R	L	**L**
Roads	L,R	L,R	L,R	L	L	L,R	L,R	L,R	**L**
Urban Road Transport	L,R	L	L,R	L,R	L	L	X	L	**X**
Ports	L,R	X	X	L	X	L	L	X	**X**
Airports	R	X	X	L,R	L	L	X	X	**X**
District Heating	L	L	L	L	X	L	L	L	**X**
Water Supply	L	L	L	L	L(a)	L,R	L	L	**L**
Agriculture, Fishing, Hunting, Forestry	L,R	R	L,R	L	L	L	L,R	X	**X**
Electricity	L	X	X	L	X	L,R	L,R	L	**X**
Commerce	L,R	L,R	L	L	X	L,R	L	X	**X**
Tourism	L,R	L,R	L,R	L,R	L	L	L,R	X	**X**
Security/Police	L,R	L	L	X	L	L,R	L	X	**X**
Fire Protection	L	L	L,R	L	L	L	L	L	**L**
Justice	R	X	X	X	L	X	X	X	**X**
Pre-School Education	L	L,R	L	L	L	L	L	L	**X**
Primary and Secondary Education	L,R	L,R	L (b)	L	L	L	L,R	L,R	**X**
Vocational and Technical Training	L	R	L	L,R	L	L	L,R	X	**X**
Higher Education	R	X	X	X	L	X	L,R	X	**X**
Adult Education	L,R	L	L	L,R	L	L	L	L	**X**
Hospitals and Convalescent Care	L,R	L,R	L,R	R	X	L,R	L,R	R	**X**
Personal Health	L,R	L,R	L	R	X	L	L	L,R	**X**
Family Welfare Services	L,R	L,R	L,R	L	L	L	L,R	L	**X**
Welfare Homes	L	L,R	L	L	L	L	L	L	**X**
Housing	L,R	L,R	L	L	L	L,R	L	X	**L**
Town Planning	L	L	L	L	L	L,R	L	L	**L**

Source: Adapted from Coughlan and de Buitleir (1996: 6–7)

L = Local Governments;

R = Regional Governments (including state governments; departments in France; provinces in Italy)

(a) Scotland only

(b) Mainly primary

Broadly speaking, Irish local government financing has progressed through three stages. The first period was prior to the mid-1970s when a significant proportion of local government revenue was generated through local mechanisms, in this case domestic rates. This stage was followed by an attempt to generate revenue through local service charges, while the current situation is characterised by the return of a centralised funding system which followed the introduction of the local government fund in the late 1990s. Since the abolition of the domestic rates tax system in 1978 and agricultural rates in 1982, local government has been dependent on central government for a substantial proportion of its funding. At the same time, successive governments have failed to deliver on their commitment to adequately compensate for this lost rates revenue, which significantly reduced local government's ability to generate income independently of central government. Local government may generate revenue from commercial property rates but the maximum permissible rate set by central government limits its value. Moreover, the decision in 1997 to abolish domestic water charges represented a further diminution of the independence of local authorities. (Callanan, 2004: 72)

A local government fund consisting of government grants and motor tax receipts has been in operation since 1998. While most of this money can be spent in theory on any programme at the discretion of the local authority, in practice most of the money has to be disbursed on what may be termed "inescapable demands". For example, a local council cannot decide unilaterally to abolish the planning department (in the unlikely event that it would wish to) in order to save money for other activities. Rather the law not only requires that local authorities provide a planning service but it also specifies the standard of service, i.e., that all planning applications must be processed within eight weeks. Such "inescapable demands" exist in almost every service area, nor are local authorities generally consulted when these requirements are set out in national legislation. After all of these demands are collectively met through the various sources of revenue open to local authorities (including the local government fund), very little remains for discretionary financing. As a result of these increased fiscal demands, local authorities frequently have no option but to increase charges, or commercial rates, or both.

Table 13.2 Local Governments Income Receipts 1977-2002

The figures in this table are indicative and not directly comparable due to changes in accounting practices over the years.

Revenue Source	*1977* %	*1983* %	*1991* %	*2002* %
Rates	34	12	21	24
Government grants	46	65	61	47
Other	20	23	18	29

Source: Adapted from Dollard, 2003: 328

As shown in Table 13.3 overleaf, Ireland's proportion of local authority taxes to total tax is one of the lowest in the OECD.

All the evidence shows that local authorities do not have adequate resources. The most recent analysis available (Indecon, 2005) identified a number of increased demands on local authorities in a number of service areas in upcoming years. For example, an increase in housing maintenance costs will arise from ongoing government investment in new housing stock, together with increased costs associated with managing enhanced public water and sewerage systems. After considering different models for estimating the future expenditure of local authorities, the report finds that current expenditure is likely to increase significantly in the period up to 2010, and given the current funding sources, projects a growing shortfall between expenditure and revenue. Depending on expenditure assumptions, Indecon's estimate of the future funding gap ranges from €415.9 million to €1,513.9 million for 2010, a considerable shortfall by any measure. Although the report emphasises that economy measures and increased efficiency will not by themselves plug this gap, the government has rejected outright the proposals for new tax revenue for local councils, although it will implement the proposed recommendations on efficiency savings.

The establishment of the local government fund in Ireland reflects to a certain degree a move away from specific funding towards more discretionary "block" grants, common in many countries but any discretionary spending here is, in practice, often more theoretical than real on account of the "inescapable demands" explained above. In addition, a significant proportion of central government financing still comes in the way of "specific grants", i.e., earmarked for particular purposes.

Table 13.3 Comparative Local Authority Taxes as Percentage of Total Taxation, 2001

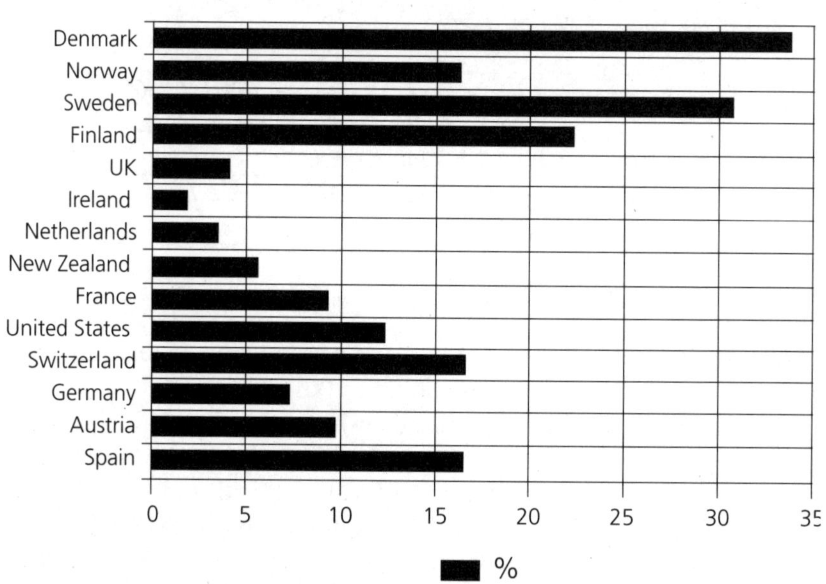

Source: Adapted from Organisation for Economic Cooperation and Development, 2003: 25

Increasing Dominance of Central Government

An excessive degree of central supervision and control of local government activities has always been a feature of the Irish system. Moreover, its pervasiveness is arguably increasing, in breach of the EU's principle of subsidiarity. Detailed regulation and supervision of local government activities is well established within the administrative tradition, and legislation is often supplemented by more detailed statutory instruments, ministerial regulations, circular letters, "guidelines" and other material which generally set out the details of implementation in a prescriptive manner. The problem of excessive central control was recognised by central government a decade ago in the last white paper on local government reform, (Department of Environment, 1996: 7) but little has been done since to tackle the issue in any comprehensive way. The net result is a lack of a "policy space" to adapt national legislation that is better suited to local needs. (Institute of Public Administration, 2004: 24–5)

The Irish system contrasts starkly with most other systems of central supervision of local government, which tend to adopt a more "hands-off" approach. In fact, there is an increasing realisation in many European countries that central government is poorly equipped to deal with area-based challenges that often do not fit neatly into sectoral boundaries as society becomes increasingly diverse, and which require instead a coordinated and concerted effort at the local level. As a result, the preoccupation of central government in countries like Sweden, Denmark and Finland over the past 25 years has shifted fundamentally away from formal controls and detailed and prescriptive rules and regulations towards a greater emphasis on advising, influencing, negotiating and bargaining with local authorities, as well as ensuring the legality of decisions. Most countries have formally structured arrangements to discuss in advance those budgetary or legislative decisions which will affect the operation of local authorities with central government bodies. One example is the "Central-Local Partnership" in Britain, where ministers and central government officials and local government political representatives and officials meet regularly to discuss new legislation and policy initiatives that will fall to local authorities to implement. Such a tradition of central-local relations differs radically to Ireland which lacks any comparable framework for information sharing between local and central levels of government.

IRELAND'S COMPLIANCE WITH THE EUROPEAN CHARTER FOR LOCAL SELF-GOVERNMENT

While Ireland has both signed up to and ratified the European Charter for Local Self-Government, the box below clearly demonstrates the very limited extent to which Ireland is complying with its principles.

For example, Article 3 of the Charter states that "Local authorities shall within the law regulate and manage a substantial share of public affairs under their own responsibility and in the interests of the local population". Such is unequivocally not the case in Ireland if one considers the narrow range of Irish local authority functions, compared to their counterparts abroad, as illustrated in Table 13.1. Given the prescriptive nature of regulation of local government activities in Ireland, local authorities also do not carry out their functions "under their own responsibility". Furthermore, central government has consistently allocated substantial powers to local, regional and national quasi-public agencies that are unelected.

Article 5 provides that "Changes in local authority boundaries shall not be made without prior consultation of the local communities involved, possibly by means of a referendum". While some consultation with communities often takes place, the extent of any "consultation" is frequently very limited. For example, the creation of the three new Dublin counties was presented merely as the redrawing of administrative boundaries and was not accompanied by any major public consultation exercise or referendum.

With regard to organisational autonomy, Article 6 of the Charter provides that "Local authorities shall be able to determine their own internal administrative structures so they can adapt them to local needs". This autonomy however is not the case in Ireland where central government retains a significant statutory role. In addition, Article 8 provides that "Administrative supervision of local authorities shall be proportionate and normally aim at ensuring compliance with the law or constitutional principle". Again, Ireland does not comply.

In 2001, a senior delegation from the Council of Europe's Congress of Local and Regional Authorities of Europe (CLRAE) visited Ireland to assess the state of Irish local democracy. Part of the delegation's remit was to assess the extent to which Ireland complies with the provisions of the European Charter. The CLRAE report observes that local government in Ireland appears to be more controlled by detailed central government regulations than is usually the case in non-common law countries and recommended that this system be systematically reconsidered and where appropriate, either abolished or replaced by statute law. (Congress of Local and Regional Authorities of Europe, 2001a: 12, 15) The report similarly concludes that "it is doubtful whether the prolific use of regulations is in harmony with the spirit of the [European] Charter [of Local Self-Government]". (Congress of Local and Regional Authorities of Europe, 2001b) This conclusion finds considerable support in Ireland, where one of the key recommendations of the Democracy Commission (Harris, 2005) cited the need to devolve power to local government and enhance the role of democratically elected councillors.

Ireland's Compliance with the European Charter of Local Government

European Charter of Local Government	Ireland's Compliance
Article 2 of the Charter states that "The principle of local self-government shall be recognised in domestic law and, where practicable,in the constitution."	Article 28A of the Constitution does provide a formal constitutional basis for local government but it does not recognise the principle of local self-government.
Article 3 Local authorities shall within the law regulate and manage a substantial share of public affairs under their own responsibility and in the interests of the local population.	In Ireland this is not the case Additionally, central government has consistently allocated substantial powers to local, regional and national quasi-public agencies that are unelected.
Article 4 The basic powers and responsibilities of local authorities shall be prescribed by the constitution or statute law; a) The basic powers and responsibilities of local authorities shall be prescribed by the constitution or statue law; b) Local authorities shall have general competence; c) Powers given to local authorities shall normally be full and exclusive and not undermined or limited by national or regional authority.	Ireland is in compliance in relation to a and b, though primarily through statute rather than constitutional provision. Ireland is not in compliance in relation to c.
Article 5 Changes in local authority boundaries shall not be made without prior consultation of the local communities involved, possibly by means of a referendum.	While there is often some consultation with communities, it is considered to often be poor. No referendums.
Article 6 Local authorities shall be able to determine their own internal administrative structures so they can adapt them to local needs.	Ireland is not in compliance. Central government retains a significant role, through statute.
Article 8 Administrative supervision of local authorities shall be proportionate and should normally aim only at ensuring compliance with the law or constitutional principle.	Ireland is not in compliance.
Article 9 (a) Local authorities shall be entitled, within national economic policy, to adequate financial resources that they may freely dispose of within the framework of their powers; (b) These resources shall be sufficient to meet their responsibilities and diverse and buoyant enough to keep pace with the cost of carrying out their tasks; (c) Local authorities shall have the power to determine the rate of local taxes and charges; (d) As far as possible, grants to local authorities shall not be earmarked to finance specific projects.	a) Local authority taxes as a proportion of the total tax take in Ireland is one of the lowest in the OECD. b) Local authority resources are not adequate or buoyant enough to meet their responsibilities. c) The financial autonomy of Local Authorities is strictly constrained. d) Discretionary finance is theoretica rather than real because of demands. Some funds also specifically earmarked.

The Future of Local Government

Despite the limited scope that increased centralisation affords for action at local level, many local authorities in recent years have become more proactive in a number of areas including environmental awareness (working with local schools and businesses to involve more people in recycling), tourism promotion and local economic development and employment. Local councils have thereby clearly demonstrated their capacity to take on new responsibilities and challenges, but such initiatives must be accompanied by access to new financial resources.

While there is a residual unwillingness by central government to consider wholescale devolution of functions to local authorities, best practice elsewhere reveals a wide range of options between full devolution and the current Irish level of rigid controls. For example, the principles contained in the White Paper *Regulating Better* (Department of the Taoiseach, 2004) could be applied to democratically-elected councils as well as businesses, effectively granting local councils more discretion in terms of their activities, and in particular how they carry them out. One method of advancing this agenda is to differentiate for local councils those areas where nationwide uniformity is desirable and where local authorities must continue to operate on an "agency basis" (i.e., have no discretion) from those areas where discretion exists to adapt policies, plans and programmes to local circumstances as is the case in France. This distinction in services would bring greater clarity to what is currently a rather ambiguous situation in Ireland.

It should also be possible to extend the right of democratically-elected councils to formally scrutinise and hold accountable the operations and activities of public bodies and agencies at local level. This engagement is already underway in the field of policing through the new Joint Policing Committees, where local councillors, community representatives and local gardaí come together to discuss community policing needs in local areas. The rationale behind such a "scrutiny" process is the opportunity it affords elected members, as democratically-elected representatives of the local population, to bring enhanced accountability to public bodies operating in their area. Such a role is already recognised in Section 64 of the Local Government Act 2001, but the structure needs to be put on a stronger legislative footing in order to make a real impact, since in practice there are frequent difficulties in getting representatives from relevant agencies to agree to attend meetings of local councils. As happens internationally, the "scrutiny" role could also be extended to areas like education and schools (especially the Department of Education, which essentially delivers a local service), health (Health Service Executive), public transport (CIÉ, Dublin Transport Authority), economic development (Industrial Development Authority, Enterprise Ireland), tourism (Fáilte Ireland) and other agencies operating at local level.

Q13.2 How far are these levels of government subject to free and fair electoral authorisation, and to the criteria of openness, accountability and responsiveness in their operation?

As is the case at national level, the three main political parties in Ireland continue to dominate local elections with Fianna Fáil in a pre-eminent, albeit declining, position. At the same time there has been a severe decline in turnout in local elections over the last thirty years. The PR-STV system used for local as well as national and European elections is judged to be a free and fair one, providing a more representative outcome than would be afforded by other systems such as first-past-the-post, although the system does foster a tendency to focus on the narrow concerns of individual constituents rather than broader policy objectives. The insertion of a specific provision for local government (Article 28A) into the Irish Constitution following a referendum in 1999 provides a formal constitutional basis for local government and ensures that council elections take place every five years. Prior to this provision, it was not uncommon for central government to postpone local elections for lengthy periods.

LOCAL GOVERNMENT ELECTIONS

As with national elections, one-party pre-eminence – namely that of Fianna Fáil – has been a prominent feature of Irish local government, although the percentage of first preference votes in local elections for that party has declined from 45.5 per cent in 1985, to 38.9 per cent in 1999 and 31.8 per cent in 2004 – this translates to a drop of 135 seats in less than 2o years. (Coakley and Gallagher, 2005: 469) Depending on their timing, local elections can provide an opportunity for mid-term judgement on the government of the day and in 2004 the loss of 80 seats (9 per cent) for Fianna Fáil was such a judgement.

Political control of local government is achieved through either winning an outright majority of seats in the council or by negotiating a power-sharing arrangement with one or more other parties or independents. Control means access to the relatively powerful positions of chairs of committees and to membership of committees and external agencies as well as ensuring a dominant influence on the council's policy-making areas such as planning and infrastructure. Following the 2004 elections, Fianna Fáil controls just 26 per cent of the mayor/deputy mayor positions, while winning 34 per cent of council seats. Fine Gael did better with 41 per cent of the posts and 33 per cent of seats as did Labour with 21 per cent of posts and just 11 per cent of seats. Non-party/independent candidates and minor parties tend to do better at local elections than at national elections. In the 2004 elections non-party/independent candidates accounted for 12 per cent of the mayor or deputy positions. (Kenny, 2004: 16)

Local elections provide considerable opportunity for turnover and new faces in politics. After the 2004 poll, there were 292 new members of the 34 county and city councils which represents a turnover of 33 per cent. (Kenny, 2004: 9)

Turnout

Up to 1999, the overall decreases in turnout in local government elections reflect a decline of almost 20 per cent over a period of 32 years. (Kenny, 2003: 107) An exception was the dramatic increase in turnout in the June 2004 elections which coincided with both European Parliament elections, as was also the case in 1979 and 1999, and perhaps more significantly a controversial constitutional referendum on citizenship. (See Section One for more detailed discussion of this referendum). Kenny (2004: 8) notes that the most interesting aspect of the changed pattern between 1999 and 2004 was the resurgence in turnouts in Dublin and its commuter belt which challenges the traditional perception that local elections are "essentially the preserve of the local population'.

Table 13.4 Local Elections 1967 – 2004

Year	*Turnout*
1967	69.0
1974	61.1
1979	63.6
1985	58.2
1991	55.1
1999	49.5
2004	58.7

Source: Adapted from Institute Public Administration 2005: 431

Electoral System

PR-STV (Proportional Representation–Single Transferable Vote) is the electoral system used in Ireland for local as well as national and European elections. (See Q 5.4 for discussion of PR-STV). The evidence suggests that this system encourages a more engaged relationship between elected councillors and their constituents and independent commissions in both Scotland and Wales have recently recommended it as the system best suited for local government. Critics of the system in general emphasise the way in which PR fosters personalism, i.e., that votes tend to be cast on the basis of personality rather than political principle or ideology, and also assert that it can contribute to a climate of political corruption. All of these concerns apply at the local level.

Impact on Policy-making Function

Elected councillors formally retain the final decision over "reserved functions" including many of the key policy frameworks within which officials must work. There have also been significant reforms since the mid-1990s resulting from the *Better Local Government Report* in 1996 designed to enhance their policy role. In practice, however, a significant number of councillors display little interest in policy issues. One reason for this is the electoral system, which at the end of the day effectively prioritises the individual good over the common good. At the same time, PR-STV involves multimember constituencies which offer voters a choice of candidates from the same party at election time. Rivalry is thereby typically more intense between candidates from the same party and in the absence of any differences in policy platforms, candidates who can point to having "delivered" for constituents enjoy an advantage. This situation generally results in local councillors who tend to be preoccupied with operational matters affecting individual constituents, and who in some cases display less concern for the general good of the overall locality. It also allows them to be largely passive on policy matters, with a tendency to rely on council officials to take the lead on policy making. (Quinlivan, 2003: 5–6)

The ability to look beyond individual fiefdoms and employ a county / city-wide perspective was part of the rationale behind the proposed directly elected mayors who would be elected by the county and city "at large" rather than specific electoral areas or wards. At present, however, the current electoral system continues to contribute to a frequent policy vacuum on county / city-wide issues which can only be filled by the county / city manager or officials.

Councillor/Elector Ratio

A number of questions arise about the role of elected councillors in local decision-making processes and their relationship with the citizens who elected them. Ireland is unusual in that the distance between elected councillors and their electorate is substantially greater than any other Member State of the EU with the exception of Britain (see Tables 13.5 and 13.6). The Democracy Commission's recent report notes that "Ireland's high number of constituents per council can impact negatively on experiences of local democracy to the extent that it makes local government remote from the people and is among the factors reducing the likelihood of participation". (Harris, 2005) At the same time, the number of electors per councillor varies significantly; for example, in County Leitrim there are 1,117 electors per councillor, while in County Cork there are 5,784 electors per councillor, and in Dublin City 6,717 electors per councillor. This considerable disparity stands in opposition to the principle of political equality enshrined in Article 16.2.3 of the Constitution.

Social Representativeness of Local Authorities

The pattern of elected representation of the population in the chambers of local authorities broadly reflects that at national level, although local authorities do provide more opportunities for special interest groups and minorities to be directly represented. For example, women, younger people and employees in the private sector are in general underrepresented, while remarkably few councillors work for US multinationals, even though these employees represent an increasingly large section of the workforce. (See Q 11.4) Most councillors are either self-employed (e.g., businessmen or farmers) or employed by the state (e.g., teachers), or retired.

Dual Mandate

The 2003 Local Government Act which banned the dual mandate was unquestionably a major political reform, albeit one which met with a great deal of political resistance before finally coming to pass. Given that 138 of the 226 members elected to the Dáil or Seanad in 2002 were members of local councils, the reform clearly creates the space for wider participation of the population in electoral politics. At least theoretically, frees TDs to focus on national issues; allows local councillors to focus on local demands; and helps to diminish the strong role of personalism in Irish politics. However, an inappropriate degree of potential for interference in local politics by national politicians continues to exist, as the Local Government Act 2003 explicitly affords TDs and senators continued access to local authority documentation and information. (Kenny, 2003: 114)

OPENNESS, ACCOUNTABILITY AND RESPONSIVENESS

> *An influential but little-known facet of local government is formed by the layers of committees, boards, authorities and partnerships to which councils have nominating rights. This array of bodies might be termed "secondary representation" in that councillors take part on the respective boards as an extension of their primary local authority mandate. Indeed the activities of some of the organisations are little known within the local government sector and often escape the attention of the otherwise knowledgeable local press.* (Kenny, 2003: 112)

The complex interrelationships and considerable levels of opaqueness described in the above quotation patently militates against openness and transparency.

County/City Manager System

Unlike many local government systems elsewhere in Europe, Ireland has a council manager system of local government, wherein every county / city council has a county / city manager who acts as chief executive. Under legislation the elected members have reserved functions while the county / city managers are granted executive functions. Reserved functions generally pertain to policy matters and the creation of a policy framework within which the managers and officials must work. Managers are appointed by the Local Appointments Commission for a seven-year term. Their role in decision making has largely removed political responsibility for controversial decisions from councillors (Collins and Cradden, 2004) as has the Waste Management Act 2001 which allocated significant decision-making powers to the city / county manager on the selection of sites for waste management facilities.

There is some anecdotal evidence to suggest that many councillors were quite happy to be taken "off the hook" on problematic decisions such as the location of waste management facilities or Traveller halting sites, even if they publicly condemned the power being taken away from them. In practice, the manager reports his or her decisions to the council which has limited powers to overturn them. Councillors can, for example, overturn a manager's decision to grant general planning permission to an individual, although this power (in operation since 1955) has not always been used constructively by members in the past. (Collins and Cradden, 2004) For example, it has been used to give planning permissions for housing in areas where it should not, on the basis of objective evidence, have been granted.

The balance of power between the manager and the councillors is weighted in the favour of the former, who is appointed on a full-time basis with access to required resources and information. Councillors, on the other hand, operate on a part-time basis and, with few channels of their own, remain dependent on the manager for their information. Another significant aspect of managerial powers is his/her role as the person in direct contact with central government and the "disseminator of national policies". In practice, the non-hierarchical relationship between the manager and council leads to a state of mutual dependency which does not serve accountability. (Daemen and Schapp, 2000: 63)

Absence of a Professional Political Executive

City/county managers are the only senior public servants who must account on a monthly basis for their actions and have a reputation for "honesty and diligence". (Collins and Cradden, 2004) At the same time, they are unelected. The Local Government Act (2001) provided for the direct, popular election of chairpersons/mayors in county and city councils for a full five-year term but this provision was repealed in 2003 due to a widespread fear among many public representatives that party members would lose to protest candidates or local "characters". (Callanan, 2004: 61–3) The opposition of backbench TDs was also a key factor in the repeal, as both national parliamentarians and local councillors were opposed to creating a position that might give rise to high-profile spokespersons for local areas. In particular, many national politicians saw the position of directly-elected mayor as affording an effective platform for local politicians to emerge as competitors for a Dáil seat in the next general election. The prospect of "single issue" or "personality" candidates dominating the process (or what some alternatively called "beauty contests') was also not regarded as a positive development by either local or national politicians. The fact that the Minister who had originally pioneered the initiative in 2000-2001, Noel Dempsey, had moved to another portfolio in 2002, was not unimportant in the decision to repeal.

Recent research (Henry *et al.*, 2006) has suggested that the Corporate Policy Group (CPG), consisting of the mayor of the council and each SPC chairperson, has the capacity to evolve into a stronger political board as described above. [See Q 13.3 for further discussion of CPGs]. In particular, the CPG could play a greater corporate governance and scrutiny role in overseeing local council activities which might include: evaluating implementation of the corporate plan and operational plans; customer service reviews; performance management and financial overview; assessing stakeholder satisfaction by establishing focus groups, commissioning surveys etc; ethics; and the council's communications policy. However, the fact that party leaders rarely sit on the CPG represents an obstacle to this kind of evolution. Instead the CPG is composed of party representatives who frequently have to discuss their positions with both their SPCs and their party groups.

Integrity of the Local Government System

In October 1997 the Flood Tribunal (currently known as the Mahon Tribunal) was established to investigate "persistent and disturbing" allegations of political corruption in the physical planning process and decisions by local authorities to rezone land from agricultural to industrial or housing use. The Tribunal has found that Dublin-based local councillors (and TDs) accepted money from developers, albeit *via* a lobbyist, and that a senior local government official received a payment from developers for giving "advice". (Collins and Cradden, 2004) However, it is unclear the degree to which corruption is widespread in Irish local government. A number of cases have arisen in recent years, but they appear to be isolated incidents. (Collins and Quinlivan, 2005: 395–400) (See also Q9.4)

Forms of Consultation

The primary method by which the community can influence the decision-making process of county / city councils is by exercising their franchise in local elections. During the working term of the council, its elected members hold private consultations with constituents at public venues throughout their constituency. At these "clinics" local residents have the opportunity to discuss issues with the council members in private. Clinics are commonly held in a local hall or in a meeting room in a hotel or public house. However, there is no formal provision or requirement for councillors to hold clinics and their prevalence varies widely.

In addition to participative structures such as SPCs and CDBs, (discussed in more detail in Q13.3), local councils in Ireland have also been experimenting with alternative and sometimes innovative ways of both listening to their communities and allowing people to participate in local affairs beyond the ballot box, including such measures as surveys, setting up focus groups, and holding public meetings. Many local councils have also established youth councils under the Comhairle na n-Óg programme, where local schools elect representatives to county / city youth councils to discuss relevant issues such as environmental improvements, recreational facilities and road safety, and to make recommendations to the full council.

Information concerning services provided by local government such as housing, planning, maintenance etc. are broadly advertised in the media and at public buildings. Objections and appeals can be formally made to the council and are often investigated by independent committees.

Borough and town councils function in much the same way as city / county councils, albeit on a smaller scale. However, borough and town councils have tended to devolve many of their powers upwards to the city / county level, so that provision for community consultation and influence usually rests with the relevant city / county council. The membership of the two regional assemblies consists of county / city councillors and there are no formal structures for community involvement in decision making at this level. Community representation consequently lies with the relevant councillors who sit on the assembly on behalf of their council and its constituents.

Table 13.5 Council, Councillor and Citizen Relationships in the European Union

Country	*Population*	*Number of relevant local councils*	*Average population per council*	*Average size of council*	*Population per elected councillor*
France	59.6 million	36,700	1,600	14	118
Austria	8.2 million	2,350	3,500	17	209
Sweden	8.8 million	310	28,400	111*	256
Germany	83 million	15,300	5,400	15	350
Finland	5.2 million	452	11,500	28	410
Italy	57.7 million	8,100	7,100	12	608
Spain	40 million	8,100	4,900	8	610
Belgium	10.3 million	589	17,500	22	811
Greece	10.6 million	1033	10,300	10	1,075
Denmark	5.4 million	275	19,600	17	1,115
Portugal	10.1 million	308	32,800	29	1,131
Netherlands	16 million	548	29,000	19	1,555
Ireland	**3.8 million**	**118**	**33,000**	**14**	**2,336**
United Kingdom	59.6 million	468	127,350	49	2,603

Source: Knox, 2002: 3; * Includes deputies, elected at the same time.

Table 13.6 Local Government Electors per Councillor in Britain and Ireland

	Number of councillors	*Population*	*Number of councils*	*Average population per council*	*Population per elected councillor*	*Local government elections per councillor*
Northern Ireland	582	1.7 million	26	64,980	2,903	2,059
Scotland	1,245	5.1 million	32	153,000	4,108	3,201
Wales	1,273	2.9 million	22	128,000	2,314	1,761
Ireland	1,627	3.8 million	118	33,000	2,336	1,654

Source: Knox, 2002: 4

Q 13.3 How extensive is the cooperation of government at the most local level with relevant partners, associations and communities in the formation and implementation of policy, and in service provision?

A range of new structures was put in place at local level under the Local Government Act of 2001, with the stated purpose of restoring real decision making to local authorities and their local residents. The centralised structures and decision making that affect many important local services, such as enterprise, health and education, severely limit the potential for real involvement of either local representatives or local associations and communities in these services. At the same time, the last 20 years have seen an emphasis at local level on the development of partnerships among the public, private and voluntary sectors which mirror the social partnership model at national level. While these structures allow for more diverse composition many of the individuals, groups and agencies represented are not at all accountable to local communities. As a result, the establishment of many local development agencies has actually diluted the already-limited democratic accountability of the local public policy decision-making process without any clearly identifiable or quantifiable gain.

EXTENT OF INVOLVEMENT

Ireland's governance structure involves a large number of agencies (22 distinct types totalling 491 agencies nationwide) which operate in overlapping areas. There are three very broad levels of operation. (Ó Broin and Waters, 2007 forthcoming)

- Sub-city / county; for example, town councils, some area partnerships, port authorities and RAPID and CLÁR programmes.
- City / county; for example, city and county councils, city / county development boards, city / county enterprise boards and VECs.
- Quasi-regional; for example, regional assemblies, regional authorities, Health Service Executive regional structures and Department of Education and Science regional structures (all of whose regional areas differ).

Local governments are responsible for the vast majority (circa 90 per cent) of locally-accountable public expenditure decisions, although this disbursement represents itself a tiny proportion of overall expenditure at local level. (see Q.13.1 for further elaboration)

In an Action Programme for the Millennium, the government set out its commitment to the restoration of real decision-making power to local authorities and local people. An important step towards this goal was the proposal to establish three new kinds of entities within each city and county council – namely, strategic policy committees, a corporate policy group and a city / county development board – whose key role would be to facilitate greater interaction between local government and other public agencies and between local government, civil society and local communities. This initiative was given effect by the Local Government Act, 2001, which also provides that town councils may establish municipal policy committees.

Strategic Policy Committees

Strategic Policy Committees (SPCs) are tailored to the size, membership and administrative resources of the local authority. Consisting of a mix of local councillors and representatives external to the local authority, SPCs are required to have a minimum one-third of their membership drawn from sectors relevant to the committee's work. Their remit is to develop and review policy and to act as a forum for consultation with relevant sectors. Although the role of SPCs is to assist and advise the council which retains the decision-making authority, in practice many SPC recommendations are either adopted in full or with minor amendments only. The sectors selected for representation on SPCs include:

- agriculture / farming;
- environmental / conservational / culture;
- development / construction;
- business / commercial;
- trade union; and
- community / voluntary / disadvantaged groups.

The establishment of SPCs was intended to facilitate the discussion of strategic-policy matters among councillors with the involvement of expert or knowledgeable parties. For this reason the non-councillor places on the SPCs are usually filled from professional groups, industry groups or advocacy groups, e.g., the Construction Industry Federation and Chambers of Commerce, at least in the case of the larger authorities. Each sector (apart from agriculture and farming in the case of urban local authorities) is to be represented on at least one SPC in each local authority. The following statistics from the Institute of Public Administration's review of SPCs show the breakdown of the non-councillor places before 2004 between the various sectors.

Table 13.7 Strategic Policy Committee Sectoral Members by Category

Sector	*Number of representatives*	*% of total representatives*
Community/voluntary/disadvantaged	203	32
Business/commercial	110	17
Environment/conservation/cultural	102	16
Development/construction	75	12
Trade union	67	11
Agriculture/farming	66	10
Other	12	2
Total	635	100

Source: Institute of Public Administration, 2004: 10

Community representatives and environmental representatives, who make up almost half of the total non-councillor representatives, are nominated through the local community fora, which have been set up in each county and city council area and are open to all local community and voluntary groups active in the locality.

Corporate Policy Group

A Corporate Policy Group (CPG) comprises the mayor as its chair together with the chairs of each of the SPCs. Its function, supported by the manager, is to bring together the work of the different SPCs and to provide a forum for policy issues which transcend the remit of individual SPCs. The mayor also represents the CPG at meetings of council. Although the CPGs were envisaged as a "cabinet-style structure" (O'Sullivan, 2003: 59), it is unclear if they will establish a clear and coherent role for themselves. (See comments in Q 13.2 on the CPGs in the light of recent research conducted by Henry *et al.*, (2006))

The rationale behind the creation of SPCs (as well as the CDBs discussed below) was to replicate the success of the national social partnership agreements at local level as part of a concerted effort to develop a more participative and less centralised democracy. However, the narrow range of functions allocated to local government in Ireland in turn constrains the nature and scope of any strategic policy developed by the SPCs as it is unlikely that the relevant council will be involved in implementing it. Furthermore, instructions from central government can be so prescriptive that there is often a lack of "policy space" or alternative options for SPCs to consider.

City/County Development Boards

Following the work of an interdepartmental task force on the Integration of Local Government and Local Development Systems, chaired by the Minister for the Environment and Local Government, city/county development boards (CDBs) were established in 2000. The membership of the development boards consists of representatives from local government, state agencies and the social partners. Included in the social partners strand are members from the community and voluntary sector, the former of which are drawn from the community forum structures that exist within each county. Each CDB was required to prepare and oversee the implementation of a ten-year strategy for economic, social and cultural development that would serve as a template in guiding all public services and local development activities and effectively bring greater coherence to the planning and delivery of services at local level. An immediate positive outcome to the establishment of the CDBs was the opportunity it afforded for key players at local level to come together for the first time to engage in a process of long-term planning for each county or city. (Government of Ireland, 1998, 1999a, 1999b, 2000) However, the subsequent difficulties faced by CDBs in moving beyond this to actually devise and implement local policy priorities in a coordinated and deliberative manner lies in the fact that the key public agencies participating, e.g., Enterprise Ireland, FÁS and the Industrial Development Authority, are national organisations with little or no local autonomy. As a result, their ability to sign up to a locally-agreed strategy is severely limited. Furthermore, certain key service providers, e.g., the Department of Education and Science, are not involved, which limits the ability of the CDBs to implement agreed strategies. (Ó Broin, 2004: 37–52) Recent research on the RAPID programme, under which local authorities bring together state agencies and public service providers to coordinate services in targeted disadvantaged urban areas, has confirmed the difficulty of securing "buy-in" from some national agencies, such as the Department of Education and Science. (Fitzpatrick Associates, 2006) At the same time, it is also relatively easier to sign off on the strategy than it is to ensure that agencies actually comply with its provisions, given the fact that the CDBs have no power of sanction. As such, it remains unclear to date whether the CDBs are exerting a real influence on the work and planning activities of agencies.

Despite these concerns, CDBs have carried out innovative work and have provided a mechanism for local councillors and communities, *via* their community fora, to engage in policy discussions with local public agencies in a manner that wasn't possible before their establishment. In addition, some CDBs have provided additional mechanisms to include other stakeholders in the local policy formulation process. For example, the Fingal CDB provides a position on its board for both the Institute of Technology in Blanchardstown and Dublin City University.

Community and Voluntary Fora

The Community and Voluntary Fora were not only established as area nominating bodies to SPCs and CDBs, but also to facilitate local groups to develop and progress joint initiatives and projects in areas of common concern, and to allow for interaction, the sharing of ideas, and cooperation with other community groups working on similar issues in the area. Each forum is assigned a budget for its activities upon agreement of a work programme with the area local authority. More localised "area fora" also exist in many places, as well as subgroups devoted to specific interests. It is also generally expected in most areas that the community fora will be either consulted or directly involved in the nomination of community representatives to the joint policing committees at local level. In general the community fora are open to groups working in various capacities within local communities. Area partnerships, local drugs taskforces, RAPID/CLÁR structures also tend to have similar forum-type structures in their specific areas.

In addition to the community forum, community groups and individuals can also influence the local decision-making processes through attending the "clinic" of their local TD, who can in turn contact their local councillor. Of course community groups can also contact councillors directly, although this approach is considerably more difficult in a city such as Dublin than it is in a town council such as Balbriggan.

LOCAL PUBLIC AGENCIES

The last 20 years have also seen the establishment of a number of new public and semi-public agencies at local level in Ireland. (See Table 13.8 for details.) While their impact on local governance processes is as yet unclear, the establishment of such area partnerships, community partnerships, city/county enterprise boards, LEADER groups and RAPID/CLÁR groups has significantly increased the number of people and groups perceived to be participating in the local governance process. A process is also currently underway to bring a number of local development groups, such as LEADER companies, area partnerships and community partnerships under an umbrella organisation for each county/city area. While these new agencies have varying aims and objectives, it is possible to identify a common characteristic, namely an emphasis on the development of partnerships between the public, private and third sectors which arguably mirrors the social partnership model pioneered at national level. It could be further argued that this system is more inclusive than the previous experience of national-level service delivery, given the more diverse composition of these new agencies and organisations. At the same time, however, many of the individual groups and agencies are in no way accountable to local communities.

While it is generally accepted that locally-elected officials in Ireland have more limited powers and areas of competence than their counterparts in other countries (Quinn, 2003: 452–5; John, 2001: 25), the establishment of many of these local development agencies has in fact further diluted the already limited democratic accountability of the local public policy decision-making process.The typical composition of many of the new structures including community partnerships, LEADER programmes etc. consists of a mixture of local authority representatives, representatives of social partners, nominees of state agencies and members of the local community. The actual success rate in providing more diverse representation of the local community in these structures varies. (Ó Broin and Waters, 2007, forthcoming)

As shown in Table 13.8, the willingness to encourage broader community participation in local governance clearly exists, even if mechanisms are not always in place to ensure the widest representation of the community. Within this context, Ireland has been decidedly slow to devise and implement complementary forms of participation such as citizens' juries. Nonetheless, the inclusion of community and voluntary sectors on the CDBs has facilitated their input into the overall strategy and framework for future developments relative to their sectors. A major question remains, however, as to whether the establishment of structures to facilitate the involvement of social partners and the statutory agencies represents the development of a more inclusive decision-making process, and if so, whether this new inclusiveness represents a step towards a more democratic and accountable form of decision making. It is possible to argue that while more people are involved in the decision-making process, the process itself has become less transparent and accountable to the public as a variety of local public agencies negotiate their own relationships with each other and central government while at the same time diluting the influence of elected councillors. Furthermore, the structures that have been established often appear to be devised in such a way that their actual use depends on whether or not local governments decide the "circumstances are propitious". (Forde, C., 2004: 62)

Table 13.8 Local and Regional Public Agencies in Ireland

Organisation and number	Type (decision-making and/or advisory)	Composition of board
1. County Councils (29)	Decision making	Elected Councillors and the County Manager.
2. City Councils (5)	Decision making	Elected Councillors and the City Manager.
3. Town Councils (75)	Decision making	Elected Councillors
4. Borough Councils (5)	Decision making	Elected Councillors
5. Regional Assemblies (2)	Advisory	City and County Councillors from the constituent local governments.
6. Regional Authorities (8)	Advisory	City and County Councillors from the constituent local governments.
7. Regional Health Authorities (4)	Decision making	The composition of the HSE Regional Boards has not yet been clarified.
8. Regional Tourism Boards (7)	Decision making	Open to all living within the region but particularly those working in tourism, local governments, clubs etc.
9. Regional Fisheries Boards (7)	Decision making	Mixture of Ministerial nominations, tourism representatives, local councillors and representatives of the numerous fishing organisations.
10. Regional Drugs Task Forces (10)	Advisory	The RDTFs include representations from the following organisations: Regional Drug Co-co-ordinator of the Health Service Executive, local government representation; VEC; Department of Education and Science; Department of Community, Rural and Gaeltacht Affairs; Gardaí; Probation and Welfare Services; FÁS; Revenue Commissioners; social partners.
11. Harbour Authorities (5)	Decision making	Includes representatives of users of the harbours, local government, chambers of commerce and ministerial representation.
12. Port Companies (12)	Decision making	Board of Directors consists of representatives of employees of company, relevant local government, some individuals appointed by minister.
13. City/County Development Boards (34)	Advisory	Typical composition is as follows: local government (7), local development (6), state agencies (9) and social partners (6-8).
14. City/County Enterprise Boards (35)	Decision making	Typical composition is as follows: independent chairperson, members are from the local government (4), the other 10 are nominees of state agencies, social partners, promoters of small business etc.
5. Area partnerships (38)	Decision making	Typical composition is as follows: independent chairperson, members from the local government (3-6), nominees of state agencies (6), social partners (6) and local community (6).
16. Community partnerships (33)	Decision making	Typical composition is as follows: independent chairperson, members from the local government (3-6), nominees of state agencies (6), social partners (6) and local community (6).
17. LEADER (35)	Decision making	Typical composition is as follows: independent chairperson, members from the local government, nominees of state agencies, social partners and local community.
18. County/City Childcare Committees (33)	Decision making	Typical composition is as follows: providers nominees, members from the local government, nominees of state agencies, social partners and local community.
19. Vocational Education Committees (33)	Decision making	Typical composition is as follows: chief executive, members from the local government, nominees from teaching unions and parents.
20. Local Drugs Task Forces (18)	Advisory	Typical composition is as follows: nominees of state agencies and local community.
21. RAPID (45)	Advisory	Typical composition is as follows: local government, local development, nominees of state agencies, drugs task force and local community. Each programme also has a co-ordinator who is employed by the relevant local government.
22. CLÁR (18) Ceantair Laga Árd-Riachtanais	Advisory	Typical composition is as follows: local government, local development, nominees of state agencies, drugs task force, social partners and local community. Each programme also has a co-ordinator who is employed by the relevant local government.

Source: Ó Broin and Waters, 2007 forthcoming

DEMOCRACY BEYOND THE STATE

Fourteen: International Dimensions of Democracy

Are the country's external relations conducted in accordance with democratic norms, and is it itself free from external subordination?

INTRODUCTION AND SUMMARY

At first sight, a country's international relations may appear to have little to do with the quality of its democracy. Yet in practice such relations affect it from two quite different angles. First if the core idea of democracy is that of self-government, of control by the people of the decisions that affect their collective lives, it follows that a democratic audit cannot ignore the ways in which those decisions may be determined by institutions or forces outside the state. A country might have the most perfect internal democracy but enjoy little real self-government if most of the decisions that mattered for the lives of its citizens were taken beyond its borders. Second the quality of a country's democratic life can also be gauged by how it treats other countries and their legitimate aspirations. How strictly does it observe the international rule of law and international treaties? How fair is its treatment of immigrants and asylum seekers? How far do its policies support democracy and human rights abroad? These are the kinds of question to be addressed in this section of the audit.

In regard to the first issue identified above, we conclude that Ireland's governance is properly independent of interference and control from outside forces. To be sure, its globalised economy is dependent upon the maintenance of inward investment from abroad, but this foreign investment has, to date at least, contributed significantly to economic growth and is not experienced as substantially compromising Irish sovereignty. Similarly, the fact that Ireland, like other EU members, is subject to EU law and the judgements of the European Court constitutes a voluntary pooling of sovereignty that has been endorsed by the voters in successive referenda. At the same time, Ireland plays its part in international bodies as an equal, not a subordinate, member. Any democratic limitation therefore stems rather from a lack of domestic public interest in, and parliamentary oversight of, Ireland's international policy, though the deployment of troops abroad requires specific approval of the Oireachtas.

With regard to respect for international law, Ireland has ratified the major UN-sponsored human rights and other treaties which impact on domestic jurisdiction. An exception is the Convention on the Rights of Migrant Workers, which seeks to provide increased long-term security for migrants in respect of residence, employment and family life – aspects wherein Ireland's own policy is currently deficient. Ireland has, however, recently incorporated the UN Refugee Convention into domestic law and was commended by the UNHCR in 2003 for its overall handling of the growing numbers of asylum seekers, though the appeals system has been criticised for its secrecy and potential arbitrariness. In respect of Ireland's observance of other treaties, concern has been raised at the likelihood that the country will not meet its targets for reducing greenhouse gas emissions under the Kyoto Protocol. Overall, Ireland has a very positive record of support for the UN and its agencies. It is a major contributor to UN peacekeeping forces, especially in Africa, and has played a significant role in disarmament negotiations over the years. Ireland is also a strong supporter of developing countries, as demonstrated by its increased overseas financial aid, and by its voting record in support of resolutions initiated by the developing world. This positive image would be further enhanced, campaigners argue, if the country's overseas development strategy were more fully integrated with other policy areas, such as agriculture and trade.

Q14.1 How free is the governance of the country from subordination to external agencies, economic, cultural or political?

In terms of freedom of governance, Ireland can be said to lie somewhere close to the norm for developed democratic states. It has been a member of the United Nations (UN) since 1955 and participates in most international bodies and agencies such as the World Trade Organisation, International Labour Organisation, World Bank, World Health Organisation and more. In European terms, Ireland is a founder member of the Council of Europe and joined the European Union in 1973. Ireland is not a signatory of the North Atlantic Treaty, and thereby not a member of NATO. The Irish economy is one of the most globalised on our planet and a significant level of inward investment by multinational corporations has to date been among the contributing factors to its remarkable economic growth over recent years. All of these factors impact on the state's freedom of governance, yet it would be difficult to argue that any of them, or even all, amount to "subordination to external agencies".

MEMBERSHIP OF INTERNATIONAL BODIES

Irish membership of international bodies can be divided into two groups. The first group comprises those organisations in which elements of national sovereignty of the member countries have formally been pooled. Prominent within this group are the European Union (EU), the Council of Europe and the International Criminal Court. The second group consists of international bodies where little, if any, national sovereignty has been transferred and where each Member State retains a veto.

Any examination of the impact of such bodies on Irish economic, political and cultural autonomy needs to look first at the principles underlying membership in such organisations. The Irish state itself was founded on the principle of achieving political and economic independence, with the 1916 Proclamation, for example, demanding "an unfettered control of Irish destinies". However, as international conditions changed, the rationale for sovereign self-sufficiency eroded and Ireland, like other countries, faced up to the opportunities and challenges of interdependence, and following a long period of isolationism, the Irish government proposed joining the EEC in the 1970s. The white paper of 1972 outlined the case for joining the Common Market and, by definition, conceded some aspects of sovereignty:

> For most countries ... the real freedom, as distinct from the nominal right, to take national action and pursue policies in the economic and trading sectors is circumscribed ... by the complex

> nature of international, economic and trading relationships ... our vital interests may be affected by the policies and actions of other larger countries or groups of countries. This gravely restricts our capacity to exercise the right of freedom of action and thus represents a very real limitation on our national sovereignty. (Government of Ireland, 1972)

Ireland's membership of the EU and other international organisations can therefore be seen as part of an international trend towards the creation of interdependent relationships, which while limiting some aspects of the sovereignty of individual states, can also serve members' interests by allowing states input into decisions by other states which will affect them in any case. (Coleman, 2005)

The European Union

The European Union represents a historical development because of its unique transnational status, including its directly-elected parliament. Moreover, the EU with its treaties, its transnational executive, and parliament – with much of its political power vested in the Council of Ministers from the 27 Member States – has become part of the normal political framework wherein Irish governmental decisions are taken.

The principle is well established that where discrepancies arise between European and national law, European law takes primacy. This reality confers constitutional status on the European treaties, and pools a considerable element of sovereignty in the European Court of Justice, which is the supreme court of the EU.

In some of the EU's operations, decisions must be made unanimously, which effectively gives a veto to all Member States. In other areas, decisions are made by weighted qualified majority voting, which potentially obliges some Member States to adopt measures they would rather not in the interests of the Union as a whole. EU decisions made by qualified majority voting thereby have a potentially greater impact on the sovereignty of Member States.

Recent treaty amendments have brought with them the increasing use of qualified majority voting as the default decision-making system. This development increases the likelihood of an Irish government being obliged to accept a decision it has opposed. Consideration of such a scenario, however, also needs to take into account the practice within the EU of avoiding such scenarios. In addition, the slow decision-making process within the EU affords Member States the opportunity to express reservations about any given proposal as it works its way through the legislative process.

Finally, Irish membership of the (then) European Communities in 1973 was approved by an overwhelming majority of the people by referendum. Moreover, since membership of the EU involves a degree of subordination of domestic legislation and constitutional provisions, all additional European treaties (Single European Act, Maastricht, Amsterdam, Nice etc.) in Ireland are submitted to referendum. In this respect, the Irish people have repeatedly chosen to pool some of their sovereignty within the EU.

It can be argued, therefore, that Ireland's membership of the EU does not entail subordination to an external agency. Rather, it involves the pooling of certain aspects of state sovereignty within a structure that provides safeguards for the national interests of all Member States, which are accompanied in Ireland's case by the free adoption or rejection *via* referenda of measures involving changes to the Irish Constitution.

If viewed as an external body, a case can be made to present the EU as an entity to which Irish governance could, on occasion, be subordinate. However an equally strong case can be made for the EU as an integral part of Irish governance structures, whereby the question of subordination does not arise.

Council of Europe

Ireland is a founder member of the now 46-member Council of Europe. Unlike Irish membership of the EU, membership of the Council of Europe is not based on a national referendum. While this body is a classical international structure operating by consensus for all major decisions, it is the parent body of the European Convention on, and the Commission and Court of, Human Rights. Ireland, like all other Member States, is bound by decisions of the European Court of Human Rights. As a result, Irish governance, like that of all Council of Europe members, is subordinate to the Court.

The European Court of Human Rights continues to play a significant role in the defence and furtherance of human rights in Europe, including in Ireland. Two cases can be cited as examples, the 1979 Josie Airey case, which was crucial in securing the introduction of a civil legal aid scheme and the Senator David Norris case in 1988 which led to the decriminalisation of homosexuality in 1993. In addition, a 2002 referendum which totally abolished the death penalty in Ireland, even in time of war, was an endorsement of the protocol to the European Convention on Human Rights and Fundamental Freedoms.

It could be argued, however, that conformity with international human rights legislation does not constitute subordination to an external agency, since protection of human rights has become a core aspect of good democratic governance. In fact, the Council of Europe has done a great deal of work across Europe to strengthen the framework on human rights across the continent. This achievement is particularly evident in the fact that new accession states to the EU must first satisfy the conditions for membership of the Council of Europe, which in practice has seen the adoption of a wide range of human rights legislation by new Member States as a condition of entry.

International Criminal Court

The Rome Conference of 1998 led to the statutory establishment of the International Criminal Court (ICC) which entered into force on 1 July 2002. The ICC is the first ever permanent, treaty-based, international criminal court which has jurisdiction to prosecute genocide, crimes against humanity and war crimes. The Court is an independent international organisation with a special relationship within the UN, and was established, in part, as a response to ethnic cleansing in the former Yugoslavia and to genocide in Rwanda.

Ireland has ratified the ICC *via* a referendum to amend the Irish Constitution to allow for ratification of the ICC Statute, which was passed in 2001 with over 64 per cent in favour. In this referendum, Irish citizens collectively agreed to make themselves liable to prosecution by the ICC. As with the EU, the argument can be made that the Irish people have decided to pool an element of their sovereignty into the International Criminal Court, making it an integral part of the structures of Irish governance rather than external one. If this argument is accepted, the question of Irish "subordination" to the ICC does not arise.

The United Nations

Ireland has been a member of the UN since 1955 and participates in all its various specialised agencies.

Ireland has been an active member, dating from the 1950s when it played a key role in the negotiation of the Nuclear of Non-proliferation Treaty (NPT). Ireland has also played a significant role in UN peacekeeping missions; in August 2005, for example, only Poland within the EU had more troops deployed on UN peacekeeping worldwide. Since the first Irish mission to the Congo, 86 Irish soldiers and gardaí have died while serving on UN missions.

Ireland is party to six of the seven most significant UN human rights treaties. However, unlike both the European Court of Justice and the European Court of Human Rights, where court decisions are legally binding on EU member countries, the UN has limited jurisdiction to enforce human rights treaties within Member States. (See Q14.2)

Analysis of Ireland's voting records within the UN, including a period of membership of the Security Council, would seem to indicate an independence of action and an absence of subordination to other countries. (See Q14.4)

Other Organisations

Ireland is also a member of what may be termed the standard international organisations such as the World Trade Organisation, the World Bank, International Monetary Fund, International Labour Office, World Health Organisation etc.

All of these organisations can be described as democratic in the sense that their decisions are taken in accordance with their statutes and rules of procedure which were in turn adopted and approved by their members. The voting procedures within some of these organisations have come in for vehement criticism, particularly from countries in the global South, as being weighted towards the interests of the developed nations. Such organisations have limited means of enforcing their decisions, at least within developed economies such as that of Ireland, so the question of subordination in Ireland's case rarely arises.

IRELAND IN THE GLOBALISED ECONOMY

Ireland is now one of the most globalised economies in the world. Between 1990 and 2005, Irish exports rose from just over €18 billion to over €88 billion, with annual GNP growth rates of around 9 per cent during that time. (www.cso.ie) By way of contrast, in its first half century of independence, the Irish economy remained heavily dependent on the UK. A number of different factors combined to achieve this remarkable transformation: state policy to attract foreign investment; investment in education, most notably in technological higher education; national agreements between the social partners; the massive inflow of EU funding; and significant inward investment, notably from US-based companies.

While there is disagreement on the exact figures, Ireland has undoubtedly attracted the largest per capita share of direct foreign investment in the EU. The largest component of this investment is US led. Table 14.1 shows figures up to 2000 which illustrate that Ireland attracted far more direct foreign investment than the EU average. (Barry 2004: 12) Statistics from the Industrial Development Authority (IDA) confirm that most of the jobs created in Ireland through foreign direct investment are of US origin. (See Table 14.2)

Table 14.1 Foreign Direct Investment (FDI) Per Capita (USD), 1985–2000

	Ireland	UK	Spain	France	EU-15
1980	1,102	1,119	137	415	546
1985	1,313	1,130	233	594	688
1990	1,569	3,542	1,696	1,720	2,113
1995	3,251	3,408	3,331	3,119	3,029
2000	15,623	8,079	3,567	4,401	6,271

Source: Barry, 2004: 12, referring to FDI stock from UNCTAD (2001); population data from Eurostat.

Table 14.2 Origin of Industrial Development Authority Supported Companies

Origin	No. of Companies	Total Employment
US	473	93,331
Germany	135	10,986
UK	117	7,239
Rest of Europe	210	16,364
Asia Pacific	46	3,278
Rest of the World	29	1,530
Total	1,010	132,728

Source: Industrial Development Agency, 2006: 19

There are many reasons for US economic investment in Ireland, including Ireland's historic links with the US, the overriding need to acquire foreign capital and technical expertise, and of course the advantage to the US of locating in a low-tax regime with access to European markets. The overall effect of this overseas investment strategy has in turn moved Ireland away from its previous dependence on the United Kingdom economy, which had been a salient feature during its protectionist era.

At the same time, the present figures do underline a real dependence on the US. This dependency, coupled with US military and political power, has raised questions among the Irish public as to Ireland's independence in its political decision making, particularly in relation to issues of foreign policy. Ireland's stance on the war in Iraq and the continued use of Shannon Airport as a stopover for US troops have been two issues which have been prominent in public discourse. The protest marches against the US-UK invasion of Iraq in 2003 were also the biggest demonstrations on a foreign issue that the country has ever seen.

There is little doubt that foreign investors present in Ireland could, if they wished, collectively exercise considerable pressure on any government. Equally accepted is the fact that no Irish government would lightly embark on policies which would either antagonise such investors or discourage potential ones. This actuality can be seen as a form of "subordination" of Irish governance, but may also be seen as an example, albeit acute, of realpolitik in the current global reality. (See also Q14.4)

FOREIGN POLICY AND NEUTRALITY

Foreign policy in the first 50 years of Irish independence (1922–1972) was effectively dominated by – and often determined in respect of – Ireland's relationship with the UK. Since 1973 that centre of focus has changed to the EU, although economic, cultural, familial and other ties to the UK, coupled with the Northern Ireland question, ensure that relations with London retain a central place in Ireland's international affairs.

In Irish politics, foreign policy has rarely been a central or contentious issue. The country's largest political party, Fianna Fáil, is not affiliated with any of the major political internationals, and while Fine

Gael is a member of the Christian Democratic International and the European Peoples' Party, these engagements cannot be described as central to the party's policies. Membership of the Socialist International and the Party of European Socialists plays a larger role in the deliberations of the Irish Labour Party. Sinn Féin sits with the Group of the European United Left in the European Parliament, but once again this participation is not central to the party's decision-making process. The Green Party is probably the most influenced in terms of its domestic policies by its membership of their International.

The foreign policy of the Irish state has traditionally been left in the hands of the small, but highly professional, group of public servants of the Department of Foreign Affairs, originally known as the Department of External Affairs. It was only in 1996 that the government produced the first white paper on foreign policy in the history of the state. That it took three-quarters of a century for the state to engage in a serious public foreign policy debate underlines the muted role that the issue has played in Irish politics.

Ireland's policy of neutrality during World War Two was significantly influenced by a desire to assert full independence from the British Empire. More recently, the deployment of more than 10 armed Irish personnel abroad is subject to what has become known as the "Triple Lock" mechanism, whereby such deployment requires 1) a UN Security Council mandate, 2) a decision by the Irish government and 3) approval of that decision by the Oireachtas.

The concept of neutrality, in the formal sense of non-membership of a military alliance, remains highly popular and perceived threats to Ireland's neutrality played a part in the initial rejection of the referendum on the Nice Treaty in 2001. When the referendum was rerun in 2002, the Treaty had been amended to include greater safeguards for Ireland's neutral status.

The growing area of European Security and Defence Policy (ESDP), however, poses significant questions in terms of the traditional defence, security and foreign policy approaches of all EU Member States, whether they are NATO members, neutral or non-aligned.

The initial concept of a European Rapid Reaction Force (ERRF), consisting of up to 60,000 troops designed to intervene in major protracted crisis situations, and largely influenced by lessons drawn from the conflicts within a disintegrating Yugoslavia, is being supplanted by the Battlegroup concept, which involves smaller, more rapidly deployable, units.

Other ESDP approaches, including modular deployments in which mixed levels of military, police, court and prison service, healthcare and civil defence, NGO and other personnel, would be determined in response to a particular crisis. This evolving security/defence debate poses significant challenges to all traditional foreign and security policy approaches, including Irish neutrality.

The aforementioned European Union Rapid Reaction Force (ERRF) which became operational in 2003 is a transnational military force managed by the European Union itself, rather than any of its Member States. The ERRF is not a standing army in that units remain with their national armies when not deployed, and national governments retain the power to decide if their forces will take part in any particular operation. The duties of the ERRF have been expanded from humanitarian, rescue, and peacekeeping and peacemaking to include "joint disarmament operations", "military advice and assistance tasks" and "post-conflict stabilisation". The ERRF's mandate also allows that, "all these tasks may contribute to the fight against terrorism, including by supporting third countries in combating terrorism in their territories". The ERRF has already completed its first mission of monitoring civil unrest in Macedonia. Ireland is a party to the ERRF and is signed up under the Nice Treaty to collective responsibility for the deployments of the ERRF. At present, however, Ireland's participation can only arise where UN authorisation for military intervention is in place.

The aforementioned EU Battlegroups are a separate development within the European Security and Defence Policy. The aim of the Battlegroups project is to create several units for international intervention and tasks, extending to full-combat situations. The Battlegroups will be capable of being deployed more rapidly and for shorter periods than the already operational European Rapid Reaction Force, thereby allowing for a quicker response to international crises, in which the Battlegroups will likely prepare the ground for a larger and more traditional force to replace them in due time. In 2006, the Minister for Defence Willie O'Dea announced that the Irish government would open talks on joining the EU Battlegroups. The Minister also announced his intention to change the law so that the government could allow Irish troops to participate in some operations not subject to UN Security Council resolutions, which, if implemented, would constitute a very significant change in Ireland's military policy.

CULTURAL SUBORDINATION

Cultural policies are also an area increasingly subject to international scrutiny, as notably evidenced by the incorporation of such sites as Skellig and Newgrange as UNESCO world heritage sites. As a result, Ireland now has international obligations to protect such sites and can be called to account over failure to properly maintain them. It would be difficult to argue, however, that being held accountable for responsibilities freely entered into in any way constitutes subordination to an external agency.

Q14.2 To what extent does the government support UN and European Council human rights treaties and respect international law?

Ireland's compliance with its obligations under UN and Council of Europe human rights treaties are dealt with throughout the audit, in particular under Section Three on Civil and Political Rights and under Section Four on Economic, Social and Cultural Rights. Here, an overview will be given of those treaties which Ireland both has, and has not ratified, along with a description of the processes for ratification of, and for monitoring compliance with, UN and Council of Europe treaties.

Ireland's membership of various international organisations, principally the UN and the Council of Europe, bring obligations under international human rights law. Ireland is currently party to six of the seven major UN Human Rights treaties. At European level, Ireland has ratified all the core treaties of the Council of Europe. Alongside these treaties, Ireland's constitution contains strong human rights provisions. The precedence of the constitution in Irish law, however, can limit the effect of rights under international human rights law.

The Human Rights Unit within the Department of Foreign Affairs is responsible for: facilitating the ratification of international human rights instruments; Ireland's national reporting obligations under a number of human rights treaties to which Ireland is a party; and for coordinating Ireland's participation in international human rights fora. In addition, the Irish Human Rights Commission formally took up office in July 2001 as an independent statutory body, and possesses a wide-ranging remit to promote and protect human rights, as defined both in the constitution and in international agreements to which Ireland is a party. Periodic reports from UN and Council of Europe monitoring committees also provide an assessment of Ireland's compliance with, and breeches of, each treaty and are widely publicised.

Ireland, along with all other EU members, is party to the Kyoto Protocol which set targets and timetables for reductions in greenhouse gas emissions by developed countries. The gap between Ireland's Kyoto targets and projections based on current emission levels leaves Ireland third last among EU Member States in terms of compliance. As such, additional measures are needed for Ireland to meet its obligations under Kyoto.

INTERNATIONAL HUMAN RIGHTS LAW

Ireland plays an active role in the work of various UN specialised agencies, in the Commission on Human Rights, and on other UN fora for promoting universal standards of human rights. Ireland was a member of the Commission on Human Rights from 1997–1999 and commenced a further three-year term from January 2003. In addition, Mary Robinson, former President of Ireland, served as UN High Commissioner for Human Rights from 1997 to 2001.

Ireland's membership of the UN and the Council of Europe brings obligations under international human rights law. The major UN and Council of Europe human rights treaties to which Ireland is currently a party are listed below.

United Nations

- Charter of the United Nations
- Universal Declaration of Human Rights
- International Covenant on Civil and Political Rights
- International Covenant on Economic, Social and Cultural Rights
- Convention on the Rights of the Child

- International Convention on the Elimination of All Forms of Discrimination Against Women
- Convention on the Nationality of Married Women
- International Convention on the Elimination of All Forms of Racial Discrimination
- Convention on the Prevention and Punishment of the Crime of Genocide
- Slavery Convention of 1926 and related instruments
- Convention on the Reduction of Statelessness
- Convention relating to the Status of Stateless Persons
- Convention relating to the Status of Refugees
- Convention against Torture and Other Cruel, Inhuman and Degrading Treatment or Punishment
- Rome Statute of the International Criminal Court
- Geneva Conventions on Humanitarian Law

Council of Europe

- Statute of the Council of Europe
- European Convention for the Protection of Human Rights and Fundamental Freedoms
- European Social Charter
- European Social Charter (revised)
- European Convention for the Prevention of Torture and Inhuman or Degrading Treatment or Punishment
- Framework Convention for the Protection of National Minorities
- European Convention on the Exercise of Children's Rights

Source: www.ihrc.ie/treaties/treaties.asp

Ireland is party to six of what are sometimes referred to as the "big seven" UN Human Rights treaties. The sole exception is the Convention on the Rights of Migrant Workers and the Members of their Families. Following recent developments in immigration, the government is currently under particular pressure from human rights groups, the IHRC and the UN Committee on CERD, to ratify this Convention. (Irish Human Rights Commission and NCCRI, 2004)

Neither has it signed the Optional Protocol to the Convention on the Rights of the Child on the sale of children, child prostitution and child pornography. Thus, just two of the 25 treaties identified by the UN Secretary General at the Millennium Summit as representative of the UN's key objectives have yet to be ratified by Ireland. (See Box pages 548-9)

At European level, Ireland has ratified all the core treaties of the Council of Europe, including the European Convention for the Protection of Human Rights and Fundamental Freedoms and the European Social Charter. However Ireland has not yet ratified the Council of Europe Convention on Action against Trafficking in Human Beings, which was adopted by the Council in May 2005. (Amnesty International (Irish Section), 2005b: 21) An offence of "trafficking" does not currently exist in Irish domestic law and until this is defined as a criminal offence, Ireland cannot ratify this Convention.

In August 2006, the UN General Assembly's *Ad Hoc* Committee reached agreement on the text to create a new core human rights treaty to better promote and protect the rights of persons with disabilities. The International Convention on the Rights of Persons with Disabilities was formally adopted by the General Assembly in December 2006 and will enter into force after ratification by the necessary number of UN Member States, at which time it will become the eighth core UN human rights treaty. The Irish government has played a leading role in bringing this Convention into being.

Procedure for Ratification of Human Rights Treaties

The Irish Constitution contains strong human rights provisions. Article 40.3.1 of the constitution states that "The state guarantees in its laws to respect, and, as far as practicable, by its laws to defend and vindicate the personal rights of the citizen". This phrase has proved to be of great significance in the development of human rights law in Ireland. In particular, since the "personal rights of the citizen" are not exhaustively listed in the constitution, it has allowed the courts to play a significant role in establishing the rights of both citizens and non-citizens alike. The courts to date however have done so more readily in the area of civil and political rights than they have for economic, social and cultural rights. (See also Section Three and Section Four)

Article 29.6 of the Irish Constitution provides that "No international agreement shall be part of the domestic law of the state save as may be determined by the Oireachtas." This provision has been interpreted as precluding the Irish courts from giving effect to an international agreement if it is contrary to domestic law or grants rights or imposes obligations additional to those of domestic law. Ireland must therefore ensure that its domestic law is in conformity with the agreement in question where it wishes to adhere to an international agreement.

In adopting international treaties, different countries use different processes, whereby some states accede directly, while others ratify directly and still others sign and then ratify. Ireland employs a process of signature followed by ratification, wherein signature of a treaty signals agreement in principle but does not carry any legal obligation. With ratification, the treaty becomes legally binding.

Lengthy delays in the past sometimes occurred between signing and ratification of human rights treaties in Ireland. These delays at times reflected the difficulties involved in incorporating human rights conventions and international agreements into Irish law, while at other times they signalled a lack of political will. In recent years, Ireland has generally adopted a policy of signing international treaties only when domestic law has been amended to allow ratification to quickly follow.

However, due to the precedence of the Irish Constitution in Irish law, even after ratification the rights afforded under an international treaty might not have full effect. For example, the definition of "the family" in the European Convention on Human Rights (ECHR) is broader than that under the Irish Constitution but the definition of the family in the constitution continues to take precedence in Irish law, even after ratification of the ECHR. Therefore, while non-traditional families such as lone parents and homosexual couples have access to some family rights under the ECHR, the constitutional definition of the family in Ireland excludes lone parents and homosexual couples from entitlement to these fuller rights under ECHR.

Monitoring Compliance

Ireland has a number of state and statutory bodies charged with ensuring compliance with national and international human rights law. Foremost amongst these are the Human Rights Unit in the Department of Foreign Affairs and the more recently established Irish Human Rights Commission.

The Human Rights Unit, which was established as part of the Department of Foreign Affairs in 1996, has three main functions. First, it is responsible for facilitating the ratification of international human rights instruments. Second, it has responsibility for Ireland's national reporting obligations under the various human rights treaties to which Ireland is a party. Third, the Unit is responsible for coordinating Ireland's participation in international human rights fora, including the UN Human Rights Council which replaced the Commission on Human Rights in late 2006 and the EU Human Rights Working Group.

Ireland is obliged to submit periodic reports to the monitoring body on its progress in implementing each of the UN treaties to which it is a party. UN reports in recent years have included:

- the UN Human Rights Committee Report under the International Covenant on Civil and Political Rights, 2000;
- the UN Economic and Social Council Report under the International Covenant on Economic, Social and Cultural Rights, 2002;
- the UN Committee Report on the Elimination of Discrimination against Women, 2005;
- the UN Committee Report on the Elimination of Racial Discrimination, 2005; and
- the UN Committee Report on the Rights of the Child, 2006.

A number of reports have also been issued recently in respect of Ireland's compliance with Council of Europe human rights treaties by the following committees.

- the European Committee on the Prevention of Torture, 2002;
- the European Committee on Social Rights, 2004; and
- the European Committee on the Prevention of Torture, 2006.

The Concluding Comments published by each of the monitoring committees, highlight areas where Ireland is not in compliance with its international obligations under each treaty, along with recommendations on actions to rectify the situation.

The Irish Human Rights Commission, an independent statutory body, was set up as a direct result of the Good Friday Agreement of 1998 and is a counterpart of the Northern Ireland Human Rights Commission. Although the Commissions are independent of one another, they are charged with ensuring an equivalence of rights north and south of the border.

The Human Rights Commission Act 2000, confers a wide-ranging remit on the Commission to promote and protect human rights as defined both in the constitution and in international agreements to which Ireland is a party. Under the Act, the Commission is mandated to protect and promote:

(a) the rights, liberties and freedoms conferred on, or guaranteed to, persons by the constitution; and
(b) the rights, liberties or freedoms conferred on, or guaranteed to persons by any agreement, treaty or convention to which the state is a party.

Part of the remit of the Commission is to ensure that the rights contained in the various conventions to which Ireland is a signatory are upheld by the state. In this regard, the Commission makes submissions to UN and Council of Europe monitoring committees, such as CERD and CEDAW in 2005 and to the UN Committee on the Rights of the Child in 2006.

Only the European Court of Human Rights, which monitors compliance with the European Convention on Human Rights, has the power of legal sanction to enforce state compliance. Compliance with UN human rights treaties and other treaties of the Council of Europe largely rely instead on moral pressure being brought to bear on member states through the publication of *Concluding Comments* which highlight areas of non-compliance together with recommendations for state action.

The UN in particular has been examining its options with regard to strengthening its powers to force Member States to comply with their obligations under human rights treaties. The UN Commission on Human Rights has been criticised in recent years, most notably by the then UN Secretary General Kofi Annan, who said in 2005, "... the Commission's capacity to perform its tasks has been increasingly undermined by its declining credibility and professionalism. In particular, states have sought membership of the Commission not to strengthen human rights but to protect themselves against criticism or to criticize others. As a result, a credibility deficit has developed, which casts a shadow on the reputation of the UN system as a whole". (Annan, 2005: para 182)

A smaller standing Human Rights Council – similar to the existing councils on security and development within the UN – replaced the Commission in 2006. The upgrading of the Commission on Human

Rights into a fully-fledged council is aimed at granting human rights the priority accorded to it in the Charter of the United Nations and at strengthening the UN's ability to enforce compliance with international human rights law. The establishment of the Human Rights Council has been welcomed by the Irish government.

INTERNATIONAL ENVIRONMENTAL LAW

Ireland along with all other EU members, ratified the Kyoto Protocol in May 2002. The Kyoto Protocol is an international agreement, reached in 1997, which sets targets and timetables for reductions in greenhouse gas emissions by developed countries. The protocol extends the signatories' commitment to the UN Framework Convention on Climate Change to reduce greenhouse gases.

Before the recent boom in Ireland's economy, emissions of greenhouse gases were relatively low. However, sustained economic growth has contributed significantly to increased energy usage and a higher output of greenhouse gases.

Between 1996 and 2003 Ireland saw an increase in just about every field related to the economy, including:

- a 73 per cent increase in Gross Domestic Product;
- a 35 per cent increase of people in the workforce;
- a 26 per cent increase in total primary energy requirement;
- a 66 per cent increase in household and commercial waste; and most importantly,
- a 12 per cent increase in greenhouse gas emissions.

In addition, Ireland's carbon dioxide emissions increased by 22 per cent over this period, the most marked increase occurring in transport, due mainly to the increased number of private cars on Ireland's roads. (Central Statistics Office, 2005c: 11)

Ireland has a target under the Kyoto Protocol for 2008–2012 of a limited increase of 13 per cent in total greenhouse emissions above 1990 levels. The projected emissions in 2010, based on existing policies and measures in Ireland, forecasts an increase of around 40 per cent above 1990 levels. (Department of the Environment and Local Government, 2000b) The shortfall of 27 per cent between Ireland's

Kyoto target and projected emissions in 2010 is one of the largest of all the EU Member States, making it abundantly clear that additional measures will need to be taken for Ireland to fulfil its obligations under Kyoto.

UN Multilateral Treaty Framework: 25 Core Treaties

N.B. The seven major treaties are identified by *

Human Rights

1. **Convention on the Prevention and Punishment of the Crime of Genocide.** Ratified by Ireland 22 June 1976
2. **International Convention on the Elimination of All Forms of Racial Discrimination.*** Signed by Ireland 21 March 1968; ratified by Ireland 29 December 2000
3. **International Covenant on Economic, Social and Cultural Rights.*** Signed by Ireland 1 October 1973; ratified by Ireland 8 December 1989
4. **International Covenant on Civil and Political Rights.*** Signed by Ireland 1 October 1973; ratified by Ireland 8 December 1989
5. **Optional Protocol to the International Covenant on Civil and Political Rights.** Ratified by Ireland 8 December 1989
6. **Second Optional Protocol to the International Covenant on Civil and Political Rights.** Ratified by Ireland 18 June 1993
7. **Convention on the Elimination of All Forms of Discrimination against Women.*** Ratified by Ireland 3 December 1985
8. **Optional Protocol to the Convention on the Elimination of All Forms of Discrimination against Women.** Signed by Ireland 7 September 2000; ratified by Ireland 7 September 2000
9. **Convention against Torture, and Other Cruel, Inhuman or Degrading Treatment or Punishment.*** Signed by Ireland 28 September 1992; ratified by Ireland 11 April 2002
10. **Convention on the Rights of the Child.*** Signed by Ireland 30 September 1990; ratified by Ireland 28 September 1992
11. **Optional Protocol to the Convention on the Rights of the Child on involvement of children in armed conflicts.** Ratified by Ireland 1 November 2002
12. **Optional Protocol to the Convention on the Rights of the Child on the sale of children, child prostitution and child pornography.** Signed by Ireland 7 September 2000; not ratified by Ireland
13. **International Convention on the Protection of the Rights of All Migrant Workers and Members of their Families.*** Not signed or ratified by Ireland

Refugees and Stateless Persons

14. **Convention Relating to the Status of Refugees.** Ratified by Ireland 29 November 1956

Penal Matters

15. **Convention on the Safety of United Nations and Associated Personnel.** Ratified by Ireland 28 March 2002
16. **International Convention for the Suppression of Terrorists Bombings.** Signed 29 May 1998; ratified 30 June 2005
17. **Rome Statute of the International Criminal Court.** Signed by Ireland 7 October 1998; ratified by Ireland 11 April 2002

Disarmament

18. **Convention on Prohibitions or Restrictions on the Use of Certain Conventional Weapons which may be deemed to be Excessively Injurious or to have Indiscriminate Effects (and Protocols).** Signed by Ireland 10 April 1981; ratified by Ireland 13 March 1995
19. **Protocol on Prohibitions or Restrictions on the Use of Mines, Booby-Traps and Other Devices as amended on 3 May 1996 (with amended Protocol II).** Ratified by Ireland 27 March 1997
20. **Convention on the Prohibition of the Development, Production, Stockpiling and Use of Chemical Weapons and on their Destruction.** Signed by Ireland 14 January 1993; ratified by Ireland 24 June 1996
21. **Comprehensive Nuclear-Test-Ban Treaty.** Signed by Ireland 24 September 1996; ratified by Ireland 15 July 1999
22. **Convention on the Prohibition of the Use, Stockpiling, Production and Transfer of Anti-Personnel Mines and on their Destruction.** Signed and ratified by Ireland 3 December 1997

Environment

23. **Kyoto Protocol to the United Nations Framework Convention on Climate Change.** Signed by Ireland 19 April 1998; ratified by Ireland 31 March 2002
24. **Convention on Biological Diversity.** Signed by Ireland 13 June 1992; ratified by Ireland 22 March 1996
25. **United Nations Convention to Combat Desertification in those Countries Experiencing Serious Drought and/or Desertification, Particularly in Africa.** Signed by Ireland 15 October 1994; ratified by Ireland 26 March 1996

Source: Amnesty International (Irish Section)

Q14.3 How far does the government respect its international obligations in its treatment of refugees and asylum seekers and how free from arbitrary discrimination is its immigration policy?

The ongoing economic boom, combined with EU enlargement, has seen Ireland become a country of significant inward migration within the past decade and a far more diverse society within a relatively short period of time. The proportion of foreign-born persons living in Ireland rose from 6 per cent in 2002 to almost 10 per cent in 2006, and immigration is projected to continue at current levels of about 30,000 a year for the next five to ten years.

All migrant workers in Ireland are covered under the same key employment rights legislation as Irish nationals and non-Irish nationals living in Ireland have substantial protection under the constitution and equality legislation. Despite these protections, however, exploitation of migrant workers by employers is occurring.

Ireland's overall immigration policy framework is in a process of evolution. Present government strategy envisages a twin-track approach: the first track comprising a permanent migration system primarily focused on attracting skilled migrants to Ireland that will effectively select people as potential citizens; and a fast-track scheme of temporary workers based on sponsorship by employers, with more restricted access to permanency and family reunification. Like all other EU states, Ireland is not party to the UN Convention on the Rights of Migrant Workers and the Members of Their Families. Ireland's immigration policy is also still evolving in regard to access to Irish citizenship and/or permanent residency status, which are core elements of the successful integration of migrants.

Ireland is a party to the 1951 UN Convention Relating to the Status of Refugees. The number of applications for asylum in Ireland increased significantly between 1995 and 2000 before levelling off and then further declining after 2003. In that time, Ireland has established a functioning asylum system which has been praised by the UNHCR representative as performing more efficiently than a number of other EU asylum systems. However, a number of concerns regarding Ireland's asylum system remain.

ECONOMIC PERFORMANCE AND MIGRATION

A strong relationship exists between economic performance and migration. For example, at times of recession and high unemployment, such as during the 1950s and again during the 1980s, Ireland experienced sharp rises in the numbers of Irish people seeking jobs abroad. The economic decline in the 1950s was so severe that the high numbers leaving Ireland saw the population fall to its lowest ever level around 1961. However, the economic recovery of the 1970s saw many emigrants return and the net gain from the numbers arriving resulted in Ireland's population growing once again. (Immigrant Council of Ireland, 2005a)

It is no surprise therefore that the Celtic Tiger economy has been accompanied by net inward migration, as Ireland became an attractive country in which to seek employment. In fact, the scale of the economic boom has in turn created ongoing skills and labour shortages that have required both the Irish government and private business to actively recruit workers abroad.

The scale of increase in overseas recruitment has been dramatic. In 1999, 6,000 employment permits were issued to workers from overseas, but by 2003 this figure had risen to over 47,500. Immigration is projected to continue at current levels of about 30,000 a year for the next five to ten years and then to decline. (International Organisation for Migration, 2006)

Not suprisingly, this scale of migration has had a significant impact on Ireland's population. As already noted, the percentage of foreign-born persons resident in Ireland rose from 6 per cent in 2002 to around 10 per cent in 2006, (Central Statistics Office Preliminary Report, 2006c) and in a very short period of time Ireland has become an ethnically diverse country in which over 400,000 people are currently of migrant origin.

Given the long history of mass emigration, inward migration has posed significant challenges in recent years for government agencies and policy makers. At the same time, the Irish government has been presented with a very significant but very different set of challenges from the large increase in the numbers of people seeking asylum and refugee status here, even though those numbers have been in decline since 2003. And, while the issues of labour migration and refugees are often linked in the public mind, the issues are in fact quite separate, not only governed by different international and domestic legislation, but also posing different challenges in terms of policy.

IMMIGRATION

The European Context

It is widely known that the EU forms an important part of the context wherein Ireland's current immigration policy is being formed. Beginning in 1985 and again in 1990, Germany, France, Belgium, the Netherlands and Luxemburg negotiated a series of multilateral arrangements concerning the movement of people across their borders. These measures took effect in 1995 and quickly included other EU Member States.The most obvious effect of these Schengen agreements, as they are known, was the gradual abolition of border checks. However, Schengen applied initially only to nationals of participating EU states and did not confer the right to travel freely within the EU on non-EU nationals. The Long-Term Residents Directive, introduced in 2006, has since conferred this right on non-EU nationals who are also long-term residents of a participating EU state but Ireland is currently not participating in the Long-Term Residents Directive.

In 1997, the Treaty of Amsterdam was adopted as part of EU law both to further the Union's integration and allow for enlargement. The Schengen arrangements were accordingly incorporated into the Treaty of Amsterdam and now apply to a greater or lesser extent in 13 of the 15 Member States that formed the EU prior to enlargement. In addition, the Schengen arrangements were a prerequisite for the ten new accession states that joined in 2004 and are also a condition for all future entrants.

The two states in which the Schengen arrangements do not currently apply are the UK and Ireland. When the UK chose to opt out of Schengen, insisting on the necessity of maintaining its own border controls, Ireland also chose to follow suit. The main reason for Ireland's opting out from the Schengen arrangements is a logical one, namely to preserve the Common Travel Agreement with the UK. This Common Travel Agreement, which has been in place since the early 1950s, allows UK and Irish citizens to travel freely between the two countries without having to carry a passport. It is therefore not seen as feasible for Ireland to adopt the Schengen agreements without a

British decision to do likewise, as Ireland would then have to impose full border controls between the UK and Ireland, including between Northern Ireland and Ireland.

The opting-out by the UK and Ireland excludes both countries not just from the application of the Schengen arrangements but also from the application of any future developments in EU immigration and asylum law, except where either country decides otherwise. Ireland is thus less tied to developments in EU immigration policy than it would otherwise be and more in control of its own approach to immigration and integration.

The enlargement of the EU, with the accession of ten new Member States in 2004, provided a dramatic change in the overall European immigration picture. Its most immediate effect was to greatly increase the pool of potential EU migrants and workers.

As a member of the EU, Ireland's immigration policies distinguish between European Economic Area (EEA) and non-EEA nationals. Citizens of the EEA, which comprises the EU plus Norway, Liechtenstein and Iceland, have the unrestricted right to live and work in Ireland as long as they are either an employee, self-employed or economically independent. Non-EEA nationals are not permitted to enter into employment in Ireland unless they have specific permission to do so. The expansion of the EU accordingly expanded the pool of EEA migrants who are eligible to live, work and settle in Ireland.

To understand the effects of EU enlargement on Ireland's immigration policy, we must distinguish between the types of employment permits granted to non-Irish nationals who come to work in Ireland. Two main types of work permit have existed in recent years: work permits and work visas/authorisations. Work permits are issued for a maximum period of one year and applications are made by the employer who must satisfy the Department of Enterprise, Trade and Employment that no Irish or EEA worker is available to fill the post. Once granted, the non-EEA national recruited into the post is not allowed change employer during the duration of the permit, unless a second employer is issued with a work permit. Work visa/authorisations, however, are granted for two years, usually in high-skill areas that are in great demand, and employees are permitted to change employers during that period.

The large majority of non-EEA nationals who have come to Ireland in recent years have arrived *via* the work permit system. In

2002 for example, 40,500 work permits were issued compared with only 2,610 work visas/authorisations. (Ruhs, 2003) At the same time, the Irish government made a very significant decision in granting EU accession state nationals the unrestricted right to live and work in Ireland, *via* the Employment Permits Act 2003. As a result, 40 million new potential employees acquired the right to work in Ireland after accession on 1 May 2004. Only the UK and Sweden also granted accession state nationals immediate access to their labour markets, while all other EU Member States imposed transitional measures, restricting such access for a period of up to seven years. In 2006, four further countries – Spain, Portugal, Greece and Finland – opened their labour markets fully to the accession states, bringing the total to seven. In late 2006, however, the Irish government decided to restrict labour market access for workers from Bulgaria and Romania which joined the EU in January 2007.

EU enlargement has impacted dramatically on the work permit system in particular, which has been scaled back significantly as a result. In 2002, prior to EU enlargement, the five countries with the greatest number of permit workers in Ireland were Latvia, Lithuania, Philippines, Poland and Romania, and together these countries constituted over 40 per cent of all permit workers in that year. (Ruhs, 2003: 16) Following enlargement, Latvia, Lithuania and Poland became full members of the EU.

In response to these changes, the government introduced a number of modifications to the work permit system in the Employment Permits Act 2003. Prior to this Act, employers were free to recruit as many non-EEA workers as they wished and to employ them in any job whatsoever, provided they could provide proof that every effort had been made to recruit from within the EEA. Moreover, three out of every four permits issued over recent years have been for employment in relatively low-skilled and low-wage occupations, especially in the service sector. (Ruhs, 2005) As part of the changes brought about by the Employment Permits Act, the Department of Enterprise, Trade and Employment introduced a list of mostly low-skilled occupations which were no longer eligible for work permits. At the same time, the Department began returning applications for new employment permits for workers from outside the EEA in order to encourage employers to give preference to EEA workers.

Then, in August 2004, the Department of Enterprise, Trade and

Employment effectively excluded low-skilled occupations from the work permit system by announcing that it will only consider new work permit applications from employers who want to hire highly skilled personnel. (Ruhs, 2003)

Enlargement has thereby provided a pool of low-skill labour previously supplied *via* the work permit scheme, which has been substantially reduced as a result. As a result, low-skill workers from outside the EEA currently find it far more difficult to come to Ireland than before EU enlargement.

Ireland's Evolving Immigration Policy

Ireland's current system for dealing with immigration is a combination of historical legacies and of recent policies, some of which, although not designed for the purpose, play an active role in shaping immigration policy.

Two more recent pieces of legislation, however, are designed to create a less *ad hoc* approach to immigration. First a discussion document was published by the Department of Justice, Equality and Law Reform in April 2005 which set out its proposals for an Immigration, Residence and Protection Bill and invited responses thereon. The scheme for the Bill was subsequently published in September 2006 and referred to the Irish Human Rights Commission for review prior to consideration by the Oireachtas. The Commission's observations were sent to the Minister for Equality, Justice and Law Reform in December 2006 (See below). Second the Employment Permits Act 2006 was published by Minister of Enterprise Trade and Employment, Micheál Martin, and is already in force.

Both pieces of legislation aim to both clarify and streamline all of the administrative procedures currently governing immigration and place them on a statutory basis. Each piece of legislation also proposes a number of changes, each broadly indicative of an emerging wider policy direction. The most significant innovation in the Employment Permits Act is the replacement of work visas/authorisations by Green Card Permits, from January 2007.

Green Card Permits are available to those in occupations where the annual salary is €60,000 or more, and to a restricted number of "strategically important occupations" in the annual salary range €30,000 to €59,000. Green Card Permit holders can apply for immediate family reunification, and for permanent residence after two years residence in Ireland. Green Card Permits thus represent a significant improvement compared to the previous work visas/authorisations. (www.entemp.ie)

The proposed Immigration, Residence and Protection Bill is intended to provide a more comprehensive treatment of the entire issue of immigration and residence, dealing with the processes that arise before a person enters Ireland, during his or her stay, and upon departure, if and when that arises. The proposed Bill consequently covers visa and pre-entry clearance procedures, border controls, entry into Ireland, admissions procedures for entry for work, study and self-employment, for other non-economic purposes such as retirement, family reunification and research, proposals on residence status and residence permits, as well as proposals for removal from the state if necessary.

One of the proposed changes in the proposed Bill is to legislate for long-term resident status after five years residency in the state. Naturalisation, i.e., the acquisition of Irish citizenship, is open to non-Irish nationals after five years legal residence in the state. However, there are currently no clear criteria regarding a person's entitlement to citizenship, which is instead granted at the absolute discretion of the Minister. After eight years, non-Irish nationals can apply for permission to remain without condition as to time. However, as with the granting of Irish citizenship, the granting of such permission to remain is not automatic even after eight years, but rather at the discretion of the Minister for Justice, Equality and Law Reform.

The proposed Bill would also streamline the services of the Irish Naturalisation and Immigration Service (INIS) and increase coordination between the various departments responsible for immigration issues.

Two features of the government's strategy on economic migration in particular stand out. The first of these is the decision by the Department of Enterprise, Trade and Employment, which has responsibility for economic migration policy, to actively discourage employers from recruiting low-skilled labour from outside the EEA, as discussed above. Government policy is evolving instead towards recruiting labour from outside the EEA mainly in high-skills areas.

The second salient feature is the twin-track approach envisaged in the present strategy, comprising "a permanent migration system with a primary focus on attracting skilled people to Ireland ... which would select people as potential citizens", and "a fast-track scheme of temporary skilled labour ... based on sponsorship by employers." (Department of Justice, Equality and Law Reform, 2005d)

A differentiation of rights, such as access to long-term residency and to family reunification, based on educational qualifications and skills is also evident in current policy thinking. As such, long-term residency and family reunification are being seen primarily in the context of their importance in attracting highly-skilled migrants rather than within a broader human rights framework. (Department of Justice, Equality and Law Reform/Department of Enterprise, Trade and Employment, 2005) Moreover, their current status is not provided for in legislation and the discretionary power of officials means they are often refused, even for highly-skilled workers.

Human Rights Concerns

Human rights concerns have been voiced about the current direction and implementation of immigration policy, which is largely labour driven. These concerns generally centre on two main issues: first the consequences of the different standards of treatment for high-skills (wage) versus low-skills migrants; and second the often inadequate levels of protection afforded to migrants employed in Ireland.

International law has made an initial attempt at normalising the situation of migrants around the world. The UN Convention on the Rights of Migrant Workers and the Members of Their Families 1990 sought to standardise a series of rights and entitlements for migrant workers. However, this Convention has so far been ratified primarily by countries with considerable numbers of migrants and remains not ratified by Ireland and most other EU Member States. There are also primary human rights entitlements laid down in the UN Charter on Human Rights which, while not specifically relating to migrant workers, set out a basic minimum of rights based on principles of common humanity.

With regard to the first issue, the National Consultative Committee on Racism and Interculturalism has voiced concern that "migrant workers should not be treated as economic entities, but as people with a broad range of social, cultural, civil and political rights. The development of immigration policy must secure these rights....Immigration policy should not undermine equality.'(National Consultative Committee on Racism and Interculturalism, 2005)

The International Organisation for Migration likewise states that "Regardless of the duration of the residence and working period, migrants" human rights should be protected in accordance with the UN Convention on the Rights of Migrant Workers and the Members of their Families which entered into force in 2003.'(International Organisation for Migration, 2005) The Immigrant Council of Ireland has also called on the government to adopt an agreed set of core rights for all immigrants rather than adopting a regime of positive discrimination in favour of certain categories of worker. (Immigrant Council of Ireland, 2005b)

As it happens, the second issue, namely the often inadequate levels of protection currently afforded to migrants employed in Ireland, has received more attention in the media than the question of discrimination between high- and low-skills workers. It is important to note that all migrant workers in Ireland are covered by the same key employment rights legislation as Irish nationals. Documented immigrants thereby have the same protection under the law in regard to terms of employment, remuneration, minimum notice, working hours, unfair dismissals and right to join a trade union as Irish workers. In addition, equality legislation which prohibits discrimination on nine grounds, including race, also applies equally to migrants and Irish workers. Despite this legislation, a growing number of documented cases of exploitative employers flagrantly breaking the law continue to emerge. Among the most high profile cases have been Irish Ferries, where a Filipino beautician was being paid €1 per hour in comparison to the minimum wage onboard of €14.74, and Gama Construction, which was accused of paying Turkish workers €2 to €3 an hour and requiring them to work up to 80 hours a week. (*Irish Times*, 8 July 2005) The Migrant Rights Centre of Ireland has also recently published research highlighting the unacceptable conditions of many, mostly female, migrants employed in domestic and care work in private homes in Ireland. (Migrant Rights Centre Ireland, 2004)

The criticisms of government over the exploitation of migrant workers have highlighted two main areas of concern. The first of these is the inadequate resourcing of the labour inspectorate, which generally means that unscrupulous employers are unlikely to be caught. A key finding of the two most recent reports on immigration by the NESC (National Economic and Social Council, 2006) and IOM (International Organisation for Migration, 2006) is that international experience shows that the maintenance of labour standards within a country is a more effective means of managing migration than control of entry to the country, as enforcing labour standards reduces the demand for labour at unacceptably low levels of wages or conditions which in turn reduces supply. Enforcement of employment rights is thereby in the interests of all.

The second area of concern is the fact that under the current work permit system, the work permit is owned by the employer and is not transferable to another employer. As a result, workers who leave their employment to escape exploitation effectively become both unemployed and resident under an illegal immigration status. At present an informal system exists to confer a bridging visa upon the migrant, but such a visa is not an entitlement and is subject to the discretion of the immigration officials. Moreover, changes in the Employment Permits Act 2006 do not adequately address this difficulty.

ASYLUM

Together with the increase in non-Irish nationals coming to Ireland to work, the past decade has seen dramatic changes in the number of asylum applications here. As shown in the table below, the number of applications between 1995 and 2000 increased significantly from a very low base, before levelling off and falling again after 2003.

Table 14.3 Number of Asylum Applications per Year 1992 to 2005

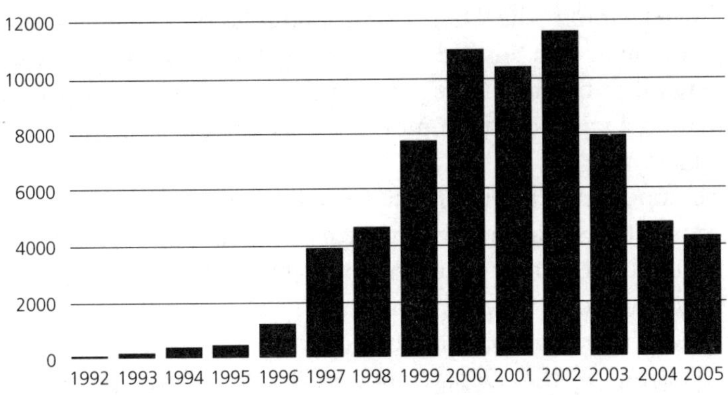

Source: Office of the Refugee Applications Commissioner, 2006: 35

Upon joining the United Nations in 1956, Ireland signed the 1951 UN Convention Relating to the Status of Refugees. The Geneva Refugee Convention defines who is a refugee and provides that a state cannot return a person to a country where they will be at risk of persecution. The European Convention on Human Rights Act 2003, which has been incorporated into Irish law, also stipulates that nobody can be returned to a country where she or he faces a real risk of torture, inhuman or degrading treatment.

Hungarians fleeing the Soviet invasion during the 1950s, and Chileans and Vietnamese fleeing war and persecution in the 1970s were among the first refugees who found safe haven in Ireland. Since these groups were invited by the Irish government, usually at the request of the United Nations High Commissioner for Refugees (UNHCR), they were not required to prove their refugee status on arrival. The numbers of applications for refugee status were so low during these years that a written procedure was not put in place for processing claims for refugee status until 1985. Even then, the numbers were so low that the procedure allowed the Irish authorities to consult with the UNHCR on every case. However, this procedure suddenly proved unworkable when the number of applications for asylum increased markedly during the 1990s.

It is important, however, to put Ireland's recent experience in context. Despite the increase in the number of asylum seekers, Ireland still receives only a small fraction of the world's refugees. For example, in 2001 Ireland received less than 1 per cent of the world's approximate 12 million asylum applications. Many of the asylum seekers who have sought refuge in Ireland have come from the former Yugoslavia, the former Soviet Union, the Democratic Republic of Congo, Rwanda, Nigeria, Romania, Iraq and other countries that are clearly perceived by the general public as places where persecution, civil conflict, and discrimination against ethnic minorities were, or still are, widespread. (www.amnesty.ie)

At the same time, the significant increase in the relative number of asylum applications presented a very real challenge to the government and the civil service, which up to the mid-1990s simply lacked both the institutional and policy infrastructure required to deal with the surge in applications. For example, in 1996, only four people worked in the asylum division of the Department of Justice, Equality and Law

Reform. Since then, significant institutional and legislative measures have been taken which together form the basis of Ireland's current asylum system.

OUR CURRENT ASYLUM SYSTEM

Upon initial arrival in Ireland, asylum seekers are housed in temporary hostel accommodations in Dublin. However, a policy of dispersal, introduced to address the shortage of available accommodation in Dublin, means that asylum applicants are likely to be sent, shortly after arrival, to accommodation centres around the country.

Together with the introduction of dispersal, the Irish government has a policy of direct provision, under which asylum applicants who arrived in Ireland after April 2000 are not entitled to full social welfare payments. Instead, assistance is provided in the form of full-board hostel accommodation, including three meals a day.

In addition, asylum applicants receive €19.10 per adult per week and €9.60 per child. These payments have remained at the same level since their introduction in 2000, and asylum seekers are prohibited from working during their asylum application. If they are caught working, they may be fined or imprisoned and, under proposals in the Immigration Act 2003, their applications for asylum may be deemed withdrawn.

Under the Refugee Act 1996 and its amendments, applications for refugee status are heard by the Refugee Applications Commissioner, who considers "first instance" applications, and a Refugee Appeals Tribunal. (*Irish Times*, 6 June 2005) The Refugee Appeals Tribunal is responsible for considering and deciding appeals against negative recommendations of the Refugee Applications Commissioner.

Asylum applicants whose applications for refugee status have been refused and whose appeals have proved unsuccessful face the possibility of enforced deportation by the state.

HUMAN RIGHTS CONCERNS ON ASYLUM

A number of issues of concern have been raised with respect to our current asylum system.

Poverty and Social Isolation

Concern exists that the current policy of locating asylum seekers in remote areas, and affording them a minimal level of subsistence, encourages isolation and depression, contributes to stigmatisation, and mitigates against the integration of refugees.

Many EU countries already allow asylum seekers to work under certain conditions, and an EU Reception Directive, which took effect from 6 February, 2005, allows some access to work for asylum seekers. All other EU Member States, except Ireland and Denmark, are participating in this Directive.

The Working of the Refugee Appeals Tribunal

The Refugee Appeals Tribunal has been the focus of much debate and criticism in recent years. The 35 members of the Tribunal are appointed by the Minister for Justice, Equality and Law Reform. There is no independent selection procedure, nor interview, and while members must have at least five years of legal practice experience, no knowledge or experience in asylum law is required. In addition, members are paid on a fee-per-case basis. This policy, which is currently being tested by judicial review, differentiates the Refugee Appeals Tribunal from others such as the Employment Appeals Tribunal or the Equality Tribunal whose sitting members are either paid per day or are salaried civil servants. It is furthermore argued that a fee-per-case basis provides a financial incentive to conclude proceedings speedily and maximise the number of cases heard per day. Applicants whose cases have been turned down by the Appeals Tribunal can take their case to the High Court for judicial review, although this avenue is limited only to complaints on procedure and the High Court cannot re-examine the facts of the case. Nonetheless, the high number of cases of judicial review successfully taken against the Tribunal led the Master of the High Court to conclude that many of the Tribunal's decisions were not evidence based. (*Irish Times*, 6 June 2005)

A culture of secrecy is also perceived to surround the workings of the Tribunal, together with a widespread perception that said secrecy is being used to mask a lack of consistency in the decisions of its individual members. The Tribunal furthermore has a policy of not publishing its decisions and has until recently refused to allow lawyers for asylum applicants access to its prior relevant decisions. This latter procedure has been found by the High Court to be in breach of applicants' rights to fair procedures under the constitution and in contravention of the European Convention on Human Rights. (*Irish Times*, 8 July 2005)

Largely in response to these concerns, the draft Immigration, Residence and Protection Bill published in September 2006 contains a proposal to abolish the Refugee Appeals Tribunal and replace it with a new body, to be called the Protection Review Tribunal, composed of full-time personnel.

Deportation

Deportation is a tool of last resort in the enforcement of immigration and asylum law in relation to asylum seekers, economic migrants and overstay students. In the public mind, however, deportation is seen most often as an asylum issue, given the fact that, due to the difficulties and expense associated with deportation, many countries favour sanctions against employers as a means of enforcing the law for immigrants rather than the pursuit of individuals in breach of the conditions attached to their work permits or work visas/authorisations. As a result, deportation in international practice is most often used in cases where asylum applications have been denied.

The government's powers of deportation are legislated for under the Immigration Act 1999. The decision to issue a deportation order only arises when the procedures outlined have been exhausted. According to the Act, the Minister for Justice, Equality and Law Reform also has discretion at this stage in the process to grant humanitarian leave to remain. In making such a decision, the Minister has to have regard to provisions within the Act which include taking into account the person's age, duration of residence in the state, employment prospects, any representations made by or on behalf of the person and any other humanitarian considerations. Concern has been expressed that the Act gives the Minister almost unlimited discretion at this very late stage in the process over who he or she allows to remain in the country and who shall be deported. Concern has also centred on the lack of transparency on how decisions are made at this late stage. The charge has also been made that media support, together with the support of a politician, can be crucial determinants in avoiding deportation, regardless of the merit of the case.

Media Representation of Asylum

A further concern in regard to asylum relates to media representation. A recent study has shown that media images of asylum in Ireland have been overwhelmingly negative. (Devereux, *et al.*, 2005) In a content analysis of newspapers covering the period 2002 to 2004, the study found that fully two-thirds of stories on asylum focused on negative portrayals. Such portrayals included, for example, presenting the quest for asylum as an inherently illegal process; presenting asylum applicants as a financial, moral or cultural threat to Irish society; or focusing on the criminal behaviour of some individuals seeking asylum. Such an overwhelmingly negative portrayal of asylum is a real cause for concern, carrying as it does the power to significantly influence public perceptions and public debate.

Institutional Racism

A final concern relates to what is known as institutional racism. Institutional racism refers to the fact that many of the major institutions in society, such as the educational system, the police, healthcare institutions, welfare systems, sports organisations etc. tend to function within long-established rules and practices that find their base in mainstream culture. Immigration, however, changes the population which is served by these institutions, which in turn requires that institutions alter their practices to ensure they are sufficiently accessible to, and do not discriminate against or exclude, migrants. In understanding institutional racism, it is important to realise that the fact that certain rules may be discriminatory does not mean that the person charged with their implementation is necessarily racist. Nevertheless, it is essential that policies be adopted that ensure against exclusion and discrimination.

In a recent report, Amnesty International, in association with the Irish Centre for Human Rights at NUI Galway, conducted an examination of the safeguards in place within four government departments to ensure against institutional racism. The report concluded that clear examples of discriminatory laws and policies continue to exist across the departments studied. Furthermore, the departments examined included the Department of Justice, Equality and Law Reform which plays the foremost role in Ireland's asylum system. (Beirne and Jaichand, 2006)

AN INTERIM ASSESSMENT

Despite these real concerns, Ireland has received international praise for its rapid response to the challenges of having become a country of asylum.

Writing in 2003, the UNHCR Representative in Ireland wrote, "The government has quickly and effectively since 1997 established a functioning asylum system....Today Ireland's asylum system is performing at greater efficiency than a number of other EU asylum systems. ...The emphasis on refining asylum legislation, establishing and building institutions, streamlining procedures, training staff, implementing a reception programme, drafting an integration policy, and contributing to the development of European instruments on asylum, has all taken place in the space of five years. During this period Ireland has maintained high protection standards, by virtually shunning the practice of detention, by sensitising staff to the needs of children and women, including the determination of cases involving gender-related persecution. A free legal aid scheme was agreed with the Legal Aid Board, and safeguards in procedural aspects of refugee status determination have been fair." (Prutz Phiri, 2003: 119, 124) This overall view is however, contested as overly positive by Irish NGOs working directly with refugees and those seeking asylum.

In December 2006, the Irish Human Rights Commission, in its observations on the Scheme of the Immigration, Residence and Protection Bill, expressed a number of specific concerns. First, that prison is not a suitable place of detention for asylum seekers and other immigration related detainees who are attempting to enter the state or who are subject to removal orders. Of particular concern is the negative impact on children whose parents are detained in prisons on immigration related grounds and who are then placed in the care of the Health Service Executive. Second, the Commission noted that the Scheme of the Bill proposes to mix asylum and protection issues with general provisions on the immigration of non-Irish nationals. The Commission expresses concerns that doing so creates potential legal uncertainty for the status of protection applicants and may impede access to the protection determination process. Finally, in its observations the Commission expresses its concern that there is a large element of ministerial discretion maintained over immigration related decisions allowing for exceptions or exclusions on grounds such as the security of the state, public security, public policy, public health or the public good. Likewise, organs of the state including immigration officers, members of the Garda Síochána, and staff of the Health Service Executive are charged with making decisions on important issues of human rights. (www.ihrc.ie)

INTEGRATION

Immigration is a topic of interest not only in Ireland but internationally. For example, UN Secretary General, Kofi Annan, in 2002 identified migration as a priority issue for the international community. In response, the governments of Sweden, Switzerland, Brazil, Morocco and the Philippines established a Global Commission on International Migration (GCIM) which was launched by Kofi Annan in December 2003. The Commission's Report which was published in October 2005 identifies integration of immigrants into their chosen society as an essential focus for future policy. (Global Commission on International Migration, 2005)

Within the EU, the European Programme for Integration and Migration, funded by a consortium of foundations, is currently in operation. This programme aims to open up debate and encourage broader commitment to the development of constructive integration policies at the EU level and to engage the widest possible range of societal stakeholders in this process. The programme identifies the need to encourage positive public attitudes towards investment in integration policies as being of paramount importance, given the difficult conditions that high levels of questioning, fear and insecurity in many Member States currently create for effective integration. The EU Commission is also seeking an open method of coordination to attempt to secure support for a community development policy, as it also recognizes that economic conditions are likely to guarantee further migration. As a result, integration is seen as the key "to enable immigrants to feel part of society."(European Commission, 2001)

Of particular interest is an International Comparative Citizenship Project, run by the Carnegie Endowment's International Migration Policy Program, which reported in 2000. (www.ceip.org) This project explored the role of citizenship as an agent of cohesion and division across established democracies. The project looked at questions including the criteria for admission for immigrants; the terms of their residence; the basis for their inclusion (or marginalisation); their rights and duties; and the requirements of citizenship. The project concluded that failure to define proper and fair membership rules risks creating different, and almost by definition unequal, classes of membership in societies which will in turn eventually affect societies adversely. It identified four primary areas of importance:

- access to Citizenship;
- dual Nationality;
- political Integration; and
- social and Economic Integration.

Issues of citizenship, in particular, are fundamental to the way a nation approaches its integration policies. Access to citizenship and/or permanent residency are a prerequisite for immigrants to feel they have a long-term future in their chosen country. The denial of this long-term security also mitigates against effective integration policies in other areas. In Ireland, the Citizenship Referendum in 2004 put the issue of access to citizenship firmly on the public agenda and further developments in immigration and asylum policy promise to reshape the concept of Irishness and the definition of Irish citizenship in the years ahead.

Q14.4 How consistent is the government in its support for human rights and democracy abroad?

Ireland has a very positive record in supporting human rights and democracy abroad, and there is also ample evidence of Ireland's commitment to supporting international law. This evidence is seen in support for UN peacekeeping, particularly in Africa; in financial contributions to UN agencies; in recent increases in overseas aid and commitment to reaching the Millennium Development Goals; in support for strengthening the UN's role in disarmament and human rights; and in Ireland's record during its period of membership of the UN Security Council in 2001-2002.

HUMAN RIGHTS BEYOND THE STATE

In 1996, the government produced the first white paper on foreign policy in the history of the state, which identifies four priority areas for Ireland's foreign policy: peacekeeping, disarmament, human rights and development. (Department of Foreign Affairs, 1996)

Irish Foreign Policy Goals

Following on from the 1996 white paper on foreign policy, the Department of Foreign Affairs' Strategy Statement lists the following broad goals as constituting the cornerstones of Irish foreign policy.

1. Work to achieve the full implementation of the Good Friday Agreement and the sustained operation of all its institutions, promoting cooperation, mutual understanding and respect between both traditions on the island, between North and South in Ireland and between these islands.
2. Pursue Ireland's foreign policy in accordance with the ideals enshrined in the constitution and in conformity with the principles of the United Nations Charter, through the development of our bilateral relations with other States, our participation in the European Union's Common Foreign and Security Policy, and our active and principled participation in international organisations.
3. Promote and protect Ireland's interests at the heart of the European Union as it continues to evolve and enlarge, including through the further development of our relations with our current and future EU partners.
4. Promote Ireland's trade, investment and other interests, including its culture, in close cooperation with other departments, state agencies and the private sector, ensuring that the state's network of diplomatic and consular missions adds real value to this task.
5. Make a substantive and effective contribution to achieving the Millennium Development Goals, and to poverty reduction and sustainable growth in developing countries, through the policy and programmes of (Irish Aid), and by working for a just and stable international economic system.
6. Protect and support the interests of Irish citizens abroad, maintain and strengthen links with people of Irish ancestry, and provide a modern and efficient passport and consular service.

(www.foreignaffairs.gov.ie)

As can be seen, support for both the United Nations and the European Union feature prominently in Ireland's foreign policy, as does an emphasis on supporting human rights abroad. In addition, the UN Millennium Development Goals are given a central place in Ireland's development policy.

This commitment to the UN and to the international human-rights agenda derives both from a pragmatic acknowledgement of the importance of a regulated world order in which the interests of even the smallest states are guaranteed and protected, and from a genuine identification with the ethical foundations of the UN. (Connolly and Doyle, 2005) The evidence which shows Ireland's commitment to the UN and to the promotion and protection of human rights abroad will now be considered.

THE GOOD FRIDAY AGREEMENT

The relationship between Ireland and the United Kingdom has undergone a remarkable transformation within the past three decades, whereby the two governments now regard one another as allies rather than as antagonists. (British Council Ireland, 2005) Central to this change has been the settlement reached on the constitutional position of Northern Ireland, involving the two governments and the political parties in Northern Ireland, in the Good Friday Agreement of 1998.

The changing relationship between Ireland and the UK can be traced back to the Sunningdale Agreement in 1973, through the Anglo-Irish Agreement of 1985, to the Good Friday Agreement. Over this period, Ireland's policy has been stated as broadly having been a twin-track approach aimed at persuading London to allow Dublin input into the Northern situation on the one hand and to reduce the threat from paramilitary violence on the other. (O'Kane, 2001) Both of these objectives can now be claimed to have been met. The Good Friday Agreement creates a framework of institutions in which Dublin plays a role and the strategic shift on the part of both republican and loyalist paramilitaries to end political violence and engage with the institutions set up under the Good Friday Agreement has transformed the situation within Northern Ireland.

A key component in the Agreement was the move by the Irish government to remove the constitutional claim over Northern Ireland contained in Articles 2 and 3 of the Irish Constitution. Sectarian divisions between the communities in Northern Ireland, however, remain to be reconciled. (See also Q1.3)

The positive role which the Irish government has played in bringing about the Good Friday Agreement, along with the commitment of current Taoiseach, Bertie Ahern, is acknowledged in the high level of public support in Ireland for the government on this issue.

IRELAND'S RECORD WITHIN THE UN SECURITY COUNCIL 2001-02

A recent analysis has been carried out on Ireland's voting record within the UN General Assembly during the period 1990–2002. (Young and Rees, 2005) During this period, resolutions on Palestine and the Middle East, apartheid, and colonialism made up 38 per cent of all resolutions. Issues of human rights and disarmament made up another 31 per cent. The analysis shows that over the period, Ireland was the EU state most likely to vote in support of resolutions raised by the global South.

Ireland's progressive stance in support of developing countries explains in part the country's high standing within the General Assembly, as evidenced by Ireland's election to the UN Security Council in 2001-02. Ireland's membership of the Security Council placed it in a high-profile position which required it to take a public position on a range of international issues. A recent independent analysis of Ireland's record within the Security Council concludes that "Irish diplomats displayed a consistent support for multilateralism, for the UN system, and for a humanitarian and human-rights based approach to international relations." (Connolly and Doyle, 2005: 382)

The Iraq issue dominated the Security Council during Ireland's term, during which Ireland opposed US policy on issues such as the widespread use of sanctions against Iraq and on whether a second resolution was required to attack Iraq. All of Ireland's decisions during its term on the Council were consistent with its publicly-stated support for the continuation of weapons inspections and opposition to a unilateral attack on Iraq.

Upon leaving the Security Council and following the commencement of the US war on Iraq, the Irish government was more publicly muted in its opposition to the US, although pressure of domestic public opinion would later impel the government to distance itself from Washington's approach. However, in common with other European countries including France, Irish airspace and facilities, in particular Shannon airport, remain available to the US.

Ireland's standing within the UN was also evidenced by the appointment of the Irish Minister for Foreign Affairs, Dermot Ahern, as special envoy for UN reform by the UN Secretary General, Kofi Annan, in 2005.

Other instances of Ireland's support for democracy and human rights include support for a draft resolution promoted by Arab states supporting the principle of land for peace between Israel and the Palestinians – a draft resolution vetoed by the US; opposition to the ending of the arms embargo to Ethiopia and Eritrea in 2001; and ensuring a larger UN peacekeeping operation in East Timor against the wishes of the permanent members of the Security Council. Ireland also opposed a US-backed plan for a constitutional settlement on the constitutional position of Western Sahara, which would have almost certainly resulted in the integration of Western Sahara into Morocco. Instead, Ireland took a principled stand based on the rights to self-determination of the people of Western Sahara. (Connolly and Doyle, 2005)

IRELAND'S ROLE IN UN PEACEKEEPING

Ireland by law can only participate in overseas military missions which have been mandated by the UN, and approved by both the government and the Oireachtas. In practice, Ireland's overseas military involvement throughout the history of the state has been limited to participation in peacekeeping missions under the UN mandate.

Indeed Ireland has, by international standards, a commendable record in supporting UN peacekeeping. In August 2005, only Poland and France within the EU had more troops deployed on UN peacekeeping worldwide than Ireland. (United Nations, 2006) And only Ireland and Sweden, among developed states, currently provide significant numbers of troops under UN command in Africa. This latter fact can be taken as a measure of Ireland's commitment to international peacekeeping in Africa. (Connolly and Doyle, 2005: 366)

Ireland's longest-standing contribution has been to the UN peacekeeping mission in the Lebanon, to which Ireland provided troops from 1978 until late 2001. Around 400 members of the Garda Siochána have also served with UN missions around the world, while eighty-six Irish personnel have died while serving as UN peacekeepers.

Moreover, the presence of Irish peacekeepers in places like Liberia, Kosovo and Bosnia clearly cannot be said to result from Ireland's narrow economic interests. (Connolly and Doyle, 2005: 366)

IRELAND AND DISARMAMENT

Ireland has a strong track record of promoting international nuclear disarmament, having played a significant role in the negotiation of the Non-Proliferation Treaty in the 1950s. In addition, Ireland, along with the governments of seven other nations, launched the New Agenda Declaration in 1998, which called for an unequivocal commitment by the nuclear weapon states to the total elimination of their nuclear weapons, coupled with the immediate work on the practical steps and negotiations required for its achievement. The New Agenda Declaration concluded that "the proposition that nuclear weapons can be retained in perpetuity and never used – accidentally or by decision, – defies credibility. The only complete defence is the elimination of nuclear weapons and assurance that they will never be produced again." (Joint Declaration, 1998) The issue of nuclear proliferation has assumed increased importance with the testing of nuclear weapons by Pakistan in 1998 and North Korea in 2006.

Ireland was also one of the core group of states which pursued the negotiation of the Convention on the Prohibition of the Use, Stockpiling, Production and Transfer of Anti-Personnel Landmines and on their Destruction, concluded in Oslo in 1997. Ireland was the first state to ratify the Convention in December 1997 and contributes bilaterally and multilaterally to mine clearance and mine rehabilitation projects in mine-affected countries.

Ireland also participated actively in the 2001 United Nations Conference on the Illicit Trade in Small Arms and Light Weapons in All Its Aspects. The Program of Action from the Conference adopted a range of national, regional and global initiatives to reduce the indiscriminate proliferation and sale of millions of illegal small arms and light weapons, especially in Africa, Asia and Latin America. However, a proposed legally-binding Arms Trade Treaty, which would ban arms transfers if they are likely to contribute to human rights violations, fuel conflict, or undermine development, has yet to be agreed by UN member nations.

IRELAND'S ROLE IN OVERSEAS DEVELOPMENT

The government's Overseas Development Assistance programme is managed by Irish Aid, formerly Development Cooperation Ireland, which is a division of the Department of Foreign Affairs. Since its inception in 1974, the Irish Aid programme has maintained a strong focus on Sub-Saharan Africa, with programmes in six "Programme Countries", namely Lesotho, Mozambique, Tanzania, Ethiopia, Zambia and Uganda. In March 2003, East Timor became the seventh Irish Aid Programme Country, and the first outside Sub-Saharan Africa. A large number of Irish NGOs are also involved in development, including Concern, Trocaire, Goal, Oxfam Ireland, Action Aid Ireland, Christian Aid, Afri, and the Irish Red Cross. Of these, the largest are Concern, Trócaire and Goal.

Approximately one-third of Ireland's overseas development aid is invested in large-scale multilateral aid projects, much of which is channelled through the United Nations aid system. In addition, Ireland's emergency assistance in response to natural disaster, famine and war, is channelled through non-governmental organisations (NGOs) and international organisations such as UNHCR (United Nations High Commissioner for Refugees), UNICEF (United Nations Children's Fund) and the International Committee of the Red Cross. As a result of the growth in its overall aid budget, Ireland at present is significantly increasing its support to these and other UN agencies.

As stated earlier, Ireland has also given the UN Millennium Development Goals (MDGs) a central place in its development policy. The UN Millennium Development Goals were adopted as a UN Resolution in September 2000, and all 191 UN Member States, including Ireland, have pledged to meet the goals by 2015.

UN Millennium Development Goals

1. Eradicate extreme poverty and hunger
2. Achieve universal primary education
3. Promote gender equality and empower women
4. Reduce child mortality
5. Improve maternal health
6. Combat HIV/AIDS, malaria and other diseases
7. Ensure environmental sustainability
8. Develop a global partnership for development

(United Nations Millennium Declaration, 2000)

Much of the media and public attention around the MDGs has focused on the eighth goal, wherein governments have pledged to relieve debt, increase aid and allow poorer countries fair access to markets. Much of the focus in Ireland has similarly been on the government's commitment to reaching the Millennium Goal pledge of 0.7 per cent of Gross National Income in overseas aid. The country average internationally is 0.4 per cent, while Denmark, one of 5 countries already above the UN target, scores highest at 0.96 per cent. The Irish government meanwhile is committed to reaching the 0.7 per cent target by 2012. (Government of Ireland, 2006)

To achieve this target, Ireland's aid budget has already quadrupled since 1997 to around 0.4 per cent of GNI. Optimistic projections for economic growth predict the 0.7 per cent figure could represent as much as €2 billion by 2012. (*Irish Times*, 8 April 2005) Such levels of expenditure are a very significant increase on anything that Ireland's development agencies have heretofore administered, and the government is currently in the process of adapting the framework for the delivery of Ireland's overseas aid in order to deal with the scale of funding increases. Sceptics within the development community are concerned to ensure that Ireland's target of 0.7% is met, in the light of a stepping back from an equally strong commitment by government in 2004.

More Than Aid

In 2005, the government launched a process of public consultation aimed at preparing a white paper on Ireland's programme of Overseas Development Assistance (ODA). This process followed quickly upon reports of the Ireland Aid Review Committee in 2002 and the OECD Development Assistance Committee (DAC) Peer Review Group in 2003, both of which examined the structures and processes within government for ODA, and resulted among other things, in a refocusing of Ireland's funding to a smaller number of UN agencies. The white paper itself was launched in September 2006.

A radical shift in international thinking has occurred within development agencies and donor governments, whereby overseas aid is now seen as just a single element of a much wider set of issues which need to be addressed. As a result, other issues such as trade, investment, migration, environment, security, and technology policies are regarded as of equal importance.

These interrelationships of once disparate issues are reflected in the white paper submissions. For example, both Dóchas, the umbrella body for Irish development NGOs, and Trócaire have called on the government to develop greater policy coherence across departments to ensure the effectiveness of Ireland's development goals. Trócaire's submission cites trade, environment, finance, migration and economic policy as instances where inconsistencies between government policies may have a detrimental impact on developing countries. A specific example given is the conflict between Ireland's ODA programme and the EU agricultural policy in which Ireland participates, whereby Irish farmers may well actively contribute to development aid projects in their own community, while simultaneously campaigning to retain maximum EU subsidies. This kind of a conflict can also be said to represent a political dilema not just for the Irish, but for the wider developed world as well.

A second example of inconsistency is the disconnect between the primary objective of Ireland's ODA programme to eradicate poverty, and the priorities of the EU's aid programme, which has seen the proportion of its aid going to the world's poorest countries actually fall from 70 per cent in 1990 to less than 29 per cent in 2001, as EU aid shifted to countries in Eastern and Central Europe. (Trócaire, 2005: 28) While no funds have been actually withdrawn from EU aid programmes, it is clear that the emphasis on Central and Eastern Europe has not facilitated the growth of such programmes in the poorest countries in the face of the refusal of EU Member States to increase the EU budget. (Dóchas, 2005)

The Commitment to Development Index

The fact that aid is only one factor in spurring development in poorer nations is illustrated by the "Commitment to Development Index" (CDI), developed by the Centre for Global Development (CGD). (See Table 14.4) The CDI ranks rich nations according to how their policies help or hinder social and economic development in poor countries by assessing seven major domains of government action: foreign aid, trade, investment, migration, environment, security, and technology policy. Ireland's overall ranking in 2006 was 13th out of 21 countries assessed. The Dutch government meanwhile has recently adopted the CDI as one of its external performance standards for development.

Table 14.4 Commitment to Development Index 2006

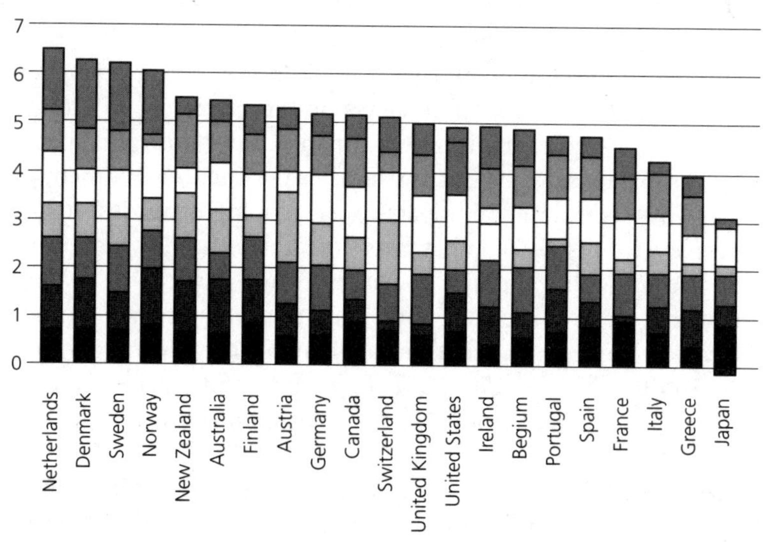

Source: www.cgdev.org

Analysis of the individual categories which make up the index shows that Ireland is particularly strong in the area of aid, where it ranks in the top five of 21. (Table 14.5)

Further analysis of aid performance reveals that Ireland's foreign aid programme is particularly well-designed and delivered. For example, Ireland ranks first in the "no tied aid" category, whereby foreign aid must be spent in the donor country, usually to the benefit of the donor at the expense of the recipient country. Ireland's overseas development programme does not involve the use of "tied aid".

Ireland also ranks first in the category which donates to "relatively poor countries with more democratic governments", and second in the category of donations to large average project size, which maximises economic uses of resources. However, the overall aid contribution at 0.39 per cent of GDP (ranking 9) brings down the Irish performance somewhat, and it remains to be seen how the government commitments to reaching the agreed 0.7 per cent contribution (as percentage of GDP) by 2012 will effect Ireland's overall ranking on the CDI.

Ireland performs well in the environment sector, coming in second place, in line with its modest heavy-industrial base. However, Ireland at the same time hinders developing countries, by providing large subsidies to its fishing industry.

Table 14.5 Aid Scores 2006 Commitment to Development Index

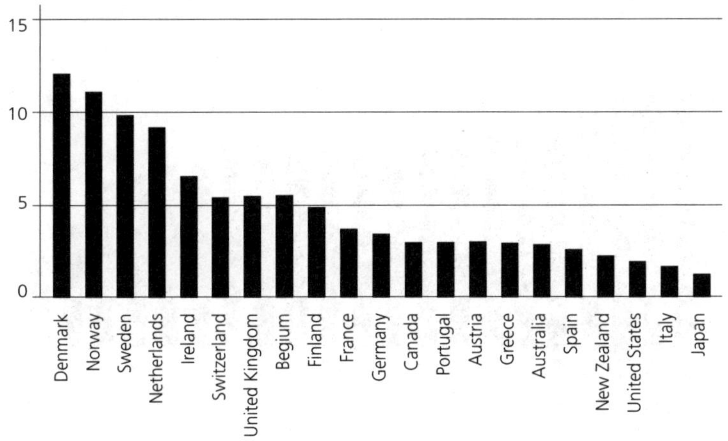

Source: www.cgdev.org

Ireland also performs poorly in the area of investment, which looks at investment strategies by higher-income countries to poorer or developing countries that transfer technologies, perform training and development functions and contribute to economic growth. Ireland itself has benefited enormously from this kind of inward investment, but is a laggard rather than a leader in direct outward foreign investment in developing countries, coming last of 21 developed nations in this category. Two main reasons are cited for Ireland's poor performance: first, its failure to provide political-risk insurance through a national agency which would lessen the risks for private investors in an otherwise economically or politically less favourable environment; and second, its policy of allowing double taxation of corporate profits on such ventures. (See Table 14.6)

Migration is a category where Ireland again scores relatively poorly – 11 out of 21. The main reasons cited here are the small number of foreign students from developing countries studying in Ireland, and the relatively small number of unskilled foreign workers from developing countries who live in Ireland.

Ireland's other weak performance spot is trade (ranked 18 out of 21), whereby protective policies towards agricultural products and subsidies to farmers (all located under the overarching EU protectionist umbrella), mean that Ireland, in effect, actively works against trading efforts by developing countries.

Table 14.6 Technology Score 2006 Commitment to Development Index

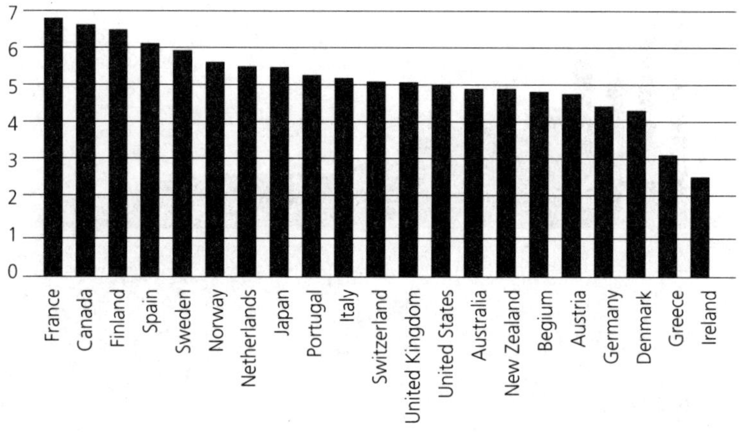

Source: www.cgdev.org

GENDER-BASED VIOLENCE

Ireland has taken a lead in addressing the issue of gender-based violence around the world. Gender-based violence as a "weapon of war" has been evident in almost all recent conflict zones, e.g., Sierra Leone, Rwanda, Darfur, Bosnia and Kosovo. In Rwanda in 1994, for instance, it is estimated that between 250,000 and 500,000 women were victims of rape. Over ten years on, 67 per cent of the survivors are now HIV positive. A consortium of Irish human rights, humanitarian and development agencies, including Irish Aid, are currently undertaking a study to examine the capacity of Irish-based organisations to respond to gender-based violence, particularly in conflict situations. (Irish Consortium on Gender Based Violence, 2005)

NORTH/SOUTH GLOBAL INFLUENCES ON HUMAN RIGHTS AND DEVELOPMENT

The initial thrust of the World Trade Organisation (WTO), and more particularly of its General Agreement on Tarrifs and Trade predecessor (GATT), was to urge poorer countries to open their markets to the developed world's exports, even as those same richer countries progressively closed their markets to exports from the South, most notably in agricultural goods. This situation was further complicated by generous export subsidies from both the US and the EU for their own agricultural exports, a practice known as dumping.

While this imbalance is slowly changing, opinion remains divided as to whether or not bodies such as the WTO can be utilised by the South to achieve greater global trade justice. In the meantime, EU and US agricultural export subsidies are being phased out, partly as a result of pressure within the WTO from the G3 – Brazil, South Africa and India – and other groupings.

Ireland's positive international reputation on development has been partly undermined by its strong protectionist stance on EU subsidies for agricultural production and exports – which reflects to some degree its internal conflict of interests.

RENDITION

One issue which has placed the Irish government in a very difficult position from a human rights standpoint has been recent allegations concerning the use of Shannon Airport as a "stopover point" for CIA rendition flights.

A Council of Europe investigation in 2006 into alleged secret detentions and unlawful inter-state transfers involving Council of Europe Member States revealed a network of US detention sites and transfers in countries around the world, in which Ireland is charged as having played a part.

According to the Council of Europe report, the Irish Government had stated that there was "no reason to investigate the presence of American aircraft" since the United States had given diplomatic assurances that rendition flights were not passing through Shannon Airport. However, the report goes on to indicate that, despite diplomatic assurances to the contrary by the United States, CIA rendition flights have been refuelling at Shannon. (Marty, 2006)

The Irish Human Rights Commission, which has researched the issues in conjunction with the European Parliament, has also found that there have been "repeated and credible reports that US aircraft were being used to secretly transport prisoners to destinations where they were at risk of torture, inhuman or degrading treatment, a practice commonly described as "rendition", and that a number of the aircraft concerned had landed frequently at Irish airports, in particular at Shannon airport." (Irish Human Rights Commission, 2006: 1)

Conclusions

Ireland has undergone significant social, economic, cultural and political change during the last two decades or more.

Dynamic and sustained economic growth has led to a level of wealth, as expressed in conventional GDP terms, unprecedented in the country's history. As a result Ireland has become, for the first time in modern history, an attractive destination for immigrants, resulting in dramatic changes in religious, cultural and linguistic diversity.

The Good Friday Agreement has provided a constitutional agreement between the Irish and British governments, based on overwhelming support across the island, on the status of Northern Ireland. This has saved lives, encouraged inward investment and engendered a new sense of optimism, albeit lessened due to ongoing difficulties in implementation.

Ireland's democracy has evolved against this backdrop of a society in the process of transformation and it is the state of this democracy which we have sought to capture in the detailed analysis of the preceding chapters. Our goal in this final chapter is to summarise the findings of the audit by listing what we have found to be the main strengths and weaknesses of Irish democracy, together with those aspects "in flux" where a definitive judgement would be premature. Liberal democracy such as ours is a form of government which is never completely realised. Rather, it must continue to evolve by both leading and responding to changing conditions. These include demands by citizens for greater control over, and participation in, decisions affecting them, the increasing complexity of social and economic organisation, social relationships and the effects of globalisation.

STRENGTHS

Public Commitment to Democratic Values

Democracy starts with the individual citizen, and Irish citizens demonstrate a relatively high level of satisfaction with the way Irish democracy is developing, compared both with five years ago and with the European average today. Irish people also profess a belief in an individual's ability to influence political decisions and in the duty to vote. Irish people have an egalitarian concept of democracy and support the realisation of social and economic rights through Irish law. A high degree of consensus, moreover, exists around attitudes to democracy across social class, gender and age. However, the belief in an egalitarian society combined with the high level of satisfaction with how Irish democracy works is rather a paradox in view of the very high level of inequality in Irish society by comparison with our European neighbours.

Social Partnership

Ireland has developed a distinctive system of social partnership which has currently evolved to include a wider range of interests and organisations than would generally be the case elsewhere. A significant proportion of the Irish adult population are involved to some degree in the social partnership process, making it by far the most important measure by which conflicting interests are reconciled and government policy influenced.

It is, however, important to note that the role of the fourth pillar, the community and voluntary sector, is confined to a consultative/ advisory role at the invitation of the government and, moreover, many public representatives perceive themselves to be marginalised from an important site of decision making.

Electoral System

The electoral system of proportional representation, using a single transferable vote in a multiseat constituency system (PR-STV) is largely representative; opposition parties are free to organise and voting and electoral procedures are safeguarded in the constitution and in law. Ireland's party system is generally effective in forming and sustaining governments in office and does not fracture along religious or ethnic lines.

Rule of Law

On the whole, the rule of law is applied and enforced consistently throughout the country. Citizens are largely well-protected by the law and, while there is public anxiety about crime, the overall crime rate is low by international standards. The constitution guarantees due process and a fair trial for those charged with criminal offences and the judicial system is effectively independent of the government. Citizens have ownership of the constitution in that every change therein requires a referendum.

Throughout the history of the Republic of Ireland, the military have been securely under the control of the civil authorities, and their occasional deployment among the civilian population has been uncontentious, due to the strict policy of "police primacy". The Irish military is a major contributor to UN peacekeeping forces and has played a significant role in disarmament negotiations over the years.

Freedom of the Media

Ireland has one of the highest levels of press freedom in the world. Irish people read more news when compared with many other European countries and this proclivity supports a considerable diversity of choice in newspapers, both national and local, despite the unusual degree of concentration of press ownership in Ireland. The press has also had considerable success over the years in uncovering and publicising wrongdoing in public life. Along with a retrenchment of the freedom of information (FOI) best-practice environment, only relatively recently instituted, journalists up to now have had to operate within what they regard as unduly restrictive libel laws. Proposed defamation legislation to include the establishment of an independent press council may address this latter issue. However, it is legitimate to question whether the libel laws are an adequate explanation for the media's failure, at the time, to uncover the public corruption which recent tribunal findings revealed was extensive, during the 1980s in particular.

Civil and Political Rights

Ireland has a strong system for the protection of civil and political rights, wherein Irish citizens enjoy extensive rights to freedom of movement, expression, association and assembly. In recent years, Ireland has put in place a framework of legislation and institutions to promote and monitor human rights, including the Irish Human Rights Commission and the Equality Authority.

Ireland is relatively open to migrants. In comparison with the votes won by overtly anti-immigrant and racist parties in some other

European countries, explicit anti-immigrant and racist policies have hitherto attracted minimal electoral support in Ireland.

Ireland's Interaction with International Organisations

There is ample evidence by international standards of Ireland's genuine commitment to supporting international law and human rights abroad. To wit, the UN Millennium Development Goals play a substantial role in overseas development policy; Ireland has a commendable record in supporting UN peacekeeping; it has a track record of promoting international nuclear disarmament at the UN; and it has maintained an independent stance while on the UN Security Council from 2001 to 2002. Moreover, the Irish government played a lead role in the recently concluded UN Treaty on the Rights of the Disabled. Pragmatism does occasionally take precedence: for example, Ireland's stance on the war in Iraq gave rise to significant and demonstrated public disquiet.

WEAKNESSES

High Levels of Poverty and Inequality

By international measurements there is a growing inequality in Irish society in parallel to its growing wealth. In Europe, it has among the highest "at risk of poverty" rates and the lowest rates of expenditure on social protection. Notwithstanding the substantial decrease in the numbers experiencing consistent poverty, this level of inequality represents a failure of our democratic system, particularly in view of the public's clearly-expressed preference for an egalitarian society. Furthermore, while internationally committed to the provision of social and economic rights, the absence in Ireland of a human-rights orientation in the framing of, and access to, public services exacerbates the inequities which arise from income inequality, which is itself an outcome of political decisions that limit redistribution. Many politicians and public officials are wary of enforcing and protecting through law those rights to public services such as health, education, housing or disability services. Examples of policies which have negative impacts on vulnerable groups include a deterioration in the provision of public social housing; a smaller proportion of the population eligible for free medical care; lower levels of investment in education per capita than many other EU countries, particularly at primary and preschool levels, accompanied by state subsidy of private education, most markedly at second level; tax policy favouring those who can afford to invest most in pension provision; a continuation of tax and welfare poverty traps; and an almost complete absence of resources for civil and legal aid for social and economic redress.

Lack of Representativeness in Public Life

The long-standing disadvantaged position of a number of groups in Irish society is further reflected in their poor representation in, or indeed their absence from, the structures and institutions of public decision making. Those from poorer socio-economic backgrounds are underrepresented in important areas of public life including politics. Ireland also has a dismal record when it comes to the representation of women in politics; nor are women adequately represented in the judiciary, gardai, military, senior levels of the public service, including health and education, or the media. By way of contrast, women are far more likely to be victims of domestic violence and continue to be seriously disadvantaged in economic terms and in employment. Members of the Traveller community who also continue to suffer systemic discrimination and high rates of poverty and social exclusion are either totally absent from or scarcely present in political office; nor are they adequately represented in the ranks of the judiciary, the gardai, military, or the media.

Voter Registration and Turnout

There are serious deficiencies in the system of voter registration, which is outdated and inefficient and disadvantages those living in more deprived areas and those citizens lacking a fixed address. Ireland, too, shares a serious problem with western democracies, namely that of declining voter turnout. Voter turnout at the 2002 general election was the lowest ever recorded for a parliamentary election in Ireland, and there is a relatively low participation rate among those living in disadvantaged communities and young people. Voter turnout for local, European and presidential elections is generally much lower still.

Declining Participation in Party and Representative Politics

A substantial number of Irish people believe that party political activism is a waste of time. This belief is further reflected in the relatively small proportions of people who are active in politics, which has in turn become a major preoccupation of all political parties at the present time and a feature of politics not confined to the Irish context. There are many reasons for this decline, among them the perception that the policy differences between political parties have been reduced almost to vanishing point. How this decline in such a central institution of representative democracy is to be addressed is one of the key challenges facing us.

Parliamentary Oversight

Significant weaknesses are to be found in parliamentary oversight of central government and the legislative process itself. This shortfall is even more marked in relation to the explosive growth over the past decade or so in the number of non-elected public bodies, currently circa 500, that deal with core public activities. Many of these bodies are extremely significant in the public functions they perform, the scale of public expenditure they control and their sheer size as public sector employers: the Health Services Executive (HSE) is a prime example. Furthermore, no public appointments commission exists, such as is found in other countries, to ensure the impartiality of appointments to the boards of these bodies, a number of which are also not subject to freedom of information legislation.

Imprisonment

By European standards, imprisonment in Ireland is overutilised as a response to crime, particularly for low-level non-violent offences. The age of criminal responsibility also still remains one of the lowest of any country in Europe. In addition, a highly disproportionate number of those living in disadvantaged areas and of members of the Traveller community are in prison. Ireland has also been criticised internationally for using prisons in inappropriate ways, such as for holding people with severe mental illness, for immigration-related detention, and for incarcerating children alongside adult prisoners.

Limited Scope and Independence of Elected Local Councils

In Ireland, the trend towards centralisation of power has gone perhaps further than in any other European country. The prerogatives and responsibilities of elected councillors have been simultaneously eroded over the past decade or more from three different directions.

Statutory obligations determined by central government are increasingly extensive and regulated in detail, and leave little discretionary finance for local decision making. The absence of a broadly-based and equitable local tax is also a severe hindrance to local development of services in a wide range of areas. This has been accompanied by the loss of local functions to non-elected public bodies, which are subject to little public accountability. Finally, the strengthened role of council manager has given the chief executive of city and county councils a competence in decision making which has further eroded the political responsibility of elected members. Initiatives under recent legislation to establish effective social partnership bodies for local authorities with an emphasis on longer-term planning, such as county development boards and strategic policy committees have been broadly welcomed as an attempt to reverse the centralising trend but have done little to address the limited autonomy of elected local government itself.

Church Influence

Rights to practise religion and culture are protected in a number of international human rights instruments to which Ireland is a party and the free profession and practice of religion are also guaranteed under the constitution. However, a Catholic ethos and influence continues to predominate in important areas of public life and is at odds with an increasingly multicultural and secular society. For example, the very limited availability of non-religious schooling, particularly at primary level, means that parents in Ireland effectively cannot choose secular schooling for their children. This is notwithstanding the fact that those who do not profess any religion are now more numerous as a proportion of the population than any single minority religious group.

IN FLUX

Public Management and Delivery of Services

A number of systems for improving public management have been put in place. However the necessary positive outcomes have not as yet shown through in the delivery of front-line services and considerable concern continues over the capacity for long-term planning and gaps in expertise.

A new social partnership deal has just been concluded which

details economic and social policy for the next ten years in areas as diverse as pensions, housing, and regulation of the labour market. At the same time, there is an increasing reliance by those who can afford it on private provision of public services, which is underpinned by state policy to promote the provision of public services by the private sector.

Despite significant legislative and administrative reforms, arrangements for consulting public-service users on issues of service delivery are less well developed and any consultation is only done in a relatively piecemeal fashion compared with best European practice. In general, consultation is better at local than at national level, although surveys paradoxically show that services by local authorities have a low public-satisfaction rating.

Policing

The Garda Siochána Act 2005, the most comprehensive review of the Irish police since 1922, provides for the establishment of a Garda Inspectorate to monitor the performance of the police and a Garda Siochána Ombudsman Commission to investigate complaints against the gardai by members of the public. Furthermore, a number of positive initiatives have been taken in recent years including: an independent human rights audit of the gardai; the appointment of ethnic liaison officers; a change in the entry requirements for the police to encourage more applications from ethnic minority groups; the appointment of liaison officers to the lesbian and gay community and provisions for the first time for community policing structures. Issues of continued concern as these reforms are implemented, include the essentially-political nature of appointments to senior positions, the absence of a police board and concerns over resourcing of the Ombudsman Commission

Immigration

Ireland's recent economic success has been accompanied by net inward migration. While improvements in the legislative framework are underway, the current absence of a comprehensive policy framework on immigration means that a substantial number of migrant workers face an insecure future, are unable to live together with their partners and children, and are unable to access the basic employment rights to which they are entitled under existing Irish law. A number of human rights concerns which likewise remain unaddressed include a differentiation of rights – such as access to long-term residency, to family reunification and to freedom of movement in the labour market – on the basis of educational qualifications and skills; and the absence of clear criteria regarding a person's entitlement to citizenship and/or long-term residency rights, which are instead granted at the "absolute" discretion of the Minister for Justice, Equality and Law Reform.

Asylum

Ireland, which has recently incorporated the UN Refugee Convention into domestic law, was commended by the UNHCR in 2003 for its overall handling of the growing numbers of asylum seekers. Concerns remain, however, including: the use of prison as a place of detention for asylum seekers and other immigration related detainees; the negative impact on children whose parents are detained in prisons on immigration-related grounds; the large element of ministerial discretion maintained over immigration-related decisions; and the extent to which immigration officers, members of the gardai and staff of the Health Service Executive are charged with making decisions on important issues of human rights.

Rights of Children

Following a period of intense lobbying by children's rights advocates, the government in November 2006 announced its intention to hold a constitutional referendum on the rights of the child in early 2007. This measure is deemed necessary as the constitution has been interpreted as presently granting a higher value to the rights of parents than to the rights of children.

Accountability and Integrity

Recent decades have seen an unprecedented reform of the legislative and administrative framework governing the openness and accountability of politicians and public officials. These measures include legislation to prevent corruption, financing of political parties and elections; legislation on conduct and responsibilities of ministers and senior civil servants; establishment of various ombudsman offices; a standards in public office commission; and freedom of information legislation. Nonetheless, there are important indications that change at these levels has not yet become part of public culture, as evidenced by a continuing culture of secrecy, together with weak systems for identifying wrongdoing and imposing sanctions. Consider, for example, the recent retrenchment of FOI, the lack of any whistle-blower legislation, and a continuing shortage of detailed statistics on corruption. Moreover, there are continuing problems with adequacy of mechanisms for controlling election expenditure and following up on breaches of the legislation.

Where to from here?

As we argued in the Introduction, the purpose of this first systematic assessment of the condition of Ireland's democracy is to inform public discussion and debate about the direction in which our country is moving, and to identify the key points where the ongoing reform of public life needs strengthening. The health of our democracy is a matter of concern to all our citizens but especially to the political parties, those in government, the media and the associations of civil society, and to those engaged in education at all levels. We commend this report and our conclusions to them and trust that our findings will add weight to those who are campaigning to improve the quality of our democracy.

Bibliographical Note on Contributors

CONTRIBUTORS

JOHN BAKER works in the Equality Studies Centre, School of Social Justice, University College Dublin. *Author of Arguing for Equality* (1987) and a coauthor of *Equality: From Theory to Action* (2004), he has also been active in equality-related organisations and campaigns

ELAINE BYRNE is a policy analyst at the United Nations Anti-Corruption Unit. She has recently finished her PhD on Nineteenth and Twentieth Century Political Corruption in Ireland. She is the lead researcher for Transparency International's National Integrity System Country Study on Ireland.

MARK CALLANAN is a lecturer with the Institute of Public Administration in Dublin. His research interests include local government and comparative subnational government. He is coeditor of the standard text on Irish local government, *Local Government in Ireland: Inside Out*.

CATHAL COLEMAN is attached to the School of Politics and International Relations at University College Dublin. He has recently completed a PhD on the concept of subsidiarity and is currently working on political corruption and on new research in deliberative and direct democracy.

TOM CLONAN is the Irish Times Security Analyst specialising in defence and security issues. He also lectures in communication theory at the School of Media, Dublin Institute of Technology and is a retired army officer.

FIONA CROWLEY is Research and Legal Manager with Amnesty International's Irish Section, with responsibility for the Section's research and lobbying agenda on domestic and intergovernmental human rights issues of concern to the organisation.

TOM GORMLEY is a lecturer in Industrial Relations and Human Resource Management at University College Dublin. He is currently working on his PhD, the central topics of which are are workplace partnership and deliberative decision making.

TONY KINSELLA is an author and commentator specialising in international relations. His current focus is on the evolving global society where force, or the threat of force, can no longer be seen as an effective tool of state policy. In 2005, he coauthored *Post Washington*. He is a regular contributor to *The Irish Times* and other publications.

OLIVE MOORE works as Coordinator of Amnesty International Irish Section's Human Rights Based Approaches Initiative, a project working to promote and advance human rights based approaches in Ireland. Olive is currently undertaking a PhD in Human Rights and Development.

GRAINNE MURPHY has worked with TASC as a researcher for the past two years on the Democratic Audit Ireland project and is coauthor of *Outsourcing Government: Public Bodies and Accountability* in 2006.

AOIFE NOLAN is a Lecturer in Law and an Assistant Director of the Human Rights Centre at Queen's University, Belfast. Her primary areas of research are economic and social rights, children's rights, international human rights law, public interest law and comparative constitutional law and has published on these subjects.

LÚGHAIDH Ó BRAONÁIN is currently completing his PhD on the use of the new media in Irish political campaigning at the Department of Communications in Dublin City University.

DEIRIC Ó BROIN is Director of NorDubCo, a regional think tank based in Dublin City University. His research interests are urban politics and local governance. He recently edited, with Peadar Kirby and David Jacobson, *Taming the Tiger – Social Exclusion in a Globalised Ireland.*

DAMIAN TOBIN is lecturer in Business and Management at the Centre for Finance and Management Studies, School of Oriental and African Studies (SOAS), University of London, where he specialises in Distance Learning. His main area of research deals with the topics of corporate governance, the state sector, and transition economies with particular emphasis on China.

TOM WALL is an independent consultant and lecturer on industrial relations issues and is a former Assistant General Secretary of the Irish Congress of Trade Unions. In 2003-04, he conducted research on social partnership from which he obtained a Master's Degree with UCD.

ROBIN WILSON is the former director of the think tank Democratic Dialogue. He is completing a PhD at Queen's University on consociationalism and the travails of politics in Northern Ireland and is co-author of the *Power to the People? Assessing Democracy in Northern Ireland*, a publication of the Democratic Audit Ireland project.

AUTHORS

IAN HUGHES has worked as a research scientist, as a lecturer in physics and science communication and in academic management. He has worked with TASC over the last two years as Senior Researcher with the Democratic Audit Ireland Project. He coauthored *Public Perspectives on Democracy* published in 2005.

PAULA CLANCY is the Director of TASC – A Think Tank for Action on Social Change and Director of the Democratic Audit Ireland Project. Her publications cover areas from media and politics to community arts to gender. She is coauthor of *Outsourcing Government: Public Bodies and Accountability* published in 2006

CLODAGH HARRIS is a Lecturer with the Department of Government at University College Cork. Her research interests include active citizenship and democratic participation. She was Coordinator of the Democracy Commission Project (2004-2005) and edited the Report of the Democracy Commission *Engaging Citizens*, published in 2005.

DAVID BEETHAM is Professor Emeritus, University of Leeds, Fellow of the Human Rights Centre, University of Essex, and Associate Director of the UK Democratic Audit. The method of democracy and human rights assessment which he pioneered has been used in many countries around the world.

Appendix 1

FURTHER ACKNOWLEDGEMENTS

In addition to the individuals and organisations named in the Acknowledgements, we would like to express our thanks to the following people who contributed to this study by peer review and/or attendance at expert seminars/roundtables, and in many cases by supplying additional valuable input. It is important to note that all the individuals listed below contributed in an individual capacity.

Maura Adshead, Department of Politics and Public Administration, University of Limerick
Noeline Blackwell, Free Legal Advice Centres
Laurence Bond, Equality Authority
Teresa Brannick, School of Business, University College Dublin
Kathleen Cavanagh, Irish Centre for Human Rights, University College Galway
Denise Charlton, Immigrant Council of Ireland
John Coakley, School of Politics and International Relations, University College Dublin
Alpha Connelly, Irish Human Rights Commission
Maria Cronin, Irish Business and Employers Confederation
Catherine Cosgrove, Immigrant Council of Ireland
James Doorley, National Youth Council of Ireland
Roland Erne, University College Dublin Business Schools
Nicky Gallagher, Office of the Ombudsman for Children
Yvonne Galligan, Centre for the Advancement of Women in Politics, Queen's University Belfast
Brian Harvey, Social Researcher
Mark Kelly, Irish Council for Civil Liberties
Sallyanne Kinihan, Irish Congress of Trade Unions
Kathleen Lynch, School of Education, University College Dublin
Yvonne McKenna, Volunteer Centres Ireland
Brian McKevitt, Standards in Public Office Commission

Aidan Moore, Standards in Public Office Commission;
Aogán Mulcahy, School of Sociology, University College Dublin
Kevin Murphy, Former Ombudsman
Muiris MacCarthaigh, Institute of Public Administration
Tim McCarthy, Department of Government, University College Cork
Aodh Quinlivan, Department of Government, University College Cork
Orla O'Connor, National Women's Council of Ireland
Colm O'Cunacháin, Amnesty International (Irish Section)
Siobhan O'Donoghue, Migrant Rights Centre Ireland
Seán O hÉigeartaigh, National Economic and Social Forum
Damien O'Mahoney, Cork City Council
Paul O'Mahony, Department of Occupational Therapy, Trinity College Dublin
Peter O'Mahony, Irish Refugee Council
Nora Owen, Former Minister for Justice
Damian Peelo, Irish Travellers Movement
Aileen Pyne, Cork County Council
Kevin Rafter, Sunday Tribune
Christopher Robson, Gay and Lesbian Equality Network
Eamon Ryan, TD, The Green Party
Tom Ryan, Association of Municipal Authorities of Ireland
Donal Toolan, Forum of People with Disabilities
Gerard Whyte, School of Law, Trinity College Dublin
Maev-Ann Wren, Economic Consultant

Bibliography

Acheson, N., Harvey, B., Kearney, J. and Williamson, A. (2004) *Two Paths, One Purpose: Voluntary Action in Ireland, North and South*, Dublin: Institute of Public Administration.

Amárach Consulting (2004) *Quality of Life in Ireland 2004 Report, A Study for Diageo Ireland*, available online at www.amarach.com.

Amnesty International (2003) *Mental Illness: The Neglected Quarter*, Dublin: Amnesty International Irish Section.

Amnesty International (2004) *Annual Report 2004*, London: Amnesty International Publications.

Amnesty International (2005) *Human Rights for Human Dignity: A Primer on Economic, Social and Cultural Rights*, Oxford, UK: Amnesty International Publications.

Amnesty International (Irish Section) (2000) Briefing to the UN Human Rights Committee on Human Rights Concerns, available at www.amnesty.ie.

Amnesty International (Irish Section) (2004) *Justice and Accountability – Stop Violence against Women, Summary Report*, available online at www.amnesty.ie.

Amnesty International (Irish Section) (2005a) *Stop Violence against Women*, Dublin: Amnesty International, Irish Section.

Amnesty International (Irish Section) (2005b) *Our Rights, Our Future, Human Rights-Based Approaches in Ireland: Principles, Policies and Practice*, Dublin: Amnesty International, Irish Section.

An Garda Síochána (2004) *Human Rights Audit: Report from Ionnan Management Consultants*, available online at www.garda.ie.

An Garda Síochána (2005) *Public Opinion Survey 2005*, available online at www.garda.ie.

An Garda Síochána/Police Service of Northern Ireland (2004) *A Cross Border Organised Crime Assessment*, Northern Ireland Office/Department of Justice, Equality and Law Reform Joint Publication and Department of Peacekeeping Operations.

An Garda Síochána Complaints Board (2004) *Annual Report 2003*, Dublin: Stationery Office.

An Garda Síochána Complaints Board (2005) *Annual Report 2004*, Dublin: Stationery Office.

Annan, K. (2005) *In Larger Freedom: Towards Development, Security and Human Rights for All, Report of the Secretary-General*, New York: United Nations.

Arriaga, X.B. and Oskamp, S. (eds.) (1999) *Violence in Intimate Relationships*, Thousand Oaks, CA: Sage Publications.

Bacik, I. (2002) "Women and the Criminal Justice System" in P. O'Mahony (ed.), *Criminal Justice in Ireland*, Dublin: Institute of Public Administration.

Bacik, I. and O'Connell, I. (1998) *Crime and Poverty in Ireland*, Dublin: Round Hall.

Bacik, I., Kelly, A., O'Connell, M. and Sinclair, H. (1997) "Crime and Poverty in Dublin: An Analysis of the Association between Community Deprivation, District Court Appearance and Sentence Severity" in I. Bacik and A. O'Connell (1998), *Crime and Poverty in Ireland*, Dublin: Round Hall.

Bacon, P. & Associates in association with F. MacCabe (1999) *The Housing Market: An Economic Review and Assessment. Report Submitted to the Minister for Housing and Urban* Renewal, Dublin: Stationery Office.

Bacon, P. & Associates in association with F. MacCabe (2000) *The Housing Market: An Economic Review and Assessment. Report Submitted to the Minister for Housing and Urban* Renewal, Dublin: Stationery Office.

Bacon, P. & Associates in association with F. MacCabe and A. Murphy (1998) *An Economic Assessment of Recent House Price Developments: Report Submitted to the Minister for Housing and Urban Renewal*, Dublin: Stationery Office.

Baker, J., Lynch, K., Cantillon, S. and Walsh, J. (2004) *Equality: From Theory to Action*, London and New York: Palgrave.

Banisar, D. (2004) *The freedominfo.org Global Survey: Freedom of Information and Access to Government Record Laws around the World*, available online at www.freedominfo.org/survey.

Barclay, G. and Taveres, C. (2002) *International Comparisons of Criminal Justice Statistics 2000*, Statistical Bulletin 05/02, London: RDS Communications and Development Unit, Home Office.

Barry, F. (2004) "Export Platform FDI: The Irish Experience", *EIB Papers*, 9/2.

Beetham, D. (2006) *Parliament and Democracy in the Twenty-First Century: A Guide To Good Practice*, Geneva: Interparliamentary Union.

Beetham, D., Bracking, S., Kearton, I. and Weir, S. (2001) *International IDEA Handbook on Democracy Assessment*, Stockholm: International IDEA.

Beetham, D., Bracking, S., Kearton, I., Vittal, N. and Weir, S. (2002) *The State of Democracy: Democracy Assessments in Eight Nations Around the World*, The Netherlands: Kluger Law International.

Beetham, D., Byrne, I., Ngan, P. and Weir, S. (2002) *Democracy under Blair: A Democratic Audit of the United Kingdom*, London: Politico's Publishing UK.

Beirne, L. and Jaichand, V. (2006) *Breaking Down the Barriers: Tackling Racism in Ireland at the Level of the State and its Institutions*, Dublin and Galway: Amnesty International (Irish Section) and the Irish Centre for Human Rights.

Bourke, S. (2004) *Taking the Free Speech Temperature*, Dublin: School of Communications, Dublin City University.

Boyle, R., Humphreys, P., O'Donnell, O., O'Riordan, J. and Timonen, T.V. (2003) *Changing Local Government: A Review of the Local Government Modernisation Programme*, Dublin: Institute of Public Administration.

Boyle, R., O'Riordain, J. and O'Donnell, O. (2002) *Promoting Longer-Term Policy*

Thinking, CPMR Discussion Paper No. 22, Dublin: Institute of Public Administration.

Brady, C. (2006) "Who Edits the Editor?" *Village* (19 January 2006).

Brandenburg, H. and Hayden, J. (2003) "The Media and the Campaign" in M. Gallagher, M. Marsh and P. Mitchell (eds.) *How Ireland Voted 2002*, Basingstoke: Palgrave Macmillan.

Brennan, N. and McDermott, M. (2004) "Alternative Perspectives on Independence of Directors", *Corporate Governance: An International Review*, 12/3 (July).

Bresnihan, V. (2001) *Out of Mind, Out of Sight: The Solitary Confinement of Mentally Ill Prisoners*, Dublin: Irish Penal Reform Trust.

British Council Ireland (2005) *Britain and Ireland: Lives Entwined*, Dublin: British Council.

Broadcasting Commission of Ireland (2006) "BCI Completes Review of Ownership and Control Policy in Advance of Radio Licensing Advertisements", available online at www.bci.ie/news_information/press44.html.

Browne, H. (2005) "Tiger-talk is Cheap", *Village* (8 December 2005).

Byrne, E. (2006a) "Ireland" in *Global Corruption Report*, Berlin: Transparency International.

Byrne, E. (2006b) "A Brief History of Irish Corruption Law", *TIQ Quarterly Ireland*, Issue 3, Dublin: Transparency International Ireland.

Byrne, I. and Blick, A. (2006) "Home Truths" in S. Weir, *Unequal Britain: Human Rights as a Route to Social Justice*, London: Politico's.

Byrne, R. and McCutcheon, J.P. (2001) *The Irish Legal System*, 4th edn., Dublin: Butterworth.

Byrne, R., Kennedy, M., Ní Longain, M. and Shannon, G. (2003) *Law Society of Ireland: Employment Law*, Oxford: Oxford University Press.

Callanan, M. (2004) "Local and Regional Government in Transition" in *Political Issues in Ireland Today*, N. Collins and T. Cradden (eds.) Manchester: Manchester University Press.

Carey, T. (2005) *The Annual Report of the Mental Health Commission including the Report of the Inspector of Mental Health Services*, Dublin: Mental Health Commission.

Casey, J. (2000) *Constitutional Law in Ireland*, 3rd edn., London: Sweet & Maxwell.

Central Bank (2004) *Compendium of Irish Statistics 2004*, available online at www.centralbank.ie.

Central Bank (2006) *Compendium of Irish Statistics 2006*, available online at www.centralbank.ie.

Central Statistics Office (2003a) *Third Quarter 2002: Quarterly National Household Survey. Voter Participation and Abstention*, available online at www.cso.ie.

Central Statistics Office (2003b) *Census 2002, Vol. 6: Occupations*, Dublin: Stationery Office.

Central Statistics Office (2004a) *Women and Men in Ireland 2004*, Dublin: Stationery Office.

Central Statistics Office (2004b) *CSO Quarterly National Household Survey, Crime and Victimisation Quarter 4, July 2004*, available online at www.cso.ie.

Central Statistics Office (2004c) *2002 Census of Population, Volume 11 Irish Language, March*, Dublin: Stationery Office.

Central Statistics Office (2005a) *Measuring Ireland's Progress 2004*, Dublin: Stationery Office.

Central Statistics Office (2005b) *Quarterly National Household Survey: Equality, Fourth Quarter 2004*, available online at www.cso.ie.

Central Statistics Office (2005c) *Environmental Accounts for Ireland 1996–2003*, Dublin: Stationery Office.

Central Statistics Office (2006a) *Survey on Income and Living Conditions (EU-SILC) 2005*, available online at www.cso.ie.

Central Statistics Office (2006b) *Quarterly National Household Survey*, Quarter 3, available online at www.cso.ie.

Central Statistics Office (2006c) *Preliminary Report on the Census 2006*, Dublin: Stationery Office.

Centre for the Advancement of Women in Politics (2004) *Independent Gender Equality Audit and Fianna Fáil Gender Equality Action Plan 2004–2014*, available online at www.qub.ac.uk/cawp/research/FiannaFailreport.pdf.

Chubb, B. (1982) *The Government and Politics of Ireland*, 2nd edn., London: Longman.

Cichowski, R. (2000) *Sustaining Democracy: A Study of Authoritarianism and Personalism in Irish Political Culture*, Centre for the Study of Democracy, CA: Irvine.

Clancy, P. and Murphy, G. (2006) *Outsourcing Government: Public Bodies and Accountability*, Dublin: Tasc@NewIsland.

Clancy, P., Hughes, I. and Brannick, T. (2005) *Public Perspectives on Democracy in Ireland*, Democratic Audit Ireland Project, Dublin: Tasc.

Clinch, P., Convery, F. and Walsh, B. (2002) *After the Celtic Tiger*, Dublin: The O'Brien Press.

Clonan, T. (2000) "The Status and Role Assigned to Female Personnel in the Irish Defense Forces", (dissertation), Dublin: Dublin City University.

Coakley, J. (2003) "The Election and Party System" in M. Gallagher, M. Marsh, and P. Mitchell (eds.) *How Ireland Voted 2002*, Basingstoke: Palgrave Macmillan.

Coakley, J. (2005a) "The Foundations of Statehood" in J. Coakley and M. Gallagher (eds.), *Politics in the Republic of Ireland*, 4th edn., New York: Routledge and PSAI Press.

Coakley, J. (2005b) "Society and Political Culture" in J. Coakley and M. Gallagher (eds.), *Politics in the Republic of Ireland*, 4th edn., New York: PSAI Press.

Coakley, J. and Gallagher, M. (2005) *Politics in the Republic of Ireland*, 4th edn., New York: Routledge and PSAI Press.

Coakley, J., O'Caoindealbhain, B. and Wilson, R. (2006) *The Operation of the North-South Implementation Bodies*, available online at www.democraticdialogue.org.

Coleman, C. (2005) *Subsidiarity and European Union: A Conceptual Analysis*, PhD thesis, School of Politics and International Relations, Dublin: University College Dublin.

Collins, E. and Sheehan, B. (2004) *Access to Health Services for Transsexual People, Equality Research Series*, Dublin: The Equality Authority.

Collins, N. and Cradden, T. (eds), (2004) *Political Issues in Ireland Today*, Manchester: Manchester University Press.

Collins, N. and O'Shea, M. (2000) *Understanding Political Corruption*, Cork: Cork University Press.

Collins, N. and Quinlivan, A. (2005) "Multi-level Governance" in J. Coakley and M. Gallagher (eds.), *Politics in the Republic of Ireland*, London: Routledge.

Combat Poverty Agency (2006a) *Making Poverty the Policy Priority in Budget 2007, Submission to the Minister for Social Affairs and the government*, Dublin: Combat Poverty Agency.

Combat Poverty Agency (2006b) *Analysis of Budget 2006, February*, Dublin: Combat Poverty Agency.

Comhairle (2006) *Resource Database for Voluntary and Community Sectors*, available online at www.cidb.ie.

Committee on Members' Interests of Dáil Éireann (2000) *Report of the Results of an Investigation into a Complaint Concerning Deputy Denis Foley*, available online at www.irlgov.ie.

Community Workers Cooperative (2005) *Government Censures Dissent: Funding to the Community Workers Cooperative Axed*, press release, 25 January 2005.

Comptroller and Auditor General (2005) *Annual Report of the Office of the Comptroller and Auditor General 2004*, Dublin: Stationery Office.

Conflict Archive on the Internet, *Half the Battle: Understanding the Impact of "The Troubles" on Children and Young People*, Chapter 3: Deaths of Children and Young People in The Troubles, available online at http://cain.ulst.ac.uk/index.html.

Congress of Local and Regional Authorities of Europe (2001a) *Congress of Local and Regional Authorities of Europe Report on Local Democracy in Ireland*, Doc. CPL 8(4) Part II, Strasbourg: Council of Europe Publishing.

Congress of Local and Regional Authorities of Europe (2001b) *Congress of Local and Regional Authorities of Europe Recommendation 97 on Local Democracy in Ireland*, Strasbourg: Council of Europe Publishing.

Connaughton, B. (2005) "The Impact of Reform on Politico-Administrative Relations in Ireland: Enlightening or Confusing Roles of Political and Managerial Accountability?", paper presented to the 13th Annual NISPAcee Conference, Democratic Governance for the XXI Century: Challenges and Responses in CEE Countries, Moscow, Russia, 19–21 May.

Connolly, E. (2005) "The Government and the governmental System" in J. Coakley and M. Gallagher (eds.), *Politics in the Republic of Ireland*, 4th edn., London and New York: Routledge and PSAI Press.

Connolly, E. and Doyle, J. (2005) "The Place of the UN in Contemporary Irish

Foreign Policy" in M. Kennedy (ed.), *Obligations and Responsibilities: Ireland and the United Nations 1955–2005*, Dublin: Institute of Public Administration.

Connolly, J. (2004) *Developing Integrated Policing*, Dublin: Blanchardstown Community Policing Forum.

Constitution Unit (2004) *Nations and Regions: The Dynamics of Devolution, Devolution Monitoring Programme Quarterly Report*, Northern Ireland Report 21, November, London: UCL.

Corcoran, F. (2004) *RTÉ and the Globalisation of Irish Television*, Bristol: Intellect.

CORI (2003), *CORI Socio-Economic Review 2003: Achieving Inclusion, Policies to Ensure Economic Development, Social Equity and Sustainability*, Dublin: CORI.

Corrigan, C. (2002) *Ireland Background Report: OECD Thematic Review of Early Childhood Education and Care*, Dublin: Department of Education and Science.

Coughlan, M. and de Buitleir, D. (1996) *Local Government Finance in Ireland*, Dublin: Institute of Public Administration.

Coulter, C. (2002) "Politicians still want a say in judicial process", *The Irish Times*, 11 April 2002.

Council of Europe (1950) *Convention for the Protection of Human Rights and Fundamental Freedoms*, available online at www.convention.coe.int.

Courtney, J. (2004) *Elections*, Canadian Democratic Audit Series, Vancouver: University of British Columbia Press.

Crotty, W. (1998) "Democratisation and Political Development in Ireland" in W. Crotty and D. Schmitt (eds.), *Ireland and the Politics of Change*, Harlow: Longman.

Crowley, F. (2003) *Amnesty International Summary Report: Mental Illness, The Neglected Quarter*, Dublin: Amnesty International (Irish Section).

Daemon, H. and Schaap, L. (2000) 'Ireland: associated democracy', in Daemon H. and Schaap L. (eds), *Citizen and City: Developments in Fifteen Local Democracies in Europe*, Rotterdam: Centre for Local Democracy.

D'Art, D. and Turner, T. (2005) "Union Organising, Union Recognition and Employer Opposition: Case Studies of Irish Experience", *Irish Journal of Management*, 26/2.

Dáil Debate (2006) Vol. 16, No. 1, 25 April.

Daly, Y.M. (2004) "The Changing Irish Approach to Questions of Criminal Justice", *Cork Available online Law Review*.

Dell, G. (2005) "A Primer on the UN Convention against Corruption", *TIQ Quarterly Ireland*, Issue 4.

Democratic Unionist Party (2004) *Devolution Now: The DUP's Concept for Devolution*, policy paper, available online at www.dup.org.uk.

Department for Justice, Equality and Law Reform (2005) "Address by Minister to an Information Seminar for Ethnic Communities on Garda Recruitment", National Consultative Committee on Racism and Interculturalism (NCCRI), 6 October.

Department of Communications, Marine and Natural Resources (2004) *Public Service Broadcasting Charter*, Dublin, available online at www.dcmr.gov.ie.

Department of Communications, Marine and Natural Resources (2004), *Public Service Broadcasting Charter: June 2004*, available at www.dcmnr.gov.ie/Broadcasting/Public+Service+Broadcasting+Charters/.

Department of Education and Science (1999) *Ready to Learn: White Paper on Early Childhood Education*, Dublin: Stationery Office.

Department of Education and Science (2005) *Key Educational Statistics*, available online at www.education.ie.

Department of Environment and Local Government (1996) *Better Local Government, A Programme for Change*, Dublin: Stationery Office.

Department of Environment and Local Government (2000a) *Homelessness: An Integrated Strategy*, Dublin: Department of Environment and Local Government.

Department of Environment and Local Government (2000b) *National Climate Change Strategy*, Dublin: Stationery Office.

Department of Environment, Heritage and Local Government (2002a), *Homeless Preventative Strategy*, Dublin: Departments of Education and Science; Environment, Heritage and Local Government; Health and Children; and Justice, Equality and Law Reform.

Department of Environment, Heritage and Local Government (2002b) *Dual Mandate to End*, press release, 18 December 2002.

Department of Environment, Heritage and Local Government (2005) *Annual Housing Statistics Bulletin*, available online at www.environ.ie.

Department of Finance (2006) Progress *Report on the National Development Plan*, Dublin: Stationery Office.

Department of Foreign Affairs (1996) *Challenges and Opportunities Abroad: The White Paper on Foreign Policy*, Dublin: Stationery Office.

Department of Foreign Affairs (2005), *Strategy Statement of the Department of Foreign Affairs, 2005- 2007*, available online at www.foreignaffairs.gov.ie.

Department of Health and Children (2001a) *Youth Homelessness Strategy*, Dublin: Stationery Office.

Department of Health and Children (2001b), *Quality and Fairness: A Health System for You,* Dublin: Stationery Office.

Department of Health and Children (2003a) *Audit of Structures and Functions in the Health System*, Dublin: Stationery Office.

Department of Health and Children (2003b) *Report of the National Task Force on Medical Staffing*, Dublin: Stationery Office.

Department of Health and Children (2005) *Health System Achievements, October*, Dublin: Department of Health and Children.

Department of Justice, Equality and Law Reform (2002) *Value for Money and Management Audit of the Citizen Traveller Campaign and the Preparation of a Report on Financial Position*, Dublin: Department of Justice, Equality and Law Reform.

Department of Justice, Equality and Law Reform (2005a), "McDowell Announces Government's Nominees for Garda Ombudsman Commission", press release, 15 December 2005.

Department for Justice Equality and Law Reform (2005b) *"Address by Minister to an Information Seminar for Ethnic Communities on Garda Recruitment"*, Seminar organised by the National Consultative Committee on Racism and Interculturalism (NCCRI), Dublin, 6th October.

Department of Justice, Equality and Law Reform (2005c) "Government Decision Will Transform Situation in Relation to Women on State Boards", press release, Minister of State Frank Fahey, available online at www.justice.ie.

Department of Justice, Equality and Law Reform (2005d) *Immigration and Residence in Ireland: Outline Policy Proposals for an Immigration and Residence Bill – A Discussion Document*, Dublin: Stationery Office.

Department of Justice, Equality and Law Reform (2006) "International Women's Day 2006", press release, 8 March, available online at www.justice.ie.

Department of Justice, Equality and Law Reform and Department of Enterprise, Trade and Employment (2005) *Joint Submission to the EU Green Paper on Economic Migration*, April 2005, Dublin

Department of the Environment (1996) *Better Local Government – A Programme for Change*, Dublin: Stationery Office.

Department of the Taoiseach (1999) *Reducing Red Tape: An Action Programme of Regulatory Reform in Ireland*, Dublin: Lloyds of Dublin on behalf of the Department of the Taoiseach.

Department of the Taoiseach (2002) *Towards Better Regulation: A Consultation Document*, Dublin: Department of the Taoiseach.

Department of the Taoiseach (2004) *Regulating Better: A Government White Paper Setting Out Six Principles of Better Regulation*, Dublin: Stationery Office.

Department of the Taoiseach (2006) *Towards 2016: Ten-Year Framework Social Partnership Agreement 2006–2015*, Dublin: Stationery Office.

Deutsch Karlekar, K. (ed.) (2005) *Freedom of the Press 2005: A Global Survey of Media Independence*, New York: Freedom House, Rowman and Littlefield Publishers Inc.

Devereux, E., Breen, M. and Haynes, A. (2005) "Smuggling Zebras for Lunch: Media Framing of Asylum Seekers in the Irish Print Media", *Etudes Irlandaises*, 30/1.

Dochas (2005) *Submission to Development Cooperation Ireland: Public Consultation on the Future of Ireland's Official Development Assistance Programme*, Dublin: Dochas.

Dollard, G. (2003) "Local Government Finance: The Policy Context" in M. Callanan and J. Keogan (eds.), *Local Government in Ireland – Inside Out*, Dublin: Institute of Public Administration.

Donoghue, F. (1998) "Defining the Non-profit Sector: Ireland" in L.M. Salamon and H.K. Anheier (eds.), *Working Papers of the John Hopkins Comparative Non-profit Section Project*, No. 28, Baltimore: The John Hopkins Institute for Policy Studies.

Donoghue, F., Prizeman, G., O'Regan, A. and Nöel, V. (2006) *The Hidden Landscape - First Forays into Mapping Non-profit Organisations in Ireland*, Dublin: Centre for Non-profit Management, Trinity College.

Dooley, E. (2001) *Homicide in Ireland 1972–1991*, Dublin: Stationery Office.

Dooley, S. (2003) Statement to the Joint Committee on Communications, Marine and Natural Resources, Sub-Committee on Information Communications Technology, Wednesday, 4 June 2003, available online at http://broadband.oireachtas.ie/JC13_Page04.htm.

Dooley, S. (2005) "Comments to meeting of the Democracy Commission", 17 May 2005.

Doyle, J. and Connolly, E. (2002) "Can We Draw Comfort from the Recent Election" in *Racism in Ireland*, available online at www.dcu.ie/alumni/summer02/p8.html.

Drudy, P.J. and Punch, M. (2005) *Out of Reach Inequalities in the Irish Housing System*, Dublin: Tasc@NewIsland.

Dublin City Childcare Committee (2006) *Childcare Audit and Needs Analysis 2006*, available online at www.childcareonline.ie.

Dublin Rape Crisis Centre (2002) *The SAVI Report: Sexual Abuse and Violence in Ireland*, Dublin: Liffey Press.

Eagleton, T. (2002) *The Truth About the Irish*, Dublin: New Island.

Earnest, D.C. (2003) *Non-citizen Voting Rights: A Survey of an Emerging Democratic Norm,* paper presented to the 2003 annual convention of the American Political Science Association, Philadelphia, 28 August 2003.

Educate Together (2005) *Shadow Report by Educate Together on the First National Report to the United Nations Committee on the Convention on the Elimination of all Forms of Racial Discrimination by Ireland*, Dublin: Educate Together.

Eivers, E., Shiel, G. and Shortt, F. (2004) *Reading Literacy in Disadvantaged Primary Schools,* Dublin: Educational Research Centre.

Ejohr, T. (2006) *Inclusive Citizenship in 21st Century Ireland: What Prospects for the African Immigrant Community?*, Dublin: Africa Centre.

Elgie, R. and Fitzgerald, P. (2005) "The President and Taoiseach" in J. Coakley and M. Gallagher (2005) *Politics in the Republic of Ireland*, 4th edn., London and New York: Routledge and PSAI Press.

Elliott, S. (1999) "The Referendum and Assembly Elections in NI", *Irish Political Studies*, 14.

EPIC Project (2006) *Election Process Information Collection*, joint project of IIDEA, UNDP and IFES, available online at www.epicproject.org.

Equality Authority (2002) *Implementing Equality for Lesbians, Gays and Bisexuals*, Dublin: Equality Authority.

Equality Authority (2003) *Schools and the Equal Status Act,* 2nd edn., Dublin: Department of Education and Science, Equality Authority.

Equality Authority (2006) *Annual Report 2005*, Dublin: Equality Authority.

Eurobarometer (2002) *Eurobarometer 56, Public Opinion in the European Union*, Brussels: European Commission.

Eurobarometer (2004) *Eurobarometer 61, Public Opinion in the European Union*, Brussels: European Commission.

Eurobarometer (2006) *Eurobarometer 65: Public Opinion in the European Union*

National Report: Ireland, Spring, Brussels: European Commission, available online at www.europa.eu.int/comm/public_opinion.

European Commission (2001) *Communication from the Commission to the Council and the European Parliament on an Open Method of Coordination for the Community Immigration Policy*, Brussels: European Commission.

European Committee for the Prevention of Torture and Inhuman or Degrading Treatment or Punishment (2002) *Report to the government of Ireland*, available online at www.cpt.coe.int.

European Committee for the Prevention of Torture and Inhuman or Degrading Treatment or Punishment (2003) *Report to the government of Ireland on the Visit to Ireland Carried Out by the European Committee for the Prevention of Torture and Inhuman or Degrading Treatment or Punishment*, Strasbourg: CPT/Inf.

European Commission Against Racism and Intolerance (ECRI) (2001) Second Report on Ireland, Strasbourg: Council of Europe.

European Court of Human Rights (1996) *Goodwin v UK Judgment*, available online at http:www.echr.coe.int.

European Monitoring Centre on Racism and Xenophobia (2006) *Migrants' Experiences of Racism and Xenophobia in 12 EU Member States: Pilot Study*, Vienna: EUMC.

Europol (2005) *European Union Organised Crime Situation Report 2005*, The Hague: Europol.

External Advisory Committee on the Defence Forces (2002) *The Challenge of a Workplace*, Dublin: Defence Forces Printing Press.

Fahey, T. (ed) (1999) *Social Housing in Ireland: A Study of Success, Failure and Lessons Learned*, Dublin: Oak Tree Press.

Fahey, T., Hayes, B.C. and Sinnott, R. (2005) *Conflict and Consensus: A Study of Values and Attitudes in the Republic and Northern Ireland*, Dublin: Institute of Public Administration.

Fahey, T., Nolan, B. and Bertrand, M. (2004) *Housing, Poverty and Wealth in Ireland*, Dublin: Institute of Public Administration and Combat Poverty Agency.

Fanning, B. (2002) "The Political Currency of Racism, 1997–2002", *Studies*, vol. 91.

Fanning, B., Mutwarasibo, F. and Chadamoyo, N. (2003) *Positive Politics: Participation of Immigrants and Ethnic Minorities in the Electoral Process*, Dublin: Africa Solidarity Centre.

Farrell, D. (1999) "Ireland: A Party System Transformed?" in D. Broughton and M. Donovan (eds.), *Changing Party Systems in Western Europe*, London: Pinter.

Farrell, D. (2001) *Electoral Systems: A Comparative Introduction*, Basingstoke: Palgrave.

Farrington, D. and Morris, A. (1983) *Sex, Sentencing and Reconviction*, British Journal of Criminology, Vol. 23.

Feldman, A., Ndakengerwa, D.L., Nolan, A. and Frese, C. (2005) *Diversity, Civil*

Society and Social Change in Ireland: A North-South Comparison of the Role of Immigrant-Led Community and Voluntary Sector Organisations, Dublin: Migration & Citizenship Research Initiative, Geary Institute, UCD.

Ferriter, D. (2004) *The Transformation of Ireland 1900–2000*, London: Profile Books UK.

Fine Gael and Labour Party (2005) *A New Departure for Social Partnership: Agreed Statement by Fine Gael and the Labour Party*, Dublin.

Fitzgerald, G. (2003) *Reflections on the Irish State*, Dublin: Irish Academic Press.

Fitzpatrick Associates (2006) *Evaluation of the RAPID (Revitalising Areas through Planning, Investment and Development) Programme*, report prepared for the Department of Community, Rural and Gaeltacht Affairs, Dublin.

Fitzpatrick Associates Economic Consultants (2006) *Review of the Implementation of the government's Integrated and Preventative Homeless Strategies, Submitted to the Minister for Housing and Urban Renewal*, Dublin: Stationery Office.

Fleming, S. (2005) *Tax Policy in the Context of a Newly Regulated Charity Sector*, address by Seán Fleming TD, Chairman, Joint Oireachtas Committee on Finance and the Public Service, at the Irish Charities Tax Reform Group 14th Annual Conference, Dublin.

Forde, C. (2004) "Local Government Reform in Ireland 1996–2004: A Critical Analysis", *Administration*, 52/3.

Forde, M. (2004) *Constitutional Law*, 2nd edn., Dublin: First Law Ltd.

Fowler, J. (2006) "Education, Education, Education" in S. Weir, *Unequal Britain: Human Rights as a Route to Social Justice*, London: Politico's.

Freedom House (2000) *Religious Freedom in the World: A Global Report on Freedom and Persecution*, Washington, DC: Centre for Religious Freedom.

Free Legal Aid Centre (2005) *Access to Justice: A Right or a Privilege? A Blueprint for Civil Legal Aid in Ireland*, Dublin: FLAC.

Gallagher, J. and Marsh, M. (2002) *Days of Blue Loyalty: The Politics of Membership of the Fine Gael Party*, Dublin: PSAI Press.

Gallagher, M. (2005a) "The Constitution and the Judiciary" in J. Coakley and M. Gallagher (eds.), *Politics in the Republic of Ireland*, 4th edn., London and New York: Routledge and PSAI Press.

Gallagher, M. (2005b) "Parliament" in J. Coakley and M. Gallagher (eds.), *Politics in the Republic of Ireland*, 4th edn., London and New York: Routledge and PSAI Press.

Gallagher, M. and Komito, L. (2005) "The Constituency Role of Dáil Deputies" in J. Coakley and M. Gallagher (eds.), *Politics in the Republic of Ireland*, 4th edn., London and New York: Routledge and PSAI Press.

Gallagher, M., Laver, M. and Mair, P. (2005) *Representative Government in Modern Europe: Institutions, Parties and Governments*, 4th edn., London: McGraw Hill.

Gallagher, M., Marsh, M. and Mitchell, P. (2003) *How Ireland Voted 2002*, Basingstoke: Palgrave Macmillan.

Galligan, Y. (2003) "The Candidates" Perspective" in M. Gallagher, M. Marsh and P. Mitchell, *How Ireland Voted 2002*, Basingstoke: Palgrave Macmillan.

Galligan, Y. (2005) "Women in Politics" in J. Coakley and M. Gallagher (eds.), *Politics in the Republic of Ireland*, 4th edn., London and New York: Routledge and PSAI Press.

Gannon, B. and Nolan, B. (2005) *Disability and Social Inclusion in Ireland, Joint Report of the National Disability Authority and the Equality Authority*, Dublin: Economic and Social Research Institute.

Geary, J. (2007, forthcoming) "Employee Voice in the Irish Workplace: Status and Prospects" in P. Boxall, P. Haynes and R. Freeman (eds.), *Employee Voice in the Anglo-American World*, Ithaca, NY: Cornell University Press.

Gilland Lutz, K. (2003) "Irish Party Competition in the New Millenium: Change or Plus Ca Change?" *Irish Political Studies*, 18.

Global Commission on International Migration (2005) *Migration in an Interconnected World: New directions for action*, Geneva: United Nations

Gogan, S. (2002) *Unmet Legal Aid in Ballymun*, Dublin: Ballymun Community Law Centre.

Golder, M. (2003) "An Evolutionary Approach to Party System Stability", paper presented at the 2003 Annual Meeting of the Midwest Political Science Association, Chicago, USA.

Government of Ireland (1972) *The Accession of Ireland to the European Communities*, Dublin: Department of External Affairs.

Government of Ireland (1998) *The First Report of the Task Force on the Integration of Local Government and Local Development Systems*, Dublin: Stationery Office.

Government of Ireland (1999a) *The Second Report of the Task Force on the Integration of Local Government and Local Development Systems - Preparing the Ground*, Dublin: Stationery Office.

Government of Ireland (1999b) *The Third Report of the Task Force on the Integration of Local Government and Local Development Systems - Strategic Policy Committees: Guidelines for Establishment and Operation*, Dublin: Stationery Office.

Government of Ireland (2000) *The Fourth Report of the Task Force on the Integration of Local Government and Local Development Systems - A Shared Vision for County/City Development Boards*, Dublin: Stationery Office.

Government of Ireland (2006) *White Paper on Irish Aid*, Dublin: Department of Foreign Affairs.

Government Publications Office (2003) *Commission on Financial Management and Control Systems in the Health Service*, Dublin: Stationery Office.

Grace, E. (2005) "Corporate Governance: Ireland", *Corporate Finance* (June supplement).

GRECO (2001) *First Evaluation Round: Evaluation Report on Ireland*, Strasbourg: Council of Europe.

Gregory, J. and Lees, S. (1999) *Policing Sexual Assault*, London and New York: Routledge.

Haran, P. (2006) *Report of the Legal Costs Working Group*, Dublin: Stationery Office.

Hardiman, N. (1998) 'Inequality and the Representation of Interests' in Crotty W. and Schmitt, D., *Ireland and the Politics of Change*, London and New York: Longman.

Harkin, A.M (2001) *Equity of Access to Health Services: Some Relevant Issues in an Irish Context*, Dublin: Institute of Public Health.

Harris, C. (ed.), (2005) *Engaging Citizens: The Case for Democratic Renewal – The Report of the Democracy Commission*, Dublin: Tasc@NewIsland.

Harvey, B. (2002) *Rights and Justice Work in Ireland: A New Baseline*, York: The Joseph Rowntree Charitable Trust.

Haughey, C. and Bacik, I. (2000) *Final Report: A Study of Prostitution in Dublin* (unpublished), Dublin: Trinity College Dublin Law School and Department of Justice, Equality and Law Reform.

Haynes, A., Devereux, E. and Breen, M. (2004) "A Cosy Consensus on Deviant Discourse: How the refugee and asylum seeker meta-narrative has endorsed an interpretive crisis in relation to the transnational politics of the world's displaced persons", Working Paper WP2004-03, available online at http://www.ul.ie/sociology/pubs/wp2004-03.pdf.

Health and Safety Authority (2005) *Health and Safety Authority Newsletter* (summer).

Health Services Executive (2006) *Leas Cross Nursing Home Report*, Dublin: Health Service Executive.

Heeks, R. (2000) *Government Data: Understanding the Barrier to Citizen Access and Use*, Manchester: Institute for Development Policy and Management.

Hegarty, M. (2006) "Equality Proofing – A Local Development Strategy" in D. Jacobson, P. Kirby and D. O'Broin (eds.), *Taming the Tiger: Social Exclusion in a Globalised Ireland*, Dublin: Tasc@NewIsland.

Hegeland, H. and Neuhold, C. (2002) "Parliamentary Participation in EU Affairs in Austria, Finland and Sweden: Newcomers with Different Approaches", *European Integration online papers*, vol. 6 (June 2002), available online at www.eiop.or.at/eiop.

Henry, L., Kendlin, H., Maher, N., O'Callaghan, M., O'Donoghue, C. and Woods, B. (2006) *Corporate Policy Groups: Review, Analysis and Recommendations*, A Paper for the 2005/2006 Leadership in Local Government Programme, Dublin: Institute of Public Administration.

Hogan, G. and Whyte, G. (2003) *The Irish Constitution*, 4th edn., Dublin: Butterworths Law (Ireland).

Homeless Agency (2004) *Making it Home: An Action Plan on Homelessness in Dublin 2004–2006*, Dublin: Homeless Agency.

Homeless Agency (2006) *Counted in 2005: Periodic Assessment of Homelessness in Dublin*, Dublin: Homeless Agency.

Honeyball, S. (1989) 'Employment Law and the Primacy of Contract', *Industrial Law Journal*, 18/2, 97–108.

Honohan, I. (2005) 'Active citizenship in contemporary democracy', in Harris, C. (ed), *Engaging Citizens: The Case for Democratic Renewal in Ireland - Report of the Democracy Commission*, Dublin: Tasc@NewIsland.

Horgan, J. (2001) *Irish Media: A Critical History since 1922*, London: Routledge.

Horgan, J. (2004) *Broadcasting and Public Life, RTÉ News and Current Affairs 1926–1997*, Dublin: Four Courts Press.

Howard, P. (1996) *The Joy*, Dublin: O'Brien Press.

Humphreys, G. and Craven, C. (1997) *Military Law in Ireland*, Dublin: Round Hall Sweet & Maxwell.

Humphreys, P. (1998) *Improving Public Service Delivery*, CPMR Discussion Paper No. 7, Dublin: Institute of Public Administration.

Humphreys, P. (2002) *Effective Consultation with the External Consumer*, CPMR Discussion Paper 23, Dublin: Institute of Public Administration.

Humphreys, P., Drew, E. and Murphy, C. (1999) *Gender Equality in the Civil Service*, Dublin: Institute of Public Administration.

International IDEA (2002) *The State of Democracy: Democracy Assessments in Eight Nations Around the World*, Stockholm: Kluber Law International.

International IDEA (2004) *Elections in the European Union: A Comparative Overview*, Stockholm: International Institute for Democracy and Electoral Assistance.

Immigrant Council of Ireland (2005a) *Background Information and Statistics on Immigration to Ireland*, Dublin: Immigrant Council of Ireland.

Immigrant Council of Ireland (2005b) *Summary Analysis and Initial Response to the Government's Proposals for an Immigration and Residence Bill*, Dublin: Immigrant Council of Ireland.

Indecon (2005) *Review of Local Government Financing*, Dublin: Department of the Environment, Heritage and Local Government.

Industrial Development Agency (2006) *Annual Report 2005*, Dublin: IDA Ireland.

Information Commissioner (2004a) *Annual Report 2004*, Dublin: Stationery Office.

Information Commissioner (2004b) *Review of the Operation of the Freedom of Information (Amendment) Act 2003*, Dublin: Stationery Office.

Information Commissioner (2005) *Report of the Information Commissioner to the Joint Committee on Finance and the Public Service for the Purpose of Review of Non-Disclosure Provisions*, Dublin: Stationery Office.

Ingle, R. (2006) 'Meet the Producers', *Irish Times*, 4 March 2006.

Inspectorate of Prisons and Places of Detention (2004) *Annual Report 2003/04*, Dublin: Department of Justice, Equality and Law Reform

Institute of Public Administration (1970) *The Devlin Report A Summary: An Abridged Version of the Report of Public Service Organisation Review Group, 1966–1969*, Dublin: Institute of Public Administration.

Institute of Public Administration (2004) *Review of the Operation of Strategic Policy Committees*, Dublin: Institute of Public Administration.

Institute of Public Administration (2005) *Administration Yearbook & Diary 2006*, Dublin: Institute of Public Administration.

Institute of Public Administration (2006) *Administration Yearbook & Diary*, Dublin: Institute of Public Administration.

Institute of Public Health in Ireland (2001) *Inequalities in Mortality 1989–1998: A*

Report on All-Ireland Mortality Data, Dublin: Institute of Public Health in Ireland.

International Federation of Journalists (2005) *Media Power in Europe: The Big Picture of Ownership*, available online at www.ifj.org/pdfs/EFJownership 2005.pdf.

International Human Rights Commission (2006) *Observations on the Criminal Justice Bill 2004 (Youth Justice)*, submitted to Minister for Justice, Equality and Law Reform, available online at www.ihrc.ie.

International IDEA (2003) *Handbook on Funding of Political Parties and Election Campaigns*, Stockholm: International Institute for Democracy and Electoral Assistance.

International IDEA (2004) *Voter Turnout in Western Europe since 1945*, Stockholm: International Institute for Democracy and Electoral Assistance.

International Labour Organisation (1949) *Right to Organise and Collective Bargaining Convention*, Geneva : International Labour Organization.

International Lesbian and Gay Association (2004) *ILGA World Legal Survey: The State of the Laws*, Brussels: International Lesbian and Gay Association.

International Organisation for Migration (2005) *Comments by IOM on the European Commission Green Paper: An EU Approach to Managing Economic Migration*, Geneva: International Organisation for Migration.

International Organisation for Migration (2006) *Managing Migration in Ireland: A Social and Economic Analysis*, Dublin: NESC.

Inter-Parliamentary Union (2004) *A Guide to Parliamentary Practice*, Geneva: IPU Secretariat.

Inter-Parliamentary Union (2005) *The Participation of Women and Men in decision-making: The Parliamentary Dimension*, Data sheet No.6 24-27 October, available online at www.ipu.org.

Inter-Parliamentary Union (2006a) *Parliament and Democracy in the Twenty-First Century: A Guide to Good Practice*, available online at www.ipu.org.

Inter-Parliamentary Union (2006b) *Database on Women in Politics*, available online at www.ipu.org.

IPSOS MORI (2006) *Irish Civil Service – Customer Satisfaction Survey Report 2006, Research Study Conducted for the Department of the Taoiseach*, Dublin.

Irish Consortium on Gender Based Violence (2005) *Gender Based Violence: A Failure to Protect*, Dublin: Joint Consortium of Human Rights Humanitarian and Development Agencies and Development Cooperation Ireland.

Irish Council for Civil Liberties (2002) *ICCL Background Paper on the 30th Anniversary of the Establishment of the Special Criminal Court*, available online at www.iccl.ie.

Irish Council for Civil Liberties (2003a), *ICCL Submission to the Joint Oireachtas Committee on Finance and the Public Service*, Dublin: Irish Council for Civil Liberties.

Irish Council for Civil Liberties (2003b) *Policy Paper on Police Reform – Why Patten Should Be Applied Here and How This Can Be Achieved*, available online at www.iccl.ie.

Irish Council for Civil Liberties (2003c) 'ICCL Welcomes Garda Complaints Board's Call for Independent Investigation', press release, 19 November 2003.

Irish Council for Civil Liberties (2005) *Submission to the CEDAW Committee*, available online at www.iccl.ie.

Irish Council for Civil Liberties (2006) *Equality for All Families*, Dublin: Printwell Cooperative.

Irish Defence Forces (2006) *Defence Forces Policy on Interpersonal Relations in the Defence Forces*, available online at www.military.ie.

Irish Examiner (23 December 2004) 'Prison Costs – System Not Giving Value for Money'.

Irish Examiner (7 February 2005) '95% of Rape Cases End without a Conviction'.

Irish Examiner (10 February 2006) 'Garda Bosses Discuss Gay and Lesbian Equality'.

Irish Human Rights Commission (2004a) *Observations on the Proposed Referendum on Citizenship and on the 27th Amendment to the Constitution Bill 2004*, Dublin: Irish Human Rights Commission.

Irish Human Rights Commission (2004b) *Observations on the Disability Bill*, Dublin: Irish Human Rights Commission.

Irish Human Rights Commission (2004c) *Observations on the Garda Bill 2004*, Dublin: Irish Human Rights Commission.

Irish Human Rights Commission (2005) *Making Economic, Social and Cultural Rights Effective: An IHRC Discussion Document*, Dublin: Irish Human Rights Commission.

Irish Human Rights Commission (2006) *Response to Minister for Foreign Affairs in Relation to the Transfer of Persons to Locations Where They May Be Subjected to Torture, Inhuman and Degrading Treatment*, Dublin: Irish Human Rights Commission.

Irish Human Rights Commission and the NCCRI (2004) *Safeguarding the Rights of Migrant Workers and their Families*, Dublin: Irish Human Rights Commission and the National Consultative Committee on Racism and Interculturalism.

Irish Independent (17 October 2003) 'Libel Laws in Breach of Basic Human Rights'.

Irish Independent (12 April 2004) 'U-turn on Widows' Cuts Should Be First of Many'.

Irish Prison Service (2005) *Annual Report of the Irish Prison Service*, Dublin: Irish Prison Service.

Irish Refugee Council (2003) *Asylum in Ireland: The Appeal Stage*, Galway: Irish Centre for Human Rights.

Irish Times (6 November 1997) 'Spring's Influence Can Be Seen throughout North Kerry'.

Irish Times (25 May 1998) 'Government to Consider Means of Overcoming Poll Restrictions'.

Irish Times (12 March 1999) 'UUP Has Blocked Establishment of Institutions It Agreed Last Easter'.

Irish Times (22 April 2000) 'Few Have Lawlor's Record of Handling Ethical Issues', 22 April 2000.

Irish Times (11 May 2000) 'Foley Admits He Breached Ethics Act', 11 May 2000.
Irish Times (20 May 2000) 'Politicians Respond Feebly to the Crisis Within', 20 May 2000.
Irish Times (24 May 2000) 'Motion to Suspend to Foley Approved', 24 May 2000.
Irish Times (13 June 2001) 'Second Nice Poll Likely after Election'.
Irish Times (2002) 'Election 2002' available online at www.ireland.com.
Irish Times (2 July 2002) 'Law to Stop Travellers Occupying Land without Consent is Enacted'.
Irish Times (24 July 2002) 'Constitutionality of Trespass Law Queried'.
Irish Times (31 August 2002) 'RTÉ is Still Looking for a Secure Financial Haven'.
Irish Times (16 November 2002) 'Binchy Calls for Trespass Law Repeal'.
Irish Times (22 November 2002) 'Backbench Unrest is Easily Cured'.
Irish Times (1 March 2003) 'Higgins, Howlin Remain Resolute'.
Irish Times (2 June 2003) 'Two-tier System of Care, Propped up by a Contract to Die For'.
Irish Times (5 June 2003) 'Without Seismic Reform, Healthcare Will Remain in Permanent Crisis'.
Irish Times (12 June 2003) 'When is Buying Votes Not Buying Votes? If You Do It Early Enough'.
Irish Times (20 October 2003) 'Threat of Legal Action Used to Silence Journalists'.
Irish Times (21 October 2003) 'Caught between Free Expression and Protecting Citizens from Unjust Attack'.
Irish Times (23 October 2003) 'Press Council Must Be Independent of State and Papers'.
Irish Times (10 February 2004) 'Majority Have Confidence in Fairness of Garda, Poll Shows'.
Irish Times (1 March 2004) 'O Neachtain Delighted by FF Nomination Decision'.
Irish Times (27 May 2004) 'McDowell Creating Divided Society'.
Irish Times (1 June 2004) 'Opinions Differ on Practice of Co-opting Family'.
Irish Times (28 October 2004) 'Shortt Seeks Damages for Prison Ordeal'.
Irish Times (2 November 2004) 'Names of Dead on Kerry Electoral Register'.
Irish Times (25 January 2005) 'Anti-poverty Group Criticises Funds Withdrawal'.
Irish Times (5 February 2005) 'Ethics Commissions Seeks Legal Advice on Leech Investigation'.
Irish Times (12 February 2005) 'Ruling May Improve Access to Civil Legal Aid'.
Irish Times (17 February 2005) 'Bill on Nursing Home Charges Unlawful'.
Irish Times (12 March 2005) 'Waiting Times for Free Legal Aid Fall'.
Irish Times (8 April 2005) 'Ireland's Aid Targets'.
Irish Times (29 April 2005) 'A Missed Opportunity to Advance Equal Rights'.
Irish Times (23 May 2005) 'McDowell Wants Movement on Child Abuse Issue'.
Irish Times (6 June 2005) 'Looking for Fairness and Consistency in a Secretive Refugee Appeals System'.
Irish Times (18 June 2005) 'Gama Secure 70% of PAYE Relief Scheme'.
Irish Times (24 June 2005) 'Takeovers Spell Good News for Regional Media Organisations'.

Irish Times (8 July 2005) 'Asylum Tribunal Must Disclose Findings'.
Irish Times (13 July 2005) 'Society Urges Closure of Irish Lapdancing Clubs'.
Irish Times (26 July 2005) 'Accept Irish Citizenship While You May'.
Irish Times (26 July 2005) 'If You Go Down to the Woods Today'.
Irish Times (24 September 2005) 'Election There to Be Won by Opposition'.
Irish Times (18 October 2005) '147 Juveniles Placed in Irish Prisons'.
Irish Times (21 October 2005) 'CAB Recovered Close to 19m Last Year'.
Irish Times (22 October 2005) 'Curtin Appeal Begins on Monday'.
Irish Times (24 October 2005) 'One Third of Candidates to Be Women by 2014'.
Irish Times (27 October 2005) 'Church Role in Schools Must End'.
Irish Times (28 October 2005) 'Court Reserves Judgment on Challenge by Curtin'.
Irish Times (3 November 2005) 'Reality of Church Role in Schools'.
Irish Times (25 November 2005) 'Awards Night: Minister on Hand for Hospitality Awards'.
Irish Times (21 December 2005) 'Whistle-blower's Privilege Circumscribed'.
Irish Times (1 January 2006) 'We Need Law to Protect the Whistle-blowers'.
Irish Times (24 January 2006) 'Glad to Be Gay: Teachers Stand Up for Their Rights'.
Irish Times (27 January 2006) 'TDs Want Changes to EU Services Directive'.
Irish Times (4 February 2006) 'Prisoners in Irish Jails to Get Postal Vote'.
Irish Times (13 February 2006) 'Same Sex Couple Seek Date for Court Hearing'.
Irish Times (24 February 2006) 'TV3 Says It Might Pull Out of Licence Fee Scheme'.
Irish Times (20 July 2006) 'The Number is Up for Present Constituency Boundaries'.
Irish Times (27 September 2006) 'Ahern to Face Dáil Questions over 50,000 Loan Not Repaid'.
Irish Times (12 October 2006) 'Irish Social Transfers Among Lowest in OECD'.
Irish Times (13 October 2006) 'Nally has Sentence for Killing Traveller Quashed'.
Irish Times (14 October 2006) 'Economy the Real Trump Card'.
Irish Times (14 November 2006) 'Judgment is Evidence of Invisible Status of the Child'.
Irish Times (15 November 2006) 'Major New Mental Health Law Long Awaited'.
Irish Times (16 November 2006) 'Estimates to Include 1 Billion of Extra Spending'.
Irish Times (13 December 2006) 'Ahern Defends Plan for Nursing Home Care'.
Irish Times (20 December, 2006) 'The Moriarty tribunal findings'.
Irish Traveller Movement and Combat Poverty Agency (2002) *Travellers in Education: Strategies for Equality*, Dublin.
John, P. (2001) *Local Governance in Western Europe*, London: Sage Publications.
Joint Declaration (1998) *Joint Declaration by the Ministers for Foreign Affairs of Brazil, Egypt, Ireland, Mexico, New Zealand, Slovenia, South Africa and Sweden – Towards a Nuclear-Weapons-Free World: The Need for a New Agenda*, New York: United Nations.

Katz, R.S. (2001) 'The Problem of Candidate Selection and Models of Party Democracy', *Party Politics*, 7 (May 2001).

Kavanagh, A.P. (2005) 'Bin Charges Disputes, Personality Politics, Sinn Féin and Increased Local Election Turnout', paper presented at the PSAI annual conference 2005, Belfast.

Keena, C. (2004) 'On the Paper Trail', *Irish Times*, 3 April 2004.

Keenan, O. (2001) 'From Delusion to Ambition: Creating a New Agenda for Children in Ireland' in K. Lalor (ed.), *The End of Innocence: Child Sexual Abuse in Ireland*, Cork: Oak Tree Press.

Kellaghan, T., McGee, P., Millar, D. and Perkins, R. (2004) *Views of the Irish Public on Education: 2004 Survey*, Dublin: Educational Research Centre.

Kelly, D. (2003) 'Power Corrupts and Absolute Power…', *The Thunderer* (20 December 2003).

Kelly, L. and Regan, L. (2003) *Research Report on Rape Cases Attrition Rates in Europe*, London: Child and Woman Abuse Studies Unit, London Metropolitan University.

Kelly, M. (2005) *Immigration-related Detention in Ireland, A Research Report for the Irish Refugee Council, Irish Penal Reform Trust and Immigrant Council of Ireland*, Dublin: Human Rights Consultants.

Kennedy, C. (2003) 'Domestic Violence: How We Answer Their Cries for Help', *Cork Online Law Review 2004*, available online at www.ucc.ie/colr/.

Kennedy, F. (2000) *Cottage to Crèche: Family Change in Ireland*, Dublin: Institute of Public Administration.

Kennedy, F. and Sinnott, R. (2006) 'Irish Social and Political Cleavages' in J. Garry *et al.* (eds.), *Irish Social and Political Attitudes*, Liverpool: Liverpool University Press.

Kenny, L. (2003) "Local Government and Politics" in *Local Government in Ireland – Inside Out* Callanan M. and Keogan J. (eds) Dublin: Institute of Public Administration

Kenny, L (2004) "A commentary on the Local Government Elections 2004" in *From Ballot Box to Council Chamber: A Guide to Ireland's County, city and town Councillors 2004-2009"* Kenny, L (ed) Dublin: Institute of Public Administration

Kilcommins, S., O'Donnell, I., O'Sullivan, E. and Vaughan, B. (2004) *Crime, Punishment and the Search for Order in Ireland*, Dublin: Institute of Public Administration.

Kilkelly, U. (2005) *The Children's Court: A Children's Rights audit*, Cork: UCC.

Kirby, P. (2006) "Agenda for Action" in D. Jacobson, P. Kirby and D. O'Broin (eds.), *Taming the Tiger: Social Exclusion in a Globalised Ireland*, Dublin: Tasc@NewIsland.

La Porta, R., Lopez-De Silanes, F., Shleifer, A. and Vishny, R. (2000) "Investor Protection and Corporate Governance", *Journal of Financial Economics*, 58/1.

Laffan, B. (2001) "The Parliament of Ireland: A Passive Adaptor Coming in from the Cold" in A. Maurer and W. Wessels (eds.), *National Parliaments on their Way to Europe: Losers or Latecomers?*, Baden-Baden: University of Cologne.

Laffan, B. and Tonra, B. (2005) "Europe and the International Dimension" in in J. Coakley and M. Gallagher (eds.), *Politics in the Republic of Ireland*, 4th edn., New York: Routledge and PSAI Press.

Laver, M. (1998) *A New Electoral System for Ireland?*, Dublin: Policy Institute, Trinity College Dublin.

Laver, M. (2005) "Voting Behaviour" in J. Coakley and M. Gallagher (eds.), *Politics in the Republic of Ireland*, 4th edn., New York: Routledge and PSAI Press.

Law Reform Commission (2006a) *Consultation Paper: Legitimate Defence*, Dublin: Law Reform Commission.

Law Reform Commission (2006b) *Consultation Paper on Legal Structures for Charities*, Dublin: Law Reform Commission.

Law Society of Ireland(2002) *Charity Law: The Case for Reform: A Report by the Law Society's Law Reform Committee*, Dublin: Law Society of Ireland.

Law Society of Ireland (1991) *Report on Civil Legal Aid*, Dublin: Law Society of Ireland.

Law Society's Law Reform Committee (2006) *Rights-Based Child Law: The Case for Reform*, Dublin: Law Society, available online at www.lawsociety.ie.

Lehmbruch, G. (1984) "Concertation and the Structure of Corporatist Networks" in J. Goldthorpe (ed.), *Order and Conflict in Contemporary Capitalism*, New York: Oxford University Press.

Lijphart, A. (1997) "Unequal Participation: Democracy's Unresolved Dilemma", *American Political Science Review*, 91/1.

Lines, R. (2005) *Living in the Past: The Americanisation of the Irish Prison System*, Dublin: Irish Penal Reform Trust.

Lipset, S.M. and Rokkan, S. (1967) "Cleavage Structures, Party Systems and Voter Alignments: An Introduction" in S.M. Lipset and S. Rokkan (eds.), *Party Systems and Voter Alignments: Crossnational Perspectives*, New York: Free Press.

Lodge, A. and Lynch, K. (eds.) (2004) *Diversity at School*, Dublin: Equality Authority.

Lynch, K. and Lodge, A. (2002) *Equality and Power in Schools: Redistribution, Recognition and Representation*, London: Routledge/Falmer.

Lynch, K. and Moran, M. (2006) "Markets, Schools and the Convertibility of Economic Capital: The Complex Dynamics of Class Choice", *British Journal of Sociology of Education*, 27/2, 221–35.

Lyons, P. (2006) Irish Opinion Poll Archive, Dublin: Trinity College Dublin, available online at www.tcd.ie.

Mac Carthaigh, M. (2005) *Accountability in Irish Parliamentary Politics*, Dublin: Institute of Public Administration.

Mair, P. (1993) "Fianna Fail, Labour and the Irish Party System" in Gallagher M. and Laver, M. (eds), *How Ireland voted 1992*, Dublin and Limerick: Folens/PSAI Press.

Mair, P. and Weeks, L. (2005) "The Party System" in J. Coakley and M. Gallagher (eds.), *Politics in the Republic of Ireland*, 4th edn., New York: Routledge and PSAI Press.

Marsh, M. (2000) "Candidate Centreed but Party Wrapped: Campaigning in Ireland under STV" in S. Bowler and B. Grofman (eds.), *Elections in Australia, Ireland and Malta under the single transferable vote: Reflections on an embedded institution*, Ann Arbor: University of Michigan Press.

Marsh, M. (2005) "Parties and Society" in J. Coakley and M. Gallagher (eds.), *Politics in the Republic of Ireland*, 4th edn., New York: Routledge and PSAI Press.

Marsh, M. and Benoit, K. (2002) "Campaign Spending in the Local Government Elections of 1999", paper presented at the Annual Conference of the PSAI, Belfast, October 2002.

Marty, D. (2006) *Alleged Secret Detentions and Unlawful Inter-state Transfers Involving Council of Europe Member States*, Strasbourg: Committee on Legal Affairs and Human Rights, Council of Europe.

Massicotte, L. (2000) "Second Chamber Elections" in R. Rose (ed.), *International Encylopedia of Elections*, Washington, DC: CQ Press.

Maurer, A. (2001) "National Parliaments in the European Architure: From Latecomers" Adaptation towards Permanent Institutional Change?" in A. Maurer and W. Wessels (eds.), *National Parliaments on their Way to Europe: Losers or Latecomers?*, Baden-Baden: University of Cologne.

Maurer, A. and Wessels, W. (eds.) (2001) *National Parliaments on their Way to Europe: Losers or Latecomers?*, Baden-Baden: University of Cologne.

McCarthy, C. (1977) *Trade Unions in Ireland: 1894–1960*, Dublin: Institute of Public Administration.

McCullagh, C. (2002) "The Social Analysis of the Irish Prison System" in P. O'Mahony (ed.), *Criminal Justice in Ireland*, Dublin: Institute of Public Administration.

McDonagh, M. (2003) *Freedom of Information in Ireland: Five Years On*, available online at www.freedominfo.org/.

McGauran, A., Verhoest, K. and Humphreys, P.C. (2005) *The Corporate Governance of Agencies in Ireland: Non-Commercial National Agencies*, Dublin: Institute of Public Administration.

McGee, E. (2005) "Communicating with a Multi-ethnic Ireland", *Irish Times*, 26 November 2005.

McGinnity, F., O'Connell, P.J., Quinn, E. and Williams, J. (2006) *Migrants' Experience of Racism and Discrimination in Ireland*, Dublin: Economic and Social Research Institute.

McGuinness, C. (1993) *Report of the Kilkenny Incest Investigation*, Dublin: Stationery Office.

Mee, J. and Ronayne, K. (2000) *Partnership Rights of Same-sex Couples*, Dublin: Equality Authority.

Meehan, E. (2000) *Free Movement between Ireland and the UK: From the "Common Travel Area" to the Common Travel Area*, Dublin: The Policy Institute, Trinity College Dublin.

Mesquita, J. (2006) "New Life for Health?" in S. Weir, *Unequal Britain: Economic and Social Rights as a Route to Justice*, London: Politico's.

Migrant Rights Centre Ireland (2004) *Private Homes: A Public Concern. The Experiences of Twenty Migrant Women Employed in the Private Home in Ireland*, Dublin: MRCI.

Minister for Enterprise, Trade and Employment (2003), Speech to Dáil Éireann, 20 March 2003, available online at www.entemp.ie/press/2003/200303a.htm.

Mitchell, J. (2005) *The European Union's "Democratic Deficit': Bridging the Gap between Citizens and EU Institutions*, available online at www.euorg.org.

Mitchell, P. (2003) "Ireland: "O What a Tangled Web..." - Delegation, Accountability and Executive Power" in S. Kaare, W.C. Müller and T. Bergman (eds.), *Delegation and Accountability in Parliamentary Democracies*, Oxford: Oxford University Press.

Molina, O. and Rhodes, M. (2002) "The Past, Present, and the Future of a Concept", *Annual Review of Political Science, 5*, 305–31.

Montague, P. (2002) *Lessons of Election 2002 for Irish Campaigners*, available online at www.montaguecomms.ie/research/research.pdf.

Moran, B. and Price, V. (2005) *Gender Balance on Air (Radio Teilifís Éireann) - Project Summary Report*, Dublin: RTE and Department of Justice, Equality and Law Reform.

Morgan, D. (1997) *The Separation of Powers in the Irish Constitution*, Dublin: Sweet and Maxwell.

Morgan, D. (2003) "Selection of Superior Judges in Ireland", delivered at Conference on Judicial Reform: Function, Appointment and Structure, held by the Centre for Public Law, University of Cambridge, 4 October 2003.

MORI Ireland (2004) *Trust in Public Institutions – A Preliminary Report*, Dublin: MORI Ireland.

Mulcahy, A. and O'Mahony, E. (2005) *Policing and Social Marginalisation in Ireland*, Combat Poverty Agency Working Paper 05/02, Dublin: Combat Poverty Agency.

Mulgan, R. (1997) "The Processes of Public Accountability", *Australian Journal of Public Administration*, 56/1.

Murphy, K. (2002) "Good Governance - A Personal Perspective", address by the Ombudsman at University College Cork, 27 September 2002, available online at http://ombudsman.gov.ie.

Murphy, M. (2006) "The Emerging Irish Workfare State and its Implications for Local Development" in D. Jacobson, P. Kirby and D. O'Broin (eds.), *Taming the Tiger: Social Exclusion in a Globalised Ireland*, Dublin: Tasc@NewIsland.

Murphy, R.J. and Farrell, D.M. (2002) "Party Politics in Ireland" in P. Webb, D. Farrell and I. Holliday (eds.), *Political Parties in Advanced Industrial Democracies*, Oxford: Oxford University Press.

National Centre for Partnership and Performance (2004) *The Changing Workplace: A Survey of Employees' Views and Experiences*, Report of the Forum on the

Workplace of the Future, 2, Dublin: National Centre for Partnership and Performance.

National Consultative Committee on Racism and Interculturalism (2005) *Submission on the Green Paper on an EU Approach to Managing Economic Migration*, Dublin.

National Council on Ageing and Older People (2001a) *Community Care Services, Ageing in Ireland Fact File No. 6*, available online at www.ncaop.ie.

National Council on Ageing and Older People (2001b) *Long-Stay Care, Ageing in Ireland Fact File No. 7*, available online at www.ncaop.ie.

National Crime Council (2005) *Domestic Abuse of Women and Men in Ireland*, Dublin: National Crime Council in Association with the ESRI.

National Disability Authority (2005a) *The Education for Persons with Special Educational Needs Act 2004*, available online at www.nda.ie.

National Disability Authority (2005b) Submission to the Democracy Commission, Dublin.

National Economic and Social Council (2005a) *The Developmental Welfare State*, Dublin: National Economic and Social Council.

National Economic and Social Council (2005b) *Strategy 2006: People, Productivity and Purpose*, NESC Report No. 114, Dublin: National Economic and Social Council.

National Economic and Social Council (2006) *Migration Policy*, Dublin: NESC.

National Economic and Social Forum (2002) *Equity of Access to Hospital Care*, Report No. 25, Dublin: National Economic and Social Forum.

National Economic and Social Forum (2005a) *Early Childhood Care and Education*, Dublin: National Economic and Social Forum.

National Economic and Social Forum (2005b) *Care for Older People*, Dublin: Government Publication Office.

National Economic and Social Forum (2006a) *Creating a More Inclusive Labour Market*, NESF Report 33, Dublin: National Economic and Social Forum.

National Economic and Social Forum (2006b) *Improving the Delivery of Quality of Public Services*, Report 34, Dublin: National Economic and Social Forum.

National Economic and Social Forum (2006c) *NESF News, Newsletter of the National Economic and Social Forum*, 6/2 (Winter).

National Women's Council of Ireland (2002) *Irish Politics, Jobs for the Boys!: Recommendations on Increasing the Number of Women in Decision Making*, Dublin: National Women's Council of Ireland.

National Women's Council of Ireland (2003) *Women and Poverty*, NWCI Factsheet No. 2, available online at www.nwci.ie.

National Women's Council of Ireland (2004) *Women in Politics and Decision Making*, available online at www.nwci.ie/politics.html.

National Youth Federation (2004) *National Youth Poll 2004*, available online at www.nyf.ie.

Nestor, S. (2000) *International Efforts to Improve Corporate Governance, Why and How*, Paris: OECD.

Netherlands Institute for Multiparty Democracy (2004) *A Framework for Democratic Party Building*, The Hague: Netherlands Institute for Multiparty Democracy.

Nolan, A. (2007, forthcoming) "Ireland" in M. Langford (ed.), *Social Rights Jurisprudence: Emerging Trends in International and Comparative Law*, New York: Cambridge University Press.

Norman, J., Glavin, M. and McNamara, G. (2006) *Straight Talk: Researching Gay and Lesbian Issues in the School Curriculum*, Dublin: Centre for Educational Evaluation, Dublin City University.

Norris, D. (1999) Seanad Debates, 29 April 1999, available online at www.irlgov.ie.

Northern Ireland Life and Times Survey (2005) available online at www.ark.ac.uk/nilt.

Ó Cinnéide, S. (1998) "Democracy and the Constitution", *Administration*, 46/4.

O'Brien, M. (2005) "Magazines and Periodicals: Off the Shelf" in H. Shaw (ed.), *Irish Media Directory and Guide*, Dublin: Gill and MacMillan.

Ó Broin, D. (2004) "An Emerging System of Local Governance? A Review of Policy, Practice and Prospects for the Future", *The Journal of Irish Urban Studies*, 2/2, 37–52.

Ó Broin, D. and Waters, E. (2007) *Assessing Local Democracy in Ireland – Governing Below the Centre: Local Governance in Ireland, Democratic Audit Ireland*, Dublin: Tasc@NewIsland.

O'Connell, P.J., Clancy, D. and McCoy, S. (2006) *Who Went to College in 2004? A National Survey of New Entrants to Higher Education*, Dublin: Higher Education Authority.

Ó Cuanachain, C., Reidy, A. and Power, C. (2004) *The Electoral Amendment Act: The Implications for Fundraising and Campaigning by Non-profits*, Dublin: Public Communications Institute.

O'Dea, P. (2002) "The Probation and Welfare Service" in P. O'Mahony (ed.), *Criminal Justice in Ireland*, Dublin: Institute of Public Administration.

O'Donnell, C. (1952) "The Source of Managerial Authority", *Political Science Quarterly*, 67/4, 573–88.

O'Donnell, I. (1998) "Crime, Punishment and Poverty" in I. Bacik and M. O'Connoll (eds.), *Crime and Poverty in Ireland*, Dublin: Round Hall Sweet & Maxwell.

O'Donnell, R. (2000) "Public Policy and Social Partnership" in J. Dunne, A. Ingram and F. Litton (eds.) *Questioning Ireland – Debates in Political Philosophy and Public Policy*, Dublin: Institute of Public Administration.

O'Donnell, S. (2003) "News Consumption in Ireland and the European Union", *Irish Communications Review*, 9.

O'Donoghue, C. and McDonough, T. (2006) "The Heart of the Tiger: Income Growth and Inequality" in D. Jacobson, P. Kirby and D. O'Broin (eds.), *Taming the Tiger: Social Exclusion in a Globalised Ireland*, Dublin: Tasc@NewIsland.

O'Kane, E. (2001) "The Republic of Ireland's Policy towards Northern Ireland:

The International Dimension as a Policy Tool", *Irish Studies in International Affairs*, 13.
O'Mahony, P. (1997) *Mountjoy Prisoners: A Sociological and Criminological Profile,* Dublin: Irish Penal Reform Trust.
O'Mahony, P. (2002) "Punishing Poverty and Personal Adversity" in P. O'Mahony (ed.), *Criminal Justice in Ireland*, Dublin: Institute of Public Administration.
O'Reilly, E. (1988) *Masterminds of the Right*, Dublin: Attic Press.
O'Reilly, E. (2004) *Review of the Operation of the Freedom of Information (Amendment) Act 2003*, available online at www.oic.gov.ie/en/Publications/SpecialReports/.
O'Reilly, E. (2005) Address by the Ombudsman and Information Commissioner at the FLAC Conference: Public Interest Law in Ireland – The Reality and the Potential, 6 October 2005.
O'Sullivan, T. (2003) "Local Areas and Structures" in *Local Government in Ireland – Inside Out,* Callanan M. and Keogan J. F. (eds) Dublin: Institute of Public Administration.
O'Toole, F. (1995) *Meanwhile Back At the Ranch: The Politics of Irish Beef,* London: Vintage.
Oasis (2006) Information on Public Services: An Irish eGovernment Resource, available online at www.oasis.gov.ie.
Office of the Information Commissioner (2005) *Annual Report 2005,* Dublin: Stationery Office.
Office of the Ombudsman (2001) *Nursing Home Subventions – A Report to the Dáil and Seanad in Accordance with Section 6 (7) of the Ombudsman Act, 1980,* Dublin: Office of the Ombudsman.
Office of the Ombudsman (2002) *Redress for Taxpayers, A Special Report by the Ombudsman to the Houses of the Oireachtas*, available online at www.ombudsman.gov.ie.
Office of the Ombudsman (2006a) *Serving the Public: Has the Modernisation Agenda Delivered?*, available online at www.ombudsman.gov.ie.
Office of the Ombudsman (2006b) *Annual Report 2005*, Dublin: Office of the Ombudsman.
Office of the Refugee Applications Commissioner (2006) *Annual Report 2005*, Dublin: Office of the Refugee Applications Commissioner.
Onyejelem, C. (2005) "Multiculturism in Ireland", *Irish Review*, 33 (Spring).
Organisation for Economic Co-operation and Development (2001) *Regulatory Reform in Ireland: Governance*, OECD Reviews of Regulatory Reform, Paris: OECD.
Organisation for Economic Co-operation and Development (2003) *Revenue Statistics 1965–2002*, Paris: OECD.
Organisation for Economic Co-operation and Development (2004a) *Early Childhood Education and Care Policy: Country Note for Ireland*, Paris: OECD.
Organisation for Economic Co-operation and Development (2004b) *Review of National Policies for Education: Review of Higher Education in Ireland,* Paris: OECD.

Organisation for Economic Co-operation and Development (2005a), *National Accounts of OECD Countries*, Paris: OECD.

Organisation for Economic Co-operation and Development (2006) *Starting Strong II: Early Childhood Education and Care*, Paris: OECD.

Parliamentary Question (2003) Response to Parliamentary Question: Prison Place Costs, 25 March 2003, available online at www.iprt.ie/ proceedings/print/712.

Pavee Point Travellers Centre (2005) *A Review of Travellers' Health Using Primary Care as a Model of Good Practice*, Dublin: Pavee Point, Primary Health Care for Travellers Project.

Pavee Point Travellers Centre (2006) *Pavee Point Factsheet: Distribution*, available online at www.paveepoint.ie

Peters, B. (2001) *Equality and Quality: Setting Standards for Women in Journalism, IFJ Survey on the Status of Women Journalists*, available online at www.ifj.org/ pdfs/ws.pdf.

Pollak, A. (1999) "An Invitation to Racism? Irish Daily Newspaper Coverage of the Refugee Issue" in D. Kiberd (ed.), *The Media in Ireland: The Search for Ethical Journalism*, Dublin: Four Courts Press.

Power Commission (2006) *Power to the People - The Report of Power: An Independent Inquiry into Britain's Democracy*,London: The Power Inquiry.

Prutz Phiri, P. (2003) "UNHCR, International Refugee Protection and Ireland" in C. Harvey and U. Fraser (eds.), *Sanctuary in Ireland*, Dublin: Institute of Public Administration.

Putnam, R.D. (2000) *Bowling Alone: The Collapse and Revival of American Community*, New York: Simon & Schuster.

Quinn, B. (2001) *Maverick: A dissident view of broadcasting today*, Dingle: Mount Eagle Publications.

Quinn, B. (2003) "Irish Local Government in a Comparative Context" in M. Callanan and J.F. Keogan (eds.), *Local Government in Ireland – Inside Out*, Dublin: Institute of Public Administration.

Quinlivan, A. (2003) *Local Democracy After the Dual Mandate*, Paper Presented at the Annual Conference of the General Council of County Councils, Cork, 31 May.

Report of the Forum on Broadcasting (2002) available online at www.dcmnr.gov.ie.

Reporters without Borders (2004) *Ireland – 2004 Annual Report*, available online at www.rsf.org.

Reporters without Borders (2006) *Press Freedom Index 2006*, Paris: Reporters without Borders.

Riordan, P. (1994) "Punishment in Ireland: Can We Talk About It?" *Administration*, 41/4.

Roche, D. (1992) "Irish Local Government: Controlled to a Virtual Standstill" in K. Rafter and N. Whelan (eds.), *From Malin Head to Mizen Head: The Definitive Guide to Local Government in Ireland*, Dublin: Blackwater Press.

Roche, W.K. (2006) "Social Partnership in Ireland and New Social Pacts", *Industrial Relations: A Journal of Economy and Society*, 45/3.

RTÉ (2005) *RTÉ: Information on Payments to Ten Most Highly Paid On-Air Broadcasters for 2003*, available online at www.RTÉ.ie/about/pressreleases.

RTÉ (2006) "Regulator's Code Tightens Credit Rules", RTÉ News (www.rte.ie), 25 July 2006.

RTÉ Programme Maker Guidelines (2002) available at www.rté.ie.

Ruddle, H. and Mulvihill, R. (1999) *Reaching Out: Chartable Giving and Volunteering in the Republic of Ireland*, Dublin: National College of Ireland.

Ruddock, A. (2005) "The Tide is Turning", *The Guardian* (London), 5 December 2005.

Ruhs, M. (2003) *Emerging Trends and Patterns in the Immigration and Employment of Non-EU Nationals in Ireland: What the Data Reveal*, PLACE: The Policy Institute, Trinity College Dublin.

Ruhs, M. (2004) *Ireland: A Crash Course in Immigration Policy*, Washington, DC: Migration Policy Institute.

Ruhs, M. (2005) "Managing the Immigration and Employment of Non-EU Nationals in Ireland", Studies in Public Policy 19, Dublin: The Policy Institute, Trinity College Dublin.

Scarrow, S. (2005) *Political Parties and Democracy in Theoretical and Practical Perspectives: Implementing Intra-party Democracy*, Washington, DC: National Democratic Institute for International Affairs.

Second Report of the Co-ordinating Group of Secretaries (1996) *Delivering Better Government*, Dublin: Government Publications.

Seymour, M. (2004) "Juvenile Justice in the Republic of Ireland", prepared for the Thematic Working Group on Juvenile Justice, European Society of Criminology, available online at www.esc-eurocrim.org.

Seymour, M. (2006) *Alternatives to Custody*, Dublin: Business in the Community - Ireland in association with the Irish Penal Reform Trust.

Share, P. (2003) Community Studies Lectures 2003–04, Institute of Technology, Sligo, Sligo.

Shaw, H. (2005) "Radio: The Audio Boom" in H. Shaw (ed.), *Irish Media Directory and Guide 2006*, Dublin: Gill and MacMillan.

Shleifer, A. and Vishny, R. (1997) "A Survey of Corporate Governance", *The Journal of Finance*, 52/2.

Simon News (2002) No. 5 (March 2002).

Sinnott, R. (1995) *Irish Voters Decide: Voting Behaviour in Elections and Referendums since 1918*, Manchester: Manchester University Press.

Sinnott, R. (2005) "The Rules of the Electoral Game" in J. Coakley and M. Gallagher (eds.), *Politics in the Republic of Ireland*, 4th edn., New York: Routledge and PSAI Press.

Standards in Public Office Commission (2002) *Guidelines for Dáil General Election 2002*, Dublin: Standards in Public Office Commission.

Standards in Public Office Commission (2003) *Review of the Electoral Acts 1997–2002,* Dublin: Stationery Office.

Standards in Public Office Commission (2005a) *Civil Service Code of Standards and Behaviour,* Dublin: Stationery Office.

Standards in Public Office Commission (2005b) Press release concerning Minister Martin Cullen, 15 February 2005.

Standards in Public Office Commission (2006) *Functions of the Standards in Public Office Commission*, available online at www.sipo.gov.ie/en/AboutUs/Functions/ (accessed 28/2/2006)

Statesman Journal (2005) "Profound Effects Likely on U.S., Mexican Elections", 30 January 2005.

Stewart, J. (2005) "Incomes of Retired Persons in Ireland" in J. Stewart (ed.), *For Richer, For Poorer: An Investigation of the Irish Pension System*, Dublin: Tasc@NewIsland.

Sub-Committee on European Affairs (2002) *First Report of the Sub-Committee on European Affairs*, available online at www.irlgov.ie.

Sub-Committee on European Affairs (2005) *Second Annual Report on the Operation of the European Union (Scrutiny) Act 2002 (1 January 2004 to 31 December 2004)*, available online at www.irlgov.ie.

Sunday Business Post (30 July 2000) "September Will Be Worse for Charlie'.

Sunday Business Post (25 December 2005) "Judges: Male, Middle Class and Dublin-born'.

Sunday Independent (13 February 2005) "How Myers Tackled the Single Mothers "Issue" and Became a National Hate Figure'.

Sunday Tribune (15 August 2004) "There Is Still No Separation of Party Politics and the Judiciary'.

Sunday Tribune (22 October 2006) "Sunday Tribune/Millard Brown Survey".

Sunday Tribune (12 November 2006) "For Mad, Sad or Bad Children – Nothing Changed'.

Task Force on Active Citizenship (2006) *Together We're Better: Background Working Paper*, available online at www.activecitizen.ie.

The Belfast Agreement (1998), *Constitutional Issues 1 (vi)*, available at www.nio.gov.uk/agreement.pdf.

The Economist (14 October 2004) "Why Worry".

The Electoral Commission (2005) *An Audit of Political Engagement 2*, London: The Electoral Commission and The Hansard Society.

The Wheel (2006) *Implementation Updates*, available online at www.wheel.ie.

Tierney, J. (2006) "The Importance of the Local in a Global Context" in D. Jacobson, P. Kirby and D. O'Broin (eds.), *Taming the Tiger: Social Exclusion in a Globalised Ireland*, Dublin: Tasc@NewIsland.

Tovey, H. and Perry, S. (2003) *A Sociology of Ireland*, Dublin: Gill & Macmillan.

Tovey, H. and Share, H., (2003) *A Sociology of Ireland*, 2nd edn., Dublin: Gill & MacMillan.

Transparency International (2004) available online at www.transparency.ie.

Transparency International (2005) *Report on the Transparency International Global Corruption Barometer 2005*, Berlin: Transparency International.

Travers, J. (2005) *Interim Report on Certain Issues of Management and Administration in the Department of Health and Children Associated with the Practice of Charges for Persons in Long-Stay Care in Health Board Institutions and Related Matters*, Dublin: Stationery Office.

Trócaire (2005) *Towards an Integrated Government Policy for Development Cooperation: Submission to the White Paper on Development Cooperation*, Maynooth: Trocaire.

Tupman, B. (2006) "The Politics of Policing Transnational Crime in the European Union", University of Exeter Politics Department, available online at www.ex.ac.uk/~watupman/undergrad/Neilson/.

Tussing, D. and Wren, M-A. (2006) *How Ireland Cares: The Case for Health Care Reform*, Dublin: New Island.

United Nations Committee on the Rights of the Child (2005) *Consideration of Reports Submitted by State Parties Under Article 44 of the Convention, Second Periodic Report of State Parties due in 1999 – Ireland*, available online at www.unhchr.ch.

United Nations Human Rights Committee (2000) *Concluding Observations of the Human Rights Committee: Ireland*, 24/07/2000, UN Doc. a/55/40, Geneva: Office of the High Commissioner for Human Rights.

UNCTAD (2001) *World Investment Report*, Geneva: UNCTAD.

United Nations (2003) *Global Illicit Drug Trends 2003*, Vienna: United Nations International Drug Control Programme, available online at www.unodc.org.

United Nations (2005) *Committee on the Elimination of Discrimination against Women Concluding Comments and Recommendations on Ireland,* New York: United Nations

United Nations (2006) *Monthly Summary of Contributors of Military and Civilian Police Personnel*, Peace and Security Section of the Department of Public Information, New York: United Nations Department of Peacekeeping Operations.

United Nations Children's Fund (UNICEF) (2002) *A League Table of Educational Disadvantage in Rich Nations*, Innocenti Report Card, Issue 4, Florence: United Nations Children's Fund.

United Nations Development Programme (2006) *United Nations Development Programme 2006 Annual Report: Global Partnership for Development*, New York: United Nations.

United Nations Millennium Declaration (2000) *United Nations General Assembly Resolution 55/2*, New York: United Nations.

Village (9 March 2006) "Workers and taxpayers hit by builder subcontracting'.

Village (1 July 2005) "Speedy Amendments to Garda Bill Undemocratic'.

Visser, J. (1998) *Concertation – The Art of Making Social Pacts*, Report on a seminar on social pacts, Brussels, 1998.

Walsh, D. (1997) "Keeping it Trivial Is the Surest Way to Stay Out of Trouble, *Irish Times*, 7 June 1997.

Watt, P. and McGaughey, F. (eds.) (2006) *How Public Authorities Provide Services to Minority Ethnic Groups, Northern Ireland, Republic of Ireland, Scotland - An*

Emerging Findings Discussion Paper, Dublin: NCCRI.

Weeks, L. (2004) 'Independents in Government: A Case Study in Ireland', Paper presented to European Consortium for Political Research 2004 Joint Sessions of Workshops '*New Parties in Government*', Upsalla, Sweden.

Weir, S. (2006) *Unequal Britain: Human Rights as a Route to Social Justice*, London: Politico's.

Whelan, C.T., Nolan, B. and Maître, B. (2005) *Trends in Welfare for Vulnerable Groups, Ireland 1994–2001*, Policy Research Series, No. 56, Dublin: Economic and Social Research Institute.

Whyte, G. (2002) *Social Inclusion and the Legal System*, Dublin: Institute of Public Administration.

Wickham, J. (2006) *Gridlock: Dublin's Transport Crisis and the Future of the City*, Dublin: Tasc@NewIsland.

Wilford, R., Wilson, R. and Claussen, K. (2007, forthcoming) *Assessing Democracy in Northern Ireland*, Dublin: Tasc@NewIsland.

Wilkinson, R.G. (2005) *The Impact of Inequality: How to Make Sick Societies Healthier*, London and New York: Routledge.

Wilson, M. (2006) *Views on Organised Crime in Northern Ireland: Findings from the January 2006 Northern Ireland Omnibus Survey*, Belfast: Northern Ireland Statistics and Research Agency, Northern Ireland Office.

Wilson, R. and Wilford, R. (2006) *The Trouble with Northern Ireland: The Belfast Agreement and Democratic Governance*, Tasc Pamphlet Series, Dublin: Tasc@NewIsland.

Wood, D. M. and Young, G. (1997) 'Comparing Constituent Activity by Junior Legislators in Great Britain and Ireland', *Legislative Studies Quarterly*, 22:2.

Working Group on Domestic Partnership (2006) Options Paper Presented by the Working Group on Domestic Partnership to the Tánaiste and Minister for Justice, Equality and Law Reform, Dublin : Dept of Justice, Equality and Law Reform.

Working Group on the Jurisdiction of the Courts (2003) *The Criminal Jurisdiction of the Courts*, Dublin: Stationery Office.

Wren, M-A. (2003) *Unhealthy State: Sixty Years of a Sick Society*, Dublin: New Island.

Young, H. and Rees, N. (2005) "EU Voting in the UN General Assembly", *Irish Studies in International Affairs*, 16.

YouthNet (2003) *Research into the Needs of Young People in Northern Ireland Who Identify as Lesbian, Gay, Bisexual and/or Transgender*, Belfast: Department of Education.

Zappone, K. (ed.) (2003) *Re-thinking Identity: The Challenge of Diversity*, Dublin: Joint Equality and Human Rights Forum.

Index

Emboldened page ranges refer to chapters; italicised page numbers refer to tables; entries refer to the Repubic of Ireland unless otherwise indicated.

Support TASC

A Think Tank for Action on Social Change

> *'the limited development of think tanks is a striking feature [of Ireland] for such bodies could do much to focus new thinking about the country's future democratic and political development'*
>
> (REPORT TO THE JOSEPH ROWNTREE CHARITABLE TRUST, 2002)

Ireland almost uniquely in Europe has relatively few think tanks of any kind and, prior to the establishment of TASC, none whose sole agenda is to foster new thinking on ways to create a more progressive and equal society.

Your support is essential – to do its work TASC must keep a distance from political and monetary pressure in order to protect the independence of its agenda. If you would like to make a contribution to TASC – A Think Tank for Action on Social Change, please send your donation to the address below

DONATIONS TO:

TASC
A Think Tank for Action on Social Change
26 Sth Frederick St, Dublin 2.
Ph: 00353 1 6169050
Email:contact@tascnet.ie
www.tascnet.ie